You Can't Say That: Memoirs

Ken Livingstone was born in South London. When he left school he wanted to spend the rest of his life working at London Zoo and never expected or wanted to be a politician. But with no vacancies at the zoo, he ended up instead in the political jungle working with bizarre beasts, many of whom are now fortunately extinct. At his first-ever council meeting he introduced a pensioners' travel pass. Later he built council homes, cut fares, met the IRA, championed equalities and lost his job when the GLC was abolished. This might have been enough for one political life, until he decided to do it all over again as Mayor of London, putting two fingers up to Tony Blair in the process. He still lives in London.

Praise for *You Can't Say That*:

'Absorbing.' Andrew Neather, *Evening Standard*

'A fascinating and informative portrayal of London and British politics during the latter half of the twentieth and into the twenty-first century. It is also leavened by Ken Livingstone's sharp wit and lack of deference.' *Morning Star*

KEN LIVINGSTONE

You Can't Say That

MEMOIRS

faber and faber

First published in 2011
by Faber and Faber Limited
Bloomsbury House
74–77 Great Russell Street
London WC1B 3DA

This paperback edition first published in 2012

Typeset by Faber and Faber Limited
Printed and bound by CPI Group (UK) Ltd, Croydon, CR0 4YY

A CIP record for this book
is available from the British Library

ISBN 978–0–571–28041–4

FSC
www.fsc.org
MIX
Paper from
responsible sources
FSC® C101712

To Emma, for it all

Contents

Illustrations

1

The Lambeth Walk

1945–1962

My parents' relationship was the most important thing in both their lives, and they remained passionately in love until my father's unexpected and shocking death at the age of fifty-six. They married in Wandsworth on 31 July 1940, just eight weeks after they had first met at a music hall in Workington. My mother, Ethel Ada Kennard, was a dancer who was part of a three-woman act called the Kenleigh Sisters. My father, Robert Moffat Livingstone, was in the audience one night with two shipmates on shore leave from the merchant navy. Having had enough drink to boost their confidence, the sailors waved and winked before passing a message to the three women to join them for supper in the local fish-and-chip shop.

Ethel, shy and easily embarrassed, was appalled when Bob started singing to her the Bing Crosby hit 'I Have Eyes (to See With But They See Only You)'. 'I wanted the ground to open and swallow me up,' she said later. But for all her embarrassment it was love at first sight. She told John Carvel, who wrote a book about me in the 1980s, *Citizen Ken*, 'It was a lovely number. And he really meant it. We were meant to meet.' They each left the fish-and-chip shop that night to phone their respective fiancés and tell them that they had found someone else.

As Ethel was on tour, and Bob at sea, it was possible for them to meet on only three occasions before they got married in the summer of 1940, both aged twenty-five. The years that followed were difficult. Bob was on duty for long periods of time. Following

Hitler's invasion of the Soviet Union in the summer of 1941, he worked as a ship's master on the perilous Arctic Sea convoys of arms shipments to Murmansk in northern Russia. Prime Minister Winston Churchill and President Franklin Roosevelt had decided that the Soviet armies should be sustained at all costs in their titanic struggle against the Nazis. Dad's affection for Russians dated from his visits to Murmansk. Their generosity to him when they had so little themselves left a deep impression.

The British navy's resources were stretched thin and the human cost of the convoy system was brutal. Nazi submarines would lie in wait and many sailors' lives were lost. Dad was incredibly lucky to survive the torpedoes that struck his ship as a U-boat worked its way along the line of ships, sinking each in turn. Had Dad been in the vanguard he would surely have died, but after the first ship sank sailors on the other vessels gathered by the life rafts to wait for the inevitable torpedo strike. After days adrift in the appallingly cold conditions of the Arctic Sea, Bob was rescued and invalided out of the service. He went to live with Ethel in the small flat her mother rented in Streatham. He had barely met his mother-in-law before the marriage. Dad had no idea what lay in store for him.

My grandmother, Zona Ann Williams, was born in 1888, a year before the creation of the London County Council (LCC), and grew up in South London around Balham and Tooting. As a boy I was mesmerised by her sanitised tales of life in nineteenth-century London. Nan was one of seven children (only five of whom survived) and raised under a regime of strict Victorian values. Life was not easy for her, but she experienced nothing like the crushing poverty that afflicted poorer London families just a couple of miles north in the slums of Kennington.

Nan turned her back on her family as a teenager when she came home late one night and was savagely beaten by her father. She packed her belongings and left to work in the pubs that serviced the theatrical trade she idolised. She fell pregnant by her future husband Charles Kennard, a painter and decorator raised by his grandparents in Eastbourne.

The shame of being pregnant and unmarried was such that to her dying day Zona never admitted her secret to anyone, including her children. Only after Nan's death did my mother discover that she had changed the dates on her wedding certificate to hide her disgrace.

I was told my grandfather was blown to bits by a German shell in Flanders just two months before the birth of his second child, my uncle Ken, but the truth is more complicated. Zona insisted he was a wonderful man with a constant smile, but the fact that he did not marry her until two months after my mother was born suggests he was not as committed as she later convinced herself he was. Within two weeks of the outbreak of war he had enlisted in the 6th Battalion of the Dorsetshire Regiment, but his rebellious streak landed him on charges six times in three years. He was dispatched to France two years later on 3 July 1916, where he was wounded in the Battle of the Somme. He was jailed twice, once for twenty-one days for being absent without a pass, drunk and lying to an officer. A seven-day sentence followed, this time for being absent without leave for two and a half days and for 'missing a military tattoo'.

Uncle Ken always insisted that my grandfather died because our soldiers were sent forward to certain death so that their bodies would fill the enemy trenches and allow British tanks to pass over their corpses. In 2005 Ancestor Incorporated suggested it was more likely that my grandfather, having committed yet another offence against the regulations, was sent to the front line by his commanding officer simply to avoid the delay and expense of a court martial. Whatever the truth, Private Charles Joseph Kennard of 142 Hartfield Road, Wimbledon, died at Arras on 16 May 1917, aged thirty-two.

*

Zona never took up with another man. Turning inward, she devoted herself to raising her two children in a succession of rented rooms in South London. Having fallen out with her parents, Nan was far too proud to go to them for help so she lived on her war widow's pension and the wages she earned from occasional shop work. Mum recalled trips to local markets just as they were closing and the food was sold at half price, saving enough money to buy a bottle of cheap port, which was Zona's favourite tipple. Mum was left with rotten teeth, though Nan did pay for them all to be taken out and replaced with dentures as a twenty-first birthday present.

Nan was determined that Ethel was not going to 'skivvy' for a living so she planned for Mum to fulfil her own dreams of a career on the stage. By skimping and saving, Zona was able to enrol Mum in ballet lessons and she performed well in several competitions. In a less class-ridden time Mum might have joined a professional ballet company, but instead had to settle for a job as an acrobatic dancer touring provincial music halls with the famous names of the day: Donald Peers, Tommy Trinder, Two-Ton Tessie O'Shea and Cecil Lyle, the 'Great Illusionist', who daily sawed Mum in half. When Mum joined the company, Nan found her lodgings in Reading. It was the first time fourteen-year-old Ethel had been away from home so she cried herself to sleep in her one-room digs. The next day she met Jo and Nan, two other girls in the show. They became close friends and formed the Kenleigh Sisters, doing tap-dancing routines, ballet and the kind of back flips and balancing manoeuvres that are now part of modern gymnastics. The three of them shared digs throughout my mother's fifteen years on the stage and they remained firm friends for life.

Uncle Ken did well in his local LCC school and would have stayed on had there been enough money. Instead he left at fourteen and went to work for Mr Campbell, a local tailor and leading figure in the Streatham Tory party who represented the constituency on the

LCC. My uncle spent his life in both the rag trade and, apart from one brief interlude, the Tory party. In 1949 Winston Churchill's son-in-law, Duncan Sandys, was parachuted into this safe parliamentary seat which had been nurtured by Campbell for years. My uncle was so angry at this that he resigned from the party and got Dad to write to the local paper complaining about the treatment of his employer. I remember Mum anxiously asking Dad, 'Are you sure we won't get into trouble for doing this?' Uncle Ken was right to be outraged as Sandys completely neglected his constituency, appearing only once every five years when he was driven through Streatham in an open car waving to the voters on the Saturday before polling.

My uncle's views were so right-wing that he joined Oswald Mosley's fascist Blackshirts in the 1930s and when he died in December 1986 I discovered he was a member of both the Tory party and the far-right National Front at the same time. Becoming more intolerant with age, he went through the *Radio Times* and *TV Times* each week with a marker pen obliterating any programme listing that included black or Irish people, gays, lesbians or David Frost. For the last five years of his life, when I was leader of the Greater London Council (GLC), he so hated my politics that we had no contact. Uncle Ken's social life revolved around the pub at lunchtimes and almost every evening. He spent so much on drink that he never saved enough to buy his own home. It was in the pub that he met each of his three wives, an unusual number for the time. He married first just before he left to fight in Burma in the Second World War. His girlfriend had lied that she was pregnant, so on his return the marriage was annulled. His second wife, Pat, was the love of his life but after marrying him she was diagnosed with TB and died a few years later. He outlived his third wife, Vi, by a few years. With no children of his own he doted on me, his only godson – until I joined the Labour party.

*

Although Mum's childhood was tough within the claustrophobic cocoon my grandmother wove around the family, Dad had been denied even this kind of support. His father was a shipping clerk working in the Argentine before Dad's birth in 1915. According to our aunt Attie, my grandfather was 'high up in the railways'. So that their second child, if it was a boy, might evade the national service that Argentinian law required of all males born in the country, my grandparents and their daughter Cathy came back to Dunoon in Scotland for the birth, returning immediately to Argentina, where they lived for the next seven years. In 1922 they returned to Dunoon permanently, though by then the family was disintegrating as Dad's mother was very ill and Grandfather was having an affair. Only after Dad's death did Aunt Cathy talk of his devotion to his mother and the anger he felt towards his father. He never once discussed his own family with me or my sister; it was as though his life had begun only when he met my mother.

Catherine, Dad's mum, finally died aged forty-nine when he was sixteen. My grandfather, who was called Robert Moffat like his son, moved out of the family home and at the funeral shook Dad's hand, said, 'Good luck, son,' and walked away. Dad never saw him again. We never discovered when or where he died. Aunt Cathy had just married her fiancé Leo McCloud and the newly-weds took Dad in to live with them.

Dad did well at Dunoon grammar school but had to leave early to work, cutting timber on a local estate. In 1932, as Cathy's family started to grow, Dad joined the merchant navy at seventeen as a deck boy. While Mum travelled the length and breadth of Britain appearing at music halls, Dad travelled the world, working side by side with men of all races and religions in the harsh conditions of the merchant navy. He had none of the racism so common in those times.

Given their ghastly childhoods, it's not surprising my parents threw themselves into a devoted lifetime commitment to each other. In their love they found all they had missed as youngsters, but when it came to raising my sister and me they were prisoners of their pasts.

My nan Zona so immersed herself in her children that she feared losing them to marriage. Boyfriends and girlfriends were disparaged and scared off. Once Nan so wound up my uncle that he smashed his fist through the glass door of the living room. The world outside was portrayed as a dangerous place and the family was the only thing of value. Estranged from her own family and constantly moving on after rows with landlords, she clung desperately to her children – even keeping Mum away from school for company and hiding behind furniture when the school truant officer came knocking.

When Mum told Nan she was engaged to Bob, she was given a long lecture. Nan warned he must have a woman in every port. Nan phoned Cathy, probing for details, but she could find nothing to dissuade Mum from marrying Bob and so instead made his life as difficult as possible.

Nan suffered from violent mood swings, a possessive nature and a viciously wounding tongue. Today she would have therapy and a fistful of pills but in the 1940s no such prescriptions were available. This was the emotional nightmare that awaited my father as he moved into Nan's flat to convalesce after the sinking of his ship. He soon decided to join Mum on tour and was taken on by her company to play minor stage roles. For Mum the world of dance had been exhilarating and liberating. Freed from the grasp of her mother and the bleak digs, she toured Britain with good friends earning twice the average wage.

My parents' stage careers ended when Nan's arthritic kneecap was removed and Mum had to look after her for months. When she tried to go back on tour, wartime regulations forced her to work in a local munitions factory where she loathed the grinding work and the coarse language.

*

My parents had decided not to have children, but one night in September 1944 Dad ran out of condoms. With words Mum never forgot Dad assured her, 'It can't matter just this once, Eth.' If condoms had been sold in packets of four rather than three I wouldn't be here. I was also lucky Mum had not been killed in an air raid as she so loathed the discomfort of the shelters that she took the risk of sleeping in her own bed during the final blitz on London in the winter of 1944.

I was born at home a few minutes after midnight on 17 June 1945, though Dad claimed he heard my first cry a few minutes before the clock chimed. As is common in dancers, Mum's labour was short but she wanted a girl and was appalled at how ugly I looked, with no hair and a huge mass of yellow pus in my eyes because the midwife hadn't cleaned them properly. By coincidence the first Labour leader of the LCC, Herbert Morrison, was born with the same condition and lost the sight of one eye. Mum told John Carvel, 'I thought he looked ugly so I used to put the blankets over his head and tell people not to disturb him. He looked terribly ill for the first few weeks, but was lovely by the time he was six months.' Mum couldn't produce milk, so I was bottle-fed from birth.

My earliest memory is of Mum coming home from hospital in February 1948 with my newborn sister Linda, whom I adored. Her arrival coincided with an epidemic of gastro-enteritis which killed many infants, including the sister of the BBC presenter John Humphrys. When I caught it the doctor said I had no chance of surviving and the important thing was to prevent the infection spreading to Linda. While Mum cared for Linda, Nan saved my life. I remember lying on cushions in the armchair while Nan spoon-fed me back to health. Nan and Mum were quite matter-of-fact when recalling this crisis. It was a few months before the start of the NHS and in those days there was nothing unusual about a child dying. I often listened to men and women of my parents' generation talking about childhood friends who had died simply because their parents could not afford medical care. I recovered but remained thin and weedy throughout my school days, so Mum and Nan were over-protective, worrying about my 'delicate' nature and my summer colds. I was fussy about food, and Mum often had to cook something separate for me or wash tomato sauce off baked beans before I would eat them. At secondary school I was the smallest boy out of over 400 in my intake, and only when I started work did I put on some height and weight.

In 1957 Mum spent weeks in hospital being nursed through a hysterectomy complicated by massive fibroids. She and Dad were in awe that all this treatment was free. Without the NHS Mum would not have survived and it was the only policy of the post-war Labour government that my parents supported. Recognising the impact the NHS had on ordinary families, the Tories knew they had to support it or have no hope of returning to power.

21B Shrubbery Road, Streatham, the flat where I was born, was in the respectable Tory-controlled Borough of Wandsworth and the Streatham constituency was one of a handful of inner-London seats which stayed Tory during Labour's 1945 landslide. When I returned to visit the house thirty-five years later I realised how small it was. Two bedrooms, one large enough for only a single bed and wardrobe, and a kitchen in which it was almost possible to stand in the centre and touch all four walls, off which was a scullery ventilated by a gap between wall and ceiling which opened to the elements. Then there was the immaculately kept front room, the largest in the flat but used only at Christmas and on the rare occasions when anyone visited. It was also where bodies would be laid out in the event of a death. Forbidden as a child to enter the room, I would peer through the glass door at this oasis of cleanliness and quiet. This was my little world and I felt secure in it. While Dad was away Mum used me as a hot water bottle and in the mornings Nan would come in with steaming, sweet tea, which I called 'tuppatea'. On their regular cinema trips Mum and Dad shared one layer from a box of Milk Tray chocolates and I would wake up to find that they had left me the coffee crème, a real treat in the days of sweet rationing.

Uncle Ken was fighting the Japanese in Burma so Nan took over his small bedroom and I lay in a padded orange box by my parents' bed. For the first six years of my life Dad escaped this claustrophobic environment by working on fishing trawlers and in the merchant navy. Every few days a postcard would arrive from somewhere in the world with a little message while Nan continued to disparage the Scots in general and Dad in particular. Mum hated the fact that Dad was away so often and when he came home his hands were cut and scarred from handling the hooks and nets on the trawlers. He switched to working on cross-Channel ferries and on one trip he took Linda and me along, but as we didn't have passports we had to stay on board and could only imagine what exciting adventures lay beyond the harbour at Calais. I would be twenty-one before I went abroad.

*

As I was blissfully unaware of the ongoing hostilities between Nan and Dad, my early memories are happy ones. Shrubbery Road was off the busy Streatham High Road so there was no question of being allowed outside the front door to play, but I would sit for hours at the window looking at passing rag-and-bone men and police officers coming and going from the police station opposite. We would wrap our food scraps in newspaper and go into the courtyard at the back of the police station to feed the pigs the police were rearing to help with the food shortage. Living opposite a piggery meant that lots of flies invaded the flat, and strips of sticky flypaper were always hanging from the ceiling. Mum would lift me up to watch flies struggling to escape their doom. This was in the days before television.

Linda and I were the only children living in our flats and it wasn't until I started school that I met any others. As Mum often worked during the day and Nan was disabled by her missing knee-cap, my horizons were confined to our little flat with the occasional walk round to Sunnyhill Road to peer through the windows of the milk-bottling plant or play on Streatham Common. Sometimes we ventured further afield. I remember the excitement when, aged three, I caught my first glimpse of the sea as our train pulled into Brighton. Evenings were spent clustered around the radio listening to the adventures of PC49 and Dick Tracy. Once a week came the luxury of bathtime, soaking in the tin tub filled with hot water from the kettle. Winter fog, smog and snow made the flat even more cosy and I would peer out of the window waiting for Uncle Ken to return from selling cloth in the East End in the hope that he had brought me another tin cowboy, Red Indian or jungle animal. After I'd spent the evening making plasticine figures, Mum or Nan would read me to sleep with Tarzan adventures from the books of Edgar Rice Burroughs.

There were none of the educational toys we now take for granted and the only books at home were my uncle's Tarzan and cowboy paperbacks. Nan talked to me all the time so at least I developed my verbal skills. Nan wasn't a convert to Dr Spock's child-centred theories, and took great pleasure in telling all and sundry how she potty-trained me by rubbing my nose in the mess I once made on the floor. She said I never did it again.

*

My parents only attended church for weddings or funerals, but Nan and Mum often went to spiritualist meetings. This did not prevent my mother ensuring I got a place at St Leonard's, the local C of E primary. To show what a polite little boy I was she dropped her handkerchief from her purse during the interview with the headmaster so that I could dutifully lunge forward and pick it up. Sir Reg Goodwin, the Labour leader of the GLC when I was first elected, had also been to St Leonard's, though we had little else in common.

Mum and Nan taught me the alphabet, but there was no academic tradition in our family. My parents' only ambition for me was to get a job with a pension, something no one in our family had ever achieved. Nan even discouraged me from bothering with homework. My first day at St Leonard's was in a class of forty-eight children sitting in ordered rows. When Mum picked me up my teacher said, 'He's a perfect little Christopher Robin,' and told her how I had stood in front of the rest of the class, entertaining them. Teaching was still by rote as we chanted the alphabet and our times tables. We were told we lived in the largest city on earth (although we had just slipped into second place behind New York) in the most advanced country at the heart of the greatest empire in human history. Other peoples and countries might one day be raised up to our level, even the Americans – a line often repeated in my secondary school. The wall was covered by a vast map of the world on which imperial red was the predominant colour, even though India and Pakistan were already independent. The school was confined to a small site with separate boys' and girls' playgrounds, each not much bigger than a substantial living room, so there was no physical education and on the rare occasions that a trip to the local swimming baths was organised I was excused because of my constant colds.

Shortly after I started at St Leonard's Mum, Dad and I moved to an LCC flat of our own. From the age of seven I walked to the local bus stop and made the two-mile trip from Brixton to Streatham un-accompanied. My parents weren't worried as in those days passing adults didn't hesitate to intervene if they saw children either misbe-having or getting into danger, though I was kept home during the 'great smog' which killed 12,000 Londoners in December 1952.

Our new three-bedroomed flat at 23 Irby House was a recently built extension to the Tulse Hill estate, a much sought-after part of the LCC's post-war housing programme. My parents were over-joyed finally to have a place where we could be alone as a family, and Linda and I had our own bedrooms which started to fill with the toys that came with the end of rationing and post-war restric-tions. The pair of us loved exploring Brockwell Park and the local bombsites. Apart from washing up my daily chore was to get up first, clean out the ashes from the grate and light the fire. Central heating was a distant luxury and in winter there was often ice in-side our windows. On the rare summer days when it was really hot we went to Brockwell Park Lido, where Dad impressed us with his swimming skills.

Our neighbours all seemed to be called Henry, George, Albert, Agnes, Gladys or Bessie and respectable working-class values were reinforced in our house by the *Daily Express*. Mothers obeyed the weekly rota which demanded that they scrubbed the stairways on their hands and knees. My parents did not swear and there was lit-tle bad language outside the home. Conversation was polite to the point of being stilted, as is well captured in Mike Leigh's 2004 film *Vera Drake*. There was no discussion of politics or religion outside of the immediate family, and no discussion of sex anywhere.

What was discussed was the war, which had changed the lives of a generation. Men who might never have left their towns before found themselves on the other side of the world and women who had never worked outside the home filled the jobs those men left, producing the munitions they fired. Every aspect of Britain's class system was challenged during those six years of social upheaval. My parents felt the war had robbed them of the best years of their lives, but for others who were lucky enough not to be in the front line the war freed them from grinding poverty or menial work and widened their horizons.

The war anchored all our lives. Endless films, books, radio and later TV programmes ensured that the war was relived and debated on a daily basis. The games we played on local bombsites involved shooting Germans and Japanese, although the ritual slaughter of American Indians ran a close second. My mates and I pored over pictures of British prisoners tortured by their captors. For my generation Nazism was the defining reference point for pure evil.

I am still proud that for eighteen months Britain stood alone against the greatest political and moral evil in human history, and that the country survived the power of the Nazi war machine. Cordell Hull, President Roosevelt's Secretary of State, said in his memoirs: 'Never had I admired a people more than I admired the British in the summer and autumn of 1940. Even their children seemed to realise that upon their indomitable spirit depended not only their own fate, but also that of the whole democratic world.' We wondered if we could equal our parents' sacrifice if we ever faced such a challenge. Our respect for them meant there was no question of forgetting the two minutes' silence on Poppy Day. Everything stopped at 11 a.m. on 11 November, even the traffic in the middle of a working day.

I dreaded the compulsory national service which loomed over my future with endless warnings that 'national service will beat *that* out of you' whenever I was bad. As any sentence for misconduct while in the army was added to your two-year stint I feared that with my lip I might never get out. Fortunately the Tory government abolished the draft shortly before I became liable.

*

My parents gave me a clear sense of right and wrong and the gift of guilt, which overwhelmed me whenever I misbehaved. After I stole a small dictionary from W.H. Smith I hid it in my room for years, convinced that people would know it was stolen just by looking at it. On a visit to one of Mum's friends I swung from a branch that snapped off in my hand and was made to feel embarrassed. My idea of an exciting adventure was when a friend and I went into adjacent phone boxes and spent tuppence phoning each other. This was my first ever phone call. When King George VI died in 1952 my sister and I were firmly told that we had to be sombre all day, with no running or shouting.

The strictest rule of all was the ban on entering our parents' bedroom. There was the occasional glimpse through the opening or closing door but no question of crawling into bed with them. On Sunday mornings my sister and I would wake up to a Wagon Wheel, a piece of fruit and a glass of milk which we had to consume in silence before we let ourselves out to play on the local estate while our parents had the morning to themselves.

Looking back, it's easy to criticise my parents for not being more tactile but my Mum had seen Nan cry only once in her life – after Nan had all her teeth taken out. My parents had been raised at a time when medical advice was that children should be left to cry in their prams rather than be cuddled or they would never be tough enough to survive. Children were seen but not heard. The American baby expert of the interwar years, John Watson, advised parents to break the spirit of children as a horse is broken, and at the same time the British government advised that children should be locked in their bedroom at night with the father keeping the key to prevent the mother going to the child when it cried. Linda and I were not raised in this brutal fashion but the 1950s were still a time when boys were definitely not supposed to cry and I insisted that Mum and Dad didn't kiss me goodbye when they came to school for fear of being laughed at. I found it liberating when men later began to show their feelings in public.

Initially my sister and I were each other's best friend, although Nan stirred up trouble because she thought Linda was Dad's favourite. As we entered our teens with our own sets of friends, we rowed and fought. One nasty trick of mine was to sit behind Linda on the bus and tie her pigtails around the handrail so she would have a struggle to get off the bus at our stop. As Linda told John Carvel, 'You could never get your own back if he decided to show you up. Nothing embarrassed him.' Linda also recalled, 'We were always brought up as equals. There was never any question that Ken was more important than I was because he was a boy. Mum's opinion was never any less important than Dad's and Dad always did the housework. I don't think Ken has ever felt superior to women, the way a lot of men did.'

Sex remained behind a closed door in our sheltered little world. Mum stopped our mixed bathtimes when I was seven and I really had no idea about this mysterious world of reproduction until I was in secondary school. There was never anything on the radio relating to sex, and even our first television portrayed an unnaturally sanitised world.

Before the first Clean Air Act was passed in 1956 most Londoners heated their homes with coal fires that produced a great deal of smoke, and with over a million manufacturing jobs in the city the fine black soot in the atmosphere demanded an endless round of cleaning. At the end of winter came the great spring clean during which everything was taken down and washed: the water would be black. Visits from friends or family unleashed another bout of cleaning and thus were discouraged, given the work involved. Callers were usually kept engaged in a long conversation at the front door rather than being invited in. It was not until I had my own flat with wave after wave of visiting friends and overnight guests that I realised how strange this was.

In today's London, with a vast array of cuisines on offer, it's hard to believe that we put up with the monotonous post-war diet that included liberal quantities of corned beef, Spam and bread and dripping. Europeans had mayonnaise and real orange juice, but we made do with salad cream and orange squash. The ritual of the Sunday roast hung over childhood like a promise of indigestion. Around nine o'clock on Sunday morning Mum would get up to put the cabbage on to boil and a chunk of mutton into the oven with the potatoes. By midday the cabbage would have simmered into an unrecognisable green mass made edible only with large quantities of HP Sauce. After masticating our way through the vast pile of food we all fell asleep in front of the radio to be woken in time for tea by Liberace tinkling away on the ivories. It was not until I went to work in South Kensington that I discovered the exotic foods we now take for granted, and I feel that I didn't have a good meal until Chinese and Indian restaurants spread across the city. (When she was in her mid-seventies Mum came to live with me and complained, 'The carrots could have done with another hour, dear.')

*

Like most South Londoners we used local facilities and trips by bus 'up to London' were a rare adventure reserved for Regent's Park Zoo, the Tower of London, the Monument or Madame Tussaud's. Like tourists in their own city, my parents never visited the same place twice.

The cinema played a big part in our lives. Nan regaled us with the plot-lines of all the great movies from the twenties and thirties. For a generation unable to visit the overseas graves or memorials of the relatives they lost in the war, a trip to the seaside was a big treat and so film brought the whole outside world into their lives even if it was only in the form of Hollywood sets. Nan was determined that my arrival would not interrupt their thrice-weekly visits to matinees, so they took along a tin of condensed milk and if I started to cry my dummy would be dipped in the tin and stuck in my mouth. I grew up with a love of cinema and a set of bad teeth. When we were older, the whole family would go to the Astoria in the evening, thinking nothing of joining a queue round the block for the second showing if the first was full, and later walking home eating a bag of chips in the crisp night air. At the end of every film the audience stood rigidly to attention while the National Anthem was played.

This routine was killed off by the arrival of our first television in 1955. My parents' opposition to public ownership meant they weren't prepared to buy a TV until the advent of commercial television allowed them to do their bit by supporting free enterprise. Apart from Mum's daily small bets on the horses, our family was not interested in sport – other than in the football pools, which led to a discussion every Sunday lunchtime about what we would do if we won the £70,000 top prize. Dad's dream of buying a small Scottish island and living in splendid isolation filled my sister with horror.

Through satellite TV and the internet today's children have access to more information than presidents or prime ministers did in Victorian times, but in the 1950s the outside world intruded on us only dimly. My earliest political memory is of the Pathé Newsreels at the cinema reporting that the war in Korea was dragging on; but the death penalty was one issue we were all conscious of, as our parents argued the rights or wrongs of the hangings of Derek Bentley and Ruth Ellis. I couldn't understand how Ruth Ellis could have killed the man she loved and I remember the gentleness with which Dad explained Ruth's act: 'Sometimes you love someone so much you don't want anybody else to have them.' I valued that moment because my father spoke to me as an adult rather than as a child. Our parents protected us by hiding the unpleasant but I wanted to be treated as a grown-up and was frustrated when they shielded me too much.

My heroes were two spacemen (they weren't yet called astronauts). Every week I eagerly waited for the *Eagle* comic to continue Dan Dare's endless struggle against the evil Mekon. Dan Dare was the firm-jawed, clear-eyed honourable Englishman who never panicked. On radio's *Journey Into Space*, set in the distant future of the 1960s and 70s, Captain Jet Morgan led the first British expedition to the moon (without an American in sight) and went on to defeat the Martian invasion of Earth. Andrew Faulds, the actor who played Morgan, later became a right-wing Labour MP who denounced the left in general and the GLC under my leadership in particular.

Although in some years I qualified for free school meals (so joined the queue of boys waiting until paying pupils had eaten first), Mum and Dad always scraped together enough to have a week or two by the seaside at Camber Sands or Seasalter on the Kent coast, and once we had acquired a car we went to Dunoon in Scotland to see Auntie Cathy. There were no motorways, and we had to leave at the crack of dawn to reach Carlisle by midnight, when the four of us would sleep in the car. My sister and I drove our parents mad by arguing for most of the journey before reaching Dunoon by the ferry across the Clyde in time for lunch. I loved the massed pipe bands and caber tossing at the Cowal Highland Games, but I didn't like it when Cathy's brother-in-law, Uncle David, embarrassed me by insisting I sit on his lap. Forty years later I discovered that my cousins had been sexually abused by him. They never told their parents, and it was only after one of them died that his wife told me how he had broken down and told her what his uncle had done to him. The secrecy about sex in 1950s Britain enabled paedophiles to operate with impunity.

*

Dad found work as a window cleaner on the shop fronts of Streatham High Road and after a few years managed to buy an old car to carry the ladders. In the evenings he worked as a stagehand, shifting scenery at the Streatham Hill Theatre. This was one of the largest theatres in Britain and as plays finished their West End run it was often the first port of call on their national tour. Dad got complimentary tickets for Monday-night performances and I was the only kid I knew who regularly went to the theatre. My pocket money came from a paper round, but I got a much better job one panto season when Hughie Green played Ali Baba and paid me thirty shillings a week to act as his stooge. This involved struggling into a woman's corset every night while pretending I had never seen one before.

Mum worked as a cinema usherette but when her babysitting arrangement broke down I had to go with her every evening for a week to watch Bill Haley in *Rock Around the Clock*. I was bored out of my skull. Mum also worked in the local baker's, and on Saturday mornings at Freemans catalogue-shopping headquarters. Linda and I were left alone in the house with strict instructions not to answer the door to anyone. My parents took on this burden of work because they wanted to buy their own home. Two or three 'slum-dwellers', as Mum called them, had moved on to our estate and she feared that this was the start of a long decline. However, Mum and Dad found the £4 a week they put aside for the deposit only kept pace with the increase in house prices. Eventually the estate agent arranged to loan them £100 to top up the £400 they had saved, and we moved two miles down the road to West Norwood. Having grown up during the Depression, Mum and Dad saw debt as something frightening and from the moment they took out their mortgage in 1957 they worked all hours in order to pay it off as soon as possible.

While Nan was babysitting us one evening she complained of a terrible headache. I tried to stay awake because she seemed so ill, but I eventually fell asleep on the end of my bed. I woke in the morning to be told that Nan had suffered a stroke and was in hospital. After she recovered she came to live with us and, following the death of Auntie Pat, Uncle Ken and his bulldog also moved in.

*

I was in my final year at St Leonard's when Aunt Pat died of TB. My parents told me that I shouldn't talk about her death at school, almost as though it was a matter of shame. Eight years later a chest X-ray revealed a TB scar on my lung. I presumed I had contracted it from Aunt Pat, but my immune system defeated it. Pat's death might have been a factor in what became my worst year at school as I sat in the back row giggling with the other boys doomed to fail their 11-plus. One day that summer we were in the Streatham milk bar with one of Dad's friends, who was proud his son had got into grammar school, while my parents said nothing about me. Mum took me aside and said that Dad couldn't bring himself to say where I was going because I had failed my 11-plus.

Despite this my parents felt I might have a second chance in the brand-new, eight-storey Tulse Hill Comprehensive, although with half a dozen grammar or fee-paying schools in the same catchment area it was comprehensive in name only. The thirteen forms in each year were rigidly streamed by ability. The top three were deemed to have academic potential and the bottom seven were expected to learn vocational skills in the twenty-six school workshops. The remaining three were intermediate ability classes, most of whose members were expected to sink down rather than rise up, and I was placed in the bottom one. Clifford Thomas, the headmaster, had been deputy head at Dulwich College and believed that if he imported a public-school ethos boys would be dragged up by their bootstraps.

Philip Hobsbaum, my first form master and English teacher, was an extraordinary man: a bearded, East-End-born secular Jewish socialist with a volcanic temper. After Cambridge he worked for a theatrical agency before becoming a brilliant, charismatic teacher who brought out the best in any child. In the 1950s, when racism and sexism were the norm, and women were expected to confine themselves to housework, he challenged traditional views and stereotypes and seemed almost revolutionary to us. While other classes sat in rows, he would sweep the chairs and desks to one side to stage an impromptu play or mock trial. The main wall was rapidly covered by a class newspaper. Philip later told John Carvel: '[Ken] was highly articulate and very friendly, a marvellous communicator. I thought he would have a future in journalism or advertising rather than politics. At the age of eleven he had great ability to get his points across and he was unflappable. He would always turn aside any aggression from other boys with a joke.' Philip introduced me to politics, too. Recalling a school visit to watch the House of Lords in session, he said that I was 'completely at home there, not at all in awe of institutions or being on strange territory'.

Late 1956 was an interesting time. During my first few weeks at Tulse Hill School, Britain, France and Israel invaded Egypt to prevent that country nationalising the strategically important Suez Canal and my parents and uncle were consumed by anti-Americanism when the US forced Britain into a humiliating withdrawal. At the same time Russian tanks rolled into Hungary and President Eisenhower was re-elected, while black Americans resumed their long struggle for civil rights. We debated all these issues at school, and in the first speech of my life I denounced Britain's Suez adventure: our biggest foreign policy disaster until the war in Iraq nearly fifty years later. When Philip staged a mock general election he decided I should be the Liberal candidate. When I asked Dad what I should say in my election speech, he told me, 'Just take a bit of the Labour policy and a bit of the Tory policy.' One consequence of my growing interest in politics was that it allowed me to row with Dad almost every evening at dinner time.

Although Philip taught me for only a year, he transformed my academic prospects by encouraging me to read – among other books, *Nineteen Eighty-Four* (the most important book in forming my political beliefs) – and at the end of my second year I was one of only two boys in my class to be promoted to the academic stream. Now being taught alongside middle-class students, I stayed friends with my old classmates from estates in Lambeth and Clapham. Hobsbaum went on to teach Seamus Heaney and other writers at Queen's University Belfast and was appointed Professor of English at Glasgow University, where he encouraged successful writers including the Booker prizewinner James Kelman. When I became leader of the GLC in the early 1980s, Philip came to see me at County Hall. I expected an old white-haired bear of a man to come hobbling into my office and was amazed to realise that Philip was only about ten years older than me and was quite small. By then the author of several books, he had retained his Jewish roots and told me how he had been beaten up on his first day at grammar school by a boy shouting that Jews killed Christ.

*

While Philip had awakened an interest in politics and armed me with some facts with which to challenge my parents, I was a long way from any coherent beliefs. Mainly I was arguing against things as they were, rather than proposing any alternatives. My social attitudes reflected the prevailing moralising ethos of the time. In his diaries, Tony Benn describes how the chaplain at the RAF training camp where he was stationed in 1945 led a debate about whether sex outside marriage could ever be justified. The conclusion was that it couldn't be, and this was still the prevalent view in the 1950s as my friends and I struggled to come to terms with puberty and hormones. There was no sex education provided by the school or our parents and absolutely nothing helpful on television. As in so much else, Orwell's *Nineteen Eighty-Four* changed my outlook as I read about Julia and her normal sexual appetites. My classmates shared my amazement that a woman might actually desire sex. Only later did I discover that Orwell had created a woman of the kind he wanted rather than one he knew.

Our parents warned us about 'Dirty Old Men'. This did not stop boys getting free equipment for their bikes by going into the back room with one of the shop assistants in the bike shop at Herne Hill. Mum wouldn't let me have a bike because it was 'too dangerous', so I could only guess what horrors happened in the bike shop. My attempt to change Mum's mind by practising on my friend's machine failed when I crashed into the front of a car and staggered home covered in blood.

My other inspirational teacher at the school was Raymond Rivers, who taught biology from my third year. His belief in the rigour of scientific method and determination to challenge anything unproven set the pattern that I hope I have lived up to. He was a committed atheist at a time when that could be a problem for teachers, who were required to state their religion when applying for a post, and declaring for anything other than the Church of England could influence the Appointments Committee. Raymond was a critic of the faux-public-school ethos of the headmaster, who tried to drive him out by removing him from his form class. This petty decision was reversed after boys asked their parents to sign a petition. I always believed Raymond's iconoclasm and atheism were part of a socialist worldview and it was a shock when after a gap of forty years he came to lunch at City Hall and told me he was a lifelong Tory and a strong supporter of Mrs Thatcher. Fortunately he was also a strong supporter of the congestion charge.

*

Raymond stimulated my fascination with biology, in particular with reptiles and amphibians. Starting with one newt and a few tadpoles caught in Brockwell Park, my bedroom rapidly turned into a miniature version of the Zoo's Reptile House. All four walls were lined with three tiers of aquariums and vivariums containing tropical bullfrogs, newts, salamanders, snakes, lizards (including two monitor lizards nearly a metre long) and an alligator which Mum worried would escape and eat our dogs. I couldn't resist taking my pets into the baker's where Mum worked to scare the staff but the only time my passion for reptiles involved any real danger was when a friend went on holiday and asked me to look after his poisonous Formosan vipers. He left me the serum which had to be administered within minutes of a bite to avert paralysis and possible death.

The heated tanks turned my bedroom subtropical, with rich smells wafting through the house. The worst moment was when the alligator passed a fishy stool into its eighty-degree water, where it gently simmered all day while I was at school. We came home to find the overpowering stench of alligator poo. I often forgot to put the lid back on the jam jar of bluebottle pupae and several hundred would hatch in the heated room and Mum would arrive home to be greeted by a huge cloud of bluebottles orbiting the light bulb. She stopped cleaning my room.

My interest in astronomy was fuelled by Patrick Moore's TV programme *The Sky At Night*, and Dad was as excited as I was when we went along to the newly opened Planetarium in Baker Street. At a time when society valued academic achievement more than celebrity no one thought it surprising that the lecturer was the Astronomer Royal. I also became closer to Dad when we spent several Sunday mornings mixing concrete to build my first pond.

I still hung around the streets with friends, but spent more time at London Zoo. I loved Guy the Gorilla, sometimes throwing him a bar of milk chocolate which he would delicately unwrap and slowly eat. Fifteen years later when he died under anaesthetic while having dental work I felt guilty and didn't complain when the zoo banned the public from feeding the animals.

Saturday afternoons were often spent at a pet shop in Tooting, chatting to the owner George Boyce about his imported reptiles, his Rotary Club activities and his Tory beliefs, but London's leading pet shop was Palmers, by Camden Town tube. Before laws regulated the keeping of dangerous animals you could buy a lion cub for £5 and in 1960 they had a young gorilla on sale for £1,200. I stood in front of its cage for ages fantasising about stealing it.

*

There were worse problems at home than those caused by my menagerie. I was too young to realise that Dad had the patience of a saint and it's hard to believe how he tolerated years of withering sarcasm from Nan and her attempts to poison my relationship with him. Another cause of strife was that Uncle Ken had promised to set up a joint firm with Dad to sell cloth to London tailors and this was why my parents bought a house big enough to accommodate Nan and my uncle. As interest rates rose my parents struggled to make ends meet and with Uncle Ken's failure to establish the business they weren't getting the income they had been promised. Finally, they told Uncle Ken and Nan they would have to leave. There followed several more rancorous weeks in the house before Uncle Ken moved in with the woman who would become his third wife, taking Nan with him. Now realising, at last, what Dad had been going through, I switched loyalties even to the extent of locking Nan out of the house when she went to the outside privy. With relationships completely severed it would be four years until Uncle Ken came to tell us that Nan had lost her sight after another stroke and had only a few months to live.

Things were also not going well at school. Although Tulse Hill produced the actors Ken Cranham and Tim Roth, *Guardian* journalist David Hencke and the poet Linton Kwesi Johnson, the school had grown to its maximum size of 2,300 boys and it became a more brutal place. In an interview with my biographer Andrew Hosken, a former pupil called John Land said, 'They used to say that if you could survive Tulse Hill School, you could survive anywhere.' Another pupil, John Harris, recalled, 'The cane was used quite regularly in the school . . . certainly bullying did happen and I learned to deal with that,' and remembered seeing older boys hanging a science teacher out of the window of the first-floor laboratory by his braces. Hosken also quotes Ian Scott, who recalls that I was one of those boys 'with a ball of string and an apple core half covered with frog spawn in his pocket'.

In the 1950s schools had several periods of games and PE each week, but I was still smaller and weedier than other boys in my class and never managed to jump over the horse or shin up the ropes. In cross-country running I came in ahead of only one incredibly fat boy. Our PE instructors behaved like the worst kind of British Army sergeant-majors, believing that if they humiliated you often enough you would eventually succeed, but all they did was destroy any interest I might ever have had in sport.

I started to play truant from school with the friends I had left behind in the sixth stream, hanging out in the derelict windmill in Brixton Hill. In school I would skip lessons and hide in the library, reading books about natural history and, for the first time, about politics. In my fourth year I was bottom of the class and forged my report to hide my lack of progress from Mum and Dad.

Mum told *Woman* magazine in 1985, 'I remember saying to Bob I don't know what will become of him because he didn't like school. He wasn't interested in going out with girls, or going to football. He wasn't interested in anything except his pet lizards and friends

– always wanted to be the boss. No, you couldn't say he was all that popular when young.'

I was one of the few boys in the fifth year who wasn't made a prefect, which probably had something to do with a speech I made at the school's open day when we debated the motion 'School Days are the Happiest Days of Your Life'. I opposed the motion and attacked the price of the school uniform, which was only available from Thomas's at Herne Hill, who had been granted a monopoly. Parents complained that school uniforms did not last as long as they should. There were rumours that there might be a relationship between the headmaster and the firm, based on no more evidence than their shared surname. Uncle Ken said it was made from overpriced low-grade wool. When I repeated this in my speech there was a burst of applause from the parents in the audience but I later learned that the staff had discussed whether or not I should be asked to leave the Debating Society.

In those days only one child in twenty in Britain went to university and my parents had no such expectations for me, although my sister was doing better, having passed her 11-plus and gone to a grammar school. When the time came for O levels I passed in only English Literature and Art. Two further attempts added only Geography and English Language, and so when summer term ended in 1962 I joined my dad on his window-cleaning round and started looking for work in the small ads of London's three evening newspapers.

My school days had not been happy and it hurt that I had not been made a prefect. I was glad to leave, but I knew I had wasted my opportunities and was embarrassed that Linda was doing so much better at her grammar school. For all my daydreams about being a famous scientist or another David Attenborough I feared I didn't have the ability or self-discipline to turn them into reality.

2

Into Africa

I was willing to help Dad on his window-cleaning round, but with chilly early autumn mornings and chapped hands I soon realised that window cleaning wasn't for me. I was passionate about animals, but neither London Zoo nor Gerald Durrell's zoo in Jersey had vacancies so I became an apprentice animal technician at the Chester Beatty Research Institute attached to the Royal Marsden hospital in Fulham Road. My first weekly pay packet contained six pounds and five shillings, but the job also came with a pension, so fulfilling my parents' ambition for me. They were delighted. At the job interview the company secretary graphically mapped out my life, saying I would start pension contributions at eighteen, I would retire at sixty-five and most likely die by sixty-eight (then the average male life span). As, of course, it was unthinkable that I would ever leave a job with a pension, I sat on the bus each day calculating that I would make the same journey 26,000 times before I retired.

The animal unit had eight or nine teenagers and five adults. The boss, Charlie Smith, had a robust approach to management. If I made a mistake he would grab me by the ear and drag me to see what I had done wrong. Everyone knew their place and we saw nothing odd about this. The work was repetitive and dull but I was also working with women. Tulse Hill School had been a boys-only institution, with male teachers, so the transition to work was exciting. Women technicians had a separate tea room as it was felt men and women shouldn't mix. The teenagers were all virgins as women didn't in general have sex with someone unless they were going to marry them. If a woman slept with a man because he promised marriage and reneged she could theoretically sue for breach of promise under the Married Women's Property Act 1882 because her marriageability was damaged. (The 1882 Act remained in force until 1970.) Men expected the woman they married to be a virgin but didn't believe the same rule should apply to them. We heard lurid tales of brides who had hysterics on their wedding night after seeing a penis for the first time. (In 1973 a friend was present as a doctor asked a man why he hadn't brought his wife to hospital when her breast cancer was so obvious. 'What kind of pervert do you think I am? I've never seen my wife naked,' the man replied.)

Films such as *Saturday Night and Sunday Morning* and *Room at the Top* added to our fear as we watched lives ruined by pregnancies and illegal abortions. Many friends got married out of sheer sexual frustration rather than love, or as the Rolling Stones put it in 'Sittin' on a Fence': 'they just get married 'cos there's nothing else to do'. All my schoolmates did so by their early twenties. I hated the way men talked about women and began to prefer female company. When I did have girlfriends we faced the problem of where to go to be alone, as parks were still patrolled by keepers on bikes ensuring that moral standards were upheld.

Old hands at work scared new recruits with tales of haemorrhoids being operated on next door in the Royal Marsden. We listened to horrific tales of people limping to the toilet and screaming with pain for days following surgery, wondering how long before it was our turn, unaware that with the advent of better diets and over-the-counter creams we were unlikely to have to face the ordeal.

That time now seems like another world – shabby, dull and dingy. Travelling to work, everyone dressed in shades of grey, with colour a rare exception. Young men were sent home from City firms for daring to wear a pale blue shirt instead of a white one. Yet we were just a couple of years away from the explosion of music, fashion, lifestyle change and psychedelia that would be known as the Swinging Sixties.

Realising what I had thrown away at school, I started evening classes at Norwood Technical College and got O levels in Human Anatomy, Physiology and Hygiene and an A level in Zoology. As my interest in politics grew the local library became a haven where I pored over *The Economist*, the *New Statesman* and the daily papers.

From a wholly working-class Tory background I was suddenly surrounded by a very left-wing environment at work. Of the technicians I worked with, all bar one were Labour supporters. Their influence combined with the dramas unfolding in the world outside changed my politics for ever.

The seminal event was the Cuban missile crisis of October 1962. Following President Kennedy's blockade of Cuba we talked about the real possibility of full-blown nuclear war and what we would do in the four minutes left to us if the air-raid sirens sounded. Our virginity narrowed the range of options. My workmates wanted at any cost to avoid catastrophe but I was angry that the US could unilaterally blockade Cuba for introducing missiles when they had already surrounded the Soviet Union with nuclear bases.

*

If Cuba was the worst crisis of the times, the Profumo scandal was the most bizarre. It's hard to imagine the impact the affair had on how we viewed our rulers and betters. There was a code of silence in the media about the sexual shenanigans of the upper reaches of society. The establishment could lead lives of debauchery as long as it was hidden from the masses.

Apart from the odd society divorce in the 1950s nothing prepared us for stories of nude bathing and orgies at Cliveden, the country seat of the *Observer*'s editor David Astor. The news that

Christine Keeler had been sleeping both with John Profumo, the Secretary of State for War, and with a Soviet spy unleashed a media storm. MPs pretended to be shocked that a minister had lied to Parliament and pontificated about the threat to national security. Papers reported rumours of sex parties where a cabinet minister was seen naked except for a hood and some honey smeared over his genitals, which were inserted into a jar full of bees. For Middle England the real scandal was not that Profumo shared Keeler with a spy but with a black man, 'Lucky' Gordon.

Centuries spent persuading us that the great and the good were born to rule and were of higher moral calibre were blown away that summer of 1963. Radio and television had until then been polite to the point of obsequiousness. All that now changed as programmes such as *Beyond the Fringe* and David Frost's *That Was The Week That Was* used satire to debunk the self-serving image of the governing class.

*

When I got home on Friday 22 November there had been nothing to suggest that this day would change my life. Mum gave me my dinner on a tray so I could go into the living room and catch the end of the BBC's news round-up with Cliff Michelmore. The television came on just as the phone rang on Michelmore's desk and after a moment's silence he relayed the news that President Kennedy had been pronounced dead. I went and told Mum and Dad but Mum thought I was joking. The BBC replaced its scheduled programmes with sombre music and ITV was forced to do the same after a storm of protest from viewers as they began the scheduled episode of *Emergency Ward 10*.

We spent the rest of that evening glued to the television as details of the assassination came through including the arrest of Lee Harvey Oswald. We didn't take seriously the suggestion by some in the American media that this could be a Soviet plot and Mum was more concerned that Vice-President Johnson looked like an American gangster. That weekend became a crash course in American politics for the hundreds of millions watching and, although I didn't realise it at the time, it started an obsession with politics that would change the course of my life. Because Telstar, the first US communications satellite, had recently been launched we were getting US television coverage almost as it happened and there was a feeling that the whole world was watching these events unfold. The following day over dinner we watched as Jack Ruby shot Oswald live on television, an event Mum dismissed as 'just what you'd expect from Americans'.

Although I was critical of Kennedy over the Cuban missile crisis I was devastated by his death. He had grown in office and in his final year as president I had been moved by the stand he'd taken on civil rights, and with the nuclear test ban treaty it seemed that Kennedy might bring the Cold War to an end. I was also impressed by the way his brother Robert dealt firmly with the Southern segregationists. The powerful imagery of Kennedy's funeral both set in train the legend of the modern Camelot, as it was intended to do, and drove my interest in politics.

*

Back in Britain, my political allegiance was settled not just because the Tories imploded but because a dynamic young leader took over the Labour party. Harold Wilson embraced classlessness and meritocracy and promised the modernisation of Britain. He dominated the politics of the time as Tony Blair did thirty years later, but, unlike Blair, Wilson was grounded in the Labour movement and did not believe that the private sector was always superior to the public one.

I literally trembled with excitement as Labour won the 1964 election, believing that Wilson would transform Britain and abolish poverty. My rows with Dad increased due to his cynicism about Wilson's motives but as the Labour leader began to disappoint me I drifted leftwards, never forgiving him for dashing the hopes he raised – which led to the return of the Tories six years later. Each generation in turn is seduced by leaders who promise so much and deliver so little, creating a cynicism which destroys the hope that parties can transform society. Perhaps it's part of growing up, but I never again invested so much hope in a politician.

I consumed books on the USA past and present and believed in the ideal and promise of America. I followed the 1964 American election contest between Johnson and Barry Goldwater (the G. W. Bush of his day). I was addicted to *Slattery's People* (the *West Wing* of 1965) in which Richard Crenna played the minority leader in a state senate. I was gripped as he dealt with local problems and politics and thought what a great job that would be.

Another hero – an unlikely one for a young atheist like me – had been the octogenarian Pope John XXIII who, after decades of reactionary leadership in the Catholic Church, was elected as a stop-gap in 1958 but had gone on to transform the church until his death in 1963. One hundred years ago the Catholic Church was hostile to democracy, signed a treaty with Mussolini and did not oppose the rise of Hitler in Germany. Catholicism impacted on our family because Auntie Cathy married a Catholic and had to promise that the children would be raised as Catholics. As my cousins left Dunoon in search of work they stayed with us in London, bringing tales of religious bigotry between Scottish Catholics and Protestants.

The first sign of change was when John XXIII appeared on the balcony overlooking St Peter's Square and, unlike his predecessor Pius XII, opened his arms wide to include the crowd in his blessing. He convened the second ever Vatican Council, unleashing reform as the bishops and cardinals debated the role of the church.

He struck a blow against anti-Semitism by absolving Jews of the murder of Jesus Christ. He began a dialogue with other faiths and ended the ban on Catholics even entering a Protestant church. One ex-Catholic friend assured me that before John XXIII any Catholic tourist who wandered into a Protestant church while sightseeing was automatically excommunicated from the church. He set up a commission to review the ban on contraception and in the last months of his life began to address the role of women in the church. All this was resisted by the Curia, the bureaucrats who run the church, so when showing visitors around the Vatican John XXIII joked, 'I'm only the Pope around here.'

The Swinging Sixties had also arrived while these exciting political changes were going on. I no longer spent lunchtime in the museums of South Kensington but strolled the King's Road appreciating the receding hemlines. As a fan of Bond books I read that he had olives for breakfast and, seeing them for the first time, I thought it would be sexy to do the same. I found them disgusting. My conservative moral values were under assault. I still felt that promiscuity was a bad thing but would have made an exception for myself had the chance arisen. Sadly, any chance of romance was dramatically reduced by my herpetological hobby. In all the Saturday afternoons I spent chatting to other reptile enthusiasts in George Boyce's pet shop, only one young woman ever came in and she was dating another collector. I was undoubtedly a bit of a geek, very ungroovy and still living with my parents, so I was quite shocked when Mum announced, 'Now you're working you can stay out all night if you want,' to which Dad replied, 'I don't know about that, Eth.'

Different rules applied to my sister. Linda's pregnancy at sixteen was the death knell for my priggishness. As kids we had been best friends but grew apart in our early teens. We knew our family was slightly weird and suspected that Mum and Dad preferred our two dogs to us as their love was unconditional and they didn't answer back. But Linda and I reacted differently to our family. I decided I did not want kids, but she escaped the family by creating her own as soon as she could, getting married and having two adorable children. She created a happy, child-centred family which owed nothing to our rather Victorian upbringing.

Nowadays teenage pregnancy is commonplace but in 1965 it was a very different story. Mum went on endlessly about what the neighbours would think and the shame Linda had brought on us. Given Mum's own illegitimate birth and uncle's annulled marriage, double standards were certainly at work. Dad was much more supportive and I was firmly on Linda's side.

It would be five years before Linda got a council flat, so her husband Malcolm moved in with us and with the birth of Maxine and then Terry the house was a livelier and happier place, if also a more cramped one. I joined Malcolm on his Friday-night South London pub crawls. The house vibrated with pop music as the Beatles, the Stones and Bob Dylan changed how we thought and lived. Their music was more of a challenge to Conservatism than any of the politicians with the exception of Roy Jenkins, the Labour Home Secretary, who liberalised censorship, divorce, abortion and homosexuality.

*

Uncle Ken came to say Nan was dying and we went to see her on Christmas morning. I was distraught to see that the woman who had been such an influence on my life (as well as having saved it) was blind, frail and barely able to leave her bed. For the three months remaining to her we took turns to sit with her but I was warned not to say I was a Labour supporter as the shock might kill her, so we talked of her childhood, the wars, and her hero Sir Winston Churchill.

Dad had always forgiven Nan because of her difficult life, but on her last night before she slipped into unconsciousness she told Dad she was sorry for the way she had treated him. As we followed the hearse to the crematorium everybody in the streets stopped and took off their hats, as was the custom in those days. Like Herbert Morrison, Nan was born the year before the LCC was created and died as it was absorbed into the Greater London Council.

That autumn Ian Smith's racist government in Rhodesia declared independence to prevent black majority rule. In every other colonial rebellion, British troops had been sent to restore order, but Wilson feared there would be a backlash if he sided with black Africans against our white 'kith and kin'. I had furious rows with friends who didn't believe black people were ready to govern themselves or shouldn't be allowed to govern whites. These rows brought me closer to the Ghanaians I worked with at Chester Beatty and for the first time I had black friends.

Although I was still a bit of a prig, I was changing. I no longer wished to spend my life safely accumulating a pension, so I quit work to hitch-hike through Africa with my best friend Mick Towns. I had read *The Year of the Gorilla* by George Schaller and wanted to reach the remote area on the Uganda–Rwanda border where these gentle animals lived. We planned to travel along the coast of North Africa to Cairo and get a boat up the Nile to Uganda, though in the end our journey took a rather different course. Neither of us had left Britain before so we rushed to get our passports and injections to inoculate us against various diseases. We were not helped by the Labour chancellor Jim Callaghan, who introduced an emergency budget measure which stopped anyone from leaving the country with more than £50. While it was possible to have two weeks' holiday in Spain with that sum, we wondered how far we would get before our money ran out.

We knew nobody who had hitch-hiked in Africa and so we relied on books and magazine articles. The only advice from Mick's dad was to look out for the amazing rolls the French made with real butter. They were called 'croissants', he told us.

*

We spent the morning of Wednesday 28 September 1966 packing our rucksacks, which weighed well over 50lb each, and then the whole family, including Linda and baby Max, piled into Dad's car for the drive to Dover to see us off. Arriving in Calais too late to hitch a lift, we spent our first night under canvas. The local police who were observing us thought it was hilarious when I fell backwards into a ditch as we tried to erect the tent.

The warnings we'd heard that French drivers rarely gave lifts were confirmed as we wasted two days trying to get one. My diary records that those who did pick us up included a man armed with a gas spray gun in case he was attacked and a woman who worked in educational TV. 'Girls are very confident here,' I wrote. 'One who gave us a lift just turned round and said everyone would think Mick was homosexual because of his long hair. I was stunned at her frankness.' The weather was terrible, and I was shocked that northern France was so run down and ramshackle. I wrote, 'We can see the price France must pay for President de Gaulle's nuclear madness.' (France had been conducting tests on nuclear weapons in the deserts of Algeria since 1960.) Older women were invariably dressed in black and 'the girls are nowhere near as pretty as in London; they also lack mini skirts and it now seems odd not to see girls' knees'. The further south we went the more people stared at Mick's hair.

Disabled war veterans were everywhere and France seemed much more backward than Britain. 'The toilets are very awkward and often lack wash basins. The French don't bother about flies and only flick them away when they get near their eyes or nose,' I wrote. But I didn't know then that President de Gaulle had cut military spending by 40 per cent and redirected the money into a massive programme of investment which would result in France leapfrogging Britain by the end of the decade.

From the outside, houses appeared to be in terrible condition, but inside they were impeccable, as we discovered when a young man who gave us a lift took us to meet his mother-in-law. She fed us a wonderful home-cooked meal and I discovered, and immediately copied, the French habit of eating each item on the plate separately. After the meal we sucked Eau de Vie (80 per cent alcohol) from sugar cubes.

The weather and the scenery improved in the Loire valley with sandbanks on the gentle river, beautiful châteaux set in the hills and cave houses carved into the rocks. In a local café a grizzled old French communist invited us to try a glass or two of Vouvray and told us of his time in the French Resistance and what it was like to cut the throats of the Nazi occupiers and their collaborators.

We finally gave up hitch-hiking and took the cheap midnight train to Bordeaux. The train was packed and we stood for the whole journey, arriving at three in the morning. Someone gave us a lift straight to the Spanish border. We crossed over near San Sebastián. The campsite was four kilometres out of town and 300 metres up a hill, but the view was fantastic and it was dark enough for me to see the Milky Way with the naked eye for the first time in my life.

*

In Madrid we stayed at a campsite which was 'very sandy, and full of large ants and loud-mouthed Americans'. I was shocked at the oppressive presence of Franco's armed fascist police and the sheer number of civil war veterans with missing limbs standing around selling cigarettes from small trays. 'The people are stunned at our clothes and Mick's hair, they seem to be about two years behind in fashion and six months in records. The girls don't kiss except on the cheek from very close friends. They don't understand the idea of a political opposition and have not heard the name of Russian premier Kosygin. The whole population seems to live in a walled-up world which nothing penetrates.

'The zoo must be the worst in Europe. But delicious food, squid and onions, cold hake with bowls of sauce, veal in its own juice, cold potatoes and mayonnaise, cold omelette, fruit salad in red wine.' My Spanish was so rudimentary that when I ordered a beer the waiter brought me a pear on a plate. 'Madrid is full of delightful little fried-fish shops (octopus, prawn, whitebait and dozens more). The highest building is only 32 storeys. Mick loves Madrid and wants to live here permanently.'

On our way to Granada we got separate lifts and on reaching La Carolina at nine that night I could find nowhere to sleep. Mick had the tent with him, so I decided to walk twenty-five kilometres to Bailén, the next town. I didn't know that Mick was in the tent behind a hedge five feet from where I was dropped off.

'It was raining very lightly but after two hours I was near collapse, a vast blister covering the whole of my heel. But I got a lift from an Algerian. He wore a heavy gold bracelet, had jasmine-scented breath – most odd. He had a portable record player alternating between the Beatles and a horrible Arab dirge. Arrived in Granada two in the morning, holed up in a local garage until it stops raining at six, when the whole street became alive with bats.'

I stayed in a cheap hotel and explored the Alhambra palace with the beautiful 'snow-capped Sierra Nevada mountains which give a glorious backdrop to the blazing white Arabic city'. Mick arrived in time to catch Françoise Hardy on TV. 'She sang five songs all told, which is three more than I had ever seen in the UK. I just can't understand why we never see her on British TV. She is so much better than any other girl singer.'

The wildlife was beginning to fulfil my hopes. The walls in southern Spain were covered with lizards and fat geckos. I caught one but it dropped its tail and escaped. I crawled around looking at the red and black beetles, massive grasshoppers and giant locusts but my favourite species was the red and grey hummingbird hawk-moth which fed through its two-inch-long proboscis as it hovered before flowers. The ponds of the Alhambra were filled with edible and marsh frogs. 'Very few birds, they eat them all here and their place is taken by bats.'

Homosexuality was still illegal in Britain. We met many gays from many countries, but they had the sad quality of exiles. Mick (better-looking than me) seemed to attract them. 'One queer American asked Mick if he'd like to wrestle in the grass,' I wrote.

At Gibraltar we 'arrived late at night and took beds at the Toc H youth hostel, run by an old boy of seventy-four called Jock, which was full of Yanks and Aussies (all very decent). Mick had the misfortune to take the bed with the bugs.' With its population of 20,000 squeezed in and around narrow traffic-congested streets, Gibraltar reminded me of Brixton with sunshine. St Michael's Cave was full of stalactites and we learned that there are thirty miles of galleries inside the rock dating back to 1799 with bizarre English names like the Great North Road. We climbed halfway up the rock to see the monkeys. One of them gave me a rabbit punch when I tried to stroke its baby.

Everything was very expensive so we went to Smokey Joe's for our meals, which consisted of chips and grease with everything. There were no licensing laws and in one pub 'the owner was the most extravagant queer I have ever seen and the two girls behind the bar might have been boys. When we left the owner gave Mick an extra big wave.'

The Sudanese embassy official said we could not travel through southern Sudan to Uganda because of the civil war (which continued into the twenty-first century) but three trekkers from the youth hostel said they were going across the Sahara desert on a lorry route from Colomb-Béchar in Algeria down to Niamey in Niger and then on to Ghana.

I had read about people trying to cross the Sahara and dying. In 1948 three Frenchmen tried to walk eight miles there after their car stalled and they'd all died. A decade earlier, an Englishwoman had died of thirst a few miles from In Guezzam, on the Algeria–Niger border, which she could have seen if she had climbed further up the rock on which her body was found. But an eighteen-year-old London taxi had sailed across the desert without any problems and travelling in November the temperature would be a relatively bearable mid-nineties Fahrenheit in the shade (if we could find any). Since our original plan had been scuppered, we decided to risk it.

*

We left Gibraltar with Stanley Barker, an Aussie, on a ferry to Tangier. 'We took a hotel room after much haggling. Left the light on all night to discourage the bedbugs but a few still appeared. The Casbah is very dirty, has a large traveller population of self-conscious misfits and real "don't-cares" (they all talk about hash as though you are abnormal not to take it). One Norwegian became the third person to ask me if I was an Aussie because of my accent. The Arabs insistently offer hash or boys or girls or dancing or an illegal exchange rate.

'Sat on the Rabat road in blazing sunshine for three hours before getting a lift from a Yank with a young Swedish girl in tow. The van was made out like a house but the weight of us caused it to expire and we had to get out at a tiny little town where we waited twenty-four hours before another lift. The walls were covered with geckos and the ground was alive with millipedes, lots of cattle egrets, lots of dead horses around. Got a lift from a Moroccan called Dadi who said that Moroccan boys were very nice. We've just heard that Prince Charles had broken his nose at rugby, it quite put us off our food. Mick's got bumps like golf balls from gnats or maybe bed-bugs.'

Morocco was a medieval dictatorship under King Hassan, whose security services had murdered the exiled opposition leader Mehdi Ben Barka in Paris. 'The coins are interesting. Pre-1963 show a big-nosed, fez-wearing Hassan whereas the 1965 coins show a remarkable likeness to Kennedy.'

From Fez, we travelled to Oujda and then into Algeria. 'The lifts come in fits and starts going 40k one day and 400 the next. The scenery in Morocco was very barren and sunny but here in Algeria it is very green and rainy. The weather broke two days ago after a long drought and everywhere is under about six inches of water. The night before last we spent an hour looking for a site to pitch the tent on the road to Algiers but the road is surrounded by orange orchards all of which have become orange ponds. I managed to fall back into a great mass of sticky mud and emerged with bi-coloured jeans. That night we had to camp on a lay-by with noisy traffic rumbling by, all in all not our best night . . . large number of oranges for breakfast and after shivering in the icy wind all morning we got a lift into Algiers. I had my torch stolen by one of the passengers.' This was, I should say, the only time on our trek that anybody stole from us.

At the youth hostel we caught up with Stan and Dave, another Australian. The place was full of Australians, Americans and a host of Europeans. 'Long, loud discussions on contraception in India lasting into the night. The travellers here all sleep with their money at the bottom of their sleeping bags. The habit is catching and we have become very distrustful. Harry, the American, asked Dave if he knew where the bathroom is. Dave's response was I don't know about the bathroom but the shithouse is out the back. The hostel treats everyone like kids with lights out at 10 p.m., which is odd because half the people are over forty. We went to see the botanical gardens where the ponds are full of painted frogs [*Discoglossus pictus*], all males, brown, grey, spotted, striped, all fat as butter and don't swim away when we pick them up. The zoo was as bad as Madrid's. A large jam jar with holes punched in the top and stuck down with Sellotape contained a pink horned viper. The attendant said he'd rather I put the jar down.

'The Algerians are a good bunch and on the whole quite cheerful. Things are as expensive as in Europe and we are still waiting to reach the places where people tell us you can live on a shilling a day. A letter I sent home from Tangier cost one shilling and sixpence, the price of a cheap meal. We manage to pass ourselves off as students and get cheap meals (chicken and haricot beans) at the university. Criticism of the regime is very open and we could see only one picture of President Boumedienne and only one Vive Le President sign. There are a lot of right-wing nationalist Arabs around. One chap told us that the British were hated because there has been no action against Smith in Rhodesia but English students are good because they dislike Smith.

'We went to the local Palestine Liberation Centre, which is full of poor deluded idealists who think that Jordan will give back their chunk of the West Bank for a Palestinian state. They believe that Kennedy was killed by the Jews because he was going to help with the liberation. I gave one of my "all men must live in peace" turns, then sat back and read the *New York Times* while Mick and Stan kept at it for an hour. We all parted amid handshakes and smiles.'

All I knew about the Palestinian issue was Israeli propaganda from the film *Exodus*. I did not know that the Palestinians had been driven off their land into refugee camps and this was my first chance to hear their story. I wasn't persuaded of the Palestinians' case but an image that stayed with me was of a young man telling me his father had gone back to look at the house he'd been forced to leave and as he stood outside the new Jewish owner abused him until he left.

My diary goes on: 'One of the Aussies has just returned from Colomb-Béchar having been halfway through the Sahara. He says the French are still in control of the interior of Algeria and there's much more traffic than he thought. The cars and lorries always stop and there are loads of little villages where people give travellers eleven days' hospitality according to the Koran or something. All the guff about how hot it is in the day and how little water there is is way off the mark, so Mick and I are now much happier about our prospects of getting through.' Fortunately for us we didn't take the route via Colomb-Béchar as there were many landmines in the desert near the border, and three Brits were blown up by them soon after we left.

'Left Algiers on 8 November and got a lift to Blida, where we picked up another lift from an old FLN member who is now chief of electricity supply in the Djelfa area. When we reached Djelfa he took us to a local carpenter's shop where he met up with all his old comrades in the FLN guerrilla army. We sat around in a large circle with a bottle of Ricard and one glass. Each person would have the glass in turn and down it in one go. Each time the glass started a new circuit the amount of water in the Ricard would be reduced. He translated the tales the Arabs recounted of their long violent struggle against the French. As the Ricard came round with less and less water I kept making excuses to go to the loo just before it reached me. This was to no effect and I have no recollection of how we got to our hotel room. The next morning we waited until twelve o clock when he dragged us off for a couple of beers and two steaks each before setting off on the road to Laghouat.' The café the Arab took us to had an open-plan toilet in the middle of the floor. This consisted of a hole in the ground surrounded by a metre-high wall. People were quite happy to relieve themselves while custom-ers dined at the tables pressed against the wall. I decided to wait.

'The driver drank bottles of beer consistently as we drove through the day and to reassure us that his drinking had no effect on his driving he stopped the van and with 100 per cent accuracy shot a succession of beer bottles out of the sky as we threw them up for him.'

At Laghouat, a large oasis with acres of date palms, he put us up in his house. His garden was filled with orange trees and huge toads (*Bufo mauritanicus*, to be precise). These creatures must have been here for millennia before the Sahara became so extensive, I thought, as there is no way they could have made it across the desert from oasis to oasis.

'The next morning we soon got a lift to Ghardaïa. The rains had been very heavy and the car stalled twice in the streams that cov-ered the roads. We camped that night – our first in real desert, but I was awoken when a large cockroach fell on my face. Then a lift in the back of a lorry down to In Salah. After El Goleh the tarmac gave out and we hit the rough old earth track. You spend the day being bounced a foot or so into the air and by the end of the day my bottom felt like a squashed tomato. That night we all climbed into the back of the lorry and I tried to sleep in an Arab cloak and found it most cold until I slept sitting up with my arms around my knees. The driver let us eat from the communal bowl of spiced soup with bread and grapes to follow. Eight of us had to share only three spoons but we didn't dare insult the driver by refusing.

'In Salah is very depressing due to its desolate and grubby nature. Just a few palm trees and a filthy little market with dried meats and dates all covered with swarms of flies. We camped in the shelter of a garage as there was a medium-sized sand storm for a couple of days. The heat was terrible in the day but we kept fairly warm at nights. Our presence attracted some large stag-beetles, but there was nothing else to be found in the place. The shops are all identical, they sell three kinds of jam, sardines, cheese spread and corned beef. We get bread from a baker's which everyone crowds around at opening time and pushes and fights to get into (queues don't exist outside of Britain).' Because of the heat we were able to pour the corned beef from the can onto our bread. 'You would just lie in the shade', I wrote, 'until evening and then go to sleep. Sometimes it was too much of an effort to talk. I write much slower and seem to be unable to apply myself to anything. It's 4.30 and the sun is setting so the flies will go away soon.

'After two days a couple of lorries drew up and agreed to take us all south for free (Stan was still with us). The scenery was quite depressing with huge blackened mountain gorges and endless stretches of sand. The gorges of Arak were impressive, a narrow twisting road ran alongside a small stream banked by sand and a considerable amount of greenery. The second night we camped in a flat sandy area surrounded by sharp cruel mountains in a perfect circle about seven to ten miles across. There was a small central peak which I climbed in the last rays of the sun. When I got to the top the sun had set. The whole thing was like the surface of the moon and I could have been standing in the centre of a small crater. Sometimes the mountains seemed pink or blue but it may be the high flint content which reflects the sunlight. The sand is red and sometimes the black mountains form a line between the blue sky and red sand. There were a large number of antelope droppings and hoof prints. The place was covered in snake tracks (sand viper?) and I caught a little gecko scuttling along the dunes which froze in the torchlight. It was almost translucent.'

Then my diary records: 'On the third day I had my bad bout of diarrhoea.' This got worse by the hour and the following morning I was passing crystal-clear green mucus laced with blood and was too weak to walk. This was clearly dysentery, which meant that for forty-eight hours, although I was drinking a lot of water, I couldn't retain any of it. I was losing weight so rapidly that my watch band was hanging off my wrist. As we were at least a day from the next town – Tamanrasset – I didn't think I was going to make it and lay there thinking, I'm only twenty-one and I'm going to die without having done anything worthwhile.

The lorry driver was now really worried. He bundled me into his cab and after driving for a short distance suddenly did a ninety-degree turn off the road, driving straight into the desert. Eventually we saw a barbed-wire fence stretching the length of the horizon with a door in the middle of the fence and a bell. After twenty minutes a jeep full of French legionnaires appeared. They took one look at me and led us to the French military post at In Ekker, which was a base for the French nuclear test programme. The French army doctor gave me twenty-six pills to take on day one and sixteen pills each day for three days and said we had better stay until I had recovered.

It seemed to work. 'The two-day rest was very good and we had showers and free food and drink and a nice clean compound of houses like an old Western fort.' The legionnaires, who I discovered earned only £3 a week, were getting ready to evacuate at the end of the year as the French were moving their nuclear test programme to the South Pacific and turning the whole area over to the Algerian government. It is a nice irony that I owe my life to the French nuclear programme.

A legionnaire gave us a lift to within a hundred kilometres of Tamanrasset and we hitched a ride in a jeep for the rest of the way. We passed through the town of Tit and found our first praying mantis, gold-flecked, along with our first scorpions – about two inches long, coloured yellow and grey-green. At Tamanrasset two young air-traffic controllers (with only two planes a week, they weren't very busy) let us stay in their house for a few days. No one was allowed to leave the town before 23 November as President Boumedienne was due to visit and they wanted to make sure the place didn't look too deserted. 'As it's cooler we spend our time sitting in the house playing cards and chess with one trip out each day to check for lorries and buy the usual bread and sardines. At night all the non-natives go to the local hotel (we don't, as it's expensive), nothing else happens, except for the once a week showing of *Zorro* in the local school.'

The big day arrived. 'The President drove through today and everyone was tidied up for the occasion. In his wake he brought a BBC man looking very British and a *Pravda* reporter. The BBC man bought us about ten shillings' worth of food, which is very helpful as we didn't have a single Algerian coin left. The next day we went to customs and spent six hours waiting for our lorry (the customs went mad and looked in everything, even Mick's vitamin pills). Before we left three peace corps workers from Ghana came through and gave us the USA mid-term election results.' The Democrats had done badly with huge Republican gains. I said it was depressing that Ronald Reagan had been elected governor of California, but one of them assured me that it would be great because 'Reagan is so reactionary that within six months he'll create a revolutionary situation'. Unfortunately this was wildly optimistic. They advised us to get the train from Kano to Lagos. We promised to see them in Ghana.

*

As we crossed the border into Niger 'the temperature grows (hottest yet, almost unbearable between noon and 3 p.m.). We came to a vast forest of thorn trees (all flat-topped due to the wind) with just a few tiny leaves. We saw our first gazelle (a bit like a Grant's) and a lone wolf. The water holes are listed as good but as the water was green we stuck to our own.' The lorry driver allowed us to top up from his water supply, which was carried in whole goat skins called gherbas.

Along the way we came across 'quite a lot of Tuaregs on their camels with huge long swords. Some of them wear brightly coloured pouches and very highly coloured turbans which have just a slit for their eyes.'

Fortunately we got to Agades before my next bout of dysentery announced its arrival with stomach cramps. Several locals helpfully carried me to the town's 'hospital', where an injection worked quickly. The doctor invited us to stay in the hospital hut, which had two wooden beds. Before we lay down I flashed the torch over the cracks between the planks and discovered thousands of bedbugs lined up side by side squeezed between the planks waiting for their next meal. We slept in our tent.

'The town centre', I wrote, 'has a large depression where everyone goes to defecate while vultures hop around looking for anything edible. Very large black and red wasps here . . . Today is Sunday and the African who is driving us to Kano tomorrow took us to see the local races which were the same as in Britain except at the last race the horses galloped off into town with the crowd following, screaming and shouting. Afterwards the driver gave us some couscous and a bit of vile cheese-flavoured, rock-hard biscuit. All the food had sand in it.

'On the trip down to Zinder the vegetation picked up a lot and we left the desert behind. Found the largest scorpion and stone-like crickets. The savannah is pale green and dry, with low spiky trees everywhere. Saw a Patas monkey on the horizon and lots of ground rodents with long bushy tails.

'We were twenty-five miles south of Agades when suddenly the car swerved off the road and went chasing after three adult ostriches and about twenty of their young. All the Africans jumped out to catch the young ones. I was chasing after one with an African just in front of me when the ostrich turned round and ran into my feet. As the others that had been caught were destined for the pot I insisted on keeping Horace, as we decided to call him. He is about two feet high to the top of his head and we feed him banana, to-mato, oranges and bread. He walks around at the end of a rope, pecking everything in sight. When we get to Accra we hope to give him to the zoo.

'We resumed the journey to Kano. The bloody driver of the jeep was driving too fast at night and knocked down a camel which for-tunately got up and hobbled away. We pulled up at the Nigerian border and slept there until it opened. The next morning the im-migration officer was very British and only gave us a five-days visa as we didn't have much money.

'We arrived at Kano at 9 a.m. Hot, dry, very crowded, open gut-ters on each side of the street, Agama lizards everywhere, females grey with yellow on head, males bright red head, red and blue tail. Small head frills. Scales very rough. They were on every wall and unbelievably fast. There were no flies in Kano. The begging is ter-rible, all the time, all the people.

'We stopped at the Paradise Hotel, ten and six a night, filthy bath and bog.' Every square inch of my body had a mosquito bite in the morning. 'Horace slept in the corner of the room, which became very hot and shitty. De-ticked Horace and gave him a shampoo. Left him to dry on my bed but he crapped and it ran right through the mattress. Mick chewed lettuce while I held his beak open.'

We had arrived in Kano just a few weeks after the massacre of every Ibo man, woman and child by the Hausa majority and there were still bloodstains all over the walls and pavements. 'We met some Brits behind the counter at Barclays who told us that on the night of the killings they didn't see anything. The next morning things were bad (one whole trainload of Ibos were made to get off and all were hacked to bits). The result was chaos and the trains were held hostage by Eastern Region, which means now there is only one train a week instead of one a day. The Ibo blame and hate Britain for it all as the Hausas love Britain and the British government kept supporting the undemocratic regime.

'We had to pay £2.18 shillings for the train to Lagos. The ticket man called us to the front of the queue to give us tickets. We also had to keep answering the question why, as white people, we were travelling third class. The next morning we set off with Horace in a towel. The platform was crowded and we had to fight for a place after a panic caused by the train leaving too soon.' I remember that we had loaded up with bread and bananas as the journey would take over twenty-four hours. Every single square foot of the train was occupied, with people sitting on the roof and hanging on at the end of each car. The only way we could get in and out of the carriage if we wanted a pee was by stepping from armrest to armrest and then hanging off the end of the carriage. At one point while I was relieving myself, the train suddenly emerged from the jungle into a field filled with women who collapsed laughing at the sight of me hanging off the back of the train peeing into the air.

Most of the people getting on were Yorubas, who were terrified that if they didn't get out of Kano quickly they would be the next ethnic minority to be massacred. The mood on the train was incredibly tense until we passed out of the Hausa-dominated north.

Horace had the capacity to produce as much guano as the entire bird population of Trafalgar Square, so by the time we went to sleep our little corner of the train was pretty disgusting. I was woken up in the night as we pulled into a station. The man opposite had kicked off his sandals, which was unfortunate, as that was the spot where Horace had decided to relieve himself and the man didn't have time to clean up before he slipped them back on and got off the train.

*

We had read the old official English colonial guide to Lagos, at the time a city of just 364,000 people (today there are nearly eight million), which warned us: 'Dress for Europeans by day consists of long trousers, white shirt and long sleeves, a tie and a head covering. On official occasions a jacket or dinner suit is worn.' It also warned us that 'Lagos does not offer any tourist attractions which would make a trip to the outlying country worthwhile'.

My diary notes that 'the train arrived at Lagos at 4.30 p.m. the next day and we got a bus to the beach where we pitched our tent. Horace caused a big stir.' The beach was occupied by two local religious prophets (one had a monkey on his shoulder) who conducted services with their attendant nuns intermittently through the day and night. To our amazement the American Harry appeared and invited us to camp with his friends Stewart and Alan, who had parked their little French 2CV along the beach. 'Horace promptly crapped on Harry's groundsheet. Everywhere in Africa the whites discuss bowel movements. Lizards scuttled around the holy men's compound. Transparent pink crabs come out in their thousands. Swimming all the time but at night algae emitting blue light cling to your body.' One evening I decided to go for a swim after everyone had gone to sleep, so I was naked. One of the religious leaders came down to the beach with all his white-clad nuns and was obviously waiting for me to finish swimming before they began their ceremony. I kept swimming in the hope they would go away but in the end I couldn't do anything except emerge and walk past them in acute embarrassment.

When I tell people we spent a week on a Lagos beach leaving our possessions in the tent as we explored the city, returning to find nothing had been touched, they can't believe it. But what was striking about Africa then was the optimism and confidence people had in the future. Mick and I never felt threatened or at risk: everywhere people were welcoming and incredibly hospitable.

I wrote home to my parents: 'There are some relatives of people at the Chester Beatty we will stay with while we potter around in Ghana. Then we hope to get a job for about three months and get the boat back home (for about £49 on a passenger boat, third class, it might be cheaper on a cargo boat if we can find one). I didn't write from Kano because things are not yet back to normal after the killings two months ago. On the Sahara crossing Mick and I did nothing but talk about what we were going to eat when we get home: fishcakes, rissoles, fish and chips, chicken, shepherd's pie, bubble and squeak and a vast Chinese meal. Out here we eat bread and tinned sardines or corned beef, cooked yam, lots of oranges and endless banana sandwiches. We sold Horace yesterday to a children's school (they could only afford thirty shillings but as it's a good home we didn't mind). I would have liked to bring him home but I don't think we could ever have house-trained him and the export licence for animals is pretty steep. We have just got our visas so we hope to leave for Ghana tomorrow. I've got some addresses and with a bit of luck we will be able to sponge over Christmas.'

Mum replied, 'We were pleased to hear you found a good home for Horace. Linda was hoping you would bring him home with you, can you imagine what the dogs would be like and what about the garden?' Dad added, 'I suppose you are quite up to date with all the recent events in Rhodesia. It's been quite exciting politically. Harold has had a field day in the news during the crisis . . . I rather envy you at the moment. Mum and I are both quite proud of what you have achieved so far. Hope you manage a decent job together . . . lots of love from everyone and a special true blue greeting from Dad.'

Alan Gough, a friend from work, wrote, 'The Rhodesia crisis as you probably heard is now at a head . . . your findings of how the coloured people are treated by the white gods out there I have found invaluable only this morning, to quote you in a very heated argument on the present crisis. It never fails to surprise me how at times like these some of one's closest acquaintances turn out to be shit houses. You will be interested to hear, and I might add also delighted, in the past few months I have become a confirmed atheist, surprised? I spent many hours on reading the work from the Dead Sea Scrolls and have visited the Masada exhibition that is now in London. So that's one up to you. Eh?'

My diary continues: 'The next morning we left for the lorry park at the railway. After a two-hour wait we piled in the back of a flatbed truck with several mothers and carsick children. The road to the border was red with dust with low forest and palm trees. We passed small villages made of corrugated iron and mud.' We were driving along the coast road passing from Nigeria through Dahomey and into Togo. 'The land became more sandy, more palm trees appeared and we saw a long procession of drum-beating villagers at a fishing village in which the huts were on stilts in the sea water cut off from the beach. At Lomé we slept on a filthy beach with pigs and sand crabs, one of which got in my sleeping bag.

'The beaches in Ghana are more like the south seas with long log fishing boats and crashing blue seas only marred by the continual stops for police checks.' This was eighteen months after the military coup overthrew President Nkrumah and I wrote home that 'things here are rather wobbly at the moment, the old government (all one man of it) left the economy in a terrible state and as a result the prices are the worst we have seen since we have left England, we don't do bad though and we live off pressed pork from communist China at two shillings and ninepence for a big tin. At night we wander around the markets and buy a bellyful of yam and banana. We are staying in a peace corps hostel which only costs four shillings a night and is the best place since home – real baths, toilets and very clean. The only drawback is the enormous cockroach that emerges from under the bath and scuttles around the floor until you get out of the bath and then dives back under it. We are going to go upcountry for a couple of weeks to see the old, untouched forests. When we get back to Accra we will try and get home unless we get some work, which is highly unlikely as the government likes to restrict the number of whites employed here as they might be accused of being imperialist lackeys by Mali. Also whites send all their money home which causes an economic crisis. All the people here are very friendly though (one Ghanaian rushed out of a bar and gave me a pint of beer as I was English and then spent an hour telling me how he hates the Russians as they ruined his country).

'The hostel is set on a hill behind an embassy with Agama lizards everywhere. In Lagos my attire of jeans and T-shirt provoked horror among the white swine and some natives, just not on. It's odd for the local people to be exposed to the open shirts we were wearing as they don't normally see them on whites, and the whites don't usually mix with locals. The locals find our navels funny (one yam-seller reached across and stuck her finger in mine to see if it was real). There was a terrible gap between black and white in Lagos, neither side knows the other. At the High Commission in Lagos I told a British official we were planning to go into the jungle, he replied, "You realise that you would be travelling with Ghanaians, don't you?" The people in Ghana don't beg very much but they are still friendly with exchanging addresses.

'Yesterday we hitched out to the Volta dam but didn't get there as an Indian from Kaisers, the big steel firm, picked us up and took us to his gliding club. He gave us a huge meal in the flat which used to belong to Hanna Reitsch [Hitler's female pilot] until Nkrumah was thrown out when she fled to Germany. She was very close to Hitler in the war and flew the first manned doodlebug. That flat was like a palace. After coffee Mick went up in a glider but before I could go up a terrible storm came and Mick had to come down pretty quick. One parked plane was torn off the runway and smashed to bits so I guess I was quite lucky not to be up at the time.

'We went to Aburi botanical gardens. On the trip we saw the fantastic view from the escarpment and Nkrumah's palace. Mick kicked over a pile of logs to reveal a black snake but by the time I caught up with him it had slithered away. Saw our first soldier ants. The undergrowth alive with insects with frogs living in the shade of rotting palm tree segments. One huge tree is the sole remnant of the original rain forest.

'Bad planning in Ghana is almost beyond belief. China factory without a clay supply, sugar cane factory without water, bottle factory running with vast inefficiency causing overpricing, tarmaced roads to the villages in which Nkrumah's relatives lived.

'Met Ron from Enchi and Jeff [the peace corps workers we met in the desert]. They drove along to Saltpond past the small Arab slave forts and the amazing beaches with fishing boats. Stopped at Jeff's bungalow. Club Beer is vile. That night I wandered round the bungalow with a dim hurricane lamp until I caught a toad. Inebriation gave the toad the advantage.'

We stopped in Tarkwa, where we ended up in conversation with two local girls outside a bar one evening. They complained about the English 'come-on'. One said it's almost a dormant, slow approach, followed by an all-of-a-sudden 'bang'. '"Are they joking? I'm never sure," said one girl. "How did the English ever propagate!" the other asked. We explained to them about the grim side of the Englishman's approach to sex and the vulgar, unsophisticated approach of the US male.

'We left Accra on the twentieth and went with some peace corps geologists to Enchi (population 150) which is miles into the jungle. On the way up we saw a black cobra and ran over another brown, yellow and red snake which didn't get off the road in time. At Enchi we went off into the jungle with a geological gold survey group and two guides (it took four hours to move three miles) and saw the most unbelievable number of butterflies of every colour, shape and size, centipedes, millipedes, tarantulas, land crabs, small lizards and three frogs in a gold panning pit. Mick bought a squirrel. We called him Hubert. He eats oranges and bananas. He was in very bad condition at first but after twenty-four hours' sleep and some food he is beginning to look respectable. He has a black and brown peppered coat and a ringed tail.

'Enchi is very small but has a large bar-cum-dancehall open to the air. Everyone is dancing "highlife" [a slow, suggestive shuffle]. The four of us would sit in the corner and Ron would get his man-servant to find his girlfriend and arrange to meet secretly so as to protect her from being overcharged by the shopkeepers if they know she is sleeping with a white man. The second night at the bar Ron's girlfriend came and sat down and I thought she wanted to sleep with me but she was only making suggestive Nigerian dance signs. Back at Ron's caravan we all had our photo taken while she kept rubbing Mick's arm (Mick was most disturbed).

'Mick and I slept in the tent outside the caravan but first I had to evict three toads and one skink which were living under my pillow. We slept under mosquito nets for the first time. At night the air is full of glow worms. In the morning the mist is so dense it hides even the nearest fields. That day Alan and two bushmen took us into the deep bush a half-hour's drive on the logging roads, and then straight off into the bush, which was dark, damp and muddy. A green trail at first giving way to a stream of muddy water. We were taking rock chippings everywhere to test for gold. We only went two and a half miles but it seemed like ten. I was unsuccessful in my attempt to lure a frog by imitating its call. On the way out of the bush one of the bushmen pushed me to one side and slashed down with his machete to cut the head off a venomous puff adder. It was perfectly camouflaged, so I was about to tread on it. He wrapped it up in a large bandana and carried it on his head while it still writhed. We had it for dinner, it tasted a bit like chicken. We passed three hunters who called Mick "madam" as they assumed he was my wife.

'We came to a small village with a central tree about forty feet high, full of nests which were round bundles of twigs with the entrance underneath. The birds were brilliant yellow with black heads and tails. The back was brownish yellow. Finches? The whole tree was alive with them (at least sixty nests) twittering and chirping. The village chief has protected them. At Samreboi there is a plywood plant and a large British community (all drinking) plus reports of a huge frog. Huge spreading trees with some branches having fallen to the ground and rotted. There is nothing but these for a long stretch and it is completely sunless inside the jungle.

'We spent Christmas at Asankrangwa with the Salzmans, a young American couple who gave us vast amounts of food (though I did have to decapitate the Christmas chicken for them) and the local native palm wine which tastes good provided it is drunk down in one gulp. We told the Salzmans about our home life and British inefficiency. Then a long conversation about how the peace corps wants its volunteers to mingle with the community and why this doesn't occur.

'The rain forest is all around now, huge spreading trees with lots of weaver birds nesting in them. We also found singing termites, a big mob of them get on a dried leaf and jump up and down in time causing an audible noise yards away. This was happening everywhere in the jungle and there may be a connection with the driver ants as they seem to be out in force with the soldier ants sitting upright with pincers in the air forming a double line through which the workers storm at a fair old pace.

'On Boxing Day we went into the jungle on our own and got lost and ended up walking over a tree bridge following one of the palm wine trails (each morning the natives tap the palm trees to get the sap, which is neat palm wine).

'After Christmas we set off to Kumasi at five in the morning and reached [peace corps worker] Ollie Olson's house at 11 a.m. The road up to his house was lined with vast plantations of cocoa and we slept and read until Ollie and Will Reiser [another peace corps worker] arrived at 8 p.m. I was traumatised when I accidentally killed two geckos I hadn't seen in the door hinges. The next morning we all piled into a jeep and drove forty miles west to Adobewora. The road was pretty bad and by the end was two wheel tracks with a two-foot gully running down the middle. The camp was in a clearing with a caravan and four tents. Sand flies started on Mick the moment we arrived. That night we had yam chips and a spinach substitute made from the middle leaf of the cocoa plant. We had the usual good rows with a right-winger called Michael James on Vietnam and Bobby Kennedy. I found a vast caterpillar with a nasty line in venomous spines and another one encased in spun silk with bits of wood and leaf attached a bit like the British caddis fly larva. One night in the caravan a large mantis flew onto my leg. We put it in a large jar and fed it a grasshopper which it ate bit by bit, licking each leg clean and then discarding it with a disdainful flick of its wrist. The next night we went out with Paul [another peace corps worker] and his carbide lamp after a short, sharp downpour, to look for a tree bear (hyrax, a guinea-pig-size relative of the elephant) which makes a howling screech which builds up into a frenzy lasting a full minute which is usually answered by another or one of the huge flying squirrels which glide from tree to tree or a bush baby which makes a hideous shriek. We wandered into a cocoa plantation when the lamp gave out. This was just as a bush baby started to call so we couldn't find it.

'We left Adobewora to return to Kumasi for New Year. A cowherd had left his cattle in the front garden of Ollie's house. Ollie had a vast New Year's Eve meal in preparation and lots of beer to consume. Mr Boateng, his friend Charles [relatives of my friends at Chester Beatty] and three other Ghanaians as well as Ollie's 'wife' all went round the market to buy cassava for the party. The party revealed the intense right-wing attitude of the Ghanaians who had contempt for anyone less lucky than themselves. But we spent a pleasant evening listening to 'Harbour Lights' and reading Bertrand Russell's *Why I Am not a Christian*. The next morning Ollie took me to the cultural centre to see the drums, gold ornaments, Ashanti stools and carvings. Later I went to meet my work colleague Jacob's uncle. After a beer he took me to meet Jacob's mum and then on to his chicken farm. He drove very slowly as he was plastered, but he took me to his house where we had some Martell brandy.'

*

I received a letter from George Boyce, the pet-shop owner:

I was sorry to hear about your unwelcome enteric condition during your trip across the Sahara and your equally nauseating experience at the Peace Corps party. The latter intestinal upset was, as you suspected, no doubt caused by the native beer, although I would suggest not so much by the beer but by the amount of local saliva that is expectorated into the beer to encourage this revolting mixture to 'work'. Well Ken, to be serious for a while, has the effort been worthwhile. You have certainly covered a vast area of Africa at a nominal cost, experienced the 'seamier' side of life and encountered illness without the benefit of a national health service. I imagine that experiences such as these must have the effect of helping to mature ones outlook. All the 'lads' and 'lasses' at the shop have asked me to convey to you their best wishes for your continued success in the termination of your journey. To these felicitations, Ken, I would add those of my own and of course Doris. Yours as ever, George.

My diary continued: 'Returned to Accra and the peace corps hostel where a young Ghanaian wanted to know if I was a Russian spy and if I was really English why didn't I have a big nose. His brother had just arrived in Brixton and didn't seem to like it, but we then discussed freedom and I spent an hour assuring him that many people at home think like I do. As he left he clasped my hand and said, "You are a plain man, you carry your heart in your hand."

'We went to visit another of Jacob's relatives, Mr Adjety, who showed us round his furniture factory. He took us to meet his friends, the director of the state farming corporation, the secretary general of the TUC and the ex-minister of agriculture. The meal was foufou, which tastes of potato with the texture of chewing gum, and rabbit in hot peppers followed by much beer and a long conversation on the Nigerian problem and sex in Kumasi.

'We were invited to the Deputy British High Commissioner's house and he and his wife were a marvellous and unpretentious couple with lots of kids. After dinner the kids went off to play football while I stayed to talk politics and play a little golf. The oldest daughter Dawn drove nine of us in a Mini to a party of self-conscious teenagers, playing the Beatles' 'Tomorrow Never Knows'. Mick takes an unnecessarily harsh attitude to the white kids out here when really they aren't to blame for being so cut off from the average man.

'Went out to a small village eight miles past Aburi at the invitation of the local chief. The chief's secretary had sent out the wrong date however and we just sat and discussed the price of cocoa for half an hour and left (Mick made his intentions to the chief's daughter embarrassingly clear!). The next day I checked the shipping lines and spent the rest of the day in the library while Mick ran aground on his plans for the chief's daughter. On Tuesday we left for Saltpond and got in about noon and went down to the beach straightaway. An endless line of coconut palms stretching off into the mist and a beautiful blue sky and sea with great white cresting waves pounding in. Lots of shells and urchins, puffer fish, moray eel and turtle. That evening went to sleep after a nice chat on foreign policy.

'On the way back to Accra in Castle Road was a very large pond swarming with dragonflies of red and blue, a bird of unimaginable blue swooped over the pond and back, a large black bullhead-like fish sat looking up at me. Everywhere large frogs, possibly *Occipitalis*.

'Next day we went to Tema harbour very early and checked all the ships, even Russian ones, for a passage home. All negative. We were guided round the docks by an ex-Liverpool barber who insisted he could give Mick a fine haircut. On Saturday we were surfing again and then down to the town. In one bar a Negro said he was happy to talk to white men as white people don't go to the Negro bars. In another we listened to music from the VC10 band, the Balingo dance was a seduction one which leaves nothing to the imagination and caused one old dear to drag her youthful partner out of the dance. There was a huge roar of approval from the crowd. One Englishman said, "I must admit I'm rather embarrassed at being in an African bar."'

*

We never found a ship, as all the berths were booked months in advance, so we went home the way we came, across the desert. Everyone in the hostel warned us to leave soon as there was about to be an army coup in Togo and the border would close. We said our goodbyes, exchanged addresses, told everyone to visit if they came to London and set off just as the Harmattan began. This is the cold, dry wind that sweeps cruelly across the desert. The nearest West Africa gets to a winter. Suddenly the sea water is cold and the waves are stronger.

My record of our return journey is fairly brief. 'The bridge over the Volta had been completed so no more ferry crossings were needed. The guy who gave us a lift in his jeep ran into a buzzard which we thought was dead so we stuck it in the back with us to eat later but alarmingly it suddenly woke up and with a large, sharp beak, started taking lumps out of everything within reach so we let it go. Walked through Lomé the next morning and reached the Dahomey border at midday and got a lift to Cotonou in an old mammy wagon which broke down three times before it got to Porto-Novo, the capital. After trying at youth hostel went in search of an English teacher called Dave Mills. His headmaster, very nice, drove us to his place. Long discussion about the rights and wrongs of giving Africa a European culture.

'We got to Lagos and booked the train to Kano, this time the journey took forty-six hours as the train broke down and had to be repaired. Very few lizards now in Kano given that it's cold and dry. Streets are full of dust, your nose cakes up, lips crack and you need glasses to keep dust out of your eyes. Street sellers make huge omelettes, two feet across, filled with vegetables. You just buy as much as you want.'

We arrived in Niger and looked up our peace corps contacts Jack Little and Victoria Soucer. 'They have to really rough it: no lights, mud huts for girls, grass huts for men, lots of diarrhoea and dysentery. Victoria is working on the social status of women and Jack is trying to improve the peanut crop. After coffee at Jack's two Frenchmen invited us round to their place where a party was in progress with roast lamb which ran with blood in the French tradition and Scotch. After the party we went round to the house of a local French peanut factory owner (who hated Negroes). Jack did not see any hope for Niger except as a cattle producing country but the Hausas consider it beneath them to herd cattle. He doesn't have a high regard for the French way of independence. He thinks there is a love/hate relationship between the French and the African civil servants, who are going to take over when and if the French ever go.

He saw the French owner of the peanut farm kick his manservant. After blaming the Cold War on Truman I crawled into bed about 2 a.m. Next morning at 6 a.m. after coffee, peanuts, dysentery and a Terramycin tablet we went with Vicky and her friends to Zinder.

'As we continued north we saw several large monitor lizards, two or three foot long. We walked out of Zinder past the main water supply, a small lake filled with African lilies and two dead donkeys. Camped at the roadside for the night near three dead cattle and lots of bones. Wind is now stronger and quite cool and very dry. The next day we got a lift on a lorry with thirty-five other people which stopped every ten miles for emergency check. After a day without food in freezing wind and chasing another ostrich we arrived at Agades. The change in the place is stunning. Everything is dry and sandy. All the plants have gone. We got on a lorry going all the way to El Goleh. We passed a vast number of cars (seven) of people going south, mainly Aussies, Swiss and Germans. We got stuck in the sand quite a lot. One of the goats on the lorry died and the driver cut it up and gave us a leg.

'We carried on north until just outside Arak we came across the memorial to the Arabs who died fighting the French in Algeria. It's just a few stones but with an amazing mountain backdrop and a green flag on top. Every lorry circles it twice as their way of showing respect and the ground is now worn smooth.

'We arrived in Algiers and went back to the hostel to discover that the toilet still hadn't been cleaned. The next morning we booked up to go steerage in the hold for £7 each on the boat to Marseilles. I went back to the botanical gardens and collected some of the painted frogs to take home [where they lived happily in my garden pond]. They were still the same specimens in the same gullies that we had seen in November. The boat left at seven in the evening and took twenty-three hours to cross in terrible seas that seemed to be rising and falling so violently that we had to lie flat to stop being seasick. We were in the prow of the boat which was very crowded with Algerians who had had too much to drink. Fortunately we slept on the hatch cover so we were above the vomit.

'From Marseilles we got the train to London via Paris for 166 francs, which left us with just 20 francs in total. We didn't hang around as we both wanted to get home as soon as we could and had run out of money. Northern France was ice-bound, and the Channel was cold and beautiful and I felt quite emotional as the cliffs of Dover came into view.'

Customs viewed us with suspicion and asked if we had ever tried hash. They searched through everything and were surprised to discover our collection of desert rocks and frogs.

We took the train to Victoria and I arrived home at 3.30 on a cold February afternoon in time for tea. Everyone said how well I looked, but I felt very tired. The dogs barked briefly and then ignored me.

3

Years of Upheaval

1967–1971

Africa changed me. What struck me in those very different cultures was what I had in common with them. And the Westerners I had met were graduates, but I held my own in our debates about politics and life. The nerdy English boy with no expectations except a pension now wanted something else, but I had no idea what it might be.

Just after my return from Africa Chester Beatty Research opened a unit in Sutton with the aim of finding a cure for childhood leukaemia. I was really excited when Alan Gough, head of the animal unit, took me back as his deputy. This was my first position of responsibility and it was a job I believed in. At the time, a diagnosis of leukaemia in a child was a death sentence. Researchers were divided into rival camps. One believed the cure lay in conventional chemo and radiotherapy, but our unit believed in stimulating the immune system to defeat the cancer. We took the cancerous white blood cells of children and injected them into sheep whose immune systems killed the cells. Then we took sheep antibodies, injecting them into the child to attack the cancer. The improving techniques triggered longer and longer remissions.

Each day in the main hospital I passed angelic children all doomed to die unless we found a cure. Seeing the children, I knew we were justified in experimenting on animals if it saved their lives and I got angry when people said the life of a rat was as important as that of a human. Eventually chemo and radiotherapy did prove to be better, and anti-vivisectionists might argue that our work was wasted, but along the way we developed our understanding of the human immune system and so helped discover treatments for other diseases.

Late one Friday a doctor rushed into our unit claiming he had found the virus that causes leukaemia, but we had been handling that virus for months, sucking up body fluids containing the virus from the mice we experimented on through small pipettes. All of us had got a mouthful at one point or another, so after a worrying weekend we were much relieved when he admitted he was wrong.

*

During my travels I couldn't believe how little of the original West African rain forest remained and how seldom on our journey we had seen anything much more exotic than a rat, so instead of keeping amphibians as pets I decided to try breeding them in captivity in case they became extinct in the wild. I was the first person to breed the frog *Hymenochirus curtipes*, a central African dwarf frog, in captivity after the Natural History Museum gave me a pair. They were completely aquatic and by chance I did not have an aerator bubbling away in the tank when they mated. The male grabs the female from behind and they swim upside down, scattering sperm and eggs which hang by microscopic threads from the surface film. They need still water to breed, so had an aerator been in the tank the eggs would have sunk to the bottom and died.

I first got in touch with the Natural History Museum as a schoolboy when I discovered twenty-four albino frog tadpoles in a local garden. Only a handful had ever been found before so I had visions of breeding them and making a bit of money. But they all died in the bitter winter of 1962–3. The preserved frogs I'd brought home from Algiers went into the museum's collection.

Professor George W. Nace at the University of Michigan at Ann Arbor was establishing a frog bank so with each breeding success I dispatched a packet of live amphibians to America. Nace asked if I would like to work in his unit but I had fallen in love and wanted to marry, though by the time she turned down my proposal I had given up frogs for politics. Mum was so worried I would never marry that she taught me how to cook.

*

Nineteen sixty-eight was arguably the most dramatic year in Western politics since the Second World War; it certainly changed my life for ever. By 1967 I had become disillusioned with Wilson for his spinelessness against the white racists in Rhodesia and for failing to devalue the pound and protect jobs in British industry, but this was nothing compared to my growing anger at the US aggression in Vietnam. In 1945, after the Japanese wartime occupation ended, the communist leader Ho Chi Minh set up an independent republic in what was then French Indo-China and asked for American support. Instead the US and Britain restored French colonial rule. After eight years of war the French were defeated at the battle of Dien Bien Phu but the US thwarted Ho's victory by threatening to use nuclear weapons unless Vietnam was split between a communist north and a US puppet state in the south. The people the US supported were a small Vietnamese Catholic elite who had collaborated with the Japanese occupation. The cynicism of the US has never been more clearly expressed than in President Eisenhower's autobiography *Mandate for Change*, which was published in 1963: 'I have never talked or corresponded with a person knowledgeable in Indo-Chinese affairs who did not agree that had elections been held as of the time of the fighting possibly 80 per cent of the population would have voted for the Communist Ho Chi Minh as their leader rather than Chief of State Bao Dai.'

The 1954 peace deal brokered by Russia and Britain promised a free cross-border vote on reunification in 1958 which would determine the future of the whole of Vietnam. The US backed the Southern regime in refusing to allow that vote, so Ho Chi Minh started fighting the corrupt and brutal President Diem. Buddhist monks protested by burning themselves to death. The lack of support for Diem's regime led President Kennedy to authorise an army coup against it, and the Diem brothers were executed in 1963 by the colonels who took over. The military regime in South Vietnam only survived because it was propped up by the US. President Johnson refused to accept that Ho Chi Minh was the popular choice to lead the country so the US rained death on its people north and south of the border, bombing and shooting civilians in vast numbers. Many US troops slipped into drug addiction and committed atrocities against innocent civilians. The news media reported what was going on, and support for the war in the US declined while the world watched in horror as images of napalmed women and children and destroyed villages appeared nightly on television.

My views on foreign policy were crystallised by the book *From Yalta to Vietnam* by David Horowitz, which appeared as a Pelican in 1967 and demonstrated the lengths to which the US would go to overthrow governments to secure economic advantage. The US propped up brutal dictatorships as long as they could siphon off wealth or use land for military bases while claiming to defend democracy from communism. This book did more than any other since *Nineteen Eighty-Four* to make me a socialist. Ironically, the author became a rabid neoconservative in the 1980s and today runs a project that accuses left-wing academics in the US of supporting Islamic terrorism.

By 1968 I had decided to join the Labour party, but changed my mind when Home Secretary James Callaghan, a man devoid of any liberal instincts, pushed a bill through Parliament denying Kenya's

Asian population entry to Britain. When Duncan Sandys had negotiated independence for Kenya earlier in the decade he had given
Kenya's Asian minority British passports in case they were ever dis-
criminated against. As Kenya began denying their economic and
civil rights Sandys, ratting on his promise, demanded we rescind
their right to come to Britain. With the *Mail* and the *Express* whipping up hysteria Wilson capitulated for fear of alienating voters.
TV commentator Brian Walden, who had been Callaghan's parliamentary private secretary at the time, told me that as Callaghan
saw him going into the No lobby in the House of Commons he
said, 'If you go through that door your political career is finished'
– as indeed it was. There were thirty-five Labour rebels: a mixture
of left-wingers like Michael Foot and honest right-wingers who ab-
horred racism (Roy Jenkins found a reason to be absent). I was so
disgusted I put off joining the Labour party and in Labour's leadership election in 1976 I supported Michael Foot rather than Tony
Benn because Benn had voted for Callaghan's bill.

Meanwhile the drama continued to unfold in Vietnam. On 30
January 1968 Viet Cong guerrillas overran the main South Vietnamese cities and occupied the grounds of the American embassy
in Saigon. Although driven back by US troops, their courage and
sacrifice exposed the lie that Ho Chi Minh had no support in the
south. The respected US television newscaster Walter Cronkite's
reports demolished the claims of Johnson that the US was merely
defending an independent country from a communist invasion.
The Vietnamese were fighting for independence just as Americans
had done in 1776 against King George III.

The US General Westmoreland (who insisted that Vietnamese didn't value human life as we do) demanded another 206,000
troops to add to the half a million already losing the war. The response of US voters was far less belligerent and Johnson won the
Democratic primary in New Hampshire with just 49 per cent while

the anti-war Senator Eugene McCarthy got 42 per cent. Then Senator Robert Kennedy announced that he would run for the Democratic nomination. Faced with losing to the man he most loathed, Johnson announced his retirement.

The left didn't trust Robert Kennedy, who had been a right-winger in his twenties and early thirties. His decision to run only after Johnson had been weakened by McCarthy confirmed suspicions that he was driven purely by ambition. I disagreed. As Attorney General in his brother's government he had been changed by the civil rights struggle, and after his brother's assassination he took up the cause of America's poorest citizens, both black and white. McCarthy was too cool and intellectual to connect with ordinary people. The American feminist Gloria Steinem knew she was right to support Kennedy when she watched McCarthy ruffle a small black boy's hair and then wipe his hand on his trousers. She was reminded of the cold, pinched-faced banker who denied her father a loan. With Robert Kennedy in the race I felt there was a chance a president could be elected who would change the world. It would be forty years before I felt that way about a US candidate again.

For young people the prospect of electing Kennedy was too far off to wait for and demonstrations against the war filled the streets in cities around the world. Chanting 'London, Paris, Rome, Berlin, we will fight and we will win', students staged public protests and occupied their campuses – most dramatically in France, where they were marching against both the war and the autocratic General de Gaulle. And the young marched against racism in the US and South Africa. This generation, raised with the sound of their own music, began to experiment with sex and drugs even though they still risked expulsion if the opposite sex stayed overnight in halls of residence.

In Britain, radical youth alienated by Wilson turned to activists like Tariq Ali and his magazine *Black Dwarf*, which denounced both the Soviet Union and the US. Tariq was also the public face of the International Marxist Group (IMG), but its marches and occupations were insignificant compared with the upheaval in France, where the student protests were transformed when the communist-led trade unions called a general strike. Paris and other French cities were brought to a standstill, with brutal conflicts between police and protesters. De Gaulle flew to meet French generals and get their backing to break the protests, and mobilised the conservative French countryside against the left.

The protests collapsed and there was a swing to the right in a snap general election but attention had already shifted to what was happening behind the Iron Curtain. In Czechoslovakia the communist reformer Alexander Dubček came to power committed to humanise and democratise the communist system. Having already rolled back Khrushchev's de-Stalinisation programme, Brezhnev and the Soviet leadership were terrified that reform might threaten them and began to issue veiled threats. Student demands for reform in Poland were brutally crushed.

In America the establishment feared the Reverend Martin Luther King's campaign against racial discrimination, which was also beginning to tackle issues of class and the war in Vietnam. These movements coming together threatened change on a scale unseen since President Roosevelt's New Deal. The FBI under J. Edgar Hoover was obsessed with King and black radicalism. If King's murder by James Earl Ray on 4 April 1968 was part of a conspiracy it remains unproven, but I believe it was the threat he posed to the powerful that led to his death.

The ghettos erupted in anger at the assassination of their best hope and greatest leader. In 1968 most police forces were white and racist and horrific indiscriminate shootings by the police followed King's death. In the heart of the black ghetto in Indianapolis Robert Kennedy made a powerful plea for unity between black and white. Kennedy was the only politician capable of bridging the racial divide in America, which was reflected among his supporters, the white working class and poor blacks who won him the California primary on 5 June. Just after midnight, shortly before he went to thank his followers, he took a call from Mayor Daley of Chicago pledging his support at the Democratic convention. As Daley was the crucial power broker in US politics, this was the turning point which would have taken Kennedy to the White House but the extremist paranoia that led to the death of Martin Luther King was about to claim its second high-profile victim as Kennedy was shot three times by Sirhan Sirhan, a Palestinian Christian incensed at the support America had shown for Israel during the recent Six-Day War. In the space of two months the hope of change in America had been extinguished for a generation.

President Johnson had agreed to peace negotiations with the Vietnamese but just as he was under maximum pressure to end the war he was let off the hook by the decision of the Soviet Union to invade Czechoslovakia and brutally snuff out Dubček's attempt to create 'Socialism with a human face'. While a quarter of a million Russian and other Soviet bloc troops marched into Prague, Chicago was convulsed by violence as peace campaigners besieged the Democratic convention. Vice-president Hubert Humphrey defeated Eugene McCarthy for the nomination, but he was a poor campaigner and Republican Richard Nixon squeaked into the White House. The powers that be relaxed, after a worrying year, confident that it would be a long time before any force arose to challenge them. The peace negotiations in Vietnam dragged on for four more years, allowing President Thieu to continue looting Vietnam until he finally loaded his plane with gold and fled to the UK, where he lived the rest of his life in luxury in Surrey.

*

Throughout this year I was an observer glued to the TV, hoping that a new politics would be born. I got involved only once, one evening when I joined an anti-war march down Charing Cross Road, but by the end of the year I could see that all the challenges to the status quo had been defeated both at home and abroad. In order to achieve change I knew I had to join the system and change it from within. Challenges from outside the establishment had more chance of success if there were sympathetic people working on the inside for the same goals. I agreed with Daniel Cohn-Bend-it, a leader of the French student protests, when he said, 'We must begin the long march through the institutions.' He later became a Euro MP for the German Green party.

Race became a bigger issue in the UK when Tory MP Enoch Powell's 'rivers of blood' speech, arguing against immigration, triggered racist attacks in London. Black bus conductors and others were verbally and physically abused. But Labour's position on race was not much better. London Labour MP Bob Mellish actually complained of immigrants 'pouring off the banana boats'. In a cabinet subcommittee meeting Richard Crossman recorded: 'Ever since the Smethwick election [where local Tories won the seat from Labour at the 1964 election with the campaign slogan 'If you want a nigger for a neighbour, vote Labour'] it had been quite clear that immigration can be the greatest potential vote loser for the Labour party if we are seen to be permitting a flood of immigrants to come in and blight the central areas of all our cities.' The biographer of Labour minister George Thomas quotes Home Secretary Frank Soskice warning that 'if we do not have strict immigration rules our people will soon all be coffee-coloured'. Our Labour party was not unique. Australian Labor party leader Arthur Calwell supported Australia's 'whites only' immigration laws with the slogan 'Two Wongs don't make a white'.

My local MP John Fraser, it has to be said, defended the black community in Brixton although this lost Labour some voters in highly marginal Norwood. A local party member objected to the song 'Young, Gifted and Black', saying, 'If they want to be integrated they shouldn't go on about how good it is to be black.' John's Tory opponent wanted to ban all immigration, repatriate blacks to the West Indies and bring back hanging and birching for young offenders. Fortunately he was convicted of embezzlement shortly before the 1970 general election and replaced by Peter Temple-Morris.

For all its imperfections I never thought of joining any party other than Labour. Ollie Olson, one of the peace corps volunteers I had met in Africa, came with his wife Diane to Britain to avoid being drafted to Vietnam, moving in with us while he got a work visa. Ollie and Diane's main interest was photography so I joined them at a Cartier-Bresson exhibition followed by a May Day concert in the Royal Festival Hall – the first time I had been to a concert. We also discovered the Academy Cinema in Oxford Street with its repertoire of foreign-language films. Ollie was helped by John Fraser, who was an approachable and unpompous man, so finally in February 1969 I overcame my doubts and joined the party: a rare example of a rat boarding a sinking ship. I was happy to work with the Marxist splinter groups on issues where we agreed but I believed we could achieve more if we could radicalise the Labour party.

If I had had friends in the party I would have joined earlier, but like many other working-class kids I lacked the confidence to join when I knew no one. Fortunately Norwood Labour party had a dynamic full-time agent in the shape of Eddie Lopez, the son of a Spanish musician, who happened to share my taste in music. His much-put-upon wife Brenda didn't seem to mind as the two of us listened to Cream on enormous headphones in their front room. Eddie had given up his career as an accountant to turn Norwood into a safe Labour seat. So far things hadn't gone too well, with Labour wiped out in the 1967 GLC elections and the Tories winning fifty-seven of the sixty Lambeth Council seats in the 1968 borough elections. The tide of Tory gains was so unexpected that one Tory victor in Vauxhall demanded a recount as he'd only stood because there was no chance of him winning. With a general election due in two years, John Fraser's chances looked slim.

Many members had left in disgust at Wilson's 1966 wage freeze and failure to condemn US aggression in Vietnam. At my local branch meeting I was the first new member for a year and only the third person in the dozen present who wasn't a pensioner. Bill Adams, the chair, joked, 'Make sure he doesn't get away.' I was lucky to have an open-minded MP and an agent who didn't fear new members meant trouble. Just two miles up the road the Vauxhall Labour party had fewer than fifty members (compared to 750 in Norwood), all of whom were either former councillors or their relatives. The agent, Elsie Boltz, was employed by Vauxhall MP George Strauss to head off challenges to his incumbency. New members were neither sought nor encouraged.

Within two months I was elected to the General Management Committee (GMC), the Executive Committee and the Local Government Committee and became chair and secretary of the local Young Socialists – there was only one other member. The others had left to join Paul Foot in the Trotskyist International Socialist Group led by Tony Cliff. Small revolutionary parties were more exciting, but I believed in radicalising the Labour party.

This was a new world, and I was consumed with an exhilarating round of committee meetings, canvassing and fund-raising and arguments about how John Fraser should vote on Secretary of State for Employment Barbara Castle's 1969 anti-trade-union White Paper 'In Place of Strife'. My first speech to the GMC denounced Wilson for trying to cure the economy by curtailing trade unions instead of devaluing the pound sooner and cutting military spending to balance the budget. I wrote my speech out line by line but

I was shaking so much I couldn't see the words and had to lean against the wall to stop trembling. I was applauded and party chair Vic Matthews said it was the best maiden speech he'd heard at a meeting in a long time. I was on cloud nine for days and was determined to spend the rest of my life as a Labour activist. I hoped to get elected to the borough council but guessed that would take years.

*

One issue about which I was in a minority was the war in Biafra. Having seen the aftermath of the genocide in Kano, I believed that the Ibo people had the right to independence. But Wilson sold arms to Nigeria to protect our oil interests so the Ibo state was crushed and dismembered by the corrupt military regime.

My confidence grew as I helped draw up policies for the borough council election manifesto and select candidates for the GLC election, which was when I first met Tony Banks. Tony worked for the engineering unions' left-wing general secretary Hugh Scanlon, but lost my vote by ignoring policy issues and announcing, 'I have nothing to offer you but my youth.' Instead I voted for a pensioner who was attacking what he called RIP: rent, interest and profits. Tony was selected and went on to win the GLC seat for Hammersmith.

While canvassing for the GLC election I first met the lawyer Victor Mishcon. He had defended Ruth Ellis and would later handle Princess Diana's divorce and try to keep Jeffrey Archer out of prison. Victor was the son of a rabbi who had fled Poland before the First World War and was a talented member of the Labour group at County Hall as well as serving on Lambeth Council. He was not standing again, but took the time to get to know and encourage me. He left his chauffeur-driven Bentley out of sight while canvassing with me in the slums of Brixton.

Although the Labour party was in decline, the events of 1968 had radicalised many young people and I recruited pupils who had started the Schools Action Union (SAU). Most came from private and grammar schools and their head teachers threatened to expel them if they went on strike. Eddie Lopez let them meet in our local HQ and I lobbied Labour school governors to prevent them being expelled.

With under 200 members, mainly in London, they were all pupils with the exception of Max Hunt, a teacher with a Ho Chi Minh beard. As a Maoist, believing the world was on the verge of revolution, he opposed my attempts to recruit members into the Labour party. We didn't know then that 1968 was a once-in-a-lifetime upheaval rather than the beginning of a new world, so Max insisted that we should prepare for armed struggle.

Tariq Ali of the IMG believed Brixton could be a 'revolutionary base area', and the American Black Panther party had formed a small chapter in Brixton. The local police had a grim reputation, with tales of prisoners being savagely beaten in the cells to extract confessions. At the Lambeth Community Relations Council, the police community liaison officer admitted there was nothing he could do because 'it isn't possible to have glass cells'.

I saw the local police at work on a Panther march protesting against police brutality. With a hundred people on the march (fewer than the police who were present) everything stayed peaceful until a drunk started shouting and lunged at one of the Panthers, who didn't hit back. Police ignored the drunk and arrested the Panther. The case was heard by Judge King-Hamilton, a notorious reactionary, who handed down a prison sentence.

My best recruits from the SAU were Paul and Kevin Moore, who both became Lambeth councillors, with Paul serving as vice-chair of transport during my GLC administration and on the Transport for London (TfL) board when I became mayor. But the long march through the institutions was not as exciting as immediate revolution, with Max organising paramilitary training to prepare for armed struggle. He wanted us to assemble at 10 p.m. one night for a forced march to Brighton, warning we would have to climb over back-garden walls because during a revolution troops would control the streets. Max warned that if anyone broke a limb they would be left behind, as would happen in a real revolutionary war. On the appointed night most SAU members joined me at my local, the King's Head, in West Norwood for our regular Saturday-night singalong.

The SAU was united only by a loathing for Jack Straw, then president of the National Union of Students. Alarmed that pupils might be attracted to revolutionary politics, the NUS set up a rival National Union of School Students but they needn't have bothered as Max's eccentric Maoism drove most SAU members away. The remainder split into pro-dope or anti-dope factions and were never heard of again.

*

After the experience of Reagan and Thatcher and the collapse of the Soviet Union, it's hard to understand why so many believed we were on the way to socialism in our lifetimes. But we grew up in the 1950s when Russia beat the US to launch the first satellite, put the first man in space and for a time had dramatic economic growth, with Soviet leader Nikita Khrushchev predicting they would over-take the US by 1980. Who were we to know any better? We also lived with our parents' memories of the Great Depression, the cre-ation of the welfare state and the nationalisation of basic industries. Africa and Asia had thrown off colonialism, America was losing in Vietnam and the anti-apartheid struggle was a rallying point for youth worldwide. As a reformist I believed the state could manage things better and that capitalism needed firm regulation to prevent its excesses. As in Russia in 1917 and China in 1949 people only turned to revolution when they had nothing to lose but their lives.

This was why so many were caught up in left-wing groups debating the way forward, studying Trotsky and Lenin or Mao Tsetung. I believed naively that Mao's cultural revolution was trying to prevent Chinese communism developing into a bureaucracy like Stalin's in the Soviet Union. We now know that in reality Mao was leading a violent coup against his comrades in the Party to regain the predominance he had lost following his failed Great Leap Forward in which millions starved to death.

Left-wing groups argued, fought, fused and split. Each believed they knew the correct way forward and if others would follow everything would be possible. What had more impact on most young people in fact were bands such as Love and Cream. We argued about the meaning of Beatles compositions and Dylan's lyrics and the songs of Jacques Brel as sung by Scott Walker (banned by the BBC as they dealt with prostitution and homosexuality). In cinema a new generation of directors challenged convention with *Easy Rider*, *2001* and *If*. Robert Altman's *M*A*S*H* captured the lunacy of war, and I wanted to live my life in the anarchist style of the doctors portrayed by Donald Sutherland and Elliott Gould.

Almost every weekend we marched against the war or apartheid, but the really massive demos were organised later by the TUC against the anti-union laws being proposed by Ted Heath's new Tory government following Labour's defeat at the 1970 general election. They were run with military precision as hundreds of thousands marched and the trade union stewards put the left-wing factions firmly in their place at the back, just ahead of the lesbian and gay groups. It was a heady experience: with numbers like this how could we fail?

*

In the midst of all of this excitement things deteriorated at work, where the management were proposing redundancies. Along with other workers in the unit I joined the Association of Scientific Workers (about to be absorbed into Clive Jenkins's union ASSET, then to become ASTMS). After a rowdy meeting with management we organised a one-day protest strike. It did not stop the redundancies, but John Fraser got media coverage by raising it in Parliament. I was told I would not be promoted further and should look for another job.

I had already decided to leave as I had gone as far as I could. Working in the unit imposed a degree of isolation. Every day I had to change into medical whites, walk through fluorescent disinfectant and, except for meal breaks, spend the day alone with thousands of mice. Apart from it being lonely work, the disinfectant turned my feet bright green, which girlfriends found off-putting.

My mentor at Chester Beatty had been Tom Connors, a charismatic research doctor whom I hero-worshipped, and it was he who encouraged me to go into politics. I had worked on and off for him over eight years and felt proud when he phoned me at home to say he was hung-over and asked me if I would conduct his experiments. After I left I followed his career as he made the biggest single cancer breakthrough of the last fifty years. Before Tom's work, testicular cancer was almost inevitably fatal. Today 97 per cent of cases are cured because he saw the potential of a drug that others hadn't noticed. For forty years he was the leading specialist in chemotherapy, making Britain the world leader in anti-cancer drug development. Connors founded Cancer Research UK and was the first non-American to serve on the top scientific advisory and oversight committees of the National Cancer Institute, US, which advised the American president. I last saw him when I was running for mayor. He had been diagnosed with prostate cancer and joked, 'I'm hoping to live long enough to find a cure!' Sadly, he didn't.

*

Eddie Lopez tapped up a few members to raise money to employ me to sign up postal voters for the general election, which was expected in October 1970. When Wilson called it for June I took my annual holiday to work on the election. Eddie and I worked through the night assisted by the Moore brothers and other members of the SAU. Ted Heath's Tories secured a surprise 31-seat majority, although John Fraser was just able to fend off Peter Temple-Morris at Norwood by a margin of 631 votes.

Having spent everything trying to win the election, the party now had no money to employ me. I wanted to work with children and the previous year, just up the road in Streatham, Philippa Fawcett Teacher Training College had changed its admissions policy to include men (one of whom had burned himself to death in support of the Russian invasion of Czechoslovakia). There was an acute shortage of teachers so virtually everyone who applied was accepted. I enrolled in Social Biology with the goal of teaching science to non-academic kids. At the first seminar the lecturer took ten minutes to gently build up to the proposition that there were different classes in society. There were gasps from many of the Home Counties students who had never lived in a big city before. I realised the curriculum was not going to be intellectually challenging.

Andrew Hosken's biography *Ken* records: 'Livingstone attended Philippa Fawcett so infrequently during this three-year course that several former students interviewed for this book were convinced, wrongly, that Livingstone had dropped out after a year without obtaining his teacher training certificate.' My worst attendance record was on the drama course. The first lesson at 9 a.m.

on Monday involved lying on the floor pretending to be a flame. I decided that drama wasn't for me. Marks towards the teacher's certificate were awarded half from the final exam and half from students' best twelve pieces of coursework, so I did thirteen pieces of coursework which were graded A or B and decided to leave it at that while concentrating on getting elected to Lambeth Council.

Labour ran Lambeth from 1934 until the Tory landslide in 1968 but the leadership had grown unimaginative, exercising a tight grip on the party in order to keep left-wingers out. The Labour leader Alderman Archie Cotton and most of the old guard died within eighteen months of losing to the Tories. Eddie Lopez was determined that the next Labour council should be more radical, particularly as the Tories were running the borough better than the old Labour regime had done. The Tory leader was Bernard Perkins, talented and liberal-minded, who started a five-year plan to expand public services, increased house building and cracked down on bad landlords. Housing was at the top of the political agenda following the TV drama *Cathy Come Home*, which depicted a young family torn apart and its children taken into care because of the lack of housing. At the 1970 election the Tories' housing spokesman, Peter Walker, spoke in Lambeth and promised to build more council houses than Labour. I ran a housing campaign demanding more homes to prevent us reverting to Labour's poor past performance.

John Major was the best of the new Conservative intake and was promoted to chair the Housing Committee, but some backbenchers were openly racist so Perkins expelled them. Their factional leader was then arrested buying dope in a set-up by a drug dealer offended by his racist speeches.

As a member of the Local Government Committee I threw myself into drafting the manifesto. After Wilson's 1970 defeat there was an influx of university-educated younger members and we were determined to do better than the Tory council. A local pensioner campaigned for the right of OAPs to travel free on buses between the rush hours and this became an issue when the Tory council gave free travel for only the poorest old people, so we promised free off-peak bus travel for all Lambeth's pensioners.

As an awkward twenty-five-year-old I found it embarrassing knocking on doors in the 1971 borough elections and pleading 'Vote for me'. Because of the good record of Major and Perkins we were not certain to win but the national swing against the new Heath government in 1970 did it for us. We did not expect the landslide which handed John Major his first defeat. The 57–3 Tory majority on Lambeth Council was transformed into a Labour majority of 51–9. The average age of the Labour group was halved and only eight Labour members had ever served on a council before.

The Labour group launched into a vicious struggle between left and right in which I was an enthusiastic participant. The left elected Charles Dryland as leader over Vauxhall's Ewan Carr, but Ewan beat me to chair the Housing Committee. I was elected as vice-chair. Under John Major Lambeth had a reputation for innovation but our plans for an increase in house building were hampered by an overstretched building industry and spiralling construction costs. My area of responsibility was to improve the service to tenants in our 28,000 homes.

The state of today's council housing is the end result of thirty years of selling off the best properties and not allowing councils to build new homes to cope with waiting lists. What remains is mainly flats on large estates that have become a last resort for single parents and the unemployed. In 1971 council tenants comprised much the same mix of working- to middle-class families as society in general. In Lambeth the vast majority of them were in employment, with rent arrears never more than 2 per cent, and there were few sink estates except those deliberately maintained as such by the council as a deterrent.

We had six of these in Lambeth. The three worst, truly appalling places, were reception centres for homeless families. I was stunned when I visited Louisa Court and Lennox Buildings, Victorian slums of one- and two-bedroom flats used for families who often had five or six children. The local school could not cope with such numbers of especially needy children. Middle-class families who became homeless were often housed quickly on ordinary estates, so these halfway homes were used by council officials as a dumping ground for poorer families they feared might drag down better estates. After months or years tenants who 'conformed' were allowed to move to slightly less appalling conditions in 'intermediate accommodation' at Ferndale Court, Edward Henry House and Black Prince Road. Provided they maintained a good rent record, they might after a number of years be considered for better council housing.

We were determined to end this punitive approach and it was my job to get people out of these dreadful blocks, but housing department civil servants were opposed to the new councillors' policy. It made their lives easier to concentrate difficult tenants in a few blocks they could ignore. They didn't care that children's early lives were blighted. It took two years to overcome obstruction and empty the three reception centres.

I also wanted tenants to get involved in managing their estates, but had my first setback when some of them asked to see the terms and conditions of the residential caretakers so they could check that they were doing their job. As the caretakers' wages were paid from their rents this wasn't an unreasonable request, but the deputy director warned that the unions would strike if I agreed to it. I was in a vulnerable position. The bureaucrats had colluded with the unions to block the first step in transferring power to tenants. Ewan told me I was on my own and my enemies in the Labour group would exploit the issue if the unions did strike. I backed off and still regret that I did.

The officials also resisted our new policy on empty homes. Councils left properties empty for years before demolishing them to build new housing, but ripped out toilets and smashed holes in the roofs to prevent squatting. Before the election I had been in contact with people from the housing charity Shelter and local squatting groups and now I met them with housing officials. We agreed that squatters would form a housing association and we would pass them empty homes to use until we needed them back for demolition. With the size of the housing programme there would always be a flow of properties to re-house squatters from the properties they had to vacate. The squatters were delighted, as were local residents, who didn't want derelict properties on their streets. Although the housing officials hated it there was nothing they could do and in the years that followed thousands of people lived in what would otherwise have been empty homes.

*

I was exhilarated by my new role but I was stretched to my limits. Of the new members under thirty, only two of us did not have a university degree. I was faced with an avalanche of committee reports, technical documents and Acts of Parliament which I had to master. Until then I hadn't even known the difference between revenue and capital budgets – now I was notionally in charge of the revenue budget for managing 28,000 council homes. To get on top of the job I skipped college and was in the town hall day after day questioning officers and picking the directors' brains over lunch. During an early committee meeting I overcame my insecurity enough to ask officers to explain a technical term. A long-serving Tory said, 'I'm glad you asked that. I never understood what they were talking about.'

My mentor was housing director Harry Simpson, who had a passionate commitment to solving London's housing crisis. He set out to teach me what I needed to know, deluging me with books and reports and taking me to the annual housing conference in Scarborough as he had done three years earlier with John Major. The Tories were elected on a promise to stop building housing but Harry had shown them the conditions in the worst of the privately rented housing, which often had an entire family to a room and another one trying to live in the attic. The Tories changed their policy. When Harry died, the then prime minister John Major became patron of the charitable trust that established a housing library in his memory.

The other great officer at Lambeth was chief architect and planner Ted Hollamby. After working for the Miners' Welfare Commission he joined the architects' department at County Hall, where he lost the battle to build the Thamesmead development as a series of villages separated by the streams that ran through the site. He came to Lambeth and turned a backwater into a pioneering department. He passionately believed that council housing should be as good as if not better than private housing, and some of his estates are still the most sought-after in the borough. His hero was William Morris and at his own expense he bought and painstakingly restored Morris's Red House in Bexleyheath, now owned by the National Trust.

We got on really well, except that I wanted things done overnight and Ted's nature was to go over the details of every development until it was perfect. He later became the first chief architect and planner for Thatcher's London Docklands Development Corporation. Although I opposed the LDDC taking over the GLC's role, I knew it would be better with Ted leading the development and at the GLC I agreed to fund the Docklands Light Railway he wanted. Before he died in 1999 he wrote to me urging me to stand for mayor.

I was having the time of my life finding my feet in local government, but the same could not be said for Charles Dryland, the new leader. I realised he and I had very different views on the night of my election when he said, 'Think of this as though you have just been elected to the board of a medium-sized company with an annual budget of £13 million.' Dryland relied on senior officers rather than giving councillors real control of the machine. Although elected with the votes of the left, he was a middle-of-the-road economics lecturer, who drove around in a bright red convertible sports car.

Lambeth Council was riddled with management-speak and some councillors lost sight of politics as they droned on about 'information flows', 'system theory', 'critical path analysis' and 'forward planning rationalisation'. We improved services, but the bureaucracy grew still more rapidly. In 1967 Lambeth had 3,600 manual workers and 1,800 white-collar staff. Seven years later the number of manual workers was the same, but the white-collar staff had doubled. The biggest growth was in management services (now human resources), which quadrupled in size. Another big increase was in social services. In 1987, twenty years before the tragedies of Victoria Climbié and Baby P, I wrote: 'New working practices encourage social workers to model themselves on the professions with elaborate career structures and a detachment from their clients. This meant that much of the increase of staff was consumed in internal management systems and failed to lead to any improvement in the service provided to the public' (*If Voting Changed Anything They'd Abolish It*, p. 24).

Charles Dryland gave me my first lesson in how leaders succeed or fail. With no firm principles, he flip-flopped between left and right, alienating both wings of his own party. The changes we made happened despite his leadership rather than because of it. As well as free bus travel for pensioners and closing halfway homes, we also gave schoolchildren free milk after Mrs Thatcher, then education secretary, abolished it. Dryland's handling of government-imposed rent increases for council tenants was a disaster. He made all the right noises about opposing the rise in rents, only to collapse at the last minute and vote with the right wing to implement the increase. At the next annual general meeting of the Labour group he came third in the election for leader, losing out to David Stimpson, a hard-working Labour right-winger.

The sexual revolution also had its effect with one of the newly elected right-wingers trying, with little success, to initiate wife-swapping parties among the councillors. Perhaps it was because I was a geek or too left-wing, but I was never invited. He also complained that, having gone for treatment at one of the council's clinics for sexually transmitted diseases, he was given a number, whereas he wanted everyone attending the clinic to be referred to by name. We didn't bother to check if the public wished to give up their anonymity in the waiting room, but we did introduce free contraception for all. The media said we were encouraging promiscuity, but with Lambeth's teenage pregnancy rate it didn't need much encouragement. The bureaucracy undermined the policy by limiting the issue to twenty condoms a month per couple on the grounds that no one had sex during a woman's period or more than once a day.

*

Sex was also an issue at Philippa Fawcett, where overnight guests were banned from the halls of residence. They didn't object to us having sex, but said that guests would use electricity and water which was paid for by the ratepayers, which might be an illegal use of public money.

I had been elected secretary of the college's student union and fell in love with its president, Christine Chapman, a bubbly, bossy, energetic and assertive twenty-five-year-old who lived in the halls of residence. I was twenty-six and felt ridiculous sneaking out of her room before the cleaners arrived. At the principal's annual sherry party for the student union executive I turned up late into an atmosphere you could cut with a knife. Christine had got into a row with the principal about overnight visits and loudly announced that I was stopping with her that night and asked what they were going to do about it.

The rules were set by a committee with equal numbers of staff and students but chaired by the college principal, who had a casting vote in the event of a tie. One of the lecturers on the staff–student council failed to turn up at the next meeting so the students had a majority of one. Following an excruciating appeal from the principal begging us not to take a decision, as she feared the Inner London Education Authority might take us to court, our resolve held: the ban on guests was lifted and never mentioned again.

Such prudery may sound odd, given the reputation of the Swinging Sixties, but the promiscuity of the day was only for a small elite with the rest of us looking on in envy. In 1974, although the incidence of sexually transmitted diseases had more than doubled during the last decade, it still stood at only a quarter of a million. Similarly, although attendance at family planning clinics had trebled, little more than a million people made use of them. In the 1970s, with the birth-control pill widely available and Aids, genital warts and herpes well below the horizon, everyone, including me, started having a good time.

4

I Wanna Be Elected

1971–1974

Although he didn't agree with my politics, Dad was always very proud of my achievements. When I became vice-chair of the governors of Norwood Girls School in 1970 as a Labour party nominee he kept the school prospectus because my name was in it and the following year when I was elected to the council he told everyone in the pub I would one day be an MP. The fact that I stood in Knight's Hill ward rather than the ward we lived in was a relief for Dad. Otherwise, he would have agonised about not voting Tory for the first time in his life. But he used his van to take voters to the polls for me. After all the rows, Dad and I were finally enjoying a better relationship.

Dad gave up window cleaning to deliver supplies to launderettes and had more time at home instead of working two jobs to pay off the mortgage. Mum and Dad bought a run-down cottage in the Lincolnshire village of Welbourn, close to Mum's former dance partners who lived in Lincoln. They planned to retire to the cottage after selling the house in London, and to open a small kennel business.

At weekends Dad repaired the cottage while Mum worked on the garden, coming back to London on Monday evenings. I got home late one Monday in September to find the house dark. The phone rang and I heard the shock in Mum's voice saying that Dad had had a heart attack and was in Lincoln hospital. I was stunned as Dad was always healthy, and had only ever taken time off work once, when he had flu. Mum and Dad were both heavy smokers, but Dad was addicted to the extra-strength cigarettes that used to be given to sailors, as well as to the very strong tots of rum which helped them get through the appalling conditions at sea. After the war he rolled his own using extra-strength Sailors Old Shag. When Mum tried one of Dad's roll-ups it nearly choked her.

As Mum rang off I was convinced Dad was going to die. That night Christine could not lift my fear that these were the last days of Dad's life. When I got to Lincoln I couldn't believe he looked so healthy, even questioning whether he'd really had a heart attack. I began to hope he might pull through but some days later he had a much worse attack and was rushed to Sheffield. I got there at midnight on Sunday to find Dad looking far more frail. He had always been very fit and it was shocking to see the tubes keeping him alive. I found the night-shift doctor, not much older than me, and asked her if Dad was going to die. She said, 'Yes, most probably tonight.' I've always been grateful for her honesty because I had to get Mum through the next few hours. Linda arrived in the middle of the night with Malcolm and the children.

Dad hung on, defying the doctor's prediction. In the days that followed we never went further than to walk round the hospital grounds. As we sat with Dad he could only sip a few drops of water and say a few words. Next day Malcolm took the kids back to London and Aunt Cathy arrived. The surgeons were so impressed that Dad was still alive they decided to try open-heart surgery. They told us that it was a long shot, but because it was Dad's only chance we agreed.

We kissed Dad before he went under the anaesthetic, fearing we were saying goodbye for the last time, while Mum just prayed the surgery would work. Dad never regained consciousness but in the hours that followed the surgeons were amazed at the tenacity with which he clung to life. We spent the long hours with Mum saying that Dad would have to take it easy when he got home and every other thing we could think of to keep her going.

Just before midnight on Tuesday the nurse asked us to come to the intensive care unit, which was at the other end of the hospital. On the long walk Mum kept saying that perhaps Dad had woken up but Linda and I knew that he had died. Mum collapsed on hearing the news, but recovered enough to say goodbye and kiss him for the last time. 'Kiss your father goodbye,' she told us. She had to be given a sedative to sleep.

We wanted Dad's body sent back to London for a funeral all his friends and family could attend but we couldn't afford it because an undertakers' racket allowed them to charge for a body passing through each county from Lincoln to London. Linda and I registered the death and organised the funeral in Sheffield for the following Friday.

A funeral is bad enough without having to hold it in a city where you have no friends. Catholics know how to celebrate the life of a loved one but the Church of England service at Sheffield crematorium with Linda, Cathy, Mum and me, four old friends and a vicar with no idea who Dad was, felt like passing through a supermarket checkout. Dad's ashes were scattered later in the rose garden at West Norwood cemetery with the family present.

Mum and Dad wanted to die together because each dreaded surviving the other. This was Mum's worst nightmare. They were both fifty-six when Dad died and she would wait twenty-six years to join him. Night after night she cried herself to sleep, unable to accept that 'he died when so many evil people carry on living'. For the rest of her life she relived her time with Bob and I often found her dancing alone, saying she could feel that Dad was with her.

Mum went to spiritualist meetings and started 'getting messages' from the other side. As an atheist I was disparaging but some messages contained uncanny details of obscure incidents from the past, one medium telling Mum that Dad did not want her to buy the bike she was thinking of acquiring. Mum had forgotten a bad biking accident twenty years earlier. I also couldn't explain why, while she was staying with Aunt Cathy, Mum woke at four in the morning to find Cathy sitting on her bed saying her son Ken had appeared before her and waved goodbye. Six hours later Ken's wife phoned to say that he had died of a sudden heart attack at the age of forty-six.

Mum sold up to go and live in the cottage as she and Dad had planned. Her decision was made easier when, after her first day back at work at the bakery, the shop was robbed and the staff were held at knifepoint.

I had suppressed my own grief so I could help Mum but I was constantly overwhelmed, remembering the rows with Dad during my adolescence. It was unbearable that the relationship we had begun to settle into had been snatched away. Like Dad, Mum was proud of me and over the years I could afford to take her to good restaurants and on holidays, but I never got to do that with Dad. There wasn't a day I didn't think about him, and he often appeared in my dreams. Only after his death did I really appreciate his remarkable strength, gentleness and patience. I assumed the pain would lessen but it was twenty years before it began to fade. My generation were taught that boys don't cry and real men hide their feelings, so my grief remained private as I threw myself into work. Dad's early death taught me not to play safe. I would take risks.

*

I didn't need encouragement from Eddie Lopez, my friend and the local Labour agent, to stand for the 1973 GLC election. Because Lambeth meetings were in the evening and the GLC meetings were in the daytime it meant I could serve on both bodies. It wouldn't be possible to do a normal job as well but with the allowances from both I could get by. The 92 seats on the GLC were identical to the 92 London parliamentary constituencies. As long as they had a home in London, GLC candidates didn't have to live in the constituency they represented at County Hall (unlike borough councillors, who had to live in the borough they served), and there were no rules preventing people standing for both their local borough and any GLC constituency, but it was certainly easier for me to represent Norwood at County Hall because it was one of the four constituencies in Lambeth.

Given Eddie's popularity with the membership, the only obstacle was my opponent, a hardened, Trotskyite revolutionary called Ted Knight. A Strand Grammar School boy, eleven years my senior, he had lived his whole life in the area. He joined the party in the late 1940s and got caught up with the tiny cells of British Trotskyists. Although they eventually split into the Socialist Labour League (SLL, which became the Workers Revolutionary Party), the Socialist Review Group (which became first the International Socialist Group and then the Socialist Workers Party) and the Militant Tendency, and some had even met Leon Trotsky, in the late 1940s they were all working in one secret faction inside the Labour party. In this heady atmosphere young Ted spent eight years of his life working for the revolution under surveillance by MI5 and Special Branch.

Ted was still a teenager when the Labour party expelled him in the mid-1950s for his involvement with the SLL and his father, who worked at the Ministry of Defence, was questioned by Special Branch. Given this background, Ted was secretive and protective of his private life. It was only in 1969, after Ron Hayward replaced the reactionary Sarah Barker as the Labour party's national agent, that it became easier to rejoin the party, Hayward saying that 'our problem wasn't reds under the beds but reactionaries in the cupboard'. When Ted was interviewed by the national party sub-committee Hayward joked that it wouldn't be long before he saw Ted on the panel of parliamentary candidates.

Eddie took a gloomier view, predicting that Ted would try to take over the party and suspecting that he might still be a member of the SLL, which was led by the autocratic Gerry Healy. Ted didn't find it easy getting along with the young radicals either. His impeccable haircut, immaculate clothes and class-based approach to politics had little in common with the casually dressed, younger Trotskyites and refugees from the Schools Action Union who had established the Chartists, another small Trotskyist group who mixed politics with music and believed the left had to embrace issues of race, feminism and homosexuality – which Ted considered to be diversions from the 'real' class struggle.

In *Ken*, Andrew Hosken quotes the Chartist Keith Veness: 'They [Ted and I] were the odd couple, you couldn't find two people more different in lifestyle behaviour, outlook and everything else. Ted's a nice guy once you batter down the defences. He's quite old fashioned and gentlemanly in a way, and that's something you can certainly never accuse Ken of being.' Along with Chris Knight and Graham Bash, Veness tried to take over the South Suburban Co-op with young socialists getting their membership book and their dividend just so they could go to the stores once a year to try to vote out the managers.

Ted was readmitted to the party too late to fight the borough elections and I first met him on the night I was selected. When I thanked him for his support he looked me in the eye and said, 'Well quite frankly, comrade, there wasn't anything better on offer.'

In 1983 Ted told John Carvel that he viewed me as 'basically a Wilson supporter, probably with some influence from people like Crosland, if he was actually ever considering what Crosland was writing, which I doubt . . . I think it was quite useful for Ken to have somebody closely arguing with him who had very clearly defined views on matters of Labour party and socialist policies, someone who had actually gone through the schools of Marxist training.'

Hosken in 2008 quotes Ted as saying, 'At first, he was somewhat naïve . . . what I was able to bring about was an understanding that if you are going to succeed, then you have to build a base; you had to build allies and you have to organise to win.'

Given his hopes of overthrowing capitalism, Ted was very law-abiding, believing socialists had to be incredibly careful in their personal lives. At two o'clock one morning he was giving me a lift home from a council meeting and took a wrong turning. As there was no one in sight, I suggested we take an illegal right-hand turn to get back on course, but Ted insisted on going round the one-way system again.

Ted set out to take control of the party with hard-line motions intended to split the broad-left consensus. He proposed support for the communists in Vietnam but was surprised to find every-one agreed with him, so he demanded withdrawal of British troops from Northern Ireland, which did indeed split the party. Like most members I was glad Wilson sent troops into Northern Ire-land in August 1969 to protect Catholics from a police riot by the Protestant-dominated force. So I opposed Ted's motion, which was defeated.

The Heath government destroyed this consensus when troops killed four civilians on a house-to-house search in the Cath-olic Falls Road. The local army commander at the time, Colonel Michael Dewar, wrote in his book *The British Army in Northern Ireland*: 'The Lower Falls operation changed everything . . . The PIRA [Provisional IRA] grew from fewer than one hundred activ-ists in May–June to roughly 800 in December 1970.' In the police riot during the summer of 1969 Catholics joked that IRA stood for 'I Ran Away', but following the introduction in August 1971 of internment without trial for suspected terrorists the IRA was over-whelmed by new recruits and the cycle of violence began. Heath took a pro-Unionist line, but Reginald Maudling on his first visit to Belfast as Home Secretary, said, 'What a bloody awful country. For God's sake bring me a large Scotch,' as he boarded the plane home.

Although the IRA started a bombing campaign it wasn't until 6 February 1971 that they killed a British soldier. Five months later Heath introduced internment, with British troops and Protestant police kicking in the doors of Catholics at dawn, rounding up hundreds of men they suspected were in the IRA, and carting them off to prison without trial. Thirteen were tortured using the same methods used against British POWs in the Korean War.

Sixteen civilians were killed in 1970 but by 1972 that figure had risen to 249, and 149 soldiers and policemen were also murdered. Although many of the civilians killed were Catholic victims of loyalist death squads, the British media concentrated on IRA terrorism. In Derry on 30 January 1972, the infamous British army killing spree known as Bloody Sunday left fourteen unarmed Catholics dead.

In the Dublin *Sunday Business Post* twenty-five years later a soldier's written record, made just days after the killings, was finally published: 'A group of some 40 civilians were there running in an effort to get away. [Another soldier] fired from the hip at a range of 20 yards. The bullet passed through one man and into another and they both fell . . . A Catholic priest ran across to the bodies shouting about giving the last rites. He was clubbed down with rifle butts . . . I remember thinking . . . that no one would ever know about it.'

Lord Chief Justice Widgery conducted an inquiry with a clear steer to exonerate the troops. In America funding for the IRA tripled, in Australia dockers refused to unload British ships and in Dublin the British embassy was burned to the ground. In the Commons Bernadette Devlin, a republican MP, slapped Maudling across the face. Now I could see that Northern Ireland was, as Ted claimed, a remnant of the British Empire, I stopped supporting the presence of British troops and realised there would be no peace in Ireland without the political involvement of the IRA.

Ted also made the running when Heath changed the law to force councils to increase rents by £1 a week although the average wage was less than £20 a week. To sweeten the pill, Lambeth was in line for a big increase in government funds to build new council housing. I was prepared to accept the rent increase if it meant we could cut the council's waiting list more quickly. Once again I changed my mind after hours of debate with Ted, who believed that a nationwide campaign against the rent increase might bring down Heath. My ward had over a thousand council homes so we called a public meeting with the hall laid out with 1,200 chairs ready to receive the angry tenants. Ted was in the chair with me and two other councillors on the platform. Eventually two men and a dog arrived and sat in the middle of the hall. Ted decided the meeting should go ahead anyway and the four of us harangued the two men and their dog, who couldn't even slip away unnoticed. Fortunately they were members of the Communist party and used to long boring meetings.

A couple of weeks later we were due to select our candidate to fight the 1973 GLC election and as nobody took County Hall very seriously my only competitor was Ted. Increasingly as mentor and rival we worked together and Ted withdrew, wryly admitting that Eddie Lopez had it sewn up for me. Eddie was such a good agent that I was worried when he moved to Exeter, but he left me a detailed plan for the GLC election. I was also nervous when Ted was narrowly elected chair of Norwood Labour party as I hadn't voted for him, but he came up with a brilliant idea for raising funds for the election by distributing leaflets all over neighbouring Bromley claiming to be a Rates Reform Group asking for jumble. We were deluged with good-quality jumble, almost forced on us by grateful Tory voters who thought the rates were too high and didn't realise they were contributing to my campaign. At our annual dinner the guest of honour Barbara Castle was given a brutal introduction by Ted for supporting Wilson's anti-union laws. She replied in kind and never forgave him. Years later at the annual Labour party conference as she walked by Ted she looked at him and uttered 'Bastard'.

*

My main area of concern lay in what the GLC could do to improve housing. In inner London one family in five shared their home with another family and two out of five did not have their own bathroom, hot water supply or lavatory. In Lambeth we still had walk-up blocks of flats with communal bathrooms and toilets on each floor. The London Labour party had a radical manifesto to take over all private rented housing in London and double the size of the council-house building programme. They also proposed to freeze bus and tube fares as a step towards free travel and cancel the plans to build three vast motorway rings around London as well as promising that the Labour boroughs' free bus passes for pensioners would be extended to the Tory boroughs.

Labour had great fun when Heath, after being caught in traffic one evening, angrily demanded to speak to the Tory GLC leader Sir Desmond Plummer, unaware that he was in a shower in Tokyo. After being berated for several minutes, Plummer pointed out that he had little power over traffic but would be happy to deal with the problem if Heath increased the GLC's transport powers. The call was front-page news and rumbled on for days. Thirty years later I lobbied Blair unsuccessfully for these powers, just as Boris Johnson continues to do as I write.

Just before the election the Tory GLC changed the motor-way ring plans and proposed to put a six-lane elevated motorway through Norwood, demolishing 1,100 homes, blighting another

1,200 and running through our three parks. Bizarrely my Tory opponent, Peter Malynn, voted for this even though the route went through the safest Tory wards in the constituency.

This was my first environmental campaign and I wanted to make it the centrepiece of the election but Ted said it would only interest 'middle-class environmentalists' and he wanted to stick to class issues. When 700 people turned up at the two meetings we'd called, Ted changed his mind and even agreed that our posters in Tory areas should say 'Save Norwood from the M23 – Vote Livingstone' without mentioning Labour.

Bill Livingston, a genial middle-of-the-road Tory, had represented Norwood at County Hall on the LCC and the GLC but had now decided to retire. The Tories put out an election leaflet warning that I was no relation to Bill, just a dreadful 'Red under the bed'. Labour won the GLC by 57 seats to the Tories' 33 and 2 Liberals. In Norwood, the Tories' last-minute Red scare had no impact and I won 54 per cent of the vote. Tony Banks invited half a dozen newly elected members to meet in St Stephen's Tavern in Whitehall just before the first Labour group meeting. Two of the six were Dr Stephen Haseler and Douglas Eden, who eventually defected to the SDP, so it wasn't much of a left caucus. Sir Reg Goodwin, who had been leader during opposition, was elected unopposed and the real struggle was over who would be his deputy.

Our little caucus supported Illtyd Harrington, a bearded, flamboyant, lovable rogue. He had been chosen as candidate for Dover at the 1964 general election but the Labour leadership had overruled the local party. The reason was that during the late 1950s and early 1960s all new Labour candidates were vetted by MI5, who then reported to Labour's deputy leader George Brown and national agent Sarah Barker in a London restaurant whether the candidate might be a threat to national security. As some in MI5 (Peter Wright of *Spycatcher* fame, for one) believed Wilson was a Russian agent, the left-wing, CND-supporting Illtyd had no chance. This secret vetting stopped after the 1966 election but helps explain why most Labour MPs were so moderate. Illtyd won the deputy leadership contest, and at the same time Jack Straw was elected deputy leader of the Inner London Education Authority (ILEA). Despite his undermining the SAU, I went along with the decision of Tony's caucus to support Jack.

*

The County Hall building is a vast Edwardian monolith, so imposing and intimidating that some Labour members felt that just getting elected was an advance for socialism. With 1,200 rooms, 1.2 million square feet of office space and twelve miles of corridors it was such a maze I often got lost. County Hall itself housed 7,000 staff with another 28,000 in locations around London, with 60,000 staff at London Transport and over 50,000 in the ILEA.

The building was designed by Ralph Knott, a twenty-nine-year-old architect, following a competition in 1908. As the largest local authority in Europe the Tories of the day felt they needed a building that reflected the grandeur of their position. The main floor with its members' offices and council chamber was the grandest of all with fittings of imported oak, Portland stone and Italian marble. The chairman's 'throne' was carved from a petrified oak dredged from the Thames. The entrance to the members' floor was up a grand ceremonial staircase barred to members of the public. The longest corridor stretched for more than a quarter of a mile and some mornings the fog would leak in from the windows and obscure the end of it. There was a conscious attempt to mimic Parliament with a members' terrace, bar and restaurant (with subsidised prices) looking out over the Thames towards the houses of Parliament. GLC meetings started with a prayer from the chairman's personal chaplain. We abolished this but couldn't stop the outgoing

Tory chairman insisting on a prayer for the last time. The chaplain got his revenge when he said, 'I have been told to be brief so I shall simply beseech Almighty God to watch over those who have chosen to walk a crooked path.'

The plush surroundings and seductive treatment of members went back to the beginning of the LCC. The first elections in 1889 saw senior Tory and Liberal MPs elected to serve in both institutions and they expected to be treated as if they were in Parliament. By 1973 members of the GLC were looked after better than MPs. All members had an office and committee chairs had personal assistants, typists, chauffeur-driven cars, constantly restocked drinks cupboards and access to the royal box at the Royal Festival Hall. Proceedings in the chamber mimicked those of Parliament and we were 'Honourable Members' rather than mere councillors.

The Labour group had been dominated by wealthy middle-class members and our intake changed that, but some members developed an air of self-importance and forgot why they had been sent there. When chief whip Harvey Hinds proposed to allow waitresses in the members' restaurant to use the nearby 'Lady Members' toilet he only just won the vote.

The Tories had millionaire property developers such as Horace Cutler, the amiable Willy Bell who owned several blocks of Manhattan and Lena Townsend, whose childhood had been spent on a houseboat on the Nile with a second houseboat for the horses. Lena was an unworldly, one-nation Tory who when leader of ILEA chaired the panel that appointed inner London's head teachers. She was convinced that all men in suede shoes were homosexual, so no one committing this sartorial gaffe was ever appointed. I wore a blue safari jacket and suede shoes to match. I can only imagine what she thought of me.

One Tory I got on with was David Avery, an ex-MI5 officer who loved telling how there was a knock on his door one evening from a Special Branch officer who interviewed him as a suspected homosexual and therefore a security risk. The officer revealed that the source of this allegation was the MP Duncan Sandys, who had noticed that David 'smoked his cigarettes like a woman'. When David had persuaded the officer he was not a homosexual he got the reply 'Well, I am.'

With so many committees at County Hall there was a job for every Labour member. I was appointed vice-chair of the Film Viewing Board but I only learned about this in the papers after Sir Reg Goodwin's secretary mistakenly wrote to the retired Tory Bill Livingston offering him the job, which he mischievously accepted. The GLC's Film Viewing Board was the court of appeal for films which had been banned by the British Board of Film Censors (BBFC), a voluntary body appointed and funded by the film industry. The chair of the GLC board was Enid Wistrich, who, like me, opposed censorship on principle, so we embarked on a round of meetings to collect the evidence to justify ending film censorship for adults. We met the British Film Institute, the police, the BBFC, the Arts Council, film critics, churches, unions, cinema owners, the Home Office and Mary Whitehouse's Festival of Light as well as anti-censorship campaigners. While this went on we watched films submitted by companies appealing against bans or extensive cuts.

As I loved film I was disappointed with the rubbish we had to see. I had to sit through works such as *The Porn Brokers*, *Is There Sex After Death?*, *Sex Farm*, *School Girls*, *Big Zapper*, *White Slavers*, *The Sex Adventures of the Three Musketeers*, *Heat*, *Toilet Talks*, *Teenage Love* and *Snow White and the Seven Perverts*. We were paid £10 per film watched by the GLC, so this was the largest committee of the council, but the decisions it made depended on who bothered to turn up. The Tories opposed even the mildest sex scene whereas the Labour members got very worried about violence.

GLC rules said we should uphold the ban on films which 'tended to deprave or corrupt', but each member had their own idea of what was depraved and corrupt. *Blowout*, a French film about four men eating themselves to death, was banned by the BBFC because it showed a woman masturbating on the exhaust of a Bugatti, but two Tories from Bromley, Joan Wykes and Jean Tatham, said this was the most disgusting film they had ever seen because of the flatulence it featured. Try as we might we couldn't convince Joan and Jean that flatulence was not depraved or corrupting.

Frank Smith was another Bromley dinosaur who believed that depravity in 1970s Britain was on a scale unseen since Caligula. He was sometimes so outraged that he watched the film twice, taking Mary Whitehouse along for a repeat showing. The right-wing press warned that our liberal approach would undermine public morals. A *Times* editorial damned us for passing a documentary about the murderer Charles Manson with an X certificate, claiming that Londoners, obviously not as sophisticated as *Times* editorial writers, might mimic Manson's crimes.

The only occasion I compromised was during the first kung-fu film I had to endure, *Fist of Fury*, ninety minutes of windpipe smashing, head-crushing and groin-kicking to a soundtrack of grunts and groans. The distributor wanted the X certificate reduced to an AA so that teenagers could see it. I worried about violence in films, but also knew that about a hundred producers of kung-fu films with X-certificate ratings would all appeal if we gave in on *Fist of Fury*. We left well alone.

Enid's study found no conclusive evidence linking criminal or violent acts to the viewing of sexually explicit or violent films, but there was some evidence that violence in TV Westerns and crime series could lead to an increase in such behaviour by young men. Our work was to no avail. By the time the council voted on Enid's report the early radical phase of the Labour GLC was over and seventeen Labour members, including Reg Goodwin, voted with the Tories to carry on censoring.

Eight years later as leader of the GLC my opinion had been changed by feminism and by some disturbing films that celebrated sexual violence against women, so we did not overturn the BBFC bans, but after the GLC was abolished the BBFC was given legal standing. Funded by the film industry, the BBFC was reluctant to challenge Hollywood's obsession with violence and one censor who suggested cutting sexual violence against women was forced out of her job. Under Hollywood's pressure the goalposts constantly moved to permit ever more realistic violence. When *Basic Instinct* was released in 1992 the BBFC cut the scene where Michael Douglas anally rapes Jeanne Tripplehorn but within a decade that scene was being shown after the 9 p.m. watershed on Channel Five.

*

The GLC election took place just weeks before my final teacher's certificate exam but with the teacher shortage the bar was set low enough for 98 per cent of students to pass. So low, in fact, that, having studied sociology as my main subject and finding the sociology questions boring, I answered psychology questions instead. Although I hadn't studied psychology I still passed, and was offered jobs by Croydon and the ILEA but the government had by then introduced attendance allowances for councillors, so I could make £2,000 a year as a GLC member. Christine and I decided that she would teach for the next four years and I would throw myself into politics and see how far I could get at County Hall.

We set about implementing our manifesto with enthusiasm: house building increased, private landlords were bought out, fares frozen and plans for the three motorway rings scrapped. But the old guard had not given up and the veteran Labour member Dame Evelyn Dennington, ably supported by Andrew McIntosh, one of the new members who was emerging as an effective advocate for the right, fought to save part of the motorway plan at the Cambridge roundabout where the North Circular Road meets the A10.

The GLC was in a different league from Lambeth Council in that it discussed major regional and national issues. Twenty years after the catastrophic floods of 1953 the Heath government finally gave the go-ahead to build the Thames Barrier with the GLC in charge. No barrier of comparable size had ever been built in Britain so three civil engineering firms formed a consortium. The consortium was given no incentive to finish either on time or on budget, so the cost rose from £60 million to £600 million. By 1977 the completion date was being put back by a month every month so the new Conservative GLC leader, Sir Horace Cutler, offered a bonus (or bribe, some might say) to everybody from the chief executive to the tea lady if it was finished by a fixed date. To no one's surprise the delays ceased.

The government also took the lead on airport capacity. In 1960, an inquiry had found that people living near Heathrow were subjected to more noise 'than they can reasonably be expected to tolerate'. Worried that Paris or Amsterdam might overtake London as Europe's busiest airport, Wilson set up the Roskill Commission to investigate the possibility of building a third London airport to relieve the pressure on Heathrow and Gatwick. This vastly expensive and long-running planning inquiry eventually proposed a new airport in Buckinghamshire at Cublington.

One member of the commission, Colin Buchanan, proposed an alternative in the Thames Estuary at Foulness near Maplin Sands on the Essex coast, which, he argued, would regenerate London's East End. This idea had been proposed in the 1930s, revived in the 1950s and again in the 1960s. Heath ignored Roskill and plumped for Foulness. In 1973 he gave the Maplin Development Authority (MDA) a budget of £250 million, proposing to open the first runway by 1976, a second in 1980 and two more to follow. To see off the challenge from the port of Rotterdam Britain would build Europe's largest seaport next to the airport and a new town of 300,000 people to provide the workforce at both ports. There would be an eight-lane motorway and high-speed rail line whisking people into a revamped St Pancras station.

Labour's shadow environment secretary, Tony Crosland, was sceptical. Of the party's national leaders he was my hero, a gifted economist who I hoped would succeed Wilson. I was in awe when he came to lunch at Lambeth with myself and Ewan Carr. He confessed he had been more interested in foreign policy and had not paid much attention to housing until he was given the environment job. He rehearsed the arguments against the new airport. Foulness means 'place of birds' and a fifth of the world's Brent geese wintered there, presenting real risks as aircraft can suck birds into their engines and crash. He also believed it would hasten the closure of existing ports and speed the decline of the East End of London.

The whole story is brilliantly captured in *When the Lights Went Out*, Andy Beckett's history of the 1970s. He quotes Tory environment minister Geoffrey Rippon telling the Commons in 1973 that 'Maplin is necessary to maintain Britain's position as one of the world's great centres of international aviation' – the same nonsense we heard when Gordon Brown decided to build a third runway at Heathrow. The economic case was demolished by Alan Walters (later economic adviser to Margaret Thatcher) and in the Commons both the Tory right-winger Norman Tebbit and the Labour maverick Tam Dalyell opposed the idea. The Tory majority was cut to 9 votes.

The estimated cost of the project quadrupled to £1 billion, amid speculation that it could rise to £2 billion. The opening date slipped back to 1983. Crosland invoked the image of the Soviet Union by nicknaming Maplin 'Heathograd' in July 1973. Twelve months later, Heath was out of office and Crosland cancelled it. The BNP later revived the idea and in 2008 my successor as mayor, Boris Johnson, paid Doug Oakervee (the project director who oversaw the building of Hong Kong airport) to investigate the Maplin idea. He concluded it would cost £40 billion.

*

The film board was a good apprenticeship in the ways of County Hall but my real interest was housing. I was a member of the Housing Management Committee, chaired by Marie Jenkins. There was widespread agreement that she was out of her depth and had to go, so I put my name forward for election to the Leaders Panel, a small group of backbenchers who met with the whips and the leader to allocate jobs.

Paddy O'Connor, our deputy chief whip, said they had been told I was 'a troublesome little bastard' but as I was at County Hall full-time I had made more impact than most other new members. Most of my speeches were about housing and even those who were suspicious of me accepted that I knew what I was talking about.

According to Hosken, Illtyd Harrington recalled that I 'was a strange character, he sort of loped around; that's how he worked. He was rather hesitant. I wouldn't say shy, but he wasn't abrasive either. He had a rather nice, rather vicious, South London sense of humour.' Reg Goodwin's political adviser Peter Walker told Hosken I was 'a political obsessive . . . Politics was a cult for him as it would have been for me if I hadn't had kids! He didn't come from great wealth; he was working-class. He had a good feeling for coalitions but it didn't mean to say that he was as confident as a lot of people.'

I was the only left-winger to be elected to the panel. When we met, Goodwin proposed I should be vice-chair of the Housing Management Committee under the new chair, Tony Judge, a former policeman who edited the *Police Federation Journal*. From the right of the party, Tony was the star of the new intake and

Goodwin's preferred successor. Judge admitted knowing nothing about housing but we agreed the GLC didn't work very well and a lot of members were not up to the job. We became good friends, disagreeing only on the issue of hard-to-let flats. I thought we should persevere with the waiting list but Tony put first-come, first-served ads in the evening papers. This led to long queues of young people outside our housing offices with the unintended side effect that a lot of left-wing graduates moved into old working-class estates, thus radicalising the local Labour parties.

The biggest change in the leadership was the departure of Jack Straw. After his year as deputy leader of the ILEA, the right felt he spent too much time pursuing his political career and the left that he was too cautious, but before we could vote him out he became political adviser to Barbara Castle and resigned.

The GLC had a quarter of a million homes, some of them dating back to Victorian times, and modernisation meant moving people out and renovating those homes, but it would take twenty years to work through the backlog and it didn't change their external appearance or layout. Tony Judge asked me to visit all the estates in the programme and come up with new ideas.

As I slogged around London I decided we couldn't ask tenants to wait twenty years to have modern amenities and in twenty years they would still look run-down from the outside, however much we spent internally. (With the election of Thatcher, twenty years would indeed pass before demolition began.) I proposed, and it was agreed, to give everybody a modern kitchen, gas-fired central heating, double-glazed windows and burglar-resisting front doors while we prepared to replace the worst estates with new homes.

*

Things were also going well at home. Mum was in the cottage in Lincolnshire, spending a lot of time with her old dancing friends.

Christine was teaching at Southwark's most difficult school and we moved to a small basement flat by West Norwood station. Although I was twenty-eight and Christine twenty-seven, we had to pretend to Christine's parents that we weren't living together. Only I could answer the phone at night or in the morning in case Christine's mum or dad called. When we stayed with them I shared a room with her brother. Mum was less prudish, though when we stayed at her cottage she left the light on in a third bedroom so the neighbours wouldn't know we were sleeping together. Ken Phipp, our new Labour agent, warned me that older members disapproved of our living in sin. We had always planned to marry and after Christmas 1973 we did so in the register office at Groby on the outskirts of Leicester, where Christine's parents lived, with only our immediate family as witnesses.

I loved all the little rituals of making our first home together. The bus to County Hall left from outside our front door, which was handy, though it would have been better if the drivers hadn't switched on the engines to warm them up at 6 a.m. A home of our own meant a whirlwind of friends coming and going, parties and endless political debate. I would have been happy to become a council tenant but without children we had no chance. The flat was damp in winter. Christine developed a worrying cough so we started looking for a place to buy. As we didn't have years of savings with a building society we needed a letter of recommendation from our MP, John Fraser, assuring them we were respectable, honest and hard-working in order to get a mortgage. When Eddie moved to Exeter he had sold his home to my old peace corps friend Ollie and his wife Diane. They decided to split up so we bought Eddie's old house – a four-bed Edwardian terraced house by Brockwell Park – for £13,000. Christine insisted that we paint the house before I built a pond.

The first few years were tight. The GLC allowance was about the same as the average wage and although inflation reached 25 per cent in 1975 the Labour government refused to increase the allowance for the next five years, effectively halving its value during that period. One way we saved money was by getting a lift with Uncle Ken and Aunt Vi as they drove to Lincoln to spend Christmas with Mum. This was two months after the Arab–Israeli war of 1973 and petrol prices soared, so because Uncle Ken had heard that the most economical speed was 20 mph we did exactly that from Brixton to Lincoln, starting at noon and arriving at 8 p.m. Ken refused to stop anywhere on the way.

*

One thing that helped my confidence was membership of the Area Health Authority (AHA) for Lambeth, Southwark and Lewisham. Heath had pushed through the biggest reorganisation of the NHS since it was set up in 1948, taking away local councils' community health responsibilities (and the GLC ambulance service) and giving them to hospital managers and consultants who favoured their own hospitals and started the long decline in community health care. Barbara Castle as Labour's new Minister of Health left the Tory changes in place and didn't even remove the Tories who had been appointed to chair the new AHAs.

As the Lambeth, Southwark and Lewisham AHA covered Guy's, St Thomas's and King's College teaching hospitals it was the largest AHA in Britain and top-heavy in consultants quite happy to slash community health care so that they got the lion's share of resources. Heath's social services secretary Sir Keith Joseph had appointed an arrogant, waistcoated property developer with no knowledge of the NHS or South London to chair our AHA. He resigned after a few meetings, complaining he didn't feel comfortable that members expected to vote. Barbara Castle ignored the wishes of the three local Labour councils and imposed Sir Kenneth Younger, a pleasant former MI6 officer and Labour minister from the Attlee government.

Under Sir Kenneth meetings were better-tempered and unlike the property developer he actually used the NHS. At one meeting he announced he was having major surgery the following month. At our next meeting the consultants were embarrassed when we had a minute's silence in honour of Sir Kenneth, who had died from septicaemia because the operating instruments had not been properly sterilised. Sir Kenneth had obviously received no special treatment.

The committee was frustrating because we didn't have the votes to protect community health services from the depredations of the consultants, but it was my first contact with big business. As the most prestigious AHA in Britain, leading businessmen had been appointed to it by Keith Joseph. Five years earlier I would have been in awe of them, but watching them in action I wasn't terribly impressed. My particular favourite was the then chairman of Nat-West, Sir John Prideaux. Tall, grey-haired and distinguished, with a deep voice and confident manner, he struggled to keep up with the speed at which we conducted business on the committee and it dawned on me that he was the chair of the bank mainly because he looked the part. As I banked with NatWest I considered moving my account, but guessed that the other banks were chaired by similar characters and just hoped the bank was really being run by brighter and sharper people further down the pecking order.

I believed I could achieve more at the GLC, so rather than looking for a parliamentary seat I wanted to spend the rest of my life at County Hall. Given my showing in Labour group elections, I dreamed of following in the footsteps of Herbert Morrison and becoming group leader. I couldn't believe how well things were going and on sunny days I would stride to work through Brockwell Park feeling that life couldn't get any better. But it did when Nixon was forced to resign over the break-in at the Democratic party offices at Watergate, and the following year the Vietnamese army swept through South Vietnam, forcing the US to flee and finally achieving independence for their country after thirty years of dreadful war.

My only setback had been in not getting elected chair of Lambeth's Housing Committee but I hadn't been ready for the job, so it was good that I didn't win. Now I'd learned enough to win arguments with officers at both Lambeth and the GLC. Notwithstanding my worries about the management of my bank account, everything else in my life seemed to be going just right. I had no idea how wrong I was.

5

Our Friends in the North

1974–1979

The election of David Stimpson as Lambeth Council leader in 1973 marked the end of our radical phase. David promised Charles Dryland that he could be chair of the Housing Committee if he supported him in the second ballot after Dryland was eliminated. Dryland asked for the same assurance from the left's candidate Mike Petrou, but we made the mistake of rejecting it. We felt that if Dryland wasn't up to being leader he shouldn't be inflicted on our tenants. Dryland's small group of supporters held the balance of power and had we done the deal we could have consolidated our hold on power and replaced Dryland the following year. I remembered this eight years later when centrists had the power to make Andrew McIntosh or myself leader of the GLC.

Dryland froze me out but my campaign against bad landlords in the borough continued. The reclusive Gerson Berger family owned a thousand run-down homes using the profits from them to fund a fundamentalist religious sect. Lambeth housing officials did not want to take these homes over because of the cost and work involved, so they asked Dryland to exclude the press and dozens of Berger's tenants from the committee hearings. He failed and the committee rejected the officers' concerns and agreed compulsory purchase orders. That was the end of any relationship I had with the chief officers. Officers then got Dryland to secretly stop passing empty homes to the homeless and started wrecking them. The Family Squatting Group now had 300 people in the hundred homes we had passed to them. But for Dryland, they might have had a great deal more.

The officers also obstructed the closure of our three Dickensian halfway homes. I promised the seventy-six families in Edward Henry House they would be moved after a flood in November 1973, and damp-ridden Ferndale Court with its baths in the kitchens had 500 children sleeping four to a room. Families were supposed to be moved after two years but many had just been left to rot. The third block at Black Prince Road was no better.

Lambeth's middle-class welfare officers feared that black people, single parents and the unemployed lacked 'good home standards' and should be kept in these old properties. When I argued we should drop this subjective process we were told that the GLC was to blame because it would only accept nominations into GLC homes of 'acceptable' tenants. At the GLC, on the other hand, officers said this policy was specifically at the request of the London boroughs. I never discovered who was telling the truth.

Nothing would happen unless I forced the issue so I resigned as vice-chair of housing in December 1973. With the row in the papers and the next Lambeth Council election five months away, Stimpson took the issue out of Dryland's hands. Hosken's interview for *Ken* with the then senior housing officer, Tony Bird, confirmed that my resignation 'did force the council to move the families out of the halfway homes . . . and tenants' lives were transformed'.

Ted and I worked to replace Stimpson and I was elected chair of the committee to write our manifesto and vet candidates. I opened the process by consulting widely and, believing it was up to the local members to decide their candidate, by ensuring that no one, left or right, was barred. (Left-wingers had been barred in the past but Ted and I refused to allow those on the left to use the same methods to block right-wingers.)

Ted and I encouraged working-class members, who feared they might not be up to it, to stand by promising that we would support them. For the first time we had more than just the token black face so one right-winger proposed not using photographs of the candidates. We hoped to gain Tory-held seats but there was a swing to the Tories and we lost two wards. Stimpson offered me the chair of housing if I did not stand against him for the leadership but I refused. He comfortably defeated me and excluded Ted and myself from chairing any Lambeth committees. This led to his downfall when he ran out of competent right-wing chairs.

Colin Blau, the third chair of housing in three years, faced mounting criticism about the vandalised empty homes and police kept having to clear the gallery during public meetings. We had set up elected neighbourhood councils to consult with them, but when they began complaining officers refused to meet them or answer their letters. This fed public anger and one of the neighbourhood councils elected a Maoist majority, so Stimpson closed down the lot. The Maoist paper's headline proclaimed 'Livingstone: traitor, careerist and scab'.

The more criticism there was from the public, the more Stimpson's clique embraced the council officers. A housing officer risked his career to tell me that lettings cards for new council homes had 'whites only' written on them in pencil. I was surprised as Harry Simpson had resisted pressure from Labour councillors in the 1960s to keep black families out of new homes, always asking for this to be put in writing, knowing they wouldn't dare do it. Blau had been replaced by Malcolm Noble, who had been at college with me. I told Noble where the files were but nothing happened, so I gave the story to the *South London Press*, who printed the evidence.

The officer responsible for the 'whites only' marking was suspended and Noble admitted he had casually raised the issue with the director of housing, who had told him nothing like that could possibly be going on. Apparently, neither bothered to check. The NALGO representative Bill Pitt staunchly opposed disciplinary action, waffling about 'putting the past behind us', and the officer was merely reprimanded for 'mismanagement'. At the next AGM Noble beat me by just one vote for chair of housing and Ted was only five votes short of defeating Stimpson. In 1981 Bill Pitt was Liberal candidate in the Croydon North West by-election and virulently attacked my record as GLC leader.

*

While Stimpson drifted to the right (with Blau and Noble he eventually defected to the SDP), local Labour parties were being radicalised by the changes unleashed by the Swinging Sixties. The first Women's Liberation Conference at Ruskin College, Oxford, in February 1970 had attracted derisory newspaper coverage which became more hostile when feminists disrupted the Miss World contest later that year. The first edition of *Spare Rib* appeared in July 1972, co-edited by Rosie Boycott (who, twenty years later as editor of *Esquire* magazine, appointed me as restaurant critic and later became Boris Johnson's food adviser).

Feminism was split between socialist feminists who focused on the Labour movement and radical feminists whose extreme wing envisaged a world without men. Labour responded with the 1975 Sex Discrimination Act and an Equal Opportunities Commission. The Equal Pay Act reduced the pay gap between men and women from 35 per cent to 24 per cent during the 1970s.

Although Parliament legalised gay sex it remained socially unacceptable, as the Labour MP and medical doctor David Owen made clear in a speech saying that legalisation should not discourage gay men from seeking a cure. Gay politics erupted out of its Soho closet in November 1970 when the Gay Liberation Front (GLF) held a protest against police harassment. The GLF's first meeting at the London School of Economics two months earlier had attracted hundreds of supporters, including John Lennon and David Hockney, via its magazine *Come Together*. By 1972 the GLF had split into several groups, one of which later came to Brixton to stand against John Fraser in the October 1974 election, when their candidate mortified traditional Labour party members by parading on a horse and coming to the count in a coffin to symbolise the death of democracy. He polled 223 votes. I had picked up a more tolerant approach on gay issues because Mum had worked with gay people throughout her dancing career and she always made clear to me and Linda how nice she had found them.

Two activists from early GLF meetings had a huge influence in London politics. Angela Mason, first director of Stonewall (the lobbying group for lesbian and gay rights), advised me as mayor, headed Tony Blair's Women and Equality Unit and became a Labour peer. Peter Tatchell had a more confrontational approach, asking the Royal Parks to allow the first Gay Pride march in July 1972 to end in Hyde Park. The snotty reply was that 'the Royal Parks are for families, not homosexuals'.

University-educated radicals and feminists were joining the Labour party and changing its working-class ethos. Mary Evans was the loudest and funniest, with her unerring ability to wind Ted up with her criticism of trade unions. Ted felt that raising issues of housework and childcare during strikes played into the bosses' hands, but Mary pointed out women had waited too long for change. It was not until 1979 that the TUC issued their 'Equality for Women within Trade Unions Charter'.

I met Mary when she was campaigning for the homeless. A strong critic of Dryland – he provoked uproar when he asked, 'Why are you young women so aggressive these days?' – Mary wanted the council to provide free sanitary protection but Stimpson delayed the issue, saying he would ask the Association of Municipal Authorities (AMA) to make this national policy. Stimpson had to put up with a chorus of sexism in the AMA Labour group, where one leader asked if his pipe tobacco should also be free, but he had dragged the issue out until the reorganisation of the NHS removed our powers to do this.

Before the arrival of the GLF in Brixton my only contact with gays had been the expat Brits Mick and I had encountered in Africa and a couple of Mick's friends who ran a florist's in Whitechapel. I got involved when an ILEA college proposed a course for social workers about problems faced by gays. The Tories screamed that this was 'homosexuality on the rates' and Jack Straw, who chaired the Further and Higher Education Committee, stopped the course, saying he wasn't ready to see ratepayers' money spent in this way.

The GLF wanted a grant of £17,997 to support their advice service but George West (a survivor from the old Labour regime) waged holy war against the sodomites. I pointed out that the world was changing and San Francisco's police chief marched in the annual Gay Pride rally (alongside Harvey Milk who in 1977 became the first openly gay man elected to public office in America). But West won easily after a homophobic rant warning that homosexuals wanted to 'force it [sic] down people's throats'.

I took up the case of the schools inspector who was told to resign as his boss didn't know the difference between a gay man and a paedophile, the boss saying he 'had no idea what it was these people did'. Committee chair Stanley Mayne overturned the decision and helped me win my first breakthrough on gay issues when the GLC Labour group voted by 31 to 6 to recognise the newly formed staff Gay Society.

*

The Heath government was coming apart at the seams. The miners' strike of January 1972 – the first time since the general strike of 1926 that the National Union of Mineworkers had declared a strike – was very successful, attracting support from dockers and other workers, and in early February Heath declared a national emergency and introduced a three-day week. They struck again in February 1974 and Heath again brought in a three-day week. So when a snap general election was called on 7 February, with the poll set for the 28th, I took charge of canvassing in Norwood. Opinion polls predicted a Tory win, since they hoped to capitalise on fear of the militant unions, but on the canvassing returns we were getting a swing of 4 per cent to Labour in Norwood. Unlike today, when people change their mind on their way to vote, political loyalties were stable. If one person in a house was Labour, then usually so was everybody else. Seats changed hands because disillusioned loyalists stayed home. Norwood's Tory wards showed a big increase in 'don't knows'. I so enjoyed organising elections that I would have loved to work as a Labour agent while serving on the council, but this was against party rules.

Wilson squeaked back into power but I had no expectation his government would do anything interesting and I wasn't disappointed. The recession triggered by the oil embargo following the 1973 Arab–Israeli war saw inflation reach 26 per cent and the government started cutting spending and services. As the biggest local-government spender, the GLC was in the Treasury's sights.

*

The GLC manifesto that Labour had produced in 1973 was both radical and costly. We had increased house building and frozen fares, but Goodwin had no leadership skills. He had gone to the same primary school as me and, like Ted, to Strand Grammar for his secondary schooling. A devout Christian, he had worked as a taster in his father's tea company before a twenty-eight-year career as general secretary of the National Association of Boys Clubs. His devoted wife, Lady Penelope, drove him around at election time in an old Ford Prefect. They lived in a cottage on the South Downs, but Reg kept his right to serve on the GLC by renting a Southwark council flat. This could not be used against him by the Tories as Horace Cutler, the leader of their GLC group, also lived outside London in Gerrards Cross, while occupying a London Transport flat.

Goodwin's idol, Dr Alfred Salter, an early Labour pioneer in local government, had built homes so energetically that 98 per cent of housing in Bermondsey was council property. Bermondsey Labour party was controlled by the brutal Bob Mellish, Harold Wilson's chief whip, who as chair of the London Labour party ruled London Labour politics with a rod of iron. In 1946 Mellish had beaten Goodwin to succeed Dr Salter as MP by packing the selection meeting with dock workers, but he allowed Reg to continue his career at County Hall as he posed no threat to himself. In the 1967 GLC election only eighteen Labour members were elected, eliminating stronger personalities, otherwise Goodwin would never have become leader. A local journalist wrote that he was like 'a monk welcoming one to his retreat'. But some found Goodwin's modesty preferable to the devious ways of Harold Wilson. He detested his coarser colleagues and when he joined the Labour table in the members' dining room swearing stopped and conversation turned to polite generalities.

Goodwin preferred the company of senior council officers and his personal staff, who treated him with affection. In a break with the past he appointed a political adviser, Peter Walker, a twenty-seven-year-old party employee who persuaded Goodwin to cast off his waistcoat and stiff-collared shirts. He told Andrew Hosken that he was 'a man from the 1930s living in the 1970s'.

John Carvel records a less kindly assessment from Harvey Hinds, the Labour chief whip:

Reg was a hermit. He lived entirely within himself. And as a leader he was weak. He was the prey to the last person who got into his room before the decision had to be taken . . . he was a man of integrity, but a recluse, a sphinx, who couldn't socialise, couldn't talk to people, had to be bludgeoned into actually receiving anyone into his room. I almost had to make an appointment with his secretary to see him . . . upon entry, he would be at one end of the room, deep in papers, and eventually he would look up. Then he would be absolutely courteousness itself – do sit down, can I get you a cup of tea – but there was always the impression of actually intruding on private grief to walk into the room and bring him in contact with the reality of the political situation.

Goodwin hated the competition for his ear and often retreated to the County Hall chapel to avoid competing egos. Hosken quotes Illtyd Harrington saying that '[Goodwin] found it very difficult to get off his knees and come upstairs to make a few decisions . . . You could never get an opinion out of him; he would always smile. He looked rather like someone who would have made a second deacon in a Methodist church.'

New members could not work out what Goodwin's politics were. He had written much of our radical manifesto in 1973 but had prospered under right-wing leaders. After six months, however, we discovered exactly where he stood on the left–right spectrum. Reg Prentice, MP for Newham North East (who eventually defected to the Tories), was involved in a fight about whether the government should lift the penalties imposed by the District Auditor on Clay Cross councillors who had refused to increase rents. Prentice argued they should be left to rot while Dennis Skinner, MP for the area, led the fight to have their penalties removed.

Dr Stephen Haseler and Douglas Eden, two GLC members (who, bizarrely, had come to our small left-wing caucus six months earlier), persuaded Goodwin to sign a round robin calling on Harold Wilson to back Reg Prentice which they then released to the media. Goodwin looked a complete fool when Wilson copied his reply to the press:

At a late hour last night an unsigned letter arrived in this office addressed to Mr Wilson and purporting to come from you. In order that he might see who the sender/s were he was referred to an annexure with a list of persons prominent in local government together with a small number of prospective parliamentary candidates.

Mr Wilson well understands that you would have been concerned at [the decision to support the Clay Cross councillors] though since it occurred nearly two months ago it is difficult to understand why it has not been raised with him earlier. He would have been glad at any time to discuss the matter with you . . . I am asked to say that letters from you to Mr Wilson would be welcome at any time, by which he means letters, not a 'round robin' cooked up by a number of people with little interest in Clay Cross and less in unity and success of the party . . . your authority is devalued by association with some of the signatories in the annexe to the letter . . .

Mr Wilson would, however, like you to know that should any members of your GLC Labour group step out of line . . . he will not write, either individually or as part of a consortium, a dissociatory letter with copies to all your colleagues.

Goodwin relied heavily on the GLC's new director general, Sir James Swaffield, who had been secretary to the Association of Municipal Authorities with real influence over government policy, and was head and shoulders above the usual run of local government chief executives. After the election Maurice Stonefrost was appointed comptroller of financial services. Following an impressive council career he had run the Chartered Institute for Public Finance and Accountancy. Stonefrost was intense and passionate while presenting his arguments in a relaxed and charming way.

Our problems were compounded by a mish-mash of responsibilities, some of which should have been transferred to the London boroughs. The GLC was supposed to be a strategic regional authority but the Tories had refused to devolve powers to it from government and so it failed to capture the public imagination. Finally, our manifesto was written during a boom, without working out what it would cost or who was going to pay.

Inflation was soaring, which was the reason for the 85 per cent rate increase in our first budget. County Hall had spent twenty-five years borrowing for post-war reconstruction (mainly homes), leaving us with a debt of £1.6 billion. This was six times our annual budget and these old debts, originally at 3 per cent interest, were being refinanced at 13 per cent. Goodwin took his committee chairs to a secret meeting in Aldermaston, where Maurice warned that banks would not lend to us unless we scaled back our spending plans.

If Maurice had come to the Labour group we could have questioned him, challenged his assumptions, and might have agreed a way forward without tearing ourselves apart, but Goodwin proceeded by stealth. When the group met on 10 June 1974 he proposed an immediate 12 per cent public transport fare increase. He deeply regretted this but felt 'a thoughtful public would understand it'. Feeling that it was being bounced, the group was more angry than thoughtful and things got worse when news of the secret meeting at Aldermaston slipped out. To Goodwin's annoyance the group rejected the increase by 31 votes to 25.

At the Labour group meeting on 22 July Dame Evelyn Dennington, chair of the Transport Committee, proposed without warning an immediate 20 per cent fare increase. I pointed out group rules meant a previous decision could only be discussed again within six months if two-thirds of the members present agreed, and I challenged Goodwin to call such a vote, which he lost. I felt an almost physical wave of hatred directed at me from Goodwin's supporters as the meeting broke up amid obscene abuse. Newham's Tom Jenkinson bellowed at me, 'I'd like to kick your arse all the way back to fucking Lambeth.'

The issue was raised again after the October general election, when we were told that unless Goodwin got his way he would resign. Demanding a 36 per cent fares increase as well as cuts in every committee budget, he said taking this difficult decision now would save our house-building programme. He won the vote by 46 to 9. Two months later Goodwin forced through an increase in council rents of 12 per cent, now claiming that *this* would save our housing programme.

When Illtyd Harrington presented Labour's second budget in February 1975 the increase in rates was 80 per cent (nine-tenths of it due to inflation). The average London householder was paying £40 a year to the GLC, but if we had not increased rents and fares or made cuts it would have been £55 per year. In other words, we had torn ourselves apart and dumped our manifesto to save the average householder 30p a week, while families saw their fares increase by 35 per cent, a quarter of a million council families had to pay increased rents, and 2,000 jobs were cut while unemployment rose. And while the average householder saw an annual saving of just £15, Shell paid £240,000 less on its South Bank headquarters than it otherwise would have.

*

Gladys Dimson, chair of housing, had spent two years increasing new house building and taking over private rented accommodation but her most difficult task had been to persuade the thirty-two London boroughs to agree a Strategic Housing Plan (SHP) for the whole city. There was bitter opposition from Tory boroughs amid fears that more council housing would bring in Labour voters and black families. But as the environment secretary Tony Crosland prepared to make the SHP legally binding, Goodwin proposed cuts in our housing programme.

Crosland's political adviser David Lipsey told me Crosland had got the Treasury to fund the programme with a £150 million loan, so I was surprised when Goodwin proposed a £50 million cut. Goodwin claimed the banks would refuse to lend and his reduction had the support of the government. I relayed word for word my conversation with David Lipsey, effectively calling Goodwin a liar to his face. Ina Chaplin, who had known Goodwin for thirty years, whispered, 'You've really upset Reg. I've never seen him look so furious.' But all I could see was his usual immobile, sphinx-like stare into the distance.

As we deferred the decision in order to clear up what Crosland really wanted, Goodwin made a bitter personal attack on me, claiming I had gone behind his back. We would now take this decision at the 1975 annual meeting, where Goodwin was seeking re-election as leader. We were so poorly led that ILEA leader Sir Ashley Bramall sounded out members to see if they would support Goodwin's removal. Although Bramall was on the right of the party he was at least competent, but I couldn't persuade the left and we didn't have the votes.

After Goodwin was re-elected unopposed he proposed that Gladys Dimson be replaced by Richard Balfe, but his reasoning for the £50 million housing cut had changed. He now argued that to carry on building would increase the rates in the run-up to the next GLC election in 1977. Balfe promised to find £50 million of 'savings' without cutting the housing programme. By now the group was so demoralised it agreed to sack Dimson and cut the housing programme. The following afternoon Goodwin demanded I agree to support future cuts as well as rent and fare increases or be sacked as vice-chair of housing management. I refused and returned to the back benches, where I spent the next two years working with our scientific department to report on environmental issues, proposing that all committee reports should include an environmental assessment alongside the financial and staffing implications. My report was never published on the grounds that it would add to costs.

Goodwin told the group that the cuts 'could well mean the difference between Labour winning power in 1977 with a modified housing programme or Labour losing with a higher but unacceptably expensive housing programme'. In the next two years increases in fares and rents were so big that Goodwin could freeze the rates at 1975 levels. By the 1977 GLC election house building had reverted to the level we had inherited from the Tories.

*

The left was in a minority on the Labour party's London executive, chaired by Bob Mellish, but gained ground at each year's London party conference. Goodwin was furious that I continued to criticise his policies and at the meeting to discuss the next increase in fares Jim Daly, the chair of the Transport Committee, proposed and won a vote in the Labour group that 'Ken Livingstone should not be allowed to speak [at GLC meetings]'. Daly was incandescent when I ignored this decision and following a visit to Moscow he waxed lyrical about the benefits of a council with no dissidents. When Daly defected to the SDP in 1980 he gave as one reason 'the undemocratic and intolerant nature' of the Labour party.

I was becoming better known among party members thanks to Camden Labour leader Frank Dobson, whose council provided the best services in London. His radicalism was clear when anarchists led by the writer Jenny Diski asked him to support the setting up of a free school in derelict buildings at King's Cross for local kids who had dropped out. Frank gave Jenny a £20,000 grant, provoking fury among ILEA members who couldn't distinguish between fee-paying and free schools.

In early 1975, with an economic crisis looming, the Wilson government embarked on a policy of cutting council spending. In May Tony Crosland made a speech in Manchester warning councils that 'the party is over'. In response, Frank Dobson convened a London-wide conference in July to set up Labour Against the Housing Cuts and I became its secretary. The campaign widened to defend all services and went national as Labour Against the Cuts, producing a newsletter and sending speakers all over the country. As the other campaigners had young families, I was usually the one who was sent. Although it was Crosland's department making the cuts he was clearly doing his best to minimise the damage and I still hoped he would succeed Wilson.

*

With the cuts and with council powers being sucked up to Whitehall my hopes of a life doing good works at County Hall crumbled. (Under Thatcher and Blair the marginalisation of local government continued.) I decided to stand for Parliament and threw my hat in the ring for Hampstead. Ben Whitaker became Hampstead's first Labour MP in 1966, when the actor Peter O'Toole hired a coach with Guinness on tap and went round the pubs of Kilburn promising a free drink and a ride to the polling station for anyone voting Labour. The seat was won in 1970 by Tory MP Geoffrey Finsberg who increased his majority in 1974 while the rest of Britain swung to Labour. Some locals put this down to snobbery as our candidate, Tony Clarke, was a postman. I suspected it was because Tony was on the right of the Labour party and we would only win Hampstead with a radical candidate.

The selection process in 1976 was a two-horse race between myself and Vincent Cable, a senior Foreign Office diplomat and a former president of the Cambridge Union. The party was split down the middle and although we never had a cross word I thought even then that he should be in the Liberal party. I won by 24 votes to 20 and Vince became a senior economist at Shell before being elected as a Liberal Democrat MP in 1997.

As I supported a wealth tax, a handful of members resigned. At my first Hampstead dinner party I chewed my way through a bouquet garni under the impression that it was a stuffed vine leaf, compounding the gaffe with the excuse that this was not standard fare in Lambeth. One member wrote to the national party urging them to overturn my selection:

His education is sketchy. I understand he went to a College of Education and we all know how low the standard is at some such places which I think I would describe as schools for nannies. This is a great pity when one thinks that there were in the running for the candidature two PhDs, a QC and several other graduates of reputable universities such as Oxford. I am not suggesting that every Labour candidate should be a graduate: merely that to win a constituency with as sophisticated an electorate as Hampstead we need a candidate with clear intellectual ability . . . the attached article of mine shows the disastrous result . . . when we had a postman as a candidate . . . this selection has been a clear use of Ovid's line: '*Video meliora proboque, deteriora sequor*' (I see the better things and I approve, I follow the worse). If the NEC refuse endorsement . . . there might be a chance of a left-wing candidate who is not a fool being chosen . . .

At County Hall Tony Banks started plotting to take over the Labour group at the election in 1977. We made a few gains, and the brightest star among the new members was Greg Dyke, representing Putney, who joined our caucus of left-wing candidates. Sadly, he didn't win Putney but went on to change the face of breakfast television with Roland Rat. Although there was no chance of the left winning, the *Daily Telegraph* alarmed Middle England with the headline 'Shock wave of Marxism hits GLC elections', warning that 'Formidable gains by the left . . . have split constituency organisations and sent a shock wave through the Labour party . . .

it has brought quiet jubilation to Marxists and other left-wing candidates.'

Tony was the boss and I was the apprentice as we schemed and planned. Tony's political career started a decade earlier than mine as a Liberal candidate for Lambeth Council in 1964 but as he claimed to be only two years older than me he couldn't have been legally qualified to stand. I assumed he had taken a couple of years off his age but when I said this to his wife Sally after his death in 2006 she smiled and said 'and the rest'. His other endearing vanity was wearing platform shoes to hide his small stature. His *Daily Telegraph* obituary described him as 'brash, hyperactive and witty, with a dapper, not to say dandyish appearance'. His love of animals had made him a hard-line vegetarian and his long commitment to Chelsea FC wasn't diminished when as MP for West Ham he had to support them as well. On entering the House of Lords in 2005 he applied for the title of Lord Banks of the Thames, though he ended up as Baron Stratford.

Tony seldom mentioned that he was the son of a senior diplomat in Poland and had grown up in an exclusive block of private flats on Streatham High Road where Dad cleaned the windows, a fact Tony made me promise not to reveal. We shared a passion for animals and he'd had a Saturday job in the Brixton Arcade pet shop from which I'd bought amphibians in the late 1950s, though when I gave him a large Asiatic toad as a present Sally was not too pleased.

An astute political operator, Tony was political adviser to the Minister for Overseas Development, Judith Hart, and then worked for the Association of Broadcasting and Allied Staffs. Tony would have been our candidate for leader had the left won control of the Labour group at the 1977 election, not just because he chaired the General Purposes Committee but because as head of research in the Amalgamated Engineering Workers he coordinated links between left-wing unions and was well connected with anyone who mattered on the left. He played a key role in organising Tony Benn's leadership campaign following Wilson's resignation in 1976, and expected eventually a job in Benn's cabinet if successful, with the aim of succeeding to the Labour leadership. Unfortunately, Benn came fourth in the first round and dropped out to support the eventual runner-up, Michael Foot.

I spent hours in Tony's office while we organised the campaign to prevent former CIA spy Philip Agee and Mark Hosenball (a journalist who had exposed CIA crimes and the intelligence eavesdropping activities at GCHQ in Cheltenham) from being deported. When Labour Home Secretary Merlyn Rees eventually deported them in 1977 he assured the House of Commons this was not done to appease the US, but requests made under the Freedom of Information Act have since revealed that Henry Kissinger made a secret visit to London the week before the deportation decision. Lord Denning, in his judgment of the case, said in words that now seem comical: 'In some parts of the world national security has been used as an excuse for all sorts of infringements of individual liberty. But not in England.'

Tony relied on me to analyse opinion polls and voting trends, which showed that the Tories would win the GLC and our seats would be lost, so we moved to safer seats. None of us wanted to leave our current seats but party members agreed it was important that as many left-wingers as possible should survive to continue the fight. Tony took Douglas Eden's constituency of Feltham after I assured him it was safe, but the swing was worse than expected and Tony lost, though he never blamed me. Tony also took my advice when he stood as MP for Watford. I told him he would win it as long as the Tory lead nationally was under 6 per cent but after the 'winter of discontent' Mrs Thatcher led the Tories to a 7 per cent lead and Tony lost. He had to wait until the 1983 election to get into Parliament.

I was luckier. Paul Moore's group the Chartists had members in Hackney North and Stoke Newington, whose retiring GLC member Dr David Pitt had been a friend of mine since his doomed campaign in Clapham to be the first black Labour MP. Hackney North's General Management Committee was on a knife edge after an influx of younger members like Kate Hoey, who was in the IMG when she was elected NUS vice-president (and made life as difficult as possible for Jack Straw). She told me she had been subject to a smear campaign that she had been involved with the 'Stoke Newington Eight' (better known as the Angry Brigade who had tried to assassinate Robert Carr, Ted Heath's employment secretary), but there was no truth in this; we became such good friends that she let me use her holiday home in Portugal.

*

Stoke Newington was more diverse than my old seat of Norwood, with a large black and Asian community as well as the largest Orthodox Jewish community outside Israel or New York. Ashley Bramall, who had investigated many disputes in the local party, warned me that only an Orthodox Jew could understand the schisms among the factions. I was amazed to see one group demonstrating against the existence of Israel and the politics of Orthodox Judaism remained a mystery, although I developed a passion for lunches of smoked salmon and cheesecake. One young man said he would only vote for me if I agreed to support Israel, right or wrong. As I wouldn't ask anyone to support me, right or wrong, I declined.

This religious and racial mix was a prime target for the National Front (forerunner of the BNP). As anger with Labour mounted, the NF grew and on a march in Wood Green I had to stop Christine pushing through the police cordon protecting the NF marchers. The Labour party decided to ignore the NF but the Chartists and I disagreed and all my campaign literature explained that the NF was a fascist party and a threat to democracy. The NF was registering support on old estates where people felt neglected by both council and government as they watched their jobs go with the closure of the docks and the collapse of manufacturing. The government complacently assumed they would find work in other parts of London.

Hackney Council had a poor record on housing and with cuts by the government and the GLC many estates were run down. While half the NF support was racist, the rest was a protest against neglect by Labour. Time after time locals told me, 'I was going to vote for the NF but I'll vote for you because you've called in person.' I even found one elderly black woman on a poor estate intending to vote for the NF in the hope they would send her back to Jamaica. With the unpopularity of Callaghan's government in 1977 I was by no means certain to be elected to the GLC, particularly as the Communist party ran Monty Goldman against me. Local Trotskyist groups with a deep loathing for the Communist party followed Monty around with a megaphone reminding local voters of the Stalin–Hitler pact of 1939.

With only a small local Labour membership there was no chance of a full canvass until our local MP David Weitzman said he was retiring. Kate Hoey begged me to drop Hampstead and stand for MP in Stoke Newington. Almost certainly I would have been selected, but although I could have represented Stoke Newington on the GLC as well as becoming its MP it would have been very messy. Also I couldn't do that, given how hard people had worked to get me selected in Hampstead. Kate also got a phone call from Jack Straw, sounding out his chances in the seat, followed by a deluge of letters from wannabe MPs, so we sent them our canvassing schedule and invited them to join us. Every night and weekend we had eighty ambitious canvassers, which allowed us to run such a strong GLC campaign that the Tory candidate complained that we were being unreasonable by campaigning so hard as this meant all parties would have to start doing the same thing, 'which would mean unnecessary work for everyone'.

The former Conservative MP for Lancaster, Humphrey Berkeley, came to canvass for us. He supported the legalisation of homosexuality and demanded sanctions against Rhodesia, which cost him his seat when local Tories refused to campaign for him. Now in the Labour party, he realised he wouldn't be selected as the Labour candidate for Stoke Newington but still turned up to help and drove me back home across London at the end of each day, regaling me with stories about his attempts to expose Jeffrey Archer's dodgy dealings.

While we were waiting for the count at Hackney Town Hall news came that the NF had won 5 per cent of Londoners' votes, and although they had done badly in Hackney North, in three wards in Hackney South they would have won seats had it been a borough council election. Although I had the third-best result in London, it was Labour's worst night overall since 1968. The Tories were back in control of the GLC, winning 64 seats to our 28.

*

With the Labour group decimated, Goodwin had to give me a job as opposition spokesman on housing development. No one anticipated the ferocity of the new GLC leader Horace Cutler's attack on housing. He immediately cut the building programme by two-thirds to just 2,000 a year and sold off all GLC land to prevent future house building. Cutler sold all new council homes in marginal constituencies rather than let them to families on the waiting list. Although intended for families on Hounslow's waiting list, homes on the new Brentford Dock estate (very convenient for White City studios) were sold to BBC staff.

Some of the Tories were so virulent that George Tremlett, the new chair of housing, and I became quite close. When Andrew Retter, the newly elected Hayes and Harlington Tory, asked, 'When are we going to stop housing niggers?' George replied, 'We don't use language like that here.' Retter said, 'They do where I come from.' When the GLC's chief valuation officer invited George to join the housing department's Masonic lodge he declined.

The GLC had a large house-building department and one of Richard Balfe's worst decisions under the previous regime had been to appoint Tory activist Denshore Dover as its director. Dover believed housing 'should be provided by private developers [only]'. The District Auditor produced a highly political report criticising an overspend of £1.5 million on thirty-six contracts (which was nothing compared to cost overruns by private developers) and Cutler used this to stop all building by the department. Dover was sacked after he became a Tory MP two years later and sued the GLC for wrongful dismissal. How he expected to work full time for the GLC while being an MP was never explained, but he dropped the case in exchange for a year's salary. Thirty years later his career ended following revelations about his expenses claims as an MEP.

Margaret Thatcher had succeeded Ted Heath as Tory leader in 1975 and Cutler's policies were a foretaste of how right-wing a government led by her would be. They united the Labour group after its years of division. Cutler's worst act of vandalism was to close the GLC nursery where the trees for London's parks and streets were grown. The saplings there were bulldozed to increase the site's value to developers.

*

In the three years following my selection in 1976 I threw everything into winning Hampstead: fund-raising, voter-registration drives and energising the party. I believed that hard work, as John Fraser had shown in Norwood, could turn a Tory marginal into a Labour seat. Christine and I sold our house in Lambeth to Tom

Jackson, the postal workers' union leader, and for the same price bought a flat in West Hampstead. The difference between living north and south of the river was amazing. It was not just swapping the Co-op for Waitrose, but in South London lives are built around the timetables of buses and British Rail trains. Now we could walk to the tube and a train would come along every few minutes. Initially I felt hemmed in in North London, the roads seemed narrower and each house had an extra storey, but I soon acclimatised and South London began to seem almost too roomy. One thing I never adjusted to was the difference in pubs. I'd come of drinking age in sparsely occupied saloon bars with an older clientele where you could meet for a quiet pint. In Hampstead pubs were young, funky and heaving.

Two local activists who helped me win the parliamentary nomination were Neil and Margaret Fletcher from Kilburn, where the long-serving councillor was a paedophile. Although no one could prove this, council leader Roy Shaw made certain that Albert Skinner never held any post of responsibility. As I had moved out of Lambeth and wouldn't stand again Neil and Maggie organised my local selection for Camden Council as Hampstead was in the borough, with Neil as one of the other candidates. Skinner left the Labour party to run as an independent, claiming that the Labour party had been taken over by extremists, but we held the ward. One reason for the Tory gains across London was that Thatcher outflanked the NF on immigration with a television interview in January 1978 in which she said, 'People are really rather afraid that this country might be swamped by people with a different culture ... we do have to hold out the prospect of an end to immigration, except, of course, for compassionate cases.'

Thatcher won the support of Enoch Powell, though was denounced by church leaders, political opponents and, anonymously, by some in her shadow cabinet, but she achieved her desired effect as the Tories moved from level-pegging with Labour into an 11-point lead. With racist votes swinging behind Mrs Thatcher, the NF's hopes withered. In the three South Hackney wards where they had led twelve months before, the resurgent Tory vote kept them in second place.

Against the wishes of Roy Shaw, I was elected chair of the Camden Housing Committee, succeeding Tessa Jowell. I won because our candidates had found widespread dissatisfaction at the slow and bureaucratic nature of the housing department. After the frustration of watching Lambeth's housing policies implode I knew what to do. I commandeered an office inside the department, appointed a personal assistant and to the horror of senior officers became a full-time chair, writing my own committee reports when officers dragged their feet.

It was exhilarating to be running something again, getting up early to go to the town hall. Previous chairs had a weekly meeting with the director of housing but I worked directly with second- and third-tier officers who took the day-to-day management decisions. The best of these jumped at the chance to get quick decisions rather than ploughing through bureaucracy and waiting weeks for the Housing Committee to decide. With constant pressure I humanised the way we treated homeless families, cut the number of those in bed-and-breakfast accommodation in the borough to under twenty and passed empty homes to a short-life housing association. Wanting to work with the trade unions, I met the local branch of NALGO (the main union representing local government white-collar staff) and asked them for suggestions, but was disappointed when they said it was not their job to propose changes and they wished simply to respond to management proposals.

Camden had the best social services, libraries and council housing in London and Frank Dobson, the previous leader, and his successor Roy Shaw ensured that the housing department had the funds to keep the stock in better repair than Lambeth. We were building 2,000 new homes a year, at which rate families on the waiting list would all have been housed within a decade. The problem was that Camden didn't have enough land and the architects' department was planning to build homes over railways. Constructing concrete rafts on stilts over railway lines is expensive and time consuming, so I proposed that instead we take over badly managed private rented accommodation and modernise it. As well as preserving the character of our streets, this would give families access to gardens.

I was having a real impact on housing policy and had a good chance of winning Hampstead, so Christine and I decided to take Mum with us on our first holiday to the USA on one of the new bucket-flight deals. We exchanged our flat with a family in Connecticut. Mum got a bit bored watching a meeting of the New Haven town council, which I couldn't resist attending, but using the house as a base we travelled through Boston up to Maine and down to New York. The volume and quality of goods in the shops made it feel like we had come to the capital of a great empire, but the crime was so bad that many tourists did not use New York's subway. A holiday is the quickest way to reveal hidden tensions and I discovered Christine and Mum really didn't like each other, although they had kept it from me for years.

*

The election of Thatcher as Tory leader led to complacency in Labour ranks as they assumed she would be a weak candidate and alienate middle-of-the-road voters. Jim Callaghan had a good press but his record as Chancellor of the Exchequer was dismal and as Foreign Secretary non-existent. A reactionary Home Secretary, he opposed the progressive reforms of Roy Jenkins and supported violent police attacks against anti-Vietnam war protestors in the

Grosvenor Square riots in 1968. After entering Number 10 he immediately sacked Barbara Castle, whose past affairs offended his moral code, and immigration minister Alex Lyon for letting 'too many' immigrants into the country: an unpleasant reminder of the time when Callaghan had stripped Kenyan Asians of their British passports in 1968. Eddie Lopez had warned me about his pomposity and arrogance. When Labour canvassers called at his Lambeth home for support at council elections he replied, 'That will depend on the quality of the candidate; send them to see me.'

There was a poll bounce in Labour's favour when he replaced Wilson as prime minister because the first year of wage policy allowed a flat £6 increase, which was higher than inflation. The second year of wage policy saw a cut in living standards as inflation rose to 18 per cent while wages only went up 9 per cent, and this was a factor in Labour's wipeout at the 1977 GLC election.

With a general election on the horizon, no one was surprised that the third year of wage policy from August 1977 saw earnings rise by 14 per cent as inflation slowed to 8 per cent. As living standards rose, Callaghan's poll ratings soared ahead of Thatcher's and the parties were neck and neck. This seems surprising in retrospect, given the common depiction of the 1970s as a time of national decline with Britain teetering on the brink of ungovernability, but history has been rewritten to justify the destructive forces unleashed by Thatcher in the 1980s. A 1977 Gallup poll found the British to be among the happiest people on earth. In *When the Lights Went Out* Andy Beckett quotes two surveys of public attitudes for the magazine *New Society* which showed that by a margin of two to one all social classes preferred a 'pleasant life' over 'working as hard as you can for as much money as you can get'. In the seventies the pay gap between men and women narrowed, the working day shortened and annual leave increased from two or three weeks to four or five. With the arrival of North Sea oil we looked forward to a big increase in both private and public investment.

Thatcher was far from confident she could win an election in October 1978. Polls showed that if Ted Heath had still been leader the Tory advantage would have been 10 per cent greater. The public's mistrust of Thatcher reflected a widespread belief that she would provoke even more discontent from the unions than Heath had. Speaking to the Tory conference in 1976 she said she was 'look[ing] forward to discussion and consultation with the trade union movement about the policies that are needed to save our country'. In January 1978 the minutes of Thatcher's Steering Committee warned, referring to the Tory plans for union reform: 'if we told the truth about the unions we should certainly lose the election'. With the whole country expecting an autumn election in 1978 I watched Callaghan's September TV broadcast with Harvey Hinds in the members' room at County Hall. I had called a meeting of my election team in Hampstead that evening to start the campaign and was stunned when Callaghan announced he would not call an election after all. There was real anger that he had led us all up the garden path. In his memoirs Callaghan admits he made a mistake 'in allowing the speculation to build up . . . without uttering a word to cool it'. His senior policy adviser, Tom McNally, warned him that 'you'll either be remembered now as a political genius or as the man who missed the boat'.

In her autobiography, Margaret Thatcher recalls sharing the sense of anti-climax but asks: 'Would we have won a general election in the autumn of 1978? I believe that we might have scraped in . . . but it would only have needed one or two mistakes in our campaign to have lost . . . even if we had won, what would have happened next? . . . If we had been faced [with the wave of strikes] over the winter of 1978/9 it might have broken us, as it finally did the Labour government . . .'

Labour's vulnerability was Callaghan's determination to try another year of wage restraint. His first setback came when the Labour party conference rejected his 5 per cent pay policy. When Ford's annual pay deal broke this barrier, the government decided not to buy cars from them but were humiliated when Parliament voted to reject the policy. While pay rose in the private sector, Callaghan's insistence on holding the line with public sector pay ushered in the infamous 'winter of discontent'. The Tory press had a field day as council workers went on strike, huge piles of rubbish built up, grave diggers refused to bury the dead and hospitals could only deal with emergencies.

I was aware the impact the strike was having on council estates with heating cut off and lifts unrepaired, so I met with other left-wing Camden councillors and we decided to propose a local wage settlement to end the strike. The union demand was for a minimum weekly wage of £60 for a thirty-five-hour week. We had no interest in increasing the wages of senior staff so instead of the national claim we proposed a 'minimum wage supplement' to increase weekly wages of the low-paid to £60.

Many middle-of-the-road councillors were ashamed that some staff only received £45 a week and we won by one vote after accepting an amendment that the thirty-five-hour week should mean new jobs rather than more overtime. It was left to deputy leader John Mills, chair of the Finance Committee, to sort out the details. John, a bright and honest right-winger, did everything possible to carry out the decision but negotiations dragged on because the idiots in the local NALGO branch couldn't recognise a good thing when they saw it. The strike in Camden didn't finish earlier than the national dispute, but we at least we had ended the scandal of low pay among our staff.

The strike was barely over before Thatcher cobbled together a single-vote anti-government majority of 311–310 in a no-confidence motion and the general election was called for 3 May. Although I no longer expected to win in Hampstead, Geoffrey Finsberg was complacent and did not campaign for two weeks after the no-confidence motion. Local Tories panicked but needn't have worried. Our canvassing showed that the Labour vote was holding up but also that there was a small swing to the Tories.

Fear of Thatcher galvanised Hampstead party activists including writer Margaret Drabble and guitarist John Williams. At the campaign launch I was amazed that we raised almost enough money to cover the whole cost of the campaign but was told we would have raised 'even more if you weren't a candidate'. Although polls showed Labour gaining, our national campaign was more about keeping Thatcher out than providing reasons to re-elect Labour. During a walkabout with me environment secretary Peter Shore talked openly of defeat and how Thatcher would screw it up and open the way for Labour to come back.

Nothing developed my confidence as much as that election. In local government you are one of a group but as a parliamentary candidate you are on your own. Every day you are engaging with people, answering their questions, being forced to think about issues you might not have considered before and having to work out what you really believe. All this under the intense pressure of a campaign where any slip of the tongue is seized upon by opponents or journalists. Just surviving makes you feel you've grown.

The worst moment was when Kevin Moore, my ex-colleague from Lambeth Council who was helping with the campaign, drove me around the constituency's retirement homes. At one home for the very elderly the supervisor said I should start in the 'confused' room where the residents were getting ready for their weekly outing. As I walked in and announced I was the Labour candidate a frail woman on a Zimmer frame threw up her arms, screamed and fell backwards, which started the others wandering around in panic. The staff rushed in and suggested I try the 'very confused' room which was full of OAPs lying on sun beds with no sign any of them were conscious. I couldn't face rousing them in order to get their vote, so we slunk away to a cake shop to restore our spirits.

Although Callaghan was paternalistic to the point of arrogance, he was preferred as prime minister by voters over Thatcher by 44 to 25 per cent, and one of the last polls by NOP was showing a Labour lead over the Tories of 0.7 per cent. Thatcher's campaign prefigured the age of spin with her refusal to take part in a televised debate with Callaghan and her speeches being delivered to exclusively Tory gatherings. Instead of submitting to questioning by journalists she set up endless photo opportunities, including a very stilted-looking one with a new-born calf. The Tory manifesto promised to cut inflation, taxes and public spending but gave no details.

On election day Maggie Fletcher was getting out the voters and happened to knock on the door of some Irish constituents seconds before they were arrested in a counter-terrorist police operation. Ignoring her protestations, they carted her off too and threw her in the cells of Paddington Green police station for the rest of the day. We weren't allowed to contact her and she feared that if Thatcher won she might never get out. I arrived at the count knowing I had lost but not by how much. Although the swing to the Tories in inner London was over 7 per cent, it was only a 2.1 per cent change in Hampstead. If Callaghan had called the election the previous autumn we might just have pulled it off. I was determined never again to lose an election because a Labour prime minister had screwed up.

6

A Very London Coup

1979–1981

Party workers gathered at Neil and Maggie Fletcher's house (she had finally been released by the police) as news of Thatcher's victory came through. Most shared Peter Shore's view that Thatcher would be so bad that Labour would have a walkover next time but I feared that a leader with firm beliefs and money from North Sea oil would be hard to dislodge. As every GLC election had been won by the party in opposition at Westminster I expected Labour would win the GLC in 1981. One who agreed was Bill Bush, Reg Goodwin's new head of office, who was already disillusioned.

When Labour had lost the GLC election two years earlier Peter Walker went to his office after the results to find a letter from the head of personnel saying that his four-year contract as Reg Goodwin's political adviser had ended and he should leave the building immediately. Senior officers hated Goodwin having a political adviser and were horrified when Horace Cutler did the same. Peter went to pastures new so Goodwin appointed David Candler, a Labour party official who had worked for Wilson in Downing Street. But Candler was friendly with Michael Halls, the liaison officer from MI5 to Number 10. Convinced that Wilson's office was a security risk, Halls used Candler to funnel smears about Wilson to *Private Eye*. Candler's conspiratorial and ingratiating manner so alienated everyone at County Hall that he was forced out. With three years to the next GLC election, the twenty-six-year-old Bill Bush was the only credible applicant for the job. With his laid-back style, humour and radical politics we hit it off immediately. He had a soft spot for Goodwin but wanted me as Goodwin's successor. We worked together to ensure the next administration would be one we could be proud of and he let me know what was going on behind the scenes.

Another break for the left at County Hall was the retirement of Bob Mellish. The new chair of the London Labour party was Arthur Latham, MP for Paddington since 1969 and a member of the left-wing Tribune Group. The left finally had a majority on the regional executive and Arthur was assisted by the arrival of Ron Todd, regional organiser of the Transport and General Workers' Union. The London TGWU had been led until then by Bert Fry, a right-winger who ensured trade union members on the executive supported Mellish. After Bert's autocratic style Ron was a breath of fresh air, allowing union reps to express their own views without fear of being purged.

My key allies on the executive were Michael Ward, a workaholic Wandsworth councillor, Jeremy Corbyn, a NUPE regional officer, and David Nicholas, a Wandsworth councillor whose courtesy, calmness and genuine interest in others made him one of the nicest people I ever met in politics. He had the task of producing our manifesto for the 1981 GLC election.

A year earlier the *Observer* had reported that the new GLC Labour group was 'sadly lacking in obvious leadership potential if Sir Reg decides to go, and there may be a move in some London Labour parties to persuade the leading left-winger, the young and thoughtful Mr Ken Livingstone, to seek the succession'. Roy Shaw, the Camden Council leader, laughed with disbelief at this description but apart from Ted Knight and Tony Banks no one else was in the frame as the left's candidate. Fares would be the most difficult area so I asked David Nicholas if I could chair the Transport Working Party, knowing that my leadership chances would be boosted if I could find a solution to the problem. With the retirement of Bert Fry the right on the executive was led by John Spellar, the key organiser for the right-wingers who ran the electricians' union. He tried to block me by nominating Brian Nicholson, treasurer of the London Labour party and leader of the dock workers in the TGWU, but I won by a single vote.

The mood in the party was growing angry. The legacy of the Labour governments of 1964 and 1974 was small apart from Roy Jenkins's reforms and Labour lacked administrative competence let alone radical reforming instincts. Callaghan's decision to hang on to the leadership gave both wings of the party time to mobilise for a civil war. In London we also had the legacy of Goodwin round our necks although the general secretary of the London Labour party, John Keyes, still supported him.

Drawing up the manifesto was exciting and lifted the depression I felt following my defeat in Hampstead. I believed we could make the manifesto radical and (unlike 1973) properly costed. But the rest of the party were focused on the possible leadership challenge of Tony Benn and the demand that Labour MPs should be subject to democratic reselection rather than holding their seats for life. I called a meeting for all London party members at the old Hampstead Town Hall to discuss 'Taking Over the GLC' but I was the only person who turned up. At the 1979 party conference in Brighton that October I spent the week asking people I trusted to stand for the GLC, with little success. Tony Banks was convinced that the London regional committee of the engineering union had more power than the GLC.

I tried again and invited party members to a meeting on 18 October to discuss 'How the Left Could Take Over the GLC'. This provoked a furious denunciation from John Keyes, who circulated his letter far and wide, this time guaranteeing a good turnout. In gratitude I renamed it the John Keyes Annual Memorial Lecture.

Just six months before candidate selection there was at last a desire for change and I was at the centre of it. The meeting included old friends from the Chartist group, Paul and Kevin Moore, along with Graham Bash, Keith Veness and Chris Knight (who became notorious at the G20 Summit demonstrations in London in April 2009 for organising an Alternative Summit on his university campus and being fired from his academic job as a result). A few weeks later at the Tufnell Park flat of Keith and Valerie Veness, with Graham Bash and Chris Knight we decided to produce a new journal called *London Labour Briefing*. It would focus on Labour taking over the GLC and London councils but also raise issues of race and sexuality which other left-wing journals considered diversions from the class struggle. We believed the personal was political and that politics affected all aspects of our lives, not just working and voting.

The first issue appeared in February 1980 but it was the third issue that captured right-wing press interest with a piece on sexism. Media hysteria grew when the fifth issue ran articles on monogamy, multiple relationships, collective living and a piece by Chris Knight discussing his impotence. I was called to order by the Tory chair in the GLC because of the disruption I caused trying to sell it to Tories who couldn't believe anyone would mix sex and politics. The offensive press coverage drove up sales as we explored matters of race, disability, male violence against women, gay rights and alternatives to the family. An article on transvestism unleashed hysterical homophobia in the Sunday papers which coincided with the first day of the 1980 Labour party conference. One paper claimed Michael Foot was shocked at the large number of 'perverts' attending the party conference.

*

Just as things were looking up at County Hall, Camden Council was starting to fall apart. With the general election safely behind her

Thatcher stopped building new council homes and so Camden's programme ground to a halt and money for estate improvement dried up (the GLC went from building 6,000 homes a year to zero). By the mid-1980s waiting lists all over London were rapidly growing.

Thatcher's proposals to let council tenants buy their homes didn't just mean longer waiting lists, but many estates ceased to have a good social mix and became sink estates housing an excluded underclass. The simple fact is that many people cannot afford to buy their own homes and need decent accommodation for rent. Although there was an increase in building by housing associations it was barely a tenth of what used to be built by councils. Eighteen years later Tony Blair's government ignored growing homelessness and continued Thatcher's policy.

As well as trying to cope with the decimation of Camden's housing programme I faced the prospect that my career might be about to end when all Camden Labour councillors received a letter from Ian Pickwell, the government-appointed District Auditor (DA), whose job it was to monitor council spending. He believed Camden had not increased council rents enough and required an immediate increase or he would charge councillors for the 'lost' rent income. He also decided that Camden's minimum wage supplement was 'unreasonably generous . . . at the expense of the ratepayers' and planned to recover the £1 million it had cost from the thirty-one Labour councillors who voted for it.

The letter left me in a state of shock which lasted for days. Tony Blair's government eventually abolished the DA's power to fine and ban councillors for what were political choices, but that was far in the future. The bankruptcy facing councillors caused panic and bitterness, most of which was directed at me as it had been my idea. The wealthiest members were angriest; working-class councillors were more understanding because they had more in common with our low-paid workers.

The post of DA had always been a politically partisan one. In 1912 the then DA ruled that the LCC had exceeded its powers providing fruit, cod-liver oil and malt extract to schoolchildren, arguing these were not food. My first contact with the DA was when a Lambeth councillor alleged I was over-claiming my attendance allowance. Instead of asking me directly, the DA ordered a council officer to check my desk diary. The person felt guilty and told me what had happened but as I had nothing to hide I let the matter go. Ian Pickwell showed his colours when, at the same time as he was trying to bankrupt us, he decided Tory councillors in Westminster who had lost their borough £1.5 million a year by not charging businesses for refuse collection in breach of the 1936 Public Health Act had not broken the law, even though some were local businessmen benefiting from their own decision.

The Labour group on Camden Council had a rule that only allowed someone to chair a committee for two years, moving them on just as they got on top of the job. The fear gripping the Labour group allowed Roy Shaw to reassert his leadership and the left were defeated in the 1980 elections for committee chairs. Once again I returned to the back benches and went off with Christine to spend a week in Sorrento.

*

Our GLC manifesto with 70,000 words of detailed and costed proposals to solve London's transport, housing and employment problems had gone out for consultation in spring 1980. We had three options on fares. Andrew McIntosh proposed to cut them initially by 25 per cent and thereafter increase them in line with inflation (putting rates up by £20 a year for the average household). Having cut the fares I felt we should then freeze them for four years (which would cost £38 a year). Abolishing fares altogether would increase rates by £100 a year per family, though it was doubtful that we could expand the system sufficiently to cope with the extra demand.

The regional executive proposed to put all three options to a special London party conference to decide. Goodwin grumpily claimed this would cost us the election and was unhappy that so many left-wingers were on the panel of candidates. To make matters worse, the London party conference had voted by ten to one that Britain should withdraw from Northern Ireland and had asked the National Executive Committee (NEC) to allow the GLC Labour leader to be elected by the London conference instead of just Labour GLC members. The NEC did not agree to this, but Goodwin realised the game was up so he tipped off Andrew, his preferred successor, that he would resign.

The chief whip Harvey Hinds was amazed to receive Goodwin's resignation letter without any warning. *The Times* announced, 'Front runners for the leadership are likely to be Mr Illtyd Harrington, age 48 . . . and Mr Andrew McIntosh, age 47.' Only London's two evening papers reported that there might be a third candidate. The *Standard* warned readers that 'the left wing of the party is certain to nominate Ken Livingstone, 34'. The *Evening News* reported, 'There is also a strong likelihood of a left-wing candidate – Ken Livingstone . . . If there is a left-wing takeover . . . after next year's elections . . . the new leader could be ousted when extremists come to power.'

I was lying by the pool in Sorrento oblivious to all this. When I got home two days later Bill Bush phoned saying that it was a two-horse race between Illtyd and Andrew. I had missed three vital days with just ten days before the vote, but no one was campaigning as most assumed Illtyd would win, although they did not intend to vote for him themselves. I had only four sure votes. I bumped into Andrew in the gents at County Hall and was surprised that he had no idea about the views of members other than his core supporters. We agreed to share information about our supporters and we were not surprised to discover some members were promising both of us their vote.

The majority wouldn't vote for Illtyd but were not enthusiastic about Andrew. Ashley Bramall would have won comfortably if he had stood, but he was leader of the ILEA which faced a threat of abolition from Mrs Thatcher. As the ILEA got 80 per cent of its income from Westminster Council and the City of London, schools would suffer if they had to rely on resources of the poor boroughs like Hackney or Lambeth. Ashley decided that his duty was to fight to save the ILEA.

After three days I knew Andrew and Illtyd each had a third of the votes and the remaining third wanted neither. Most wanted a clear break with the Goodwin years, which doomed Illtyd, who had been his deputy. Having lined up the undecided votes I worked on Illtyd's supporters to ensure that they would switch to me if Illtyd was eliminated in the first ballot. The Monday of the vote was a hive of activity at County Hall with an unsuccessful last-ditch attempt to draft Sir Ashley. When the result of the secret ballot was announced people were stunned that I had ten votes, with Illtyd and Andrew on nine each. In the run-off between those two my supporters split two to one for Andrew and Illtyd was eliminated. In the final ballot, although Harvey and Illtyd swung behind me, Andrew was the winner by 14 votes to 13. With a day's gap between the ballots Illtyd and Harvey could have delivered me victory if they had lobbied their supporters to vote for me.

A jubilant Andrew invited everyone to an impromptu party in the leader's room. I was despondent, having come so close, and kept running over in my mind what I could have done to get that extra vote or two. My only consolation came from watching Harvey Hinds berate one of Illtyd's voters who had abstained on the final ballot. Harvey and I believed that Andrew should have no trouble hanging on to the leadership for a decade or more. Illtyd feared Andrew would share Goodwin's preference for working with senior officers of the council and Harvey took me to one side to say we should stay in touch so as to try to control Andrew as much as possible.

John Carvel recorded his astonishment that Harvey, who suffered my endless rebellions, and Illtyd, whose leadership chances I had just skewered, switched their support to me, but journalists always emphasise personality over policies. Harvey told Carvel that Andrew was 'just a very slightly cleverer version of Reg Goodwin', while I promised an open and inclusive leadership tolerant of dissent. Most politicians are loyalists who spend years supporting leaders they disagree with, but are free to be themselves during a leadership election.

For all my rows with Illtyd I liked his larger-than-life character and his wicked wit and there had been many occasions when we laughed together. Mum was fond of him because of his interest in the theatre and had been wowed when we met him and Kenneth Williams having lunch at County Hall. In his diary that day Kenneth Williams writes that he found Mum and me charming and added, 'Ken is v. attractive I must say.' Illtyd told Andrew Hosken, 'You could see that [Ken] obviously adored his mother ... I realised that he was a natural performer.' He said I had excellent timing and, 'Like all music hall artists, he was very good at dealing with hecklers. But I noticed there was something in Ken's relationship with his mother that he had to be performing and demonstrating. But no one, including me, appreciated how ruthless he was.'

*

Harvey and Illtyd could see that London was rapidly changing. The homogeneous white, skilled and prosperous city of the 1950s now had growing poverty, a million black and Asian citizens and a population that spoke over 160 different languages and dialects. Women had a bigger role at work and London was a haven for lesbians and gays fleeing intolerance in other parts of the country. New forces were changing London, and Harvey and Illtyd knew that I was in tune with them.

Although disappointed at the outcome of the leadership election, I was also amazed I had run Andrew so close. Tony Benn invited me to a party at his home on 30 May. This was the left's equivalent of a royal garden party and I felt I had finally arrived. Tony's Holland Park home was heaving with lefties and I said he also should reach out to the centre when he bid for the party leadership, but he felt that the parliamentary Labour party was much more right-wing than the GLC Labour group. I pointed out that even Andrew McIntosh felt Tony was the only credible candidate to succeed Callaghan.

Andrew was a Benn supporter at the time because Tony had not yet gone over to the hard left. Following Labour's defeat in 1979 his first moves were quite cautious. When challenged by the left at London rallies he wouldn't commit to abolishing the powers of the DA, nor to withdrawing troops from Northern Ireland, but later, at the 1980 autumn conference, his speech marked a decisive shift to the left, promising to create 'a thousand Labour peers' to break the power of the House of Lords. Following Tony's speech Andrew McIntosh said there were now no circumstances in which he would support Tony.

Andrew made me opposition spokesperson on transport and planning and accepted my proposal that we should freeze fares following the initial cut, but he suffered Goodwin's aversion to the slower members of the group. His shyness was mistaken for aloofness and he annoyed the union reps on the regional executive by using flip charts as though he were making a market-research presentation. Two factors sealed Andrew's fate that summer. Cutler had imposed a budget with a £34 million deficit for London Transport. The transport authority would be bankrupt by autumn without increasing fares by 43 per cent, closing three tube lines and slashing several bus routes. As Labour's new transport spokesman, I was hardly off the television, pointedly contrasting Cutler's policies with ours.

Press interest mushroomed after the chief executive of London Transport, Ralph Bennett, invited Cutler to lunch to discuss the crisis. As Cutler bounced out of his chauffeured GLC car and swept into LT's headquarters at 55 Broadway, he was stopped by the security guard who told him he would have to wait while he phoned upstairs for clearance. Cutler loudly announced that he was the leader of the GLC, to which the guard replied, 'I don't care if you're Mr Pastry, you can't just walk straight in here.' Cutler stormed out and was driven back to County Hall. I was in the members' dining room as Ralph Bennett rushed in to apologise, but Cutler refused to go back to lunch and later announced that he was sacking Bennett. In the end Cutler had to add £30 million to the LT budget as well as pushing through an emergency fare increase in September 1980.

The second factor that sealed Andrew's fate was his failure to win over Harvey and Illtyd. Instead of a strong policy committee Andrew preferred to deal with each issue on a one-to-one basis much as Tony Blair would one day bypass his cabinet with so-called 'sofa government'. Andrew started having meetings with comptroller Maurice Stonefrost to discuss our budget with no other Labour members present and our suspicions increased when Andrew asked Bill Bush to leave the meetings even though he was head of the Leader's Office. Throughout June and July 1980 I met with Illtyd and Harvey as our concerns grew and we discussed selection results for the candidates at the forthcoming GLC election. Of the 6 safe seats where sitting members were retiring, the left took 5 and in the 30 Tory marginals the only right-winger to be selected was Tony Judge. If Labour won the 1981 election the left would be just a handful of votes short of a majority in the new Labour group, which gave Harvey and Illtyd the power to decide the leadership. One of my supporters was Kate Hoey in Hornsey, but ignoring my pleas to stay she stood down from the GLC in order to fight Dulwich at the next general election.

Kate's loss was balanced by the selection of Dave Wetzel in Hammersmith, who, like his father, had worked on the buses as a conductor and driver. He was obsessed with Esperanto and insisted on signing all his letters 'Yours in socialism'. It took several attempts for me to persuade him to stand, as he believed the GLC was filled with living fossils. The selection of Valerie Wise was almost accidental. She had invited me to speak to her local party in Westminster about the manifesto so I challenged her to stand. With her Lancashire accent and huge glasses the initial impression she made was that she was too serious by half. Married to an optician, she was the daughter of Audrey Wise MP who had lost her Coventry seat with the fall of Callaghan's government, but underneath Valerie was very funny and became one of my closest allies.

My problem was that Ted Knight opposed a left–centre deal and harboured his own ambitions to challenge Andrew if he, Ted, was elected to the GLC. As leader of Lambeth Ted made the mistake of cutting services following Thatcher's cut in council grants, but did a U-turn when the local party insisted he reverse the cuts. Now he had to make a deeply unpopular supplementary rate increase in the middle of the year. Voters were angry and Ted was struggling, so I was not surprised when he said he would support me for the GLC leadership. The next annual leadership election would take place the day after the GLC election but, certain I now had the votes to replace Andrew, I told him it would be in the Labour party's best interests if he stood down before the election rather than be replaced afterwards, but he didn't believe Harvey and Illtyd would vote for me and never bothered to ask them.

*

In the seven years since I'd been married I had been radicalised as I was caught up in the Labour party and the new politics of race and gender. Christine had made her mark as an incredibly effective teacher who could inspire the most difficult children, but she was developing in a different direction from me. With my workaholic commitment to politics, I was out most evenings when she came home emotionally drained by work and needing comfort and support. After a lot of agonised discussion, we decided to separate and I moved out to live temporarily with Paul Moore and his wife. Andrew kindly asked how was I coping, but as politics has to be a ruthless business and I was planning to replace him I didn't want to get any closer to him and just mumbled that I could manage.

Thatcher was deliberately introducing policies to make life difficult for councils generally and the GLC in particular. Environment secretary Michael Heseltine rushed laws through to prevent councils creating new housing or transport without government permission and removed the powers of the GLC and local councils to redevelop the derelict docks of the East End, a decision that delayed the redevelopment for eight years. The government funded cuts in the top rate of income tax by slashing grants to local councils, so we got blamed for rate increases while Thatcher got credit for tax cuts for the wealthy. The new GLC administration would inherit rates at 24p in the pound, but the loss of the government grant could force us to almost treble rates by our third year in order to implement our manifesto. The *Evening Standard* did everything possible to keep the Tories in power with banner headlines screaming '£720 million on the rates – the price of a Labour victory'.

The Economist sneered, 'Labour has no clear sense of what kind of animal the GLC is. But it believes that, whatever it is, it exists to spend money.' Had anyone at *The Economist* read our manifesto they would have gained a clear sense of the GLC as a regional authority. Our plans for democratic accountability of the police, a regional industrial policy and integrated transport systems bore an uncanny resemblance to Tony Blair's when he decided in 1997 that the new mayor would have the regional powers we wanted in 1981.

*

Local London council by-election results were showing only small swings to Labour, so we weren't certain of winning the 1981 GLC election, and after eight years of achieving not very much at County Hall I had no wish to carry on in opposition. If Labour didn't win I wanted to do something else rather than make faces at the Tories, so I gave up my safe seat in Stoke Newington to challenge Patricia Kirwan, the sitting Tory in the key marginal of Paddington, which we had to win. My campaign to win the nomination was organised by the bright and hyperactive Neale Coleman. Facing what we thought would be a tough election, Neale found me a bedsit in Maida Vale in a house filled with medical students.

Paddington Labour party was well organised but its MP, Arthur Latham, lost his seat in 1979 when the local priest campaigned against him on the abortion issue. I was taken aback when Illtyd said that the priest had died and that as a candidate I would be expected to attend his funeral, which was to be conducted by Cardinal Basil Hume. I protested but the Tories would be there so I had to turn up. As Illtyd and I came up to the church door he introduced me as the Labour candidate, adding, 'We want good seats, none of your rubbish.' We were ushered right to the centre of the church and I was seated on the right of the coffin with Patricia Kirwan on the left. Never having represented a Catholic area, I still felt uncomfortable, but different religions have different expectations of politicians. In fact this was the beginning of a good working relationship with Cardinal Hume, which led to the GLC funding his work with London's homeless.

Although the party in opposition at Westminster had always

won control of the GLC, privately we were nervous. London had the biggest swing to Thatcher in the whole country in 1979 and her policies were having a harsher effect on the rest of the country than on London and the south-east. In Scotland, Wales and the north of England Labour was doing very well, but London council by-election results were showing only small swings in our favour. Nor had Cutler given up the fight.

Cutler commissioned a study into winning the 1988 Olympic Games for London. This offered a choice of holding the games at Wembley Stadium or in the derelict Royal Docks in Newham, but Wembley was not a realistic prospect as building the athletes' village would have meant concreting over Fryent Park and the 2,350 double-stacked portable housing units would have left no worthwhile legacy. In Docklands the athletes' village would be permanent housing, with a legacy of high-quality sports facilities, but it could only work with the extension of the Jubilee Line to the stadium site. The Labour group felt it wasn't possible to justify spending on the Olympics while Cutler was cutting services and increasing fares and rents.

As the 1976 Montreal games almost bankrupted the city the only serious bid for the 1988 games was from Seoul, the capital of South Korea, and the International Olympic Committee (IOC) didn't want the games to go to what was then a military dictatorship. If London bid, we would win. Cutler proposed a national lottery to raise Olympic funds and that the government should pay to extend the Jubilee Line. Cutler was calling in favours from Thatcher because for four years he had used his own money to pay for staff in her private office. But gratitude is rare in politics and his hopes were sunk when Thatcher said there was no question of spending hundreds of millions on extending the Jubilee Line, nor was she in favour of a lottery. But Cutler did pull off another sporting first. After attending the New York marathon he had decided to have one in London and bludgeoned past resistance from borough councils and London Transport to stage the first London marathon on 29 March 1981, just at the start of the election campaign.

Cutler had the enthusiastic backing of the *Standard*, which was owned by Trafalgar House boss Lord Matthews, who at an editorial board meeting told staff that their first priority was to prevent Labour winning. Mike King, their County Hall reporter, told Matthews he would have to work with Labour if we won and wouldn't be able to do so if his reporting was biased, so Matthews appointed Keith Dovkants to do the hatchet work in a series of lurid double-page spreads. On eve of poll the front page featured an explicit instruction to Londoners not to vote Labour.

Cutler promised to 'stress the ugly face of Marxism' and in his manifesto mentioned Marxism seventeen times in just sixteen pages. The *Daily Telegraph* did its bit with a leading article headed 'Will London be Marxified?', asking, 'Could the dictatorship of the proletariat . . . be imposed without a prior Communist revolution? . . . the Left is now poised to take over the leadership of the Labour Group . . . The Livingstone method is to create a self perpetuating dependency . . . Crippling rates, bad services, compulsory purchase, redevelopment and council flats . . . drive out productive citizens and businesses, and replace them by more dependants whose low incomes and high degree of social problems increase the council's entitlement to Exchequer aid. If he were to gain control, how far off would our capital's point of no return be from a "Livingstone death"?'

The *Daily Express* screamed, 'Why we must stop these red wreckers', quoting Cutler's warning that we would 'establish a Marxist power base . . . from which a concerted effort can be made to unseat the Government of the day – even Labour . . . if it puts nation before party'. Given Cutler's limited record of success, the Tory campaign concentrated on 'violent crime . . . muggers . . . drunks at discos . . . pornography . . . and legislation to restore decency'. In Parliament

Geoffrey Finsberg, my opponent in Hampstead, warned that people like me 'would not be fit to clean the boots of people like Herbert Morrison'. In his LCC days Morrison had been denounced as a frightening socialist and in his diary Harold Macmillan described him as a 'dirty little cockney guttersnipe'.

We were also fighting the election just as the divisions in the Labour party led to the creation of the Social Democratic Party (SDP) by four Labour right-wingers, David Owen, Shirley Williams, Roy Jenkins and Bill Rodgers. The polls showed that while Labour was on course to win there was huge support for the SDP. Andrew and I worried that if the SDP made the GLC election their first electoral test and were led by Shirley Williams they could win an outright majority, but the 'Gang of Four' didn't think that the GLC was worth fighting for.

The right wing of the Goodwin administration, Stephen Haseler, Douglas Eden and Jim Daly, were frustrated when the SDP ducked the GLC elections. Backed by Lord George Brown (Labour's deputy leader under Wilson) they formed the Social Democratic Alliance (SDA) in order to contest the election. On 6 March Lord Brown announced, 'The nation's capital is threatened by a Trotskyist takeover and bankruptcy.' Jim Daly was going to run against me in Paddington and Stephen Haseler against Ted Knight in Norwood. Although Daly alleged there was 'a great deal of fear' in my local Paddington party, only eight of the area's one thousand members defected to the SDP and I couldn't resist pointing out that it was only four years since Daly had voted to expel Haseler from the GLC Labour group.

Fearing a poor result, the SDP leadership told the SDA candidates to stand down. Haseler defiantly continued to stand against Ted in Norwood but when Daly obeyed his party's order, the SDA substituted Jim Spillius, 'a close friend of the Tongan royal family', to run against me. At the first debate in Paddington I explained

Labour's policies and Jim Spillius said, 'How can you follow that? I agree with every word Ken has said,' and promptly sat down. The Liberal candidate announced that he also agreed with the points I had made and droned on about how important it was to come out and vote. The sitting Tory, Patricia Kirwan, didn't disagree with any of my policies either and concentrated on her record in the constituency. Spillius whispered to me, 'I don't know what I'm doing here. This is all a terrible mistake!'

A *Standard* reporter wanted to talk 'off the record' with me, so we met at the Castle pub on the Harrow Road. He said Cutler was renting a flat owned by London Transport above Baker Street tube station. It was only thirty minutes up the Metropolitan Line to Cutler's family home and the reporter told me Cutler used the flat as a 'love nest', but Lord Matthews wouldn't run the story. The reporter wanted me to blow the issue wide open. It would appal today's spin doctors, but I wasn't interested in Cutler's private life and wanted to win on our policies. But after the election I instructed LT to invoke the terms of Cutler's lease, which specified that the flats were not to be rented as second homes.

Thames TV journalist Ed Boyle also stumbled onto Cutler's sex life when the crew turned up at Cutler's office to interview him and they found the door locked. When the door eventually opened a woman hurried out while Cutler rearranged his clothing. 'Nothing like a good woman after lunch,' he proclaimed. Journalists then had more respect for people's private lives, and Cutler could well afford to sue, but no politician would get away with such behaviour today.

Cutler's overbearing confidence was captured by his response to Boyle's question, 'What are your biggest mistakes?' Cutler grinned and said, 'The earlier Mrs Cutlers.' When my turn came for the Boyle treatment, Arthur Latham was horrified that I allowed them into my bedsit to film me playing on my (quarter-size) snooker table and feeding my salamanders but it provided nice continuity with the profile of Andrew McIntosh in which he was also depicted playing snooker on his (half-size) table.

The BBC took the GLC elections seriously and on the four Thursdays before polling day set aside an hour after the nine o'clock news on BBC1 for debates on transport, housing and industry and employment, plus a final confrontation between Andrew and Cutler. I was due to speak in the opening programme, on transport, and was incredibly nervous. This was my first big TV debate and if I blew it any chance of the GLC leadership could slip away. But with the Tories' transport record I had an easy win, and given their refusal to build council housing and rising unemployment, the debates on housing and industry also went well.

Each of the four studio audiences comprised a mixture of party members and relevant interest groups. As groups campaigning on housing or transport were critical of the Tories, this gave us sympathetic audiences but the groups invited to the Andrew–Cutler clash were ratepayers' associations hostile to our planned rate increase. Their presence and Cutler's shameless populism turned the debate into a rout with the ratepayers giving Cutler a standing ovation. It looked as though the following week's election was going to be close.

*

Polling day passed without a hitch and at Porchester Hall, where the votes were being counted, the chair of Paddington Tories, Ian Harvey (who in 1958 had been forced to resign as an MP when caught having sex with a guardsman), came up to me and said, 'Our candidate's no good so I voted for you.' As I went on stage a reporter mentioned we had won marginal Hornchurch and as my result showed a 13 per cent swing I believed we were heading for a landslide. As I stepped down from the platform two large men I had never seen before picked me up by the elbows and carried me through the crowd into a waiting car. The BBC left nothing to chance in ensuring that David Dimbleby's *Election Special* got the first interview with me. In the studio the politics lecturer and expert in election statistics Bob McKenzie tried to get me to announce that I would stand against Andrew, but I maintained the line that the Labour group had the right to hear my decision in person rather than over the airwaves.

After a round of interviews I reached Paddington's victory party in time to hear that Ted had been defeated and we had failed to capture Hampstead and Croydon North West. In local elections throughout the rest of the country there had been big swings to Labour, but we had just 42 per cent of the vote in London to the Tories' 40 per cent, which gave us a majority of only 8 in the 92-seat chamber. At County Hall in the small hours of Friday morning Michael Foot, now leading the Labour party following the previous November's leadership election, was the star guest at our victory party where he toasted Andrew with the ringing endorsement, 'It's going to be fine because you, Andrew, are in charge and you know the machine.' I stayed away because I liked Michael and knew he would ask me not to stand against Andrew. Depressed and worried, I got to bed at 3 a.m. I had expected us to win at least eight more seats and now we could be defeated if the right wing of the group abstained on key votes. Was Ted's defeat in Norwood a warning we would face similar unpopularity when we raised rates in order to cut fares? Had the press campaign against the left worked, and would this persuade Harvey and Illtyd to leave Andrew in place as leader?

Andrew must have had similar thoughts as he bounced into County Hall brimming with confidence to meet the chief officers and spell out how he intended to run the administration. The officers had been warned by Harvey that Andrew would be replaced, but gave him no sign of this. Summoning a press conference in the leader's office he announced, 'I am going to win [the leadership election]. The results of the election show that the people of London . . . wanted a Labour administration of responsible and realistic people. That is what they are going to get.' Andrew convinced the *Standard*, whose banner headline read 'The left lose out' with the strapline 'Red Ted defeated: moderates in control'. I slipped in during Andrew's press conference and waited at the back of his office as he strode off followed by the press pack to do TV and radio interviews. Harvey and Illtyd hung back and when we were alone they shut the door. Illtyd said, 'You've got it all sewn up. For God's sake don't do anything to blow it today.' They felt our lower than expected majority had been caused by Andrew's performance in the debate against Cutler and his emphasis on rate increases.

Asked by Carvel why they supported me, Harvey said, 'Ken was a leader who knew his mind and knew what he wanted to achieve . . . I was yearning for a leader who would lead . . . I saw in the likes of Ken and the young people who were just beginning to come through in my local Labour party the best hope for the future for the Labour party.' Illtyd said, 'What struck all the older politicians was the speed and efficiency of what we were looking at. We overestimated it very much. We thought we were looking at a juggernaut. We were looking at something that was sharper, younger, appeared to be crisper . . . They looked unstoppable. They appeared to be fresh, open-minded. These were attractive things to see. We had gone through a long period of appalling local government. It had atrophied . . . Things needed to be done in transport, housing, fresh ideas about planning. They all appeared to be alive, marvellously alive . . . It had flags, whistles and steam coming out of it at you.'

Harvey and Illtyd offered to make sure Andrew didn't do anything we disapproved of while I prepared for the afternoon caucus. I had invited all successful candidates from the left and the centre of the party to meet at 2 p.m. just three hours before the group AGM. I opened the meeting and suggested we consider all posts and if more than one person was interested we should have a show of hands to decide who to support. There was a moment of euphoria when I announced that the left had a majority of the group present in the room. By the end of the meeting two-thirds of the group had arrived, including two who came to tell me why they intended to vote for Andrew. Illtyd nominated me for leader, which was agreed, and then Harvey and Illtyd were also nominated unopposed to continue as chief whip and deputy leader.

Things weren't so simple when we came to committee chairs. Ted had wanted to chair finance and his defeat left a gap that was filled by Tony Hart (husband of the Tribunite MP Judith Hart, whose political adviser had been Tony Banks). Tony Banks had wanted to chair transport but changed his mind and went for arts and recreation. On the spur of the moment former bus driver Dave Wetzel threw his hat into the ring, starting a career in transport policy that would see him become my vice-chair of Transport for London when I became mayor in 2000. There was a bitter battle between Bryn Davies and Frances Morrell over who should lead the ILEA and another tussle as to who would chair public services and the fire service. A lot of vice-chair positions were contested and with only fifteen minutes before the start of the full Labour group meeting I was already emotionally drained.

Andrew's first inkling that things might not go his way was the emptiness on the members' floor as most of them were in my meeting, but he had what he thought would be a trump card: a letter from Michael Foot endorsing him as leader. Andrew gave it to the new London Labour party general secretary George Page to read out before the vote, but Page kept silent. He believed that I knew how to work the Labour party and Andrew didn't. While the ballot papers were counted the room was eerily silent and the tension unbearable. My senses were acute and I felt I was watching events from outside my own body. Two years of relentless work climaxed in the two or three minutes it took to count just 50 votes.

When Arthur announced the results I had received 30 votes to Andrew's 20 (I had been promised support by thirty-three members and never found out who the missing three were). The mood in the room was fraught and there was no jubilation as the result was announced. I nervously made a short speech about the need to work together. Andrew sat absolutely stunned and silent as we proceeded to vote for chair and vice-chair positions one by one. As each of the posts were called I nominated the person that the caucus had chosen, followed by a moment's silence during which no one else was nominated. As Andrew had not asked his supporters to nominate right-wingers for the positions, each of my nominees was elected unopposed. He had expected to adjourn if elected and take a day to form his administration. I had expected several talented right-wingers to be elected over some of the weaker candidates from the left and I now had a dangerously unbalanced administration.

The meeting was over in forty-five minutes and we had to push our way through a heaving, noisy media scrum. Journalists wanted a comment from Andrew, who was near to tears and being helped through the mob by GLC member Yvonne Sieve, shouting, 'Leave him alone.' Bill Bush rushed me off to begin three hours of back-to-back interviews. For all the mayhem around me I was able to stay calm. At forty-six Herbert Morrison had been the youngest leader at County Hall. I was still only thirty-five, but felt the last ten years in local government had prepared me for this moment. After the frustration of seeing my ideas blocked I now had the chance to demonstrate what Labour could achieve. Over the next four years we could set an example in delivering our manifesto promises and show that Labour in government could be successful.

*

That evening in Perth, Thatcher warned the Scottish Conservative Conference, 'Others have more sinister ambitions. They have no time for parliamentary democracy . . . tiny caucuses which plot and scheme to win power . . . power for one purpose only – to impose upon this nation a tyranny which the peoples of Eastern Europe yearn to cast aside.' Although equating our policies of cheaper fares and more council housing with the horrors of Stalinism was a smidgen over the top, the Tory press went along with this line.

Thatcher's nonsense was taken up by the right generally and led Frederick Forsyth to write *The Fourth Protocol*, a book in which the Soviet Union plans the takeover of Britain through a similar coup in the parliamentary Labour party. Forsyth imagined the spy Kim Philby drafting a report on the GLC to Soviet leader Brezhnev:

. . . within sixteen hours – not days or weeks or months, but sixteen hours – Andrew McIntosh was deposed . . . and replaced by a Far Left activist called Ken Livingstone of whom not more than five per cent of Londoners had ever even heard. It was a truly brilliant coup, of which Lenin himself would have been proud . . . Although a non-descript, instantly forgettable little fellow with a nasal voice, Livingstone has shown himself to be a consummate politician in the Far Left mould. A full time operator since his teens, content to live in a tiny bedsitter flatlet, devoid, it would seem, of any social, leisure or family life, he lives, eats and breathes politics twenty-four hours in every day . . . He has managed in five years to build up a personal Far Left political machine that now spans the whole country, its tendrils far beyond the confines of London . . . The Livingstone coup d'etat is the model upon which is to be based the final takeover of the Labour party leadership not before its electoral triumph but a few days after it.

As I arrived for work on Saturday morning the first thing I saw on my new desk was a pile of GLC press cuttings. Under a banner headline 'Red Ken crowned King of London', the *Sun* announced 'His victory means full-steam-ahead red-blooded Socialism for London'. The *Daily Mail* reported, 'A left-wing extremist was installed as leader . . . and last night the signs were that the Left's victory in London could be repeated up and down the country.' The *Daily Express* described me as 'The political extremist Ken Livingstone . . . for the last six years and more he has had no proper job. Instead he has acted as a professional local councillor, living on his "expenses" of about £7,000' (actually I was only earning £3,000 – not much more than the County Hall cleaners). There was an assumption in some of the press coverage that people like me shouldn't be running things and this snobbery was captured best in the *Daily Telegraph* when it complained that I had no background, no education worth speaking of, no money and 'had appointed a black man to chair the police committee'.

Given that the media had spent months warning I would become leader if Labour won, the press claims that this was a 'secret' coup were more than a little exaggerated, but that did not stop the story from entering popular mythology. With the passage of time others took a different view. Ten years later Roy Jenkins told me that 'at the time I thought what you did to McIntosh was appalling but after seeing him at work in the House of Lords I now know why you did it'.

At Saturday morning's ILEA Labour group we avoided the mistake of excluding the right wing, though the impact was undermined when Frances Morrell referred to it at the meeting as 'taking prisoners'. That evening Valerie Wise invited the left to a party at her mum's Barbican flat where the news came through that François Mitterrand had been elected the first socialist president of France. As we talked excitedly about our plans for London, I truly believed that the elections of Thatcher and Reagan would be just a temporary setback in the long march to build a better world.

7

What the Papers Say

1981

As I left my bedsit that Monday morning, 11 May, a *Standard* photographer was hiding behind the dustbins, no doubt to see whether anyone was leaving with me. By the time I got to County Hall the early edition of the *Standard* was fuming, 'The worst nightmares about the Greater London Council and its new masters on the far left seem to be coming true even faster than we had feared . . . The truth which the left will never acknowledge is that they are operating on a non-existent mandate. Labour won the election under the moderate Mr McIntosh (and small thanks he got) . . . so now it is up to the government and in particular to Michael Heseltine . . . to keep some measure of control over London's spending . . .'

The *Daily Mirror* quoted Andrew McIntosh: 'The danger to the Labour party is so great that I have decided I must expose what is going on. It's gang warfare – just like the Jets and the Sharks. The left are after personal power.' The *Sunday Telegraph*'s headline warned: 'New GLC leader promises storms'. The *Sunday Express* headlined 'New left threaten police: we are the masters now', and the *Daily Mail* had the headline 'Little Stalins', a quote from the electricians' union boss Frank Chapple. I assumed the press would soon revert to type and ignore local government, but I couldn't have been more wrong.

My first meeting was with the director general (DG) Sir James Swaffield to explain how I intended to work. No more would chief officers lobby the leader if they were unhappy with their committee's policies. I was not going to be used to thwart our manifesto by behind-the-scenes manoeuvring. With a bigger majority I would have broken up the DG's department and taken direct control of the machine, but with our small majority the right wing would have voted with the Tories to prevent me from doing this.

Next was the first meeting of the Policy Committee (PC) comprising all committee chairs and Labour group officers. I proposed that in future we would start the meetings with the council officers present to discuss issues. Then the officers would leave and the PC would make recommendations to the full Labour group to be agreed or rejected. I proposed that we abolish 'collective responsibility' so that PC members could oppose PC recommendations in full group, and if Labour members voted against us in full council there should be no disciplinary action against them. I saw no reason to continue the suspensions and expulsions that had torn the Goodwin administration apart. Members would answer to their local parties for their voting record and we agreed that any member of the Labour group could attend the PC and speak (but not vote). We also co-opted Arthur Latham and Ted Knight from the London Labour party executive to keep an eye on us. To keep everyone involved I asked each Labour GLC member to take responsibility for an area of policy.

This change meant that PC meetings were now good-humoured, no matter how intense the debates in the group, because everyone could have their say without the threat of disciplinary action and we never lost a significant vote. The exception was when Tony Banks's Arts Committee cut the Royal Opera House grant to fund community arts projects. As this had not been agreed by the Labour group, the right wing voted with the Tories to defeat us in full council. Tony was furious and some on the left wanted to discipline the dissidents but it was Tony's fault for not following the new rules and in future all the chairs made sure they did.

As well as being the right way to run a political group it saved our majority. After the election Jim Daly kept claiming he was negotiating with unnamed members planning to defect to the SDP. Harvey feared that up to seven members might go but being open and inclusive meant that only two members crossed the floor to join the sole Liberal (halving our majority from eight to four). The defectors had always intended to join the SDP but hadn't the integrity to stand under their own colours.

In 1974 Tony Judge had told me that 'the Labour party shows its contempt for County Hall in the quality of the candidates it selects', but no one could make that complaint about the new group. Harvey joked that the average age of the group had been cut by thirty years and they were impatient to end the pretensions, junketing and freeloading of the Cutler years. We scrapped the annual international holiday for the chair of the GLC paid for by the ratepayers, and the extravagant receptions at which members of the establishment had been fed and watered. As I travelled by tube, we did away with the leader's chauffeur-driven car, saving £20,000 a year, and ended the tradition of the chair of the council dressing in medieval clothes to deliver a medieval address of welcome to visiting heads of state. Porters were delighted that, unlike Cutler, I did not wish them to stand to attention as I walked by. It was more difficult to stop senior officers greeting me with 'Good morning, Leader'.

The GLC mimicked Parliament's late-night sittings with the opposition demonstrating their virility by keeping us there past midnight. As the Members Bar opened at 5 p.m., late-night sittings were usually unproductive. During the Goodwin years I had caused uproar in the Labour group by prudishly proposing that we permanently close the Members Bar as a way of shortening meetings but now I settled for a 10 p.m. closure. We decided that Londoners could book our meeting rooms in the evenings and at weekends when the building was empty. The gentlemen's club atmosphere evaporated as the building filled up with people discussing job losses, nuclear weapons, racism, sexism and the environment.

On the Transport Committee, as Dave Wetzel worked on the fares cut we did away with the complex ticketing system which involved a different fare for every station-to-station segment of a tube journey. Free bus travel for pensioners was extended to the underground and the ban on pensioners travelling free between 4.30 and 7.00 in the evening was abolished. The Tories voted against the measure on grounds of cost. The new chief executive of LT, who had been appointed by Cutler, was Sir Peter Masefield – a classic urbane, establishment patrician who was committed to public transport and had been involved in transport policy since the war. He had fagged for Lord Beaverbrook's son at Westminster School and then became Beaverbrook's personal assistant during the years of negotiation, in the face of American opposition, to organise the post-war civil aviation industry into a system of licensed national carriers.

Michael Ward and his vice-chair Valerie Wise faced stiff opposition from the bureaucracy as they struggled to set up an Enterprise Board to save and create jobs. The officers' first attempt to marginalise the policy was to give it to a section of the department that dealt with refuse disposal. The next Machiavellian ploy was to take counsel from an outside barrister who declared it was illegal to establish the Enterprise Board. It took Mike and Valerie months and many more legal opinions to reverse the original advice. Finally, officers claimed that there was no space to house the new staff and encouraged the Staff Association to object to recruiting people from outside the existing workforce.

The legal department pulled the same trick by getting advice that it was illegal to cut the price of school meals and introduce school breakfasts. The GLC had the largest legal department in Britain but it was filled with risk-averse lawyers who had come to the GLC for an easy life and they only solicited advice from barristers who were known Tories. The barristers were exclusively white and overwhelmingly male, so we added new ones to the list and insisted that no opinion could be sought without members deciding which barrister to use and accompanying officers to the meetings.

Nothing dramatised the change at County Hall more than the People's March for Jobs. Carrying the banner of the original Jarrow marchers, the 500 participants set out from Liverpool, Huddersfield and Llanelli on May Day 1981, arriving in London four weeks later on the day of our first full council meeting. I asked Valerie to plan their reception and accommodation inside County Hall. Valerie found the camp beds reserved for use in the event of a nuclear war and used money set aside by the Tories for civic receptions in order to provide food. No newspaper ever objected to the lavish GLC receptions of the past, but now journalists swarmed over the building searching for signs of damage or drunkenness.

Valerie and Michael also ended the strike at *Time Out* magazine. The owner, Tony Elliott, was a 1960s hippy who wanted to change the magazine from being a collective with all staff earning the same money into a more conventional business. The staff went on strike and Beatrix Campbell led a delegation asking the GLC to lend money to set up *City Limits*, a rival magazine. Making a loan to striking workers horrified the middle-aged lawyers and accountants among the officers, who found themselves negotiating with people so wildly attired they claimed to be unable to tell which were men and which were women, but five years later *City Limits* had repaid its loan, captured a third of *Time Out*'s readers and was only snuffed out during the recession presided over by John Major in the early nineties. When I reported the loan to the London party executive the only dissenting voice came from the print unions.

Now senior officers knew we were serious about our manifesto, and while Maurice Stonefrost relished the cultural change our director of personnel certainly didn't. Late one Friday afternoon he produced a doctor's letter stating that he was unfit for work, and took immediate retirement on full pension. By the time we discovered this on Monday morning he was gone, never to be seen again.

The DG Jim Swaffield discreetly asked the Lord Chamberlain not to invite GLC members to the wedding of Prince Charles and Lady Diana on 29 July, but our request was ignored and I received a personal invitation. The Labour group unanimously agreed I shouldn't go but asked the Palace if we could choose a couple of pensioners as London's representatives. By the time this was rejected, the press were in full hue and cry over our 'snub' to the royal pair. I spent hours explaining to one paper after another why we had declined to attend. I refused all further interviews after a while, but an Australian TV reporter told my secretary that she was prepared to sleep with me in exchange for an interview. Instead of dismissing this as funny, I should have taken it as a warning that media interest wasn't going to die away any time soon.

*

Unlike every other British city London did not have a Watch Committee of local councillors and magistrates overseeing the police. The Home Secretary was responsible for the Metropolitan Police but this 'oversight' was carried out by just one civil servant, with the result that effectively the Met were a law unto themselves. Labour's wage freeze and opposition to capital punishment had alienated the police. In 1979 I canvassed a block of police flats in Chalk Farm and found not a single Labour voter. The police's attitude towards demonstrations was that order should be preserved rather than people's right to protest. This led to the death of the Warwick University student Kevin Gately in Red Lion Square during a demonstration against the National Front in 1974 and the killing of the teacher Blair Peach at an anti-fascist demonstration in Southall in 1979. The *Sunday Times* published the names of six members of the Special Patrol Group, one of whom had clubbed Peach to death with an unauthorised weapon, but none of the officers would identify the culprit, who thus got away scot-free.

Labour's manifesto had demanded that the Met should answer to a GLC Police Committee chaired by Paul Boateng. Too much of Londoners' rates allocated to the police was spent spying on trade unionists and peace campaigners rather than putting bobbies back on the beat and tackling the crimes that mattered most to Londoners. As unemployment soared in areas like Brixton and Thatcher cut benefits, the police were used to keep the lid on society, but as pressures built Brixton erupted in rioting before the GLC election, in April 1981, and during that summer there were also riots in towns and cities across the country, most notably in Birmingham, Liverpool and Southall in West London. Locals complained that the police behaved like an occupying army.

The Met Commissioner Sir David McNee, who had regular working lunches with Cutler, now ordered that no police officer was to have any contact with GLC members. McNee resigned after an intruder managed to climb into the Queen's bedroom at Buckingham Palace, but his replacement was worse. Sir Kenneth Newman's record as police chief in Northern Ireland during the late seventies was characterised by a shift from convictions based on forensic evidence to confessions obtained by coercion in the cells. He refused to meet anyone from County Hall. Soon he was boasting that his use of snatch squads and stop-and-search had nipped many potential riots in the bud, but his hard-line approach later sparked Tottenham's Broadwater Farm riot of 1985, in which a local beat officer, Keith Blakelock, was brutally hacked to death by an angry mob. On the day after Blakelock's murder he tried unsuccessfully to avoid taking part in a TV debate with Bernie Grant and me, his handler telling the producer, 'He's not going on with those two shits.' The producer was having none of it, but this was the only time that Newman answered to London's representatives during his five-year tenure at the Met.

John Carvel writes, 'It is hard to do justice to the sheer volume of anti-Livingstone press coverage by merely recounting some of its riper examples.' I naively believed and hoped that our policies on women's rights, anti-racism and challenging homophobia would be reported fairly by a Fleet Street in which at the time not a single reporter or print worker was black, no reporter on any paper was openly gay and no woman held a position more senior than editorship of a women's page. I must have been mad. Tony Banks, who was close to Tony Benn, had seen Fleet Street's methods and urged me to ignore the Tory press. The GLC's press office simply responded to press enquiries rather than trying to set the agenda.

The right-wing press had a clear agenda. Mark Hollingsworth, in his book *The Press and Political Dissent*, revealed that the *Daily Mail* editor Sir David English had decided explicitly to make the GLC and myself prime targets. One of his best reporters, Richard Holliday, was flown back from the Middle East and sent into County Hall with the order to file six stories a day. At each morning's editorial conference Sir David would ask, 'What are we doing on the GLC today?' He would then decide which of Holliday's stories best suited the smear for that day. Cartoonists were instructed to draw pictures nastier than anything the *Mail*'s libel lawyers would allow their reporters to write. The cartoons implied that I supported the bombing of Londoners and that the GLC was funding the IRA. It's hard to sue a cartoon.

*

Because Christine and I had separated and I supported lesbian and gay rights there was intense interest in my private life. One Sunday

Mum phoned to ask why I'd had a vasectomy, which was a story that day in the *People*. What was appalling about this and other bizarre stories such as my 'ambition to be elected pope' (I was neither a Catholic nor celibate) and the claim that I imported pills from San Francisco which changed the taste of human semen to a strawberry flavour, is that they made no attempt to contact me to ask whether they were true. My weekly rubbish usually disappeared before the bin men came.

What hurt most was when they went after my family. The *Daily Mail* offered Christine £10,000 for the 'inside story' of our marriage with the promise they would 'write it up' for her. As we were still friends, we joked about making up some lewd fantasies, taking the money and splitting it. Richard Holliday and a photographer travelled to Lincoln and spoke to my mother, pretending to be doing a survey of opinions on the Humber Bridge with the follow-up, 'What does your Ken think about this?' She said what she thought of journalists and slammed the door and they slunk back to London.

On 20 August the *Daily Mail* reported three psychologists' diagnosis of my 'shocking' behaviour but the psychologists all denied the quotes attributed to them, and the president of the British Psychological Society complained that the 'irregular behaviour on the part of [*Daily Mail*] staff ... falsely brought the profession of psychology into disrepute'. The docile Press Council predictably dismissed a complaint against the *Mail*.

Richard Holliday became my shadow, and the strain of following me began to tell on his health. At first he looked stressed, with a visible tremor in his hand, and I didn't help by pointing him out to the audience whenever I spoke at public meetings. He would cringe over his notebook as they hissed him. As a person he was pleasant and a good writer, one who could have got a job on the *Guardian* or the *Financial Times*, but he mournfully explained that the *Mail* paid better and, given the size of his mortgage, he couldn't afford to leave. Eventually he was replaced by the creepier and less engaging Tony Doran.

My worst mistake was allowing Max Hastings into my bedsit. The day after I became leader the GLC press office asked me to give Max an interview for the *Standard*. He turned up while I was ironing my shirts, so his article depicted me as an austere bedsit revolutionary and spawned the *Private Eye* 'Leninspart' series. Max wrote, 'He is separated from his wife and says everything he owns is in the bedsit: a portable snooker table, a tank of salamanders, a wardrobe, a bed, a suitcase, a couple of chairs and a portable TV. He had spent the afternoon doing the ironing, with which he persisted through the early stages of our interview.' Max then quotes an anonymous Labour GLC member claiming that I was 'utterly ambitious, mean, ruthless, a brilliant organiser of caucuses'. The anonymous source goes on to claim that I had told a colleague, 'I don't need anybody. I can cope,' concluding, 'He's not interested in ordinary human relations – simply in getting to the top of the greasy pole.'

Things started to improve with the arrival at County Hall of Veronica Crichton – a tough thirty-two-year-old press officer the Labour party had sent to work with Andrew and myself during the 1981 election campaign, when she had insisted on vetting Andrew's loud ties. I liked her honesty: when I asked what she thought of the choice the group faced between me or Andrew she replied that she regretted so important a post had such a limited pool of talent to choose from, convincing me she would be the ideal person to deal with the press. But she couldn't start until the end of July, by which time the press had done its worst and our poll ratings were at rock bottom.

Veronica, who was born in Lambeth, was very sociable but intensely private (when she died of cancer in 2002 none of her friends even knew she was ill). She arrived at her desk each morning with strong black coffee and a cold tin of pilchards. She accepted the job on the condition she would not be asked to lie for us and her integrity ensured that she rapidly gained the trust of both press and politicians. She decided to stop interviews with the Tory press and concentrate on radio and television, which gave people more chance to make up their own minds. Veronica also decided that I should start doing public meetings where Londoners could question me directly. We hoped our poll ratings would pick up in the autumn with the fares cut. I was exhausted and, although we had separated a year earlier, Christine and I flew off to Hong Kong for a break.

*

On returning my first meeting was with Harrow Gay Unity, where I made the same speech about lesbian and gay rights I had been making for years. The *Standard*'s screaming banner headline was taken up by most of the press the following morning. The flavour of the coverage was captured by my nephew Terry, who rushed home from his paper round, shouting, 'Gran, Gran, the paper says Uncle Ken's a fairy.'

It was years before Chris Smith became the first MP to come out as gay, and for a politician to be outed as gay meant the end of his or her career. Cyril Taylor, Cutler's deputy leader, told me every 'queer-bashing speech I make is worth another thousand votes in Ruislip Northwood'. MPs who supported equal rights usually made clear they were not gay themselves, but I felt that to do this implied there was something wrong with being gay. Years later my Brent East Labour party agent found that many party members assumed I was gay. I received letters from lesbians and gay men who had been aware of their sexuality for years but unable to raise the subject with friends or relatives. A woman in East Anglia wrote that she was married with two children, had known all her life she was different but had never met another lesbian so could I please put her in touch with a lesbian organisation. When gay activists urged me to come out I didn't have the heart to disillusion them.

Hysteria mounted when we funded the Gay Teenage Group to research the needs of lesbians and gays under twenty-one, which was the legal age of homosexual consent at the time. Conservative rent-a-quote MPs denounced us for 'encouraging it' but the report found over half of young homosexuals had trouble at school, that one in five were beaten up, one in ten thrown out of their homes by parents and one in five had tried to commit suicide. Now the *Sun*'s editor, Kelvin MacKenzie, really was interested and set a team of reporters onto me to dig into my private life. Peter Chippindale and Chris Horrie in *Stick It Up Your Punter*, their book on the *Sun*, write, 'A minute scrutiny of his lifestyle for clues to deviancy disappointingly revealed only that he kept newts and lived extremely modestly . . . "Fucking newts!" raged MacKenzie at his hit squad. "All you can find is newts!" The team were sent out again but "Red Ken's private life was relentlessly dull."'

A year later Conservative Central Office returned to my sex life when they sent press officer Arthur Williamson to work for the GLC Tories. Williamson fixed a meeting with reporters from the *Mail* and *Telegraph* with the GLC Tory member George Tremlett to 'get the dirt on Livingstone'. The *Mail* asked, 'What we really want is something on his sex life. Is he queer? What about his women, who does he go out with? Is he a communist?' They also tried to portray me as racist. George refused when asked by Williamson to submit a question for the next council meeting which had 'been personally drafted by the editor of the *Daily Mail*, Sir David English', to imply I was anti-Semitic. Tony Doran got a Zionist group to smear me instead.

So it was back to sex. The *Sunday Mirror*'s Trudi Pacter was taken to lunch by Tory officials who told her, 'We have reliable sources who claim that Livingstone was at a gay party where he was buggered by six men in succession.' She ignored the slander. Central Office then spread a rumour that MI5 and Special Branch had a file listing the schoolgirls with whom I was involved. A *Sun* reporter said his paper had heard I met with a paedophile group above an East End pub one Friday, but I proved I had been speaking at meetings outside London every Friday evening that month. One reporter refused to move from Veronica Crichton's doorstep until she allowed him to search her flat to see if I was in her bedroom.

In fact I was by then living with Kate Allen, a Camden councillor. As we left her flat one Sunday morning, Doran, the grandly titled 'Home Affairs Reporter' at the *Mail*, got out of the car he had slept in all night and crept up beside us in his grubby coat. 'What would you like to say about the new love in your life, Ken?' We ignored him, so he went to see Christine. We had planned to divorce in three months on the grounds of two years' separation but with the *Mail* running large stories about Christine as the wronged woman she was hurt that her private life had become so public and changed the grounds of our divorce to adultery. This intrusion into an amicable separation, with no children, and no disagreements about property or money, typifies everything that is rotten about the *Mail*. When its owner, Lord Rothermere, left his wife and young children for another woman the *Mail* decided their readers did not need to be told one word about it.

I don't believe in suing newspapers. Public figures should accept vigorous criticism and it was wrong that Robert Maxwell was able to suppress news of his corruption simply because he had enough money to sue. Legal aid is not available for libel cases so by the time you get to court one or two years later you will have had to raise £100,000 in legal costs. Then there is the tricky practice of offering a settlement at the last minute. If you decline the offer, and a jury awards damages just one penny less than the newspaper offered, you have to pay their legal costs and your own, which in a major trial can mean bankruptcy. This happened when Ted Knight and I were libelled by *Private Eye*, who claimed that Colonel Gaddafi had put $200,000 into a numbered Swiss bank account for our use. I was happy to laugh it off but Ted insisted on suing. Just before the court case was due to begin, *Private Eye* offered a few thousand pounds which we accepted because we couldn't risk being landed with the costs.

I only survived the press because friends were supportive and Tariq Ali and others on the left came out strongly in my defence. At a lunch with *New Statesman* journalists they urged me not to back down and people stopped me on the street to say, 'Don't let the bastards get you down.' I also had a remarkable experience at the London School of Economics student union. I never had more than a few dozen people come to hear me at meetings, but the LSE auditorium was so packed I had to climb over the desks to get to the front. The mood was electric and I was elated for days. Back in County Hall I told people that something remarkable was happening when a council leader could get such a response.

*

Today it's hard to recall the gulf separating left and right thirty years ago which fuelled the viciousness of most of the press. Thatcher and Reagan preached a free-market triumphalism based on smashing trade unions and cutting the welfare state. In Liverpool, Manchester and Brixton the poor rebelled by rioting. The Cold War was renewed with a vengeance when Russia caught up with America in the nuclear arms race by diverting money to make more nuclear weapons. Thatcher brought American cruise missiles into the English countryside and Russian leader Yuri Andropov believed that the West was planning a sneak nuclear attack. This fed a paranoia in which those questioning Cold War policies were considered stooges of the Russians or worse.

The Labour opposition in Parliament was demoralised and uncertain how to resist Thatcher, so it was trade union and local government leaders who led the opposition. Demonised by the Tory press, we became heroes to the left. Like Benn and Arthur Scargill, the miners' leader, I went from meeting to meeting with the crowds becoming larger and more passionate. All my previous activity had been supporting the agenda set by left-wing MPs but now I was helping to set the agenda. At the Labour party conference in Brighton that October, I chaired the meeting where we assembled to cheer Tony Benn, who had failed by a handful of votes to replace Denis Healey as deputy leader. While waiting for Benn I outlined the coming battles in local government and what we had to do. As I walked back to Brighton station I was nervous. What if I got it wrong?

The most venomous press coverage was about Ireland. Since the debates with Ted I had learned a lot about Ireland from my reading, my involvement in the Troops Out movement and contact with Irish people. I believed that violence would continue until there was a political settlement, and that inevitably meant negotiation with the IRA. With the election of Thatcher, policy hardened as she set her face against negotiating, ever, denying that there was any political basis to the conflict and insisting the IRA were merely criminals and psychopaths.

Two days before the GLC election Provisional IRA member Bobby Sands had died after spending over two months on hunger strike, sparking worldwide anger and an upsurge of violence in the north of Ireland. A few weeks before his death he had been elected MP for Fermanagh and South Tyrone. Typically Thatcher refused to make any concession which would allow the IRA prisoners to call off their hunger strike, and ignored all pleas or pressure as nine other republicans starved themselves to death.

As the hunger strikers died one by one I knew that London would suffer more bombings so I called on Thatcher to treat the IRA captives as prisoners of war, as they were demanding. On 21 July I met Alice McElwee, the mother of one of the hunger strikers, who had been invited to County Hall by Labour member Andy Harris. Alice was devastated at the thought of losing her son Thomas but respected his decision and so would not agree to have him intravenously fed once he slipped into a coma. I was moved by her combination of pride in her son and fear of his death. The visit unleashed a wave of violent criticism from the Tory press. Eighteen days later Thomas McElwee died.

Thatcher's intransigence and the bombings in Hyde Park and Chelsea poisoned attitudes towards London's Irish minority who felt isolated by media hostility. Most Irish Londoners kept their heads down but a small group of republican sympathisers turned up at County Hall declaring that they intended to stay on the steps to protest against celebrating Charles and Di's wedding while 'Irish prisoners are dying'. On 29 July, while the royal couple travelled to St Paul's, they released black balloons in protest. It rapidly entered press folklore that I let the balloons off, but the first I knew about it was when I read it in the next day's papers. The protest ended when National Front thugs attacked the protesters, who took refuge in County Hall. No paper reported the attack.

A few days later I was working at night when the switchboard put through a call from the distressed mother of another hunger striker. Her son had slipped into a coma and she desperately wanted to know how much longer before Thatcher agreed to restore political status to the prisoners so she could take her son off the hunger strike. I eventually convinced her that Thatcher was prepared to see the death of every hunger striker rather than be seen to give in to the IRA. She found it hard to believe that as a mother Thatcher could do this, but she believed me and instructed the prison doctors to start feeding her son.

The cost of Thatcher's inflexibility was borne by Londoners when an IRA nail bomb exploded outside Chelsea Barracks, killing two and injuring thirty-eight. Two days later I was asked my views and replied, 'Nobody supports what happened last Saturday in London. But what about stopping it happening? People will be letting off bombs in London ... violence will recur again and again as long as we are in Ireland. People in Northern Ireland see themselves as a subject people. If they were just criminals or psychopaths they could be stopped.' I explained that the IRA was motivated by nationalism and that its members would continue irrespective of the costs to themselves or others and we needed a political solution to stop the killing. Given that the audience were mainly young Tories (I was speaking at Cambridge), my statement was quite well received.

Richard Holliday wrote up the story for the *Mail* without emphasis on that part of my speech. But a local reporter was present and sold a very different version to the Press Association. The *Sun* sent a reporter to County Hall to show me the text of the story they intended to run under the headline 'This damn fool says the bombers aren't criminals!' with the following: 'This morning the *Sun* presents the most odious man in Britain. Take a bow, Mr Livingstone, socialist leader of the Greater London Council ... he has quickly become a joke. Now no one can laugh at him any longer. The joke has turned sour, sick and obscene. For Mr Livingstone steps forward as the defender and the apologist of the criminal, murderous activities of the IRA.'

I told the reporter I hadn't said this but it didn't stop them running this fictional version. Other papers who also bought the PA's version didn't bother to check if it was true before blaring 'Mr Ken Livingstone took the side of the IRA' (*The Times*) and 'IRA bomb gang not criminals says Livingstone' (*Daily Express*). The *Daily Mail* had reported my speech accurately, so they couldn't repudiate it, but instead demanded that the Labour group remove me from office.

The *Sun*'s headline had its effect when I was attacked by two members of the National Front at a meeting in the City of London. Respectably dressed, one stepped forward saying good evening but as we shook hands his other hand swung round to spray me in the face with an aerosol can. I was partially blinded and in great pain but pulled the can to my chest. As the man slipped behind me I threw myself back against the wall and broke free. It was over so quickly that his accomplice who was acting as lookout had no time to do anything. It was only red paint but as publicity might encourage further attacks I did not report it. A group calling itself Friends of Ulster claimed responsibility and no paper condemned the violence, which would not have been the case if a Tory MP had been attacked by left-wing thugs. Three years later the young man who had attacked me came forward to apologise. His bigotry had evaporated when he went to see his new-born baby in an East London maternity ward. Looking at the black and Asian babies in the unit, he realised the stupidity of racism.

*

County Hall was now under siege from the media as the Tories called a meeting of the council and tabled a motion of censure. The media demanded my removal, but the hysteria of the press made it impossible for any Labour councillor to vote with the Tories and I survived with the vote of every Labour member. That night after a speech to Hampstead Labour party some of us went to the nearby Three Horseshoes for a quiet drink. A gang of bulky skinheads starting chanting 'commie bastards', kicking one of my supporters in the head and throwing a woman over the bar. Papers reported the incident but failed to condemn the violence, with the *Daily Express* supporting the landlord's view that it was 'only to be expected'.

I was determined not to give in to the papers by changing policy, however vile the abuse became. I knew that the moment I did bend, the editors and owners in Fleet Street would know my breaking point and I would no longer be of any use to Londoners, but six months of media venom had shaken the confidence of the Labour group. Following the launch of the SDP the collapse in support for the Labour party in London mirrored the national decline. Audience Selection polling reported that only 35 per cent of Londoners supported me with 52 per cent opposed. A poll for Thames TV found only 20 per cent thought I was doing a good job, with 47 per cent who thought I was making a mess of it. But the thousands of letters arriving at my office were split equally for and against. Many were racist or homophobic and suggested that I should 'go back to Russia'. Some contained death threats with the odd razor blade included. One retired army major on the south coast was relatively mild: 'Dear Sir, I listened to you on Radio 4 news this morning. What a slimy hypocrite you are. Yours sincerely . . .'

My favourite was:

The Rescue Mission
182 Elliot Street
Birmingham

Dear Mr Livingstone

Perhaps you have heard of me and my nationwide campaign in the cause of temperance. Each year . . . I have made a tour . . . accompanied by a young friend and assistant, David Powell . . . a young man of good family and excellent background, is a pathetic example of a life ruined by excessive indulgence in whisky and women.

David would appear with me at lectures and sit on the platform, wheezing and staring at the audience through bleary, bloodshot eyes, sweating profusely, picking his nose, passing wind and making obscene gestures, while I would point out . . . what drink and women could do to a man.

Last summer, unfortunately, David died. A mutual friend has given me your name and I wonder if you would care to take David's place on my next tour.

Yours in anticipation

Rev. David Knight

As the press hatred mounted, Bill Bush became worried about my personal safety and unsuccessfully urged me to resurrect the leader's car. The Met's Special Branch came to warn the head of security at the GLC that my movements were 'being monitored by extremist groups', but insisted that they could not provide protection as I lived in a bedsit and travelled on public transport. We didn't tell them that I also used the local launderette.

I've no doubt that the majority of the Labour group would have liked to have seen the back of me, but couldn't agree on a replacement, and there would have been a furious reaction from constituency Labour parties if the group had given in to the Tory press. If I showed the slightest sign of weakness I'd be gone, so I had to project confidence in our ability to turn things round before the next election.

One encouraging sign was when Thames TV's *Reporting London* proposed a programme on which editors from the *Sun*, *Mail* and *Telegraph* would question me live on television. Veronica and I jumped at the idea but one after another the editors dropped out. In the end only Max Hastings from the *Standard* was prepared to go head to head with me on live TV. As I left the studio Harvey phoned with congratulations and I received a flood of supportive letters from viewers. Veronica went to work fixing up more radio and TV appearances. I was also now doing public meetings at the rate of about 300 a year, including meetings with groups not usually supportive of Labour.

It was not until February 1982 that a nationwide audience got to hear me when I made my first appearance on Radio 4's *Any Questions*, then chaired by David Jacobs. The show was to be recorded in the New Forest but we were diverted to Bristol because of heavy snow. With Ann Leslie of the *Mail* and Conservative MP Jonathan Aitken on the panel I was very much in a minority and very nervous about appearing on such a well-established and high-profile programme. My only mistake was in actually answering the questions I was asked, unlike the other panellists who answered the question they would have preferred to have been asked.

By the end of the programme Bristol had been cut off by snow and so we were put up in a hotel, and in a gesture that cut across the political divide Ann Leslie offered to lend me her razor. We waited at Temple Meads station until three o'clock in the afternoon for a train back to London. Nothing is more miserable than being stuck on a platform all day in the snow but David Jacobs remained the ever-genial host and ordered two bottles of whisky to keep us warm. By the time we got to Paddington I knew all I was ever going to need to know about Ann Leslie and Jonathan Aitken. A week later David Jacobs read out listeners' comments with many people surprised to agree with my views. David concluded by saying there had not been a single critical letter.

*

My relations with London Labour MPs improved when Hackney South member Ron Brown (brother of Lord George Brown) defected to the SDP. As chair of the London group of Labour MPs he kept telling them that I had agreed to attend meetings with them, but in fact he had failed to invite me. Frank Dobson took over this role and was both friendly and helpful, saying, 'I didn't think much of the old [Labour group] leadership, you couldn't do any worse.'

But opposition was being mobilised by the slightly sinister Keep London Free Campaign. On 23 October a secret gathering of forty-five top business people including Sir Charles Forte and representatives from Cadbury Schweppes, Taylor Woodrow, GEC, Blue Circle, Tate & Lyle, Sainsbury, Allied Breweries, Beechams, Lazards, Ladbrokes and De La Rue met and raised £200,000 for the right-wing group Aims of Industry to organise a campaign for the abolition of the GLC. Many of these firms did business with us and remained anonymous behind a committee led by Lady Shirley Porter, the new leader of Westminster Council, who was said to be the twentieth-richest woman in Europe. Members of the group included writer Kingsley Amis, the philosopher Roger Scruton and Alfred Sherman, a virulent racist from Thatcher's favourite think tank the Centre for Policy Studies.

On 6 November Michael Heseltine introduced legislation to control local government expenditure. He had already demanded that councils cut spending by a further £800 million and withheld £450 million of government grants as a punishment to those who refused to do so. Of that penalty, £120 million fell on the fourteen councils Labour had won six months earlier. After four years of GLC cuts by Horace Cutler with 6,000 jobs lost, the budget he left us of £456 million was still £50 million over Heseltine's new target. Within two years Heseltine would stop all grants to the GLC, fining London ratepayers £150 million for having elected a Labour council.

That same day Bill Bush gave me an analysis of the results of the St Pancras GLC by-election, caused when one member defected to the SDP and resigned her seat to stand again under her new colours. This was the high point of the SDP and Bill's analysis showed that in a GLC election the SDP and the Liberals would win a huge majority, reducing the Labour and Tory groups to barely double figures each. My own seat would fall and Bill concluded, 'I doubt if there's a seat in London, except perhaps Brent South, where we could get you elected at the moment.'

The sheer number of attacks from all quarters was overwhelming. I was working flat out trying to keep our show on the road in the hope that the fares cut would transform our position but I had huge doubts. I knew it was right to raise the issues of race, sexism, homophobia and Ireland. I believed in them deeply, but these issues had been marginal to the political mainstream until we took them up. Politicians believed that they were vote losers to be avoided at all costs. Twenty years later Roy Hattersley told me, 'You have no idea how deeply offensive those issues were in my local Working Men's Club.' Inevitably the most difficult issues are those that affect the prejudices in our own hearts. From the perspective of the twenty-first century with former IRA members in the Northern Irish government and black, Asian, lesbian and gay ministers, society seems transformed, but in the early 1980s attitudes were different and I should have had a better strategy when I launched these then-radical policies on an unprepared public. One poll showed that my approval rating had slumped to just 18 per cent, but all that was about to change, courtesy of Her Majesty's Law Lords.

8

Here Comes the Judge

1982–1983

Our first defeat by the judges was on the issue of council house sales. Cutler had already stopped the GLC's house-building programme and, ignoring our housing crisis, Heseltine refused to allow the GLC to build even 1,500 new homes a year. Cutler had done everything possible to stop council housing being built in marginal constituencies in case it increased the Labour vote, so a new estate of 500 flats at Brentford Dock had been withdrawn from letting and passed to an upmarket estate agent to sell off, with no preference given to Londoners or those in housing need. They persuaded Cutler to keep flats empty for up to four years so as not to depress the price by putting them all on the market at once.

Fully expecting to lose the 1981 GLC election, the Tories were worried we would be able to let homes that were completed after the election, so they formed a private company to buy up homes for sale as they were built. When we won, only 418 letting homes were left (the majority in a key marginal ward in Hammersmith) and we wanted to give them to families on the waiting list. People who had bought the neighbouring homes took us to court, fearing that having council tenants as neighbours would reduce the value of their homes.

Sir Frank Layfield, Britain's most experienced local government lawyer, advised us that we might have to compensate the owner–occupiers for 'loss of value' but would win the right to let the homes. High Court judge Sir Robert Megarry made clear his attitude towards the GLC: 'Plainly those who know they are dealing with a trickster who will seek to escape by any loophole, however dishonest, must seek to tie him up so tightly that escape is impossible . . . It ill becomes a council intent on not performing its contracts to taunt the victims with their failure to foresee its untrustworthiness. This is a shabby contention.' He dismissed the needs of those on the waiting list.

*

The tube network south of the river is far less extensive than to the north, so South Londoners would see less benefit from our forthcoming London Transport fares cut. We could see this was unfair on commuters who used British Rail, so we offered BR £20 million a year to cut its fares in London by the same amount. Norman Fowler, Thatcher's Secretary of State for Transport, instructed BR not to take the money. Dave Wetzel and I went off to see him. After some pompous pleasantries over tea, he admitted there was nothing he could do to stop us cutting bus and tube fares but if BR took our £20 million he would cut their subsidy by £20 million. Tory commuters in places like Bromley would thus lose out. Most newspapers did not report this story and the *Standard*, which could have run a great campaign standing up for readers who used BR, briefly reported the meeting and never mentioned the issue again.

Taking his cue from Fowler, Bromley's Tory leader Denis Barkway took the GLC to court on the grounds that Bromley's ratepayers were getting a raw deal. Barkway never complained about Fowler's decision or attempted to change his mind so that his residents could benefit from our policy. No other Tory borough joined the suit as they shared the view of Peter Bowness, Croydon's Tory leader, that the case 'hadn't got a snowball's chance in hell'.

Control of London Transport was passed to the GLC by an Act of Parliament in 1969. This specifically stated that the GLC could 'direct the Executive to submit proposals for an alteration in . . . fare arrangements to achieve any object of general policy specified by the Council'. In introducing the Act transport minister Richard Marsh said, 'The main powers that the GLC will have . . . will be to pay grant to the Executive for any purposes it thinks fit . . . The Council might wish . . . to keep fares down at a time when costs are rising . . . It is free to do so.' Opposition spokeswoman Margaret Thatcher said at the time that, 'if the Council decided . . . to operate services which would make it uneconomic, the Council would have to provide a subsidy from the rates', to which she raised no objection. Michael Heseltine said that 'many people would argue . . . that it would be better to subsidise those uneconomic services from the rates than to put up the fares'. In twelve days of debate not a single MP said it would be illegal to subsidise fares from the rates and the bill was passed without a division.

Over the next eleven years the GLC had raised or lowered the fares subsidy without challenge. On two occasions while drawing up the manifesto I questioned our legal department to ensure that our fares cut posed no legal problem. Following our election, Dave Wetzel and Paul Moore held meetings across London to discuss how the new fares would operate from 4 October. We were also introducing fare zones at the same time and discovered that with a 25 per cent cut some fares close to the zone boundary would have gone up rather than down, and it needed a 32 per cent fares reduction to ensure all fares were cut. This increased the fares subsidy from 29 per cent to 56 per cent, reducing fares to what they had been in real terms in 1975. All related committee and council reports were cleared by lawyers.

When the fares cut was implemented in the autumn of 1981 it caused something of a furore. The *Daily Express* reported how 'cheaper fares turned rush hours into crush hour . . . staff had to work overtime to cope with the long queues for season tickets'. The

Daily Mail took a different view, reporting that the fares cut was the first stop on the way to the introduction of a full-blown Soviet-style economy. Following the cut, an additional half a million people switched to using buses and tubes, which meant the total fares income would remain almost unchanged. Car use in London was down by 4 per cent, with less congestion and, the figures showed later, fewer accidents.

In the High Court on 28 October Lord Justice Dunn and Mr Justice Phillips rejected Bromley's case that we had acted illegally in reaching our decision. The GLC was deemed to have correctly considered all the pros and cons, including the cost to the ratepayer. They added the caveat that abolition of all fares would be illegal, and Phillips judged our reduction to be at the margin of what was lawful. Bromley was ordered to pay the full costs of the hearing.

Bromley took the case to the Court of Appeal. The GLC's head of law, John Fitzpatrick, was concerned that the right-wing libertarian Master of the Rolls, Lord Denning, would be tempted to deliver one of his idiosyncratic judgments, although he was certain that, should he do so, the Law Lords would overturn it as they usually did. Denning, unable to contain himself, heard the case within a week and exercised his right to decide which judges should sit with him. In a clear sign of what was to come he chose the extremely reactionary Lord Justice Watkins and the merely conservative Lord Justice Oliver. I wasn't surprised when following the judgment John Fitzpatrick appeared in my office in a state of shock asking for a strong cup of coffee. 'Can I be frank? It was like sitting through a party political broadcast.'

Lord Justice Watkins had delivered, as Denning had no doubt hoped, the most partisan judgment of recent times:

I have no doubt whatsoever that the large reduction of fares ... arose out of a hasty, ill considered, unlawful and arbitrary use of power. As a result ... people who daily use buses and trains in London pay about 30 per cent less for the privilege of doing so . . . ratepayers of the great City, who are unlikely to gain anything from it . . . will bear the cost of . . . an astounding decision.

Those who come newly to govern people and who act in haste in wielding power to which they are unaccustomed would do well to heed the words of Gladstone . . . 'The true test of a man, the test of a class, the true test of a people is power. It is when power is given into their hands that the trial comes.'

The new leader of the new Greater London Council had hardly been put to that test when he . . . sought out the Chairman of the Executive and, as seems beyond question, told him the Council intended to put into effect forthwith a promise contained in an election manifesto . . .

Denning had decided the 1974 Tameside case, where Tories had won control of the council just in time to overturn the previous Labour council's introduction of comprehensive schools. When the Labour government took the council to court to stop them Denning backed the Tory council, pointing out that this had been an election manifesto commitment and should be respected. As the only serving judge born in the nineteenth century, memory was perhaps no longer his strong point, but his loathing of socialism had not stopped him claiming his right to free travel as an OAP.

Lord Justice Oliver's judgment avoided Watkins's grandstanding but was more damaging. He ignored the right to subsidise fares stipulated in the 1969 London Transport Act by declaring that the fares subsidy was illegal and we should immediately raise them by enough to balance our books. This was clearly nonsensical but, while we were confident that the Law Lords would overturn the judgment, we took no chances and retained one of the country's smartest barristers, Robert Alexander QC, to argue our case. With his encyclopedic knowledge of the foibles and idiosyncrasies of each Law Lord, he declined my offer to appear in court and explain the work that had gone into the evolution of the fares policy because he feared that my presence would be considered 'offensive and inflammatory' by some judges. The five Law Lords were considered the most 'liberal' among the judges: Lords Scarman, Wilberforce, Brandon, Diplock and Keith.

To our utter amazement, when the Law Lords announced their judgment on 17 December, it was worse than Denning's. Not only did they rule that there could be no subsidy at all for fares but they revived the principle of fiduciary duty: an invention by Victorian judges to prevent the Poor Law Boards of Guardians from being too generous. In 1925 Poplar councillors were found guilty of violating their fiduciary duty because they had paid equal wages to women employees. The judge then denounced them for 'the vanity of appearing as model employers of labour . . . guided . . . by some eccentric principles of socialistic philanthropy, or by a feminist ambition to secure equality of the sexes'.

Fiduciary duty had been laid to rest in 1955 when Birmingham Council lost a case contesting its right to provide free travel for pensioners and the Tory government rushed legislation through Parliament reversing the judges' decision. The decision of the Law Lords meant that all councils now risked legal challenge if anybody could show that any council had voted to improve any service by increasing the rates. This highly charged political judgment caused uproar in legal and local government circles. In his book *The Politics of the Judiciary* Professor John Griffiths wrote:

it may be . . . that the Court of Appeal and the Law Lords deliberately intervened to control the collectivist policies of the administration at County Hall because they disapproved of those policies. But . . . they seemed not to have understood what they were doing, because they did not grasp the nature of the problem of London Transport. The judgments . . . demonstrate how ill suited is judicial review to the examination of administrative policies. They show how the narrow approach of the courts . . . leads to a misunderstanding of the purpose of legislation . . . We do not know to what extent the members of the two courts sought to inform themselves of the recent developments in transport policy . . . By choosing to set . . . financial accounting . . . over the policy provisions . . . the courts were able to virtually ignore social and economic factors . . . The reason for the choice seems to have been primarily the Law Lords' strong preference for the principles of the market economy with a dislike of heavy subsidisation for social purposes . . . whether or not their lordships were politically biased, their habits of thought determined their decision.

With only four days to go before Christmas I asked Dave Wetzel and Valerie Wise to organise a publicity campaign against the judges and had a meeting with Labour MPs to see if they would propose legislation overturning the Law Lords' decision. In most cases where the courts are biased only a few individuals suffer but this decision would hit the pockets of four million passengers and wreck the city's public transport system. LT's chief executive Sir Peter Masefield said the judgment would result in a 200 per cent fare increase, the closure of 10 per cent of the tube system, redundancy for a quarter of the workforce and the axing of many bus routes. He proposed an immediate 100 per cent fare increase and the rest in August and, as all subsidy was illegal, free travel for pensioners would have to end. This would be the biggest reduction in public transport in British history, with devastating consequences for congestion and pollution in the capital.

*

The government was also in confusion. When I met the new transport minister David Howell he said government lawyers believed a 60 per cent fare increase would be enough to comply with the judgment. After the initial gloating the press realised that Londoners actually liked our new fares policy. The judges had gone over the top and faced a public backlash and mounting press criticism.

Our campaign slogan was 'Stop the Vandals in Ermine' and thirty Londoners got huge publicity by hiring judges' robes, hijacking a bus and forcing it to drive to the House of Lords with television cameras in tow. Community groups started campaigning and the first public meeting was held in Hornchurch, where I arrived just as the National Front were in retreat after seeing the size of the crowd. Local reporters said it was the largest public meeting in the borough since the Second World War (in the seat with the highest swing to the Tories anywhere in Britain in the 1979 election).

On the way home that evening I was elated: there could be no underestimating the importance of that Hornchurch meeting. Time and again people condemned the press campaign against me, unleashing waves of applause. In Fleet Street's overconfidence that they could get away with whatever they chose to invent they had overreached themselves. The tide had turned in our favour. There was a long way to go but the judges had put the ball into our hands and I wasn't going to drop it.

If we defied the Law Lords and refused to increase fares it would put the crisis in the lap of government, who would not want to increase the fares of millions of voters who used the tube, but there seemed no chance we could get a majority in the GLC to disobey the Law Lords' ruling, and every possibility the GLC Labour group would tear itself apart. The left opposed the fare increase and the right believed we had to uphold the law. In the Labour group of forty-eight only eighteen were prepared to defy the judges. There were six doubtfuls, but even if I could convince them it would still mean a tied vote of 24–24, with the chair John Ward casting his tie-breaking vote for legality. If the group voted to obey the judges and I went against that decision I would have to resign. Andrew McIntosh saw the possibility that he could regain the leadership, telling *Time Out* journalist David Rose that he intended 'to use the fares issues to try and force Livingstone to resign . . . if Ken goes against a whip I will call a special meeting of the party and move a vote of no confidence in him'.

In the following days I persuaded the six doubtfuls to vote with me. One member who would vote for legality was Simon Turney, who was in the USA, so I phoned and asked him to stay there rather than coming back. His agreement meant we could win by 24–23. When the group met the public gallery was packed with party members and Arthur Latham announced that the London party executive had voted by 25–7 to call on us to defy the Law Lords, but my hopes were crushed when Gerry Ross, one of the six doubtfuls, sent his apologies for absence. As we went through the debate it was obvious we were heading for a tied vote of 23–23 with the chair using his casting vote to obey the judges. Suddenly Arthur Edwards, from the legality camp, got up and left to fulfil a prior commitment as chief whip on Newham Council. His absence gave us a victory of 23–22 when the vote was called. The meeting was thrown into uproar with Andrew looking like a beached whale. John Carr, who chaired the GLC's Staff Committee, organised an impromptu party in his room.

The next day the chamber was crawling with reporters and television crews as I rose to propose the Labour group's policy of voting against the fare increase. Horace Cutler with his usual bluster announced the Conservatives intended to abstain as this was a mess Labour had made and Labour must sort it out. If the Tories abstained Labour could win by 24 votes to 22. (Simon Turney was still away but Mike Ward, a former 'legal', had switched his vote in our favour following the group's decision.) Cutler's announcement electrified the debate, with hours of chaos and hilarity as Labour right-wingers begged the Tories to vote with them and Cutler steadfastly refused.

The DG Sir James Swaffield stirred the pot by warning abstainers that they would be at risk of personal surcharge for the cost of the fares cut. This caused consternation in the Tory ranks, among which most had no desire to forfeit their substantial wealth for the sake of Cutler's posturing. The meeting was adjourned so that the Tories could reconsider tactics. Television started broadcasting proceedings live and the tension was unbearable as the Tories announced they still intended to abstain. Faced with the prospect that we might win, several Tories' wives were berating their husbands in the corridors, fearing they might lose their homes. Neil Davies, one of our members, had gone a sickly green so I asked others to take him to the bar to keep his mind off the subject and prevent right-wingers getting to him.

As we filed through the lobbies the Tories sat solidly in their seats as the sole Liberal and two SDP defectors joined the vote for the fare increase. In the last seconds three Tories lost their nerve, leaped up and squeezed through the closing doors to cast their vote for an increase. The GLC had voted to comply with the Law Lords by just 27–24.

*

Across London there were huge meetings to protest against the Law Lords and MPs were getting thousands of letters about the pensioners' travel pass. The next stage in our campaign was for a private member's bill introduced by Douglas Jay, MP for Battersea North, to reverse the Law Lords' decision (private member's bills test opinion but can't progress unless the government makes time available). Even though Thatcher and Norman Tebbit had stayed in the Commons to encourage the maximum Tory vote, it was to no avail. Jay's bill passed by 205–177 votes. Nearly half of London's Tory MPs abstained. We demanded that the government find time to pass the bill, but Thatcher would not give in. Tebbit was robust in replies to constituents' letters:

Dear . . .

Thank you for sending me a coupon clipped from one of Mr Livingstone's propaganda advertisements (paid for by your rates) about London Transport fares.

Don't be conned into thinking Mr Livingstone is trying to give you something for nothing. Not only did he cut fares for Londoners but he cut them for such people as foreign tourists and well paid commuters from outside London ... Until Livingstone and his weird friends took over the GLC, London Transport was becoming more efficient and sensible ... Livingstone is pouring your money down the drain in many ways. Did you know this year he has given your money to his friends in some very peculiar organisations?

– The English Collective of Prostitutes

– Lesbian Line

– London Gay Teenage Group

– A series of left-wing propaganda sheets, including £500,000 spent on the extremist publication *The Londoner* ...

Transport minister David Howell finally came to life and rushed a bill through Parliament. Instead of keeping our fares policy intact, the bill allowed us to borrow £125 million to cover money lost during the fares cut so far. This was the worst of all possible worlds: the fares would still go up, ratepayers would have to repay £125 million over the next five years and this would be doubled by government penalties for overspending. If Howell had asked me I would have told him not to waste Parliament's time. Ever since the collapse of the Goodwin administration I had favoured keeping GLC borrowing to the minimum. Maurice Stonefrost had persuaded Goodwin and Cutler to pay back GLC debt and I continued the policy, so all investment was paid for out of the rates. If re-elected in 1985, we would be in a position to pay back all of the GLC's debt.

But if we didn't borrow the £125 million we would have to pay the whole lot back in our first budget, which was due in February. Early estimates suggested there would have to be a rates increase of 90 per cent and Andrew said he would not support anything over 70 per cent. Maurice came to my rescue by exploiting the complicated grants system at the government's expense and got it down to just under 50 per cent, so Andrew had to support the budget and we didn't have to borrow anything. Surprised by Maurice's financial dexterity, the Tories lost interest when they saw there was no Labour split, and our budget was easily passed.

The GLC's complex finances and incomprehensible grants regime meant that for our first budget I was totally dependent on Maurice. With the Labour right looking for any excuse to vote it down, and most senior officers hoping for a change of leader, my fate was in his hands and some members were surprised he went the extra mile to ensure I survived. But Maurice was an honourable public servant who believed his duty was to sustain the elected administration and, like our head of law John Fitzpatrick, he was having the time of his life. Our radical politics were liberating for Maurice and John, who had suffered long periods of local government torpor. When I asked Maurice why he had gone out on a limb for us he replied, 'I saw what "they" were trying to do to you and I thought it was wrong.' I had no need to ask who 'they' were. It took me three years to get on top of our finances.

*

We still faced another big fare increase but our campaign forced the government to rule it out. The Attorney General, Sir Michael Havers (who defended the Rolling Stones after the famous drugs bust at Keith Richards's house), announced that no new fare increase would be necessary. Never in British history had a minister overturned a ruling by the Law Lords. He had no legal power to do this and it would only be possible if the Law Lords did not object, but realising their catastrophic misjudgment they kept quiet and we all pretended that the Attorney General's decision had some legal standing.

However, the shenanigans weren't over yet. Kensington and Chelsea Council challenged our budget on the grounds that it breached our fiduciary duty. Mr Justice McNeill in the High Court had no intention of repeating the Law Lords' mistake and took the opportunity to narrow the circumstances in which fiduciary duty was relevant:

. . . the issue is one for the political hustings and not for the court. It is a matter of real concern that the court, exercising the power of judicial review, is increasingly, and particularly in this case, used for political purposes superficially dressed up as points of law. The proper remedy in such matters is the ballot box and not the court . . . The remedy is in the hands of the electorate. It is only where illegality can be established . . . that judicial review can be appropriately sought. The impropriety of coming to this court when . . . political capital is sought to be made . . . cannot be overstressed . . . I regret to say that I found wholly unconvincing the affidavit of [Kensington and Chelsea's Town Clerk]. I may be unkind to him. It may be that the arguments which he put forward were not his, but those of the Party in political control of Kensington.

Four weeks after McNeill's judgment I was in trouble again, this time in a case brought by the District Auditor, Ian Pickwell, against Camden councillors for awarding a £60-a-week minimum wage. Pickwell had rushed to retain Bromley's QC David Widdicombe in the hope that he could repeat his success against the GLC. We were represented by Roger Henderson. Widdicombe relied on the precedent set in the Poplar councillors' case in 1925 and looked pretty sick as he listened to Mr Justice Forbes's decision: 'Looking back, as we do, over sixty years of progress in the field of social reform and industrial relations, some of their Lordships' observations may, with the benefit of hindsight, appear unsympathetic.' Stating that 'nothing in this judgment is intended as a criticism of Mr Pickwell personally', Lord Justice Ormrod took his case to pieces line by line and then demolished the Law Lords' fares decision, saying 'their lengthy judgments are a mine of felicitous literary expressions'. Forbes and Ormrod strengthened the McNeill judgment and made it clear that the judgment of the court should not be used as a substitute for legitimate political decisions. I had no doubt that without the uproar over the fares case Camden councillors would have been found guilty and barred from office.

The McNeill judgment meant that we could cut fares again. With the prospect of severe congestion and 3,000 extra road accidents a year in London, something had to be done to reduce the volume of traffic using the roads. John Fitzpatrick took 'soundings in the legal world' and was told we could cut fares as long as we found a different justification and it was less than the previous cut. Roger Henderson advised a 25 per cent fares cut and Jack Dromey, a TGWU official, ran the campaign to support it.

David Howell now rushed a bill through Parliament giving him the power to decide the subsidy to public transport but Roger noticed that Howell had not understood the judgments by McNeill, Forbes and Ormrod that councillors should determine fares subsidy as long as it was reasonable. We kept quiet until the bill became law and Howell realised his error but could not stop the cut in fares.

*

We had a problem with the London Transport board. Sir Peter Masefield had retired and to no one's surprise we had a poor field of applicants, including one from a student who wrote that he had filled in his application on the top deck of a bus, pointing out his experience of public transport was through using it. The new chair was Keith Bright, who was nervous about the cut without a direction from the court, so once again we were off to the High Court, where Mr Justice Glidewell and Mr Justice Nolan ruled in our favour. There was a lot of laughter in court as the judges tactfully ignored the decision of the Law Lords:

[the 1981 fares reduction] was accordingly set aside as clearly unlawful. There is no need to discuss it further other than to mention that the basis of the decision of the Court of Appeal and the House of Lords was widely misunderstood, and in many cases, was obviously misrepresented. Some of the public comments gave the misleading impression [that] the judgments were designed to thwart the wishes of the majority on the Council for political motives. Such reactions, whether based on ignorance or whatever, can only be described as total rubbish. If the Council succeeds in the present application it would be equally ignorant, or deliberately misleading, if the cry were to be: judges slash fares or – unfortunately more likely – judges increase rates. It is to be hoped that nothing like that will happen again.

In buckling down to get the best deal we could achieve, we lost support from the hard-left groups (Labour Briefing and the Chartists). Writing in *London Labour Briefing*, an angry Paula Watson charged that 'when faced with a real challenge from the capitalist establishment our representatives on the GLC surrendered . . . what is left is the small print, tiny grants to the publishers of feminist and gay magazines and the establishment of committees on . . . the rights of women and ethnic minorities. These are worthy causes but there is nothing specifically socialist about them. Any regime of pragmatic liberals could do as much.' I had had criticism from the left before but it was painful coming from old friends like Paula.

There were always rumours about Cutler's land dealings when he acquired farmland or brownfield sites and, following a private meeting with local councillors or officers, the land would be re-zoned for housing. Twice journalists told me that they were on the point of exposing Cutler for corruption but they never managed to gather conclusive evidence. Cutler now retired as Tory leader to open a mixed naturist sauna in my constituency and invited me to the opening, but when I saw that the membership charge was £50 a year for single men and only £5 for single women, I declined. Now that his term was at an end the Tory group had to choose a new leader. They included the plodding Richard Brew and the smarmy, apolitical Alan Greengross, but the one I feared was George Tremlett, whose working-class background gave him an understanding of London's problems. When I asked one Tory who he was voting for he replied, 'Not the Jew [Greengross].'

Brew won just as the Tories started to implode. Our chair of housing Tony McBrearty discovered that three members of the Tory group had formed a housing association, taken grants from the GLC and set up their own maintenance firm which seemed to be getting lots of money for not much maintenance. As McBrearty was revealing this in the council chamber, Cutler leant forward and said to Harold Mote, one of the members in the so-called association, 'You're on your own this time'.

I asked Swaffield for the papers relating to the housing association but in classic civil service tradition he would not give me the files of a previous administration. He was prepared to give them to Andrew Arden QC, an independent barrister conducting an impartial inquiry. In the year before Arden's report the drip-drip of revelations wrecked Cutler's reputation and demoralised the Tory group, who were further stunned when the Tory member Dr Mark Patterson was convicted of stealing blood from an NHS blood bank and selling it to private hospitals.

Arden passed evidence of corruption to the Metropolitan Police but with the 1983 general election campaign about to start they decided not to prosecute, using the excuse that one of the defendants, Harold Mote, was old and frail (he lived many years more). Following the revelations the Tory chief whip, Geoffrey Seaton, resigned his seat. Cutler also paid a price. Like every outgoing leader at County Hall between 1934 and 1973 he expected a seat in the House of Lords and looked forward to running a large quango. But Thatcher was furious that the scandal coincided with the general election and Cutler got nothing.

*

We were now getting a grip on the GLC bureaucracy. Michael Kaye, a PR manager in the tobacco industry (he ran arts sponsoring for the Peter Stuyvesant Foundation), had been appointed by Cutler to take charge of the South Bank concert halls. He fitted in perfectly with the old arts establishment who saw the South Bank as their domain and bitterly resented Tony Banks's plans to open up the Festival Hall to a wider audience. Tony had a long struggle to get Kaye to make space for more popular events and in the end had to suspend Kaye and his team for ignoring the Arts Committee's plans. With Kaye gone, the Festival Hall came to life and was swarming with a younger audience coming to watch free events and an exciting programme of world music.

We set up an Ethnic Minorities Committee with myself as chair and Paul Boateng as vice-chair. Herman Ouseley, who did a similar job for Ted Knight in Lambeth, became the chief officer. Two years previously Ted had a huge struggle breaking the colour bar that prevented the recruitment of black bin men and had only been able to get the unions to agree that the Brixton round would have an all-black crew, rather than having integrated crews throughout the borough. Although the GLC claimed to be an equal-opportunities employer, nothing had been done to turn that pious statement into a reality. Only 2 per cent of new lettings had gone to non-whites – until we computerised the system and removed human subjectivity and prejudice from the allocation process.

The Fire Brigade had only seven black staff out of 6,500 fire fighters. Fortunately FBU general secretary Ken Cameron persuaded his members that the brigade needed to look more like London, but the electricians' union general secretary Eric Hammond refused to help us change the situation when we discovered that only white electricians were offered overtime.

We also had a problem with the GLC Staff Association (SA) which represented the majority of County Hall's white-collar staff.

To tackle discrimination requires a breakdown of the race and sex of the workforce by department and by grade. For two years the SA's leadership wasted the time of Staff Committee chair John Carr before they agreed to a system of voluntary monitoring. Half the staff refused to return the forms; those that were returned showed that the worst departments were the white-collar surveyors and solicitors, so the SA was now in no position to oppose monitoring by management. We found that women and black people were firmly at the bottom of the pecking order; in the supplies department, for example, no woman or black person had ever reached middle management although they made up the bulk of the staff. In 1906 the department started a dining club, membership of which was by invitation only. In the years since then only white men had been invited to join it and only dining club members had ever been promoted. The SA responded that black people had not been in London long enough to work their way up the GLC hierarchy.

When we introduced a code of conduct to ban racial and sexual harassment we were stalled by the three white men who ran the SA: John Hollocks (a founder member of the SDP), Arthur Capelin (the right-wing Labour leader of Greenwich Council) and Charles Corcoran, who claimed there was no need to ban sexual harassment as 'no one has ever sexually harassed me'.

GLC staff were recruited straight from school or university, allocated a grade such as scientific, administrative, technical, clerical or manual and placed in a department for the rest of their working lives. Each year only half a dozen were promoted from one grade to another. Council members were only allowed to appoint directors (who could come from outside). All other promotions were internal, with appointments made by officers in the grade above, who were unlikely to promote anybody questioning existing policies or procedures. The result was a nightmare bureaucracy which crushed enthusiasm, creativity and originality out of bright young staff as they began their forty years' servitude inside the system.

The SA refused to change, so John Carr took legal advice. He was advised that the existing system was unlawful and discriminatory. Armed with this opinion we unilaterally imposed changes that allowed everybody, including women and ethnic minorities, to apply for jobs at all levels. The unions on the London Labour executive supported us except for the print union rep, who warned that this could have 'dangerous implications' for working practices in Fleet Street. The SA grudgingly accepted our reforms in exchange for a 1 per cent wage increase to compensate for loss of 'privileges' (in other words because white men now faced increased job competition). As Fleet Street was every bit as exclusive and discriminatory, they ridiculed our changes and the *Daily Mail* invented the idea that I had banned staff from ordering black coffee as this was racist.

Fleet Street went really bananas when we established a Women's Committee. Even in sections of the Labour party the idea was greeted with disbelief, and when Valerie Wise announced our plans during a speech in Sheffield David Blunkett, who was sitting next to me on the platform, almost fell backwards off his chair. The most venomous opposition in the group came from an odd alliance of right-wing women and Frances Morrell, who feared that Valerie might eclipse her in such a high-profile post. Valerie was only twenty-four years old when elected and was resented because of her profile as Mike Ward's deputy chair of the Industry and Employment Committee. With her capacity for work and her integrity, she became a close friend but she was constantly picked on because of her innocence and naivety.

Valerie got little support as press attacks mounted. The *Daily Telegraph* said that among her staff 'spiky hair, boiler suits and sandals were de rigueur'. *Private Eye* expanded their 'Leninspart' columns to include Olive Oyl, chair of the Wimmins Committee. A turning point came when Illtyd sat in on one of the many meet-

ings Valerie was having with women from across London to discuss
what they wanted from the GLC. Illtyd told everyone that something quite remarkable was happening as night after night County
Hall was filled with women talking, planning and debating. The
Women's Committee had exposed a real need but when we set up
a Women's Unit the Staff Association began leaking information
to the *Mail*, where Sir David English now developed an obsession
with lesbians. *Mail* readers could have been forgiven for assuming
that we had made lesbianism compulsory. When the Women's Unit
went for a weekend residential conference the hotel was invaded by
a team of *Mail* reporters who prowled the corridors looking for
'unnatural practices', and as women strolled along the beach they
were pursued by photographers with telephoto lenses.

Although the vast majority of groups funded by the Women's
Unit were providing childcare facilities some, like Babies Against
the Bomb, were controversial. A few far-left groups such as Socialist Organiser echoed Roy Hattersley's complaint that this was a diversion from the class struggle which was confusing and upsetting
to ordinary working-class families. Maurice went out of his way
to ensure that the Women's Committee was a success, and when
I discovered he'd read the works of Andrea Dworkin (a hard-line
feminist who loved to shock) I was convinced he should become
director general when Sir James Swaffield retired.

Bill Bush noticed that the GLC barely used its power to fund
voluntary organisations. When Tory-controlled Ealing Council
decided to stop funding voluntary organisations in the borough,
we stepped in and saved bodies like their law centre, leading to a
flood of interest from voluntary organisations across London. Altogether we funded 3,000 different bodies before we were abolished, and the number that failed was in single figures.

This did not stop the press having a field day and their stories were
so creative people believed they could get grants for *anything*. Un-

successful applicants included a man in the Philippines who asked for a grant for an eye operation and two women who had formed A Woman's Right to Leg Over. They applied for a grant to compile a guide that would rate men as lovers and provide information such as the cleanliness of their home. I was convinced it was a scam by the *Mail*, but the women concerned were quite serious about it.

The most internal hostility we faced came from the civil defence unit that was responsible for dealing with the consequences of a nuclear attack on London. Many of its officers had previously worked at the Ministry of Defence or the Home Office, never submitted reports to the council and would not let us see their work. They would only give us documents that we specifically requested, but without access to the files we didn't know the titles or file numbers and were in a Catch 22 situation.

The Tories assured the public that they could survive a nuclear attack if they whitewashed their windows and waited under the kitchen table or stairs for a few days. The government's booklet *Protect and Survive* said 'on hearing the all clear you may emerge and resume normal activities'. I knew in fact that if nuclear war was imminent the Queen would sign an order suspending democracy and as leader of the GLC I could choose two other members and the three of us would be whisked to safety in a bunker in Essex along with the cabinet and royal family. There, I was to give 'advice' to the military commander administering London under martial law.

To help us get the documents from the civil defence unit we appointed the journalist Duncan Campbell, an expert in defence matters who had been one of the defendants in the 'ABC' secrets trial in 1978. Along with Crispin Aubrey and John Berry, a former corporal in signals intelligence, he was prosecuted by Foreign Secretary David Owen for writing about defence secrets which were not, in fact, terribly secret at all. The Tories went apoplectic when they realised whose help we had enlisted, but we soon found out what the department had been hiding from the public for over thirty years.

Working with Illtyd, Duncan soon demolished government claims about surviving under kitchen tables. Within twelve weeks six million Londoners would be dead from blast, radiation and disease. If the million survivors moved out to rural areas food supplies would be exhausted, so troops would ring the city and shoot dead anyone trying to leave.

We published these terrible plans and opened the bunkers at West Norwood, Southall, Wanstead and North Cheam where 3,000 officials (who we named) would be based. The government was angry that money set aside for this plan would now be used by us to campaign for the abolition of nuclear weapons. We declared 1983 Peace Year and joined other cities to form the Nuclear Free Zones Movement. Polls showed a two to one majority backing us (41 per cent of Tory voters supported us with 37 per cent against).

As our poll ratings went up, tensions in the Labour group receded. As in *The Godfather*, when the mafia dons pledge their loyalty to Michael as the new head of the Corleone family, one by one half of those who had voted for Andrew as leader assured me of their loyalty. A lot of this was down to our chief whip Harvey Hinds. Described as elfin by friends and as the poisonous dwarf by Tories, he loved managing his 'little flock of sheep'. He trained as a Church of England canon but left to become a youth leader when he began to doubt God's existence. An excellent listener as members complained about this or that, his bedside manner and a drink usually did the trick.

No one had ever managed the GLC with a small majority. Three members of the group were alcoholics, though we seldom had more than one of them out of action at a time. One afternoon the chair had to use his casting vote to break a tie during a full council meeting. Looking around we noticed Neil Davies was absent, so I went to his office while Harvey checked the loos. Neil was on the floor of his office reeking of alcohol and I half-carried him to the chamber just in time for the next vote. As he wasn't aware of what was going on I sat beside him and held his hand up to the amusement of Labour members and the outrage of the Tories.

The Tories had the legal right to demand extra meetings of the council but I could decide when they would be held and always called them for Friday afternoons, knowing that three or four of the richer Tories went to the country early and were not prepared to stay in the city beyond lunchtime. I realised that nothing in politics is new when I read in Suetonius's *The Twelve Caesars* that Julius Caesar pulled the same trick when reactionaries in the senate were making his life difficult.

*

I started my day reading reports on the way to work, arriving to find a vast pile of new papers on my desk and Bill Bush waiting to get a steer on whatever had developed overnight. By now we had worked together for so long that Bill had a good idea what my decisions would be so he listed options, starting with the one he assumed I would choose, allowing me to make several decisions in just a few minutes. The rest of the day was spent on paperwork, and popping into committees and meetings where I was needed. I always had lunch in the members' restaurant to keep in touch with backbenchers (each party had its own long table).

Embarrassingly, my office was larger than the average council flat with connecting doors leading through banks of secretaries to Harvey's and Illtyd's rooms, but the most prestigious office in the building was occupied by the leader of the Tories. It had been the office of Herbert Morrison fifty years earlier and still had his original desk and a view directly onto Westminster Bridge and Big Ben. It was just along from the DG's office and some members felt I should reclaim it, but as moving would be disruptive and expensive I didn't bother.

We were getting more media coverage than the parliamentary Labour party because our agenda looked to the future. Now people started to take us seriously, and John Prescott met me with Mike Ward to talk about his plans for regional assemblies. In those days Prescott was even more manically verbose than he later became so I sat through a lunch where he sprayed me with verbs until I staggered away, physically exhausted just listening to him. A quieter presence was David Miliband, then just sixteen, who came to work in my outer office during school holidays at the request of his dad Ralph, a Marxist theoretician. David was bright and industrious and after work I would drop in to talk to Ralph and his wife Marion with David and Ed sitting wide-eyed while we discussed the potential for an English revolution.

Many foreign mayors, having picked up that something exciting was happening in London government, came to see for themselves and were amazed that I was able to move around without armed protection and didn't have a grand mansion paid for by the taxpayer. Queen Beatrix of the Netherlands was refused permission by the government to visit Brixton after the riots and settled for an afternoon discussing GLC policies with us. Another sign that the centre of gravity of British politics was well to the right of the rest of Europe came when the leader of the German SDP opposition Hans-Jochen Vogel, former mayor of Munich, spent the day with me and at the end asked, 'Why do they call you such a radical?'

Ted Knight proposed that we should start a weekly paper to organise the fightback against Thatcher. He had left the Workers Revolutionary Party on good terms with its leader Gerry Healy, about whom opinion was bitterly divided. Tony Benn's wife Caroline felt that Healy had an 'electric personality' whereas Hosken quotes Illtyd describing Healy as 'quite a frightening looking creature; he had the head of the archetypal Broadmoor psychopath – a big bullet head. But he controlled them all through . . . moral and intellectual blackmail.' According to the *Spectator* when Healy kept butting in on another party member who carried on talking, he eventually ordered him to 'stop speaking when I'm interrupting'. Jan Pallis, a WRP member, wrote to Healy in his letter of resignation, 'Goodbye, it has been very unpleasant knowing you.' Although the WRP had all the defects of a religious cult and a hard-line interpretation of Trotskyism it supported the GLC and Paul Feldman, a reporter from the WRP's daily newspaper *Newsline*, was constantly in and out of my office making sure the Labour manifesto was fully covered.

Since I had not met Healy until he was sixty-eight, I saw only a frail old man with a wealth of stories from the times when he campaigned with left-wing Labour MPs. In the 1950s at the height of the Bevanite battles he had been waiting with Michael Foot for a train back to London when Foot told him it might be necessary for the left, himself included, to leave the Labour party. Healy was able to set up *Newsline*, a full-colour newspaper, with the help of subscriptions from wealthy WRP members such as actors Vanessa and Corin Redgrave. This was good news for our press-cuttings service, who each morning had to staple together a thick wad of mostly virulent anti-GLC stories from the papers. I could always rely on them to put *Newsline*'s more positive coverage at the front. There were rumours that Healy was also financially supported by Libya's Colonel Gaddafi. Whether that was true or not, it was a fact that money from Thatcher's government helped keep *Newsline* afloat. By printing the paper in Runcorn Healy became eligible for a government grant to businesses creating jobs in areas of high unemployment.

By starting a new paper Healy was able to introduce full-colour technology half a decade before Rupert Murdoch did. Ted arranged for us to use Healy's hi-tech print shop to produce our own paper, the *Labour Herald*. We could only afford one reporter, Steve Miller, and the initial print run was just a couple of thousand as we struggled to increase sales. Now my Saturdays consisted of driving off with Ted to some northern city where we would hold a press conference followed by a rally as we recruited lefties willing to sell the paper on a regular basis.

In his book about me, Hosken not unreasonably questions whether I should have got into bed with someone whose past was so dubious as Healy's, but I was prepared to work with anyone in the struggle against Thatcher. The WRP also began to take on board a more relaxed approach to homosexuality. Healy believed homosexuality was a by-product of capitalism that would disappear after a socialist revolution, and Paul Feldman was nervous when he wrote a supportive article for *Newsline* on our lesbian and gay policies, but Healy didn't comment.

*

A cause dear to my heart was the struggle of the Palestinians, and *Labour Herald* was just nine months old when the Israeli prime minister Menachem Begin used the excuse of an attempted assassination of the Israeli ambassador to London to launch a long-planned invasion of Lebanon with the goal of driving Yasser Arafat's PLO out of a country which hosted hundreds of thousands of Palestinian refugees. For decades the Israeli government had denied that the Palestinians even existed, claiming that all Arabs were the same and therefore Palestinians should be absorbed by other Arab countries. Ted and I challenged this in the pages of *Labour Herald* and when the GLC supported a Palestinian cultural event at County Hall British supporters of Begin's government bellowed abuse from across the street.

The invasion of Lebanon was under the command of Ariel Sharon, who carried out a wider campaign than Begin had authorised, which culminated in a horrific mass murder at the refugee camps of Shabra and Chatila in September 1982. Although PLO fighters had left the camps, leaving their women, elderly and children behind, the Israeli army lit flares in the night sky so that their Lebanese Christian allies could continue their attack.

As a young man, Begin had led Betar, a militant Jewish youth movement that for a time was modelled on Italian fascism. When Begin visited America in 1948 Albert Einstein and many Jewish intellectuals warned that Begin's party 'is closely akin in its organisation, methods, political philosophy and social appeal to the Nazi and fascist parties . . . [preaching] ultra-nationalism, religious mysticism and racial superiority'. In response to the massacres at Shabra and Chatila *Labour Herald*'s cartoonist depicted Begin in Nazi regalia on a pile of Arab corpses.

We were denounced by the Board of Deputies of British Jews but this did not stop us campaigning to get the Labour party conference to recognise the PLO as the 'sole legitimate leadership' of the Palestinian people. Labour right-wingers were horrified at the prospect of recognising Arafat's PLO but George Galloway, then chair of the Scottish Labour party, got a motion onto the conference agenda. There was a huge struggle for the votes of each trade union, with Israeli embassy officials lobbying strenuously, but to no avail as the Labour party recognised the PLO by a margin of just 1 per cent. A decade later Yasser Arafat would shake hands with the Israeli PM Yitzhak Rabin on the White House lawn.

Relations with the Board of Deputies worsened the following year when Yitzhak Shamir became Israel's prime minister and *Labour Herald* interviewed Lenni Brenner, who detailed the history of Zionism's right wing led by Vladimir Jabotinsky, who died in 1940. Among his main supporters were Menachem Begin and Yitzhak Shamir, who became the operational commander of the Stern Gang, the militant Zionist group that assassinated Count Bernadotte, the

UN Special Mediator in Palestine, in 1948. Brenner argued that Nazi documents show that the Stern Gang visited the German embassy in Istanbul in January 1941 and offered to 'establish [Israel] on a totalitarian basis, bound by a treaty with the German Reich', and in exchange the Stern Gang would 'actively take part in the war on Germany's side'. Hitler rejected the offer but when Begin came to power he issued stamps to commemorate Avraham Stern.

I was shocked by the revelations in Lenni Brenner's book *Zionism in the Age of the Dictators*, about the role of Israel's respected Labour party leaders. Lenni's book claimed that the chair of the World Zionist Organisation and first president of Israel, Chaim Weizmann, wanted 'the transfer of Jewish youth to Palestine rather than . . . equal rights in Germany'. It also said that some German Zionists sent a memo to Hitler on 21 June 1933 saying that 'we too, are against mixed marriage and are for maintaining the purity of the Jewish group' and that race separation was 'wholly to the good'. That month Labour Zionist Chaim Arlosoroff negotiated a pact with the Nazis to set up a trading company, Ha'avara, to sell Nazi goods, thus undermining the boycott organised by trade unionists and communists.

The World Zionist Congress had rejected the boycott by a vote of 240–48, and Ha'avara profits apparently provided 60 per cent of all investment in Palestine between 1933 and 1939. This fitted Hitler's 1932 policy of 'Jews to Palestine' and his deputy Heydrich wrote in 1935, 'We must separate Jews in two categories . . . Zionists and those who favour being assimilated. The Zionists adhere to a strict racial position . . . our good wishes . . . go with them.' To encourage Zionists, the Nuremberg laws in 1935 allowed only two flags to be flown in Germany, the Swastika and the blue and white Zionist banner. Rabbis were ordered to conduct their sermons in Hebrew – the language Zionism had recreated for Israel – rather than Yiddish.

In the 1930s Zionists were viewed as eccentric by the 90 per cent of Jews who wanted acceptance in the countries where they lived but Brenner claimed they persuaded the UK Board of Deputies and its US equivalent not to boycott Nazi goods. While Jewish communists pressed ahead with mass demonstrations against Oswald Mosley's Blackshirts the Board of Deputies advised UK Jews not to heckle Mosley as 'Jews have no quarrel with fascism'. Some Zionists opposed Jews fighting fascism in Spain and in 1937 the Nazi–Zionist link was strengthened when Labour Zionist Feivel Polkes agreed with Adolf Eichmann to provide intelligence, support German policy in the Middle East and find oil for Germany in return for allowing German Jews to go to Palestine. In Palestine Labour Zionists began excluding Arabs from working on Jewish-owned projects or land.

With the support of David Ben-Gurion and Golda Meir, Chaim Weizmann warned in 1935 that 'the Zionist movement would have to choose between the immediate rescue of Jews and the establishment of [Israel]'. So two-thirds of all German Jews who applied to emigrate to Israel were refused. When Jews in the Warsaw ghetto sent a cable to Jewish leaders to get the Allies to bomb the death camps, US Rabbi Stephen Wise declined because he did not want to 'disturb the war effort . . . by stormy protests', and when the US Congress was considering a bill to establish a Rescue Commission Rabbi Wise testified against the bill because it did not mention Palestine.

And of course the Labour Zionists cannot be blamed for not anticipating that Nazism would become the greatest evil in human history, but however well-intentioned their motives it was a catastrophic error of judgment not to throw all the resources of Zionism into the campaign against Nazism. Those in power after the war were understandably defensive about this record. In 1953 the Israeli government sued Malchiel Gruenwald for criminal defamation when he exposed this history. The Israeli Supreme Court, quoting the view of one Zionist that the Hungarian Jews they failed to rescue were 'without any ideological backbone', ruled that it was right 'to risk losing the many in order to save the few . . . it has always been our Zionist tradition to select the few out of the many for Palestine'.

Many British Jews were traumatised by the revelations in Lenni Brenner's book. Lenni was denounced and Ted Knight and I were abused for reviewing it in *Labour Herald*. A public meeting at which Lenni discussed his book was attacked by Zionists, who hospitalised one of the platform speakers. Brenner's book helped form my view of Zionism and its history and so I was not going to be silenced by smears of anti-Semitism whenever I criticised Israeli government policies.

I was disappointed that over the years the Board of Deputies always refused my suggestion that I should meet them to answer their questions directly, but we did work together to establish a Holocaust remembrance ceremony at City Hall. I thought this was particularly important because the decline of history teaching in our schools was resulting in increasing ignorance of this most horrific crime. When questioned, many schoolchildren confused the Cold War with the Second World War, which they believed had been fought against Russia.

Representatives from all London's faiths, including Muslims, attended the ceremony, and I found it particularly moving to see Holocaust survivors standing side by side with schoolchildren who were often learning about these events for the first time. On a more personal note, the ceremony also acted as a reminder that it was the Britain of my parents' generation that stood alone against the might of the Nazi war machine, while Europe collapsed and America stood on the sidelines until forced into action by the Japanese bombing of Pearl Harbor. I never forgot that Dad almost gave his own life in that struggle or the stories Mum and Nan told me about the courage of Londoners during the Blitz.

*

In November 1982 Sinn Fein won five seats in the first election to the Northern Ireland Assembly and GLC member Steve Bundred, who was active in the Troops Out movement, persuaded a majority of Labour members to invite Gerry Adams and Danny Morrison to County Hall to discuss how the war might be ended. The next day we woke to the horrific news that the Irish National Liberation Army (a rival group to the IRA) had let off a bomb at the Droppin Well disco in Ballykelly killing seventeen people, all under the age of twenty-seven. Overlooking the fact that this was not an IRA atrocity the Tory press whipped up a demand that we cancel the invitation. The *Sun* declared, 'Red Ken Livingstone became the most hated man in Britain last night.' The press besieged our flat and we had to move in with friends. Tory MP Eldon Griffiths visited the crime scene and removed several bloodstained items of evidence including a shoe, a record sleeve and a disco light which he then brought to County Hall and left in my office.

Michael Foot asked to see me and urged us to drop the invitation and I agreed to relay his views to the group when it met the following Monday. Thatcher said it would be intolerable if the invitation was not dropped. I faced the prospect of the Labour group voting to ban the meeting and forcing me to decide to accept that decision or quit. In the end the group never discussed the issue, because Home Secretary Willie Whitelaw used his powers to ban Adams and Morrison from coming to London, claiming there was a risk of violence if the visit went ahead. I pointed out that 'it is now ludicrous . . . to claim that the six counties are part of the UK and then go and exclude its so-called citizens from entering one part of Britain – London'. Although the press was unanimously opposed, the deluge of letters I received were equally balanced for and against the visit. No polls were conducted but in that year's Radio 4 listeners' vote I was runner-up to Pope John Paul II as Man of the Year.

In complete secrecy Steve Bundred set to work organising a visit to Adams and Morrison in Belfast in the New Year. The story broke as we landed at the airport and set the press pack in hot pursuit around the streets as we toured the area. Belfast felt as though I had stepped back to the 1950s: endless grey, shabby and run-down working-class terraces. Army patrols had the habit of shooting a family's dog before they searched a home and I noticed children cowered behind their parents when they heard my English accent. I was taken to Walsh's, a bar in the Falls Road which was used to being raided by British troops. While I was there the British army arrived but had been given instructions to withdraw if they came into contact with me. As they left the owner gave me a bottle of Black Bush whiskey, saying I should come more often. That night we went to one of Sinn Fein's clubs. Two of the previous managers had been shot dead by the British army.

Adams and Morrison were amazed that I had not given in to the pressure to cancel their County Hall visit and during the two-day trip I told them that bombing London was counter-productive and that it put back the prospects of peace and a united Ireland. Adams said it was not possible for the IRA to defeat the British army, but was equally firm that the British army would never be able to eliminate the IRA. His conclusion was that there had to be a negotiated settlement and the IRA would be prepared for a ceasefire if they had a commitment for a British withdrawal in five years' time. When Blair began negotiating with Sinn Fein, inevitably they had to compromise on these demands but the tragedy is that Thatcher's refusal even to begin a dialogue meant another 1,000 people would die needlessly before the peace process began.

*

Michael Foot was under constant pressure from right-wingers in the party to 'deal with' me and it was only when Andrew Hosken's biography was published in 2008 that I discovered how much I owed to Foot's secretary Una Cooze. Hosken describes her as 'a fifty-one-year-old Trot with very strong socialist principles ... with two cats, including one named after the communist Rosa Luxemburg'. Kenneth O. Morgan in his biography of Foot describes Una as 'endlessly loyal' and 'Michael's conscience'. Hosken quotes Foot as saying, 'All the way through that time, Una was putting Ken's case well and I came round to supporting Ken later very largely because of her influence which I trusted throughout ... Una kept me informed about what was happening at County Hall.' Ten years later when I was an MP and my secretary was on maternity leave, Una covered for her while still working for Michael. She never told me about her role in my defence.

The press hysteria had raised my profile, so when the *Time Out* journalist David Rose checked the cuttings files in Fleet Street he found the only politician who had featured in more articles than me was Mrs Thatcher. One person not pleased by all this coverage was the new leader of Islington Council Margaret Hodge. Margaret had transformed herself from daughter of the millionaire steel magnate Hans Alfred Oppenheimer via Bromley High School for Girls into a leader in the hard-left Labour caucus organising the takeover of London boroughs. She asked Ted to arrange a meeting. She had a long list of requests for GLC money but her final point was to ask me to lower my profile. 'None of the boroughs can get any coverage,' she said. I replied that if she wanted coverage she only had to invite Gerry Adams to London or start a lesbian and gay committee.

I was flattered and a bit awestruck by the media attention but I was still surprised the first time someone described me as a potential future leader of the Labour party. Television interviewer Bob McKenzie chaired a debate in which a selection of Londoners questioned me (this was in 1981, just a few weeks before the crucial contest between Tony Benn and Denis Healey for the deputy leadership). As we waited to go on air McKenzie told the audience, 'I don't know if Tony will make it but I'm certain that Ken will one day.'

This was a view shared by columnist Hugo Young, who wrote in the *Sunday Times* that the Labour party in the 1990s would be led by Roy Hattersley and myself, supported by Neil Kinnock. In 2008, when the *Guardian* posthumously published Young's private notes of interviews, they included his record of a conversation with me on a train from Harrogate to London on 3 June 1982. It was our first meeting and his impression of me was as follows: 'Humorous, decent, open, extraordinarily detached, very committed of course. A good political analyst. Very adept and knowledgeable with electoral figures. Also young. One remembers he can afford to wait, unlike Benn. I think he will be leader of the Labour party before the end of the century.'

John Golding MP, the right-wing fixer on Labour's NEC, was appalled at this prospect and began organising to prevent my selection as a Labour candidate in the 1983 general election. My first contact with Golding was when I spoke to the only ward in his constituency not under his rigid control. The ward was refused permission to circulate details of the meeting to other wards. Golding's grip on his party was so tight that when he retired his wife inherited the seat.

I was asked to be the Labour candidate in Brent East by a handful of members of the Chartist group in the constituency. They had picked up that Reg Freeson was thinking of leaving Parliament to work for housing associations on regeneration schemes. Reg, described even by his friend Tam Dalyell as prickly and difficult, was a serious man. Like myself he had no interest in the gossipy, backslapping macho culture of the House of Commons, as was shown when he stood for the shadow cabinet after Labour's defeat in 1979 and came bottom of the ballot, with less than 3 per cent of Labour MPs voting for him.

He had been happiest as leader of Willesden Council in the late fifties, where he had overseen a successful housing programme. An opponent of the Vietnam war and one of the few MPs to challenge discrimination against Catholics in Northern Ireland, he also criticised Israel's invasion of Lebanon. His years as Minister of Housing under Callaghan were unhappy because he had to slash the housing programme following the IMF cuts in 1976. Reg's grandparents fled Russia and he had been abandoned by his parents at an early age and never forgave them or revealed their names. By coincidence Reg was raised in the Jewish orphanage in the same road in West Norwood where I grew up twenty years later. He was painfully shy. Susie Orbach, the daughter of neighbouring MP Maurice Orbach, worked for him in 1964 and years later her father told her that Reg had asked his permission to marry her. Not only had they never been on a date but he had never indicated any overt interest in her.

I was also approached by left-wingers from the Newham North West Labour party, where their MP was retiring. I was virtually offered the nomination on a plate. But I had lived in the Kilburn area for five years and felt at home there and having given a commitment to Brent East I urged the Newham party to consider Dave Wetzel or Tony Banks, who eventually defeated Dave for the nomination by one vote. Had I gone for Newham I would have been elected to Parliament in 1983 and most probably had to resign my GLC leadership, thus changing the whole course of my life.

Brent East had an active Labour party where the left were trying to wrest control of the council from a competent and honest right-wing leader, John Lebor. This was part of the London-wide campaign by the left to increase its influence in Labour councils, led by Margaret Hodge, who would soon be in charge at Islington. Our drive to recruit black and Asian Londoners into the Labour party had its biggest success in Brent, where over 500 Asians joined. Whether or not Reg had been thinking of retiring, the poisonous atmosphere around the selection of council candidates and the struggle to depose John Lebor changed his mind, and so Reg stayed to fight. The small Trotskyist Socialist Organiser group felt I was a mere reformer and wanted a true revolutionary leading the left, and they made a tactical mistake when they held an open left caucus to decide between me and one of their members. Although I won comfortably, and caucusing was widespread in the Labour party, this meeting was a technical breach of the rules.

The 1982 annual party conference that recognised the PLO also saw the left lose its majority on the NEC. As Neil Kinnock and I waited to do TV interviews, he said he feared Michael Foot would soon no longer be in control of the party. John Golding took the chair of the party's Organisation Committee and ordered an investigation into Brent East. Golding writes in his autobiography that he was determined the left should get the blame for losing the 1983 general election, and he also used the changes in constituency boundaries to prevent Tony Benn getting the only safe Labour seat in Bristol by packing the selection committee with right-wing trade union delegates. He also decided to draw out the Brent East selection process until the general election, at which point the NEC would have powers to impose Reg Freeson as the candidate.

Reg and I had equal numbers of supporters on Brent East's General Management Committee, with just a handful holding the balance of power. One of these was Mike Grabiner, who had considered standing himself but earned so much at BT that he couldn't afford the pay cut. He invited me to his home, where we talked over the issues and I won his support. Two of the other swing votes were those of Harriet Harman and her husband Jack Dromey, who had been the main organiser behind the strike of the Grunwick workers, a group of low-paid Asian women, in the constituency five years earlier. Jack invited me to dinner, at which he promised that both he and Hattie would support me. He had been invited to Reg's supporters group where in a moment of despair Reg talked about giving up Brent East and standing as an independent against Thatcher in her Finchley constituency. For a tribal loyalist like Jack, candidates standing against the Labour party were for ever beyond the pale and from that moment I had enough votes to win.

Golding's tactic was to stall each time Brent East asked to start the selection process. With the election getting closer, the GMC got legal advice that the party had a duty to begin a reselection process and decided by a vote of 71–4 to ignore the NEC and get on with it. Eleven days later, on 9 May, Thatcher announced she was calling a general election. In his local newspaper column Golding wrote, 'At the NEC, I move that Reg Freeson be the Labour candidate in Brent East and this is carried by 19 votes to 9! This will freeze out Ken Livingstone, the leader of the GLC, so there is bound to be a spot of bother . . .' I had the usual left-wing votes including Tom Sawyer, deputy general secretary of NUPE, supporting me at the NEC but Neil Kinnock was one of those who voted to impose Reg on the constituency party.

One or two members urged me to stand as an independent, but Jack Dromey argued strongly against this. I shared his abhorrence of people who leave the Labour party to run against it, and with Thatcher's decision to include abolition of the GLC in the Tory election manifesto I didn't want to leave just as the GLC faced its greatest threat.

9

Abolition

1983–1986

Although the media claimed Thatcher's re-election was a result of the Falklands War, the polls showed support for her government had started to increase before then as Britain emerged from recession. I was appalled that so many young men lost their lives over the Falklands and believed the dispute should have been referred to the International Court. Thatcher knew she had no chance of winning such a case, given Britain's illegal seizure of these islands while people of Latin America were winning their independence from Spain, so she ordered the sinking of the *Belgrano* to sabotage the efforts of the US government to reach a diplomatic settlement. I spoke against the war at public meetings but the fact that the Argentine government was a brutal dictatorship which had murdered tens of thousands of its own people meant there was nothing like the public opposition to the war that we were to see in later conflicts over Iraq.

Friends said I was depressed during the 1983 election, but my recollection is of night after night speaking at rallies packed with people passionate that Thatcher should not get another term. I found it hard to believe the polls predicting a Tory landslide, so as the results came I was crushed. I had failed in Hampstead four years earlier, and the manoeuvrings of Golding meant I would be forty-two before I could stand again at the next election. Thatcher intended to abolish the GLC as rapidly as possible, and since she had a majority of 140 there was no chance of preventing it in

Parliament, but I was determined to inflict the maximum damage possible on her government.

I used to say that Thatcher abolished the GLC because we were the sort of people her parents warned her not to talk to when she was a little girl. But apart from her desire to crush all opposition she was tapping into an old Tory fear of radical politics erupting out of London's heaving slums. When the City of London was given its royal charter by King John in 1215 it *was* the whole city, but as London's poor clustered around its borders the City refused to extend its boundaries in order to keep the poor from accessing its wealth.

In 1835 the government gave every major city a council, but London had to wait another fifty years. A Royal Commission in 1854 recommended that London's 170 parishes be replaced with seven large boroughs but vested interests triumphed again when the proposal was dropped in favour of creating a quango. The Metropolitan Board of Works was given powers to tackle London's problems of clean water, sewage and road building. This unelected body became a byword for corruption. The Liberals wanted a London-wide council but the cause was set back by the horrors of the Paris commune in 1871, which reawakened Tory fears of London's seething masses.

Gladstone tried again in 1883, but right-wingers in his cabinet feared a democratic London council controlling the police. When Gladstone proposed home rule for Ireland in 1886 Joseph Chamberlain, who had been a successful leader of Birmingham Council, led the defection from Gladstone's government that put Lord Salisbury's Tories in power. As part of the deal with Chamberlain, both London and rural areas were given councils. So it was the Conservative MP Charles Ritchie who piloted the London County Council Bill through Parliament.

When the new council met for the first time in 1889, the majority of members were radical Liberals, trade unionists and independent socialists. Many senior MPs stood for the LCC and held dual membership. They began a huge programme of public works and services. Lord Salisbury was horrified that his government had given birth to this and by 1894 was complaining that the LCC was 'the place where collectivistic and socialistic experiments are tried ... where a new revolutionary spirit finds its instruments and collects its arms'. Salisbury worried that the LCC was popular and was campaigning to absorb the City of London Corporation and the police. Without consulting his cabinet he proposed the creation of powerful London boroughs to take over most of the LCC's powers, but the Liberals turned the 1898 elections into a referendum on these proposals. *The Times* described the election, in which the Tories lost eleven seats, as 'a crashing defeat' and Salisbury had to settle for creating twenty-eight powerless London boroughs, leaving real power with the LCC, which in 1904 also absorbed the London School Board.

Now the LCC was led by Tony Benn's grandfather, John, campaigning for 'cheap fares for working men'. In a bizarre parallel with what happened to the gay campaigner Peter Tatchell in the same constituency seventy-five years later – he was the victim of a savagely homophobic campaign – John Benn was defeated in a parliamentary by-election in Bermondsey after a vicious campaign by a paper called the *Sun*. After the Tories won control in 1907, demands for abolition faded away until 1934, when Labour unexpectedly won control. Labour leader Herbert Morrison became popular by restarting the housing programme, humanising the Poor Laws and reforming London's hospitals along lines which prefigured the NHS. The Conservatives were not happy.

Their plans to change the powers and boundaries of the LCC were dropped when war broke out in 1939 and not revived until 1957, when the Tories established a Royal Commission which proposed the creation of a strong regional authority which would take over many powers of central government. Their campaign against the LCC was led by Roland Freeman, who had organised the successful Tory takeover of the communist-controlled National Union of Students. In 1983 he admitted that 'all our discussions turned on the fact that we couldn't win the LCC as then constituted. We wanted a GLC with the widest possible area so we would have permanent control.'

Freeman's campaign overturned the Royal Commission proposals and strengthened borough powers at the expense of the new GLC, which was also denied the devolved powers proposed by the Royal Commission. The Tories believed that the boundaries of the GLC were wide enough to guarantee a Tory majority because they included middle-class commuter-belt areas. Roland Freeman went on to lead Wandsworth Council and chaired the GLC Finance Committee under its first Tory administration.

The Tories miscalculated the boundaries, so Labour won the first GLC election in 1964, but the Tories won three of the first five. It was only after our election in 1981 that Conservative antipathy towards County Hall revived. Michael Heseltine asked his officials to examine the possibility of abolition but dropped the idea when they reported that it would be a 'nightmare', with problems arising from it long afterwards. But Heseltine had not reckoned with Thatcher who, as education secretary in Heath's government, was horrified at the high level of spending on London schools, and persuaded the cabinet to drop the idea that Metropolitan County Councils should be education authorities when they were set up in 1974.

With the 1983 election bearing down on her, Thatcher proposed that GLC abolition be in the manifesto, but was opposed by environment secretary Tom King and most of the cabinet. In their book *Beyond Our Ken: A Guide to the Battle for London*, Andrew Forrester, Stewart Lansley and Robin Pauley write,

Some of Mrs Thatcher's own colleagues were becoming uneasy about the extent to which her general view of local government . . . was becoming coloured by her deep seated and almost obsessive objections to urban socialists, particularly Ken Livingstone . . . Ministers, including Mr Whitelaw and Mr King were confident that the sheer complexity of abolition would keep it out of policy . . . They reckoned, however, without Mrs Thatcher, who seemed to see Mr Livingstone as both a political and personal threat. She set up a new committee of ministers and pronounced herself chairman . . . Ministers claimed afterwards they had no idea until the last second that [abolition was in the manifesto]. Mr Heseltine was reported to be 'dismayed' and Mr King, when first told the news on a train in Northern England, was said to be shaken and 'aghast'. But Mrs Thatcher was unconcerned. Supreme in her thinking was the final realisation of what had become a personal challenge: the removal of the power base which had enabled Ken Livingstone to taunt and defy her, to rival and, in some ways, even to better her. Even if he slipped into Parliament a repeat performance would be impossible. And if he did not she could and would wipe him off the national political map.

Thatcher also ignored the view of the people who actually lived in London. Our poll ratings had risen dramatically since the nadir of 1981 and Londoners by 45 to 43 per cent supported increasing the rates in order to fund our second fares cut. (In the 1983 general election the swing to the Tories in London was only 3.8 per cent, whereas in the rest of the country it was 5.2 per cent. The *Standard*'s poll in October 1983 after the general election showed 54 per cent of Londoners against abolition and only 22 per cent in favour.)

There had long been calls for abolition. Simon Jenkins, the *Standard* columnist, wrote in 1974: 'there is simply no gap for the GLC to fill . . . there is no new political air for it to breathe and it is dying as a result'. Cutler in 1977 commissioned an inquiry by Sir Frank Marshall, the former Tory leader of Leeds, who recommended a streamlined strategic body dealing with regional issues and taking powers from central government. This cut no ice with Thatcher, who was more influenced by Shirley Porter's Keep London Free campaign and by big businesses, which saw the chance to pay lower rates for local services if the GLC was abolished. *Private Eye* reported Denis Thatcher saying, 'That damn GLC should be abolished. Livingstone must be on his last legs.'

*

Once the Tories had been returned to power we started to plan our fightback. The GLC provided a lot of services which people were not aware of, so we decided to brand everything we did with the GLC logo. I never shared the traditional Labour aversion to polling or advertising, and when our advertising agency was bought by a firm with South African links we switched to Boase, Massimi and Pollitt, where I first met Philip Gould (who became Tony Blair's focus group guru). BMP was an irreverent and imaginative firm which created the cackling Martians that ate Smash potato mix and the Honey Monster for Sugar Puffs.

We needed to have people from their own parties to lobby Tory and Liberal peers. Over the years I had become friendly with Roland Freeman, who had been re-elected to the GLC from Finchley but had been ostracised by Cutler, who saw him as a rival before Roland defected to the SDP in 1982. As he had run the campaign to abolish the old LCC and knew where the Tory skeletons were buried, we appointed him to head our lobbying operation in Parliament along with the Conservative peer Francis Sitwell. The press office had recruited a bright young man called Harry Barlow whose first job was to crawl out onto the roof of County Hall once a month and change the figures on our unemployment banner. He rapidly shone in the campaign and went on to do my advertising when I first ran for mayor. Veronica Crichton decided that two years of relentless media pressure was enough and returned to the Labour party as director of communication and campaigns, a job she held until it was handed over to Peter Mandelson. I was sad to see her go but she was replaced by Nita Clarke, who had spent several frustrating years trying to sex up the profile of Albert Spanswick, leader of the health workers' union COHSE.

The summer of 1983 saw a hive of activity at County Hall as the machine prepared for the fight. Thatcher had appointed Patrick Jenkin to steer through Parliament the bill paving the way for abolition. He was the minister in Heath's government who had urged the public to brush their teeth in the dark during the miners' strike while leaving all the lights blazing in his own home. Amiable but plodding, he summoned Illtyd to say Thatcher was 'going to get rid of you . . . it's nothing against you personally, we have great respect for you'. I asked Illtyd what Jenkin had said and he succinctly replied: 'We're fucked.' I said, 'We'll see about that; you're too defeatist.'

*

Around this time we had a visit from Vladimir Promyslov, a conservative bureaucrat about to celebrate his thirtieth anniversary as Moscow's mayor. He had started under Khrushchev (who interfered so much that he decided whether toilet seats in Moscow should be wood or plastic). The Communist Party of Great Britain viewed me with deep suspicion because I worked with Trotskyists and wouldn't visit states behind the Iron Curtain, unlike some Labour members who came back from East Germany or Poland praising these 'workers' paradises' when they were clearly police states.

Relations with the Russian embassy froze after my first visit eight years earlier when Tony Banks and I supported the right of Russian Jews to emigrate. An official said that he would pass our views on but we never got a response and were never invited back. It was only after we declared 1983 to be Peace Year and with the Moscow mayor's impending visit that Harvey, Illtyd and I were invited to lunch at the embassy. Harvey explained to us that Viktor Popov, the ambassador, was a convivial figurehead and that one of the KGB officers at the lunch would be the one who ran the show. Part of the fun was working out who it was. After a boozy lunch, with the ambassador urging us to drink more vodka, one of the younger officials whispered that he was pleased with the way lunch had gone; they had been very worried when I became leader, he said, as they feared I was a Trotskyist.

At a nursery in Newham the mayor and his wife were appalled to see young children playing naked in the pool. In fact Mrs Promyslov wanted to spend most of her time at Harrods. We had agreed to the visit on the understanding that a morning would be set aside to discuss the issues of Jewish refugees and human rights, but I realised we weren't going to make much progress after Promyslov remarked how useful capital punishment was and wondered why Labour was opposed to it.

*

Nita Clarke had the idea that we should launch the anti-abolition campaign by visiting all the autumn party conferences. The TUC had a motion opposing abolition which was expected to be agreed unanimously, until electricians' union leader Eric Hammond delivered a rant: 'There may be enough terrorist groupies, lesbians and other queer folk in inner London Labour parties to support Mr Livingstone's antics, but there's little support in the ranks of ordinary trade unionists.' He was drowned out by booing.

The SDP conference at Salford was a problem as they had supported abolition even before Thatcher, and the conference was filled with people who had left Labour because of people like me. We had a fringe meeting but with TV following our every move just one slip of the tongue could have sunk our whole campaign. Roland met us at the train station warning that the conference schedule was overrunning and there would not be many people in the audience at our meeting. But ours was the largest meeting of the conference. My speech was a factual account of the problems that abolition would entail and a plea for devolution from White-hall. As the applause died down I knew we had won them over and as I was passing David Owen in the corridor he said, 'I hear you've been having fun with my delegates.' 'If they carry on like this we might let them back into the Labour party', I replied. 'If they carry on like that I might let you have them back,' was his riposte.

The next morning the papers were favourable to the speech I had made, and although there was no vote in the local government de-bate speaker after speaker called on the party to oppose abolition and most of them quoted my speech. Former Labour MPs who'd defected from the party rolled their eyes in disbelief that we had changed SDP policy overnight. From that moment, we had the initiative and the government was on the defensive. Even the *Daily Express* was critical of the plans when they were finally published and David Owen was the first to denounce them.

The following week we arrived at the Liberal conference in Har-rogate to find young Liberals wearing 'I'm Red Ken' badges and virtually the entire conference turned up at our fringe meeting. Liberals had always been committed to devolution and local gov-ernment, and their views on race, homosexuality and Ireland were similar to mine. The next day they voted by a large majority to op-pose abolition.

On the train to Blackpool for the Conservative conference we were all feeling tense. They had refused to rent us space for our dis-plays and when we booked a site in the local shopping centre the owners were leaned on to cancel their contract with us, but a judge ruled that our booking should go ahead. When the exhibition opened it was attacked physically by young Tories. A vice-chair of the Tory party warned that my personal safety was at risk but issued a grovelling retraction when Tony Banks asked why the party of law and order couldn't guarantee my safety at their own conference. On our team was Tory GLC member George Tremlett, who had decided to condemn Thatcher's abolition plans, unlike his group leader Alan Greengross, whose compliant silence was rewarded with a knighthood. Our reception was almost as good as at the other conferences and at the end of our meeting they had a collection to cover the costs of our visit so it would not be a burden on London's ratepayers. While the meeting was going on Nita Clarke came up behind a man bent double looking through the keyhole of the room, but when she asked if he wanted to come in Patrick Jenkin went bright red and rushed away. The GLC party stayed in the cheapest B&Bs, which caused embarrassment to two journalists who'd been critical of the GLC when they turned up at our lodgings with a prostitute each. Their articles on the GLC became more balanced overnight.

The Labour conference was a foregone conclusion and didn't match the excitement of the Liberal and SDP events. The bureaucracy kept us at arm's length and we had trouble getting exhibition space and visitor tickets. Michael Foot had announced his resignation as Labour leader shortly after the election defeat and a Labour leadership ballot was imminent. Neil Kinnock's campaign team did not want him to be seen with me and at the TUC conference his minders had steered him in a wide circle so that no photographer could put us in the same picture.

*

With petitions and letters flooding in to MPs our campaign went from strength to strength with one unit organising local activities across London, another lobbying editors and professional bodies and Roland Freeman contacting every peer who might be likely to rebel. For the first time it looked as though there might just be a chance of defeating Thatcher. Jenkin spent a year declining offers from radio and TV programmes to debate with me until polls got so bad for him that he had nothing to lose.

Jenkin had already taken the decision which would humiliate the government and end his career, and it was the only time he ever ignored Thatcher's advice. It would take until March 1986 to abolish the GLC, so to prevent us turning the 1985 GLC election into a referendum on abolition he decided simply to cancel the election. For the final year of the GLC's existence, the Tory-controlled majority on the London boroughs would take over its functions. He considered extending our term for another year but caved in to right-wingers who were appalled to think they would have to give me another year as leader. In a letter to Thatcher Jenkin wrote: 'the 1985 elections cannot be allowed to go ahead . . . abolition would be a major issue in the elections, so there would be a major public debate going on'. But it was 'probably one of the most sensitive decisions we have to take'. Thatcher's private secretary, Michael Scholar, wrote back saying that 'the prime minister prefers deferment of the May 1985 elections . . . to substitution'.

This confidential correspondence was leaked to us. I was told the letters had been removed from a man's briefcase while he was enjoying a brothel specialising in sado-masochism and bondage. They were passed to my GLC colleague Lesley Hammond. As the letters had only been copied to the cabinet, the Attorney General, the arts minister, Jenkin's deputy and Cabinet Secretary Sir Robert Armstrong, it narrowed down the field of suspects.

We received another letter after the Tory party conference. Now the circulation list included Richard Hatfield from the Cabinet Office, and speculation about whether the documents came from a cabinet minister or his private secretary continued. I told Lesley to offer the brothel owner the loan of a GLC photocopier, but the transgender owner thought it would look out of place and worry clients. Lesley reported that the second Jenkin letter had come into the brothel owner's hands at Blackpool as she followed her clients to Tory conferences so they wouldn't miss her services. She said the letters were removed from a briefcase while the man concerned was tied to a bed and unlikely to notice what was happening. As the Tories were still reeling from the Cecil Parkinson sex scandal, some Labour members wanted to tell the whole story to the press. I vetoed this on three grounds. First, we would get no more information. Second, we had a responsibility to the brothel owner. I had no doubt her life would be vengefully destroyed by the government if she was identified, just as Dr Stephen Ward had been driven to suicide during the Profumo scandal. Finally, although identifying marks had been removed from the documents before we got them, fifteen handwritten words or parts of words remained in the margin of one letter. It would take the police or journalists no time to identify the sado-masochist from these marginal notes. Quite apart from the impact on the man's family, I feared it would unleash a wave of homophobia and sexual witch-hunting. We sat on them until March 1984, when we gave them to John Carvel at the *Guardian* just before Jenkin published his bill to cancel the GLC election. When the *Guardian* published it was assumed that the leaks came from Thatcher's staff in order to distance her from Jenkin. John Carvel won the Local Government Journalist of the Year Award for his exposure of the disagreement between Thatcher and Jenkin and I was asked to present the prize.

*

With 62 per cent of Londoners now opposed to abolition, polling showed the Tories were most vulnerable on the issue of Londoners losing their right to vote. Reg Race, who had been MP for Wood Green, had come to work for us in the DG's department where he oversaw the drafting of MPs' speeches – such as the one delivered by Ted Heath who flew back from Nairobi to take part in a debate on Jenkin's 'paving bill':

It is bad because it is a negation of democracy . . . Worst of all it is the imposition by parliamentary diktat of a change of responsible party in London government. There cannot be any justification for that. It immediately lays the Conservative party open to the charge of the greatest gerrymandering in the last 150 years of British history . . . The way the government has handled the issue has achieved the inconceivable – it has mobilised the weight of public opinion behind Mr Kenneth Livingstone. Who would have thought that possible two years ago? It is an achievement unknown in the annals of local government.

The following week I saw Heath at a meeting and congratulated him on his excellent speech, to which he responded 'And who are you?'

Nineteen Tories, including four former cabinet ministers, voted against the bill while twenty others abstained. In the House of Lords the first vote saw the Tory majority reduced to 20 and the *Daily Express* cautioned, 'Be very careful about tampering with the democratic process.' The *Mail on Sunday* warned, 'What an appalling precedent is being established for the future. Here is a moderate, democratic government abolishing an election because it happens to be inconvenient. What will a more malign force do with that one in the years to come . . . This is a very bad deal – and ministers know that very well.'

Patrick Jenkin could no longer put off debating with me and so Capital Radio organised a live debate from County Hall. Almost nobody spoke in support of abolition and Jenkin was fumbling and unsure of his facts. Radio news reported, 'Patrick Jenkin seemed to have trouble coping with the quick-witted Mr Livingstone.' It was the first and last time Jenkin took part in a public debate.

Next morning as Bill Bush drove across Waterloo Bridge after dropping his son at nursery, his car was forced to stop by Special

Branch officers, one on a motorbike, two in an unmarked car. He was arrested and taken to the cells at Rochester Road police station where he was questioned for two hours before being allowed one phone call. We sent a lawyer over while we burned all but one set of the leaked cabinet papers and Tony Banks went straight to the House of Commons to raise the issue. Jenkin's denial of any knowledge of the snatch squad did not stop Jack Straw warning, 'Before Thatcherism and its authoritarian tendencies became rampant, there would not have been the climate in which the police could possibly have considered their powers to arrest and detain someone who worked for a leader of the Greater London Council. But a climate has been created by this government in which that is apparently a commonplace.'

By the time Bill was released at lunchtime, County Hall was crawling with reporters and it was obvious what had happened. Bill had heard that Sir Keith Joseph was to announce that Londoners would be allowed to elect the ILEA. Bill told ILEA leader Frances Morrell and she asked him to brief William Stubbs, the chief education officer. I had clashed with him because of his anti-union attitudes but Morrell had ignored my advice and gone ahead with his promotion. Stubbs demanded to know our source for the ILEA story but I had told Bill that the source should not be revealed to anyone, so Bill merely said he had a friend in the Cabinet Office. Special Branch, when they picked him up, asked who he knew in the Cabinet Office so we suspected either that Stubbs had betrayed us or that his office was bugged. Morrell still refused to sack him without proof which, of course, we didn't have. After the abolition of the ILEA, he worked for government until 2002 when he was forced out by education secretary Estelle Morris, in a row over A levels.

Two days later the Lords voted down the cancellation of the GLC election by a majority of 191–143, the biggest defeat for a

Tory government since the First World War. They claimed it was because the vote clashed with Wimbledon, the Henley Regatta and a Lords Test match but forty Lords who had voted with the Tories three weeks earlier were in the House and abstained. Jenkin dug a deeper hole for the government by saying 'a party from a mental hospital in the public gallery watched with a growing astonishment and a growing sense of familiarity'.

Jenkin's claim that abolition had no political motive was undermined when Thatcher's cabinet colleague Norman Tebbit, at a meeting of the London Tory party, warned that 'very dangerous people' were at work in local government 'pursuing a policy of class warfare of which Karl Marx could only dream ... Left-wing committee after left-wing committee has been set up to harass the police force ... while our police officers have been fighting crime the GLC has been fighting the police. Mr Livingstone has welcomed IRA supporters to London and he has deliberately encouraged the breaking of the law ... the aim of Labour in London is the creation of poverty and despair ... The Labour party ... represents a threat to the democratic values and institutions on which our parliamentary system is based ... it must be defeated so we shall abolish the Greater London Council.'

Jenkin reluctantly agreed to extend my administration until abolition but announced that as from midnight that day, 12 July, the GLC could not dispose of any land. We summoned the Coin Street Action Group and transferred ownership of that site to their control just a few minutes before midnight, thus guaranteeing the provision of good, affordable homes for the local community on the South Bank. Jenkin also tried to stop our advertising campaign with amendments to his bill preventing us from awarding any contract over £100,000 without his prior consent. Anticipating this, we had signed an eighteen-month contract with BMP, our advertising agency, months before. This meant that Working for London slogans appeared behind the goals at the England v. Romania football international in Bucharest but the BBC refused to continue coverage of a Test match at the Oval until our slogans had been covered up.

Jenkin didn't know that we were the bulk purchaser for all council supplies in London so his department was suddenly flooded with 250 contracts a week – for everything from school equipment to baked beans. Tory MPs despaired of Jenkin as on huge billboards and in the papers they saw BMP's work depicting Londoners caught in a vast network of quangos and unaccountable bureaucracies. Support for the GLC peaked in September, with 74 per cent opposed to abolition and only 16 per cent in favour.

Despite such massive public support, our only chance of winning was now in the Lords, where the Tory majority was enormous but soft and ill-organised. Roland Freeman recruited a Tory hereditary peer, Baron Charlie Teviot, whose ancestors had fallen on hard times. He was delighted to give up driving a bus and joined our payroll to persuade Tory lords to oppose abolition.

Reg Race and Roland took over the Labour whips' office and assembled files on every peer including many presumed dead as they hadn't been seen in the House for up to twenty years. Out of 943 peers only 413 were registered as Conservatives but half of the 'independent' cross-benchers always voted with the Tories. We hired rooms in the Lords with food and drink available so none of them needed to slip out of our sight. A fleet of thirty cars picked them up from their homes and returned them after the final vote. Baron Joe Gormley, the leader of the National Union of Mineworkers before Arthur Scargill, was about the only Labour peer who refused to support our campaign and I wasn't surprised when it was eventually revealed that he had been involved with MI5. The nonsense of a legislative chamber based on the hereditary principle was illustrated when one of our drivers phoned to say that the peer he was driving couldn't remember where he lived.

With everything to play for, I rushed from one public meeting to another. I was always tired, working up to eighty-four hours a week. On Saturdays I would be whisked by car to as many as five public meetings but excitement and adrenaline kept me going. Peter Shore suggested I resign my seat and turn the resultant by-election into a mini referendum on abolition, so along with three other members I did precisely that. The new Labour leader Neil Kinnock and his deputy Roy Hattersley gave us full support but the Tories refused to contest the by-elections and, as David Davis discovered when he did the same thing in 2007 over the issue of civil liberties, a by-election without your main opponent doesn't have quite the desired effect.

No sooner had we resigned than I was told that Neil Davies, the Labour GLC member with a drink problem, had failed to declare a financial interest in a company bidding for a lease on a shop owned by the GLC, and had pressured an officer to write the report in a way which disguised his interest. The officer writing the report had been recruited by the Tories from the private sector and didn't think there was anything wrong with this, but it was of course illegal. I was furious and asked Maurice to investigate but within forty-eight hours the *Standard* had picked up the scent and was asking questions. I was really proud that, for all the political rows and controversies, no journalist had ever suggested that anyone in my administration was lining their own pockets. Now that reputation was at risk, and the scandal might erupt during the by-elections.

The four campaigns were going well even without our opponents, but when Kinnock turned up to our first press conference there were almost no reporters present. All the tabloids put together mentioned the GLC just fourteen times in the four months leading up to the by-elections, after years of obsessively attacking us. The Tory press had been asked to minimise coverage to reduce turnout, and without stories in the papers there was nothing for radio and television to follow up on, so Nita Clarke persuaded TV-am to have me on their morning show. 'But there's a problem,' she told me. 'You can't be political because of by-election law, so you're going to be Mad Lizzie's exercise partner'. As I rolled around the floor with fitness trainer Lizzie Webb in a truly awful tracksuit at 7 a.m. the next morning, I doubted it would affect the outcome of the by-election. That did not stop the Liberals demanding equal exercise time. The following year Nita tried to arrange for me to have a walk-on part in the new BBC soap opera *EastEnders*, but after weeks of haggling the BBC decided that this would be too political and I was denied my acting debut.

When polling day arrived in late September 1984 the *Sun* couldn't resist a warning for voters by listing 42 (out of 2,073) organisations we funded such as Babies Against the Bomb, Rights of Women, Police Accountability, Red Women's Workshops, Southwark Black Workers, the Gay London Police Monitoring Group, Gay Bereavement Project, Lesbian Line and Southall Black Sisters. It poured with rain all day, often at monsoon strength, and people told me they couldn't be bothered to vote because Thatcher wouldn't take any notice. In the end I won with 78.2 per cent of the vote but the turnout was only 30 per cent.

Fortunately the GLC had commissioned a MORI poll and Thames TV a Harris poll to get Londoners' views. The results were virtually identical. In a full GLC election Labour would have won 55 per cent of the vote to the Tories' 28 per cent, giving a council with 84 Labour members, 4 Tories and 4 for the Liberals/SDP. The polls also asked how Londoners would vote in a general election with MORI giving Labour a 13 per cent lead and Harris 18 per cent, which would have meant a loss of thirty-three Tory MPs, leaving them with just twenty-three across the city. Thames TV's poll found that 61 per cent of Londoners thought I had done a good job as leader. Three years before, I had been the *Sun*'s 'most odious man in Britain' with a poll rating of 18 per cent.

The *Standard* ran one complex piece about Neil Davies and his business affairs, and the rest of the media ignored it, but as soon as I had been re-elected leader Maurice reported that there was enough evidence to refer the matter to the police and the Director of Public Prosecutions. I gave Davies Maurice's report to read and said he'd broken the law, risked damaging the administration and I wanted his immediate resignation. Protesting his innocence, he refused to go, so I proposed his expulsion from the Labour group. Unfortunately Harvey had retired, and the whips allowed the issue to drag on while the DPP decided not to prosecute because the sum involved was too small. We had a bizarre debate in which Davies's sad and embarrassing speech triggered sympathy and even excuses on the grounds of his alcoholism. The group voted to take no further action, confirming my belief that no organisation can be trusted to police its own members.

*

Thatcher's chancellor Nigel Lawson claimed that in her eleven years she introduced fifty Acts of Parliament to reduce or control council spending. The worst of these was the legislation to allow rate-capping. This was rushed through before abolition, so we expected that the GLC budget limit set by Whitehall in February 1985 would entail dramatic cuts. While I concentrated on the abolition campaign John McDonnell, my deputy leader and chair of finance, met regularly with the leaders of the Labour boroughs to plan our response to rate-capping.

I was horrified when Ted Knight announced they had unanimously agreed a proposal by Islington's Margaret Hodge that all rate-capped councils should refuse to set budgets, thus forcing the crisis into the lap of the government and opening a 'second front' to help the miners' strike. There was no chance that a majority of GLC members would refuse to set a budget. The Tories would vote for a budget set by their own government, and we would be lucky to get half the Labour group voting against. Ted said that nobody expected the GLC to be able to do this but that some Labour councils had large enough majorities to do so.

I warned them that it would not look good if the GLC fell at the first hurdle, but Hodge's strategy was agreed by eight Labour boroughs and when Labour's local government conference met in Sheffield, the strategy had become unstoppable, whatever private doubts some of the councillors had. At the national party conference that autumn the strategy was agreed without opposition from Kinnock.

The government's attack on the miners was planned before Thatcher took power in 1979 in a strategy paper by Nicholas Ridley, a right-winger who had flirted with the idea of a military coup to overthrow Wilson in the early seventies. In her first term Thatcher was not ready to take the miners on. So energy secretary Nigel Lawson built up coal stocks at power stations and Ian MacGregor, a union-busting Scottish-American, was brought in to run the Coal Board and close down unprofitable pits.

MacGregor waited until winter 1984 was over and to be certain of provoking a strike ignored consultation agreements and announced the closure of Cortonwood, a pit with a militant workforce. The following day Steve Miller, our *Labour Herald* reporter, told me that Arthur Scargill, the NUM president, intended to call a strike without holding a ballot. I said if Scargill couldn't win a ballot he was unlikely to win the strike. Steve said that Scargill believed union members didn't have the right to vote to allow their comrades' jobs to be lost.

A *Daily Mail* opinion poll of miners showed that Scargill could, in fact, win comfortably, but his closest confidant told me that Scargill believed the *Mail* had rigged the poll and that he wouldn't win. This allowed miners crossing the picket line to claim the moral high ground and the media to concentrate on the failure to ballot rather than on the Tories' anti-union strategy. Although this weakened the strike, the left threw everything into backing the miners, with an amazing response all over Britain as people raised money for the strikers and joined picket lines. We knew that this was the decisive battle of the Thatcher years and that the outcome would determine the nature of British society for the rest of the century. With the stakes so high, judges and senior police officers were prepared to bend or break any law to ensure the miners' defeat. Without legal power to do so, police blocked cars and buses taking miners and their supporters to picket lines. The BBC slanted its news coverage – in one instance showing police charging miners after they had thrown stones, whereas the miners had in fact thrown stones in response to first being charged by the police.

Although we could not use GLC funds to support them, we put on concerts and events to raise money and I travelled the country speaking at meetings and joining picket lines. The miners saw the Met as the most violent and contemptuous of the nation's police forces, but when I joined picket lines the attitude changed. 'Would you mind standing on the other side of the road please, sir?' the police would politely ask, while the miners laughed.

The strength of support meant that victory was possible and Thatcher faced defeat when the colliery inspectors debated joining the strike, because the mines would have flooded and forced Thatcher to give in. But they carried on working and, like both the striking and the scabbing miners, lost their jobs when, after defeating the strike, Heseltine closed the industry down.

*

To make it difficult for the government to set our budget we pro-
duced no budget documents until the final budget meeting itself.
Jenkin cleverly allowed the GLC an increased budget, prompting
GLC Tories to propose a budget 30 per cent lower than Jenkin's.
John McDonnell continued to insist that rate-capping would mean
real cuts.

As we approached the crunch the rate-capped councils met on
12 February, with the miners' strike in its last bitter phase, and
were advised by lawyers that 'one thing an authority must not do
is resolve in terms that it will not make a rate for 1985–6'. John
McDonnell was not present and Hodge persuaded everyone else
to agree this new line and kept it secret. This meant that only the
GLC and ILEA were being asked to try to break the law on budget
day. Ted and I had a furious row but, looking straight into my eyes,
he said, 'Trust me, Ken. We're all going illegal together. I promise
you, there's no backsliding. They can't fight us and the miners. We
can bring Thatcher down and then anything is possible.' Shaking
my head, I said there was no way the GLC would 'go illegal' when
Jenkin's budget did not require real cuts. Ted replied, 'Lambeth's
in the same position. We can get through the year. We've got £10
million unspent. But other boroughs aren't in that position. If we
don't give a lead they will collapse. Then there will be real cuts right
across London and we'll get screwed next year when they can pick
us off one by one.'

Back at County Hall Reg Race came to me with Maurice's budget proposals, which involved £30 million of purely cosmetic cuts
and £25 million of growth. I'd known John was exaggerating the
severity of the cuts but I hadn't expected to have real growth. When
I confronted John over this discrepancy, he continued to insist we
faced £140 million cuts and begged me to stop Maurice's budget
paper or 'you will have destroyed the whole fucking campaign'. I
replied, 'If these figures are right then we're going to look like the

biggest fucking liars since Goebbels.' I had no idea of the bitterness that was about to break around me or that a decade would pass before John and I got over it.

That weekend, as the London Labour conference met, GLC members received Maurice's proposals and the news that the boroughs would not go illegal on budget day. Furious rows between borough councillors and GLC members erupted as Ted attacked the GLC: 'Quite frankly, it's a bit late for some comrades to realise there are problems.' I asked Ted and Margaret Hodge to convene a meeting for all London Labour councillors to review their decision, but both refused. The final demoralising blow was the news that the miners had voted to call off their strike.

John went on LBC News. He said, 'Well, Ken is a friend and I don't want to say anything against him but there is no doubt that he has betrayed the whole campaign in order to save his political career.' Interviewed in the *Ham and High* he said, 'Ken and I may remain friends but I will never trust him again . . . we are selling the people out because those like Ken feared disqualification from office and are clinging to power no matter what. He is a Kinnock.' I boiled over and made the mistake of calling a press conference to give my side of events, which turned into a bitter attack on John. It was a stupid decision that allowed papers to divert attention from the issues of cuts in council services to the clash between John and me. David Blunkett came to London to smooth things over, but it was too late.

The GLC's budget meeting saw two days of posturing by ten left-wingers including Tony Banks and Paul Boateng. The Labour right warned if we did not agree a budget they would vote with the Tories, but this made no impact on the dissidents. Finally, at 8 p.m. on Sunday, 10 March the GLC passed a budget that was 6 per cent lower than Jenkin's limit. The next day at the London party executive, the Militant Tendency proposed that I be censured but to my surprise this was defeated by two to one. Although Ted voted for the motion, he realised the danger of a split on the left so he urged that we should 'bury the rotting corpse' and move on. Sharing Ted's concern, Gerry Healy of the WRP asked to see me and I agreed to try to keep the group from sacking John. But John took his campaign into the constituency labour parties, claiming he was the victim of a witch hunt while behaving in a way that was guaranteed to provoke one. He met the Socialist Campaign Group of Labour MPs in Parliament but when Tony Benn proposed I be invited to put my side of the case this was defeated with strong opposition to my presence from the two Militant Tendency MPs, Dave Nellist and Terry Fields.

John's chances diminished when Reg Race reported that £120 million had been found buried away in the budget. We decided that £62 million should be used to restore the cuts in our budget and gave £58 million to the rate-capped London boroughs so there would be no cuts that year. Tony Banks and Paul Boateng, who had voted with John, were embarrassed by this sudden flow of wealth but it did not stop friends within Labour Briefing cutting me out of their lives. They tried to get Mike Ward and Valerie Wise thrown off the party executive, only to see Mike and Valerie top the poll. Margaret Hodge went on the attack in *London Labour Briefing*, saying, 'Should we pay our preceptors, especially the GLC and ... police? Should we withhold our payments for ... PAYE, VAT and ... national insurance? ... What should we do about meeting our interest payments on debt ... ? Our aim must be to strengthen and support all our comrades who are in the front line, so that we can ... inflict massive damage on this government ...'

Night after night I couldn't sleep as I tried to work out how we had screwed up so spectacularly. The stakes were so high that Ted and John had no qualms in exaggerating the scale of the cuts in order to open a second front against Thatcher. Had they succeeded, Thatcher would have been weakened or even defeated and they might have changed the course of recent British history. But the miners' strike collapsed just at the moment John could no longer hide the truth about the relatively generous Jenkin budget. The row did not affect our poll ratings, presumably because it did not impact on people's lives.

In the end only Lambeth and Liverpool went illegal and their councillors were surcharged and barred from office for five years. The removal of Ted and the Lambeth Labour group came at the start of the 1986 borough elections and local voters elected a new Labour administration in a landslide. Shamefully, although no one in Labour's leadership opposed Hodge's strategy, they ruled that Ted could never stand for any office again, while Hodge became a minister under Tony Blair.

*

As Ted had feared, although there was no real reduction in council spending that year, in the following years council budgets were squeezed with huge cuts in education and social services all across London. Jenkin's tactic had worked but Thatcher still replaced him with the brighter and quicker-thinking Kenneth Baker. With no strong ideological views, he smiled a lot, sounded soothingly sincere and waved aside arguments that London would face problems after GLC abolition.

We discovered that in 1977 Baker had written: 'In recent years there has been an increasing direction by central government over local government . . . Whitehall has, quite wrongly, interfered more and more with the activities of County Hall . . . it is impossible to have a proper strategic authority in Greater London without a change of attitude in Whitehall.' He had proposed a bigger role for the GLC, a simplified fares policy (which we had introduced), coordination with British Rail (which Norman Fowler had vetoed) and a partial lorry ban (which we were trying to introduce in the face of government obstruction). He said the GLC should help create a fairer multiracial society (now he called us loony lefties for doing so). We published this stirring defence of the GLC and sent copies to MPs and the media.

When government published its abolition bill they had forgotten key GLC functions such as managing Thamesmead housing estate and Hampstead Heath, and as they were still undecided who should now manage many of our functions the bill would create no fewer than sixty-eight new powers to deal with these tasks by edict.

MPs and peers ground away at the bill line by line. Of the thousands of responses to the government consultation only 2 per cent favoured abolition and only three Tory boroughs gave unqualified support. Independent financial studies predicted the cost of abolition would be £225 million. It all led deputy prime minister Willie Whitelaw to moan, 'How do we get out of this mess without appearing disloyal?'

We commissioned satirist Ned Sherrin to write updates of Gilbert & Sullivan – the *Rate Payers' Iolanthe* and the *Metropolitan Mikado*. Mum came to the opening night of the *Rate Payers' Iolanthe* but as the actor playing me performed a graphic simulated sex scene she whispered, 'I don't think I like this very much.' We put on two GLC staff pantomimes spoofing abolition in which we dressed in ridiculous costumes with Paul Boateng clad only in a judge's wig and codpiece (I was Dick Whittington) and clips were broadcast on local television and radio while Harry and Nita came up with new gimmicks. I paraglided across the Thames. We highlighted new projects like Battersea Peace Pagoda and the world's most modern waste-transfer station at Wandsworth, but nothing compared with the opening of the Thames Barrier.

Before the barrier was completed in 1982 I was on tenterhooks during every flood warning and in its first year it was raised twice to prevent the flooding of London. The Palace told us that the Queen would like to open the barrier but GLC left-wingers wanted the longest-serving site worker or an East End celebrity to do it. I met the workforce, who warned they would form a picket line if anybody but the Queen was chosen. Thames TV asked viewers to vote between the Queen and Sir Ashley Bramall, then chair of the GLC, and the Queen squeaked in by 14,000 votes to 17.

Everything was meticulously planned, given the tragedy that had occurred last time the barrier had been used as a PR tool. As it hadn't been ready to open before the 1981 election Cutler had organised a spurious PR event to raise his profile. It had gone horribly wrong when a steel cable snapped and whipped though a site worker, cutting him in half. The media watched as both parts of his body fell into the Thames. Thankfully, in those pre-YouTube days, the footage was never seen.

Palace officials were worried we might exploit the Queen's presence with some stunt, but her opening of the barrier would guarantee global TV coverage and I was surprised the Queen was prepared to do this at the height of the abolition battle. We encouraged media speculation that this revealed the Queen's opposition to abolition. Hosken quotes Maurice Stonefrost saying that he reassured the Palace that I would be on my best behaviour if they invited my mum, as she would love to meet the Queen and be very cross if I did anything to spoil the day.

With news of my mum's involvement the *Daily Mail* rushed up to Lincoln and offered to buy her a new dress, which she declined. On the day, Mum travelled on the Royal Barge while I waited at the barrier to greet them. As they disembarked Prince Philip said to me, 'Your mother's a lively old stick.' Mum said they discussed which horses they had backed recently. When Prince Philip asked whether she was warm enough she announced, 'Oh yes, I've got a lot on underneath, dear.' The only glitch was that as the Queen pressed the button to raise the barrier, two of the seven gates became stuck in mud but freed themselves before it became obvious.

*

Lady Porter, leader of Westminster Council, was alarmed at our popularity and wrote a letter to firms asking for financial backing to oppose us. 'I am sure you understand – though many people do not – that we are in a revolutionary situation . . . regrettably the battle . . . has so far been won by the left, which is highly organised. The GLC . . . has spent about £40 million in backing groups, many of them revolutionary. A major campaign is, therefore, being set up . . . [it has] the full support of the Prime Minister . . . cheques should be sent to me for "Efficiency in local government" . . . the Prime Minster will be meeting a dozen of its business supporters . . . at 10 Downing Street . . . I hope you will forgive me for being blunt . . . and you will support us with a sum of at least four figures.'

We got a leaked copy of this letter and gave it to the press, so Thatcher cancelled the meeting. Porter's brassy personality and pushiness was coupled with a complete absence of humour, and other Tories resented the way she pushed to the front of the anti-GLC lobby. That she is one of the few people I have ever met without a single redeeming feature was shown when we both opened a children's sports centre. The children clustered around me for autographs and ignored her, so she stormed off in a huff. Seeing my driver, she marched over, berated him and said he should make the most of his job as he'd be out of work after abolition of the GLC. When we debated abolition at the annual conference of local government chief executives, she condemned them for having given me a round of applause and then berated them for being in their shirtsleeves even though it was a very hot day.

Our strategy was to propose a series of amendments to the paving bill, each of which would establish a London-wide authority to carry on GLC functions such as waste collection and recycling, and then to propose a directly elected body to oversee them all. As opposition to abolition was widespread, the amendment was proposed by a Tory MP, Patrick Cormack, and it was defeated by only 23 votes instead of the usual 140. Over 100 Conservative MPs voted against their government or abstained. In the Lords the government chief whip Bertie Denham overhauled the whips' office and both sides made a massive effort on amendments moved by rebel Tory peers Baroness Faithfull and Desmond Plummer (Tory GLC leader before Cutler). The Tories made younger peers drone on in the hope that the older peers would give up and go home, but watching the ninety-nine-year-old Fenner Brockway hanging on to the bitter end I had real contempt for peers who turned up, signed in to claim their allowance and left before the vote. When the amendment was lost by only 213–209 it had an electrifying effect on our campaign and across London people redoubled their efforts, although many had been campaigning flat out for eighteen months. The Tories suffered defeats. The Lords passed amendments to retain a London-wide waste-disposal and recycling authority and a new highways organisation and deleted the clause allowing the government to abolish the ILEA without further legislation.

Bertie Denham finally got his act together and the Tory effort matched our own as we came to the last vote on 20 June over the proposal to set up an elected London Authority. Fortunately we had dragged the committee stage out so that it coincided with Ladies' Day at Ascot and many Tory peers were damned if they were going to miss drinking champagne in the Royal Enclosure, so Denham had to keep the debate going until after the King George V Handicap at 5.30 p.m.

As the debate began the going was good to firm at Ascot and Denham looked very unhappy, knowing he had to stretch things out into the early evening to allow time for the truanting Tories to get back. Deputy prime minister Willie Whitelaw and a team of government whips prowled the paddocks of Ascot while Denham's loyalists filibustered. There were only ten amendments left with four more to be moved by our supporters, and Denham had no idea that we planned to withdraw them. The scene was described by the *Daily Telegraph*'s Godfrey Barker:

Lord Denham's face froze with horror as Lord Rochester intoned, 'Not moved.' Frowning tremendously, Lord Denham gazed over the thinned-out ranks of unsocial Tories behind. Lord Harmar-Nicholls staggered up. He announced he was disappointed that Lord Rochester was not moving. He was disappointed for 20 minutes.

Lady Faithfull rose next to the occasion. She seemed to think that the amendment had been moved. No one enlightened her. She made the speech she would have made if it had been.

Lord Thorneycroft managed 10 minutes on the importance of amendments being important.

The afternoon wore on. The air was as sepulchral as at Ascot it was rosy. The Earl of Gowrie, smooth talker, seized the Despatch Box at 4.20. He was helped through the King Edward VII Stakes by having to repeat a Commons statement to the Lords.

At 4.55 Lord Gowrie was sent 3 extra pages at the Despatch Box for his speech to give him stamina in the Chesham Stakes. At 5.29 with the King George at the off, the last three amendments came up.

'81B, Lord Irving?' called the Deputy Speaker. 'I withdraw,' replied that worthy.

'81B 2A, Lord Dean?' came next. 'Not moved,' his Lordship grunted, and ditto to 82B. At 5.35 the tapes were up on Lord Barnett and the killer amendment on the GLC.

But Lord Denham is a man of the turf. At 6 p.m. he was still looking as sick as a parrot. But as his men filibustered smoothly down the court through 6.30 then 7, his visage brightened.

At 7.20 we came to the awesome vote. One scanned Lord Denham's men: not a morning suit to be seen. But several lads in red ties never before seen in the Lords hove into view on the Government benches. Could his Lordship yet scrape home in the Denham Stakes?

'Content, 147,' intoned the Deputy Speaker for Lord Ponsonby's men: 'Not Content, 173.'

There were elements of farce during the frantic whipping. A very old peer asked a police officer if the Lords was still in the same place, as he had not attended since the Second World War, but in the end we had lost by 26 votes and from that moment I knew the GLC would be abolished. In the Commons the government allowed only seven hours' debate and mobilised their majority to reject the Lords' amendments creating a Waste Authority and a Highways Authority. On 16 July the bill received Royal Assent and became law.

For a century and a half, legislation had extended voting rights, allowing people who didn't own property to vote, giving women the right to vote, lowering the voting age, extending all these rights to local elections and of course allowing the people of London to elect their own council. For the first time in 150 years democratic rights had been rolled back, and that the unelected Lords rubber-stamped this retrograde step showed they were not prepared to constrain a Tory government, however undemocratic its actions.

*

The Labour group agreed to do everything possible to preserve GLC services, some of which (transport, fire-fighting and waste and recycling) were taken over by quangos. But our work on equalities faced extinction and thousands of voluntary organisations would only continue if a committee of London boroughs agreed to the funding by a two-thirds majority. We looked for a precedent that might save them.

Knowing they were about to lose control of Greater Manchester, in 1981 the Tories set up a trust to continue paying children's private school fees and Lord Denning had ruled this 'tombstone' funding legal. We used Denning's judgment to continue funding projects such as the reopening of the Roundhouse in Camden and to create a trust to continue funding the community groups (mainly nurseries) which so upset the Tory press.

Lady Porter challenged the legality of such continued funding in the High Court, where Mr Justice Macpherson ruled in our favour on every point of law and procedure, a judgment so convincing that in normal circumstances no barrister would have advised their client to appeal. But Thatcher had appointed a hard-line Tory, Lord Donaldson, as Master of the Rolls in succession to Lord Denning. Donaldson overturned Macpherson's detailed and closely argued judgment with a sweeping and superficial ruling. One of the judges sitting with Donaldson said he noted the decision of the Lower Court but simply disagreed with it. As we had no chance of winning in the Law Lords we gave the £78 million that was at stake to boroughs and housing associations to use for modernising council homes.

I was travelling to Sheffield for a meeting when the *Standard* published its evening edition with the headline 'Ken's £96 million for lesbians'. The train was full of half-cut football fans and police asked me to move to first class to end the chaos in the crowded buffet, where everyone had an opinion on lesbianism. Our work with the lesbian and gay community had produced the booklet 'Changing the World – a charter of reforms', which we circulated widely. Replies ranged from enthusiastic to offensive. The Royal Society of Tropical Medicine and Hygiene told us, 'We are not interested, nor is there any place for this type of material in this organisation.' The Bedfordshire Health Authority's general manager said, 'I would consider it a waste of the time of my officers to ask them to read or discuss it with a view to take any action.' The Institute of Chartered Shipbrokers said, 'We have no interest whatsoever in your apparent efforts to assist sexual deviants.' The National Council of Women of Great Britain deplored 'organisations, which by their very nature, can only contribute to the breakdown of family life'. Tory MP John Carlisle said 'to pander to these sick and depraved people as your organisation so blatantly does is a stain on the people of London'.

Each of the quangos inheriting GLC services took a different approach. The worst was the Arts Council, which took over the South Bank concert halls and immediately made two-thirds of the staff redundant while doubling the number of senior managers and increasing their pay by 30 per cent. The quango running London Regional Transport pushed through fare increases and drastic cuts in bus services and did away with most bus conductors.

The Tories created the London Residuary Body to flog off GLC assets and land. Its chair, Tory leader of Sutton Council Sir Godfrey Taylor, was paid £50,000 a year and as I was only earning £6,000 a year I was tempted to submit a claim for back pay to the government. Taylor assured me he was 'neither racist nor sexist' and so would not need our Women's or Ethnic Minority Unit. I persuaded eight Labour boroughs in London to set up the London Strategic Policy Unit to take these staff and carry on our work on equalities and policing, but when Labour lost the 1987 general election the boroughs closed the unit to save money.

We found jobs for all the staff even if they weren't necessarily jobs they would have liked. Out of 30,000, 2,000 took redundancy or early retirement; sadly, two people committed suicide under the pressure. Taylor dragged out his job for five years and sold off most of our assets and land at low prices, many to firms who funded the Tory party. County Hall was valued at £250 million, but by the time the Tories sold it six years later the property market had collapsed and the Shirayama Shokusan Corporation (owned by a secretive Japanese family) paid just £50 million for it. The London School of Economics had offered more, but Michael Portillo (the minister responsible) feared the LSE might rent part of the building for a new Greater London Authority and sold it to the lowest bidder. Shirayama immediately banned the Royal British Legion from holding its annual service of remembrance on the ceremonial staircase whose walls bore the names of staff who died in two world wars. In response to the public outcry, they said the British Legion could hold their ceremony as long as they paid the air fares for Japanese war veterans to attend.

*

Our polling numbers continued to improve. While the Labour party under Kinnock was unable to get over 40 per cent in national polls, the GLC had broken the 50 per cent barrier for only the second time (in the 1971 borough elections Labour had achieved 53 per cent). Nationally 39 per cent of people favoured unilateral nuclear disarmament, but in London it was 44 per cent. Fifty-one per cent of Londoners believed crime should be dealt with by tackling social problems, against 46 per cent nationally. The Tories had a 19 per cent lead in support for anti-union laws, but that figure was just 7 per cent in London. Support for a public transport subsidy was 10 per cent higher in London and Londoners were 5 per cent more likely to believe that Labour would keep its promises. Our support was higher among traditional Labour supporters, such as council tenants and trade unionists, but the most dramatic difference was in the middle classes. Nationally Labour came third, with only 28 per cent support among under-35s in social classes ABC1, but in London we led with 39 per cent to just 28 per cent for the Tories. Among the older middle class we also ran 10 per cent ahead of the national figures.

Thatcher would not have gone for abolition if there had been a chance of defeating me at a GLC election but since she was re-elected in 1983 with only 42 per cent of the vote she knew she was in government due only to the weakness of a divided opposition. Contrary to her assertion that there was no alternative to her policies, we proved there was and that is why we were abolished.

At the 1983 general election the Tories' lead in London was 2 per cent less than in the rest of the country. From December 1983 Labour's lead in London was 12 per cent higher than that of the Labour party nationally and that difference stayed in double figures until abolition two and a half years later. Following abolition, the Labour leadership under Kinnock dismissed our popularity as the result of a slick and expensive advertising campaign. But the advertising campaign started four months after the gap opened between Labour support in London and the rest of the country.

Nevertheless, the GLC was abolished at the stroke of midnight on 31 March 1986 (Easter Sunday). The campaign against abolition had taken over my life for more than two years. I had to sustain the enthusiasm of others, the belief that victory was possible, and when that dream failed worked even harder to preserve County Hall's legacy. I had no time to consider my emotions as I was seldom alone and slept the moment my head hit the pillow. But in the last days, as I visited departments to thank staff for their support, their courage and warmth often moved me to tears.

The last meeting of the GLC was on the Thursday before Easter and I only just got through my speech paying tribute to those who had worked for London, many for their whole adult lives. Tony Banks, chair of the GLC for its final year, arranged for a commemorative medal for each member of the council and on the way back to my office a staff member asked to see it. Realising the medal would mean more to her than it would to me, with my memories of the last five years, I asked her to keep it. As I cleared my desk the Thames TV presenter Barbara Long popped in to ask how I was; that kindness from a journalist was the final straw and tears poured down my face.

Over the Easter weekend we put on events all over London and Mum came down to take part. Shortly after I became leader Mum (then still a Tory) had stood outside County Hall thinking, 'How can my Ken be running all this?' Now she couldn't stand Thatcher and with no pressure from me had come to think that Tony Benn should be prime minister. As we moved through the crowds around County Hall she was proud of the warmth people expressed but sad that Dad wasn't there to see it.

Tony Banks decided that in the minutes before abolition at the stroke of midnight the Fire Brigade band would play Elgar's 'Nimrod' as the GLC flag was lowered on the terrace overlooking the Thames. The 50,000 people lining the bridges and embankments cheered when by accident the flag started going up again. I then went with Mum and other GLC members to the stage overlooking Jubilee Gardens for one last speech and a get-together with Paul Weller and Billy Bragg leading the singalong, then went back to my office to collect the last bits and pieces of paper and personal stuff. The pictures on the walls were mine but the frames were owned by County Hall, so we removed the pictures. As we left County Hall Mum's handbag opened and I could see she'd stuffed a large stapler inside. When I asked her why, she replied, 'I don't want that awful woman to have anything.' As the car pulled away we could see Godfrey Taylor had decided to pay overtime rates to employ builders to scale the walls of County Hall and the Royal Festival Hall at 1 a.m. to remove the logos and all signs that the GLC had ever existed.

10

Being There

Overnight I went from running the largest local authority in Europe, with six personal staff, to organising my own life from a makeshift office in Kate's co-op flat in a run-down terrace in Kilburn. I enjoyed controlling my own life again, deciding what to do, where to go and writing my own letters. I was forty-one and had been living on an attendance allowance of £6,000 a year as leader. I owned only clothes, books, records, six salamanders and a washing machine I'd bought with the fee for appearing as co-presenter on a Saturday late show with Janet Street-Porter. Sir Godfrey Taylor let me buy my office furniture and I began sorting papers for a book about the GLC.

Between abolition and the borough elections I canvassed in three crucial wards in neighbouring Tory Westminster. Neale Coleman, who had helped me get selected for Paddington, realised Labour could take 27 of the 60 seats and that two seats in Mayfair were held by independents who loathed Lady Porter. We knew Thatcher would be in the depths of mid-term unpopularity and if Porter didn't realise what we were up to we had an outside chance of electing two councillors out of the three least safe Tory wards. We selected our strongest candidates two years early in three crucial Tory wards and canvassed every voter. Ten days before polling the Tories realised something was up. True to form Porter panicked but instead of moving resources to the targeted wards concentrated efforts in her own safe seat. We won 27 seats, failing to take the crucial two by just 106 votes. We knew the Tories wouldn't let us sneak up on them again but Porter was and is a bit dim, and set in train a series of events culminating in her being surcharged £42 million for the largest fraud in local government history.

Financial worries evaporated when I sold my GLC memoir to HarperCollins for £60,000. After tax and the agent's fee the £33,000 I had left was enough for a deposit on a home and allowed me to get through to the general election. Many on the left expected Kinnock to block my selection in Brent East, but in his posthumously published papers the journalist Hugo Young records Kinnock as saying, 'Livingstone has never been a loony, but he's deeply flawed because he regards politics as "a numbers game".'

I won most of the party wards so Reg Freeson withdrew, claiming the contest was rigged. After the rate-capping row some of the hard-left Labour Briefing group switched their support to Diane Abbott, who had worked with me in Hampstead when I was the candidate, and when it was announced that I had won got up and walked out. At the next Brent East social in the local pub, my supporters and Diane's sat on opposite sides of the room; as I walked over to where my opponents were seated they jumped up and started dancing to avoid talking to me.

*

Reg was dumped by the machine because I had developed a working relationship with Kinnock. I wanted change so I would rather compromise to win than spend a life of ideological purity in opposition. That was why I had supported Denis Healey rather than Michael Foot in the 1980 leadership election, even though I was lobbied by Frances Morrell who said the left had agreed we should all phone Michael to encourage him to stand. Michael was the nicest man ever to lead the Labour party and I loved him, but I knew we would do better if led by an old bruiser like Denis. When

Hackney North's left-wing MP Ernie Roberts brought his ballot paper to our GMC saying he would fill it out in front of us following our vote on who to support, he was mortified when I made the case for Denis and almost won. Tony Benn told me he believed that had Healey won he would have appealed to the left and would have put Benn on the front bench to end the party's civil war.

The hard left hated Kinnock for opposing Tony in the deputy leadership election. But when Chris Mullin invited several left-wing and trade-union activists to his flat in Brixton after Benn lost his seat in the 1983 election, it was clear that Kinnock would be our next leader. I argued we would be better off with Hattersley, who would appease the left whereas Kinnock would pander to the right, but Alan Meale, a trade-union fixer, reported that the left-wing unions would vote for Kinnock. As we sat in Chris Mullin's garden people were stunned when Tony Banks offered to resign as the MP for Newham North West so that Tony Benn could take his seat in the subsequent by-election. Benn wisely declined. Kinnock was three years older than me but he had gone straight to Parliament without serving on a council and had refused a job in Callaghan's government, so he had no experience of running anything. In the end the hard left voted for Eric Heffer's doomed campaign and Kinnock won in a landslide.

Although Kinnock's minders steered him around me at the TUC congress, he had to face the fact that I was leader of the GLC, just as I expected him to grow in stature and be around for a long time. Through his chief of staff, Charles Clarke, we began a delicate minuet starting with lunch at County Hall. He agreed to fight abolition line by line and I promised that his shadow local government spokesman, Jack Cunningham, and his deputy, Jack Straw, would have GLC resources to support them. The relationship warmed when the left attacked me over rate-capping.

Most Labour MPs facing deselection defected to the SDP and

lost their seats at the 1983 election but Kinnock was worried that the Bangladeshi community in Tower Hamlets might purge Peter Shore. Hard-working, able and high-profile, his removal would have been big news so Kinnock got me to ask the Bangladeshis to allow him to continue as their MP. They respected Peter and were happy to keep him if it was understood that his successor would be a Bangladeshi. Kinnock was delighted and gave this assurance. I thought I got on well with Peter, whose idea it was that I resign my GLC seat and fight a by-election, so I was surprised when I read Hugo Young's account of a lunch with Peter at Café Pelican on 15 July 1986. Shore, Young wrote, regards 'Livingstone as about the most evil man to come on the political scene for many years: clever at mobilising the minorities, but a preacher and stirrer up of hatred against most established institutions. By this means he has created a radicalised class which rejects almost everything. The politics of hatred . . . This has changed the Labour party, making old compromises unavailable . . . The only hope is that a yet newer generation, post-Livingstone, is emerging that reacts against all that stuff.'

Kinnock's oratory was inspirational but now he was reined in by his advisers and given dull speeches written by staff. While waiting to go on stage at a London rally I told him he should dump their speeches and rely on his off-the-cuff skills. He responded, 'Ken, in this job I can't do that any more.' At this stage Neil kept the left happy by visiting Cuba to meet Fidel Castro and being derogatory about Reagan's henchmen on a visit to the White House, but Ted Knight did not agree with my strategy of working with Neil and after our rate-capping row I resigned as co-editor of the *Labour Herald*, which folded nine months later.

Jim Mortimer, the general secretary of the party, took early retirement because he couldn't stand Neil Kinnock, and I sounded out Neil's office to see if I could take over Jim's role but Kinnock didn't believe it would be possible to be both a candidate for Parliament and general secretary. My relations with Kinnock went into a deep freeze a few weeks after abolition when I flew to Holland to join Gerry Adams in urging the Dutch government not to deport Irish republicans back to Britain. This prompted Kinnock to send me a furious letter of denunciation. Carvel quotes Bill Bush: 'It was absolutely clear that Ken could be allowed associate membership of the family, but only if he showed complete loyalty – 99 per cent would not do. [Ken] thought that if he did nine things the leadership approved of, there would be room for one they didn't. Politics isn't like that. They won't remember or care about the nine. What they care about is the one.' Carvel also quotes a close Kinnock associate: 'We saw him as a poseur, not a realistic politician . . . he didn't understand the contempt and anger that almost all the Labour MPs felt about his GLC leadership.'

I wasn't prepared to give up campaigning about Ireland just so that I could get a job in Kinnock's government. The more I read about our history in Ireland the more angry I became. Elizabeth I's wars in Ireland butchered a third of the Irish and Cromwell's invasion killed tens of thousands more in the 1650s. I was also stirred by the brutal way in which Britain ignored the potato famine, effectively forcing hundreds of thousands of the Irish to leave their own country for work in Britain and North America. Ireland is the only country in the world which has a smaller population today (five million) than it did in the early nineteenth century (when it had eight million).

*

I decided to call my book *If Voting Changed Anything They'd Abolish It* (an old anarchist slogan) because abolition of the GLC proved their point. Most days I wrote in longhand before going off to speak at party meetings around the country. The old British Rail system was so good I could get the last train home before midnight or, when further afield, a sleeper. These meetings were part of my campaign to become party treasurer (a post traditionally held by a trade unionist, at the time the seaman's union leader Sam McCluskie). No amount of lobbying union leaders such as Rodney Bickerstaffe or Clive Jenkins could persuade the unions to give up their hold on the post and McCluskie was duly re-elected, but I won support from a majority of constituency Labour parties and was well placed to win a seat on Labour's NEC the following year.

Another setback at conference came at the hands of John Reid, later a right-wing enforcer for Tony Blair, although it was orchestrated by Neil Kinnock's office. Eighteen months earlier Peter Hain and I convened a group open to all prospective parliamentary candidates so that they could get to know each other before the election. We called the group PPC Liaison and about fifty left-wingers turned up. Initially Kinnock's office went along with this and shadow frontbenchers addressed us. Most of our liaison work was with Robin Cook, but a revealing moment came when I asked Jack Cunningham why the Labour party didn't campaign about crime. 'Our polling shows this is a Tory issue and we've decided to leave it and concentrate on the NHS,' he said.

The Labour right had always had more MPs than the left, though the centre block usually held the balance, but so many left-wingers were selected for the 1987 election that Peter and I calculated that in the next parliament, for the first time, there would be a majority of Labour MPs on the left. The right would be reduced to 27 per cent, the centre to 16 per cent (the same as the Socialist Campaign Group) and at 41 per cent the largest block would be formed by Tribunite MPs. Tony Benn had led a faction of hard-left MPs to resign from the Tribune Group and set up the Socialist Campaign Group, and Peter and I believed this damaging split needed to be healed if the left was to set the agenda about the direction of the Labour party. If Tribune and the Socialist Campaign Group worked together the left would have 57 per cent of Labour MPs. Peter and I believed that by bringing candidates together we could end this split on the left and have the left drive the political agenda. This was something Kinnock couldn't live with, so at our PPC Liaison meeting at the Labour party conference Peter and I were surprised at the large number of candidates who turned up, many from the right. John Reid attacked Peter and myself for holding meetings dominated by 'London lefties'. He proposed that PPC Liaison be wound up, which was immediately seconded and carried by a small majority.

*

After conference Kate and I flew to Nepal with our friends Merle Amory (leader of Brent Council) and her husband Paul Franklin, a member of the Chartist group. Paul and Merle had walked in the Himalayas before and wanted to return to do the trek to Everest base camp at 18,000 feet. The ideal time to do it is in October before it gets cold but after the monsoon, so that you can be certain of glorious views. On our flight on Bangladesh Airlines the little pots of jam boasted that they were 'Made out of whole Conservatives'. Kathmandu, the capital of Nepal, felt like stepping back in time to medieval England – a city of bustling open-air markets but with Buddhist and Hindu temples instead of Christian churches. Because of trade problems, there was no alcohol except for local beer made from fermented yak milk. Fortunately the British embassy discovered we were there and the ambassador invited us to drinks and agreed to organise a helicopter to ferry us out if any of us broke a leg on the trek. We took his advice and hired a guide and two Sherpas to carry most of our luggage.

We travelled by minibus to Jiri, where the road ended, and woke in our hostel at dawn to wash in freezing water from a standpipe before setting off, each of us carrying a heavy backpack. From Jiri

(6,250 feet) to our destination Kala Patthar (18,192 feet) is sixty-four miles as the crow flies but double that as the roller-coaster path ascends a total of 45,000 feet and descends over 30,000 on the way there. The worst leg of the trek was the first day, climbing 1,625 feet, descending 1,500 and then ascending another 1,000 before reaching the village of Sangbadanda at 7,350 feet by nightfall. We came straight from desk jobs with no time to acclimatise so this became the most strenuous day of my life, and I kept cursing for having agreed to come.

We stayed with a family who kept farm animals at one end of the barn with themselves in the middle and the other end reserved for trekkers, but the animals' lice had learned the route to pallid trekker flesh. Next morning we belatedly started applying insect repellent. Trekking in Nepal is a great way to lose weight, with the local diet of pasta, rice and potatoes (and dhal if you're lucky). Meat is usually only available when a yak dies of old age after a lifetime of hauling goods up and down the mountainside. Enterprising locals had erected a sign announcing 'beef steaks' but knives broke as the tourists cut the 'steak'. We stuck with the dhal. Each evening we arrived hot and sweaty at a village, often with a river rushing by, stripped off and jumped into the crystal water – but as the water came straight from melting glaciers we froze within minutes.

With practice we found the effort easier and on the 6,000-foot climb from Kenja to the Lamjura Pass the forest gave way to cooler altitudes and we passed through a moss-covered forest of rhododendrons and prickly-leaved oaks straight out of Tolkien's Middle Earth. As in Africa twenty years before, I was shocked by the almost complete absence of any animal larger than a rat. As the air grew colder we passed the mosquito line and no longer had the problem of leeches dropping onto our heads from the undersides of leaves, but we had also passed the altitude at which chickens lay and the diet was austere. But I didn't mind the lack of food and alcohol or the hard surfaces we slept on, because every day's trekking revealed the most stunning views on earth.

We went up and down a sequence of mountain ridges until we reached the valley that led to Everest. Over thousands of years the Nepalese had literally carved an existence out of the mountainside, chiselling stairways up the side of ravines and clearing every available square metre of land for rice. The town of Namche Bazaar is home to Tibetans who fled with the Dalai Lama in 1958 and in the mornings we were woken by the eerie and evocative sound of Tibetan monks calling with their long horns. Local markets catered to the steady flow of trekkers, selling hand-woven carpets and human skulls decorated with metal for use as bowls. As Tibetans leave their dead in the open to be eaten by vultures there is a constant supply of skulls for the tourist trade. The forest now consisted of black juniper, fir, blue pine and rhododendron.

Trekkers fell into two groups: those like us slowly making our way to base camp and professional climbers attempting the summit. We kept overtaking and being overtaken by the same faces as we paused every 2,000 feet to spend two days acclimatising to the decreasing amount of oxygen in the air we breathed. We regularly encountered an English vicar and his wife in their early seventies and had an intermittent debate with them about the value of religion. The professional climbers were anti-social, totally focused on their climb to the summit, kept themselves to themselves and slept apart from the dilettante trekkers.

We were cut off from news of the outside world but one village had a radio where we learned that Jeffrey Archer had resigned as vice-chairman of the Tory party after the *Daily Star* photographed a pay-off to the prostitute Monica Coghlan, starting a chain of events which thirteen years later would end his mayoral and political ambitions.

At 12,700 feet we found the luxury Everest View hotel, originally built so that millionaires could fly in to dine in the restaurant while admiring magnificent views of the eponymous mountain through its vast windows. It was empty now except for a waiter serving coffee, who said that several of its wealthy clientele had succumbed to heart attacks after walking forty minutes up the 500-foot hill from the airstrip to the hotel without having acclimatised to the altitude. The Everest View closed in 1983.

*

For many centuries local people were content to look at their mountain rather than risk their lives climbing it, and the stone huts of base camp were built by Western climbers. The peak was named in the nineteenth century after Sir George Everest, British head of the India Survey team, but Tibetans call it Chomolungma, 'Goddess of the Wind'. For Nepalis it is Sagarmatha, 'Churning Stick of the Ocean of Existence'. By now plant and animal life was sparse, with only moss and lichens clinging to rocks, and the weather so cold that pee froze as it touched the ground. But we had one last day of trekking over glaciers before we reached the ice wall which only experienced climbers tackled. We heard of trekkers who had not paid their Sherpas and guides enough money to buy proper footwear to protect them from frostbite, and at the ice wall were wooden crosses commemorating Sherpas who had died assisting climbers.

The oxygen content of the air was only a fraction of what we are used to and I couldn't walk thirty feet before the sheer pain of breathing forced me to stop and rest. My friends were all ten years younger than me so I sat and looked at the view while they struggled the last hundred feet up the pile of brown rocks to the prayer flags that mark the top of the minor summit of Kala Patthar (at 18,192 feet high it seemed pretty major to me), from where can be seen the mountains of Lhotse and Nuptse as well as Everest. As I sat and gazed at this bleak beauty I realised that it's wrong to think of earth as a planet-full of life. Few plants or animals can survive unaided at this level apart from lichen and moss, with the occasional scavenging or migrating bird and yaks brought up to graze in the summer. In the last three weeks I had climbed to the upper limit of life on earth, and less than seven miles beneath the ocean surface we reach the lower limit. Life on our planet is confined to a layer no thicker than a tissue paper wrapped around a football. Sitting up there with almost every living thing below me, I understood the great vulnerability of life on earth.

Fortunately, going down was quicker than coming up. Winter was arriving fast; hairs froze in noses and ears and early morning air was painfully cold to breathe. Halfway down at Lukla there is a small airfield with the occasional eight-seater plane to Kathmandu. The runway slopes down to a cliff edge and if the plane is not airborne in time you plunge to your death. The perimeter of the runway is marked by fragments of aircraft that have crashed so it is an airstrip to be avoided by anyone who is even slightly phobic about air travel. As our plane hurtled towards the cliff edge, some of the passengers looked as though they were about to have a heart attack and there were several shrieks as the plane fell a few feet before soaring up into the air. Four weeks with virtually no meat, no alcohol and a punishing physical regime had got me back to my teenage weight, but it was not to last. Back in Kathmandu, at the best restaurant in town, the waiter asked if I'd really intended to order three main courses.

*

As soon as we got off the plane in London, Merle phoned her office in Brent Council and I could tell from her expression that something was wrong. A head teacher had been suspended after telling an officer in Brent's personnel department she didn't want any more Asian teachers in her school. The *Daily Mail* had run a strident campaign in her defence and eventually Brent Council gave in. The pro-communist leadership of the National Union of Teachers exploited the issue by supporting the head because they loathed the NUT branch in Brent, which had a handful of active Trotskyist teachers. Kinnock's office ignored Merle's offer to brief them on the affair and denounced the council, though the issue of exactly what the head teacher had said was never resolved. This was the opening shot in a war against so-called 'loony left' councils orchestrated by the *Daily Mail* and Norman Tebbit, who was in charge of Tory Central Office in the run-up to the 1987 election.

When I was leader of the GLC, apart from my annual holidays, I spent only four days out of the country, making one trip to Amsterdam and another to Copenhagen. Now the cities and organisations who had invited me to visit them once again approached me, starting with an invitation to Israel by the left wing of the Israeli Labour movement which was organised into a separate party called Mapam. After seeing the attacks by right-wing Zionists on the GLC they organised an exhausting round of meetings with all Jewish and Arab political factions, including visits to Yad Vashem (the Holocaust Memorial), the Golan Heights, the Masada plateau and a stay on a kibbutz.

From the moment I arrived in Tel Aviv, newspaper, TV and radio interviews went well as journalists discovered I wasn't the anti-Semitic monster I'd been painted. Mapam's optimism about peace was infectious but polls showed that over 40 per cent of Israelis were in favour of the forced eviction of all Arabs living within the 1948 borders. At the farewell dinner with Mapam they were more shocked when I suggested that a second bottle of wine at a dinner for four wasn't excessive in a land where Jesus turned water into wine.

*

Back in London, Robert Maxwell asked to meet me to discuss setting up a new London evening paper to rival the *Standard*. We had

TOP LEFT: Ken's mother Ethel Ada Kennard (left) with her dance act the Kenleigh Sisters

TOP RIGHT: Bob, Ethel and Ken Livingstone, Butlins, Skegness, 1947

BOTTOM LEFT: Aged three

BOTTOM RIGHT: With his sister Linda in Brockwell Park, 1950

TOP LEFT: Aged seven
TOP RIGHT: In his uniform for St Leonard's Church of England Junior School, 1955
BOTTOM LEFT: In his bedroom in Lambeth with his clawed toads, 1969
BOTTOM RIGHT: As a student at Philippa Fawcett training college, 1970

Protesting against charging to see the dinosaurs at Crystal Palace, 1972

TOP: Selected as Labour candidate for Hampstead, 1976
BOTTOM: Canvassing with Margaret Drabble and John Williams for the 1979 general election

TOP: Labour benches, County Hall
BOTTOM: With Bill Bush and Valerie Wise, 1983

TOP: With Tony Benn and Arthur Scargill, *Labour Herald* rally, 1982
BOTTOM: Neil Kinnock visits County Hall for the first time since
becoming leader of the Labour party, 1983. Left to right: Bill Bush,
Tony Banks, Illtyd Harrington, Harvey Hinds, Kinnock, John
Cunningham, Livingstone, Nita Clarke, John Carr

TOP: Publicising fares cuts with Dave Wetzel (left) and John McDonnell, 1983

BOTTOM: Meeting the Queen at the official opening of the Thames Barrier, 1984

met during the miners' strike, after he bought the *Daily Mirror*. The meeting was set up between Nita Clarke and Joe Haines, Harold Wilson's spin doctor who was now assistant editor and chief leader writer for the *Mirror*. Maxwell had been a soldier in the British Army during the war and later an intelligence officer in Eastern Europe before building a publishing empire and becoming a Labour MP under Wilson (his major achievement was to sell himself the entire House of Commons wine cellar at a knockdown price after he became chair of the Catering Committee).

After the dubious takeover of one of his companies in 1969, he was deemed not 'a fit and proper person' to run a publicly listed company and Labour MPs worried when he bought the *Daily Mirror* (where he eventually stole the staff pension fund), but he used his wealth and charm to buy his way back into the establishment. Given that he was a bullying crook, Joe and Nita were nervous that the meeting could go badly wrong. We were escorted in his private lift to his huge and expensively furnished penthouse office which had his helicopter parked on the roof outside. (No one has ever explained how Maxwell was the only person in London allowed by the Civil Aviation Authority to commute daily by helicopter.) A dinner-jacketed waiter served slices of kiwi and star fruit. When I commented on the quality of his dry white port he remarked he was still working through the House of Commons supplies from fifteen years earlier.

Joe and Nita sat to one side while Maxwell addressed me as though they weren't there, expanding on his plans to influence politics through his paper. Out of the corner of my eye I saw Joe and Nita freeze when in answer to his question about an article denouncing Arthur Scargill, I replied, 'I'm sorry, I don't read your papers.' 'Of course not, my boy, I wouldn't expect you to,' he responded. He asked me how my struggle to replace Reg Freeson was going and then airily waved at Joe, ordering him to write an editorial saying it was time for Freeson to retire. It appeared in the *Mirror* the following week.

His private loo was filled with TVs and teleprinters reporting stock-market news and must have cost as much as a small London flat. Deciding our meeting was over, he told Joe to escort us down in his personal lift and as the doors closed Joe said, 'What do you think? Isn't he a monster?' This view didn't stop Haines writing a sycophantic biography of Maxwell when ordered to do so, to undermine a damning biography by Tom Bower.

Maxwell was determined to break the *Standard*'s monopoly with a new evening paper in which I would write a regular weekly column. For all his egomania, he assembled a good editorial team under Magnus Linklater and an eclectic mix of columnists whom he invited to lunch at *Mirror* headquarters. Grandly announcing over the starters that he never interfered in editorial policy, he then asked the gathering what they thought about Prince Edward dropping out of Royal Marines training. Several said he should be free to choose the life he wanted rather than following the family tradition of serving in the armed forces. Maxwell then loudly announced that no paper he owned would ever carry such views. I wondered about his concept of editorial non-intervention.

In a fair world Maxwell's *London Daily News* would have survived, but when the *Evening News* folded in 1980 the *Standard* made payments to newspaper vendors in exchange for an undertaking to sell only the *Standard* (this would now be illegal under competition law), so Maxwell was up against an even more ruthless rival. Lord Rothermere relaunched the *Evening News* at a cover price of 5p, for the sole purpose of breaking the *Daily News*, forcing Maxwell into a ruinous loss-making war which eventually cost him £25 million. The paper closed after five months, in July 1987.

*

Mum said Uncle Ken wanted to see me as his angina was worse and he didn't want to die without patching things up. His third wife had died and he lived alone with his Alsatian dog. Given his views on the Irish, blacks, gays and David Frost, he had broken off all contact with me when I became leader of the GLC, once even phoning the *Daily Express*, after a late night in the pub, to tell them what a horrible child I'd been. Ken lived in Lambeth and Mum never dared tell him I was a friend of Ted Knight's, whom he so loathed that he refused to pay his rates. When Lambeth took him to court, he turned up leaning on a walking stick and ostentatiously taking his angina pills and telling the magistrate about his war record in Burma. Amazingly he got away with it, but when Ted and the Labour councillors were stripped of office and the Tories took over, as an act of solidarity he paid off his arrears. He was so horrified when Labour not only won back the council but elected as its new leader Linda Bellos, a radical black lesbian, that he returned to the town hall to demand his money back.

The day before Christmas Eve we took Mum and Ken to A l'Ecu de France, an old-fashioned French restaurant on Jermyn Street. As the great and the good had left London for their country retreats we had the place to ourselves, with Mum and Ken requesting the pianist to play songs from the thirties and the war. We couldn't discuss politics or religion so we talked about the war, which was appropriate as it was in this restaurant that General de Gaulle held meetings of his government in exile over a good lunch. As I put them in a taxi Ken gave me a hug and said, 'Goodbye, laddo.' A week later, aged sixty-nine, he died of a heart attack.

As Ken spent his earnings in the pub, he had never bought his own home and all we had to do was clear his possessions from a rented house behind Brixton prison. Mum found a home for his angry Alsatian and I discovered his collection of *Bulldog*, the National Front's journal. He had membership cards for both the Tory party and the NF and he'd also squirrelled away several articles about me, his godson. Mum said, 'If only you were a Tory, he'd be so proud.'

Mum never reconciled the brother she knew before he went to fight in Burma with the man who came back, constantly reliving the war but angry that it had taken the best years of his life. In the jungle he had been so close to starving that he'd sworn never to be hungry or thirsty again. He was happiest with his dog, his Burma Star reunions and his honorary membership of the Brixton Prison Officers Club, where the wake was held after his funeral. Having criticised the harassment of two Irish prisoners inside Brixton, the reception I got was stilted, to say the least.

*

The Tories pulled ahead of Labour during the election campaign in those early summer weeks of 1987, and it was clear we were going to lose again. The campaign against 'loony left' councils eroded Labour support just as the economy was reviving. Years later a study by Goldsmiths College found that every example of alleged looniness was untrue. Islington Council had not banned 'Baa Baa Black Sheep' in nurseries, and Bernie Grant, leader of Haringey Council, had not replaced black bin liners because they were racist but because green ones were cheaper. The 'news' that schools were 'promoting homosexuality' was a complete invention. No newspaper or Tory MP ever produced evidence of any lesson where homosexuality had been 'promoted'.

Instead of exposing these lies, Labour's response was to say that the majority of Labour councils were fine and that there were just a few bad apples. Kinnock having conceded there might be some truth in the charges, the Tories gleefully wasted more of his time by demanding that he disassociate himself from this or that newspaper invention. In February of that year Labour had lost the safe seat of Greenwich in a by-election and Kinnock's press secretary Patricia Hewitt wrote a letter (immediately leaked to the *Sun*) saying this was because of loony-left councils, and urging the party to distance itself from lesbian and gay issues. Ron Todd, the Transport and General Workers' Union leader, complained about the time Kinnock wasted responding to the Tory campaign rather than concentrating on our own policies.

Because Labour was running scared in the loony-left campaign Jack Cunningham was dispatched to the London Labour party executive to tell them that the manifesto would not include a promise to restore a Greater London Council. He claimed that northern Labour MPs would not vote for this until a regional authority for the north-east was established.

I now doubted Kinnock could ever lead us to victory. He had not grown in stature and was not on top of economic policy, as was painfully revealed when Radio 4's Jim Naughtie asked him if interest rates should go up or down, provoking the response, 'I'm not going to be bloody kebabed by a question like that.' The final straw came when the journalist Duncan Campbell found that the government had lied to Parliament and, in a project code-named Zircon, was secretly planning to launch a huge new spy satellite over Russia which would give Thatcher the ability to start a nuclear war on her own without having to rely on targeting data from American satellites. As the Russians would have known the satellite's purpose, the only reason for secrecy was to hide Thatcher's megalomaniacal ambitions from the public. Escalating the Cold War just as the new CPSU general secretary Mikhail Gorbachev was trying to end the arms race could have given Kremlin hardliners the excuse to remove him.

Police raided Campbell's home and seized his work to prevent it being broadcast by the BBC, which was also raided, and Kinnock and Healey were asked to support this in the interest of national security. Kinnock could have exposed Thatcher for lying to Parliament, escalating the arms race, undermining Gorbachev, using police to raid journalists and putting pressure on the BBC, all behind the backs of the British people. But with Healey smirking in the background, Kinnock accepted the government's version of the Zircon affair and blustered that action should have been taken sooner. Thatcher had been caught like a burglar climbing out of a window with a bag marked 'swag' and Kinnock opened the car door for her getaway. As I watched I realised he was never going to be prime minister.

*

I was doing media-friendly things such as sitting in for Jimmy Young on his Radio 2 show and being a judge on the Whitbread Book Awards panel, which was a mix of professional writers and public figures including Thatcher's Attorney General Sir Michael Havers, who had once seemed radical when he defended the Rolling Stones in the 'Mars Bar trial' after the group was arrested for possession of drugs. Kazuo Ishiguro's *An Artist of the Floating World* was so outstanding that he had ten of the twelve judges' votes, but when I asked Sir Michael who he had voted for he replied, 'Not that little Jap'.

I spoke at a left-wing conference in Zimbabwe organised by the supporters of Joshua Nkomo, the leader Moscow would have liked to see in power rather than Mugabe. People at the conference were worried about the direction Mugabe was taking and feared for the future. I had expected Zimbabwe to be arid but I found it lush and beautiful. We were taken to a game reserve, where I mortified our hosts by getting out of the car to wander around in search of local lizards.

My next visit was to Australia as a guest of the Green party in Brisbane. I was greeted by an immigration officer saying, 'I'll see you at the trade union rally tomorrow, mate,' and I must be the only person to have found an Australia exclusively inhabited by Greens, communists, trade unionists, lesbians and gays. Brisbane had an atmosphere that reminded me of the 1950s under the corrupt administration of Joh Bjelke-Petersen, who held power as premier of Queensland for two decades by over-representing rural areas and under-representing the cities. He used the police to smash trade unions, banned demonstrations, prevented aborigines registering to vote and boasted that he was the royal family's favourite Australian politician.

After a week unsuccessfully encouraging an electoral deal between Labour and the Greens, I went to Sydney, where the city councillors had been sacked overnight by the Labour government of New South Wales. My hosts in Brisbane warned me that the Kings Cross district where I was staying was a dangerous haven of crime and prostitution, but it seemed tame compared with London's King's Cross.

Sydney's city council covered only the inner city, and its majority of Greens, communists and trade unionists frustrated redevelopment schemes by big business. Whereas Thatcher wasted two years fighting the GLC, in Sydney the city's councillors heard on the radio that they were no longer in office and the government had appointed a committee of developers in their place. One woman warned me not to trust Kinnock because his press officer was Patricia Hewitt, 'daughter of the most hated man in Australia', the civil servant who decided how much wages could be increased each year. I spent Easter weekend at a beautiful inland bay where thousands of expensive leisure boats bobbed unused in the water.

*

I arrived home to lunch in May 1987 with Robert Maxwell, who was despairing of Labour's chances. 'What can I do to help my old party?' he asked. I urged him to use the *Mirror* to highlight the housing problem and campaign to start building council houses again. The Tories were still hunting down the mythical schools where homosexuality was promoted. The *Sun* finally found a gay man, with a criminal record, who had been appointed as a school governor by a Labour council and the Tories were pushing through a law banning the 'promotion' of homosexuality in schools. This was courageously talked out by Battersea's Labour MP Alf Dubs, but it cost him his seat.

Instead of challenging this rubbish Labour did not even send a message of support to a lesbian and gay election rally where I read out the anti-discrimination policy which Labour had decided to forget. Failing to challenge these myths was damaging. One Labour voter told me, 'I've always voted Labour but with all this teaching lesbianism in the schools I can't this time.'

Tax was even more damaging. Labour rightly opposed Thatcher's tax cuts for the rich and promised to reverse the 2p cut in income tax in Nigel Lawson's pre-election budget. Kinnock and Hattersley were given a detailed breakdown showing that no one earning less than £500 a week would lose out under our proposals, but during an interview Kinnock slipped and said that there would be some losers. It was all the *Mail* needed for their banner headline 'Labour's lies on taxation', with a story claiming police on £10,000 a year would pay £500 more. The *Express* went further, claiming everyone would be hit by higher taxes, and although Bryan Gould, who headed the Labour campaign, kept explaining that only the richest 5 per cent would pay more it was too late. No one believed a word we were saying.

*

My campaign in Brent East was hampered by some embittered activists refusing to work because of the rate-capping fiasco at the

GLC, but the Harris poll reported a big swing in Brent East, giving me a 19 per cent lead. This coincided with a *Newsnight* poll predicting a hung parliament, with Gallup cutting the Tory lead to 4 per cent which triggered the 'Wobbly Thursday' panic when Labour closed the gap on the Tories and Thatcher started to bypass Norman Tebbit and run the campaign herself. Given these polls, we decided to send our activists into Tory marginals, a decision that almost cost me the seat.

The Tory candidate in Brent East, Harriet Crawley, was a really nice thirty-nine-year-old moderate with not a trace of racism or homophobia in her. There was sympathy when the *News of the World* reported that she was pregnant by a senior Tory she would not name. But not everyone reads beyond the headlines and one woman asked her, 'Aren't you the one having Ken Livingstone's baby?' In a sane world the Tories would have found her a safe seat but the grass roots were selecting only Thatcherite true believers and so Harriet was up for a seat she had little chance of winning. After the election she dropped out of politics. Her life was marked by tragedy when her mother died that autumn after the election in a car crash, both of her brothers were killed in a plane crash on their way to her fortieth birthday party and her second husband died in the 2004 Indian Ocean tsunami, in which she was badly injured.

The Harris poll was wrong and I arrived at the count to the news that there was a swing to the Tories in London and the south-east, with Labour making gains in the north of the country but losing seats in the south. Bernie Grant, Diane Abbott (who replaced Ernie Roberts in Hackney North) and I all suffered swings to the Tories. I squeaked home with a majority of 1,653 (4.2 per cent) while the party returned only 20 more MPs than in the 1983 Tory landslide. The leadership of the Labour party jumped on these results as proof that left candidates were unpopular, ignoring the fiasco over Labour's tax plans, Kinnock's unpopularity, the fact that they did not challenge the Tories' loony-left smears and had turned their back on a policy that would have won support in London – namely restoration of the GLC.

In seats where a Labour MP had been deselected, new candidates suffered a 10 per cent drop in the Labour vote. When I asked Harris why they got it wrong, they said the students they employed for on-street polls approached people they felt comfortable with and that this skewed the results – so in future they switched to random phone polling.

*

None of this stopped me bouncing into Parliament all bright-eyed and bushy-tailed eleven years after I'd first been selected in Hampstead. The media were obsessed with the influx of left candidates and with Labour's first four black and Asian MPs. Induction training consisted of a two-hour meeting in which Labour whips showed us the ropes. After that we were on our own. Chief whip Derek Foster warned there was a shortage of office space for new MPs and we were given a list of secretaries who were out of work following the retirement or defeat of their MPs.

One who stood out from the list was Maureen Charleson, a bright Scottish mum who had worked for the old left-wingers Ian Mikardo and Jo Richardson, hammering away on an old-fashioned typewriter with Mik correcting the punctuation, spelling and grammar of every letter. Some MPs were nightmares to work for, so I gave Maureen Bill Bush's phone number, hoping he could reassure her that I wasn't a monster. We liked each other immediately and I promised she would never need to do another job interview, as working for me was going to be interesting. Her parents were Scottish Presbyterians, so given my views on Ireland it was some time before she told them who she was working for. Charles Clarke, Kinnock's chief of staff, warned her not to work for me as she would be ostracised by Labour MPs and their secretaries.

The Fees Office explained the car mileage allowance, which was a disgrace – the more powerful your engine the greater the allowance, so MPs bought the most powerful cars and claimed £1.40 for each mile they travelled. One MP said he paid a second secretary out of the profit he made driving to and from Parliament once a week. MPs were allowed to claim hundreds of miles per month without providing any evidence of the journeys they made, but when I asked for a London Transport travelcard I was told I could only use it while the Commons was actually sitting.

As an outer London MP I had the choice of a £1,200 annual London weighting allowance, or a 'second homes allowance' like MPs from outside London. I didn't own a first home let alone a second one so I settled for London weighting. I was more interested in negotiations between the Tribune and the Socialist Campaign Group on a joint slate of candidates for the shadow cabinet elections. As Peter Hain and I had anticipated, these two groups now comprised a majority among Labour MPs. The negotiations were between John Prescott and Michael Meacher for the Tribune Group and Dennis Skinner leading the Campaign Group team. Dennis went out of his way to accommodate the Tribunites, giving them the best positions on the slate and making no demands on policy issues, so everything hinged on the decision of the Tribune Group.

Like several MPs I joined both groups in order to argue for unity on the left, but at the packed meeting of the Tribune Group several long-serving MPs who had never been in Tribune before had now joined in order to block any deal on a joint slate. Meacher, Blunkett, myself and others argued for the deal but Jack Straw said he didn't want the votes of Campaign Group members and he was supported by Gordon Brown and Tony Blair. The group narrowly voted against a joint slate. In the ninety years since Keir Hardie became the first Labour MP, this was the decisive moment for those who believed socialism could be achieved by parliamentary means. After decades of Tribune MPs posturing on the need for public ownership, action against apartheid and the abolition of nuclear weapons, they now had enough votes to lead the party; however, faced with the whiff of power, the group ran off in the other direction, and during the Kinnock and Blair years slowly became moribund for lack of interest.

11

Rise and Fall

1987–1989

The Palace of Westminster is one of the most imposing buildings in Britain. In its Great Hall, built in 1097, Charles I was condemned to death and monarchs lie in state. The rest of the Palace was destroyed in the Great Fire of 1834 but rebuilt to look medieval and imposing and newly elected MPs often think they have achieved something just by being there. But coming from County Hall, where members had adequate resources, the building reminded me of the Natural History Museum, only with live exhibits. There was a tribal quality to meetings of Labour MPs in the vast Committee Room 14, where pounding on desks and angry growling were used to silence dissidents.

Given the scandal of MPs' expenses that came to light in 2009, it is hard to believe how poorly MPs were treated in the eighties, but the big increase in allowances, funding for constituency offices and money to employ more full-time staff came only after the 2001 general election. When I arrived many members did not have an office, let alone enough money for a secretary and a researcher.

The Labour whip who allocated desk spaces was Ray Powell, a right-winger who rewarded loyalists and punished rebels. My first weeks passed without a desk as I squatted in corridors anywhere near a phone while guides pointed me out to tourists. Diane Abbott confronted Powell. He told her that she was second from bottom on the list and I was at the very bottom. But Ray was sponsored by the shop-workers' union and the government's attempt to deregulate the Sunday trading laws coincided with the opening of new offices on Millbank. Ray brazenly allocated these new offices to those of us voting against Sunday trading.

The last thing party leaders wanted was well-researched and resourced backbench MPs, so most MPs relied on the small pool of researchers in the library for briefings. But no researcher could spend days let alone weeks developing new policies. While ignoring abuses of the second-homes allowances the authorities did nothing to help MPs be effective. We were not allowed to do paperwork while waiting to speak, nor were we allowed to take a briefcase into the chamber. An international phone call had to be booked through the Commons switchboard and we were charged for it. The long-serving Welsh MP and former Northern Ireland secretary Merlyn Rees told me that in 1962 MPs could not make long-distance calls except from phone booths just outside the Commons chamber. He was allowed five minutes to speak to constituents, after which an attendant would tap on the booth as his time was up.

Louis Harris (President Kennedy's pollster) had worked for the GLC and when I said that it seemed to me American politicians were more talented than ours he replied, 'No, they are just better resourced.' I enjoyed meals with Louis as he always had great tales from the White House. He described a visit to President Carter: 'I went through the office of Hamilton Jordan [chief of staff] where a single sheet of paper rested on his desk through to Carter's office where every surface was disappearing under a sea of paper.' A major factor in Carter's failure was his inability to delegate. He even ended up deciding who could have which slots in the White House tennis courts because his aides were arguing over it.

Contrary to the myth about all-night sittings in Parliament, it was rare that anyone had to stay after 2 a.m. At my first 'all-nighter' I perched on the back row furthest from the Speaker so he couldn't see me working on my papers while a very drunk Sir Nicholas Fairbairn spoke incoherently for twenty minutes. He was followed by the equally plastered and incoherent Labour MP Ron Brown. This seemed a complete waste of time so I went home, got a few hours' sleep and came back at 7.30 a.m. to find the debate still going on. In my fourteen years as an MP I never once stayed throughout the night.

What was important were the problems people brought to my weekly surgery, which began at 5 p.m. and could go on well beyond 10 p.m. At first I held surgeries on Thursday but they were so emotionally draining I switched to Monday evening as I could cope better after the weekend. As a borough councillor and at the GLC I felt I was able to resolve most problems that people brought to me, but after eight years in which no homes were built to rent and with immigration controls tightening annually I was lucky to solve a third of my constituents' problems. One surprise was how many constituents who were on unemployment benefit were encouraged by the social security office to register as long-term sick or disabled. As Secretary of State for Employment in the previous government Norman Tebbit had been embarrassed by the Tories' failure to cut unemployment so he got the numbers down by getting the unemployed onto sickness benefit, creating a problem that is still with us today. After more than six months out of work (and watching daytime TV) it becomes almost impossible for people to get back into full-time employment.

MPs with family in London were eager to get home. Those from distant constituencies with an empty flat waiting for them treated the Commons as a social club, filling the bars and staying into the small hours. This led to two types of MPs: those who were immersed in the culture of Westminster and those who weren't. I was firmly in the latter category, though even if I'd been representing a seat far away I wouldn't have wanted to hang around the bars night after night.

It was in the bars that some Labour MPs grumbled of their loathing for 'loony-left MPs from London', whom they blamed for Labour's poor result in 1987. Gordon Brown was said by the *Independent*'s Bruce Anderson to 'hate the London Labour party in particular with an envenomed, implacable loathing'. Nor was there any doubt who Brown had in mind when he ridiculed 'sending out search parties for ever more discontented minorities'. Kinnock loyalists said my meetings with Sinn Fein had cost votes and they were furious when I raised the issue of Ireland in my maiden speech. During the election I was followed by journalists eager to exploit any slip of the tongue so I was surprised they did not report a meeting I held in Kilburn to discuss Ireland. The other speaker was Captain Fred Holroyd, an ex-intelligence officer who had condemned the methods MI5 were using to counter the IRA in Northern Ireland and who was now fighting to clear his name after trumped-up allegations of mental instability.

Fred's speech was an eye-opener. He was right-wing, loyal to Britain and had been 'army barmy' as a kid. He'd fallen out with the army because he believed that the dirty war covertly waged by MI5 against the IRA increased their support. He told the audience that he'd worked on the same corridor in Army Intelligence in Northern Ireland as Captain Robert Nairac, who had illegally crossed the border to assassinate senior IRA member John Francis Green. On his return he had shown Fred the photographs of Green's body but the gun used to kill Green was also used on 21 July 1975 when three members of Ireland's number one pop group the Miami Showband were murdered. Nairac had crossed the border with members of the loyalist Ulster Volunteer Force and stopped a coach carrying the band at a bogus checkpoint. As members of the UVF planted a bomb in the band's minibus it went off, killing two UVF members. The other UVF members (aided by two British soldiers, according to Holroyd) then murdered three band members in cold blood. They hoped this atrocity would end the ceasefire between Britain and the IRA that had been negotiated by Wilson's government. These killings, said Holroyd, were part of a campaign by rogue elements in MI5 to destabilise Wilson's government under the cloak of Operation Clockwork Orange.

Holroyd also alleged that rogue officers in the army and intelligence services worked with Airey Neave, who was Thatcher's closest confidant and shadow Northern Ireland secretary, making clear that in his view Neave knew about the dirty-war killings. My suspicions were aroused when the journalists present reported not a word of this meeting, so I decided to use my maiden speech to raise these charges in the House of Commons. If true, officers in the British army and MI5 were guilty of murder and treason.

Thatcher had denied the existence of Clockwork Orange when questioned by Labour MPs and was trying to prevent the sale in Britain of *Spycatcher*, a book by former MI5 officer Peter Wright which detailed illegal bugging and burgling by MI5 of British citizens. Although Wright was a fantasist who believed Harold Wilson was a Russian agent, he was a senior officer in MI5 who spent a lot of time in Ireland during this period.

I could not be certain that Holroyd's allegations were true, so I qualified my speech:

May I make it clear to the House that I am reporting allegations that Hon. Members have read in newspapers and that are reported on radio and television both here and abroad. They are made by intelligence officers who served at the time in Ireland on behalf of the British Government. It may well be that the allegations are all a tissue of lies, but can we imagine any other Western Government who would allow such damaging allegations to circulate month after month and year after year and not move to lance the boil? They would either deal with the allegations or demonstrate that they were untrue. The Prime Minister's day-by-day refusal to investigate what was happening in MI5 at that time can only lead a large number of reasonable people both here and abroad to believe that there is some element of truth in the allegations now circulating.

Captain Nairac was posthumously decorated after being tortured and murdered by the IRA in May 1977 and Airey Neave had been killed in a car bomb, so there were outraged protests from Tory MPs Ian Gow (later assassinated by the IRA) and Tim Yeo. Next morning's front page of the *Sun* screamed, 'Red Ken Smears Heroes'.

The next day I received a hand-delivered letter from Robert Maxwell saying: 'I'm not prepared to have someone like you writing in my paper,' and I was sacked. A day later the *London Daily News* editor Magnus Linklater phoned to say that he thought there might be a problem and was surprised to discover that I had already been sacked. In fact I was lucky because I received a cheque for the columns I had already written, whereas when the paper closed a few weeks later the other columnists spent months pestering Maxwell before they got half of what they were owed.

At Prime Minister's Questions Thatcher said my speech was utterly contemptible and demanded that Kinnock repudiate it. Kinnock said my speech was 'probably unfair', provoking outrage from the Tories. When I was called to question Thatcher her reply convinced me that the charges were true. Thatcher always stood upright, confident and in command of the Commons but now she crouched and did not make eye contact. In that moment any doubts I had about Holroyd's allegations were dispelled. Labour was warned off the issue when MI5 leaked a photograph showing former Labour cabinet minister Douglas Jay in the company of two attractive Yugoslav communists. It was MI5's way of saying, 'We've a lot of dirt on you, you really don't want to mess with us.'

In pursuing the allegations I was helped by Colin Wallace, who had also been in the intelligence services in Northern Ireland and was part of the Clockwork Orange project, but once he was deemed unreliable he had been framed and convicted of manslaughter. With his help and Holroyd's I put over 360 questions to ministers about the dirty war. I was only able to do this because the chair of Brent East Labour party Neil Grant, a teacher at the Jewish Free School, would turn up as soon as school was out to do the research for these questions. Campaigning journalist Paul Foot was also digging around, and eventually published what he'd discovered in his book *Who Framed Colin Wallace?*

There were snide press comments about my obsession with the issue but after two years civil servants searching files at the Public Record Office in Kew to answer one of my questions found a copy of the Clockwork Orange file which had not been destroyed. In his diaries, on 31 January 1990, Alan Clark records the panic in the Ministry of Defence as junior minister Archie Hamilton conceded the operation's existence in the Commons: 'Two crises occupy the department . . . the first is something to do with a "dirty tricks campaign". These are always a bore. As far as I'm concerned "dirty tricks" are part and parcel of effective government. But apparently Number 10 were misinformed by us – or so they claim.'

Following the admission that MI5 officers had tried to destabilise Wilson's government, a committee was established to investigate Wallace's insistence that he had been framed. He was cleared, but not before it was revealed that MI5 had tried to nobble the committee. The government was let off the hook when Kinnock decided not to pursue the issue. It was not until Metropolitan Police Commissioner Sir John Stevens reported in April 2003 that it was accepted that there had been collusion between police and security services with loyalist terrorists to assassinate republicans.

But all this was in the future. On 8 November 1987 an IRA bomb at the Enniskillen Remembrance Day ceremony left eleven dead and sixty injured. Most of the dead were elderly. A week later I was interviewed on LBC and unleashed a wave of outrage when I said that as in all colonial situations Britain would in the end withdraw and 'to carry on as we are, not negotiating and not actually ending the conflict . . . seems to me to be the worst of all possible worlds'. Although my postbag was broadly supportive the *Sun* screamed: 'He is in every sense an enemy of the people. A creature of poisonous malice who has no place in parliament, no place in public life, no place in any civilised society . . . Mr Kinnock should insist on his expulsion. Right now.' Kinnock announced that I had the right to be wrong but told the parliamentary party that the IRA were 'armed gangsters who commit political atrocities and spend the rest of their time in graft, corruption and protection rackets'.

Kinnock was angry, but the Ulster Defence Association decided to go further and ordered my assassination. Although this did not become public until after I became mayor, I knew something was up when I had a visit from Special Branch late one Saturday afternoon. Sir John Stevens, who was then conducting his inquiry into the way Northern Ireland was being policed, had told them that my movements were being monitored by extremist groups and I should vary my pattern of travel. The warning was so low-key that I assumed I was merely in danger of being beaten up. I always lived with that possibility and when buying a home looked for a terraced house in a straight street with good sight lines, avoiding end-of-terrace locations and side entrances. After my election as mayor the *Standard* revealed that a UDA assassin had followed me to plan the shooting but that it had been cancelled at the last minute. When I later discussed this with Sir John I got the distinct impression that a British agent on the UDA army council had talked them out of it, and when I met MI5 boss Eliza Manningham-Buller I said I would like to buy the man concerned a meal, but she never got back to me.

The government's line to the British public was that the IRA comprised only psychopaths and criminals, but in America British ministers described them as Marxist guerrillas similar to the Sandinistas of Nicaragua, presumably to wean Irish Americans off their support for the republican movement. To prevent the public forming their own opinion, Thatcher introduced a ban on broadcasting the voices of Sinn Fein leaders which led to the risible situation in which actors were employed to lip-sync over silent film images of Adams's face. But behind the scenes the government wanted to go even further and I received a leaked BBC circular to its regions declaring that 'it has already become clear that it is the government's intention to stop us carrying actuality of figures such as Ken Livingstone and Edward Kennedy, should they express direct support for any of the named organisations'.

I complained to the BBC and to the government but received evasive replies. Home Office minister Tim Renton wrote: 'As to your request for notes of meetings on this subject, I should add that it is not our practice to release notes of meetings with the broadcasting authorities.' Deputy director general of the BBC John Birt claimed: 'Despite an extensive search we have been unable to find any trace of such guidance being issued.' When I pressed him he added, 'The BBC made no formal record of its discussion with the Home Office.' But for all the denials, I received almost no invitations to appear on the BBC over the next eighteen months.

*

Although there was mostly negative press coverage about anything I did on Ireland, most of my work was on economics. A key weakness of most politicians is that they are more interested in foreign or social policy and hope somebody else will deal with economics. I believed that British manufacturing suffered from a chronic lack of investment, but I was embarrassed at a lunch with the editor of *The Economist* when I didn't have the facts at my fingertips to back up this assertion.

Contact with London's businesses convinced me that a centrally planned economy was not more effective than market forces and we needed to harness entrepreneurial talent if we were to replace declining industries with new ones, but I couldn't understand why our economy always lagged behind Germany's or what we needed to do to catch up. Fortunately help was at hand in the form of John Ross.

John was the first person from Wood Green Grammar School to win a scholarship to Oxford, where he gained a first-class honours degree and expected to spend the rest of his life as a professor until he got caught up in the politics of the 1960s. He joined the International Marxist Group and devoted himself to the revolution. He had worked for one wing of the Trotskyist Fourth International in Paris (the United Secretariat of the FI, which was led by Ernest Mandel) and in 1982 was one of those who persuaded the rest of the IMG to give up their attempt to take over the trade unions and join the Labour party instead. He caught my attention when I read his book *Thatcher and Friends*, an analysis of voting trends over the previous 130 years. It was published in 1983, just after Thatcher's landslide victory, but argued that the Tory party was in real long-term decline. He showed how the party had spread out from its base in outer London and the Home Counties to achieve its best results in the 1930s, and had been collapsing back to its core ever since. He predicted that each time the party returned to government (and each time it was thrown out of office) it would be with a lower percentage vote than the time before. The mainstream media ignored the book and the left thought it optimistic but its predictions have been borne out in every election since.

As a workaholic professional revolutionary John put life's other pleasures second to the work of building a socialist society. A statistician of formidable intelligence, he steamrollered his opponents in debate with a directness bordering on rudeness, but unlike many on the left John was seriously interested in power. He always campaigned for the maximum realistically achievable, rather than make impossible demands on the system so as to condemn others as cowards or traitors when they failed.

Three times a week John came to the Commons to discuss developments in the British and world economies with me, explaining the economic theories that gave coherence to these events. This was followed up by phone calls so long that his teenage daughters demanded a second phone to save their social lives. As well as receiving John's help I was invited to join the Ariel Road Group of socialist economists organised by Doreen Massey, the great economic geographer, with people from the GLC's industry and employment group who were rethinking socialist economic theory in the light of the stagnating Soviet economy.

*

The general election result in 1987 was Labour's second-worst since 1918 but Peter Mandelson had run Labour's campaign to show Kinnock in the best possible light. Colin Welland, fresh from writing the screenplay for *Chariots of Fire*, wrote a party-political broadcast that was directed by Hugh Hudson with a score by Michael Kamen (who wrote the music for *Mona Lisa*). It opened with a war plane flying overhead and panned away via seagulls to Neil and his wife Glenys walking hand in hand along a sunny clifftop. The broadcast was solely about Kinnock, his background and his family with contributions from Aunt Sadie and Uncle Bill. The film closed with Neil and Glenys gazing out to sea, fading to black with the word 'Kinnock' and no mention of the Labour party. It had a huge impact and became the first party-political broadcast to be repeated. But as David Butler and Dennis Kavanagh said in *The British General Election of 1987*, 'it was a stunning invocation of the Labourism of the 1940s . . . for all its technical brilliance . . . its implicit defensiveness was revealing of the party's underlying weakness . . .

its single minded promotion of the leader . . . spoke volumes about the failure . . . to establish him securely over the three preceding years, and about the party's vulnerability on policy.' Kinnock had a 'good campaign' and John Smith and Bryan Gould were unwilling to challenge him after our defeat.

Bryan Gould, a bright and amiable New Zealander, had fronted Labour's 1987 campaign well enough to be talked up as a future leader. His next step was to get elected to Labour's NEC so the press set up that year's NEC elections as a direct contest between Bryan and myself. John Ross ensured that the left groups CLPD and Socialist Action mobilised their members to vote for me at their local GMCs but with Gould's profile in the general election and the Kinnock supporters' charge that I had cost us votes, the media decided Gould would beat me. I arrived at Brighton for that year's party conference hoping I might just win and was elated when I ended up in fourth place behind David Blunkett, Tony Benn and Dennis Skinner, polling 385,000 votes to Gould's 285,000 (he was also elected to the NEC). As Mandelson had been talking Gould's chances up to the media, the result was a shock; the *Guardian* made it the front-page lead and commentators questioned whether Kinnock was going to be able to drag the party to the right.

After the results were announced I warned that ditching our commitment to nuclear disarmament could tear the party apart. The backlash was immediate with Tony Clarke (my predecessor as candidate in Hampstead) denouncing 'aspiring, immature Parliamentarians who jump on band wagons' using language 'disgraceful, immature and beneath the dignity of a Parliamentarian'. Denis Healey warned, 'I don't think the movement will forgive anyone who tries to exploit the difficulties of the argument for personal political advantage,' and picking up on a comment I'd made that Mario Puzo's *The Godfather* was a good guide to how politics works, he said such thinking had no place in our party.

Speculation revived that I might stand for leader and I was invited onto Robin Day's *Question Time* along with shadow chancellor John Smith. John was friendly and after the post-programme dinner in the bar I told him Kinnock didn't have the qualities to be a prime minister and couldn't win the next election. 'Well, we agree on that,' he said. John was honest, competent and comfortable with his traditional Labour values, and a government led by him would have created achievements to be proud of. When Tony Benn challenged Kinnock for the leadership I consulted members of the Campaign Group and found virtually all of them prepared to switch to Smith to defeat Kinnock, so I cornered John in the lobby and urged him to stand. But it wasn't his style to make a naked grab for power and he knew he was certain to become leader if Kinnock lost another election.

John did not hate the left and would have led an inclusive government. When we met in the Commons corridors he made clear his fear that as chancellor he would have endless rows with Kinnock. I met John shortly after Nigel Lawson resigned as Thatcher's chancellor, using his resignation speech to spell out how she had undermined him. John expressed his amazement at how damaging it was to have a chancellor and prime minister at loggerheads, adding, 'If I have problems with Neil, I'll need support from people like yourself.'

Because I was back in the game my opponents redoubled efforts to block my progress. I applied to be a member of the Treasury Select Committee and I wasn't surprised I did not succeed, but there were only a handful of names ahead of me on the waiting list. I kept badgering Derek Foster, Labour's amiable chief whip, who said he was happy to put me on but the appointment had to be cleared by the Leader's Office. Two years later Derek told me that Kinnock's office had blown a gasket when he put up Diane Abbott's name for approval and Kinnock only gave in when told I was the only other person wanting to go on. I never was allowed on the committee and things got so bad that in 1996 Stephen Timms, who had only been elected to Parliament in 1994, was asked to go on the committee as I was the only person left on the list.

Given my interest in economics, people wanted to hear debates between Bryan Gould, Gordon Brown and myself, but while Bryan and I had several good encounters Brown never took part. The first bid was from the Scottish Fabians, who wanted a head-to-head between Brown and myself, but Brown declined. This pattern was never broken. Although perfectly civil when we bumped into each other, never once in twenty years did Brown debate with me on general economic questions or even on the partial privatisation of London Underground when I was mayor. In my first seven years as mayor every request to meet him was declined and it was only after he became prime minister that he and I shared a platform.

*

Following the election defeat Kinnock announced a major review of all policies and seven NEC working parties were established. My first choice was defence, which was refused, but I was allowed to join my second-choice working party, economics, which was chaired by Bryan Gould. At my first meeting on the NEC we reviewed polling data about why we had done so badly at the polls, but unbeknown to committee members all the results relating to Kinnock's poor polling figures were withheld. I worried that the sniffy attitude of the media towards Kinnock reflected a long-standing prejudice against the Welsh, but even in Wales I found many local members saw Kinnock as an embarrassment.

Most Labour MPs feared we couldn't win with Kinnock but out of loyalty or ambition wouldn't do anything about it. At a Tribune meeting I said we needed to talk about the standing of the leader but they wouldn't discuss the matter and as we left the room Clare

Short said, 'I agree with you, but you just can't say things like that.' The first time I raised it at an NEC meeting Kinnock wasn't present and I was told there was no point in going down that road. The second time I raised it Kinnock was present, but this time I was shouted down by Blunkett, who blustered that what I was saying was outrageous. I found it bizarre that everybody knew Kinnock was a hindrance to winning the next election but no one was prepared to act, even though that meant another five years of Tory government.

The policy review began with a 'Statement of Democratic Socialist Aims and Values', a dull document written by Roy Hattersley urging us to accept some of the changes Thatcher had made, claiming that the market, 'where properly regulated, is a generally satisfactory means of determining provision and consumption'. Over the next two years we pored over every aspect of policy. The Eurosceptic Bryan Gould was committed to equality and strong regulation of market forces and came up with the idea of 'supply-side socialism' (a way of avoiding tax increases by borrowing to fuel growth).

Although Bryan accepted Thatcher's privatisations, he believed that BT should be the exception. Once BT was renationalised he proposed that there should be investment to create a fibre-optic cable network linking all homes, schools and businesses in the UK. This idea had been GLC policy back in 1983 after Geoff Mulgan, one of Mike Ward's bright young researchers, proposed it. But Thatcher was backing Murdoch's proposal for satellite TV so Britain failed to benefit from the hundreds of thousands of new jobs that would have come if we had been the first country to build a fibre-optic network. Gordon Brown made a rare appearance at the committee to argue against fibre optics but Bryan won with my support. As soon as conference agreed the policy review, Bryan was demoted and the fibre-optic proposal was promptly dropped.

Preparing the party to accept privatisation and keep nuclear weapons created a deep ambivalence inside Kinnock. Many left-wingers move to the right to win office so they can achieve some of what they want but Kinnock claimed he was still a socialist. With a big majority on the NEC he could have ignored Tony Benn, Dennis Skinner, the Young Socialist representative and myself but when we complained he passionately insisted, 'Everyone here is a socialist,' to the bemusement of trade union right-wingers whose careers had been spent fighting the left.

Kinnock never took on board Churchill's dictum 'in victory, magnanimity' and continued to bludgeon us into the ground even after winning vote after vote. Tony, Dennis and myself were not allowed to speak to conference and at the two conferences that took place when I was on the NEC I was put at the furthest end of the back row so TV could never get a picture of Kinnock and me in the same shot. When I went to an election meeting for Peter Crampton, our European Parliament candidate for Hull, he told me he had been offered a visit by Kinnock as long as he agreed to cancel my meeting.

*

When I told Arthur Scargill that Benn would run against Kinnock after the 1987 election he urged me to stand instead. On the train back from Chesterfield, where Tony Benn had convened a conference for all left-wing groups and trade unions, Jim Mortimer, the ex-general secretary of the Labour party, came to sit with me to say he thought I faced this responsibility and must prepare for it. Benn's leadership challenge never caught fire and at conference in 1988 he was massively defeated, but my NEC vote increased and I came third on the list. The scale of Benn's defeat meant there was no chance of Kinnock being removed before the next election but things were slotting nicely into place for my leadership challenge after Kinnock lost it.

Labour's leader was elected with 30 per cent of the votes decided by MPs, 30 per cent by local Labour parties and 40 per cent cast by the trade unions. Local party votes were decided by their activists on their GMCs and while trade unions consulted their members the votes were in the end determined by the union executives. John Ross worked hyperactively to organise support for me in the constituencies, but the key to victory lay with the unions.

I had good links with the left-wing unions. Rodney Bickerstaffe, the general secretary of Unison, had been a friend for many years and the election in 1984 of Ron Todd as general secretary at the TGWU, my own union, meant that I could count on half the trade union vote. Ron's role in shifting the London Labour party executive to the left had been crucial to my GLC leadership. The right wing in the union was formidably organised around George Wright, his opponent for the post of general secretary who had narrowly lost the election. When Wright's supporters alleged corruption Ron lanced the boil by insisting on a second election in which he doubled his majority.

Ron had built his reputation on the shop floor at Ford's plant in Dagenham and like Jack Jones before him never allowed his position to go to his head or change his lifestyle. He continued to live in the East End of London, collecting fossils and writing poetry. For some bizarre reason he had recruited the Queen Mother as a member of the union. Born in Walthamstow, he'd left school at fourteen, sweeping up in the local barber's before joining the Royal Marines at the end of the war, where he was given the job of organising the execution of Japanese war criminals in Singapore. He was firmly internationalist and one of the small group of left-wingers who, like me, supported the Solidarity movement in Poland.

Ron was appalled by Kinnock's policy review and said so publicly at a Tribune rally after Kinnock's conference speech. Ron also had a personal dislike for Kinnock: he found him crude. The key to Ron's election as general secretary had been the work of Pete Hagger, a London taxi driver who was the organiser of the broad left inside the TGWU executive and worked closely with me to ensure the success of the left inside the London Labour party. When Pete suddenly died the left lost its sense of direction inside the TGWU, but up until his death Pete was confident he would be able to deliver the TGWU vote behind any left candidate for the Labour leadership.

My problem was with the MPs, but with a two-to-one majority in local Labour parties I could get elected as long as I could persuade 25–30 per cent of MPs to vote for me. When John Ross said, 'I don't know what you're going to do about the MPs,' I told him not to worry, if it looked like I might win enough of them would come over.

Next I needed to write a book spelling out what Labour could achieve in the 1990s, so after buying a word processor and doing a touch-typing course I started getting up at four or five in the morning to work on the book before going in to the Commons. *Livingstone's Labour* was published just before the 1989 conference and exposed MI5's plots against Wilson as well as the dirty war in Northern Ireland, but it also set out what I believed was the most a radical government could achieve. It called for a written constitution with devolution for Scotland and Wales, proportional representation and an independent foreign policy to end subservience to the USA.

The book explained how to modernise the British economy. After two years of work with John Ross I believed even more firmly that the cause of Britain's long-term economic decline was underinvestment. For forty years Britain had lagged behind Germany and France in the proportion of GDP invested in research and new enterprises. When Germany reached 25 per cent a year, Britain could only manage 20 per cent.

The reason went back to the post-war Labour government, which realised it could afford to do only two of three things. After the sacrifices of the Second World War even the Tories knew that the creation of the welfare state had to be accepted, so the choice was between a worldwide military role and modernising Britain's industry and infrastructure. Attlee's government went for the military option, the maintenance of Britain's imperial grandeur, so while Germany invested in high-tech industry and modern transport Britain built nuclear weapons and fought wars from Greece in 1946 to Iraq in 2003. The result was a less-competitive economy and a series of recessions triggered by balance-of-payments crises as we spent beyond our means. If we had cut military spending to Germany's level, then in the forty years after 1945 there would only have been three years in which Britain did not have a surplus on its balance of payments.

France made the same mistake as Britain with its costly wars in Vietnam and Algeria but when de Gaulle took the decision to withdraw from Algeria he slashed defence spending by 40 per cent and used that money to match Germany's level of investment. In the decade that followed France overtook Britain as an economic power. *Livingstone's Labour* proposed that we replicate France's success by reducing our military spending to the same level as Germany's, releasing 2 per cent of GDP each year for extra investment.

This would make it possible to modernise Britain without tax increases on middle- and working-class families or increasing borrowing. Given the problems Goodwin's GLC administration had faced with debt, I opposed the party's infatuation with supply-side economics. President Reagan got away with running budget and balance-of-payments deficits because the US was a global superpower and the dollar was the international reserve currency, so they exported their inflation to those trading in dollars or buying US government bonds. It was naive to assume that Britain could get away with this and even Clinton when elected had to reduce the huge deficit he inherited.

These proposals were a good start but we needed to flesh them out and John wanted a computer with sufficient capacity to take data from the Treasury, World Bank, IMF and OECD and explore alternatives to the traditional orthodoxies. This would be the most powerful computer in Britain not owned by government, research institutes or big business. It would cost £25,000 (more than my MP's salary before tax).

Fortunately for us, advertising industry research showed that I was one of the few politicians people believed, so I was approached by the Dairy Council to advertise Red Leicester cheese alongside Edward Heath promoting Blue Stilton. This was followed by an ad for a new paintbrush made from artificial fibres (unlike those whose bristles are pulled from the backs of live pigs). But I baulked when the Coal Board wanted to follow up their award-winning TV ad in which a dog, a cat and a mouse curled up together in front of a coal fire with one in which Edwina Currie and I would be shown meeting in a hotel lounge in front of a roaring fire. The film would end just as our lips met to a soundtrack of 'Strangers in the Night'. I also decided not to dress up as Captain Bird's Eye to advertise potato waffles when I saw the list of additives they contained. People still remembered the GLC: the Comic Strip created a spoof movie starring Robbie Coltrane as Charles Bronson playing me in a struggle against Jennifer Saunders as Brigitte Nielsen (portrayed as an alien monster) masquerading as Thatcher. Kate Bush sang, 'Who's the man we all need? Ken! Who's a funky sex machine? Ken!'

This income still wasn't enough to buy the computer so I leased it on a five-year contract at £7,000 a year. My advertising income came to a dead stop in August 1990 when Saddam Hussein invaded Kuwait, as companies didn't want me advertising their goods while

I campaigned against the coming war. Fortunately by this time we were publishing *Socialist Economic Bulletin* (*SEB*) with subscriptions at £20 a year, which helped, but still left me deep in debt. Over the next decade *SEB* did original research on the British economy, accurately predicted the disaster of Britain's ERM membership and what would happen in post-communist Russia and in China, but we were shocked when we analysed the impact on the Third World of the high interest rate policies of Reagan and Thatcher and discovered that one and a quarter billion people had been pushed back into poverty because of them.

John and his wife Pat invited us to dinner and as Mum was staying with us we took her along. This was just a few days after he installed the computer in his house and he was so excited with his analysis of exchange rates that he analysed for us all evening. When I took Mum her cup of tea in the morning she wailed, 'That was the most boring night of my life.'

*

My election to the NEC was noted by the KGB and the next day Yuri Sagadak, a very personable thirty-seven-year-old journalist from *Pravda*, turned up to interview me. Small, bright, funny and very dapper, he professed to love all things English and was infatuated with Olga Maitland. After he left John and I agreed he was most probably KGB but it was only years later we discovered that he was a colonel in the organisation. Any doubts I had about Yuri's real job evaporated as he set out to cultivate me and organise my first visit to Russia in 1988.

While Yuri was quizzing me as a potential Labour leader, I was also quizzing him about his work in Indonesia in the early 1980s. When I asked how different the country would be had its communist party not been crushed by the Muslim generals in their coup of 1965, he expressed no regret about the half-million communists who were butchered, saying they were aligned with China rather than Moscow so their regime might have become a genocidal government like Pol Pot's in Cambodia.

I was also fascinated by his criticisms of Stalin and exasperation at the state of the Soviet economy. He was critical about the failings of Soviet central planning and he thought the prominence of Gorbachev's wife Raisa was a mistake as Russians did not want leaders' wives to be like America's First Lady. He was particularly pleased with himself when he wrote an article for the Soviet press describing the IRA as terrorists. The KGB were aware of just what an appalling economic mess Russia was in. When KGB boss Yuri Andropov came to power in 1982 it was he who started the reform process which Gorbachev accelerated.

I had an insight into the discipline required of an agent in a hostile country when I called at his home one Sunday to drop off an article I had written for *Pravda*. It was just after lunch and his two young boys were playing a video game on television. Yuri spoke briefly to them in Russian and they switched off the television and spent the next hour sitting perfectly still and silent while Yuri and I talked. When Thatcher expelled him from Britain the following year, he invited journalists into his house to watch while he chipped away the plaster on the walls to reveal the microphones hidden underneath.

My visit to the Soviet Union consisted of ten days of meetings to discuss Gorbachev's reforms and to look at the state of the economy. The USSR had matched America's military strength but on a smaller economic base, so there weren't the resources left to produce enough consumer goods to satisfy demand. The distortions of the centrally planned economy created ridiculous anomalies. We were turned away from an empty restaurant until my KGB guide revealed who he was, because staff were allowed to take home unused food, and without a profit motive the staff had no interest in anyone dining there at all. As bread was massively subsidised, collective farms found it cheaper to feed bread to the cattle rather than buy feed and pocketed the difference. But even with these distortions they had built half-decent computers and supersonic aircraft.

As well as visiting a bitterly cold (in August) Leningrad and a collection of ancient churches (due to a mistake in translation – I had actually asked to visit a nature reserve area) I was flown to Georgia, the only place which still had a statue of Stalin – a local boy – and where the local party officials were asserting their independence from Moscow by boycotting Gorbachev's anti-vodka drive. Folklore has it that when Georgians had to choose between being absorbed by the Ottoman or the Russian Empire they chose the one that allowed alcohol, and I could believe this after I was driven to an open-air banquet in the middle of a field with party bosses. A long table groaning with Georgian delicacies was laid out and we started a series of toasts in which we were expected to down a full glass of wine each time. After several hours the inside was scooped out of a water melon and filled with several different liqueurs. I knew I could not drink any more without becoming seriously ill so I asked to be excused and lay down in the long grass, where I immediately fell asleep. I was woken late at night by my Georgian hosts carrying my unconscious translator into the back of the car. Throughout the next day we had to interrupt meetings as he fled to the toilet.

The most interesting part of my visit was my meeting at the West European Institute. In Moscow there were institutes devoted to each region of the world where academics, diplomats and KGB officials monitored events in that region so they could provide advice to government. I sat on one side of the table with eight or nine officials on the other as we discussed the European Union and disarmament. At one point I questioned Gorbachev's naive embrace of America with the warning that even Britain, America's closest ally, was screwed when American interests required it. This provoked an intense debate in Russian for several minutes before the chair of the Institute said, 'As you can see, some colleagues here share your doubts about America's real motives towards us.'

Back in London, before Yuri was expelled he became increasingly agitated about events in Afghanistan. A decade had passed since Russia's invasion of that country and they were now withdrawing, but Russian troops were still being killed by mujahidin fighters funded by the CIA and the Saudi government. Yuri urged me to expose the nature of the mujahidin, whom he described as fanatics with no interest in Western democracy or its freedoms. He couldn't understand why we supported people he felt were psychopaths who might one day turn on their sponsors. I was uncertain whether Yuri's opinion was accurate but I wasn't going to take up an issue at the prompting of the agent of a foreign intelligence service. Given subsequent events, I now regret I didn't. Yuri made a smooth transition to capitalism and now does very well in Russia's largest investment bank.

*

The Labour party's policy review ended in the summer of 1989 with a two-day meeting of the NEC agreeing to retain Thatcher's anti-union laws, to drop its commitment to bring privatised utilities back into public ownership and to retain nuclear weapons. After each decision, Mandelson took a compliant member of the NEC downstairs to brief journalists waiting at the door, thus ensuring that his spin set the agenda. Neither Dennis Skinner, Tony Benn nor I could leave for fear of missing a vote, so just after the vote to keep nuclear weapons I asked Dennis to filibuster long enough for me to nip downstairs and put our side of the case to the journalists. I could hear Mandelson and Robin Cook behind me and as I ran down the stairs I pressed the lift button on each floor to stall their

trip so they arrived in time to see the backs of the journalists rushing to file their copy based on my account of events. In his diary
that night Benn wrote that the party had accepted the principles
'not only of capitalism but Thatcherism'.

Kinnock's supporters were attempting to deselect me in Brent
East. The hard left had lost control of my GMC, which was now run
by Kinnockites, and I faced a tough fight but Kinnock had changed
the party rules so the selection of candidates was now by a vote of
all party members. Fortunately my opponents were split between
supporters of the former Labour MP Michael Barnes and those of
local GMB union organiser Mary Turner, who was working-class
with traditional Labour values and deep roots in the constituency,
including a spell organising Brent Council's school dinner ladies.
With a secret vote of all members there was no way of knowing the
outcome, but in the end my local constituency work paid off and I
won 64 per cent of the vote.

The following month, September, *Livingstone's Labour* was published and Brian Walden spent his hour-long TV programme questioning me on its contents and my ambitions. Most interviews last
only a few minutes and Walden's was recognised as the most significant of the political interview programmes, so this was a make-or-
break encounter. I was made more nervous by the fact that not only
was a car sent to pick me up but another car followed throughout
the journey in case the first one broke down.

Introducing me as the 'acknowledged leader of the left', the interview went like a dream. He asked serious questions and I answered
them. Afterwards he told me he had been worried because my habit
of directly answering the question put to me meant he was on his
last prepared question as the interview ended. The only other time
this had happened was when he interviewed Enoch Powell.

I went straight from the studio to the Labour conference in
Brighton for a debate with Bryan Gould. For the first time in a

debate on the economy I felt on top of the subject. Given my role in opposing Kinnock's drift to the right, I hoped my NEC vote would increase. Labour was still registering only 41 per cent in the Gallup poll, with Kinnock's personal rating trailing at just 37 per cent. The next general election was expected in 1991 when I would be forty-six years old and I was ready to challenge for the leadership. What I didn't know was that I was about to be voted off the NEC, ending for ever my ambition to lead the party.

Neither I nor anyone else on the left had any inkling of what was to come until a few minutes before the results were announced, when journalists began coming up to me to say that Mandelson was briefing that the results were a sensation and I was off the NEC. I sat in a state of disbelief. There had been no warning of a shift in votes at party General Management Committees, but when the result was announced I had indeed been defeated narrowly by John Prescott. The votes for Benn and Skinner were also down, and in the debates that followed Kinnock won convincing majorities for all his policy changes. The press were told that Kinnock was 'doing cartwheels' and Gerald Kaufman said that my defeat was the 'cherry on the ice-cream sundae'. That evening Ron Todd and I were leaving the same meeting and he drove me to my next one while expressing his disgust with Kinnock's gloating response to my defeat.

When I went back to read the history of the struggle between left and right in the party, it seemed obvious that there was only ever a swing to the left in the first couple of years after Labour governments were thrown out of office. The longer Labour was out of power, the more momentum the drift to the right gathered as the party became increasingly desperate to win.

The left was in turmoil, but what hurt most was that I had been removed not by Kinnock but by the rank and file of the party who were losing confidence that we could win with a radical programme. John Ross was distraught, blaming himself because he hadn't picked up the shift – but neither had our opponents. I tried to reassure him by pointing out that being defeated in an internal election doesn't carry the consequences that many socialists face in other countries – imprisonment or even death. I stood again each year during my time as an MP but usually came in just behind Jack Straw. In the following three years, first Dennis and then Tony were thrown off the NEC and Kinnock faced no further serious challenge. He had convinced the party to move decisively to the right in order to defeat Thatcher.

12

Back to the Wilderness

1989–1994

For twenty years I had been a workaholic activist, putting almost everything second to the pursuit of political change. Now aged forty-four, my life had been turned upside down by my NEC defeat and I knew I would have to change pace and get on with the rest of my life. I had put off buying a home so I could write *Livingstone's Labour*, but finally bought a terraced house in Cricklewood just before my eviction from the NEC. After nine years I now had a garden again, although it was a wreck, but being left on the back benches meant I had time to create a restful wildlife-friendly area. I called it the Kinnock Memorial Garden. I had also started to worry about Mum. When Kate and I visited her in Lincoln there was never any food in the house and we would buy lots of frozen ready meals and canned goods, knowing Mum couldn't bear to see them go to waste. Mum moved in with us – we had bought a larger house than we needed with that in mind. Friends said they couldn't imagine their parents living with them and although we started taking Mum to the cinema and round to friends' dinner parties she complained that I was out so much that she might as well be back in Lincoln. Eventually she moved to sheltered housing in Woking to be near my sister, her children and grandchildren.

My sister and I responded differently to our childhood. While Linda escaped at the earliest opportunity to create her own family with four wonderful children, my memories of childhood left me with no desire to bring up a family and I worried I might not be a good parent. And I was so busy pursuing my political ambitions that the choice had never arisen. If someone had told me I would go on to have five children I wouldn't have believed them.

The mother of my first two children was Philippa Need, a journalist on the *Ham and High* I had known for twelve years. She first interviewed me at the London Labour party conference in March 1977 and covered the Archway Road motorway inquiry where Ted Knight and I supported the opponents of the scheme. The inquiry regularly collapsed into chaos and on one occasion the chairman climbed out of a window onto the roof to escape local residents. I followed, trying to persuade him to come back, when Michael Howard (later leader of the Tory party), who was presenting the pro-motorway case, appeared on the roof crying, 'Don't throw him off!' For a reporter the inquiry was a godsend.

Philippa also reported on Camden's Housing Committee, and our paths crossed again when she worked for Thames TV and TV-am while I was leader of the GLC. We had become good friends. Now in her mid-thirties, she was very keen to have children although she had failed to find the right partner and felt the clock was ticking. We had never been involved romantically but I knew her well enough to know she would be a wonderful mother and so I said I would like to be the father of her children. I would be around taking an interest in them and supporting them emotionally, but Philippa and I agreed that I would not be living with them. We knew it would be a circus if the media reported our arrangement, and children should be able to grow up in privacy irrespective of the profile of their parents, so we didn't make it public when Georgia was born in 1990 and Lottie in 1992.

In the years that followed I loved taking the girls swimming, to the zoo, the Natural History Museum or the Italian café at Golders Hill Park. Slowly more and more people at their schools and in the local community learned that I was their father and it says a lot about people's basic decency that none of them tried to sell the story to the papers. As luck would have it, shortly after Lottie's birth Mr Right for Philippa did come along in the form of Mike Hutchinson (another journalist at the *Ham and High*), an intelligent, warm, funny, erudite man. Confident enough to accept the situation, he happily let me continue contact with the girls. Mike and Philippa then had a third daughter, Bertie.

*

Politics changes without warning. As I listened to the news that Saddam Hussein had invaded Kuwait I had no idea how this would take over my life as the anti-war movement mobilised opposition to the American-led invasion. The only good to come from Saddam Hussein's invasion was my eldest son Liam. I became friends with Jan Woolf, another member of the committee to stop war in the Gulf. Jan was a political activist like her husband, from whom she was separated. They had decided not to have children, but Jan had changed her mind and we agreed to have a baby. The domestic arrangements were the same as with Philippa's children and I was soon struggling around the zoo and museums with all of them, who were making their own strong bonds with each other. Ten years later when Emma Beal and I had Thomas and Mia, all three families began holidaying together with all of us packing off every summer to Devon, Derbyshire, Greece, Spain or France.

We made no announcements of the birth of my first three children but they weren't secret or hidden away and when I took them on tours of the House of Commons or City Hall people either did not notice or did not care. Once I took the three of them to lunch at the Chinese restaurant at County Hall, where the journalist Tom Baldwin was holding forth on the other side of the restaurant but he never wrote about it. Georgia went to secondary school just as I became mayor and as no one believed I was her father I turned up at the school gates to take her and her friends out for the afternoon and ended up signing autographs for some of the parents. Such visits meant that eventually thousands of people knew of my first three children.

When the Thatcher government introduced legislation to prevent single women receiving artificial insemination on the NHS, I watched with disbelief as David Blunkett spoke in support of it. After the obligatory comment that he had nothing against lesbians he explained that women didn't have a right to raise a child without a father being present. But he was so backward on sexual politics he would never understand my domestic arrangements, and I knew I'd be wasting my breath if I challenged him.

*

As 1990 wore on Nigel Lawson's economic policies took their toll. With unemployment and inflation rising, Labour had poll leads of up to 20 per cent and Kinnock's personal rating reached 44 per cent. The poll tax was the final straw that broke Thatcher's back. After all the years of attacking council spending she believed the Tories had finally come up with a method that would work – replacing the rates with a flat poll tax in which virtually everybody paid the same, whether rich or poor. Hundreds of thousands of people took their names off the electoral register to avoid the tax and 'won't pay' campaigns got under way, culminating in a huge protest at Trafalgar Square where police assaulted the demonstrators who then set fire to the shop on the south-east corner that is now a branch of Waterstone's. I was one of several MPs who refused to pay, but when I was eventually summonsed my defence that evidence from computer records was not admissible in court was ignored by the magistrate. Eventually the High Court ruled in favour of another poll tax resister who had mounted the same defence. This gave the government a hook on which to repeal the poll tax.

When Michael Heseltine challenged Thatcher for the Tory leadership in November 1990 I was just leaving the House of Commons as the result of the first ballot came through. As I walked out of the main entrance a crowd had gathered, and when I announced she hadn't won there was an eruption of cheering. Having known John Major since Lambeth, I believed that the shift from Thatcher to Major would be a bigger change than from Major to Kinnock but most Tory MPs, including Thatcher, had mistaken John's polite and unassuming manner for agreement. The first time I met John after he had entered the cabinet as Chief Secretary to the Treasury I asked, 'Given how left-wing you were in Lambeth, how do you put up with all this right-wing crap from Thatcher?' 'You know me, Ken, I haven't changed. One day I will be able to do what I want.' Sadly for him he had inherited a party on the edge of a mental breakdown.

One Tory MP I knew from GLC days was the über-Thatcherite Edward Leigh, chair of the No Turning Back Group and the last MP to get into her room to beg Thatcher to stay. He was amazed when I told him how progressive John had been in Lambeth and decided to vote for Heseltine instead. After Major's victory, we were chatting behind the Speaker's chair and Leigh was in despair that the Thatcher revolution was over. Neither of us could have anticipated that Tony Blair would eventually accept so many of her policies. Kinnock's office didn't bother to ask Tony Banks or me what we knew about John, and several months were wasted as Labour spin doctors tried to depict him as a hard-line Thatcherite while the rest of Britain warmed to him as a decent man. As John was their only chance to avoid defeat Tory MPs rallied around him, and when at Prime Minister's Questions I was called there was a rumble of groans and disgust which stopped when I raised the stabbing to death of the young black Londoner Roland Adams (not far from where Stephen Lawrence would be killed nearly three years later).

John Major's response was a robust denunciation of racism which prompted Labour MP Joan Lester to say, 'He handled that better than Neil would have done.'

In his brief year as Chancellor of the Exchequer John made a catastrophic error which did immense damage to the economy. In the run-up to the creation of the euro, countries agreed to lock their currencies into a fixed exchange rate and pro-European MPs were keen that we should do the same. As the pound was already overvalued it would have helped manufacturing if we had joined at a lower rate. *The Economist* argued for a rate high enough 'to make British firms squeal' (to increase productivity). This miscalculation locked Britain into a long recession which continued into 1992. Years later when I told my bank manager what a nice person John Major was he recalled his sleepless nights dealing with the many firms that had gone under and said he could never forgive him.

Kinnock and John Smith had agreed that Labour's first budget when they returned to power would increase pensions and child benefit, paid for by an income tax increase on earnings over £50,000 and the introduction of National Insurance contributions on earnings over £21,000 (effectively a 9 per cent tax increase). This would have been good for the poorest and those earning between £7,000 and £20,000 a year would have been no worse off. Most Labour constituencies were in Scotland, Wales or the north, so this looked like a fair deal but in London and the south-east, where wages (and the cost of living) were higher it would hit many more voters and even more were not that far off the £21,000 figure.

Twice I wrote articles for *Tribune* warning that this would be a problem and raised it in the parliamentary Labour party meeting, but Labour's budget was set in stone. Once the run-up to the election started the Tory press massively exaggerated the situation so that many people assumed they were going to be paying more tax even when they would be better off. I used my *Sun* column to spell out the truth, but after I'd submitted it I got a phone call from the deputy editor saying that it wouldn't be fair on my Tory opponent for them to run my column during the campaign.

No government anywhere had ever been re-elected during a recession and I believed that Labour would win a small majority or at worst that we would have a hung parliament. My local party had rallied round, particularly as members canvassing in the 1990 borough election had found lots of voters saying they would vote for me but not for the Labour council. Two years later, defending a majority of just 1,653 votes, I faced a tough fight against Damian Green, who had been a fervent Thatcherite, telling us we should love the poll tax. He disappeared for a year after the poll tax fiasco, only to reappear as a committed supporter of John Major. As a Catholic, he was strongly opposed to abortion and with Brent East having the largest proportion of Catholic voters anywhere in England, the Society for the Protection of the Unborn Child (SPUC) made the constituency their number-one target. They flooded the area with activists and literature with horrific pictures of aborted foetuses along with the warning that I was 'A leading pro-abortionist. He voted to allow abortion up to birth for handicapped babies and for some other reasons . . . he also voted to allow human embryos to be used as guinea pigs to test drugs and in other experiments' (a rather dishonest description of the practice of allowing stem cells from embryos to be used to help find a cure for currently incurable conditions). Help came from the unlikely figure of Cardinal Hume, who opened a homeless centre in Brent East at the start of the campaign. I was in the packed audience as the prelate devoted most of his speech to praising my work with him during my time at the GLC. Tories in the audience were furious.

Anne Harradine was my full-time agent and although this was her first election she had covered all our bases in her preparations. She was clever and down to earth, with a great sense of humour, making her the ideal agent for a constituency with so many strong personalities. After years of dealing with a vast volume of casework I didn't expect to lose but thought it would be a tough fight. But from the first morning as I handed out leaflets at Dollis Hill tube (in a Tory marginal ward) I knew from the mood of the voters that I was heading for a big win.

Unlike MPs who refuse to debate with opponents, I enjoy the fight and agreed to eight debates. Because a close result was expected we had lots of fringe candidates including Anne Murphy from a mad Marxist sect claiming to represent the communist party. She was a thirty-year-old social worker whose election address said, 'We want to overthrow parliament and the rest of the capitalist state,' and went on to call for 'the right of the population to arm itself' with 'workers defence corps – our class organised to defend our class – and undermine the bosses' armed forces'. She demanded 'workers in Britain must take sides – for the IRA, against the British army'. Her response to every question was that nothing can be achieved 'until we smash the state'. My meetings were well attended with a block of SPUC activists ensuring intense debates about abortion, but people were bemused when in response to questions about unrepaired pavements, Anne would deliver her rant about the need to smash the state first.

Labour feared I might say something that could be exploited by the media so there was always a Labour party official present at each meeting. Given that we had an independent Irish republican candidate, I knew the liveliest meeting would be at the local Irish centre. The official was horrified as the first questioner demanded to know why I didn't support the right of the IRA to let off nail bombs on the streets of London. As I explained I wasn't in favour of killing people to achieve political goals, the mad Marxists in the audience started booing and shouting me down. As BBC and ITV cameras were present, the official started looking sick. When I explained that Gerry Adams was in favour of a negotiated peace, someone in the audience screamed, 'Don't name-drop with us!' Damian Green couldn't believe what was going on and Anne Murphy launched into another tirade about the need to smash the state. The official rushed off to warn HQ but the whole meeting was so unbalanced that TV couldn't show any of it.

There was one-near disaster in the campaign. Our safest ward was the vast South Kilburn estate where the Labour vote had been 95 per cent in 1971 but had now declined to 70 per cent. Like most estates under the Thatcher regime, South Kilburn had been neglected while having to absorb the homeless and single-parent families. Unemployment was rife, with horrific levels of unreported rape, and the playgrounds were littered with used syringes. A huge proportion of my casework came from this ward and when Labour won the 1997 election we finally got the money for major improvements. But back in 1992 we decided to have a local campaign HQ on the estate and get the turnout back up to reasonable levels. I had now become friends with John Lebor, the former Brent Council leader the left had driven out in 1982. John drove me around the constituency in his expensive car and on our first call in South Kilburn he said he'd better stay with the vehicle rather than follow me to HQ, but I reassured him his wheels would be perfectly safe as everyone would assume such a posh car could only belong to one of the local drug lords.

This local strategy worked, but a teenager who lived in the flat we were using as the estate HQ was reading our canvassing returns to find out who was out during the day so he could burgle their homes. We discovered this when one of our local activists, who was HIV positive, turned up and found him burgling his flat. When we confronted the lad we discovered he had previously been accused of rape so we decided to close the local office. Somehow the *Daily Mail* got wind of the burglary (and the HIV status of our activist) and it was a mad rush to close everything down before they turned up on the activist's doorstep. While this was going on Susan Tully, the *EastEnders* actress who played Michelle Fowler, was doing a walkabout with me in Kilburn Square. She was immediately mobbed, but over the heads of the crowd I could see Anne Harradine in her car packed with election paraphernalia whisking our activist off for a break somewhere the *Daily Mail* couldn't reach him.

A week before polling day I was debating with Damian Green. He was completely depressed as polls were giving Labour national leads of 6 and 7 per cent, but at that very moment Labour was taking a huge risk with the biggest rally the party had organised in modern times, at a cost of £100,000. Sheffield had been chosen as the venue because it was a Labour bastion not blighted by ultra-left groups who might embarrass the party, and every Labour MP except for a handful such as Tony, Dennis, Bernie Grant and me had been invited.

The organisers seemed to have drawn on Leni Riefenstahl's propaganda film of Hitler's Nuremberg Rally – *Triumph of the Will*. Her film opens with Hitler in a plane descending on Nuremberg like a god, and at the rally he stands alone on the raised podium surrounded by Nazi flags and an adoring crowd gazing up at him. Presidential candidates in other countries often strike similar iconic poses but we don't elevate our leaders to superhuman status. The sheer numbers and the militaristic layout gave the Sheffield rally an electrifying atmosphere which built up as the huge screens showed live footage of Kinnock's helicopter flying him in. As he entered Sheffield Arena 10,000 Labour members went wild. Adulation at meetings is intoxicating and Kinnock was swept away by his emotions, shouting out 'Well, all right! Well, all right! Well, all right!' as Glenys desperately tugged at the back of his jacket to get him to stop. The rally continued with Kinnock standing alone on a tall podium delivering his speech against a backdrop of Union Jacks.

Robin Cook turned to John Prescott, whispering that the whole thing was making him feel uncomfortable. 'It worked for Hitler,' John replied.

*

A week later John Major's government became the first in British history to be re-elected during a recession, and although many blamed the Sheffield fiasco I believed the major factor was that we had proposed tax increases, a measure which would have pro-longed the recession. Later that summer the Labour government in Australia was also re-elected when their Conservative opponents repeated the mistake of proposing tax increases during a slump. We might have won the election with John Smith as leader or even with Kinnock without tax increases, but the combination was lethal. The tax proposals had been devised three years earlier while the economy was booming and no one in the leadership felt the need to review the policy in the light of current economic realities.

In Brent East the swing to Labour was four times the national average and Labour had a good result in London as a whole, which may have been because Kinnock was now promising to establish a Greater London Authority in County Hall which would take over the powers of the City of London. A bigger factor may have been that the recession had been much more severe in London than the rest of the country.

As Labour MPs gathered for the opening of Parliament the gloom and despair was overwhelming. If we couldn't defeat the Tories during a recession when could we ever do so? Many Labour MPs' health took a turn for the worse. The flesh fell away from Kinnock's face like someone suffering from cancer and I got psoriasis. Kinnock resigned and it was obvious that John Smith would be elected; the only issue was who would run against him. After

Benn's challenge for the leadership, Kinnock changed the rules so no one could stand unless 20 per cent of MPs nominated them. Previously only two MPs had been required but now it was impossible for the left even to enter the contest. Although John Smith reduced the number of nominations required to 12.5 per cent, this still leaves our party as one of the few in any democracy where access to national leadership is so tightly restricted. In Britain there is no chance that an outsider like Barack Obama could fight his way to the top.

Throwing my hat in the ring with Bernie Grant as my running mate gave me a platform for ten days, but even the Socialist Campaign Group couldn't unite behind me and Bernie. Some on the left wouldn't vote for me because I supported proportional representation and others disagreed with my criticism of our proposed tax increases. At one point it seemed that John would be elected unopposed, with even Bryan Gould unable to get the 20 per cent he needed to mount a challenge. I phoned John to warn him that this would look bad and he said he would ensure Bryan got enough nominations to allow a contest, which Bryan duly lost by ten to one. Bryan was demoted to deal with arts in the new shadow cabinet with the big prizes going to Blair and Brown. After a while Bryan resigned from the shadow cabinet to argue that Labour should adopt a full-employment policy, but realising the grip of the right on the party he met the MPs he was working with to tell us he had decided to leave politics and return to New Zealand. I thought he was being unduly pessimistic when he warned that if Labour won the next election it would be the most right-wing Labour government in history. When John Smith asked me why Bryan was quitting I said, 'I don't think he believes any MP who is anti-Europe would ever get a job in a government you lead.' John agreed it would be unlikely for a strongly anti-European MP to have a job in any Labour government.

At a meeting of all London's Labour MPs to discuss our expenses, I was amazed when Bernie said he had used the second-homes allowance to buy a property in his constituency although he lived in neighbouring Wood Green. Bernie used the house for his advice surgeries and as the local party HQ. Labour officials urged outer-London MPs to do the same. I told the Labour party that even if this was legal I wasn't prepared to do it. Some MPs admitted they had used the allowance to buy homes their relatives lived in or even holiday homes. When I told one MP I had opted for London weighting he laughed, saying, 'You've lost £50,000.' I thought this was particularly galling as I had actually bought a home in my constituency, and run up a huge debt funding research so I could do my job properly.

The Fees Office said I was one of 'a few MPs not claiming the Additional Costs Allowance' (to give it its proper name) and 'it was introduced because MPs' pay is so low' and 'it is a private matter between the House of Commons and its members and is not referable to the Inland Revenue'. MPs were not required to submit evidence of mortgage or rent payments or running costs, nor were there any rules about the amount of time they had to spend in either home. The ACA had been set up as a way of increasing MPs' pay without a public row and we were being encouraged to use it by the whips and House of Commons authorities. Tories were also encouraged to claim. Michael Portillo was told (by the Tory whips) that he was letting the side down by not pocketing the allowance.

*

Although I knew now I would never lead the Labour party I could still have influence in the area of economic policy. Our computer now contained full economic data for every country in the world since 1945 and for the major economies going back a century and so John Ross and I continued to produce *SEB* until I was elected mayor in 2000. Although its circulation was small it was read in the IMF, the OECD and even the Treasury under the Tories.

Our research showed that the most important factor in the success of any nation was its level of investment. This was not the prevalent view among economists at the time but when we produced a detailed analysis of our arguments Gordon Brown told his shadow Treasury team they had to read it. An early disagreement with Brown came as I pressed for devaluation of the pound and a cut in interest rates to assist industry, whereas Brown resolutely defended the high exchange rate that Major had negotiated.

Labour gloom lifted when the attempt to sustain the overvalued pound in the ERM collapsed and the chancellor Norman Lamont was forced to increase interest rates to 15 per cent. When the increase was announced there was panic among the Tories' secretaries and researchers in the Commons as many of them faced ruin trying to pay their mortgages and this led directly to pressure on Tory MPs, who were soon phoning the chancellor's aides with dire warnings about the electoral consequences. That evening Lamont announced Britain's humiliating withdrawal from the ERM and Labour soon had a 20 per cent lead with John Smith on course to become prime minister.

Parliament still had to agree the treaty paving the way for the rest of the European Community to adopt the euro, even though John Major had negotiated a British opt-out clause. President Mitterrand of France and Chancellor Kohl of Germany believed the euro would drive the process of creating a federal Europe along American lines, but in America people can move from state to state easily because they have one official language and the government redistributes wealth from rich to poor states. In Europe language barriers make it difficult for people to work abroad, and the European Commission budget was too small to allow it to redistribute wealth. The American states all had separate currencies until the dollar was introduced after the civil war. A common currency should have been the last stage of European integration, but once the euro was introduced and Britain stayed outside the currency, it weakened our manufacturing still further. As over half our trade is with Europe, why would anybody choose to manufacture goods in Britain knowing that however efficient their firm a shift in exchange rates could wipe out their profits overnight? Staying outside the eurozone was a factor in the loss of over a million and a half jobs in British manufacturing. The economic pain of our ERM membership permanently soured people against the idea of the euro, but I had no objection to joining at a rate low enough for our manufacturing to prosper.

*

After meeting former Israeli Mossad agent Ari Ben-Menashe I started to investigate Mark Thatcher's international arms dealings and discovered he had been used by Carlos Cardoen, a Chilean arms dealer who supplied weapons to Iraq. The agent contemptuously dismissed Thatcher's role as little more than topping up the drinks while the deals were being done. But the case had its sinister side: Jonathan Moyle, a British reporter investigating these deals, was murdered in Santiago with a lethal injection in his heel and his body was then posed to make it look like an auto-erotic asphyxia accident. The British embassy did nothing to assist the parents or help expose the crime. When I raised the matter in the Commons the Tory deputy Speaker told me privately that the problem with Thatcher was that 'she wanted to abolish the welfare state for everybody except her own son'. A short while later I was appearing on TV with Carol Thatcher just after it was revealed that Mark was a multimillionaire. She looked shocked, and said, 'I don't see how that could be, he's never done a day's work in his life.'

I began getting all sorts of media work, from appearances on *Have I Got News for You* to joining Michael Parkinson's weekly radio slot on LBC with Charles Kennedy and Jerry Hayes. Parkinson made it sound like people chatting in a pub rather than engaging in dull point scoring and it was all the more revealing for that. Michael had the confidence not to need to interrupt when the exchange was going well. Charles Kennedy was often late, and as Lib Dem health spokesman begged us not to reveal that he was smoking on air. An ex-Labour member who switched to the SDP, he only agreed to stand for Parliament in an unwinnable seat where the Liberals had previously won 9 per cent of the vote. To his amazement he won easily to become the youngest Member of Parliament at the age of twenty-three. Because he never took himself seriously and was prepared to crack jokes at his own party's expense, Paddy Ashdown never pushed him forward although he was an obvious future leader and was once introduced at a Lib Dem conference as 'the man who would be king, but hasn't yet decided whether he would prefer to be a rather amusing game show contestant'. Although I didn't share Charles's passion for the music of David Bowie, we became good friends and trusted each other enough to discuss our private lives, confident that nothing would go further.

When Rosie Boycott became editor of *Esquire* magazine she gave me the job of restaurant critic. Although I like my food, I am no expert on what might be in the sauce or the finer points of expensive wine, but Rosie didn't worry. 'Our readers are mainly white men in the south-east with more money than sense who just want to know where to go for a good meal.' As I would be recognised in restaurants, Rosie had a firm rule that I always had to pay for the meal, but out of the hundreds of restaurants I visited the only one where the waiter put the bill on my table and said, 'It's up to you whether you pay this or not, sir,' was in Harrods, where I'd taken Mum for lunch. I paid, though Mum thought I was mad.

My lightweight spouting on topical events or a plate of food was one thing, but I certainly didn't expect a call from Kelvin MacKenzie, editor of the *Sun*, to talk about me doing a weekly column. As the 'most odious man in Britain' I walked through the barbed-wire barricades around Fort Wapping with some scepticism, but Kelvin had cleared it with the paper's owner Rupert Murdoch and promised he would never change anything I wrote unless the lawyers said it was libellous. I was amazed how Murdoch had transformed the newspaper culture. In contrast to the boozy ethos of Fleet Street, there was an alcohol ban – except in the editor's office. Kelvin said he had been showing Norman Tebbit the new plant and offered him Coke or orange juice only to be told, 'You must be fucking joking!'

I agonised not because the paper had been so vile about me but because the left had boycotted all the Murdoch media after he smashed the print unions five years earlier. When *If Voting Changed Anything* was published the *Sunday Times* offered me £40,000 to serialise it. The only other bid was from the *New Statesman* for £400 and to the horror of the publishers – I had a veto over the decision – I insisted on taking the *New Statesman* bid. Dennis Skinner said I was mad. 'You should have taken the money and given it to the print unions.' I decided to do the column and there were some rumblings on the left but Kelvin also got flak from *Sun* readers, one of whom wrote: 'I hope you and all your family die of Aids.' True to his word, he never changed my columns but occasionally ran an editorial denouncing them.

*

The quality of the *SEB* research and my obsession with economics began to be noticed. When Lynn Barber interviewed me for the *Independent on Sunday* she wrote, 'He is obsessed with economics . . . in fact he talks so much about it that I eventually wailed,

"This is terribly boring – can't you talk about gay rights or Ireland or something?'" *SEB* had been noticed further afield and following the collapse of the Soviet Union the general secretary of Moscow's trade unions came to see me in the summer of 1992 and asked if they could borrow John Ross for a few weeks, as they had no one in their organisation who understood how market economies worked. John and I were happy to agree but neither of us realised that John would be in Moscow for eight years and that there would be a Russian version of *SEB*. John continued to work for me via phone and fax and I visited Moscow once a year.

After the coup against Gorbachev that allowed Yeltsin to seize power, John had predicted there would be consequences for workers in the West. With the end of the communist threat the worst excesses of capitalism were no longer reined in. John predicted a further erosion of trade union power, a rolling back of the welfare state and a rapid widening of the gap between rich and poor. As bad as this was for workers in the West, for people in the former Soviet Union it was a catastrophe. Instead of a transition to democracy and the rule of law under Gorbachev, Yeltsin's total privatisation of all the state monopolies allowed the most ruthless and crooked to become billionaires overnight and Russia sank into the sort of institutionalised mass corruption that had accompanied the growth of capitalism in nineteenth-century Britain and America.

In Russia change was rapid and volatile. One year the exchange rate would allow us to go to the best restaurants, the following year I would have to watch every penny. When Yeltsin took power the average life span of a Russian man was seventy; eight years later it was fifty-seven as overnight millions of jobs were wiped out and with no prospect of ever working again suicide soared and millions drank themselves into an early grave. People in their thousands stood on street corners selling their treasured possessions in order to eat. Visiting a university professor in his home I saw he had stacked a pile of potatoes around the television in the hope that they would see him through the winter. Many Muscovites were shocked at the flourishing of pornography and the growth of organised crime. There was a wave of murders in which pensioners were dumped on the streets with a bullet in the head because someone wanted their home. A society undergoing massive upheaval is not like a Western democracy where politicians carry on regardless of their errors. As each of Yeltsin's opponents miscalculated, they were swept aside by the rush of events and on each visit to John I found him advising someone new. Our Russian *SEB* urged Yeltsin to drop neoliberal economics and copy the success of China's economic reforms, where strong state regulation of the banks guaranteed higher levels of investment.

This tragedy unfolded not because Yeltsin was a drunk but because he took the advice of economists from the White House, the IMF and the World Bank, who recommended so-called 'shock therapy' in which the economy was privatised virtually overnight. Under communism production had been centralised so, for instance, all brown shoes were made in one factory complex, all ballpoint pens in another and so on. The producers of most commodities held a monopoly, so privatisation simply transferred power into the hands of oligarchs who, with no competitors, raised prices to make massive profits. Yeltsin himself awarded licences like a medieval monarch: his tennis partner, for example, was given the right to import cigarettes duty-free. The mayor of Moscow had sold properties in Moscow to himself and threatened to sue when I said that in Britain he would be facing a prison term.

Apart from economic illiteracy, Yeltsin's biggest problem was his election on the same day by the same voters who had elected the Russian parliament. The Speaker and leader of the Duma was Ruslan Khasbulatov, a Chechen economist a decade younger than Yeltsin. The Western media depicted Ruslan as a hard-line Marxist but when I met him in his grand office he seemed no further to the left than Robin Cook. Like Robin, he had a sharp tongue, finding it impossible to hide his contempt for Yeltsin's finance ministers, whom he dismissed as 'economists in short trousers'. Since the Duma tried to moderate the worst excesses of Yeltsin's bungled privatisation, Western politicians and pundits urged Yeltsin to (illegally) dissolve the parliament as a way of ending this deadlock about what form the new Russian constitution would take.

The Duma met in a building known as the White House, and Ruslan was so impressed with John Ross's work that he gave him free run of the building. My second visit to Ruslan in September 1993 almost ended in disaster when the plane in front of ours crashed on landing. We were already over the runway and knew something was wrong when our plane suddenly lurched almost vertically up. After a diversion to Helsinki I arrived back in Moscow and was taken to the White House where the mood was tense as Yeltsin was expected to use the army against the Duma. I brought a motion from the House of Commons signed by over 100 MPs opposed to the illegal abolition of the elected parliament. Ruslan welcomed me and read out the motion, at which the members rose and applauded.

After two days of meetings I was back in London (writing an article for the *Guardian* opposing Yeltsin) when John phoned to say the coup was about to start and he was still inside the White House and he had been given a gas mask. He remained in and around the parliament over the days that followed as thousands of Muscovites formed a human barrier between the Duma and the troops. Support for Yeltsin started to erode and the troops were beginning to drift away when Vice-President Aleksandr Rutskoi, who had been Yeltsin's running mate but had turned against him, took a mad gamble and tried to take over the television station. Yeltsin seized on this mistake, which was portrayed as a counter-coup, and dozens of civilians were shot dead by troops waiting inside the television centre, while tanks shelled the parliament building.

Instead of allowing Russia to evolve via the rule of law and the ballot box, Yeltsin established the precedent of using force to solve political conflict. America and Britain supported him and only the *Guardian* among British newspapers was opposed to his coup. At the next presidential election in 1996 the economic chaos was so bad that Yeltsin was expected to lose to the communist Gennady Zyuganov. The IMF obligingly made loans to Russia during the campaign and television coverage was 90 per cent pro-Yeltsin with barely a mention of Zyuganov. John arranged for me to have a one-to-one interview with Zyuganov for the *Guardian* but when I urged him to adopt the Chinese economic model he said, 'We don't have enough Chinese,' and laughed. This left me with a fear that a Zyuganov government could well fail to turn the situation round.

The oligarchs poured a fortune into Yeltsin's campaign but he had a stroke after the first ballot was announced and took no further part in the campaign. When after the second round of voting it was announced that Yeltsin had 53 per cent of the vote, everybody was convinced the result had been rigged and that Zyuganov had beaten Yeltsin by around 8 per cent. Zyuganov should have called his supporters onto the streets until Yeltsin was forced from office as the Egyptian president Mubarak would be fifteen years later but the communist party hesitated, the moment was lost and Russia continued in chaos. Now the West bemoans Putin's rule but they did not object when Yeltsin set out on this authoritarian path. Russians notice the double standards, and aren't terribly impressed with Western complaints.

*

With John away in Russia, my link to his colleagues was through Redmond O'Neill, a workaholic who combined a charming Tiggerish quality with formidable intelligence. Mark Watts, who later came to work on the mayoral campaign, describes seeing Redmond for the first time in a dingy room in Sheffield: 'He gave the most incredible talk, taking in the Russian revolution, the fall of the Berlin Wall, the re-composition of the European left and Yugoslavia, all delivered in full-throttle, forceful Redmond style, while obsessively pulling up and then pushing down his socks throughout his talk.' Redmond linked up with television journalist Marc Wadsworth to set up the Anti-Racist Alliance (ARA) in response to a string of racist murders in south-east London, of which the most notorious became that of Stephen Lawrence. I became co-chair of the committee, many of whose members had been trying to establish black sections in the Labour party for years. Kinnock had always been against the idea of black sections, as was clear when he visited a GLC exhibition commemorating the life of Paul Robeson in 1985. After announcing that Robeson would never have supported black sections, Kinnock was told by Robeson's son that 'my father always supported black self-organisation'. Eventually black sections were agreed without causing the end of civilisation.

Although he had expelled Militant, Kinnock saw no contradiction in allowing Peter Hain and Glenys Kinnock to become high-profile supporters of a Trotskyist front organisation when the Socialist Workers Party revived the Anti-Nazi League as a rival to the ARA. The ARA had considerable success but was torn apart by infighting which culminated at a meeting where I ruled that ARA employees couldn't vote on their annual pay increase, which prompted Wadsworth to lash out and smack me in the mouth. At the meeting convened to vote on his dismissal, half of the committee argued it wasn't acceptable for a black man to be sacked by whites with the others saying that colour was irrelevant to the case. Wadsworth survived by one vote with the white members and the black members split equally into the two camps. Most who supported Wadsworth dropped out of political activity but it was during this dispute that I first met and grew to respect Lee Jasper, Atma Singh and Kumar Murshid, who firmly rejected the idea that a white person couldn't sack a black employee if there were good reasons for doing so.

At the annual meeting of the ARA both Wadsworth and I were voted out. Diane Abbott took over as chair, but realised the ARA was broken beyond repair and with Lee, Atma and Kumar set up the National Assembly Against Racism, which I supported.

*

Just at the time I was bumped off the ARA, *Guardian* cartoonist Martin Rowson said there was a vacancy among his fellow trustees on the council of the Zoological Society of London which runs London and Whipsnade zoos as well as research and conservation programmes around the world. The zoo remained one of my favourite London places, and I jumped at the chance to serve on its council a mere thirty-two years after failing to get a job there. I was even more thrilled when after a few years I became vice-president of the ZSL for a term.

Since its creation in 1828 its council had been dominated by the great and good from Prince Albert to the Duke of Edinburgh. It was still the world's leading zoo but when my parents first took me it was a 'collection' aiming to 'have one of everything'. With the loss of the world's wild places and threatened extinctions of species it has become a leader in captive breeding programmes, but after a disastrous attempt at Disneyfication the zoo faced financial crisis and closure. The fear of personal bankruptcy saw most of the establishment figures quit the council to be replaced by academics, naturalists and conservationists. The zoo was hauling itself back into the black and increasing the emphasis on breeding and conservation. After the point scoring of Parliament it was a pleasure to sit on a body discussing how to save endangered species and educate visitors about environmental problems.

I arrived just as ZSL started planning its Web of Life house and became involved in the plans to build a large aquarium in Docklands. It surprised me that Britain, with its maritime heritage, had no world-class aquarium. Aquaria elsewhere in the world still had the 'collection mentality' of early zoos, so we planned to build the first conservation-led aquarium, hoping that it would change the others for the better. The architect Will Alsop came up with a breathtaking design and we could have brought a million tourists a year to Newham, the most deprived borough in Britain. But the Millennium Fund was exhausted, or as Chris Smith put it when I lobbied him in his new role as culture minister, 'The money's all gone to the Welsh and Scots.'

I was struck by the contrast with the short-termism of political debate when we discussed whether or not to buy a male Indian elephant. Having been vital in agriculture, Indian elephants are in decline as they are replaced by tractors. But buying one is a seventy-year commitment and the elephant house was too small. To start elephant breeding, we needed a larger enclosure and with no chance of getting permission to grab a chunk of Regent's Park or demolish the existing elephant house, which is a listed building, in the end they had to be moved to Whipsnade, where they bred with enthusiasm. By the time this decision was taken I had become mayor, but that did not stop Simon Jenkins in the *Standard* bewailing the fact that it was the end of elephants in London and demanding that I do something about it.

The zoo's problem was that its old animal houses and cages had become Grade II listed buildings, so we were unable to replace them with the modern buildings the animals needed. It cost twice as much to adapt an unsatisfactory listed building as to demolish and build from scratch, and while English Heritage enthusiastically campaigned to have our buildings listed they didn't cover the extra money we needed as a result of the listing. The heritage lobby really erupted when the zoo moved penguins from its world famous Berthold Lubetkin-designed pool. As soon as the penguins were in their new home their health improved and breeding increased but this didn't stop the heritage lobby complaining that even if it was bad for their health the penguins should move back to the Lubetkin pool.

*

With John Smith's election as Labour leader the old hatreds declined and members were happy with his leadership. John concentrated on attacking the Tories and avoided the introspection of the Kinnock years. Although Peter Mandelson had become an MP, his influence on the party evaporated as John had no time for him or his methods. Not everyone was happy with John, as *Daily Mirror* political editor Alastair Campbell wrote: 'I see the real divide as between "fanatics" and "long-gamers". The long-gamers . . . believe Labour has time on its side. There is no point . . . wasting energies and risking the Tory theft of ideas, in a period that will be forgotten by the next election. But what makes the fanatics frantic is that the party does not know what it is for, other than to oppose the government . . . There is little sense of the party finding itself a wider role.' Campbell listed Gordon Brown, Jack Straw, Tony Blair, Frank Field and Kim Howells as the fanatics with John Smith, Frank Dobson, Robin Cook and John Prescott as the long-gamers.

When Jack Straw raised the issue of ditching Clause Four, the article in Labour's constitution that sought 'to secure for the workers by hand or by brain the full fruits of their industry and the most equitable distribution thereof that may be possible upon the basis of the common ownership of the means of production, distribution and exchange, and the best obtainable system of popular administration and control of each industry or service', Smith slapped him down but the fanatics succeeded in changing the way Labour elected its leader. They knew their chances of grabbing the leadership would be improved if the trade union leaderships were stripped of their role in deciding their unions' vote. In the end, after an impassioned and incoherent speech from John Prescott at the 1993 conference, the rules were changed so that the trade union votes for leader would be cast not by the union executives but by the individual members. While the 'fanatics' complained about the undemocratic nature of the block vote they were quite happy with the rule that gave MPs a veto over who could be the leader. After the vote John made clear there would be no more introspective debates and that he was drawing a line under further rule changes. This led to rumours that Tony Blair was despairing that the party had not changed enough, and was considering resigning and returning to the law (rumours later confirmed by Peter Oborne in *The Triumph of the Political Class*).

On the morning of Thursday, 12 May 1994 I was getting ready to go to work when Kelvin MacKenzie phoned to ask if I would write an obituary as John Smith had died suddenly. Kelvin said that the news was being held back until his daughters were notified but the *Sun* had a source in the hospital. I was devastated. John had always been kind and when we appeared on television he would take me out for lunch beforehand to make sure we understood each other's positions. He got on well with the left and told the party's general secretary Larry Whitty, 'I've got to get away from this business of treating people like outcasts.' Having been barred from standing in the leadership election, I was torn between John's enthusiasm for Europe and Bryan Gould's criticism that our economic policies were not radical enough. Although I voted for Bryan I told the journalist Andy McSmith that with John winning, 'It will be like the liberation of Europe having a personally secure man in charge.

I am sure I will go on disagreeing with him. I shall keep banging on about defence cuts but it will be a whole different atmosphere.'

I was asked to come in to the BBC's parliamentary broadcast centre in Westminster, where a whole floor was given over to the newsroom. The reporters were as devastated as I was, but Mandelson arrived and started to work the room. Consigned to outer darkness by John, Mandelson had seemed lonely and depressed, but now he crackled with energy as he explained to reporters the process for electing the next leader and that it would be either Blair or Brown. Mandelson was back in the game.

*

There was genuine grief as people, recognising John's depth, integrity and intelligence, realised what we had lost. He was one of the few politicians people instinctively liked and trusted. The European elections were already under way so the party deferred the leadership contest until they were over. Once again no one from the left would be allowed to stand, and the contest had an orchestrated feel in which Prescott and Beckett played their part while not rocking the boat.

It was unclear whether both Blair and Brown would stand and when I bumped into Mo Mowlam, Frank Dobson and Chris Smith I asked which of the two they would choose. All three jumped down my throat with passionate warnings not to vote for Brown, yet all three would be discarded by Blair by the end of his first term. When the Socialist Campaign Group met, Falkirk West MP Dennis Canavan made a strong plea for Brown and denounced Blair as no better than a Tory. But the majority felt that Brown as shadow chancellor had been deeply reactionary. As well as dropping our commitment to increase pensions he defended remaining in the ERM at an overvalued rate and opposed calls for the pound to be devalued. He was also personally hostile to many on the left and had refused to debate important issues. In the Commons tea room I plonked down at a table with three right-wing northern MPs who were trying to decide between Blair and Brown and when I suggested we find out who Mandelson was supporting and go for the other guy they all laughed and agreed.

But within twenty-four hours polls showed that Blair would beat either Brown or Prescott. Brown stood down, but skilfully extracted from Blair a deal which Tony conceded and which would fatally weaken his premiership. Once again I briefly threw my hat in the ring although I knew I had no chance of getting the backing of enough MPs to stand. But I did get a revealing insight into the schisms at the top of the Labour party while chatting with Prescott on a train journey back from a campaign meeting. Prescott described the way in which economic policy had evolved during John Smith's two years as leader, with Smith having to chair meetings at which Robin, Gordon and Prescott slugged it out. Brown usually opened with some reactionary view that was challenged by Prescott and Cook until finally an exasperated John Smith would ease Brown towards a compromise.

Blair won 57 per cent of the vote on 21 July 1994. Alastair Campbell's diaries reveal that Blair told him about his plans to drop Clause Four as early as 11 August as well as his wish that Labour's policies should be acceptable to those who had defected to the SDP. Blair had already decided to send his son to a grant-maintained school rather than the local Islington comprehensive. Had all this been known in advance, Blair would have lost. Even with most newspapers backing his campaign and standing against two relatively weak candidates he only got half of the trade union vote. Had the 'fanatics' failed to change the leadership election rules nine months earlier he might well have lost. In the *Guardian* I warned that Blair would be the most right-wing leader in our history. I had no idea of just how right wing he would turn out to be.

13

Charlatans and Spin

1994–1997

With the election of Blair, control freakery returned to the Labour party with a vengeance. John Smith's two years in charge now seemed like a lost age of tolerance and open debate. Blair's inner circle consisted of Brown, Mandelson and, despite his views on 'fanatics', Alastair Campbell, a group lacking any experience of running a council committee, let alone a government department. Blair's effortless rise – Scotland's best private school, Oxford, the Bar and then being parachuted into a safe Labour seat at the age of thirty – was even more remarkable given that he was rejected when he tried to get a seat on Hackney Council in 1982.

In contrast, Brown's life was steeped in every committee and struggle in the fractious Scottish Labour party. Raised as a son of the Manse in the Presbyterian church with its devotion to duty and aversion to indulgence, he accompanied his father on visits to the poorest parishioners every Saturday and by age eleven was writing in his school magazine about 'what I would do if I were prime minister'. As a high achiever, he took part in an experimental programme to accelerate his education, arriving at university at the age of fifteen where he lost the sight of one eye in a rugby accident and was confined to bed for months while doctors battled to save the other. Avoiding local government, after a spell as a TV researcher he was selected for a safe Labour seat and, like Blair, was elected to Parliament in 1983.

If there is a Labour aristocracy, then as Herbert Morrison's grandson Peter Mandelson is it. He grew up round the corner from

Harold Wilson, played with his sons and took a teenage diversion through the Young Communists before rejoining the Labour party. He worked as a researcher for Albert Booth, Labour's shadow transport minister, when he helped plan the GLC's 1981 fares cut. He was elected as a Lambeth councillor in 1979, but as Ted Knight was leader there was no question of a job for him and, citing his disgust with Ted's leadership, he did not seek re-election. The only memorable event of his three years in local government was when his friend Roger Liddle urged him to defect to the SDP and in full view of Labour councillors pressed a membership form into his hand. Staying with Labour, he worked as a producer on Brian Walden's London Weekend Television before the NEC appointed him as director of campaign and communications in 1985 (by one vote over my former press officer Nita Clarke).

He persuaded Labour to adopt modern campaigning and advertising methods of the kind we had used at the GLC, but his politics were reactionary, even by the standards of the new Labour right that was emerging under Kinnock. Parachuted into a safe Labour seat with which he had no connections at all, it was rumoured that he had left his campaign job in despair at Kinnock's inability to win. In the two years before the 1992 election he advised the BBC on how to defend the licence fee and wrote a weekly piece in the *People*. (It was described by Paul Foot as 'the worst political column written in a popular newspaper'.)

The really interesting member of the inner core was Alastair Campbell. Born in Yorkshire to a Gaelic-speaking vet from Tiree and a mother from Ayrshire, he studied modern languages at Cambridge. After winning a competition in the sex magazine *Forum* he took a job writing for them as the 'Riviera Gigolo'. He went from local papers to the *Daily Mirror* but in 1986 was hospitalised after a nervous breakdown fuelled by alcoholism. Following a long period of depression, he returned to work at the *Mirror* where with the support of his partner Fiona Millar he became political editor under Robert Maxwell. A close friend to Kinnock, he was also devoted to Maxwell and after Maxwell drowned and the *Guardian*'s Michael White joked 'Captain Bob, Bob, Bobbing', Campbell punched him in the face. He then worked for Rupert Murdoch as political editor of the short-lived *Today* newspaper. Never forgetting his roots, he remains a passionate supporter of Burnley FC and like myself is a huge fan of Jacques Brel.

In three years these four would be running Britain, but as they plotted to secure their hold on the party and win the election their weakness was not just their lack of experience of government, but of running *any* organisation – public or private. Blair promised to continue the work of John Smith whereas in fact he despaired at John's leadership. The apparatchiks of New Labour, as the party had been rechristened by the quartet, were obsessed with American politics and seemed to regret being born British rather than American, preferring to watch *The West Wing* than question Denis Healey and Tony Benn about how to handle problems with the civil service. For lessons Blair looked to President Clinton in particular, and his view that 'achievement was less important than definition in the information age'. Blair copied Clinton's technique of running against his party's traditions, such as distancing himself from black activists like Jesse Jackson and what he characterised as the 'tax and spend' policy of past Democratic presidents.

Over that summer of 1994, Blair plotted with Campbell to junk the commitment to public ownership in Clause Four of Labour's constitution so as to win the support of the right-wing media. Much of Blair's first year as leader was wasted drafting a new statement of principles, which disappeared without trace as soon as the PR exercise was completed. Running against his own party consumed time that should have been spent preparing for government. Instead of deciding where he wanted Britain to be in a generation and working out how to get there, three years were wasted in gestures and media stunts.

Like Genesis in the Bible, Clause Four's stirring words captured Labour's soul and defined its principles. The Archbishop of Canterbury does not believe that God created the universe in seven days but sees no point in replacing the powerful words of Genesis with a turgid account of Big Bang theory. Party members looked on bemused as this navel-gazing exercise rolled on.

Mandelson debated the issue with me at Brent East and talked eloquently about 'new forms' of public ownership. As we were driven back to the Commons by his enthusiastic researcher Derek Draper, I warned that the inherent tensions between a chancellor and prime minister could be avoided if they shared one set of economic advisers. Mandelson said I needn't worry as he had 'never known two politicians [who were] such close friends as Blair and Brown'.

Most party members had no desire to change Clause Four but, not wanting to rock the boat, they didn't fight back. However, there was panic among the 'fanatics' when they saw the humiliatingly low return of ballots in the party vote on the issue. Party officials were taken off other work to phone members and ask them to return their ballot paper in order to give Blair his victory on a passable turnout. Campbell records that *Daily Mail* boss Sir David English was in raptures, whereas a morose Arthur Scargill told me, 'This isn't the party I joined.'

What really demoralised members was Blair's decision to send his son Euan to the Catholic London Oratory school in Fulham rather than the local Islington comprehensive which was later made famous in 2009 when visited and praised by Michelle Obama. Blair's limited understanding of comprehensive schools was revealed during dinner with Tom Sawyer, general secretary of the Labour party, when he and Cherie were shocked to discover that Tom sent his kids to the local comprehensive. Alastair (whose partner Fiona campaigned in defence of comprehensive education) opposed Blair's decision. Blair agreed it would boost the local school if Euan went there but would not change his mind. MPs from all wings of the party were shocked and disgusted. Almost without exception Labour MPs sent their children to local comprehensives because the existence of selective schools disadvantaged the majority. Another shock followed when Blair began to eulogise Margaret Thatcher's record.

This praise of Thatcher, his choice of an exclusive religious school and his willingness to fly round the world at the behest of Murdoch to address his senior executives took a toll on party members, but the desperation to win after sixteen years of Conservative rule kept them quiet. In his diaries Campbell records the anger of Kinnock in July 1998 when the Kinnocks joined him on holiday in France. After Kinnock's jibes about the Oratory and the absence of policy on Europe, Campbell describes the former leader's 'cheek muscles flexing like they do when he's close to totally losing it . . . hand movements getting wilder and then the heavy sarcasm. Mimicking Blair, Kinnock said "Oh Margaret Thatcher . . . not such a bad person, quite a radical . . . you had to admire her determination and her leadership" – that's what the fucking leader says . . . radical my arse. That woman fucking killed people.'

Glenys Kinnock complained that Blair didn't have 'a line on Africa'. 'It's not just Africa,' Neil chipped in, 'they haven't got a line on Asia, Australasia, any continent you mention.' He went on to complain that Blair couldn't deal with education because he had

chosen to send his own son to the SS Waffen Academy . . . He's sold out before he's even got there [on] tax, health, education, unions, full employment, race, immigration, everything, he's totally sold out. And for what? What are we FOR? It won't matter if we win, the bankers and the stockbrokers have got us already, by the fucking balls, laughing their heads off . . . How am I supposed to feel when I see you set off halfway round the world to grease [Murdoch] up . . . you'll get his support and then you'll get the support of a few racist bastards, and then you'll lose it again the minute you're in trouble.

The accuracy of Kinnock's analysis as recorded by Campbell is remarkable.

When Alastair pointed out that he had worked for Murdoch, Kinnock replied that 'the difference is you've got courage and bottle and you tell these fuckers what you think. Tony won't do that.' Years later Sir Robert Armstrong, Cabinet Secretary to Thatcher, Major and Blair, recounted how they each responded when told they were wrong. With Thatcher there would be an explosion, Major would look hurt but Blair would say, 'I actually think I agree with you.'

*

This relatively benign phase of Blair's leadership was about to change. Bill Morris, who had succeeded Ron Todd as TGWU general secretary, complained about a 'creeping intolerance', and newspapers said Blair had 'gone ballistic' when Leeds North East chose an Islington councillor, Liz Davies, a Labour Briefing supporter, as a candidate for this marginal seat. Living in Islington, Blair was aware of the struggles on the council where Liz had campaigned against the closure of nurseries and other cutbacks. Instead of accepting a diversity of views in the party three Islington councillors, including James Purnell, alleged that Liz had incited violence at a council meeting when the public protested against the closure of adventure playgrounds. Liz was summoned to Labour's Disputes Committee, who recommended the NEC reject her selection but gave no reason for their recommendation. When the matter was debated at the 1995 party conference, Blair put Clare Short up to smear Liz, implying that she was outside Labour's broad church. Leeds North East Labour party was suspended and its officers expelled.

Eventually Liz received an apology from Purnell in a High Court settlement (long after she was stripped of her candidacy). Purnell and the others made contributions to Jeremy Corbyn's general election fund in lieu of paying her damages.

Local parties' freedom to select their own candidates for Parliament had been eroded in Kinnock's time. After losing the Glasgow Govan by-election Labour's NEC gave itself the power to replace candidates they felt would not survive media scrutiny in a by-election. Now Blair decided that only candidates acceptable to him would be endorsed. Fortunately he only looked at marginals and ignored candidates in seats considered hopeless. (On the night of Labour's landslide in 1997, a panicked Mandelson ordered party officials to assemble files on the new MPs who had not been subject to the rigorous vetting of those in marginal seats.)

Blair also began a purge of councillors with many years' experience. A purge of Labour's Euro MPs followed, with party members being denied the right to re-select them. Twenty-four of Labour's MEPs were critical of Blair so he rigged the selections to ensure only three of them were re-elected. The rush to remove left-wingers led to a shift in the social class of Labour's elected representatives. Instead of local wards and GMCs choosing people based on local knowledge and experience, candidates now had to fill in long application forms demanding that they list their management skills – a bit much given that none of the 'big four' had ever managed so much as a snack bar. The result was a cull of those who lacked university education and a big reduction in working-class councillors, both black and white.

In contrast to the integrity of John Smith, Blair's team had no compunction about the use of smears and dirty tricks. The first shocking example of this was in the Littleborough and Saddleworth by-election in July 1995, where, in a failed effort to get the Labour candidate Phil Woolas elected, New Labour circulated leaflets falsely claiming that the Lib Dem candidate was 'soft on crime and high on drugs' and would allow unlimited immigration into Britain. I was particularly appalled as I had campaigned for Woolas when he stood for president of the NUS. I criticised these tactics at the time and wasn't surprised when fifteen years later Woolas was thrown out of Parliament for repeating these dirty tricks with smears that his Lib Dem opponent supported terrorism.

I had known Joy Johnson, the head of news programming at the BBC, as a local Hampstead Labour activist since 1976 and watched her rise through television news. She was now in charge of news coverage and of the running order of the nightly bulletin. Although Joy was a solid socialist Blair offered her Mandelson's old job as head of communications and campaigns and I was the only one who warned her not to take the job. As well as losing her influence at the BBC, she had no background in campaigning and her left-wing politics would make it impossible to work with Blair. I also feared that Mandelson would interfere. But she was a fan of Gordon Brown and hoped to use her position to support him. I was so concerned that even I considered seeing Blair to warn him it couldn't possibly work but I needn't have worried as, on her first day in HQ the national agent, Margaret McDonagh, told her, 'I'm going to get you out of this job.' Realising her mistake, Joy started keeping a diary as insurance.

After a few months Blair said that it wasn't working and that they needed to discuss her departure. 'I understand you're keeping a diary,' he enquired nervously. She got a generous severance and agreed not to publish unless New Labour briefed against her. I urged her to publish anyway but she stuck to her agreement, which is a pity, as it is a hilarious record of the jealousies in the inner circle, depicting a besotted Mandelson, a flattered and flirtatious Blair and Prescott expressing his discomfort and disgust through his body language.

Blair's next stage in tightening his grip was to replace chief whip Derek Foster, who had allowed MPs to disagree with the party line without punishment. The real power of the whips is their advice to leaders on whom to appoint to junior posts in government and opposition. Ambition is the discipline that keeps people in line. Whips did not usually waste their breath on serial rebels like me. (The only real thuggery I ever witnessed among whips was the Tory whip David Lightbown pinning a fellow Tory MP up against a wall, slapping him across the face and reducing him to tears, but Lightbown is the sad and lonely exception who was found dead in his flat surrounded by empty bottles of booze.)

Derek was forced to make way for Donald Dewar (in exchange for a promise, never honoured, of a cabinet job). My only experience of Dewar was before John Smith's death when I popped into the tea room where John, Donald and Hilary Armstrong were chatting at a table. I bounced over to say, 'You'll never believe this, I've just come from my surgery where this impeccably dressed, middle-class, middle-aged woman turned up to say, "I've just one piece of advice to give you, Mr Livingstone. If you want to achieve your political ambition you must learn the lesson of Mr Heath and forsake all sexual activity."' John and Hilary fell about laughing, but there was a significant pause before Dewar's lips turned up in a thin smile.

First elected in 1966, Donald was tall, bent and scruffy with the air of a vulture about to pick over your bones. After his wife left him to marry Derry Irvine, who became Tony Blair's Lord Chancellor, Donald never remarried, immersing himself in books and politics. He was respected as a master of the detail of Scottish devolution and stuck to his beliefs even when unpopular locally, supporting abortion and reducing the age of homosexual consent to sixteen. Nevertheless he was a disciplinarian, and committed to Blair's New Labour project – the ideal chief whip for a leader intolerant of dissent. Immediately whipping got tougher and when I tried to enter the lobby to vote against the party line on one issue, the Labour whips formed a physical barrier to prevent me crossing until I took a run at them.

Things changed as soon as Donald took over and I was summoned to the first of a series of meetings where he complained whenever I wrote or spoke out of line. Journalists were briefed that I was in danger of being sacked as a Labour candidate, including one occasion when I was at the zoo. When the TV cameras turned up I was interviewed in front of the vulture cages. Realising that if I gave Donald half a chance to expel me he would do so, we began two years of elaborate sparring in which I pushed to the limit without crossing the line. I tried to get to know Donald, but when I asked if he had seen any good films lately he dourly replied, 'I haven't been to the cinema since *The Sound of Music*.'

My worst spat with Donald was caused by Mo Mowlam, who took me to lunch to pick my brains when she took the shadow cabinet brief on Northern Ireland. She had never met Sinn Fein and I offered to be a sounding board between her and Gerry Adams. She didn't understand Sinn Fein and as paramilitaries they also saw things differently. After the 1992 general election the IRA had switched its strategy to blowing up targets in the City, which told John Major this couldn't continue, so on 15 December 1993 Major unveiled the Downing Street Declaration which he had negotiated with the Irish government. This led to an IRA ceasefire on 31 August 1994. Unfortunately Major's overall majority of 21 at the 1992 election had been reduced to single figures by defections and by-election defeats and he depended on the votes of the Ulster Unionists in any confidence motion. This meant Major couldn't bring the IRA into a peace process without losing his majority.

Adams needed to be involved in the peace process if the ceasefire was to hold so Sinn Fein told me they wanted Labour to give Major a promise not to bring his government down on a confidence motion in order that the peace process could move forward. I pointed out there wasn't a cat in hell's chance of such an undertaking succeeding but it showed the scale of misunderstanding between politicians used to parliamentary procedures and those used to fighting a guerrilla war. After eighteen months with no progress the IRA renewed their campaign with a bomb in Canary Wharf on 9 February 1996 followed by the bombing of Manchester that June.

Mo was prepared to take risks and Adams needed to carry all the IRA with him. In October 1996 Jeremy Corbyn and I met Sinn Fein leaders in the House of Commons. When it was leaked to newspapers that we had met the IRA's Army Council – which we had not done – I said on the *Today* programme I suspected the leak came from MI5 officers getting involved in politics again. MI5 issued a denial, which pointed the finger of suspicion back at New Labour and led to an unpleasant meeting with Donald Dewar, who believed I had been responsible for the leak and blew his top.

I couldn't tell Donald that I had been passing messages between Sinn Fein and Mo – who was actually sitting on the opposition front bench at the same time as I was meeting Sinn Fein – as Mo would have been instructed to stop. My relationship with Donald was now poisonous but Mo was grateful I had covered her back; she came round for dinner with her partner Jon and later supported my campaign for mayor. I was still passing messages to Mo from Sinn Fein's Mitchell McLaughlin in the election. She urged Blair to give me a job on her Northern Ireland team after we won the 1997 election, a request he sensibly refused as my presence would have made negotiations with Unionists impossible. (On 15 November 1998 the *Sunday Times* claimed that MI5 passed a file on my contacts with Sinn Fein to Blair when he became prime minister, and this was why he did not give me a job.) As peace talks started I decided anything I had to say could only make matters worse and I took a private vow of silence.

*

Although my relationship with Donald was bad, it was nothing compared to the rancid hostility from the ghastly little careerists now flooding into the party in the hope of jobs. Most had spent years infighting in the National Union of Students and the National Organisation of Labour Students, indulging in ballot rigging and smearing opponents. This was bad enough in student politics but these attitudes were damaging at a time when we needed enthusiasm and commitment from the membership. Living together, socialising and operating through their own caucuses, they did immense damage to the Labour party. They were like a clone of the Militant Tendency that Kinnock had expelled years before. When Labour's headquarters staff moved into Millbank Tower I coined the term 'Millbank Tendency' to cover Blairite party officials and their ex-student foot soldiers. This prompted a visit by an outraged Derek Draper, who complained that it was insulting to equate the two 'Tendencies'.

In fairness, Derek was the most human of the Millbank hordes. He at least held some traditional Labour values. In 1988 he'd invited me to a student meeting in Manchester and several of us had gone back to his flat for a drink, where I was stunned to see a life-size portrait of his hero Roy Hattersley pinned on the wall. Either Derek was the only student in Britain whose pin-up was Roy or I had stumbled on a bizarre homoerotic cult. Youthful allegiances shift rapidly, and after arriving as a researcher in Westminster he became a dedicated follower of Mandelson. He was soon running the official New Labour magazine, *Progress*, but he was never prepared to reveal who bankrolled this flashy publication. I liked Derek, recognised myself in this nerdy political obsessive and understood how being at the centre of power as Mandelson's right-hand man went to his head. Eventually caught claiming he had access to ministers, he resigned and left Britain to become a psychotherapist, but on his return he supported my campaign to become mayor.

Simon Fletcher was also from student politics, leading an occupation at the City of London Poly where he graduated in Politics and Government with the highest pass marks in the poly's history. He worked on Tony Benn's archives and served briefly on Camden Council but decided to do better things with his life than decide which services to cut next on this flagship New Labour council. As secretary of London Labour Left he worked with Redmond O'Neill and was on my side in the ARA split. When we had a Labour government I would need more help to be effective so I employed him as a researcher to work alongside Maureen Charleson.

*

I coped with the early years of New Labour because I was having a lot of fun outside Parliament. As well as being paid to eat by Rosie Boycott, I appeared as myself with Neil Pearson in the Channel 4 comedy show *Drop the Dead Donkey* along with the Tory MP Teddy Taylor, who appeared only on condition that he could lecture the studio audience about the evils of Europe during a break in filming. As well as annual appearances on *Have I Got News For You* I played myself in a TV mini-series called *A Woman's Guide to Adultery* opposite Amanda Donohoe and Theresa Russell. After spending twelve hours repeating the same half a dozen lines just to get four minutes of usable film I was bored out of my skull and decided that actors really earned their money.

Alan Clark and I were asked to co-host a late-night TV politics show but he was furious I had accepted a fee of £500 per programme. 'Bloody fool, we could have got a grand at least,' he said. He told me how the civil service isolated Thatcher from her right-wing supporters and was interested in the way we had organised the GLC to prevent that kind of isolation. Everything was fine until we filmed the pilot and Alan suddenly stopped being controversial and opinionated and came out with the standard party line. The programme was dropped but Alan got back into Parliament. Whenever Alan saw me in the Commons with a woman he would bear down, oozing charm and uttering an aristocratic version of Joey Tribbiani from *Friends*' 'How YOU doing?' I was surprised to get on well with Norman Tebbit, but at least we shared a working-class background and despair about the drift of John Major's government to the point where he pinned me up against a wall and demanded, 'When are you going to get rid of this bloody awful government?'

I also liked the millionaire zoo owner John Aspinall, who was more right-wing than Tebbit and had sat around with Lord Lucan and James Goldsmith fantasising about a coup to overthrow Harold Wilson, but he stood as an independent against Michael Howard in 1997 so he wasn't all bad. On the day of his finals at Oxford he decided to go to Ascot instead, making enough money to open his own gambling club, which sustained two zoos with a remarkably successful record in captive breeding. I was introduced to him by the journalist Tom Baldwin, who liked the idea of two people from political extremes who shared a love of animals. When the local council tried to close his zoo on health and safety grounds I gave evidence on his behalf. Much against his political judgment, he donated to my mayoral campaign on his death bed.

I particularly enjoyed a dinner party with John Aspinall, Alan Clark and Jimmy Goldsmith, where we were guests of Carla and Charles Powell. Alan Clark nibbled the ear of the woman sitting next to him as his wife sat at the other end of the table. Charles had been Thatcher's private secretary from 1984 and recounted his struggle to talk her out of her plan to give all four million Hong Kong Chinese British passports so they could flee the communists and come to Britain, where they would transform cities like Liverpool.

Out of the blue the rock band Blur asked me to do a monologue for their track 'Ernold Same' on *The Great Escape* album. A song about a sad, dull man with a boring life needed a dull, nasal mono-tone, and when John Major declined I jumped at the idea. I liked Blur's singer Damon Albarn: he was pleasant, polite and without any prima-donna traits. We later worked together fighting the abo-lition of student grants and opposing the invasion of Iraq. The only problem when I joined them for a live gig at Wembley Arena was the noise from the mass of ecstatic Blur fans. 'Ernold Same' is a fair-ly quiet piece and I couldn't hear the music to know when to start speaking my lines, so the band riffed until I plunged in and began.

I didn't realise it at the time, but these activities changed Lon-doners' perception of me. Throughout the 1980s my public face was purely political but in addition to the light entertainment work the *Standard* ran humorous bits about my interest in natural his-tory and gardening. Through after-dinner speaking I reached the business community that had been so hostile a decade before. But there were limits and when asked by the tobacco lobbying organisa-tion to be their spokesman in Parliament I replied that they were responsible for the death of my father and they wrote back saying, 'We seem to have touched a raw nerve.' Too bloody right. The lob-byists were clearly preparing for a change of government.

*

Nothing leaked from the circle around Blair so Labour MPs had no idea what plans were being laid for the next government. News-paper interviewers commented on his eagerness to please and his lack of class politics led to embarrassing incidents such as that in-volving the touchy-feely Australian priest Peter Thomson who was talked up as Blair's moral guide. New buzzwords like 'stakeholder economy' I dismissed as vacuous rubbish, prompting a visit from Derek Draper to warn that it was unacceptable to be critical of such an exciting new concept. Alastair's diaries show that Brown shared my scepticism. 'It was pretty clear that Gordon Brown did not believe in the basic stakeholder economy at all,' writes Campbell on 17 January 1996, adding, 'Brown used the term in a way that made it sound like a disease.'

When Blair and Brown announced there would be no increase in income tax, keeping Thatcher's tax cuts for the rich, I assumed this was a ploy to win the election. It never occurred to me they really believed in these allowances for the wealthy. Many Labour MPs expected Blair to take up the ideas in Will Hutton's book *The State We're In*, which set out economic and political reforms to make Britain like a modern Scandinavian social democracy, but Will told me there hadn't been any interest from Blair.

As Blair sucked up to the Tory media through 1996, I assumed that he and his team were at the same time drawing up a strategy to modernise our economy. Our work at the *Socialist Economic Bulletin* proved that the biggest factor in economic success was investment. The British industrial revolution happened because we were the first nation to invest as much as 7 per cent of annual GDP in our industries, giving Britain a hundred years of global domination. After the civil war in the USA investment there reached 19 per cent of GDP, driving growth which ensured an American-dominated twentieth century. After 1945 western Europe caught up with the USA, led by West Germany with 25 per cent of its GDP invested (Britain lagged behind at only 20 per cent). Japan became the second-largest economy in the world when its investment peaked at 38 per cent of GDP. I dusted off the argument I had first made in *Livingstone's Labour* that we should cut military spending to the European average so that we could switch an additional 2 per cent of GDP to investment.

Given the sophistication of John Ross's economic database, we would have been delighted to carry out some analysis for Blair but we were never asked, and Alastair reveals in his diaries their lack of real preparation, in contrast to their obsession with the daily news agenda. As early as 3 January 1995 Campbell says that he warned Jonathan Powell, brother of Charles and Blair's chief of staff during his premiership, about the short-termism dominating Blair's office. A year into Blair's leadership, Alastair notes on 17 July 1995, 'it remained a big problem that we didn't have an economic message easily understood by party and public'. The nearest Labour came to an economic strategy was in the need to accept 'competitive tax rates in an enterprise economy' and rejection of Labour as a party of 'tax and spend for the sake of it' – although exactly when Labour had increased taxes just 'for the sake of it' was never made clear.

There was further outrage among Labour MPs when it was announced that Blair and Brown would follow the Tories' spending plans (which Ken Clarke described as eye-wateringly tight) for the first two years of a Labour government. Denis Healey, who knew how long it takes to gear up an increase in spending, was contemptuous of their naivety. Campbell reveals that discussions on independence for the Bank of England were under way two years earlier but just eleven weeks before the general election he records Brown as saying he 'did not believe we had to campaign on the economy', and the only reference to the key issue of whether or not to join a single currency is on 12 December 1996, when, Campbell records, '[Blair] was determined to be pro-single currency but they had to understand just how awful the press were'.

Knowing his plans would have little support, Blair neutered the party so that he could ignore criticism. Instead of conference making and voting on policy he proposed a National Policy Forum dominated by ministers and party officials who would prepare policy documents for discussion at the conference, where delegates would not be allowed to amend them. Blair also wanted to stop party members electing MPs to the NEC, thus removing Diane

Abbott and other left-wing MPs. Now only MPs could vote MPs onto Labour's NEC. Other party members could elect six people to the NEC as long as they weren't MPs. New NEC posts were created for other office holders so that NEC approval became a rubber-stamp exercise and conference was in effect silenced.

Trade union votes were lined up to support these changes with promises that union leaders would have real access and influence over ministers, but Blair had no intention of honouring this deal. His contempt for union leaders is shown in Alastair Campbell's diary on 7 July 1995. After a meeting with union leaders, 'Blair complains "They just weren't serious people" . . . he called them "you guys", then it was "listen, you guys", then it was "for heavens sake, you guys"'. Two days later Alastair describes the T&G conference, after which Blair 'was almost speechless with rage. "These people are stupid and they are malevolent. They beg me to go to their conference and then stitch me up, and then they get all hurt and pathetic when I say what I think. They complain that we want to distance ourselves and then give us all the evidence why we should distance ourselves. I have no option but to go up there and blow them out of the water. I'm finished with these people," he said, "absolutely finished with them."'

Blair's attitude to unions was shared by the Millbank Tendency and reflected a contempt for working-class people who hadn't been to university and who also had the temerity to challenge the bright young careerists who'd recently joined the party. Blair also imposed a new code of conduct for MPs, making it easier for them to be expelled from the party on ill-defined grounds such as 'bringing the party into disrepute'. My new researcher Simon Fletcher told me, 'They're closing the Labour party down.' My hope was that once in office pressure from MPs and the need to tackle Britain's problems would force Blair to be more radical.

Twice during 1996 Margaret Hodge (now a Labour MP) came

to me saying I should see Blair about a job so I had to decide whether I wanted to be part of the struggle inside Blair's government or else to campaign from the back benches. I didn't want any misunderstanding so I sent Blair a letter analysing Labour's polls since 1945, showing that, contrary to his belief that splits and rows led to Labour's defeats, the decline in our vote was most dramatic when our economic policies failed. In February, just before the start of the 1997 election campaign, I was ushered into his office. He was alone. When I asked if he had sent Hodge he laughed and said no, she lived just round the corner from him and thought that gave her the right to talk to others on his behalf. He was pleasant but left most of the talking to me as I explained what needed to be done with the economy. Our only disagreement was his belief that a Labour government could be more radical in a second term. I said my experience in local government was of being ground down by bureaucracy and the media so that it's best to push big reforms at the start.

The meeting seemed to go well and he brought it to an end by saying, 'I would like to have you in my government but I can't make any promises' as he already had too many people jostling for too few places. A few days later Mandelson, bemused that I'd approached Blair, discussed how I could help squash the inevitable press stories that Blair would be undermined by the left once in government. We didn't have long to wait. I was installing a pond on a friend's allotment when Mandelson (who couldn't believe I was not out canvassing) rang, saying the papers were about to run a 'left coup' story and he needed my sycophantic comments in the *Observer*, where they duly appeared on 6 April. The rest of the campaign was uneventful. My members went to work in the marginals so I wandered around Brent East with a megaphone. Realising they would finally be rid of the Tories, a carnival mood developed among people on the streets. Labour only expected to gain 60 seats but I campaigned in seats we hadn't won for a generation, such as Tony McNulty's

Harrow East, where I turned up with the *Dad's Army* actor Clive Dunn to do a walkabout in the town centre.

Unusually, Brent Council opened postal votes the day before the May Day poll. In the past they had always been an accurate guide to the final result. Now they showed I had won two-thirds of the vote on a 14 per cent swing from the Tories. Labour was on course for its biggest ever majority, but when I phoned Blair's campaign team they didn't bother to pass it on to him.

*

Labour was indeed elected with its largest-ever overall major-ity, 179, as the nation returned 418 of our MPs to Parliament. As the scale of our landslide became clear people were ecstatic but as Friday turned into Saturday and I didn't get a call from Blair my sense of disappointment grew. The following Tuesday, when Brown announced he was giving the Bank of England independence to set interest rates, I realised I wouldn't have lasted long as a junior minister. The decision would favour the financial sector and under-mine the country's manufacturing base. In 1931 the government imposed a low interest rate of 2 per cent which ended the Depres-sion and was continued by the post-war Labour government. But since 1951 interest rates in Britain were usually set around 2 per cent higher than those of our major competitors, a real blow to our exporters. When Ken Clarke, who represented a manufactur-ing area, became chancellor in 1993 he understood this and kept refusing the requests of the governor of the Bank of England to increase interest rates. This led to a fall in unemployment, brought the pound down to a reasonable level and allowed our firms to re-capture some of their lost markets, leaving a better economy for Labour to inherit.

The exchange rate started increasing before the election and Brown's decisions pushed it higher, so one and a half million manufacturing jobs have been lost since 1997. The over-strong pound also fed obscene excesses in the City's financial institutions, leading to an unsustainable property boom and overheating London's economy.

Brown and Blair knew there would be strong opposition to this policy so they announced it the day before Labour MPs met for the first time. A sign of how MPs were to be managed came at the first meeting of the parliamentary Labour party, which was moved outside Parliament so TV could broadcast the standing ovation as Blair entered and delivered his sound-bite-laden speech; but the TV crews were ordered to leave before MPs questioned Blair. Dennis Skinner and I led the attack on the Bank of England decision but our points were ignored and the meeting was told it had to end because photographers had come for pictures of Blair surrounded by women MPs in the notorious 'Blair's Babes' photo.

Donald Dewar was replaced as chief whip by Nick Brown but once again I was blackballed for the Treasury Select Committee, although Nick did put me on the Northern Ireland Select Committee. After ten years of being kept off every committee, several MPs saw my name and assumed it was a typing error. Now I was on a committee with Unionist MPs who had denounced me for years. The committee was chaired by the former Northern Ireland secretary Sir Peter Brooke (Marlborough, Balliol College and past president of the Oxford Union). He was a consensual one-nation Tory who wanted to produce unanimous reports, which meant lengthy debates about points that divided the Unionist parties. The Official Unionist Roy Beggs and the DUP's Peter Robinson wouldn't vote until the even more hard-line and erratic Jeffrey Donaldson announced how he was voting. The worst meetings were when the commissioner of the Royal Ulster Constabulary, Sir Ronnie Flanagan, gave evidence. He survived by answering at interminable length until no one cared what he said as long as he stopped. I joked with

Peter Brooke that if we asked the time he would take at least an hour to reply.

Blair's ban on members electing MPs to the NEC was too late to stop one last election under the old rules. For eight years I had been runner-up or third behind Jack Straw, and with Gordon Brown standing down I expected Jack to win and was amazed when he withdrew to allow Mandelson to stand for the first time. Blair said his project would be complete when Labour learned to love Mandelson, and with Blair's popularity they expected the party to fall into line. Peter Hain stood as the soft-left candidate and several months of rallies and articles in the left press and the *Guardian* followed as tension mounted. I went on holiday to Seattle in August 1997 leaving Simon to run my campaign – a real baptism of fire. His daily call had him excited or depressed as endorsements built up. Most papers assumed Hain or Mandelson would get a seat, dismissing my challenge as the last gasp of the hard left, but the *Guardian* and *Tribune* came out for me even though Hain was chairman of the *Tribune* board.

The conference hall was packed as we waited for the result at the annual conference in September. In the minutes before the announcement London Labour party general secretary Terry Ashton whispered, 'You've pissed all over him.' Mo Mowlam and Neil Kinnock were wheeled out to sit supportively on either side of Mandelson but the roar of delight as I beat him spoke volumes about the party's doubts about Blair. A delighted Stephen Pound, just elected at Ealing North, clapped me on the back but as we were live on TV he was later berated by the whips. That night in the bar Stephen tried to make amends with a tray of champagne but he tripped and the champagne went down the whips' trousers instead of their throats. I was amazed by the number of right-wing MPs who had voted for me. Michael Cocks, Jim Callaghan's chief whip, who worked with John Golding to defeat Tony Benn in 1983, said:

'Things have got so bad in this party I had to vote for a cunt like you.' When I thanked Gordon Brown for standing down I could tell he was delighted that Mandelson had lost.

Audrey Wise went round conference warning about plans to cut benefits for single parents by £6 a week. I was one of several MPs who lobbied Harriet Harman, who honestly explained that the Tories had left two problems behind: the cut in single-parent benefit and a cut in housing benefit to private tenants living alone. Unable to get enough money from Brown to deal with both problems, she decided to prevent thousands of private tenants being evicted while she fought to help single parents the following year. When I asked why she hadn't announced the good news about single tenants, she said Downing Street didn't want to draw attention to policies helping the poorest.

I had a similar response when I cornered Jack Straw, the new Home Secretary, in the Division Lobby to ask what he was doing about the tens of thousands of refugees whose applications (some going back fifteen years) had been rejected but who had not been deported. The Tory Home Secretary Michael Howard had lost control of the system, with deportations barely in double figures each year. At the asylum processing centre in Croydon a room was so full of fading applications that rats were nesting in them. The only way to deal with this chaos was by offering an amnesty for those already here (which could be blamed on the Tories) and starting afresh with a new and fair system. Jack was sympathetic but knew Downing Street would fear the *Daily Mail*'s reaction.

Years later Tessa Jowell told me that as health minister she commissioned hard-hitting adverts to reduce teenage pregnancy using language young people would understand. The ads were rejected by Number 10 as they would alienate the *Daily Mail*. Teenage pregnancy in Britain is still the highest in Europe.

*

A few weeks after the Labour party conference Blair invited me in for a one-to-one chat. When he asked how I thought the government was doing after six months I didn't pull any punches. 'Much worse than I expected,' I told him, and detailed my disappointment that he had stayed within Tory spending limits and had not used the Tories' phoney budget figures to increase tax on those earning over £100,000 a year. I also thought he was mistaken not to hold a referendum on joining the euro as his poll ratings were so high he could pull it off. 'Do you really think that?' he replied. I responded, 'You're never going to be this popular again; it's your best chance.' When he asked if I was interested in serving in his government I said, 'I don't see any point in being in your government as everything is run from the centre. Ministers aren't allowed any responsibility and I couldn't have Alastair Campbell vetting my speeches.'

Blair's pleasant demeanour evaporated, his face hardened and although I can't remember the exact words he used, it was along the lines that if I obstructed his reforms he would destroy me. Seven years would pass before I had another meeting alone with him. Redmond O'Neill was waiting anxiously with Maureen and Simon. 'You're well out of it,' he said with relief. I didn't know until Paddy Ashdown's diaries were published that Blair wanted Paddy to join the cabinet so I assume his interest in giving me a job was to pre-empt complaints from Labour MPs for bringing in a Liberal.

Parliament reassembled for the vote to cut child benefit for single parents. Given the sound economy we didn't have to do this, but it showed the press and bankers that we were prepared to be brutal and by forcing Labour MPs to vote for something they knew was wrong it set a pattern by which Blair could get away with anything.

Harriet went through the humiliation of being unable to answer repeated challenges from John Humphrys on the *Today* programme: 'Are you doing this because you have to or because you want to?' She was also left isolated on the front bench, leading

Labour MP Martin Salter to complain that Brown should have had the courtesy to sit next to Harriet as she carried out his policy. Even worse were the images on television showing Blair holding a lavish party for celebrities at which Noel Gallagher of Oasis was plied with champagne while the MPs voted to make single parents' lives worse. Privately MPs complained about having to vote for something they knew was wrong, but few of them were prepared to damage their career prospects. Some were in tears as they had to walk past Tory Peter Lilley, the former social security minister, who thanked them for finally carrying out the policy he started. Margaret Beckett told him to 'piss off'. By the time I spoke I was angry enough to ask, 'When is this government going to pick on someone bigger than they are?' knowing it would annoy the macho Millbank Tendency. Next morning the *Today* programme reported that I faced having the party whip withdrawn from me, but the trauma the vote caused meant that Millbank decided not to make me a hero.

*

The NEC was very different from the one I had served on a decade earlier. Blair had little interest in the work of the committee, often leaving after he had delivered his report, which diminished the relevance of NEC proceedings. In November 1997, when the Bernie Ecclestone affair blew up, I believed Blair when he said the delay on banning cigarette advertising at Formula 1 motor races had nothing to do with Ecclestone giving £1 million to Labour. Ecclestone's warning that the ban could lead to the loss of many jobs would have struck a chord with any Labour leader. I said this on *Newsnight* but added that there should be an investigation. Phyllis Starkey, an über-Blairite MP, ran around the tea room getting Labour MPs to sign a letter to the whips demanding that Diane Abbott (who had said the same thing) and myself should have the whip withdrawn from us. I started referring to her as Phyllis Stasi. She didn't talk to me for years. The whips took no action, perhaps because MPs were joking about Downing Street becoming a Berni Inn or perhaps because Blair had not been honest. Andrew Rawnsley in his book *Servants of the People* reports that Blair agreed with Ecclestone to keep the size of the donation secret. The party's accounts simply recorded a donation of 'more than £5,000'.

Ecclestone won Blair over by having him driven round Silverstone while the crowds waved Union Jacks at him. No one told Frank Dobson or Tessa Jowell, who went ahead with plans to ban tobacco advertising. An alarmed Ecclestone asked Jonathan Powell to arrange a meeting with Blair, even though the Labour party were seeking a further donation from him, and he brought along Max Mosley, who had also made a donation to Labour. Blair did not check Ecclestone's claim that the ban would cost 50,000 jobs and £900 million of exports. Following the meeting Blair told Frank to exempt Formula 1 from the ban, without mentioning the donation.

Now journalist Tom Baldwin asked Downing Street if there had been donations by Ecclestone, at which point an appalled Frank was told about the £1 million. He replied, 'Cor, fuck me.' Blair referred the matter to Sir Patrick Neill, chairman of the Commission on Standards in Public Life, and was shocked to be told the money should be returned and no more donations sought. When the story broke, Brown was asked on the *Today* programme if Ecclestone had given money. He answered: 'I have not been told and I certainly don't know what the true position is.' But Gordon had indeed known, and is described by Rawnsley as leaving the interview 'in a red mist which staggered even those who had long endured his titanic tempers'. Brown raged, 'I lied. I lied. My credibility will be in shreds. I lied. If this gets out, I'll be destroyed.'

Interviewed by John Humphrys at the time, Blair claimed, untruthfully, that Ecclestone was told Labour couldn't accept further donations and that the issue had been referred to Sir Patrick Neill *before* there was any media interest. Drawing on his amateur acting career, he climaxed with a wounded claim that 'I am a pretty straight sort of guy'. When the truth was revealed in Rawnsley's book in the autumn of 2000 and Tories demanded Brown's resignation, he wriggled as Jon Snow pointed out 'these are the sort of weasel hair-splittings the Tories used to go in for'. Brown supporters briefed the press that when Blair told him about the donation he said, 'What the fuck are we doing taking money from someone like him?'

*

In the wake of the Ecclestone affair Labour party general secretary Tom Sawyer was working with ministers to draw up new election expenditure laws. I proposed there should be a £5 million limit on general election spending by each party to stop dodgy deals with big business. When Tom insisted we needed £25 million to run a campaign I said this was wasted on newspaper and billboard advertising in a pointless 'arms race' with the Tories when most voters treated all our claims with scepticism. Tom got his way and Blair's continued fund-raising culminated in the police investigating the 'cash for peerages' scandal. New Labour received more money from big business than trade unions, including donations from Enron, Railtrack (who were bidding to take over part of London Underground) and Raytheon (an arms firm breaching labour laws in the US and actively selling land mines. It still received an £800 million contract from the Ministry of Defence.) By 1999 the Labour party conference was attended by 1,500 party members and trade unionists and 18,500 lobbyists or journalists.

The NEC should also have taken my advice on the order of candidates at the 1999 Euro election. They put Richard Balfe, Reg Goodwin's chair of housing at the GLC from 1975 to 1977, in third place on the list for London-wide seats so he was certain to win. Since his GLC days he had continued to drift to the right and bragged to me that expenses and allowances in Brussels were so generous that 'I haven't had to cash my salary cheque for ten years'. When I proposed moving Balfe down and one of the women up the list the NEC got really angry, making me suspicious that the party was favouring Euro MPs who diverted funds into party coffers. I lost the vote, but following a row about Euro MPs' expenses Balfe defected to the Tories.

My worst clash on the NEC came when I described Brown's 1998 budget as cowardly because it failed to shift the tax burden from working- and middle-class families to the rich. Blair complained about my use of the word 'cowardly', which I said was a bit much, given that a very senior official inside Number 10 told Rawnsley that Brown had psychological flaws. There was embarrassment in the room as Blair denied this, although everyone round the table knew it was true.

There were some issues where I thought Blair was right. In 1991 I had been the first MP to call for military intervention to stop Slobodan Milosevic when he unleashed troops against the Slovenes and Croats. I had been appalled at the failure of Major and Clinton to stop Milosevic's ethnic cleansing of Bosnian Muslims so I was delighted that Blair took a firm stand when Milosevic started on the Kosovans. The left was split on whether or not the West should intervene and, as in Bosnia, the lack of any strategic Western interests, such as oil, meant Blair had to go out on a limb to push for America's support. The debate in Parliament was one of the few occasions where Tony Benn and myself were on different sides of the argument.

*

The *Evening Standard*'s right-wing politics had softened with the appointment of Max Hastings as editor the previous year so I wasn't surprised to get a phone call from Gaynor Wetherall, associate editor on the paper's *ES* magazine, asking if I would write a weekly restaurant column. I was invited to lunch by Adam Edwards, editor of the magazine, at Kensington Place, the local restaurant for *Standard* hacks. When I arrived with Simon, Edwards wasn't there due to a hangover and Gaynor had brought her colleague Emma Beal, who as office manager dealt with the difficult columnists and their extravagant expenses claims. Gaynor and Emma made it clear that they expected me to take *ES* staff to lunch on some Fridays when they had little work to do.

I also used the column to pay for lunch with Labour activists representing various left-wing groups who were organising the election of left-wingers to the constituency section of the NEC now that Blair's rule change was in place. Although many of them couldn't stand each other, they were all delighted to discover they could meet at restaurants like the Red Fort rather than a gloomy room in a pub. Redmond came into his own as my unofficial liaison officer, bringing together the mutually loathing groups on the left with the more mainstream Labour Reform group, which was chaired by Andy Howell (the son of Denis Howell, one of Wilson's ministers).

*

Blair's changes were squeezing the life out of the party. The London party conference was only allowed to meet every two years and was rigidly managed and cut down to a quarter the size of the pre-Blair years. We used to discuss more or less everything except foreign policy, but now party officials censored local manifestos and wards found their councillors banned from reselection on spurious grounds. Christine Shawcroft, a councillor in Tower Hamlets for twelve years and a popular local teacher, was not allowed to stand again in 1998 even though she had been a member of the London

Labour party executive and had stood for the NEC several times in the trade union-controlled women's section.

For the left to win NEC seats we needed high-profile candidates like Christine, Pete Wilsman (a leading light in the Campaign for Labour Party Democracy) and *Tribune* editor Mark Seddon, but no one better symbolised the challenge to Blair than Liz Davies, who had been stripped of her Leeds North East candidacy. Redmond worried this might be a step too far but I believed that just as members backed me rather than Hain so they would support Liz as the best way of putting two fingers up to Blair.

Journalist Paul Routledge reported that the Downing Street Political Unit was running a slate called Members First, headed by the *EastEnders* star Michael Cashman, whose character had participated in the first gay kiss in a British soap opera and who went on to become an MEP, against our Grassroots slate (as we called it). The *Guardian* editorial urged members to vote for the Grassroots slate, so prompting a flood of Blairite letters to the paper. Although it breached rules banning personal attacks, Tom Sawyer issued a press release accusing Liz Davies of slurs and innuendo against party staff but on the *Today* programme he had no answer when I reminded him that the Blairite James Purnell and others had had to apologise in the High Court for smearing Liz. Sawyer alleged that Liz and Mark Seddon had been responsible for Thatcher's election even though both were doing their O levels at the time whereas Tom, as a union official, had been organising pickets in the 1978–9 winter of discontent. New Labour's Siôn Simon, writing in the *Spectator*, likened Liz Davies to a spy and a prostitute. Kinnock accused Liz of conducting 'politics with a perpetual sneer' and 'sour sectarianism' while dismissing Mark as a dupe of the left.

Instead of using the respected Electoral Reform Society to conduct the NEC ballot Labour employed Unity Security Balloting Limited, a company established by right-wing trade unions. To no one's surprise there were leaks about how the vote was going. Blair threatened to deselect any candidate who queried USB's conduct of the ballot publicly, and all complaints were dealt with internally and in secret by USB. As Liz Davies put it, 'Any complaints about the process would be known only to USB and not to Labour party members.'

We raised just £3,000 for our Grassroots campaign but the Blairites paid £125,000 for newspaper ads and members received an identically worded letter of support from their MPs (unless, of course, their MP was one of the few who were supporting us). The Blairites employed a phone canvassing company who were given party membership lists and a script saying 'the party wants you to vote for the Members First slate'. We discovered that all this was paid for by the right-wing Amalgamated Engineering and Electrical Union.

There was an eerie silence on the conference floor as the results were read out with Mark topping the ballot and the Grassroots slate winning four of the six seats, including Liz Davies in fourth place. I was in the press gallery briefing journalists on the significance of Liz's triumph as Alastair Campbell walked past, saying, 'Don't over-spin, Ken.'

*

Mum was now too frail to travel, though she still managed to get to the betting shop every day, but it was a shock when she had a heart attack. She wanted to leave hospital to get back to the horses but loved that the nurses gave her a glass of sherry every night. Her doctor said she needed to go into a nursing home and I was dreading trying to persuade her when my sister Linda phoned to say she had died peacefully in her sleep.

Life seems to give flesh a dimension that disappears with death, and when Linda and I arrived at the morgue to see her she looked more like an Egyptian mummy in the British Museum than the mother I had loved for fifty-two years. The pain was nothing like as bad as when Dad died. Mum had lived long enough to be proud of what I had achieved and we'd had time together as adults, going to restaurants and holidaying together, so I didn't feel cheated of time as I had with Dad. The saddest of those trips had been when Linda and I took her to see the war memorial at Arras, where Grandfather's name was enshrined with thousands of others whose bodies had never been found. Even though Mum's eyesight was no longer good enough to make out his name at the top of the memorial, she was still so glad to have come at last, and I felt real anger thinking of the hundreds of thousands of wives and children who had never been able to visit their menfolk's graves in the decades after the First World War. The government that sent so many young men to their deaths never put in place a scheme to cover the cost of a visit to the war cemeteries at a time when it was beyond the means of their widows.

Linda took charge of winding up Mum's affairs but we were sad that after a life in which Mum and Dad had always worked hard there was so little to show for it. A few thousand pounds left over from the sale of her house, a few bits of inexpensive jewellery and some knick-knacks and mementoes – including the card Dad had sent me on my first birthday while he was at sea:

My dear Kenny

To wish you very many and very happy returns and all the luck and happiness in the world throughout your life. I hope you will always keep this card because I feel very proud to be sending this birthday card to my own son on his very first birthday and I hope we shall always spend all our birthdays together.

Always your loving

Dad.

14

Turn Again, Livingstone

1997–2000

The idea had been around for years when the *Standard* started a campaign for London to have a directly elected mayor and was supported by Michael Heseltine and Tony Banks. The *Standard*'s columnist Simon Jenkins (who backed GLC abolition) lobbied Blair, who opened a bottle of whisky and said, 'Persuade me.' Architect Norman Foster, another supporter, invited Blair to dinner to explain how the mayor of Barcelona had transformed his city. Finally, in April 1996 Blair was persuaded, and promised that London would have a mayor. Frank Dobson, the shadow cabinet member responsible for local government, didn't agree, so unlike the proposals for Scottish and Welsh devolution, no preparatory work was done until after the 1997 general election.

Like Frank, I thought the idea was barmy, just another example of New Labour's obsession with all things American. I pointed out that over fifty American mayors were in prison for fraud. It was my intention then to change Labour's economic policy from within Parliament. Jeffrey Archer's profile and wealth made him the Tory front runner and, in the absence of anyone else, TV and radio programmes often hauled me in to debate with him.

Blair wanted a businessman as Labour's candidate, with BA's Bob Ayling and Richard Branson of Virgin in the frame. Polls put Branson as the most popular choice, followed by me and then Archer. Even if I wanted it I knew Blair would not let me run. I told Simon Fletcher, 'They won't let me run but the stronger my position the more difficult for them to run some ghastly little Millbank clone. They will have to go for someone like Frank Dobson.' If Frank had announced then that he was standing I would have campaigned for him.

I argued that Londoners should have a choice between a mayor or an elected council but Blair was terrified of recreating the GLC so it was a 'mayor or nothing' vote in the London-wide referendum on whether there should be a mayoralty. My old friend Jonathan Rosenberg, a manic activist from Paddington, was appointed by Trevor Phillips (a TV producer and presenter) and Lord Toby Harris (a former leader of Haringey Council) to run a Vote Yes campaign. Driving a bus around London blasting out 'London Calling' by the Clash, 'Camden Town' by Suggs and 'It's a London Thing' by Scott Garcia, Jonathan soon realised he was expected to promote Trevor Phillips as the New Labour candidate.

I was endlessly debating with Archer on radio and TV as well as speaking to London organisations and firms. Archer had an ebullient quality and saw the mayoralty as a chance to wipe his murky slate clean. Only five years older than me, he was old-fashioned enough to be my father, often recoiling at my bad language. When I'd read his novels *Shall We Tell the President?* and *First Among Equals* the absence of bad language, violence and gratuitous sex left me thinking he was writing books for his mother.

Archer was being pursued by *Newsnight*'s Michael Crick, who had written an unauthorised biography of him. Contrary to Archer's assertion that his father was a colonel in the Somerset Light Infantry with a distinguished record of service, Crick revealed his father as a bigamist and fraudster on a grand scale. Born in Mile End in 1875, he had married a widow and been elected as a Tory to Stepney Council although he lived in Ilford. After serving just two years he disappeared without a trace, having exhausted his wife's funds. He reappeared in New York, claiming to have served in the

First World War, and was convicted of fraud after raising funds ostensibly to provide artificial limbs to servicemen. Many frauds, convictions and marriages followed before Jeffrey was born in 1940.

Archer's childhood was public knowledge because from the age of nine his mother wrote a weekly column in the local paper regaling Weston-super-Mare with the adventures of 'Tuppence', as she called him. After winning a scholarship to Wellington School, Archer worked hard to outperform his fitter and brighter peers but was never made a prefect (probably the only thing we have in common) and left school with only three O levels. He taught PE at Vickers Hill, a private boarding school, where he impressed with his organisational and inspirational qualities. Crick recalls student Bruce Dakowski saying, 'Boys died for Jeffrey – he had that kind of charisma . . . it was very easy for boys to fall under his spell and overachieve for him.' After failing to complete the induction course for the Metropolitan Police, Archer was elected to the GLC as its youngest member in 1967, earning a small income on the side filling in other members' attendance claims forms for a 10 per cent commission. Elected as the MP for Louth, he resigned from Parliament in order to avoid bankruptcy and began a successful career as a writer.

The media had fun with New Labour's failure to find a credible candidate. The first television debate, in the autumn of 1997, was chaired by Trevor Phillips with Archer and myself joined by Darcus Howe and the leader of the City of London Corporation, Michael Cassidy. As we waited for the audience to vote I realised I actually wanted to win. From that point on, although I expected to be vetoed by Blair, I fought to win. When John Prescott presented his White Paper on the powers of the mayor to the Commons, Speaker Betty Boothroyd couldn't contain herself as I said, 'Let me be the first to congratulate the deputy prime minister for placing before Londoners this radical and exciting new job opportunity.' Prescott's initial smile faded.

A *Standard* NOP poll on 27 April 1998 showed 66 per cent of Londoners would vote for Richard Branson, 55 per cent for me with Glenda Jackson at 47 ahead of Dobson on 30. As a household name and London's transport minister, Glenda might have won if New Labour had rallied behind her, but the Millbank Tendency never took women seriously and desperately searched around for a convincing man.

In the referendum all thirty-two boroughs voted in favour, ranging from 84 per cent in Haringey to 57 per cent in Bromley, giving an overall majority of 72–28 per cent of London voters, but the turnout was only 34 per cent. A BBC poll showed I had pulled ahead of Richard Branson by 33 to 32 per cent – Branson's vote went down as more people travelled on his trains! The following morning the *Standard*'s front page predicted the Labour fight was between Glenda Jackson and myself. The new Labour assault turned nasty with future MP Siôn Simon writing in the *Daily Telegraph*: 'Livingstone is now twisted with the bitterness of failure . . . is neither cuddly or competent; an unpleasant man and a bad politician, he is not fit to be mayor of Trumpton . . . The mayoral primary offers an opportunity for Livingstone . . . to be destroyed forever as a political force. This is a prize too valuable, an opportunity too golden, to ignore. So come on Dobson, do it for Britain. Strap on your dusty old six gun . . . and send Red Ken up to the political Boot Hill he should have been consigned to years ago.' Labour MP Gerald Kaufman was more succinct. 'I'd rather vote for Jeffrey Archer or even Saddam Hussein than Ken Livingstone.'

*

Simon Fletcher, the trade unions and CLPD organised brilliantly for the diminished London Labour party conference in June 1998. Only one person voted against the proposal that any candidate nominated by ten constituency Labour parties would automatically be on the shortlist. Blair ignored the conference decision and the Labour party announced that candidates should apply to and be 'examined' by the NEC.

As a member of the NEC I went to the first meeting of Labour's National Policy Forum at Warwick University. Although a very New Labour affair, it was chaired by Robin Cook, who got a round of applause when he endorsed me for mayor. Just how controlled the Policy Forum was became clear in a session held in a hot stuffy room. I proposed we sit outside in the shade of the trees on campus. A murmur of approval was crushed by the presiding New Labour official who said no one had agreed we could leave the room. I pushed it to a vote but only the sole black delegate supported me so we continued to sweat.

Although fully committed to New Labour (Mandelson was the best man at his wedding), Trevor Phillips took me to lunch. I said he was a good television producer but he had never run anything or had any experience of local government and I suggested we run as a team with him as deputy mayor. As I didn't want to leave Parliament, I would serve one term to re-establish city government. The mayoral powers were limited so like any minister I could do the job while remaining as an MP. Trevor went off to sound out Downing Street, later phoning to say he'd been shaken by the strength of opposition and that I was going to have to persuade Blair.

I phoned Blair's gatekeeper Anji Hunter, who was friendly, but when she called back I could tell she'd been shocked by Blair's response: 'He doesn't think there's any point in meeting you.' I told Blair's PPS Bruce Grocott I thought Blair had misconceptions about me and pointed out that MPs have a right to see their party leader. I got my meeting in a room filled with staff and made my pitch about what I would do and how I would work. We discussed the mayor's powers, the timing of the election and the threat of Archer. The meeting was cool but I gave reasonable answers to

Blair's points and he said, 'I need to think about this and I'll get back to you.' As the months went by without any response, I realised you could spend a lot of time with Blair without realising that he didn't agree with a word you were saying.

Londoners were by now noticing the Millbank Tendency's arrogance. Press stories on who Labour would choose to fight Archer always had a comment from a 'Labour party' or 'Downing Street' source saying I would not be allowed to stand. Londoners knew it should be up to them to decide who was going to be mayor, not party bureaucrats. A *Standard* poll in October 1997 showed 74 per cent of Londoners opposed my being vetoed and a year later in a *London Tonight* poll it was 91 per cent. In interviews I joked, 'Of course I won't be allowed to stand,' until Tony Benn forcefully said that I must stop saying this. I took the point and started talking about Londoners' right to decide.

Evening Standard editor Max Hastings agreed to publish my response to the government's White Paper in which I argued for more powers to be devolved from Whitehall and for the mayor to have the ability to introduce a congestion charge. Max invited me to the boardroom for lunch, saying, 'I hope you're not a vegetarian.' 'You know I'm not, I've been writing a restaurant column in your magazine for months,' I replied. 'Oh I never read the magazine,' he airily said, confirming my view that he was more interested in setting London's agenda than in the marginal bits of his paper. He was less preoccupied by London's waste and recycling, I discovered, than by the prospect of Archer running the city. 'I'll have to vote for you,' he moaned.

John McDonnell and myself were the only rebels put on the committee to oversee the bill establishing the Greater London Authority, so even if we voted with the opposition the government would win. The bill was the longest piece of legislation since the Government of India Act seventy years previously. How little planning had gone into the mayoralty was shown by the 1,392 amendments the government made to its own bill.

With still no word from Blair, Simon and Redmond set up a 'Ken's Right to Stand' campaign with Harry Barlow from GLC days and John McDonnell as chair. I worked the after-dinner circuit so we were funded by businesses paying for a humorous speech about why I should be mayor. Max enjoyed reporting New Labour's travails and when I asked the *Standard* for a reduced rate for advertising they agreed, the adverts becoming a story in themselves with each paid for by readers' donations. When I received a cheque from Sir Alec Guinness it felt like I'd been endorsed by the Jedi Council. Labour MPs and researchers had to be more circumspect and quite a bit of money was put anonymously under my door or in my pigeon hole at the House of Commons.

On the GLA Bill Committee Liberals and Tories opposed the many clauses allowing government to overrule the mayor, but these clauses were not inserted to control me. Rawnsley writes in *Servants of the People* that it was taken for granted by the inner circle that I would not be allowed to stand, quoting Blair in early 1999: 'Ken will burn himself out, won't he?' although Harriet Harman warned Blair in autumn 1998 that I would romp the selection unless something was done to stop me. Rawnsley explains the apathy thus:

The lack of urgency in Downing Street flowed in large part from the belief that the easy solution was to break [Ken's] legs. Gordon Brown, Peter Mandelson, Alastair Campbell, Philip Gould, everyone of account around Tony Blair, believed they could simply prevent Livingstone being a candidate . . . The same view was taken by Margaret McDonagh, the party's general secretary . . . Officials at Millbank had already drawn up a charge sheet of heresies and disloyalties to use to exclude Livingstone. Campbell, an especially aggressive proponent of blocking Livingstone, contended that whatever short-term controversy this caused would be much less damaging than the years of mayhem he would create as mayor.

The ex-whip Ray Powell had become so disenchanted with New Labour that he offered me the file the whips had kept on Neil Kinnock recording his 'heresies and disloyalties' in the 1970s.

While Alastair backed Tony Banks and Mandelson promoted Trevor, Paul Boateng said he would not be a candidate 'come hell or high water' and Mo Mowlam made her position clear with a big hug for me in front of the photographers at the launch of *Turn Again Livingstone*, John Carvel's second biography of me. To my surprise Carvel quoted a Downing Street source: 'Tony [Blair] likes him. They can have an amiable chat . . . he will always have regard for somebody who is a good communicator. He feels it is a terrible waste. He's rather depressed about it.' Siôn Simon was not in the least depressed, writing in the *Spectator* that I had spent my 'entire political life nuzzled into the porcine underbelly of the Scargillite, Trotskyite, fellow travelling, sinister, ultra hard left. He lives there still . . . A close colleague from his GLC days, still a committed left-winger, described him as "the most odious, duplicitous, lying snake I have ever encountered".'

Blair told Mo that the mayoralty could be a stepping stone to higher things for her but she said, 'I'm not a Londoner' and it was 'a shitty job' sandwiched between central and local government. The lack of power led Bob Ayling and Richard Branson (asked to stand by both Downing Street and Max Hastings) to turn it down. Other names kicked around in Downing Street were Delia Smith, Alex Ferguson, Martin Bell and Joanna Lumley. The Tories had similar problems with Chris Patten, who said he didn't want to be 'whinger-in-chief for London'. The TV personality Giles Brandreth and the ex-minister David Mellor turned it down, leaving the Tory former transport minister Steve Norris as the only serious challenger to Archer.

*

As 1998 became 1999 Simon Fletcher's workload became impossible and Redmond suggested that we take on Mark Watts to help out. Mark had interviewed me for his student dissertation on the GLC but was so quiet in the office it was a while before I realised how ferociously clever he was. He was just twenty-seven then, and had met Simon in Young Labour and worked for Nottingham South MP Alan Simpson after failing as a graphic designer on the Campaign Group newspaper. His ambition had been to work for me ever since reading *If Voting Changed Anything* when he was nineteen. On his first day Simon gave him a vast pile of unopened letters and Maureen started him on the photocopier while I said his vegetarianism wouldn't last, given that he could now join us on my weekly restaurant review. Mark recalls things were 'definitely a bit anarchic compared to later years. A journalist would phone up and Ken would just lean back, look mischievous and respond, while Simon held his head in his hands. Redmond would come in for long discussions about the minutiae of the selection campaign while Ken looked bored and finished his paperwork. Everyone did what Maureen told them to do. Once a week we would go for a cracking meal courtesy of the *Evening Standard*. I was cured of vegetarianism within three weeks.'

We took a gamble and called a public meeting at Westminster Central Hall through an ad in the *Standard*, but as it was February and the National Union of Rail, Maritime and Transport Workers (RMT) called a rail strike that day I worried about the turnout. We hired a small hall but the booking office said they were getting so many enquiries they moved us to a room for 400 people. We turned up an hour early on a miserable evening with the strike still on to find the room already full. I was elated as we switched to the 2,000-seat Great Hall which had hosted the first meeting of the United Nations. The TV networks interviewed me live as the vast crowd marched up the grand staircase behind me.

The hall was almost full as we listened to the novelist Beryl Bainbridge, comedians Jo Brand and Mark Steel and my old teacher John Ryan, now seventy-one, who said, 'He was not a rebel with me. He was wonderful at reciting Shakespeare . . .' Nicholas Watt in the *Guardian* wrote, 'Officials from Millbank looked on in horror at the volume of his supporters. "In a city of six million it's a sad sign for the left if they can only muster a thousand people," one party spin doctor spluttered.'

We went back to Parliament to celebrate in the Pugin Room with actor Neil Pearson, who was organising our fund-raising. Maureen was ecstatic, whispering she 'would crawl over broken glass for Neil', but she worried we had taken in so much money that she might be robbed on the way home. I invited Simon and his partner Gaby Kagan back to my place, where we continued drinking and watched Al Pacino play the mayor of New York in the film *City Hall*. Our next fund-raiser was at the Hackney Empire with Arthur Smith, Kevin Day, Phill Jupitus, Billy Bragg and Jo Brand.

The following month Trevor Phillips (who is black) claimed my offer of deputy mayor was 'racist, arrogant and patronising' and announced he was standing after all. He won the support of David Aaronovitch, who described him as 'woolly, compromising, unpunctual but having the right skills for the job'. But Downing Street went cold when it discovered that Trevor was sending his children to a private school in Harrow even though schools in the borough were rated highly. At a fund-raiser in Harrow, local members complained that in all his years there Trevor had done little to help with the practical jobs expected of members in any election.

*

As well as a directly elected mayor Blair decided there should be a London Assembly of twenty-five members with limited powers whose job would be to scrutinise the mayor's administration.

Fourteen of the members would be directly elected on a first-past-the-post basis for different chunks of London. The other eleven were elected by proportional representation from party lists so that the party composition of the whole Assembly represented how Londoners had voted.

A panel chaired by MP Clive Soley started sifting Labour candidates for the Assembly. Of 230 party members who applied 136 were rejected, including Christine Shawcroft (later elected to the NEC), Geoff Martin (a union official with twenty years' experience) and Teresa Pearce (then a member of Labour's National Constitutional Committee and now an MP). All were rejected on the grounds they 'lacked life experience'. Scottish MP Anne Begg said candidates 'lacking in life experience didn't mean you were lacking in life experience, it meant you must fill that part of the form in'. Imagine the uproar if candidates for the Scottish Parliament had been excluded by a Londoner. Most black and Asian candidates were excluded, including Tower Hamlets councillor Kumar Murshid, Labour party ethnic minority officer Raj Jethwa and Peter Herbert, the chair of the Society of Black Lawyers. Most who appealed were rejected without even a meeting to put their case.

*

Blair's attention turned to Wales, where he was determined that Rhodri Morgan, the popular choice to be Welsh leader, should be stopped even though he was not particularly left-wing or the centre of any controversy. Blair had been put off by Rhodri's dishevelled home and offended when Rhodri's mother-in-law called him Lionel Blair. Blair's candidate Alun Michael couldn't get selected in any constituency so Blair made him number one on the top-up list of candidates. To make Alun leader Blair imposed an electoral college, saying this was the same method used when he became leader, but in the national electoral college trade unions had to ballot all their members. In Wales this rule was suspended and the Amalgamated Engineering and Electrical Union cast their vote for Alun Michael without a ballot. The ubiquitous USB Ltd ran the ballot with early leaks showing Alun had narrowly won, but only because of the AEEU. Labour MP Paul Flynn wrote, 'The Labour party in Wales is ashamed of itself. We are preparing our own catastrophe.'

The first elections of the Welsh National Assembly and Scottish Parliament took place on 6 May 1999. In Wales the Rhondda, Llanelli and Islwyn, the safest seats in the province, all fell to Nationalists. At the general election we had won 34 of the 40 constituencies; now only 28 of the 60 seats stayed Labour, and our vote only went up in Rhodri's seat. Results were poor in Scotland, too, where Dennis Canavan went independent when banned from standing and held Falkirk West in a landslide. Two days earlier Nick Raynsford, Minister for London, had told the Commons we would select our mayoral candidate by one member, one vote. As I watched the results come in I told Simon and Maureen, 'At least they won't be pulling that stunt [the block vote] in London.'

*

Philip Gould told Blair I was ahead of Frank by an unbridgeable margin and only Mo could beat me. As Mo wouldn't stand I had to be eliminated before the ballot. Downing Street's dirty tricks unit got to work. On 9 June Jan Woolf answered a knock on her door to find a *Sun* reporter saying they had been told I was the father of Liam. She shut the door but two days later the *Mail on Sunday* and *The Times* appeared with the same line. The *Mail on Sunday* returned the next day and while Jan said she had nothing to say six-year-old Liam made me proud by sticking his head round the door and saying, 'Haven't you got anything important to write about like wars or poverty?'

I was told by the *Mail*, 'It's your friends in the Labour party who are saying this.' On 13 June 1999 the *Sunday Mail*'s Black Dog column reported, 'Individuals have alleged Mr Livingstone is the father of an eight-year-old [*sic*] boy from a past relationship with an attractive Labour activist. The ever helpful anonymous muck spreaders were even ready to supply the name and address of the mother and child.' On Friday 18 June Jan's bank told her someone had illegally accessed her account. My bank manager warned me that attempts had also been made to break into my account and he introduced a password so that telephoned requests for information would have to go through him.

On Saturday 26 June the *News of the World* tried its luck and turned up on Jan's doorstep, but then there was nothing further until Saturday 10 July when the *Sunday Times* rang to say it intended to run the story about my child based on information from sources in Downing Street. Believing we were talking off the record, I said if the reporter would name his source I would issue a writ for malicious libel (which I'd erroneously believed I could do if the issue were not the truth of the allegation but whether it was motivated by malice). The *Sunday Times* splashed my comment on the front page. Having been exposed as behind these dirty tricks, Downing Street and Millbank went into public meltdown and denial.

The *Sunday Times* article stated, 'One source with connections high up in the Labour party and close to Downing Street briefed a journalist from the *Sunday Times* last week with full details about the mother of the child, a six-year-old boy, including her address and details of an alleged settlement with Livingstone.' This raises the question of how 'Downing Street sources' could have known there were transfers from my bank account to Jan's (to pay Liam's nursery fees) without illegally accessing my account. Journalist Tom Baldwin told the *Panorama* programme that a 'senior cabinet minister' leaked him a document with 'one particularly nasty incident when I was provided with a name and address of someone associated with Ken Livingstone's private life'. None of this affected my poll ratings and it didn't worry Alan Clark, who loudly announced in the members' tea room, 'I'll be voting for you to stop that cunt Archer.' Cardinal Hume put it more elegantly when he called me over to where he was talking to Tory MP Edward Leigh and a few Labour MPs and announced to their astonishment, 'I'm really looking forward to voting for this man next year.'

*

By mid-July 1999 Blair had given up on Frank (who said rumours he might run were the work of 'anonymous liars') and again asked Mo to stand, but she wanted the Foreign Office. I took Margaret McDonagh to lunch to make my pitch about what a wonderful candidate I would make. I was a bit nervous when I turned up at the Tate Gallery restaurant but as I slipped into charm mode the fire alarm went off and we were all thrown out into the street. We settled for a sandwich back in her office under the suspicious gaze of the bureaucracy.

I'd had good coverage in *The Face* and *NME* and Simon persuaded me to do a photo shoot for *Vogue*'s millennium issue. When they phoned the Labour party and asked them to let me know about the shoot they were told there were many more fashionable Labour MPs they should photograph instead. Simon worried when I returned and said the shoot included scantily clad models.

Nick Raynsford phoned Blair in August 1999 and was encouraged to stand. Nick had decided to run at a dinner with Max Hastings, who desperately wanted a candidate he could support against Archer. As Nick had the support of twenty Labour MPs as well as John Prescott he wasn't put off by a poll in the *Sunday Times* showing that 41 per cent of London Labour councillors wanted me, 22 per cent Frank, 9 for Nick, 6 for Glenda, 5 for Phillips and 2 for Tony Banks. Toby Harris chaired Nick's campaign, advised by former Liberal Des Wilson, who came up with the slogan 'Time to Get Serious'. Nick announced his candidacy on 30 September, the Thursday of the Labour party conference, after confirming with Frank the day before that he wasn't standing.

Nick's launch was successful, promising a congestion charge and lashing out at 'publicity seekers or dilettantes'. He said 'until a relatively short time ago Ken didn't believe there should be a mayor of London. He described the whole idea as barmy. So frankly I find it difficult to believe he is fully committed to it.' But he supported my right to stand. As Nick and I were being interviewed on David Frost's Sunday morning programme the *Sunday Telegraph*'s readers were learning that Frank had decided to stand after all. Nick didn't believe this but couldn't get hold of Frank. When Nick did reach him Frank said his arm had been twisted by two trade unionists from the AEEU who had 'mugged' him outside conference. Rumours claimed Margaret McDonagh warned Frank he was to be sacked as health minister and this would be a wise career move. Number 10 was in chaos as Blair switched his support to Frank. Nick's campaign team were so angry at his shabby treatment that they wanted him to fight on, particularly as Frank had also opposed an elected mayor. But party loyalty prevailed. Nick withdrew and at Blair's request became Frank's campaign manager. That same day, Alastair Campbell writes in his diary, Blair was still undecided whether or not to bar me.

I hadn't worried about Nick, who came over as a polite, clean young man you wouldn't mind your daughter marrying, but was devastated by Frank's decision. The media made Frank front runner, bookies made him favourite and I thought he would win. I had become excited about what I believed I could do for the city, so there was real gloom in my office at the news.

My gloom evaporated on 15 October when a *Standard* ICM poll showed that, if I stood as an independent, I would win with 43 per cent to Archer's 25 and Frank's 23. Asked who should be Labour candidate, 50 per cent chose me, with 16 and 15 per cent for Glenda and Frank, respectively. Earlier that year ex-GLC Staff Committee Chair John Carr warned me that Blair knew that if he banned me I would never voluntarily leave the party to run as an independent. I was so angry to have my loyalty used against me in this way that I started rumours to the contrary. Alastair records that by 3 November only he and Mandelson were still in favour of a veto: '[Blair] felt we would do real damage to ourselves if we blocked him now, that we would lose lots of members, and not just on the hard left.'

Rawnsley records:

Most trenchantly against Livingstone . . . was Gordon Brown . . . Brown argued with Blair that to let Livingstone be the candidate would compromise the authenticity of the government. They had to keep New Labour 'pure'. When Blair replied that he had become queasy about using the veto, he and Brown got into one of their shouting matches. Brown railed at the prime minister that 'at any cost' Livingstone had to be stopped 'whatever it takes'. He told Blair to show some spine . . . other influential voices implored him to let Livingstone run. Philip Gould, originally a blocker, had turned 180 degrees. He lamented to Blair that they should have had a strategy either to 'incorporate' Livingstone or to 'destroy him'. But it was too late for that now. Blocking him would divide the party with 'terrible' electoral consequences. Margaret McDonagh had also stood on her head. She told Blair that the party might haemorrhage 10,000 or more members in London. Dobson also warned Blair against giving Livingstone the martyrdom he was seeking as a springboard to run as an independent.

Simon had warned me they might pull the electoral college stunt used in Wales. The NEC had already written to all constituency Labour parties saying there would be a one-member, one-vote ballot for the party's 68,000 London members and Nick Raynsford had announced it in the Commons, but now McDonagh swung the NEC behind an electoral college.

I had no objection to tens of thousands of trade unionists voting but in the national electoral college MPs (representing the party in Parliament with millions of votes behind them) also had a third of the vote. If there was to be an electoral college in London it should obviously comprise the 1,200 Labour councillors who would have to work with the new mayor. But McDonagh's scam was that London's 57 Labour MPs and 14 Assembly candidates would share one-third of the votes. This meant one MP's vote was worth 1,000 ordinary members' and 10,000 trade unionists'. Unlike members and trade unions the MPs and Assembly candidates' votes would be public, so those who valued their career prospects would vote for Frank. The next day the *Independent* reported an anonymous Millbank source saying, 'We want to see Ken's blood on the carpet. This is the way to do it.'

Mark calculated my lead among members and trade unionists was still enough to win even though Sir Ken Jackson of the AEEU (Tony Blair's favourite union leader) would vote for Frank without a ballot of members. The two Co-operative parties were part of the trade union block of the electoral college. The one in North London balloted their members and I won with 57 per cent of the vote. The South London Co-op only had 450 members and its committee of fourteen decided on the chair's casting vote they would give their 50,000 votes to Frank after the charade of consulting store managers. They also allowed Frank's campaign HQ to be based in their London office. If only Keith Veness had been successful in his bid to take over the South London Co-op in the 1970s! Millbank expected the GMB union to deliver a vote for Frank, but having been treated so contemptuously for so long they didn't feel indebted to Blair and decided to ballot their members without any recommendation to support Frank.

The left usually opposed unions being forced to ballot because it helped the right, but now the positions reversed, with Blair supporting a trade-union fix and the left demanding ballots. The key would be if, after all their years of opposition to ending the block-voting system, the London region Transport and General decided to ballot. Simon and I had a rare disagreement when I jumped the gun in favour of balloting whereas he wanted to wait until the London region T&G met the next day. Barry Camfield, the London T&G organiser, let me address their committee and asked me to wait outside 'for a few minutes'. After an hour of heated debate I was told they would call a ballot. I went on to win by 85.8 per cent to Glenda's 7.3 and Frank's 6.9. When the T&G conveyed the news to Downing Street the response was, I am told, 'Fuck. Who was second?' 'Glenda.' 'Fuck.' 'Dobbo's third.' 'Oh, God.'

*

We still had the ritual of the vetting panel, which had been set up when the plan was to ban me from standing. Candidates had to fill in a long application form laden with management-speak and puerile questions about 'life experience'. It had been twenty-six years since I'd last applied for a job and I had no experience of polishing a CV so I got a friend who had applied to be chief executive of a major charity to let me copy their application, replacing the words 'chief executive' with 'mayor'. When I appeared before them on Tuesday, 16 November the vetting panel complimented me on the professionalism of my submission.

Downing Street had told journalists I would be on the shortlist but there was still a huge scrum of journalists outside Millbank Tower. I told them that I would swear an oath of loyalty on the bones of a saint or pull a sword from a stone if I had to. Sitting under a huge portrait of Clem Attlee, Clive Soley's eleven-strong panel was dominated by people from outside London. Curtains were drawn to prevent journalists taking photos of me being grilled by the panel and in this oppressive and gloomy atmosphere my confidence drained away as proceedings dragged on. Given Blair's decision to allow me on to the shortlist, I couldn't work out why they were droning on unless they planned to dine out on this for the rest of their lives.

They wanted me to support the partial privatisation of London Underground. Contrary to the promises when Thatcher abolished the GLC, the tube had been starved of investment for years, and the extension of the Jubilee Line was botched by uninspiring managers. In 1998 Prescott had announced it would take £7.5 billion to modernise the Underground but with a public–private partnership (PPP) there would be no increase in fares or taxes.

It was too good to be true. Since then the cost had risen to £15 billion and breaking up the maintenance department into three separate organisations had proved to be a recipe for disaster on both financial and safety grounds. The privatisation of British Rail had been a catastrophe but Railtrack, the company now responsible for the mainline railway infrastructure, wanted to take over 40 per cent of the tube work, replacing track and signalling. Following the Paddington rail crash in 1999, resulting in 31 deaths and 227 injuries, I wanted Railtrack – whose shoddy maintenance of the signals on the line was responsible – kept well out of the Underground. When I met Sir Steve Robson, the senior civil servant responsible for rail privatisation, he told me Brown wanted to privatise the whole tube network and Prescott wanted to keep it public so they came up with a compromise which transport professionals believed to be the worst of all worlds. Sir Steve moved on to the board of the Royal Bank of Scotland, from which he was sacked during the financial crisis.

PricewaterhouseCoopers was paid by government to compare the costs of modernisation and somehow arrived at the ridiculous conclusion that it would cost £15.5 billion if done by the public sector but only £12.5 billion under PPP. Brown was right not to trust tube bosses and I planned a purge if I won, but most of the companies bidding had had big cost overruns and project delays. The way to modernise the tube was through new management with a record of delivery and to issue bonds on the money markets. There was no way I was going along with PPP and the panel wound themselves up because I wouldn't agree to support it in advance, whatever they might put in the manifesto. They kept sending me into a small ante-room whilst they argued among themselves.

Twenty years earlier the London party had been free to draw up the GLC manifesto but now it had to be agreed by Blair, Brown and each government department. The panel seemed unaware that this undermined the whole concept of devolution. I said that if I couldn't agree with the manifesto I would withdraw my candidacy. This was an honest offer but the panel thought I was trying to blackmail them and went berserk. I had assumed a candidate would be selected by Christmas, so my standing down would leave plenty of time for reselection. In fact they intended to put off announcing the candidate until February with the manifesto not appearing until a week before polling day. I left them arguing among themselves as I was due to speak at a meeting called by the tube unions to oppose the public–private partnership idea. Hours slipped by with no word from the panel.

Alastair Campbell wrote about that day:

I was at the dentist for three hours, then back to more discussions on Ken. We had got the broadcasters lined up for 5 pm but it was clear there was a problem . . . Ken refused to say he would support a manifesto that included PPP. There was a clear case for blocking him . . . Clive Soley was for blocking him straight away whereas Ian McCartney wanted the party to see we were bending over backwards to be fair to him. But the hacks were all hanging around outside and it was beginning to look a bit farcical . . .

About 8 pm Soley finally went out and said that Ken would have to come back on Thursday . . . TB was pretty exasperated. Our famed so called news management was looking pretty ropy . . . We had really fucked this from start to finish . . . it was a dreadful day, the best part of which was probably the dentist.

Simon thought I had been too hard on the manifesto issue and needed to let them off the hook. He and Redmond drafted a statement in which I said 'I will stand on the manifesto agreed by the Labour party' but pointed out that 'devolution means the issue of how we regenerate the transport system is a decision for Londoners . . . I have no doubt that the views of Londoners, the London Labour party membership and the mayoral candidates will be fully taken into account in agreeing Labour's manifesto for mayor.'

The following day Alastair writes:

Queen's Speech day, and Ken fucking Livingstone was leading the news. I think what I hated as much as anything was that we looked so incompetent. It was like something out of the 80s . . . GB and I had another go at TB, said that whatever [KL] signed up to, he would just shift afterwards . . . GB felt Livingstone had to do more than just go for saying he would support [PPP], he would have to retract what he had said. [TB] had spent 30 minutes with Frank, who had said there was no way he would stand if Ken was blocked . . . There was some merit in that happening and getting both of them out. Lance came in with a statement from Ken which said he would support the manifesto and not withdraw halfway through if he was not happy with it. This felt like some of the nonsense Neil had to put up with the whole time . . . At one point [TB] said to me 'Would you mind refraining from just sitting there and shaking your head?' He felt the statement made it very difficult to block him . . . GB said if he won . . . our transport policy is dead.

On Thursday there was a larger media scrum including two people in gorilla suits. Simon's statement should have been enough to resolve the issue but it went on for hours with me leaving the room while they argued. I was lying on the floor in an ante-room with a headache when Margaret McDonagh came in and said, 'It's time to get really serious now. If you're still prepared to stand on the Labour manifesto the panel will accept your candidacy.'

*

The panel's decision to allow me to stand triggered an orchestrated torrent of attacks and smears from the prime minister down. Blair gave interviews in which, conveniently forgetting Labour's economic incompetence, he blamed me (with Benn and Scargill) for Labour's election defeats. Labour MPs were lined up to denounce me in the papers. Bernie Grant claimed I was a 'dodgy character' and Paul Boateng, under the headline 'Why good old Ken should stay part of London's history', questioned my fitness to be mayor. Two days later the two of us came face to face stark naked in the gym and without saying a word he gave me a sheepish grin and a friendly punch on the arm. He knew I would understand he'd had to do it if he was to become the first black cabinet minister.

Margaret Hodge wrote an article deploring my 'incompetence', which was rich given her record of mismanagement in Islington and her decision to ignore allegations of child abuse in Islington children's homes which were later proved to be true. Chris Smith was slightly gentler, saying, 'I like Ken Livingstone a lot. But I can't help feeling that he won't provide that seriousness of purpose that London requires.' Chris showed a real skill for airbrushing me out of the GLC when he said, 'I saw the triumph of Andrew McIntosh and Dave Wetzel in putting forward the Fares Fair policy . . . We all fought to save the GLC from abolition.' The spectacle of those who had worked with me at the GLC lining up to denounce me led Roy Hattersley to pour scorn on them for their hypocrisy. I was most shocked when Nita Clarke, my GLC press officer, who had been up to her neck in all my escapades, penned the most poisonous article of them all.

In her diary Oona King, at the time occupying Peter Shore's old seat at Bethnal Green, recalls a summons to see Alastair, who said she must write an article denouncing me. Heather Rabbatts, chief executive of Lambeth Council, wrote about the terrible mess she had inherited in the borough, which she blamed on 'those who shared Ken Livingstone's core beliefs', although I had left the council seventeen years before she took over. A year earlier on *Question Time* when asked who should be mayor of London she had chosen me.

Blair and Brown held meetings paid for from party funds and, ignoring the rule banning personal attacks, claimed that I would be a disaster as mayor. The largest was an invitation-only meeting of 1,400 members at the Institute of Education. Brown had written in that day's *Standard* that I would drive jobs and investment from London but Blair had to tone it down when he was greeted by a slow handclap, saying, 'I can see this is going to be a lively meeting.' Brown denounced my support for tax increases on the rich. When questions began, the dam broke. Fawning enquiries provoked boos and hisses and Blair was floored with, 'When Ken wins, what are you going to do after all the slagging off you are doing on Frank's behalf?' Under an editorial asking 'Doesn't Mr Blair have a country to run?' the *Guardian* said Blair's behaviour 'is becoming embarrassing. Not only does it reek of control freakery; it also smacks of a loss of perspective from the man at the top. The prime minister has better things to do with his time: he should start doing them.'

As these meetings continued Glenda warned, 'When are they going to learn that the more that Ken is seen to be out of favour with the party leadership, the stronger he becomes?' I felt as if I was in the eye of a hurricane – an island of calm in a sea of fury. I went from one supportive meeting to another, couldn't walk down the street or get on a bus without people coming over to encourage me and often give money for the campaign. Blair and Brown were still getting an easy press but the tide had turned. This was only a few months before Blair's humiliation when he was slow-handclapped at the Women's Institute and the fuel blockade which brought Britain to a standstill as tanker drivers protested about fuel prices. My campaign was the first chance for those disillusioned with New Labour to register a protest.

*

In the opposition camp, stories of Archer having sex with his mistress Sally Farmiloe in a car park during a Conservative ball in Mayfair had not prevented William Hague from endorsing him as a candidate of 'probity and integrity', but Archer had to withdraw finally when a friend who had provided evidence in his 1987 libel case against the *Daily Star* admitted he had lied. (Archer had taken half a million pounds in damages in that case.) Archer went to prison for perjury. After Shaun Woodward and Archie Norman refused to stand, and ruling out Seb Coe because 'William wants to keep him nearby' as chief of staff, the new Tory candidate was Steve Norris. Archer had been due to conduct an auction at the annual Press Ball at the Park Lane Hilton, and Millbank made sure that Frank was substituted. Campbell recalls: 'I had a stack of calls from people telling me he had been absolutely dreadful. This thing felt worse by the day.' John Walsh in the *Independent* described the scene:

Looking more than usually like a Cleethorpes butcher auditioning to become the new Cap'n Birdseye, he told pointless little jokes about Archer ('He's Lord Archer of Weston-super-Mare, you know. He's the only seaside peer that Larry Grayson's never performed on – Hallo!') And, emboldened by the gasps of incredulity, explained to the meeting why he should be mayor of London despite being from Yorkshire. Correctly noting that this was a ball and not a political rally, the assembled hacks grew restless. Dobson ploughed on with a little joke about a train driver who always diverted his train via Halifax because 'he were always one for t'brightlights'. The hacks sat open mouthed as they digested the fact that this smug and hairy government stooge was treating them like an audience at a working men's club. 'Get off!' yelled a voice. 'Bring on Ken!' shouted another. Dobson ploughed on with a charming tale about a urine-scented lift. The audience broke into open revolt at Dobson's fourth repetition of the words '. . . which reminds me of a little story . . .' They banged their heads on the tables, shook their fists, screamed for his removal and summary evisceration.

Campbell writes, 'I told Dobbo about the dreadful *Mirror* poll but he showed no sign of wanting to pull out.' And on 25 January 2000: 'TB was in a real state about Livingstone. Frank had refused to come out. His pride was at stake and that was that. Also Mo was not willing to push him too hard.' The following day Blair and Campbell met Frank and Janet Dobson 'to try to persuade him to pull out. Frank said he was convinced it was moving his way, but I said there wasn't much evidence of that . . . All the evidence suggested Frank wouldn't win, and Mo might . . . Frank was adamant that he could do and she would do no better. Between us, TB and I must have tried eight or ten times, but he wouldn't move . . .'

Journalists and politicians including myself gossiped that Frank seemed depressed and a story appeared in the *Sunday Times* that a minister had said Frank was 'on the verge of a breakdown . . . resented being run by Millbank and . . . had been press ganged by Tony Blair into seeking a job he never really wanted anyway'. The minister claimed that at Margaret McDonagh's urging 'cabinet ministers had been asked to telephone Dobson and be nice to lift his spirits'. I mistakenly responded to this by saying no one would be happy with these poll ratings. Frank claimed I had started the rumour and said I was 'lower than a snake's belly'. He joked that he looked pained was because he was suffering from backache caused by carrying a big bag of Prozac around.

The ballot to choose Labour's candidate took place in February 2000. Harry Barlow gave over his advertising agency offices in Fitzrovia to run our campaign and we were overwhelmed with Labour members wanting to help. Many hadn't planned to support me but were disgusted by Millbank's tricks. Frank's team had the addresses and phone numbers of members but when Glenda and I asked for them we were told Frank hadn't been given a list. Labour members received two glossy mailings on Frank's behalf in the first three weeks so the press wanted to know how he got the list. Nick Raynsford kept popping up on the *Today* programme and because he wasn't prepared to lie made matters worse. *Panorama* revealed that Euro MP Richard Balfe (then still in the Labour party – just) had got the list from Millbank and passed it over to Frank's team. Next Millbank said three unions that would have voted for me (MSF, RMT and ASLEF) were late paying their party subscriptions. But they had always paid at year end without losing their right to vote and had they been voting for Frank I'm sure this wouldn't have happened. In the RMT postal ballot I received 2,788 votes to Glenda's 155 and Frank's 163.

Even with the loss of these unions' votes I was still ahead owing to my lead among party members. Our phone canvassing put this at two to one and a poll in the *Independent* confirmed that I had 63 per cent of the members' vote with Frank on 25 and Glenda on 12. More remarkable, asked if I should stand as an independent if Frank won, 45 per cent of party members said yes. In a postal ballot of party members in Tooting I won by 66 per cent to Frank's 23 and Glenda's 11. In their book *Nightmare! The Race for London's Mayor* Mark D'Arcy and Rory MacLean report that Dobson's team knew they 'needed to win the votes of around 35 per cent of the party membership in London – and their canvassing showed they were well behind'.

Realising they couldn't win without fraud, Dobson's supporters – without his knowledge – encouraged MPs to call on party members to collect their ballot papers. Members could vote by phone or post. When MPs or their staff turned up on the doorstep helpfully offering to collect ballots, members innocently handed them over. The MP could then open the envelope, reseal it if it was for Frank, but if for me they could use the identity code and phone the vote in for Frank. The worst example of vote theft was by Southall MP Piara Khabra, who boasted that he personally had collected 300 ballots. After I was readmitted to the party in 2004 one Labour MP told me 'that was only the half of it'.

After the election D'Arcy and MacLean revealed that Millbank had flown in two Democrats from the Clinton machine to advise. Bob Mulholland was an organiser from California but the other (never named) was described as 'stratospherically high' in the Democratic party. They attended the morning campaign meetings in Millbank and advised it was not worth attacking my policies but to look into my private life, saying, 'It's always drugs, women or money.'

All the candidates were denied the right to have observers present while the vote was counted. My campaign worker Neale Coleman's wife Jill Selborne had a friend inside Millbank and kept me posted on how the vote was going. The voting theft switched 10 per cent of the members' vote (over 3,000) to Frank. Blairites often relied on the scam of collecting Labour party postal votes and signing up non-existent members in order to rig party elections. Some went on to steal real postal votes in the Midlands, but were caught and sent to prison. I was on a train after a meeting in Croydon as voting closed on Thursday, 17 February and minutes later Jill phoned to tell me Frank had won by 3 per cent, although it would not be announced until the following Sunday. I immediately phoned Alan Rusbridger at the *Guardian* to tell him the result.

Cold with anger, I was determined to make New Labour pay. If they got away with this fraud, what would they do next? Without the ballot theft I would have won narrowly. Had all unions been allowed to vote and forced to ballot their members I would have won easily. Even with the vote theft, 21,082 party members were recorded as voting for me and 14,042 for Frank. Among the trade unionists I had 74.6 per cent and Frank 14.1. The MPs and Assembly candidates had voted for Frank by 64 to just 9 for me, but their votes were worth 1,000 party members'. In total 108,106 members, trade unionists and MPs had voted with Frank winning 22,275 to my 74,646. Glenda had 11,185 votes but Frank was declared winner by 51.5 per cent to 48.5 per cent.

*

On Friday 18 February my former agent Anne Harradine phoned to say Blair wanted to meet me and Frank separately at Chequers on the following morning. I was due to take my niece and nephew to the zoo but Anne came back to say it was OK for me to bring them. So with Simon we piled into the official government car that whisked us out to the Chilterns for the ten o'clock meeting. Blair was casually dressed like myself in jeans, trainers and an open-necked shirt and accompanied by his trusted adviser Sally Morgan. He invited Simon to join us and we sat around a coffee table in the Tudor drawing room of the prime minister's country seat while my niece and nephew explored the gardens.

Blair and Sally said they didn't know the result, which was true and says a lot about the incompetence of Millbank. He said if I had won he would support me and hoped I would stay in the party if I'd lost. He asked what I would do if Frank won. I explained that, in fact, Frank had won by 3 per cent, but with Frank 'there's no way we will win London'. I believed he would lose to Steve Norris, therefore Frank had to be prevailed upon to stand down. Blair said, 'I can't tell him what to do.' I replied, 'It's going to be very bloody and I'm not going to lift a finger to help.' There followed the usual inconclusive conversation about the PPP on the Underground and then we got on to the policies I would follow if I became mayor. After fifty minutes Blair brought the meeting to an end, saying, 'We will have to get together again very quickly.'

The next day Frank was unveiled as victor at Millbank Tower. Journalists had gathered outside our house so I announced the result was 'tainted' and urged Frank to step down. Intending to say nothing to divert attention from Millbank stewing in its own juice I said, 'I will spend the next week listening to Londoners before deciding on my next move.' With that I took my nephew and niece to the cinema, avoiding the scrum by jumping in a minicab. The press noticed I was carrying a couple of videos so my local Vidbiz store manager 'received countless phone calls from tabloid press enquiring to what videos you had rented from us . . . I'm sure I have no need to tell you which particular newspaper bothered me the most, promising free advertising by mentioning our name in an article if I would divulge the titles of the two videos . . .'

At Millbank, Andrew Rawnsley's question to Frank set the tone. 'Have you spoken to the prime minister this morning? Did you thank him for fixing the election for you?' For the next forty-five minutes Frank struggled to discuss policies but the media were only interested in the ballot, particularly the complaints about the conduct of the ballot by USB. A gleeful Steve Norris said, 'No wonder Ken Livingstone is furious – an old socialist, finally defeated by an electoral system that would not be out of place in North Korea.' Jubilant Blairites told journalists I might be given a minor job in International Development, laughing that I could spend a few years visiting refugees in Africa.

Monday's *Standard* had an ICM poll with 61 per cent wanting me to go independent. If so I would win half the vote to Frank's 22 per cent and Norris's 15. Carlton TV's phone poll found that 93 per cent of the people who phoned in wanted me to stand. Frank said Millbank officials were 'prats' as Millbank and Frank's team struggled for control of the campaign.

Brentford constituency Labour party called on Frank to stand down and Glenda said Millbank also wanted Frank out so Simon Fletcher came up with a 'Stand Down, Frank' campaign. Within a fortnight 23,000 party members phoned Millbank to complain about the result and volunteers handing out Vote for Frank leaflets were shocked by the anger of Londoners who refused to take them or threw them back in their face.

John Prescott asked to see me, so Simon and I went to his Commons office, where we were joined by Margaret McDonagh. After two hours in which John spoke for two-thirds of the time we only agreed on a statement that we'd had 'a very comradely discussion about the forthcoming London elections and their implications'.

All my close friends urged me to stay in the party. Redmond feared that if I went independent a vicious campaign could defeat me. The mood on the streets was overwhelmingly for me to stand but my Brent East party voted unanimously for me to stay and rejected a call for Frank to stand down. I was surprised when Audrey Wise stopped me in the Commons and said I should stand as an independent and I was amazed when Ron Todd phoned to say all his neighbours in Barking said I had to stand and he believed I should as well. That Audrey and Ron with a lifetime of party loyalty were saying this was a shock, but I was even more shocked when Oona King told me that she had had to vote for Frank but that I should go independent.

BBC's *Question Time* invited the candidates and myself to be grilled by David Dimbleby. Millbank was further embarrassed when Simon picked up an email encouraging loyalists to 'clap, cheer and jeer at the right points'. Frank agreed to appear just two hours before the programme was due to start but waited in a separate room from the rest of us. Frank challenged me during the programme: 'I'm not going to stand down, no matter how much you and your friends organise within the Labour party to have a go at me about it. I will not change my mind . . . Are you going to support me or are you going to stand separately? Go ahead, make my day.' Thinking I might rise to the bait, the audience burst into applause but were disappointed as I droned on about giving 'the Labour party time to sort out the mess . . . Londoners are angry. It's not about my career or Frank's career. It's about Londoners' right to decide who to vote for.'

Dimbleby pinned me down about my promises never to leave the party. 'That is why this is the most difficult decision of my life. I don't want to break my word, but at the same time I am being deluged by people in London.' Susan Kramer, the Lib Dem candidate, thought I should make my mind up: 'Are you in or out? It's time to put up or shut up.' She had a point, and afterwards I told Dimbleby the mood of the audience had helped me decide. The audience's contempt for Frank was unfair, groaning even when what he said on other issues was right. Our private polling showed that in the five months New Labour had managed Frank's campaign they had reduced his popularity rating by 24 per cent, with 45 per cent of Londoners now saying they disliked him. In the taxi home I told Simon I was going to stand and wanted to announce soon. Redmond and other friends still believed the press would turn against me, that I wouldn't be elected and would then lose my seat in Parliament. They still hoped to persuade Frank to stand down but I knew they would all back me as an independent.

That Saturday morning, 4 March, at the lesbian and gay hustings chaired by the BBC's Evan Davis at the National Film Theatre, the other candidates refused to have me on the platform. From the audience I said it was a sign of how far London had come that there was no homophobic candidate on the platform. Green party candidate Darren Johnson had the advantage of being gay but Steve Norris stole the show with a stinging attack on the bigotry of the *Mail*, calling its editor Paul Dacre 'a fuckwit'. Afterwards Simon and I went to the Royal Festival Hall café to meet Neale Coleman and Jonathan Rosenberg, who wanted me to go independent immediately. Simon had planned a Stand Down, Frank rally for Monday but Jonathan said, 'People were coming up to us and saying if you weren't a candidate they were simply not interested.' I worried if I didn't declare soon this support could turn to anger. Jonathan offered his experience of bus campaigning, believing that in six weeks just one bus could reach a vast number of people. Neale wanted to start on detailed policies for my manifesto.

After they left we were joined by Redmond just as I was phoned by Neale's partner Jill. Her Millbank mole said they would never allow me to be the candidate and if Frank stood down the NEC would impose somebody else. I told Simon and Redmond I wasn't prepared to carry on dissembling any longer. I loathed not being able to tell people the truth so I phoned Charles Reiss, political editor at the *Standard*, and he agreed to take an article for Monday's edition. I asked Harry Barlow to find a venue to launch the campaign at 11 a.m. He called back to say Frank was launching his campaign at that time so we put mine back to the afternoon to avoid allegations that we were trying to steal his thunder. After fourteen days of agonising the die was finally cast. I knew I was doing the right thing.

*

Monday, 6 March, the day of the announcement. On my way to the Commons I picked up the *Standard* to find that Reiss had devoted six pages to my decision, including a reprint of the 1981 interview I'd given to Max Hastings while doing the ironing in my bedsit. Half an hour later I emerged from the tube to find my phone had seventy-four messages on it (which I never did listen to). Simon, Mark, Redmond, Maureen and Harry were frantically organising the launch at the BAFTA building on Piccadilly while I avoided the press. In my *Standard* article I'd acknowledged that many people would feel betrayed by my broken promise never to leave Labour. 'I offer no weasel words of equivocation and I apologise, but I do not intend to take any lectures from those who have set new standards in ballot rigging,' I wrote.

At his launch Frank said, 'The ego has finally landed . . . he can run but he can't hide his politics. I will be tough on crime, he will be soft on crime. I will support jobs and businesses. He will drive them away.' Blair said my decision justified his earlier opposition: 'I believe passionately that he would be a disaster, a financial disaster, a disaster in terms of crime and police and business.' Steve Norris announced, 'This is proof there is a God and he must be a Tory. I'm the only candidate who can beat Ken Livingstone. Frank Dobson's campaign is dead in the water. Launched at eleven, sunk by three.'

With me unavailable for interview, rolling news built up the tension and by the time I arrived at Piccadilly Circus for a photo shoot with Eros there were hundreds of reporters present. Inside BAFTA I said the choice I faced was 'between the party I loved and the democratic rights of London'. When Frank's 'ego' jibe was thrown at me there was laughter as I said, 'I'm almost at that Buddhist plane where there is no ego any more as it has been beaten out of me by the ruthless media.' Media interviews ran one after another until all the candidates assembled on *Newsnight*. One minute before going on air we were told the *Guardian* had an ICM poll showing I had 68 per cent of the vote with Frank on 13, Norris on

11 and Kramer on 8. Three-quarters of Labour voters were for me and 48 per cent of Tories. These figures were as good as the best in the GLC anti-abolition campaign. I couldn't believe that Blair had mimicked Thatcher's mistake and allowed the issue to become one of Londoners' democratic rights. The result was a knee-jerk reaction uniting everybody with a grudge against Blair with my core vote, and I knew it would erode once the press switched attention from Frank to me, but the poll demoralised my opponents. Journalists assumed the outcome was a foregone conclusion so media interest went down several pegs.

*

Harry's office was deluged with supporters working all hours. I spent a lot of time persuading Labour councillors who wanted to resign not to do so. At Harry's the mood was happy but chaotic. Working in a rabbit warren of offices that was teeming with volunteers of all ages, we had so much post that hundreds of letters remained unanswered at the end. Emma St Giles had interviewed me for breakfast TV but left a note saying she would like to be my press officer, to which I readily agreed. Having ditched her impartiality, she had to leave her job immediately and was soon energetically trying to deal with the overwhelming media requests, strutting around with a phone on each hip and an extension to each ear switching between calls. Redmond phoned John Ross in Moscow and told him to come back immediately. John grabbed his laptop, jumped in a cab and went straight to the airport. Although John had warned me that the media would destroy me if I ran as an independent, he nevertheless threw himself into the campaign with enthusiasm.

I appealed for funds and they arrived by the sackful. The average donation was £16 and some people sent just £1 taped inside an envelope. Most of the donations were £10 or £20 accompanied by powerful opinions about the tube, buses or GLC. The radio presenter Chris Evans invited me to lunch at Zilli's in Soho, saying he was worried about the state of London. He offered £100,000 but said he would bankroll the whole £400,000 campaign if it was needed. When his donation became news Frank quipped, 'My old mum always told me to steer clear of redheads,' which led Chris to double the donation to £200,000. The story filled the front page of the *Standard*, much to the annoyance of Gordon Brown, who was announcing his budget that day. The only other big donor was Channel 5 boss David Elstein.

We now had more in the coffers than the £400,000 legal limit so I diverted donations to the Greens to pay for a *Guardian* ad where I would urge voters to cast their second preference Assembly vote for their party as I wanted City Hall to take a strong stand on environmental issues. A businessman wanted to make a big but anonymous donation as he had contracts with the government and feared reprisals but the law on this is clear and we had to decline. The same problem arose in Tower Hamlets, where we had to shred a cheque for £50,000 donated by businesses through a front organisation. More worrying was a letter from the Shirayama Corporation, who now owned County Hall, saying I could use it as my headquarters free of charge. I declined as they had plans (which I eventually blocked) to build on Jubilee Gardens.

I had visited all business organisations in London to ask what they expected the mayor to do and was amazed when the head of the CBI's London region offered to stand with me on an independent ticket. Without a party machine I could be damaged if the business community came out against me, so John held daily discussions with them. Most were already disillusioned with the government. London's business organisations were being pressured to come out against me by Downing Street, ignorant that I was consulting the business community and putting some of their ideas into my manifesto. Government assumed business would do its bidding regardless. The Chamber of Commerce invited the candidates to speak and in the vote that followed I received 42 per cent to Norris's 41 and Frank's 4. Blair could at least rely on Alan Sugar, who warned that I was 'a very dangerous character'. Max Hastings told me he got complaints from Number 10 about the *Standard*'s coverage of the election. A younger and less secure editor might have given in, but Max simply told them that the editorial policy of his paper was none of their business.

*

As expected, within a week my poll lead dropped 10 per cent but meetings were attracting crowds larger than any I had seen since the GLC and after a debate at the LSE I had trouble getting away through the crowd. Jonathan had the purple bus up and running but the spring of 2000 was the coldest for years and just ten minutes waving from the open top chilled us to the bone. My ratings settled at 49 per cent and stayed there until the end of April. Millbank was flailing around and Home Office minister Barbara Roche was humiliated by Jeremy Paxman on *Newsnight* when she refused sixteen times to name any of the businesses she alleged would leave London if I was elected mayor.

Rawnsley writes in *Servants of the People* that Blair made a last effort to persuade Frank to withdraw so Mo could be the candidate. 'Dobson, though he too knew he was doomed, had become stoically resigned to his fate and almost masochistically determined to see it to the death. "No one else will do any better. No one can beat Ken now. Someone's got to lose. It might as well be me."' Frank's mood is understandable. In *Nightmare!* D'Arcy and MacLean quote a Labour activist handing out warning leaflets to cab drivers that my congestion charge would cost them £300 a month: 'Here's what one chirpy London cabbie had to say to me . . . "Are you with that cunt Blair? – £300? – It will be worth paying it just to wipe the smile off his fucking face."'

Finally, Labour turned to the Police Federation. Thatcher built police numbers up to 28,000 but cuts in public spending by the chancellor Ken Clarke led to falling police numbers and real cuts in police allowances. Because Brown continued Clarke's spending limits police numbers were now under 26,000 and crime at an all-time high. Jack Straw planned a £6,000 pay increase for the police so the Police Federation leadership announced their support for Frank and called a meeting for all candidates at Westminster Central Hall. They hoped the £6,000 would be agreed in time for Frank to receive a standing ovation when he announced it while I would get torn apart because of GLC criticisms of police behaviour.

But Straw couldn't persuade Brown to push the measure through, so Frank had nothing to announce and was drowned out by 2,000 angry police slow-handclapping. Like Millbank, I assumed I too might have problems but there was thunderous applause as I started towards the rostrum. I defended the concept of public service, denounced restrictions on public spending and double standards between the pay of ordinary workers and the mega-rich. The response was rapturous. I had become a lightning rod for everyone who had seen through New Labour. As I sat down Norris was revising his speech, deleting all criticisms of me.

Police commissioner Sir John Stevens was there together with his new deputy Sir Ian Blair, who in his autobiography *Policing Controversy* recalls, 'I had never met Ken and could only remember the Red Ken of the 80s . . . I had named my cat after him, so that at least I could boss something called Ken around . . . I had been stunned when the police audience cheered him to the echo because he knew who they were and the other candidates did not.' Sir John asked me to come to New Scotland Yard, where we discussed the problems he faced and what we could do together to solve them. At his suggestion we were photographed for one of my election ads. When this appeared in the *Standard* Norris phoned to demand it be removed.

New Labour fell back on dirty tricks, some trivial, such as when all our phones were cut off at HQ. When I phoned to ask BT why they said the instruction had come from a Mr A. Hitler. I was completely open about my earnings and as my columns appeared in the *Standard* and *Independent* and my after-dinner speeches were often reported my income was hardly a secret. I had phoned the Parliamentary Commissioner for Standards to ask if I should register my earnings and he said that, as they were not 'contracts of employment', there was no need to do so.

Labour's MPs on the Committee of Standards and Privileges could simply change the rules. There was a complaint to the new Commissioner for Standards, Elizabeth Filkin, that I had not registered my earnings properly. Filkin asked for my response and I replied that her predecessor had said I didn't need to declare the income. I sent her details of everything I'd earned in the last two years – which involved me in a lot of unnecessary work in the middle of the campaign.

I didn't expect to hear any more about it, but on the morning of 17 March 2000 I was faxed the Standards Committee report criticising me for failing to register the income. It was to be released at noon, even though this was the first I'd heard of it; I hadn't been interviewed by the Committee, or even asked to comment on it. In *The Triumph of the Political Class* Peter Oborne points out that 'unfairness manifests itself in the contrasting treatment of Ken Livingstone and John Major . . . The complaint was not merely upheld but exploited by the Standards and Privileges Committee . . . John Major had committed the identical misdemeanour . . . Major ought to have registered his [income from after-dinner] speeches but on this occasion the Standards and Privileges Committee made nothing of the offence.'

In his study 'Regulating Westminster' Dr Robert Kaye claims, 'The committee's report is unusually descriptive and verbose. In former cases, the Committee's short response had played down negative findings. In Livingstone it revelled in them ... One would expect the Committee's report to be between four and eight paragraphs long [not] 14 ... In previous cases the Committee would simply note that the member had amended his register entry as required, in Livingstone it printed his new entry in full.'

Later I bumped into Ken Clarke, who said, 'This is your fault, now we've all got to start registering.' The damage was limited by good investigative journalism in the *Standard*, which identified the hapless stooge set up to make the complaint and followed the trail back via Smeath to Trevor. I was so angry the rules had been retrospectively changed I wanted to say so instead of apologising to the Commons, but the wording of your apology has to be agreed by the Speaker's Office. Simon insisted I make the apology so we could get on with the campaign rather than debate the rules of Parliament. I gave in and read out the brief statement the Speaker's Office had approved. When the expenses scandal broke in 2009 and the new Standards Commissioner Christopher Kelly ordered MPs to repay hundreds of thousands of pounds they complained that he was retrospectively changing the rules. They didn't say that when it happened to me.

Next, the two American Democrat fixers discovered that I put all my earnings from journalism and after-dinner speaking into Localaction Limited, a company which I set up in 1986. I had taken a £40,000 loan out of the company to buy a small terraced house in Brighton. Millbank gave the story to Tom Baldwin at *The Times* (then just a mouthpiece for Downing Street), who made it the front page lead with a two-page inside spread. *The Times* found an accountant, Ken Wild (a partner at Deloitte & Touche), who was prepared to say 'on the face of it these loans would appear to be illegal. There are certain exceptions but it is hard to see any reason how these loans would fall within these categories . . . this broke company law.' Allegations like that could land me in prison. Labour spin doctor Phil Murphy lobbied the rest of the papers to carry the story, though with little success. Nick Cohen writing in the *Observer* quoted an unnamed editor saying, 'I'll do you a deal. If you let me run the country tomorrow, I'll let you edit the *Guardian* tonight.' Labour MP Brian Sedgemore demanded a full inquiry by the Department of Trade and Industry but it took Charles Reiss at the *Standard* under an hour to discover that it was entirely legal for me to take a £40,000 loan out of a company I wholly owned and the story died. That day at a debate Frank said, 'I hope you know I'm not behind this dirty stuff.' I replied 'I know exactly who it is, Frank, and I never thought it would be you.'

*

None of this affected the campaign but Norris was now running second and moving to the left. Riding his own open-top bus, he made clear that he 'simply will not tolerate homophobia and racial discrimination at any stage of the policing process'. He still had the sense of humour we saw when he retired from Parliament 'because I want to spend more time with my money'. Now he urged Londoners: 'Vote Norris, I've got a family to support . . . well more than one, actually,' a reference to his second marriage.

Norris was endorsed by every daily and Sunday paper except two: the *Guardian*, which said nothing, and the *Observer*, which urged its readers to vote for me. *The Economist* warned that 'to give a populist such as Mr Livingstone a mandate such as this is like giving Archimedes a firm place to stand: he will try to use it to lever the whole of British politics to the left – perhaps even eventually to challenge Mr Blair's grip on the Labour party', and berated the parties for not finding a candidate to defeat me.

In the last week of the campaign the press onslaught that Redmond and Simon had feared got under way. A year before on May Day anarchists and nihilists had protested against capitalism with a riot in the city. Now groups like the Wombles (the White Overalls Movement Building Libertarian Effective Struggles, not the furry puppets from Wimbledon) promised another May Day riot just four days before the election along the lines of their 'Carnival against Capital' of the previous June. The Tory press increased tension and suggested I was behind the rioters, with shadow cabinet member Bernard Jenkin (son of Patrick) calling them 'Livingstone's Louts'.

With 15,000 police on hand there was less damage than previously but a McDonald's was trashed and photographs of Churchill's statue sporting a grass Mohican adorned the following day's front pages. Blair stomped out of Downing Street to pose by the paint-splattered Cenotaph. Steve Norris arrived complaining, 'Oh fuck, Labour are here already,' and announced that as mayor he would ban anti-capitalist demonstrations.

Frank arrived with Jack Straw but Frank's sound bite couldn't be heard over the workmen hammering away to shore up boards around the Cenotaph. The *Sun* front page pictured the riot under the headline: 'A vote for Ken is a vote for them.' The *Standard* warned that I would be 'a disastrous and embarrassing mayor ... the worst possible choice'. On Tuesday morning, with just forty-eight hours to polling day, a small group met inside Number 10 where Philip Gould reported the party's latest poll showing Dobson had no chance of winning but that Norris was only eight points behind me. The press were briefed by Downing Street that Blair had told a cabinet member that Norris is 'the new Labour candidate really' and the *Mirror* urged its readers to vote Tory for the only time in its history. After the election the *Sunday Mirror* reported, 'Mr Blair is understood to have voted . . . Norris.'

I wasn't surprised at Blair's desperation. A huge effort had gone into persuading Labour that socialism was a vote loser and only Blair's New Labour could have won the 1997 election. Blair always warned that 'the choice is not between this government and the government of your dreams, but this government or a Tory government', but Bob Worcester's book *Explaining Labour's Landslide* had shown Labour would have won under John Smith, Neil Kinnock or even the proverbial pig's bladder on a stick. For a socialist to win this election and defeat the three party machines would demolish New Labour mythology, so anything was justified to prevent my winning, even if it put a Tory in office.

In the end, it was all to no avail. As voting ended the BBC exit poll showed me ahead with 41 per cent of the vote. The election was conducted using the Supplementary Vote system, under which if no candidate receives 50 per cent of first-choice votes, second-choice votes are added to the result for the top two first-choice candidates. I had polled 39 per cent, Norris 27 and Dobson 13. Frank's voters' second choices were thus added to my votes and Steve's, giving me a 58 to 42 per cent majority.

Labour Assembly candidates had been called to a secret meeting, where Margaret McDonagh announced, 'It has been decided that we will accept the outcome of the election,' as though they were doing Londoners a favour. The final fiasco came when the electronic counting machines malfunctioned so instead of a result in the early hours of Friday morning it was Friday afternoon before the returning officer announced: 'Ken Livingstone has therefore been elected the first mayor of London.'

15

Where's the Mayor?

2000–2003

It was difficult to control my emotions as I started my speech with 'As I was saying before I was so rudely interrupted fourteen years ago . . .'. That hundreds of thousands of people voted for me was overwhelming and humbling and I hadn't expected to feel that. I meant it when I said that 'people who stood for mayor did so because they love this city and I want to draw a line in the sand between the divisions of this campaign and how we go forward to govern this city'. I looked at Frank, sad he'd been the fall guy for the control freaks he'd never had any time for. 'My old colleague and friend Frank Dobson has borne a terrible brunt of odium which was not his, but which should have rightly been reserved for the people who work behind the scenes.'

My first problem as mayor was getting away from the count. The scrum of journalists, photographers and camera crews outside the QEII centre surged forward, lifting me off my feet and trapping me against a wall before a wedge of police pushed through and carried me to a police car. One officer said, 'We've got to look after you, sir, you're the boss now.' The government had moved out of the Water Quality Commission and tarted up Romney House, an old hotel once requisitioned for wartime offices, as our base until City Hall was built. I was met by Bob Chilton, head of the transition team, and his interim staff who lined the stairs applauding.

John Prescott had appointed Bob (who worked on the GLC's anti-nuclear campaign) to assist the mayor in creating a new city government. Bob put his neck on the line to meet privately to plan the new Greater London Authority (GLA) and show me the building, including the mayor's bathroom from which the shower had been ripped out and replaced with a cheaper one on orders from a Treasury official who said it was too good for a mayor. I was too busy to identify the official or discover the cost of that decision.

Bob's team had three thick briefing files on problems awaiting the mayor but Prescott refused to give these to the candidates so I arrived to a desk groaning with paperwork. After half an hour Simon, John, Redmond, Mark, Neale, Maureen, Harry and others from the campaign team arrived for our first meeting. The afternoon had a surreal quality as my advisers grabbed offices in the east wing and began ploughing through briefing files. The transition team were miffed at having to work through my advisers.

I called a press conference. 'The drug dealer, the racist thug, the robber, the mindless yobs defiling monuments dedicated to those who gave their lives for our liberty, the corrupt; all of these people will find the new mayor distinctly uncuddly. Those who enrich our city with events like the Notting Hill Carnival or peacefully exercise their right to protest will have every protection provided by the law,' I said, but the journalists only wanted to know what I was going to do to Blair. The *Mail* announced, 'Left-wing extremist Ken Livingstone seized control . . .'; the *Telegraph* bemoaned, 'Livingstone represents the Beckhamisation of politics'; the *Independent on Sunday* warned, 'Now Ken has his eyes on Number 10'; the *Sunday Telegraph* predicted, 'unlike Giuliani, Livingstone isn't up to the job'; and *The Times* claimed that 'Putin is said to be an admirer'. Melanie Phillips speculated in the *Sunday Times*, 'So has the nightmare now come true for Sir John Stevens? . . . will his life be made miserable?' and wondered what might happen 'if the directly elected Livingstone demanded the commissioner's resignation' while warning that 'a city that has just elected Livingstone as mayor . . . has several years more pain ahead before [like New York] it grows up'. Former GLC member Stephen Haseler wrote in *The Times* that I 'could become a catalyst for nothing less than a re-ordering of British politics'.

The *Mail* and *Telegraph* were concerned about the order of precedence when the Queen attended London events. Ephraim Hardcastle in the *Mail* said, 'Courtiers spent much of Monday pondering should the queen meet him when she opens the Tate Modern . . . Ken knows about the discomfort – he's loving it.' The *Telegraph* reported that the Church of England believed I ranked above cabinet ministers but that the government insisted I was below them in the receiving line. Bob Chilton's transition team had spent a lot of time sorting this out with the Palace and I didn't give a damn. What was embarrassing when the Queen first met me to open the Millennium Bridge was that it wasn't finished. Because of millennium-related events I met the Queen four times in my first five weeks as mayor, and, realising this wasn't the best use of my time, the Palace conveyed the view that the Queen didn't expect my presence at every event in London. At the City's Guildhall lunch to celebrate the Queen Mother's 100th birthday (she was still as sharp as a pin) Margaret Thatcher made her way through the crowd to say, 'Stick to your guns. Everyone will be trying to tell you to do something else, but you must keep your resolve. You're now the leader of the equivalent of a small nation. Resolute, that's what you must be, resolute.' I thought this was a bit bizarre, remembering how she had greeted my election as GLC leader by comparing me to a communist dictator.

*

I'd become excited about what the new GLA could achieve if we got government, trade unions and business on board but I spent the final weeks of the campaign winding down expectations and

TOP LEFT: Meeting the crested newt at the Wood Green and Muswell Hill Scout Park
TOP RIGHT: Adopting a lion at London Zoo, 1984
BOTTOM LEFT: Pond dipping at Camley Street Natural Park, King's Cross, 1985 – a legacy of GLC funding

TOP: Meeting his *Spitting Image* puppet
BOTTOM: As 'Dick Livingstone' in a GLC panto, 1984

THE CAMPAIGN AGAINST THE ABOLITION OF THE GLC
TOP: With 'Stop Abolition' naval signalling
BOTTOM: The countdown

TOP: Regeneration with Bob Kiley, 2002
BOTTOM: At the launch of Crossrail with Gordon Brown, Douglas
Oakervee and Ruth Kelly, 2007

TOP: With Mayor Rudy Giuliani at City Hall, New York, 2001
BOTTOM: With Mayor Michael Bloomberg at a dinner for C40 Large
Cities Climate Summit, 2007

TOP: Opening offices in Delhi, 2007
BOTTOM: With Pramukh Swami Maharaj, Swaminarayan Temple,
Neasden

TOP: With Kelly Holmes and Sebastian Coe during the grand finale of the Olympic Torch relay at the O2 Arena, 2008. © PA
BOTTOM: Leading a line to lay wreaths in Tavistock Square for the first anniversary of the London terrorist bombings. © PA

Marries Emma at London Zoo, September 2009 ©PA

warning that for two years people would be asking what's happened to the mayor as I set up the organisation that I hoped could make such a big difference to the capital and its citizens. A new government inherits the civil service. The Scottish, Welsh and Northern Ireland assemblies inherited the Scottish, Welsh and Northern Ireland offices but senior GLC staff were either dead or retired and we were starting from scratch. No modern British politician had ever had the opportunity I was now presented with to create a new body, recruiting staff and drawing up planning, transport and environmental strategies. Future mayors would inherit the machine I created.

Photographers lurked outside the building to catch a glimpse through the windows and the *Standard*'s Hugh Muir filed a daily report on my activities (following me and my advisers when we returned to my home for a celebratory meal). The mood on the streets and tube was electrifying. People shook my hand and slapped me on the back but I worried that I couldn't deliver their expectations of sudden, dramatic change.

I was told Blair would phone me, so I was in the office early on my first Saturday morning and delighted to discover a greasy-spoon café just round the corner. Although exhausted by the campaign I was rejuvenated at the prospect of running something again. The building started to fill with Assembly members but none of them were Labour – Millbank had ordered them to keep away until they had a strategy to deal with me. I needed somebody with the ability to get on top of the nightmarish bureaucracy of the Met so I wanted Toby Harris to chair the Metropolitan Police Authority (MPA). He had survived as leader of Haringey Council and led and reorganised London Councils, the body that represented all thirty-two boroughs. I first met Nicky Gavron in the Stop the Archway Road campaign. After getting involved in the campaign against abolition of the GLC she became a Labour councillor in Haringey and after abolition led the Labour boroughs on London-wide planning issues. In that role she had set up a series of Q&As with the mayoral candidates on London issues and worked with London businesses on their demand for a congestion charge. The daughter of a Jewish refugee, Nicky had trained in psychotherapy and had the enthusiasm and imagination I wanted in a deputy mayor. When I phoned Toby and Nicky to offer them the jobs they were uncertain whether Labour would allow them to accept. Trevor Phillips, who had been elected to the Assembly, wanted them to insist on him as deputy but I said if it wasn't Nicky it would go to another party.

In the twenty-minute phone call, when it came, I congratulated Blair on the progress he was making in Northern Ireland and reassured him things would be fine. He was guarded but agreed that Toby and Nicky could take the jobs, undertook to make it happen and agreed Labour members should come into the building. First to arrive was John Biggs (an honest and competent former leader of Tower Hamlets, which couldn't be said about all of them), who refused to shake my hand. By afternoon all the parties were meeting in different parts of the building and I talked to each in turn. With only twenty-five members (nine Labour, nine Tory, four Lib Dems and three Greens) I said it was mad to replicate the paraphernalia of leaders, whips and party discipline but my plan for cooperative working was a step too far. I was intending to give Frank, Glenda, Norris and Kramer roles in my administration but as the mayoralty was based on the American concept of elected politicians being executive head rather than working through a permanent civil service we would all be finding our way in an environment none of us was familiar with. I planned to ask Frank to lead work on poverty and Glenda on homelessness so I phoned Blair's gatekeeper Anji Hunter as press rumours said Blair might make Frank Leader of the House. After asking Blair she said, 'No, you give him a job.' The next morning's papers had an interview with Frank saying he still expected me to be a disaster, so I thought sod it and didn't make the call.

*

Londoners wanted the mayoralty to work but I was vulnerable as an independent without a party on the Assembly. The Greens were supportive, but half the Labour group wanted rid of me at the next election and were circling like sharks. The others were nervous I might stitch them up. Len Duvall (former leader of Greenwich Council), Toby Harris and Nicky Gavron came into local government after I left and knew me only by reputation. I needed a consensus in which all parties took jobs – after all I had got the votes of 46 per cent of Labour voters, 33 per cent of Lib Dems and even 24 per cent of Tories. I thought Labour, Greens and the Lib Dems might come on board because they supported rebuilding services; the Tories would be harder to convince, but I hoped they would cooperate on issues like policing. I decided on monthly public cabinet meetings of advisers, heads of department and leaders of all four Assembly parties. I offered the job of chairing the London Fire and Emergency Planning Authority (LFEPA) to Graham Tope, leader of the Lib Dems, who declined, saying he wanted to be my human rights adviser (hardly a demanding role). Transport for London (TfL) was a new body created to supersede London Regional Transport; Steve Norris and Susan Kramer jumped at the chance to join the board and I recruited Dave Wetzel and Paul Moore (chair and vice-chair of the GLC's Transport Committee) and Stephen Glaister, a transport academic on the LRT board under the Tories.

But what to do with Trevor Phillips? For me he typified all that was rotten in New Labour yet he could one day be Labour's mayoral candidate. I was prepared to forget the past and let him chair LFEPA so that he could learn the ins and outs of local government and of dealing with one of the best-organised trade unions – all crucial if he was ever to be mayor. Trevor declined, saying he wanted to chair the Assembly (meeting once a week with lots of media coverage). I was appalled that he turned down a position of real influence and decided Trevor was never going to be a serious political figure. Len Duvall summed it up: 'There's two kinds of politicians, those who want to do something and those who want to be something, and Trevor just wants to be something.'

I offered the job to Val Shawcross, who had been a good leader of Croydon Council. She spent the next eight years transforming the London Fire Brigade, leading to a dramatic reduction in loss of life from fires, cutting waste and, later, organising emergency response procedures after 9/11 in preparation for a similar attack here. Another part of my coalition was the City Corporation, the body that represented the financial centre of London. In 1998 Judith Mayhew, the chair of the City Policy Committee (effectively the leader), told me the City had changed and wanted a good relationship with me. I had no desire to take over the ceremonial role of the Corporation or duplicate the Lord Mayor's role of eating and drinking for London so I was happy for our two organisations to work together. As the City had campaigned for GLC abolition there was surprise when I announced Judith would be in my cabinet (given that the City had hundreds of years resisting any democratic involvement in their own processes).

*

My idea of doing one term while remaining an MP was over. Control freakery under New Labour was so bad that even a cabinet member didn't have any freedom so I decided this would be my last political job and determined to make it work. I gave up Brent East at the 2001 election, but warned the Labour party if they imposed a candidate on the local party I would stand as an independent MP.

This allowed my local party to select my replacement. (Had I resigned my seat when I left the party and so caused an immediate by-election, Millbank would have chosen the candidate.) I carried on casework but only went into the Commons on the few occasions that it mattered: opposing air-traffic control privatisation and supporting stem-cell research.

My powers were limited but the role of mayor is recognised the world over. I saw this when Ford decided to close the Fiesta assembly line at Dagenham with the loss of 2,000 jobs. I warned at my first press conference that as the pound was overvalued and it was easier to sack workers in Britain than in Europe so Ford's cuts would hit Britain hardest. I spoke to the chief executive in Detroit and he dispatched Nick Scheele, the head of Ford Europe, to meet me and John Ross at the Hilton. He arrived in London the night the Tate Modern opened. As I left the Tate reception and looked for a cab the driver of a police riot van said, 'Can we take you anywhere?' I got in (and was lobbied about their pay rise), and will never forget the face of the Hilton's concierge as the riot van pulled up and I got out of the back.

Scheele accepted that Dagenham was about the most productive Ford plant in Europe, and with 28 per cent of European sales in the UK Ford were vulnerable to a public backlash and keen to keep me on board. Eventually we negotiated that Ford's European diesel plant would be based in London and they would fund the building of a Centre of Engineering and Manufacturing Excellence.

Another problem was Wembley Stadium, the much-needed redevelopment of which was running so far over budget that its completion was in doubt. Paul Daisley, the leader of Brent Council, warned of the effect on one of the poorest areas of London if Wembley closed. I wasn't happy that the Premier League clubs had no intention of lifting a finger to help, but I promised £26 million to upgrade rail and road links to the stadium.

As in the US system, the mayor is the chief executive so I was at my desk taking decisions and signing contracts (unlike spending all day in County Hall as GLC leader managing the Labour group) and dealing with outside organisations, building alliances around specific issues. The Assembly scrutinised my work and could change my annual budget if two-thirds of the members agreed on specific amendments. As mayor I was entitled to appoint directly twelve members of my staff, but I wanted a traditional council system and so told the Assembly I would not fill the mayoral appointments personally; instead I would leave the Assembly to find the best people possible. The Assembly agreed to appoint my policy advisers and I found funds for a scrutiny team so the Assembly had proper research support.

My first tussle with the Assembly was on my promise to ban lobbyists from access to members and staff. Invoking Lord Neill (Commissioner for Standards in Public Life), who said the ban was unfair, Trevor Phillips claimed that 'it is a human right to lobby'. He also asserted himself at the inauguration of the GLA on 3 July, saying that if I pushed 'policies not in the interest of Londoners, or choose to use the platform for other political ends we will, I promise, kick your ass'. Darcus Howe's next *New Statesman* column was headlined 'Ken's ass need fear nothing from Trevor', speculating that 'Trevor must still be in a state of deep cultural shock that the black community prefers Livingstone to him ... he resides miles from the nearest black person and still puts himself forward as a representative of the people ...' Trevor was torn between New Labour and his need for a radical image, saying Jack Straw's 'idea of Britishness ... suggests that there is only one way of being British'.

Not realising that expenses and allowances were decided by me, some Tories pestered Bob Chilton for parking spaces in the courtyard and were put out when I ruled there would be no such allocation, and no chauffeur-driven cars. Like myself, each Assembly member could have an annual season ticket for public transport. London Transport bosses' chauffeur-driven cars were withdrawn.

A luxury mayoral apartment was planned for the eighth floor of City Hall but while New York has Gracie Mansion and Paris the Hôtel de Ville – a grand palace on the banks of the Seine – I didn't want to live on the job and would have hated losing my garden at home. Living in City Hall I would have been cut off from the lives of Londoners and if an emergency required me to stay overnight a sofa would be fine. If I had a taxpayer-funded flat some Assembly members would have demanded a second homes allowance just like MPs.

*

The first sign that my hopes for consensus were naive came when the Assembly decided to appoint a chief executive. Bob Chilton explained the mayor was the chief executive and the law only required a 'head of paid service' – a glorified personnel officer but with the power to remove the mayor if he was too incapacitated to resign. Trevor pushed the idea of a chief executive to create an alternative power base inside City Hall. I saw no point in an expensive legal battle with the Assembly, given that whoever they appointed would recognise the legal position. Telling Trevor's committee what they didn't want to hear killed Bob's chance of getting the post and the process was soured when Tories leaked the shortlist. The Assembly appointed Anthony Mayer, hoping as he hadn't got the job of transport commissioner he might bear a grudge against me, but for eight years Anthony and I had such a good working relationship that the Tories got rid of him when Boris Johnson won the mayoral election in 2008.

The Assembly appointed Anne McMeel (who was one of Maurice Stonefrost's high-flying protégés back at the GLC) as director of finance. The new head of corporate services was Manny Lewis from Thurrock Council, who had the unenviable job of liaising between the Assembly and me on staffing and administration matters – as when the Assembly proposed to ban alcohol during the working day and more bizarrely rule that 'close personal familiarity (e.g. personal friendships, sexual relations or regular social interaction) . . . should be avoided'. As two senior officers had a bottle of wine each for lunch, half the couples I knew met at work and one leading member of the Assembly was already having an affair with a personal assistant I asked Manny to persuade the Assembly to see sense and accept an alternative that City Hall's 'culture . . . should be positive and should recognise that close working relationships do develop and need not be problematic'.

The Assembly's report on the congestion charge was a bad start. Instead of supporting, opposing or suggesting a different way of doing it, the report was merely a catalogue of every complaint ranging from those who didn't want one at all to the Greens who wanted a tougher version.

Relationships with the boroughs were cool because if I was successful they feared their role would be diminished. Things worsened when they nominated for one appointment a councillor who had circulated child porn. When I rejected his nomination the boroughs threatened a legal challenge but when Harriet Harman said the allegations were true the boroughs backed down.

I ran the GLC through a cabinet of committee chairs but now as the elected chief executive responsible for everything from fares policy to signing the photocopier contract a typical day switched between major planning decisions, recycling, the modernisation of the tube, meeting Minister for Trade Stephen Byers to discuss the Ford plant, TV and radio interviews, being lobbied by Assembly members on local issues and defusing staff grievances. Each day was wall-to-wall meetings and David Hayward, my diary secretary, had the worst job in London trying to juggle everyone who needed a meeting yesterday.

*

My mind hops from issue to issue easily, but I needed effective support. I had known my election team for years: Neale Coleman in Paddington; John Ross and Redmond O'Neill, who campaigned with me on Ireland and ran my NEC campaigns; Lee Jasper, Kumar Murshid and Atma Singh, who worked with me against racism; Harry and Theresa Coates from GLC days (she had been a Labour group secretary under Goodwin and typed the manuscript of *If Voting Changed Anything*); and Maureen Charleson, who had run my Commons office and house-trained the ferociously bright Simon Fletcher and Mark Watts. Not everyone had been a fan. John Duffy, my waste adviser, had been a Kinnockite who tried to deselect me in Brent East but then worked with me to get rid of corrupt Labour councillors.

In total they had worked with or for me for 152 years and nine times out of ten knew what I wanted without checking. When John and Simon wrote articles in my name no one could tell the difference. At the GLC we achieved more because I delegated rather than have everything cross my desk so I left people free to operate, confident they would tell me if they made a mistake rather than cover it up. Machiavelli's idea – that it's better to be feared than loved – is rubbish. I needed somebody to manage the strong personalities involved and Emma Beal fitted the bill exactly. Although she was never a political activist I saw her skills at propping up the editor, handling impossible and demanding *ES* magazine journalists and columnists while working to a weekly deadline and remaining sane, so I urged her to apply for the job of office manager.

The policy advisers were the point of contact for organisations wanting to engage with City Hall and their jobs were all subject to advertisement and open recruitment. The Assembly appointed Len Duvall to chair the interview panels and I sat in on the interviews for Simon, Neale, John Ross, John Duffy, Emma St Giles and Maureen, but after a week of interviews Simon (now Chief of Staff) took my place for the other posts. Redmond helped set up the administration, intending to return to party campaigning, but with his judgment and capacity for work he ended up advising on transport, liaising with all community groups and overseeing publicity.

I decided not to reopen past decisions so my Monday meetings started with my advisers reviewing progress and planning ahead. Our first problem was that Labour Assembly members wanted to stop me going to court over the public–private partnership, Gordon Brown's panacea for the modernisation of the underground system, and wouldn't join my administration unless an independent panel looked at the issue again. When Simon Jenkins declined to chair the panel, Will Hutton agreed and by October had produced a well-researched and damning indictment which Brown completely ignored.

*

Sir John Stevens was Britain's longest-serving police officer, politically savvy and a thoroughly nice man. He knew what was wrong with policing and had exposed collusion between Northern Ireland's police and loyalist terrorists, believing army intelligence officers had burgled and set fire to his office in Northern Ireland to prevent him getting to the truth. Sir John's only worry about the mayoral system was Jeffrey Archer's promise to have a desk in the commissioner's office, which he would never have allowed. Labour's continuation of Tory spending constraints meant that each month more police quit the force than joined, with numbers down from 28,000 in 1992 to 25,350 in 2000; crime was surging to an all-time high and murders were going unsolved. Crime continued to rise until 2002, when the increase in police numbers began to tell and crime started falling year on year.

With the arrival of Sir John in early 2000 the culture inside the force changed rapidly and the Met admitted that police had acted unlawfully the previous year when they harassed pro-Tibet demonstrators. Sir John resisted government pressure to switch police from catching criminals to increasing deportations. In his first year deaths in police custody were cut by two-thirds but not everything was perfect. Delroy Lindo annoyed local police in Tottenham by campaigning to free Winston Silcott (wrongly convicted for the murder of PC Keith Blakelock during the 1985 Broadwater Farm riots) and was arrested thirty-seven times, and charged with eighteen offences which were all dismissed by the courts. When Delroy was arrested for 'sucking his teeth in the presence of a police officer' Lee Jasper, my police adviser, slipped into campaigning mode and wanted to denounce the arrest until I pointed out that Lee just needed to pick up the phone to Sir John to sort it out.

Home Secretary Jack Straw didn't attack me during the election campaign as we would have to work together to tackle crime and carry out the recommendations of the inquiry into the shambolic manner in which the Met and the Crown Prosecution Service had handled the investigation of the murder of black teenager Stephen Lawrence by a gang of white youths in 1993. Police attitudes to ethnic minorities began changing when Sir Peter Imbert replaced Sir Kenneth Newman as police commissioner in the late 1980s and most police no longer saw their job as keeping the lid on black communities. After the fascist David Copeland planted nail bombs in Brixton, Brick Lane and Old Compton Street in April 1999 I was at a meeting between police and Bangladeshis and saw the trust police had built up. Although Sir John was seen as a bluff, old-style officer and his deputy Sir Ian Blair as a politically correct lefty, all three of us agreed on the changes needed. Many of the Met's officers came from outside London and had no feel for its culture, so when I became mayor we set out to recruit Londoners.

Police are understandably more interested in catching criminals than reviewing budgets, so the Met's housekeeping left something to be desired. (It had only just introduced double-entry bookkeeping, for example.) Sometimes it was impossible to know whether a bill had been paid. Officers could get paid twice for overtime and it was easier to requisition a hire car than a pen (with the hire car often returned weeks late). The police treasurer said no Home Office minister had ever asked any question about the budget other than 'How many officers will I get for this?'

I had no power to tell the Met what to do, but I did set the police budget. The Home Secretary appointed the commissioner while Metropolitan Police Authority members scrutinised the police and appointed senior officers but had no say in operational policing. MPA members jealously guarded their independence and refused to co-opt Lee Jasper as a member. More surprisingly they refused to co-opt a key adviser to the Lawrence inquiry, the Bishop of Stepney, John Sentamu (who had urged me not to leave the Labour party). The contrast with New York was stunning. Mayor Giuliani brought in outsider Bill Bratton as commissioner, pensioned off the twenty-three most senior officers, set crime reduction targets by precinct and moved police around the city to stamp out any upsurge in crime. I told Straw that policing arrangements worked better in New York but as usual he was cautious about making change.

Tony Blair would call Sir John in without me present but as he didn't have time to master the details of London policing this was not helpful. After the 9/11 attacks in New York Sir John was told to pull police from the suburbs to protect high-profile targets in central London. As a result, street robberies soared from 175 a day to 230. A year later, alarmed by a surge in suburban crime, Blair told Sir John to take police off traffic duty and put them in the suburbs and a year after that was asking him why David Blunkett and Cherie Blair had been caught in a traffic jam at Vauxhall Cross. Alistair Darling announced the appointment of a 'traffic tsar' who was never heard of again. Since there were no spare police for traffic duty, Blair introduced legislation to nationalise control of roadworks. We spent two years persuading government to give TfL power to license roadworks instead. But Blair lost interest and although this change became law it was only after I and then Boris Johnson lobbied the government to activate the legislation that they did so at the end of 2009.

Toby Harris and I did a deal with Sir John so that we could bring in outside accountants to find efficiency savings of £200 million at the Met over three years, using every penny saved to employ more police officers. Sir John said he needed 8,500 more officers to police the city properly, bringing the total to 35,000. Sir Ian Blair expanded the training college at Hendon to cope with the influx of recruits and removed the ban on recruiting migraine and asthma sufferers or people with inoffensive tattoos, dreadlocks or a motoring conviction (355 people rejected on these grounds in the last year were asked to reapply). We eventually reached 32,000 police officers and 4,000 police community support officers (PCSOs). I had to raise the council tax each year to achieve this total but in return I wanted bobbies back on the beat. For thirty years the Home Office and senior police had been saying that foot patrols were a waste of time, but what the public wanted was to see police officers on their streets. When we employed a few wardens to patrol Trafalgar Square it cut crime in the area by half. The surge in crime in the suburbs when police were withdrawn after 9/11 and the surge when the Queen Mother died and police were switched to central London for her funeral proved our case and opposition to bobbies on the beat collapsed.

*

My first meeting with Prescott was never going to be easy and was made worse because Nicky Gavron's high heels slowed us down and we arrived late. Prescott's office was filled with officials who'd come for the entertainment as he greeted me with the statement, 'I get lots of council leaders in here asking for things.' There followed ten minutes of rudeness until I mentioned the buses. Immediately Prescott was transformed and, unpleasantness forgotten, he excitedly discussed what we could do to improve them.

Just to maintain the present service TfL needed £1.8 billion extra for the next three years but after strenuous lobbying we got £3.2 billion including money to reintroduce conductors in a trial on two routes and bring in congestion charging (but if it went wrong the blame would be all mine). When challenged by William Hague to stop the congestion charge Blair told Parliament he couldn't 'see many advantages' to congestion charging but he was not responsible for my actions.

After the Millennium Eve fireworks display on the banks of the Thames Blair wanted to make it an annual event, even though there was disappointment that the promised 'wall of fire' along miles of the Thames hadn't happened (civil servants, nervous of the cost, cut it by 90 per cent without telling ministers), so I was asked to take over organising the display for New Year's Eve 2000, and I appointed Bob Geldof's company Ten Alps to organise it. London's train operating companies (TOCs) intended to stop running trains an hour before the display began and tube bosses, although answering to government, wanted to close stations an hour early. After weeks without progress Prescott blew his top and summoned the TOCs, tube bosses and me. When I proposed we have the display at eight o'clock to avoid additional costs the TOCs said they would stop trains at seven o'clock and the tube executives said 'us too'. When I proposed four o'clock the TOCs said they'd close at three. Prescott got angry but the TOCs and tube wouldn't budge and it was only after I got control of the tube in 2003 that we were able to have New Year's Eve fireworks. Assembly members launched an investigation which found government files showing that they only transferred the project to me when they realised it was going to fail. Prescott obviously hadn't been told by his civil servants.

Westminster Council also dumped failing projects on me. They announced that they couldn't afford to carry on rebuilding Hungerford footbridge after they'd spent £30 million on it without any sign of a new bridge. Anthony Mayer advised me that with the preparatory work done we could replace the ugly old bridge for an additional £16.7 million from TfL's budget. Then Westminster dropped the pedestrianisation of Trafalgar Square so we took that on too. As kids, Londoners go to the square to feed the pigeons and admire the view but except for a few hardy souls on New Year's Eve few ever return. Now we had the chance to create a world-class square just so long as we got rid of the pigeons. Bernard Rayner, the pigeon-feed seller on the square, supported by pigeon rights groups, resisted but as the pigeons carried encephalitis, paratyphoid, TB and Lyme disease public opinion swung our way.

*

By August 2000 I was exhausted but on the morning I was due to have a fortnight in Brighton I woke to find my leg swollen. My GP feared it was thrombosis and sent me straight to hospital. Waiting for the scan, I couldn't believe this was happening just as everything was going so well, and was delighted to be told it was Baker's knee, a cyst with identical symptoms to thrombosis (caused by spending too long on my knees weeding the garden).

By the time I returned from Brighton the country was facing a fuel blockade as protesters demanded a reduction in fuel duty and picketed the entrances to fuel depots. Fuel supplies at nine London bus garages would last only for the day so, while I lobbied government to access their emergency supplies, John and Redmond tried to find out why the oil companies weren't instructing tanker drivers to cross the picket line. With access to local police information we discovered that instead of angry crowds most of the pickets consisted of just a handful of men sitting around drinking tea. The oil companies made no effort to break the 'blockade' because if fuel duties were reduced, they would pocket much of the reduction rather than passing it on to customers (this was confirmed when Esso and others attempted a price increase on Friday, 15 September, the day after the protesters lifted the blockade voluntarily).

John and Redmond ran a Fuel Crisis Committee meeting twice a day. When we asked, local police cleared picket lines out of the way so if tankers were not leaving the depots it was because Britain was facing a strike by oil companies. John and Redmond phoned the oil bosses saying that if they didn't send fuel tankers out I would go on television to name them individually. While some companies cooperated, others suffered 'administrative delays' but further threats of publicity got their cooperation.

*

Transport for London brought together thirteen transport bodies – more than any other city in the world – giving the mayor power to appoint and remove members of the board and to set its policies. When London Transport was created by Herbert Morrison in the early 1930s it made the city's bus and tube network the world leader in urban mass transit. But by the 1970s it had become too bureaucratic and like all monopolies was exhibiting the arrogance spawned from knowing that however bad or expensive its services, the public had no choice but to use them. With GLC abolition that arrogance worsened, with chauffeur-driven executives oblivious to the decline in service. Thatcher's promises of increased investment came to nothing until John Major agreed to extend the

Jubilee Line to Docklands, but this suffered huge cost overruns and delays. The American firm Bechtel was brought in to ensure it would be ready in time for the opening of the Millennium Dome. It was, but trains were trapped in tunnels for up to twenty minutes at a time because of signalling failures. Businesses said that unless I reduced congestion and improved public transport firms would relocate to rival cities like Paris or Frankfurt. I had promised to sack the 'dullards' and bring in new management, so most of the dead wood took early retirement before TfL came under my control two months after the election.

At the GLC we had stopped phasing out the popular Route-master buses, of which there were just 1,935 left in 1984, but af-ter abolition the Tories replaced most of the Routemasters to save money on conductors. Bus journey times increased by a third as passengers queued to buy tickets from the driver and motorists got stuck behind them at bus stops. Anybody who could do so either used the tube or got in their car, so as well as becoming slow, dirty and unreliable, buses were being used only by pensioners, children and the poor. Then the Tories privatised the buses, the bus driver training centre was shut, wages were cut by a third and pension schemes were closed. The best drivers left and staff turnover was as much as 30 per cent a year. Now I told staff to buy back Routemas-ters, but we could only find forty-nine of them.

John Ross identified the key problem as a lack of competition, with companies not making realistic bids for each other's routes. We introduced penalties for underperformance and a bonus for improved service. A fifth of the contracts were re-let each year and there were immediate improvements. We told bus companies their profit margins should not be over 8 per cent, anti-union companies needn't bother bidding and I wanted a real increase in drivers' pay. Ten years earlier bus and train drivers had been paid the same. Now bus drivers were on £16,000 a year and tube drivers on £25,000.

Brian Souter, the owner of bus company Stagecoach, used his profits to fund a campaign to keep the homophobic Section 28 of the Local Government Act 1986 in Scotland (where it was known as Section 2a), but when I said I would not let contracts to homophobes Souter went quiet and when he wanted to sell I blocked the sale until he agreed to give £60 million of the profit to fill the hole in his drivers' pension fund.

Peter Hendy was Sir Peter Masefield's PA when the GLC cut fares back in the eighties, and went on to make millions following bus privatisation. Now he wanted to return to public service. Since he knew all the scams he was the ideal person to close them down. Another London Transport veteran was Derek Turner, who introduced London's red route system which banned parking on London's main routes during rush hour. Derek was a workaholic whose obsessive attention to detail made him the ideal person to operate the congestion charge with its complex IT system.

The most interesting candidate for transport commissioner was Bob Kiley, who had turned round the New York subway system after decades of squalid neglect and underinvestment. The TfL board spent two days interviewing eight candidates and we all (except Norris) agreed that Bob was streets ahead even though he was disadvantaged by doing the interview via a video link from New York. Bob was earning the equivalent of half a million pounds a year as chief executive of the body representing New York businesses and so we had to match that, making him the highest-paid public servant in Britain by a mile. Mark Watts's jaw dropped when Norris said, 'What with school fees and a mortgage a quarter of a million doesn't go very far and you can't even get a decent bottle of Bollinger for under £90.'

Kiley and his wife Rona flew to London forty-eight hours later. I met Bob in his Park Lane hotel and we hit it off right away. We faced weeks of negotiation about how our relationship would work but I knew he was the right person when he said he would only take the job if he could bring half a dozen people from America to help him get control of the TfL bureaucracy. He had modernised Boston's transport before moving to New York, where he spent $16 billion rebuilding the subway and laid the foundation for the city's zero-tolerance policy when he flooded the underground with police to arrest anyone travelling without a ticket. Bob rejected the idea that graffiti was a working-class art form and refused to allow trains out of sidings until the graffiti was removed (a policy we adopted in London).

That night Nicky and I took Bob and Rona to my favourite Italian restaurant, the Pavilion in Poland Street, where Bob regaled us with his tales of the CIA. Bob's life hadn't been easy. He was born severely premature in 1935 in Minneapolis and would have died if the hospital hadn't just taken delivery of the first incubator in the state. He spent the first six months of his life in it. Bob was 'forever changed' in 1974 when the car in which his first wife Patricia was driving their two small children, David and Christopher, was hit by another and exploded. Bob's wife and one son were killed instantly and Bob sat for days by his surviving son's bedside, but he was too badly burned to live.

Bob had a classic small-town American childhood until he became the president of the US National Union of Students. Leading a delegation to visit Cuba just after the revolution of 1959, he spent several hours after midnight debating on TV with Che Guevara. Bob felt he won because Che was too busy eyeing up one of the American women in Bob's party, who got very nervous. With many students around him covertly working for US intelligence, Bob finally joined the CIA in 1963 and became manager of intelligence operations, in which capacity he travelled the world, visiting eighty-seven countries, until he was promoted executive assistant to CIA director Richard Helms. When I recalled that Helms had gone to prison for lying to Congress and covering up assassinations Bob replied, 'Helms was very protective in keeping that stuff away from me.' Bob had found the CIA's legendary James Jesus Angleton (played by Matt Damon in the film *The Good Shepherd*) flat on his face outside HQ covered in blood after a drunken fall. After carrying him into his office, Helms told Bob to forget it had ever happened. Bob also spent time driving Robert Kennedy to election rallies, merrily describing him as a 'mean son of a bitch'. Bob ran for the Democratic nomination for mayor of Boston but his support for abortion and school bussing in a strongly Catholic, white city doomed his campaign, though it did introduce him to Rona, his second wife, with whom he had two sons.

By the end of the evening I knew he would become a friend as well as being our best chance to sort out London's transport problem. I became closer to Bob than any other official I ever worked with and he later told the *Standard*, 'I guess in my head there was a sense [Ken] was a man of the left, but very much a man of London, and therefore very much an urbanist . . . I found him to be very smart, very focused, very clear headed about what he felt he had promised . . . When we got to know each other a little bit – as much as one can in a weekend – personally I really liked him. Once that chemistry was there it was possible for me to seriously consider [taking the job]. If it had not been there it would have ended that Sunday. It would have been over.' Bob told the *Sunday Times*, 'He knows as much about American political history as anyone I have ever met. This is a learner. He reads, listens and watches. I don't find him a dogmatic person.'

I valued Bob's instinctive reaction to events and people. On the day the tube was transferred to our control I was on a Jubilee Line train where senior officials (who hadn't seen me) rushed around with walkie-talkies monitoring Bob's approach to the station, telling the driver to hold the train for him. As Bob got on the train

I told him what had happened and with a look that would have terrified a KGB agent he told the officials, 'If that happens again everyone responsible will be fired.'

*

A typical can-do American, Bob moved effortlessly between the public and private sectors and as Brown loved all things American and holidayed at Martha's Vineyard (where the Kileys had a summer home) I hoped Bob could persuade him to drop his commitment to the private–public partnership model for financing tube modernisation. Brown rightly didn't trust the old tube bosses to control spending. Before the election the then transport minister John Reid told me he wouldn't proceed with PPP unless it was going to provide value for money. Now we knew there would have to be a taxpayer subsidy if it was to work, and as Bob would clear out the dead wood in the management structure, there was no reason to continue with PPP. But Brown went to extraordinary lengths to avoid Bob. (Months later, at the Westminster Abbey service in honour of the victims of 9/11, Bob and I took our seats and noticed that the seat next to Bob was reserved for Brown. When he turned up and saw us he got the usher to move him to another row.)

As Bob couldn't get to Brown, I asked if Bob could meet Blair, who, fearing a row with Brown, arranged to meet him at Chequers, where Blair pored over the PPP contracts. He said that he shared Bob's concern at their complexity. After over a hundred meetings between Bob and Prescott's officials, we were close to an agreement based on Bob's alternative funding plan. The press were briefed that the government had reached a compromise with Bob but the Treasury refused to budge. An anonymous source was quoted as saying, 'Gordon Brown is not going to want to back down . . . If Kiley doesn't accept the PPP, he may as well leave his official £2 million home . . . and fly back to America.' On 17 February 2001

the *Independent* reported, 'Gordon Brown has intervened to oppose a deal whereby the state would take a controlling interest
in [PPP companies].' The *Observer* quoted Treasury sources: 'In
America, if they want to build a train line they just do it. We have
limits here. [Kiley's] just beginning to understand that.' Bob hit
back by depicting Brown as the Wizard of Oz, manipulating from
behind the scenes. Polly Toynbee reported in the *Guardian*, 'Calls
rain in from Brown's people claiming incredibly that the PPP has
nothing to do with the Chancellor.' Simon Jenkins in *The Times*
on 28 February wrote, 'The Treasury, which in 1998 said the PPP
would cost nothing, [has now] promised [PPP companies] up to
£700 million a year in subsidies for thirty-year leases . . . On 2 February . . . Whitehall conceded that Mr Kiley could redraft the PPP
bids . . . The Treasury simply ignored [the deal] . . . Shriti Vadera [a
former corporate financier and now Brown adviser] overruled the
two officials sent to implement the deal.'

The principal rail safety inspector, Stanley Hart, warned of a
'growing concern' about safety, accusing London Underground of a
'breakdown in local management control'. Hart was promoted and
replaced by Peter Hornsby, who warned that 'it is not clear who does
what, how and when', and that safety procedures do 'not provide us
with confidence that there is a safety management process in place'.

When the *Standard* broke the news under the headline 'New
York tough guy to run tube', businesses in London were delighted
that I was able to attract people who could deliver. Bob was so popular with the press that every journalist and expert was now criticising the PPP, with the exception of the *Daily Telegraph*'s Patience
Wheatcroft, a future adviser to Boris. Bob was being depicted in
the British press as some sort of Superman but he knew that his
popularity was transient: 'That can vanish in a nanosecond,' he told
me. Most of Labour's London MPs were hostile to PPP, as was
public opinion. London's businesses wanted Bob to be allowed to

do his job so I asked Anji Hunter to persuade Blair to take it to cabinet, where Brown would have been defeated, but Blair wouldn't take Brown on even when he could win. With the 2001 general election bearing down on 7 June and Lib Dems standing as 'Lib Dems Against Tube Privatisation' Blair sacked Sir Malcolm Bates, the chair of the Underground, and put Bob in his place to find a solution. Bob was suspicious it was a gimmick to get past the election, but he did his best to make it work.

*

The rail unions had gone on strike against the PPP but sensing the government's weakness they now demanded a guarantee of jobs for life to ensure the security of any staff transferred to the PPP companies. The transport minister, Gus Macdonald, ordered tube officials to concede the jobs-for-life guarantee to avoid a strike the week before the election.

We had been set up. After the election Bob was sacked as boss of the Underground network and Bates was reinstated. At my first meeting with Stephen Byers, the new transport secretary, he said, 'I'm not authorised to make any changes to the PPP.' Brown still refused to meet us but the bidding firms had him over a barrel. As they upped their demands, the Treasury had to agree. In the end the PPP contracts alone were two million words long. They filled two four-drawer filing cabinets and even Patience Wheatcroft was now opposed to the scheme. We had won a court action forcing the government to release a secret report by Deloitte, which said that the PPP was 'flawed . . . [with] no evidence part privatisation . . . was cheaper' and revealed the government was bending the calculations by £2.5 billion to make the PPP bids look better value. The only option left was start a court case to stop Brown, which would take months.

*

The London Development Agency (LDA) was a GLA 'arms-length' body with £400 million a year to spend on training, job creation and business support. As its budget was a third of one per cent of London's economy, we needed imagination to have any impact. In the rest of England regional development agencies were run by government and although I appointed the LDA board they had to work within government policy, so it was difficult to establish who was accountable to whom. Staff transferred to the LDA from English Partnerships, the government's regeneration agency, were used to setting their own agenda and many resented the change. And 80 per cent of the budget was already committed to projects started in previous years.

John Ross sifted applications for the LDA board but the law on appointments was very New Labour. The chair and majority of the board had to be business people and trade unions didn't get a look-in. I had the power to appoint the LDA's first chief executive and asked Mike Ward, who since the GLC had worked on urban regeneration and had unrivalled knowledge of regeneration schemes. A week after the election I took Mike to the members restaurant in the Commons where John Major came over to congratulate me followed by Patricia Hewitt. Patricia had advocated congestion charging and encouraged me to go ahead with the charge. Tony Banks sat across the restaurant ignoring us. I assumed he was angry I had got the job he wanted but as he never spoke to me again before his death I never found out. Mike agreed to take the job, knowing he had to live with the dual responsibility to government and mayor.

I had to draw up a twenty-year plan for the whole city, which, after a public inquiry and government approval, would be the legal planning framework for London. The first London plan had been written for the government by Professor Sir Patrick Abercrombie (the great post-war planner of new towns) at the end of the Second World War. This was one man's vision: coherent, readable, relatively short and accepted by all during London's reconstruction. By 1964 it was time for a new plan, but it became a bureaucratic exercise that generated vast volumes of leaden prose. At its heart was a plan for three motorways in concentric circles radiating outwards from the centre. The newly elected GLC under Reg Goodwin opposed the motorways and made so many amendments to the turgid, unreadable, multi-volume document that they were thicker than Abercrombie's original plan. I wanted to follow Abercrombie's lead with a readable single-volume plan explaining how London could succeed over the next twenty years. Nicky Gavron, who had chaired the boroughs' powerless London Planning Advisory Committee and was full of ideas for London's future, drove it forward but first we needed to know what was actually happening to London.

*

Abercrombie planned to rid London of slums by moving people and jobs to new towns so by 1990 London's population would be cut from 8.5 million to between 5 and 5.5 million (the stations on the Victoria Line are so small and cramped because it was designed on that assumption). By 1974 the GLC realised that emigration from London was undermining the city's economy and we ended the policy, but as manufacturing jobs disappeared people continued to leave until the population fell to 6.8 million in the 1980s.

Thatcher's deregulation of the City's financial firms started London's population growing again. The public-school old-boy network which ran the City for centuries was smashed by the arrival of hard-working American, Japanese and European bankers who didn't share the English tradition of long, boozy lunches which left them incapable of working. Many firms were now foreign-owned and the number of people employed in finance and business services rose from 18 per cent of London's workforce in the 1970s to double that in just twenty-five years as London came to equal New

York as one of the world's two greatest financial centres. This produced increasing divisions between a rich elite and a working class whose jobs were wiped out and replaced with low-skilled casual employment. I wanted to use the London plan to boost jobs in science, tourism and cultural and creative industries.

We had problems persuading government that London's population was on its way back up and that it would reach 8.5 million by 2025. John Ross was constantly meeting with civil servants who didn't want to accept this because it would mean London getting a bigger share of public spending. It did explain why London seemed crowded and run-down with a housing crisis, delays at hospital A&Es, congested roads and a creaking public transport system. For thirty years after the war while people were leaving London the government went on investing in transport infrastructure and housing, but that stopped with Thatcher, so she could fund tax cuts for corporations and billionaires.

Because the mayor would have the power of veto over council planning decisions for major schemes, developers who hadn't bothered to read my manifesto rushed to get projects like Paddington Basin and White City through before the election. In 1998 Prescott had appointed architect Richard Rogers to set up an Urban Task Force 'to identify causes of urban decline and establish a vision for our cities, founded on the principles of design excellence, social well-being and environmental responsibility within appropriate delivery, fiscal and legal frameworks'. Given the pressure on land, Rogers's team had argued that we should look at each site on its merits depending on the quality of the design, and I planned to remove the arbitrary restrictions on height and density which varied from borough to borough. The problem of each borough having its own planning rules was illustrated by the fiasco that surrounded Arsenal FC's move from Highbury to the Emirates Stadium. Islington Council insisted that it could be no more than thirty metres high, so the stadium had to be built with a concave roof. As this would channel rainwater onto the pitch, a pumping system was required to convey rainwater up the roof, thus wasting £5 million of the club's money that could have increased capacity at the local tube station.

The first planning decision I faced was for the 'Gherkin', the 180-metre-high Swiss Re building at St Mary Axe in the City, which I was happy to support. This was followed by Gerald Ronson's Heron Tower at Aldgate. After years of reducing the height of buildings to get planning permission, he was taken aback when I asked why it wasn't taller and he came back with a higher building. Most tall buildings are closed to the public but this would have a public viewing platform at the top. The developer, Irvine Sellar, had a proposal for the tallest building in Europe (over 300 metres and built on top of London Bridge station) designed by Renzo Piano, the Italian architect who worked with Richard Rogers on the Pompidou Centre in Paris. Based on the shape of a sailing ship, this will be one of the most beautiful modern buildings in the world, improving a squalid station and bringing 10,000 jobs to Bermondsey which has been mired in unemployment since the docks closed in the 1960s. As well as two viewing platforms it will have a hotel at the top and will be open to the public. The press warned that Irvine was using Renzo's name to get planning permission and would employ somebody else to put up a cheap and nasty building but from the moment I met Irvine I recognised he was a man who wanted to create a legacy that his children would be proud of and that will define the city.

English Heritage had not opposed the Gherkin (following a £10 million donation from the developer, according to Simon Jenkins in the *Standard*), but they wasted vast sums of public money opposing the Heron and Sellar towers through public inquiries which delayed the projects by years. The fanatical opposition of English

Heritage encouraged newspaper speculation that London would end up looking like Manhattan with photomontages showing the skyline obliterated by skyscrapers if all the proposed developments went ahead. This was just scaremongering, of course: only a small proportion of proposed schemes ever end up being built; architect Norman Foster told me that only one in ten of his commissions was ever completed as planning delays and recessions took their toll.

*

Alarmingly, the Met and TfL had no reserves and had always relied on the government to bail out deficits in their budgets. As such aid was no longer likely to be forthcoming, I wanted to start building an adequate cushion. In the election Frank Dobson promised to freeze the council tax and I said I would increase it to rebuild London's policing and transport, but the Labour boroughs had also promised a freeze so the scene was set for a fight. Eighty per cent of the mayor's budget went on the wages of police and fire fighters and all polls showed the majority of Londoners were prepared to pay a little more in order to have extra police on the streets. I proposed an increase of 73p a week for the average London family but the boroughs responded as though I was proposing £73. The leader of the London Councils, Sir Robin Wales (also leader of Newham), led a delegation against any increase, though at the same time they expected us to cut crime. There was a furious row when I pointed out the hypocrisy of their positions and refused to give in, explaining I had won by promising to restore policing by putting up council tax. Sir John Stevens was appalled at the Assembly's nit-picking and exploded when the Tory group tried to persuade him that he didn't need the extra money.

I needed nine votes on the Assembly to carry my budget and Toby, Len, Val and Nicky persuaded the Labour group to support a compromise of 54p a week, which meant a reduction of the planned increase of £23 million in transport spending. Tory leader Bob Neill claimed people all over Bromley were cancelling their holidays to find the extra 54p. (He laughed when I pointed out there weren't many holidays you could get for £28.) After years of seeing police numbers decline Sir John was delighted I'd promised increases year on year until we achieved the 35,000 officers he needed, and at a reception we attended he told Margaret Thatcher the good news. She came over to say how well I was doing.

*

It had been nearly a year since my election, so the annual anti-capitalist May Day riot was looming. Special Branch kept anarchist groups under surveillance and knew they intended to assemble at Oxford Circus and then rampage along Oxford Street and Regent Street smashing shop windows – this was advertised on their websites as 'The Sale of the Century'. This mayhem wouldn't help inward investment and could create a right-wing backlash. John Stevens and his senior staff met with my advisers and me to ensure the image that went round the world was not one of looted London shop fronts, so with Sir John's support I urged people to join the rival and peaceful trade-union march.

European anarchists often wore masks so it was difficult to identify them, and Sir John wanted to know where they had come from. These anti-capitalist demos were not like left-wing marches of the past. I told him the collapse of communist and Trotsky-ist parties meant that young radicals who once would have spent hours discussing the works of Marx and Lenin, joined a trade union and become part of a disciplined workers' movement now ended up as part of some loosely organised wild anarchist group. Lacking a coherent long-term class strategy, they lashed out angrily at visible symbols of capitalism. (Sir John told me he'd never expected to regret the demise of communism.) The police couldn't legally detain people for wearing masks, so officers were told to use a tactic of containment known as 'kettling'. In short, this meant sealing off an area with the protesters trapped inside it.

We knew that those planning violence would meet at a set time in Oxford Circus. In closing off the area we would trap a handful of innocent passers-by but most of those kettled would be violent anarchists or journalists reporting their violence. As I watched the police operation from the control centre in New Scotland Yard the operation went well with only forty-two arrests. Encouragingly, there were only 5,000 protesters, half the previous year's number.

A week earlier I had been about to address the Association of Chief Police Officers when Sir John told me that there had been a fire in my office. I had been receiving threats from anarchists, so we suspected this could have been deliberate. During my speech Sir John dispatched a police car to my home and immediately afterwards Sir John and I were driven to Romney House to inspect the damage. As the car sped away Sir John's protection officer asked, 'Can you think of anybody who might have a grudge against you?' I laughed. 'How long have you got?' I said.

Romney House had been given a cheap refit. Arms were falling off chairs and bits off the ceiling, so I suspected faulty wiring had caused the fire, but Sir John was taking no chances and for the first time in my life I was given armed protection. For the next week I was driven into work in an armour-plated car with windows that didn't open. The leader of the team was a youthful Sean Connery lookalike, and the staff drooled over him as he sat in my outer office. I was impressed by how discreetly the officers covered me, even when I went to the loo. As I got off a train 'Sean' was dead chuffed when a passenger remarked it was amazing that I could move about without armed guards. He was disparaging of American secret service agents ostentatiously running alongside the president's car:

'It's like saying, "Here's the target."' I was often not aware of where the guards were but when I nearly stepped under a bus one was immediately by my side saying, 'I don't know why we're bothering.' The fire had indeed been the consequence of an electrical fault, and as soon as the May Day demo was over the protection unit were given more useful work.

*

After twelve months in the job I was settling into the role of mayor. I wasn't unhappy to be leaving Parliament at the June 2001 general election, as my years there had been the least productive of my life, but I had come to love Brent East and at my last function at Queen's Park School I couldn't hold back the tears at the thought of losing that link. The rest of my life was turned upside down when Kate and I decided to part after twenty years together. Although amicable it was still sad and painful. For months no one noticed, so we issued a brief statement. Papers complained we had never given a joint interview and they only had two pictures of us together (some papers used a picture of me with another woman by mistake). True to form the *Mail* asked our neighbours if they had heard any rows or seen young women coming and going.

Blair was still determined to keep me out of the party but was facing defeat when the TGWU decided to support a motion at Labour conference calling for my readmission. He refused to allow a vote. The Labour party didn't use me in the general election of 2001, but many MPs asked me to help. Susan Kramer asked me to urge Labour voters to support Lib Dem candidates in seats where they were the alternative to the Tories, although she wouldn't call on Lib Dem voters to support Labour where they were the main challengers. In my column in the *Independent* I urged Labour supporters to vote tactically in seats which were a straight fight between the Tories and the Lib Dems and I gave the Lib Dems a letter for

Labour voters in Ed Davey's Kingston and Surbiton constituency where he faced a challenge from David Shaw, whom I despised for his smears alleging that John Smith was corrupt.

*

On 11 September 2001 I was coming to the end of a meeting in my office when John came in to tell me about the terrorist attack on the World Trade Center. I had had no briefing from the police about al-Qaeda so my first thought was that the US had paid a terrible price for its support of Israel. I phoned Sir John but co-incidentally he was on a flight to New York. Sir Ian Blair and I feared that something similar might happen at Canary Wharf. The government banned flights over London and Sir Ian diverted police to likely targets.

Since the end of the Cold War and the end of the IRA campaign emergency planning in London had been neglected. On the tube that night there was real fear because we had watched people jumping to their deaths from the burning buildings. In previous terrorist attacks we had seen television reports after the event, not watched people die in real time. I also knew that hundreds of British would have been in the Towers.

A thousand police officers were diverted to prime targets and I began meetings to help businesses improve their security. Sir John sent police to New York to identify British bodies and learn what we could. We were determined to protect London's Muslims, who were reporting verbal abuse and threats which led to the closure of three Islamic schools. In Twickenham an Afghan taxi driver was attacked and left paralysed for life. In Tooting a mosque was vandalised and gun pellets were left on the floor and there were incidents of Muslim women having their headscarves ripped off. Although dozens of Muslims had died in the collapsing towers, many US Islamophobes predicted that Islam would become the religion of Europe and warned that the declining white Christian population of America was being swamped by immigration and its leaders were submitting to 'world government'. Given the hostile press, it wasn't surprising a third of Londoners thought Muslim leaders had not done all they could to condemn terrorism. When George W. Bush invaded Afghanistan 79 per cent of Londoners feared we were more likely to be attacked if Britain joined him.

I convened a meeting of the London boroughs and emergency services which revealed that no one had anticipated the threat or had plans to cope with a similar atrocity in London. This alarmed David Blunkett, the Home Secretary, who rather than pick up the phone to me quizzed police officers 'because we are trying to make sure we get a grip of what Ken Livingstone is up to'. Nick Raynsford told Andrew Hosken: 'Blunkett was nervous about Ken being in charge of London's defence coordination for a variety of reasons to do with his past record.' Raynsford prevailed on Blunkett that I should be made the vice-chair of the London Resilience Committee, which the government had set up under Raynsford to identify every possible form of threat, likely targets, and how to deter and respond to attacks. Our time was divided between conducting war games featuring biological and chemical weapons and making decisions about where to store thousands of bodies or where to put the rubble if Canary Wharf was demolished. We ordered 5,000 body bags and 120,000 decontamination suits. Because of the role Giuliani had played in New York there was press talk about my role in the event of an attack, but New York and London are very different. Because it's not the capital the mayor is free to run New York with little interference from government, whereas in London police manage the response to a disaster without political direction. Through the Second World War and the IRA campaign police acquired real expertise and I told them I had no intention of interfering when they had to deal with disasters.

Given their likely impact on tourism, I was keen to avoid emergency-response exercises that could be broadcast round the world, but there was no way to simulate an attack on the tube without allowing the media to cover it and in May 2003 we sealed off Bank station for a poison-gas-attack exercise. Alarmingly, three hours passed before the bodies of the 'victims' were brought to the surface and the lessons learned were helpful during the bombings of July 2005.

The impact of 9/11 on tourism (which is London's second-biggest employer after finance) had been catastrophic. Overnight, theatres and cinema audiences halved, Westminster Council's commercial refuse collection volume was 40 per cent down as people avoided the West End. I went to see Patricia Hewitt, the minister responsible for tourism, and asked her to overturn the long-standing policy banning London from advertising its tourist attractions to the rest of the UK. With a speed I'd never seen from government before or since she changed the rules within forty-eight hours, and John Ross started directing the efforts of the London Tourist Board while I announced that the LDA would subsidise half a million theatre tickets. The London Tourist Board had been a sleepy institution which now needed to up its game if we were going to attract people from Britain and Europe to fill the gaps left following the collapse of American visitors.

I had to override resistance inside the LDA to divert £15 million from regeneration budgets to promoting tourism, but we recruited David Campbell, who had run Virgin Radio, Ginger Media with Chris Evans and Pepsi-Cola's marketing. He shook up the London Tourist Board, transforming it into Visit London. He was so good at marketing London that when the bombers eventually struck in July 2005 more tourists came the following year than ever before.

*

My second budget, in 2002, generated more hot air than the first. I wanted to put teams of police on our buses and reintroduce conductors but with the borough elections due the Assembly reduced my increase to 44p per week, so to get more police I had to stall £80 million in transport projects. It was now obvious that the attempt to build a big-tent consensus wasn't working as Assembly members couldn't shake off their partisan mentality. After all their talk of cooperation I was most disappointed with the Lib Dems, so I decided to use the mayoralty in the way Blair had intended. My policy advisers were effectively running the machine so I used the twelve posts I had left vacant to make them directors like those appointed by the Assembly and we started to function more efficiently.

However well things went, press whingeing continued. The *Telegraph* gave space to Simon Thurley, chief executive at English Heritage: 'Ken Livingstone makes me recoil. He is ruining London. People are tearing up their front gardens because of him. No one around here can park any more. Babies are being fumigated in their prams by this traffic policy, just so tourists can skip across Trafalgar Square.'

There was a huge difference in the press compared with GLC days. Instead of half a dozen reporters based at County Hall the *Standard*'s Hugh Muir would wander in once or twice a week to ask if anything was going on. Nick Davies in his book *Flat Earth News* records the dramatic collapse in the number of journalists covering local and regional news. Instead of well-researched regional TV and radio news teams individual reporters struggled to cover topics without research or back-up. Instead of developing real expertise on a subject, journalists relied on press releases which they had no time to check for accuracy, merely including an opposition comment for 'balance'.

I was invited to a stilted lunch at the *Daily Mail* with Sir Paul Dacre, who asked if I regretted my radical GLC policies and looked put out when I said, 'You didn't believe all those stories you wrote?' When Max Hastings retired in February 2002, Dacre turned the *Standard* into a 'mini *Mail*' by appointing as editor Veronica Wadley, who had spent most of her career at the *Mail*. I phoned to congratulate her and invited her to lunch but she said she was busy and would get back to me. Five years passed before we met. According to Bill Hegarty in the *Independent*, she immediately started reducing news coverage and 'introduced . . . a culture of fear on the editorial floor. Those retaining their jobs . . . were terrified they might be the next to walk the plank.'

Nick Davies concludes in his book on the press that the *Mail* 'more than any other newspaper . . . deals in falsehood and distortion . . . provoking justifiable complaint about unethical behaviour at three times the rate of other [papers] . . . there is a recurrent theme of invading privacy', and, he says, stories that portray black people in a good light are spiked. Davies never met a reporter from the *Mail* who did not have a 'story of black people being excluded from the paper because of their colour'. Reporters would be asked, 'Are they our kind of people? i.e., are they white, middle-class?' Or more often it would be: 'Are they of the dusky hue?'

A reporter told him he had been amazed at the openness of the racism in the office: 'You would often get people using the word nigger or nig-nog . . . it's the senior people who do it, not Dacre . . . there is definitely a racist environment.' Davies calculated that 64 per cent of all photos of black people in the paper were of murderers, muggers and rapists with language in the leader columns that 'bordered on incitement to hatred'. The Association of Chief Police Officers 'became so concerned about this kind of journalism that they . . . warned "ill-informed, adverse media coverage was heightening tensions and increasing resentment of asylum seekers"'. *Mail* journalists talk of Dacre's aggression, with one female editor saying, 'They call him the Vagina Monologue because he calls so many people a cunt. He would stalk through the newsroom . . . shouting, "What the fuck is this, you cunt, there's not a fucking brain in this office."'

Davies concludes, 'I know of nothing anywhere in the rest of the world's media which matches the unmitigated spite of an attack from the *Daily Mail* . . . Free to cripple reputations, free to kill ideas, regardless of justice, regardless of truth.' A similar picture appears in John Lloyd's book *What the Media Are Doing to Our Politics*. He quotes 'a politician' (generally assumed to be Tony Blair): 'The *Daily Mail* is an extraordinary product. It springs from the head of Paul Dacre who has the kind of prejudices and beliefs no one knows about. I won't go into them. But he is accountable to no one. He has absolute and unaccountable power.' I was to discover the truth of those words during the 2008 mayoral election.

The first sign of change in the *Standard* came on 19 March under the headline 'Ken's secret plan to keep out cars', which claimed I was 'rigging traffic lights so drivers will face a sea of red lights'. By 31 May the *Standard* saw further evidence of a plot. Under the headline 'Traffic lights rigged so car charge looks good' they claimed, 'Ken Livingstone is refusing to come clean on secret plans to rig London's traffic lights.' By 19 June they predicted 'the traffic light chaos inflicted on central London by Ken Livingstone . . . is to be extended to the inner London suburbs'. Wadley never produced a shred of evidence to support this campaign, which was dreamed up by a Tory Assembly member. This did not stop the AA and RAC jointly claiming I 'intentionally created the traffic chaos now – in order to make his congestion charging scheme more popular when it is introduced'.

Traffic congestion was bad because we were doing necessary roadworks to prepare for congestion charging by improving traffic flow on the boundary roads and pedestrianising the north side of Trafalgar Square at the same time. Derek Turner at TfL had warned me that this would cause problems but transforming Trafalgar Square after the congestion charge was introduced would mean four years of roadworks instead of two. I felt it was better to have a shorter period of disruption than a longer one that was slightly less disruptive. I also wanted to reduce deaths and as 1,700 pedestrian crossings in London didn't allow sufficient time for people to cross safely we rephased lights in order to give pedestrians another couple of seconds and increased the number of crossings by a fifth. Motoring correspondents railed against this, but never reported that we halved pedestrian deaths in eight years.

*

I had said openly that the first two years would be spent setting up the administration before people began to see results, but that did not stop Catherine Bennett in the *Guardian* dismissing my 'feeble record after 16 months in office' or Zoe Williams in the *Observer* claiming I had 'gone from dude to dud in about 18 months'. I could have spent a lot of time on publicity and media stunts but the real priority had to be establishing the administration. If reporters had bothered to spend any time investigating what we were doing they would have been better placed to make judgments but reporting had been replaced by the cycles of spin and counter-spin in which the media simply regurgitate what they are fed. Bob Crow of the RMT union didn't help when he warned that it was a mistake to introduce the congestion charge and only the business community was positive, with London First saying I had been a perfectly good, intelligent ambassador for the business community.

Wadley commissioned Keith Dovkants (the reporter who'd done the hatchet job on me in the 1981 GLC election) to review my first two years. Under the headline 'So what is the point of Ken?' he described me as a 'screaming, arm-waving and finger-pointing . . .

snapping, snarling brute . . . Raging against his own impotence, gripped by paranoia . . . facing the awful truth that what he promised he would do for London simply isn't happening.' He claimed a friend of mine had been shocked to see me looking 'completely, utterly drained'. Dovkants dismissed the improved bus services and claimed my funding of an extra thousand police posts was possible only with government money and that 'no one can recall Livingstone making an impact on fighting crime in London', warning 'if his dismal record is not improved, nothing will shield him from [the voters'] fury'.

*

The *Standard* was now, under Wadley, taking an aggressive interest in my private life. Under Max the paper had two paragraphs saying I had been seen on 'cosy dates' with a Lib Dem. In fact Emma Beal and I had embarked on a quiet relationship and it was strange to fall in love again with all the passion and intensity that comes with a new relationship. Under local government rules I had to report the relationship to chief executive Anthony Mayer, Manny Lewis at corporate services and Howard Carter, our head of law. The meeting was a strange combination of embarrassment and congratulations and none of them had ever heard of a politician complying with these regulations before.

Emma dreaded appearing with me at official functions so we wanted our first public engagement to be a friendly one. We chose the Mayor of London's St Patrick's Day Ball. Emma needn't have worried as none of the media even noticed we were a couple. Wanting our first holiday together to be as far from the British press as possible, we went to Australia and checked into a small hotel in Sydney. We went to the bar to discover that Tory assembly member Angie Bray and her husband were sitting by the window. We had a drink with them and Angie was kind enough to keep our holiday secret until after we got home. As old news, it rated barely a paragraph in the gossip columns.

Any woman wanting privacy couldn't have picked a worse year than 2002 to fall in love with me. It was the Queen's Golden Jubilee and I would need to attend all sorts of functions. Accompanying me to the Guildhall Jubilee lunch, Emma found herself sitting next to Andrew Lloyd Webber and filled the silence by telling him how much she'd enjoyed *Cats*. Even worse was the Golden Jubilee concert at Buckingham Palace, where she found herself sitting beside *Daily Mail* owner Lord Rothermere after the *Mail* had run intrusive articles about her.

Emma loved my three older children, all of whom were growing into fine young people – but they hadn't been brought up by me and as Emma and I began planning our family I worried that the legacy of my own dysfunctional childhood might affect my parenting skills. To our dismay Wadley discovered that Emma was pregnant and splashed it on the front page before we had told all our friends and family. Vanessa Feltz wrote in the *Express* that 'at baby Livingstone's twentieth birthday party, daddy will, if he's not pushing up daisies, be pushing 80 . . . He will be too decrepit to assist his progeny's childhood . . . a child is for life, not just a postscript. Stacking the odds against sharing your children's lives is desperately selfish.' Robert Kilroy-Silk wrote in the *Sunday Express*, 'It is treating children like an accessory . . . it will grow up with an embarrassing old man for a father.' I did worry about this a bit but you don't get to choose who you fall in love with or when. William Hill offered odds of 100/1 on the baby becoming mayor.

Wadley's editorial called my 'newish girlfriend, Emma Beal, a delightful woman, fondly remembered by many of us at the *Evening Standard*'. These fond memories didn't prevent the *Daily Mail*, *Mail on Sunday*, *Standard* and *Daily Express* besieging our home over the spring bank holiday and conning their way into the home of Emma's stepmother and father (who had Alzheimer's) to write a nasty piece on Emma's childhood.

The next day the *Standard* asked about an accident a month earlier at the fortieth birthday party of Emma's sister Kate where Emma's best friend Robin Hedges (who was working at the *Standard*) had fallen over a wall. The facts were simple. Emma and I had a row about her smoking and we left the party. As we reached the car Robin ran up and got involved in the row. Emma was upset with both of us and went back to her sister's, followed by me and Robin. As I reached the top of the crowded steps Robin lost his balance as he tried to get past guests at the bottom and fell into the stairwell. We waited until the ambulance had taken Robin to the Royal Free and drove home. After two hours at A&E Robin walked home to his flat. The next day Emma drove over to make sure he was OK and they went for a drink in the local pub.

As he was at home, Robin asked us to issue his statement: 'The simple fact is that I attended a party, during which I injured myself. It is false to suggest that anyone else was involved. It was just an accident.' The final edition of the *Standard* spun 'Mayor and reveller's mystery 12-ft fall', although it included a Scotland Yard spokesman saying, 'On arrival, officers found a man had accidentally fallen over some side steps by the front door ending up in the basement below. No allegations were made against any other person.' The next day the *Telegraph* quoted the police who visited the scene: 'We spoke to the man and established that he slipped on steps and fell into the basement area. We are satisfied that no crime had occurred.' The *Independent* reported, 'Mr Hedges was taken to the Royal Free hospital in Hampstead with severe bruising.'

Two weeks later on 14 June a banner headline in the *Standard* implied that I'd pushed Robin over the wall and fled before police arrived. Robin apparently suffered 'injuries to his head, shoulder, collar bone and leg . . . his body was left almost completely covered in bruises and doctors fear there is hairline fracture of his hip' after he 'plunged, head-first, the 15 feet from the top of the steps . . . four weeks after the fall the pain is still so severe that he is on painkillers and has dizzy spells'. The basis of this story came from a neighbour who claimed to have witnessed the whole incident while getting in and out of bed three times. The *Standard* added that a charity, Women's Aid, wanted me to resign because of the violent argument I was supposed to have had with Emma. The next day the *Daily Express* headline screamed how 'A party to celebrate Ken Livingstone's impending fatherhood [it was Kate's birthday party, of course] turned to horror'.

At its next meeting I told the Assembly the *Standard*'s report was 'one of the most inaccurate and distorted articles I had seen about myself'. Women's Aid denied making the statement and verified that the claims against me 'were without foundation'. I suspected Robin was under intense pressure by his employers when he told Emma he wanted legal advice to protect himself from being forced to make a statement by the *Standard*. I floated the idea with Sir Ian Blair that the police should conduct an investigation to clear the air, but he said, 'I can't imagine a worse waste of police resources.'

The *Mirror*'s Cassandra column described me as 'an over-promoted traffic warden of a man with a sickly face of a three-toed sloth having an orgasm . . . a patch of slime . . . a dreary, whining little man . . . a violent man, a dangerous, irascible, underhand, tantrum throwing, bullying, vain, self-serving, self-preserving creep . . . with anaconda like hooded eyes'. Martin Bright in the *Observer* reported, 'Old friends and enemies from Livingstone's time as leader of the GLC . . . said he had never had a reputation for violence or the mistreatment of women . . . one former colleague who sat at a desk next to Livingstone for two years said, "I have never seen him violent or threatening violence. I have never seen him incapable through drink."' Illtyd Harrington, my former deputy at the GLC, said, 'I have no great love for Ken but when I heard these reports I thought it sounded completely out of character.'

The Assembly asked me to make a statement (broadcast live on Sky and BBC News 24). I told the Assembly that three of the witnesses the *Standard* misquoted had issued statements to that effect, went through each incident at the party and made clear that 'I feel no malice towards Robin . . . He has suffered . . . not just the physical pain . . . but I suspect unrelenting and totally unacceptable media pressure on someone who should be left to recover.' Did the story 'justify four front pages of the *Evening Standard*, two double-page spreads, and several other articles which have been extremely free with the facts'? I pointed out that the neighbour, Stuart Williams,

has developed total recall of all conversations he heard, even though he announced that in an incident that lasted eight to ten minutes at most he went in and out of his bed three times . . . anyone who saw him on television yesterday could see that his recall wasn't quite as perfect as the *Standard* would make out . . . It could have occurred to Veronica Wadley when she first heard this story that it might be out of character. In the twenty-one years that I have been the focus of . . . unrelenting media attention . . . there has never been a single story linking me to violence or linking me to drunkenness. Perhaps had Max Hastings still been editor he might have paused and considered whether there shouldn't have been some more detailed investigation before they chose to run with the story.

I pointed out too that the *Standard* had described Robin falling twelve feet over a wall. Two weeks later they reported the wall was fifteen feet high. I knew the wall was ten feet high because I had measured it.

If London's evening paper can't get the height of the wall accurate within 50 per cent why should we trust anything they write? . . . The truth is editors have more power than any cabinet minister. They have the power to besmirch a reputation and end a career. Now that power should only be used with the greatest restraint. I think Londoners and the Assembly have the right to [ask] is that the case in this instance. I believe Veronica Wadley was reckless with the facts and malicious with that power. For five weeks we have had the *Evening Standard* trying to bring my mayoralty to an end, to ruin my reputation . . . and force me into a resignation. Fortunately for me Londoners decide who is mayor, not editors, or I wouldn't have been in this position in the first place. Also, given the hypocrisy of some journalists claiming that concern here is for Emma, I would like to say to those photographers and cameraman who stayed outside my front door this morning to get a picture of her, are harassing her, and nobody who is pregnant should be subject to that. Finally, I would like to thank Londoners [who] have stopped me on the tube and on the street to tell me they don't believe what they read in the *Standard* and I have their support and I thank them for that and I also say this to Veronica Wadley: this is not acceptable journalism and until we can have a proper answer from Veronica Wadley about how this story grew in the telling, the reality is that I won't believe what I read in the *Standard* and I simply warn Londoners now: don't believe anything you read about my policies or my private life in this paper until it has a new editor.

The *Standard*'s Hugh Muir told GLA press officers, 'This is going to be war'. Nick Mathiason reported in the *Guardian* that inside the *Standard*'s offices: 'Blue-suited as usual, Veronica Wadley . . . watched in silence as her biggest enemy stuck the knife into her reputation and then twisted it. Sitting on the back bench in the *Standard*'s Kensington High Street newsroom, Wadley, a former debutante, was not the only one stunned. In fact, last Wednesday morning, the whole paper's newsroom fell quiet save for the ringing of unanswered phones as hacks gawped uncomfortably at live footage on the BBC.'

Under questioning, I managed to satisfy most of the Assembly members. The Greens' Jenny Jones said, 'I think the mayor's explanation has pretty much silenced us all. It certainly appears to have the ring of truth about it . . . I hope that matters will now be closed on this.' Toby Harris and Eric Ollerenshaw, leader of the

Tory group, accepted my word but after the meeting the Lib Dem Graham Tope referred the matter to the Standards Board for England, sanctimoniously claiming, 'London's government will remain under a cloud and issues that really matter to Londoners will not be debated and discussed in public.' Tope didn't care that this would now stressfully rumble on throughout Emma's pregnancy. Tope's action was contemptible and I never forgave him. Charles Kennedy sent a very nice message wishing us luck and deploring Tope's behaviour. But the Brownite MP Tom Watson said, 'It was an extremely bizarre denial. It has raised more questions than answers.'

Wadley held back the news of my statement until the final edition. TV crews appeared at the *Standard* but she refused to be interviewed and when Max was asked who he supported he replied, 'Only a madman, having just walked away from editing a newspaper, would walk into a row between the Mayor of London and that newspaper.' When I answered questions from 150 Londoners on Carlton TV, 80 per cent voted that I was doing a good job but the *Daily Mirror* was not persuaded, describing me as a 'petty man, a work-shy dullard, a bone idle pedant . . .' The following morning Andrew Hosken of the *Today* programme reported he had measured the wall and it was precisely ten feet and one inch high, but Wadley refused to accept this and the *Standard* continued to refer to the fifteen-foot wall.

As there was nothing to hide I was quite happy to turn up and just answer any questions the Standards Board investigator put to me but Neale Coleman persuaded me that I would be mad to go without a lawyer and recommended his friend Tony Child, who had brought the successful legal challenge against Lady Porter's gerrymandering. Given the hostile nature of the investigation, I was glad I followed Neale's advice. The Board had only been established a few weeks earlier and they clearly felt that suspending me or even removing me from office would establish their reputation, so a year of nit-picking as well as harassing Emma during her maternity leave followed.

*

This wasn't the best background for Blair to decide whether or not I should be allowed back into the Labour fold in order to stand as the party's candidate at the 2004 mayoral elections. I was invited to meet Blair at Number 10 but was told to turn up at a remote back entrance where his adviser Sally Morgan told the security guard I was not to sign in. In a room with his key aides we discussed the Olympics, the congestion charge and extra policing and I lobbied for more powers and money. Blair asked for time to consider the issue of me being readmitted but I never heard anything more from him about it. I had a drink with Charles Clarke (then chair of the Labour party) but he was completely hostile to my being brought back even though the London Labour party executive had voted 9–3 for my readmission. In a column he wrote for *GQ* around this time Mandelson described me as a 'bogus individual . . . whose real identity is shot through with falseness and contradictions . . . a self-interested charlatan'.

The day the NEC met to decide my fate coincided with the Queen and Prince Philip opening City Hall almost exactly eighty years after her grandfather had opened County Hall. Just as her tour was coming to an end, Simon whispered that the NEC had voted by 17–13 to keep me out. I suspected that this was hostility from old Kinnockites combined with the fear that congestion charging would be a disaster but I felt relaxed and resigned myself to facing the next election as an independent. I hated the idea of having to raise half a million pounds for the campaign, but I'd done so before and at least we wouldn't be involved in tedious rows about the wording of my manifesto and I was glad I would not have to reconcile my beliefs with the policies of Blair's government.

16

Triumph

2003–2005

In the midst of Thatcher's 1981 recession there were empty seats on the buses and tubes so we tackled congestion with a fares cut, getting a big increase in public transport usage and a reduction in congestion as people left their cars at home. We also ruled out road building as most new roads just fill up with cars and the situation soon becomes just as bad as it was before. The price of land or of tunnelling in London is so high that road building can never solve the city's transport problems, so the only answer is to manage the existing road space better.

In 1936 New York's Mayor Fiorello La Guardia opened three new parkways (motorways, as we'd call them in Britain), saying they would solve traffic problems in New York for generations. Three weeks later they were gridlocked, so he announced he would build forty-five more miles of parkway. The Wantagh parkway extension opened in December 1938 but was soon jammed bumper to bumper. In *The Power Broker*, his biography of the road builder Robert Moses, Robert Caro says that 'traffic experts could not understand where those cars had come from. The other Long Island parkways, after all, were just as jammed as ever.' When the mayor opened the Triborough Bridge, New York's traffic engineers expected eight million vehicles a year but within three months that estimate increased to ten million and the older bridges were just as congested as before. Moses built another bridge, the Bronx-Whitestone, whose four lanes were immediately jammed with six million extra journeys but there was no reduction in congestion on the old bridges. Caro says, 'Four bridges had connected Long Island with the rest of the world and they had all been jammed. Now six bridges connected Long Island . . . they were all jammed.' No one drew the obvious conclusion, and mayors continued to build roads that were immediately congested. Fifty years later an earthquake in San Francisco demolished two elevated motorways and within three months the flow of vehicles into the city had been cut to the level of the reduced capacity. Britain ignored these lessons and began motorway building until the backlash against the GLC's plan for three ring roads in 1973, when traffic was running at 12 mph in central London. By 2000 traffic speed was down to 9.5 mph and getting slower.

The congestion charge was one of only two ideas from Milton Friedman, Thatcher's favourite economist, that she wouldn't touch with a bargepole (the other was legalising drugs). In 1952 he suggested a charge to ration road space instead of having drivers sitting in jams. This was politically dangerous and he predicted that by the time it was introduced we would have nuclear-fuelled cars. Harold Macmillan's government set up a committee to consider it but in 1964 the report was shelved. Singapore introduced a scheme in 1970 before most Singaporeans had a car and there was a small scheme in Norway but no one had introduced it in a large city where many considered driving to be a basic human right.

The idea was revived in the late 1990s by London's major employers, who warned the mayoral candidates that they would relocate to Paris or Frankfurt if we didn't reduce congestion. This was a problem that couldn't be ducked any longer and I was encouraged by Michael Snyder, deputy to the chair of the City of London Corporation's Policy and Resources Committee Judith Mayhew, to look at the Corporation's number-plate recognition system (which had prevented IRA bombers from getting into the financial district) as the basis for congestion charging.

As I pressed ahead, the new transport minister John Spellar tried to block the scheme. His fears that it wouldn't be politically acceptable were shared by my key advisers and when drafting the manifesto they pointed to the Labour government's Rocol study, which listed the difficulties, but I knew we had to tackle congestion so there was a brief row as I dropped the report in the bin and said, 'Now let's talk about how we're going to do it.' The *Standard* denounced Frank Dobson when he dropped the idea (ironically, in view of their later bitter opposition to it) but it created a dividing line between the parties with Frank and Steve Norris opposed and the Lib Dems, Greens and myself in favour.

TfL's Derek Turner, who was heading the congestion charge team, recruited two former GLC trainees, Michèle Dix and Malcolm Murray-Clark, who were passionately committed, and Bob Kiley's finance director Jay Walder had previous experience, having worked on the Singapore scheme. The project was overseen by Redmond and John Ross, who forced the team to challenge all their assumptions.

The idea was that the zone would be quite small and confined to London's central business district. People living inside the area would have a 90 per cent discount but everybody else driving in (except registered disabled drivers) would have to pay £5 per day. Payment could be made by phone, which meant we had to establish a large call centre to handle the volume. We also wanted drivers to be able to pay the charge at their local petrol station. If we misjudged drivers' behaviour there could be huge tailbacks and countless rat runs. We were further pressured by the fact that no one in central or local government had yet managed to introduce a big IT scheme without disastrous delays and cost overruns. If this failed my career was over and it would kill off the idea of road pricing for years. With so much at stake our scrutiny was intense and after one particularly brutal session Bob had to talk Derek out of resigning. It was stressful but it paid off. (When Heathrow's Terminal 5 opened in 2008 with catastrophic chaos and frustrated travellers I guessed that the highly paid BAA board members hadn't challenged those managing the project in the way we did with Derek's team.)

The call centre would have to be able to cope with the peaks and troughs of the number of calls in a day so we put a contract out to tender, but as the charge was so controversial there was only one serious applicant: Capita. Firms often run rings round civil servants in negotiations so it was a pleasure to watch Bob deal with Capita. He recruited Deloitte's Richard Granger and together they beat down their quotation pound by pound. Although Capita was the only serious bidder for the contract, Bob kept one other firm in play and Capita never realised the strength of its position.

My advisers made one last attempt to change my mind, with John Ross arguing that this was a regressive tax that hit the poor, but this overlooked the fact that the poorest in central London don't have a car. We went round the table as each of them urged me to put it off until my second term because they feared it might cost me the 2004 election. I was particularly depressed when Mark Watts, the most environmentally aware of my staff, came down on their side. After an hour I said I wasn't persuaded and we would go ahead with the scheme. Joy Johnson, my head of media, remarked, 'It's lonely at the top.' It was more than lonely as these were good friends and if I was wrong all of them would lose their jobs. I was down for a week.

There was unrelenting opposition from motoring correspondents. *The Times* warned of a 'high-tech fiasco ahead' and 'critics predict chaos'. The *Telegraph* said it was 'hard to see what this cumbersome scheme can possibly achieve'. Minette Marrin in the *Telegraph* urged us to 'ban buses instead'. Liam Halligan in the *Sunday Telegraph* claimed it 'is ill thought out, premature and will undermine efforts to introduce the scheme elsewhere'. David Mellor in the *People* said it was my 'suicide note, he's nuts, crazy'. The *News of the World*'s Michael Winner said 'Ken is off his rocker' and the *Independent* declared 'it should be cancelled'. The actors Samantha Bond, Isla Blair and Emilia Fox said it would hit the theatre trade and Joan Collins complained that 'driving into London is a daily re-enactment of the evacuation of Dunkirk', not realising she was making a case for the charge. Calling it the 'Jam Buster', the *Mirror* said, 'Ken's not daft, he will have thought it through ... at least he's trying to find a solution.' Andrew Marr called it 'a brilliant idea' and as we got close to the start a few columnists came out for the scheme.

The *Standard* under Max had said it was 'a bold start, we wish him well', but after Wadley's appointment they changed their tune completely, warning 'motorists, this is your nightmare ... an outdated lunacy', and claimed that traffic speed was now only 3 mph in central London because we were giving pedestrians a couple of seconds longer to cross the road. The London Assembly warned it was the wrong plan and asked me to delay it for two years. The business community lost its nerve, with the CBI saying 'it should be halted now'. Kate Hoey asked in Parliament what the government was 'going to do to stop Ken Livingstone's dictatorship'. Westminster Council went to court to block the scheme and lost. The public consultation exercises often had a majority opposed but in polls there had always been a majority of Londoners in favour of around 48–39 per cent, with the rest undecided. As the press campaign ramped up, the 'don't knows' increased and voters' satisfaction with my performance was slowly eroded until it was neck and neck with those who were dissatisfied. The *Guardian* was told that 'ministers plan to accuse Ken Livingstone of ... incompetence' when the scheme went wrong and the *FT* worried that 'much hangs on Mr Livingstone's unproven ability to manage this complex and ambitious project'. No one seemed to notice that bus usage had increased by 17 per cent since my election and that we were creating new routes. Texaco was the only petrol chain willing to allow motorists to pay the charge at their garages. So much for the market meeting customers' needs.

Hosken in his biography quotes senior TfL press officer Luke Blair:

There were plenty of people . . . who were terribly nervous and flapping about, but not Ken . . . a project like this needs a strong political champion . . . things had gone wobbly [but] all the way through, we got this message – look, Ken wants this to happen, just bloody fix it and get on with it – and people did . . . there are very few politicians who are so over-committed to such risky projects in that way . . . he always seems to have very much the same demeanour . . . rarely flaring up and that's a huge asset . . . to have this even temperament. Even when he's laying into someone pretty viciously he seems to do it in that same flat nasal way. In its way it's terribly powerful. More powerful than someone who keeps getting red in the face.

*

My old doctor thought my equable temperament was due to low adrenalin levels, but I had thirty years' experience with traffic schemes like the introduction of traffic lights at Hyde Park Corner in the mid-1980s, when weeks of hysterical press coverage stopped after accidents were cut by half. Derek Turner lived with similar predictions of disaster when he introduced London's red route system in the nineties. We both knew the scheme would work but expected some rat running and tailbacks which we could resolve with small adjustments. To minimise problems, I decided to start the scheme on 17 February 2003 during the school half-term holidays, when traffic was a fifth lighter. But there was nothing I could do about the fact that this was also just eight weeks after the birth of our son Tom. With the congestion charge so close I only took a week's paternity leave, so Emma and I were both exhausted. But I spent hours lying next to Tom watching him sleep and discovered that I loved changing his nappies. At Tom's birth he took a long time to cry and although the nurses said nothing was wrong we heard the concern in their voices. When they took Tom to the paediatrician on the ward below I was torn between going with him and staying with Emma, who was terrified that something was seriously wrong. We waited together, and after what seemed like hours they brought Tom back and announced everything was fine.

*

I had always been disgusted that Blair had gone along with the international sanctions against Iraq because this had cost the lives of half a million Iraqis, particularly children, over the previous decade as they were denied vital medical and food supplies. Saddam and his cronies weren't affected as they continued to live lives of luxury. Now I watched with horror as Blair committed us to joining America's invasion of Iraq, though I always assumed that Blair tried to use his influence to moderate the hawks around Bush.

In February 2003, just two days before the congestion charge was introduced, central London came to a halt as two million people marched for peace and against the coming war in Iraq. Two-month-old Tom joined Emma and myself on his first march but as I addressed the crowd a man rushed on stage and grabbed the microphone, screaming, 'No congestion charge.' Unfortunately for him Jesse Jackson was on stage at the time and his bodyguards weren't taking any risks and threw him over the fence. Not a bit discouraged, Aaron Barschak then went on to gatecrash Prince William's twenty-first birthday party dressed as Osama Bin Laden.

Planning to join Bob as the scheme went live at seven on Monday morning, I opened my front door at 6 a.m. Twenty TV cameras lit up the mob of journalists waiting outside. In the bedroom where Emma and Tom were sleeping the lights blasted through the blinds like the scene in *Close Encounters of the Third Kind* and

Emma leaped out of bed. As I walked to the tube I realised the journalists were going to follow me all day to record the end of my political career. I warned the press, 'It's going to be a long day and I'm just waiting for things to go wrong.' Picking up a copy of the *Metro* on the tube at 6.15 a.m. I read: 'Drivers were today battling through the first morning of congestion charge.' On the other side of London Steve Norris was denouncing the scheme as 'flawed and unworkable' at an anti-congestion-charge demonstration with Iain Duncan Smith at Smithfield. The *Sun* had one of its reporters follow me round in a snail costume but by mid-afternoon with the success of the scheme becoming obvious he slithered away.

As I stood before the vast bank of screens in the newly opened London Traffic Control Centre in Westminster, 7 a.m. came and went without one tailback or rat run. After an hour I told Bob, 'This is as boring as waiting for election results,' and left for City Hall, where, looking down on Tower Bridge, I couldn't see a single car crossing it. I remembered Emma's comment during the opening scene of a deserted London in Danny Boyle's *28 Days Later* – 'The congestion charge worked, then' – and I feared I had overdone it. Neale Coleman, the first of my advisers to stare in awe at the empty Tower Bridge, said, 'Oh God, what's happened here?' Television showed Kate Hoey with half a dozen forlorn protesters at Vauxhall but John Spellar phoned to congratulate me, saying, 'The devil looks after his own.' Tony Blair had forgotten to register his family car and racked up £1,000 of fines before he realised his error, but at least he didn't complain, unlike the singer Madonna who refused to register, saying she didn't want us to know where she lived.

The drop in the number of cars was twice what we expected and timetables had to change to prevent buses arriving at bus stops too early. Under Capita's contract they would receive a fee for each £5 charge collected, but with so few cars they faced a loss of £31 million a year so they forced us to renegotiate by not putting enough staff on the call centre to take the payments. Although we weren't obliged to, we had little choice other than to offer Capita an increase per payment, but they were being greedy so Bob and I warned them that if they didn't accept our revised terms we would suspend the scheme and sue them. They accepted. So much for transferring risk from the public to the private sector.

Traffic speeds returned to 12 mph, reversing thirty years of decline with a big improvement in bus reliability and making roads more attractive to cyclists, whose numbers soared. There was a 20 per cent reduction in carbon emissions and deadly nitrous oxides and particulates were cut by 12 per cent. This was the only thing in my career that turned out better than I had hoped.

But the most dramatic change was in the media. The *Daily Telegraph* said, 'What if the wretched thing works after all?' The *Sun* dismissed 'Ken's big con' and Richard Littlejohn wrote grudgingly, 'Admittedly traffic is quicker but the scheme was drawn up by sexually inadequate, Lycra-clad, *Guardian*-reading, cycle-mad control freaks at TfL.' Barely missing a beat, the *Standard* now complained 'thousands fined by mistake'! But for many journalists, after years of reporting delays, cost overruns and disasters in government schemes, there was a sense of awe that we had got it right and on time and on budget. Within ten days the polls had a majority of two to one in favour of the charge and my own ratings were up 10 per cent. I told Derek, 'You've won me the next election, but it's a year too soon.'

*

In the months that followed everything seemed to come right. New buses arrived as we replaced the clapped-out old fleet and increased it from 5,500 to 8,000 vehicles over five years, and as journey times were reduced business people and the middle classes got back on board with more people riding on buses than at any time since the

1950s. We hadn't got money out of the government to reintroduce conductors so instead we introduced police teams to patrol the buses (they made 240 arrests in their first two months).

The expansion of the police force was having an effect on the streets as well. After half a century of increases, crime started to come down. Outside London it peaked in the late nineties but in London with falling police numbers it continued to rise until 2002. The increased flow of recruits through Hendon College hit our streets at the end of 2001 but with police diverted to tackle terrorism after 9/11 a year passed before we saw the impact on the crime figures. By 2003 we had an extra 2,800 police in place – bringing the force to 28,602 and cutting street crime by a quarter and burglaries by 10 per cent – and we were able to put 135 extra detectives into the three murder squads. Sir John announced the Met had 'got it wrong' by taking bobbies off the beat. Our planned increase, including support officers, to 35,000 would allow us to introduce 630 Neighbourhood Police Teams across London.

Our Olympic bid was also going well. After the British Olympic Association's three failed bids for Birmingham and Manchester, the Israeli International Olympic Committee member Alex Gilady said, 'If you want to be taken seriously, come back with London.' The IOC insist on support of the host city's administration before accepting a bid, so abolition of the GLC effectively ruined London's chances for years. Within months of my election the BOA's Craig Reedie and Simon Clegg came to outline their work on possible sites which were similar to Horace Cutler's proposal twenty-one years earlier. As in Cutler's time a games based at Wembley would leave only a small legacy but in the East End it could be the catalyst for twenty years of regeneration. I admitted my interest in sport didn't go beyond a snooker table, but if the BOA would site the Olympics in the Docklands I would throw everything behind the bid. The IOC also required the support of government so the

BOA went off to lobby Blair, which took considerably longer than persuading me.

As Blair was preparing for war in Iraq it was left to culture and sports minister Tessa Jowell to lobby a sceptical cabinet already badly burned by the fiasco of the empty Millennium Dome, which had failed to attract either as many visitors as anticipated during the Millennium or a suitable tenant after it, and watching in horror the rising cost of the new Wembley Stadium. Even worse was New Labour's bid to stage the 2005 World Athletics Championships by building a new stadium at Picketts Lock in Enfield. I asked John Ross to find out what was happening and it took him only a few days before he reported, 'Don't touch it, it's a complete disaster and is never going to happen.' So we were not surprised when it was announced that the stadium wouldn't be ready and that the championships would have to be held in another country.

Against this background few rated London's chances very highly. Tessa's civil servants warned her London would lose and the *Observer* quoted Paul Boateng as saying 'It would be madness', while the *Sunday Times* warned 'Brown is going very hard against it' and Blair's former sports adviser James Purnell argued fiercely against. Alistair Darling was opposed because it would restrict his choices for transport spending. But Tessa worked quietly behind the scenes, slowly winning over most of the cabinet except Brown, who told her on 13 January 2003 that there would be no money coming from the Treasury. His aides then briefed the press that the bid was doomed unless London's council taxpayers found the £2.6 billion (which would increase council tax by £3 a week) and met any cost overruns. The *Guardian* reported, 'Gordon Brown will deliver a body blow to Ken Livingstone's plan to bring the 2012 Olympic Games to London.' Believing this was an attempt to scupper the bid with me getting the blame, I met Tessa on 16 January and agreed there would be a contribution from council taxpayers.

She jumped at the chance to negotiate a deal. As we left the building Jeff Jacobs, who had worked for Tessa before coming to City Hall as Anthony Mayer's deputy, laughed, 'If we end up winning the Olympics it will be down to this deal. No one will ever believe it.'

Over the next ten days Neale negotiated with Tessa's officials to draw up a proper funding package which split the £2.6 billion into three: £1.5 billion would come from a new Olympic lottery (as Cutler had wanted from Thatcher), half of the other £1.1 billion would come from the LDA and the rest from council taxpayers who would pay an extra 38p a week for ten years, or twelve years in the event of cost overruns. It helped that Jeff knew everyone in his former department and by coincidence Tessa's political adviser was my old GLC head of office Bill Bush, who had also worked for Tony Blair in Number 10. Suddenly it all looked manageable and polls showed Londoners supported the bid by 61–24 per cent. Although there was overwhelming press support, Blair kept putting off the decision until after the defeat of Saddam Hussein. Just eight weeks before the close of applications, the cabinet agreed that London should bid.

*

The other bidding cities were well ahead of us and we had just twelve months to put together a plan, so we needed someone who could do three years' work in one. The bid chair was appointed jointly by government, the BOA and me, with speculation that the favourite was the former ambassador to the US Sir Christopher Meyer. But we needed someone with the energy to work 24/7, not a diplomat. I met with Charles Allen (chief executive of Granada TV, who had run the Manchester Commonwealth Games) and Gerry Robinson (chair of the Arts Council). Either of them could have done it but both had other business they couldn't drop. Each agreed that if the games were to succeed we must keep civil servants and ministers from interfering. To me the obvious front runner was forty-two-year-old Barbara Cassani, who created the budget airline Go. Starting from scratch with just £25 million, within four years the company was worth £374 million when sold to EasyJet. Luckily she had left to write a book about the experience and was ready to start work for us immediately. I was impressed when she said she would do the job for £50,000 less than we were offering, saying she wanted to set an example to others about pay levels.

There were some raised eyebrows because she was an American but I admired the way she pulled together a formidable team with the unaffected multimillionaire Keith Mills (the creator of Airmiles and Nectar) as her chief executive, the former Olympic athlete Sebastian Coe and Charles Allen as vice-chairs, Mike Lee from UEFA to handle the press and the inspired choice of David Magliano, her head of marketing from Go. She realised that the creation of a legacy from the games, some continuing benefit from them, was crucial to the IOC and needed a post-2012 commitment of £10 million a year to run the facilities the games would leave behind. At the key meeting civil servants insisted no government could commit its successor to this so I said I would commit the mayor's office to support the facilities after the games. Horrified at seeing a decision taken rapidly, a civil servant said, 'You can't do that,' but the sports people smiled as I said, 'I think you'll find I just did.'

The bid document admitted our transport as it stood in 2003 couldn't cope with an Olympics, which gave me leverage to get money out of Brown. Most people in government dismissed the bid as a pipe dream of Blair, myself and Tessa, who joked about Brown's reluctance, saying, 'His pen was still hovering over the contract even while the plane was waiting on the tarmac to take the document to Lucerne' (IOC headquarters).

The disintegrating sports centre at Crystal Palace, which had London's only Olympic-size pool and international athletics track, was a threat to our bid. When the GLC was abolished Bromley Council had boasted it could manage a regional sports park but over the years there had been no investment in the complex, and now the leader of Bromley Council came to see me and Patrick Carter (the chair of Sport England) to say the council intended to close both the pool and the running track. This would have dealt a fatal blow to our chance of persuading the IOC we were serious about sport so I offered to take over Crystal Palace and find the resources to keep the sports centre going. If we won the 2012 games Stratford would become London's sports centre and we could then restore Crystal Palace to its Victorian splendour.

*

After two years complaining that nothing was happening the tone of the media shifted as my poll ratings went up and each day seemed to bring news of something going right, such as a cut in deaths and accidents inside the congestion zone. The seal was set on the turnaround when I reopened Trafalgar Square after eighteen months of work. Lord Foster's team had paved over the race track that used to be the street outside the National Gallery and installed a grand flight of steps down to a piazza worthy of a great world city. Some evenings on the way home I stopped to savour the atmosphere in the new square as it became a meeting point for Londoners. Even the *Standard*'s Keith Dovkants was impressed: 'As Ken speaks there is indeed an imperial quality in his bearing . . . this is the charismatic figure, a modern political legend, who trumpets his success unashamedly. And rightly so, perhaps.' What Dovkants didn't know was the spring in my step had more to do with the fact that Emma was pregnant again and even more delighted that our next baby was going to be the sister for Tom we so much wanted.

*

We had brought two cases against Brown's tube public–private partnership in the British courts, which we lost. We also took the case to the European Commission, who began investigating to see whether the PPP broke rules on state aid and competition. The government's procedural incompetence meant there was a good chance that Europe would order the government to start the process all over again. The tube bosses were so focused on the issue that management was slipping, with a 35 per cent increase in track and signal failure, a £67 million underspend in infrastructure and 6,000 people trapped for nearly two hours in breakdowns on the Victoria and Central lines. Management provoked another strike by reducing the inflation-linked pay increase unless the union agreed to a no-strike deal. Although I had no control over the tube it didn't stop *The Times* saying I was betraying Londoners by absolving myself of responsibility. I went over the heads of the tube bosses and agreed with the unions that we would put the dispute to arbitration as soon as I had control of the tube and the strike was called off. *The Times* now warned that the 'biggest disgrace of all is the capitulation of Ken Livingstone'.

I met the new transport secretary, Alistair Darling (the sixth transport secretary in five years and the twentieth in twenty-three years), and said I wouldn't drop the European case unless the government agreed to pay the full cost of the PPP. I got the impression he agreed, but when Darling complained I had not kept my promise to withdraw the European case I reminded him my condition was that the government had to meet the PPP's costs. Nicky Gavron acted as a go-between and Darling agreed we could carry over a £200 million underspend in the tube budget and £170 million contingency fund. Most importantly, Darling agreed that the 'government will provide extra money should unforeseen circumstances arise'. With the deal done, the tube was finally transferred to TfL's control in July 2003. Six years after Blair's election, work finally began on modernising the network, which was using equipment that in any other city would be in a transport museum. (On one occasion we in fact raided a transport museum to find spares.)

Bob Kiley's team calculated we were paying 20–25 per cent over the odds for the PPP work. The firms, which had been appointed by Brown's Treasury officials, were getting a rate of return of 26 per cent so the shareholders recovered their investment in the first three years of these thirty-year contracts.

The Tube Lines consortium, including Jarvis and Amey, was led by Bechtel, a family-owned American civil engineering firm with ties to the CIA (it won a lot of reconstruction work in Iraq after the invasion in March 2003). Bechtel managed the work by letting contracts and sacking firms that failed to deliver. The Metronet consortium was led by Balfour Beatty, which had a record of delays and cost overruns and was responsible for the Hatfield rail crash in October 2000. Unlike Bechtel, which had a reputation to lose, Balfour Beatty was widely criticised, particularly when its Brazilian subsidiary, according to the *Standard*, 'impoverished and displaced several indigenous communities'. Metronet included the train manufacturer Bombardier, the transport contractor WS Atkins, Thames Water and EDF Energy, who divided the work among themselves without competition. It is illegal for the public sector to award contracts without competitive tendering, but privatised firms could do as they liked and, of course, they never penalised themselves for delays or overspending. Bob called Balfour Beatty, Bombardier and WS Atkins 'three broken-backed firms with a record of failure'. Having not inspected the system before bidding, Bechtel was shocked to discover the condition of track and signalling and shut us out for a year while they recast their operation. Metronet just sailed on until they hit the buffers four years down the line.

To run the tube, Bob wanted to hire David Gunn, the man who

had run the New York subway for him, but David wouldn't take the job if it involved PPP, saying, 'You'll need a lawyer, not a train man.' Finding someone to run the tube when half of it was out of their control wasn't easy but a worldwide search found forty-seven-year-old Tim O'Toole, who had run Conrail in Philadelphia and was also a lawyer. He arrived five months before the tube was transferred to us and in that time he rode to every stop on the system, meeting thousands of staff. For Tim the key to the tube was the staff running it. The only problem was that his family didn't want to move to London and he missed them terribly, but he loved visiting Emma and me with armfuls of children's presents.

Tim's enthusiasm and openness was such a contrast to the departing tube bosses (he removed twenty-seven out of the top thirty executives) that he gave me confidence that if we couldn't make PPP work he had the ability to take over if they failed. I promised the unions we wouldn't undermine them or reduce their pay but I also said I thought wages on the Underground were already fair and my priority was improving bus drivers' wages. After years of boneheaded confrontation with the unions Tim was a breath of fresh air and by 2008 staff shifts lost to strikes were down from 59,500 a year before the handover to just 156.

With its dual accountability to government and City Hall, the LDA was more of a problem. Mike Ward encountered resistance to change from many of the inherited staff so I brought in Honor Chapman, a businesswoman from the property industry, to chair the board and asked Manny Lewis to become Mike's deputy. Manny had been appointed head of corporate services by the Assembly and had impressed me with his skill at handling the problem of being responsible to both the Assembly and myself.

The press reported that Chris Smith, Channel 4 newsreader Jon Snow, police commissioner Brian Paddick and even Steve Norris had been asked to be Labour's candidate against me for mayor in

2004. The *Daily Mail* said Peter Stringfellow and Mohamed Al Fayed (who wanted to scrap all bus lanes) were thinking of standing as independents. Although I topped a *Guardian* survey as the 'most influential figure in Britain's public services' Charles Clarke wasn't persuaded and asked Tony Banks to stand. My policy of culling pigeons in Trafalgar Square and levying the congestion charge on RSPCA vans had so annoyed Tony, a fervent supporter of animal rights, that he decided he would run against me. Long gone were the days when Tony had offered to be my campaign manager when I ran for the leadership of the Labour party. John Ross worried that Banks would spend his time attacking me with the risk that Norris might win as a result, so he encouraged Nicky Gavron to stand. Tony blew his chance by saying he would not urge voters to make me their second preference. This swung members behind Nicky, who beat Banks in both the members and trade-union sections of the ballot. MPs no longer had their own section. Sadly for Nicky, Labour's vote collapsed and she was running fourth in the polls.

*

The last thing Blair needed in 2003 was a by-election in a constituency with a large Muslim vote so when Paul Daisley, my successor in Brent East, died in June I wasn't surprised when Sally Morgan asked for a private meeting. I expected her to ask me to endorse the Labour candidate but she said, 'Tony wants to know if you'll come back and be our candidate for mayor.' Not pausing for an instant, I said yes. The projects we were now working on required big money from government and new powers for the mayoralty. If I were Blair's candidate he would have to ensure that my second term was a success. And I hated fund-raising as an independent because of the ethical complications.

Sally said it would take time to square all the players but asked me to proceed on the basis that this was a done deal. Her immediate concern was the by-election: 'We need a candidate you can support.' I was given a veto over the shortlist and asked my views on timing. I replied, 'The government is so unpopular I'd put it off until the autumn.' But it turned out to be bad advice. Sally's optimism that 'By then we might have found [Saddam's] WMDs' was misplaced. Subsequent events including the death of Dr David Kelly and the revelations of the Hutton inquiry into it meant that Labour's credibility continued to decline and the Liberal Democrat Sarah Teather won Brent East in September.

The Lib Dem tactics at Brent were as bad as Labour's in the Littleborough and Saddleworth by-election in 1995, when Mandelson used our candidate Phil Woolas to smear the Lib Dems as 'high on tax and soft on drugs'. In over twenty Lib Dem leaflets I received there was not a single sentence on Lib Dem policy or even on the joys of proportional representation. Labour's Robert Evans was attacked for spending time in Europe (not surprising for a Euro MP) and being a 'millionaire' (unlikely for a former primary-school teacher). The leaflets damned Brent Council for recycling only 6 per cent of household waste – the same figure as Islington Council where Sarah Teather was in charge of recycling! Although police numbers were now the highest ever in the history of London, the Lib Dems claimed police numbers had fallen. This campaign changed my feelings towards their party.

*

The Standards Board published its report on Robin Hedges's fall at my sister-in-law's party in the middle of August while I was on holiday. The investigating officer concluded there was no evidence to justify a hearing by the Board and that my explanation of events 'was not misleading or untrue'. The *Evening Standard* said it was a whitewash and took the opportunity to repeat the accusations over two days. Other papers buried it in their inside pages and the *Mail* refused to mention it. Lord Tope, the Lib Dem on the GLA who had referred the incident to the Standards Board, grudgingly accepted that the matter was closed.

*

Months went by without word from Number 10 about my re-admission to the party. When George Bush made a state visit in November 2003 I allowed a peace demo in Trafalgar Square with a giant effigy of Bush toppled like Saddam's in Baghdad. While the state banquet was getting under way I organised a reception for the peace movement attended by Ron Kovich, the Vietnam veteran who was the hero of Oliver Stone's *Born on the Fourth of July*. When Sally Morgan phoned I said I assumed that this would make my readmission impossible. 'We don't care about that,' she laughed.

As word spread that Blair was going to take me back Neil Kinnock went on the *Today* programme saying, 'I'm fundamentally and irretrievably against it. Ken Livingstone has only ever belonged to one party – the Ken Livingstone party. There is no possibility . . . of the Labour party being able to rely upon sufficient loyalty and commitment.' John Reid and Charles Clarke enjoyed telling me how they fought to change Blair's mind and there were furious rows with Brown, but once Nicky Gavron announced she would withdraw as Labour's mayoral candidate in my favour it was all over. When I turned up at an NEC sub-committee in January 2004 I was hugged and kissed by Mary Turner, who had been the candidate Kinnock ran against me in Brent East fifteen years earlier. John Prescott asked, 'Given you lied to us about not running as an independent, how can we ever believe anything you say?' I said, 'You can't, but we've all got an interest in making this work.' Finally Prescott asked, 'Is there anything in your private life which could be damaging to the party if it came out?' Everyone laughed as I said, 'Nothing the party didn't use against me already.'

According to Andrew Rawnsley's book *The End of the Party*, Iraq's descent into chaos after the invasion tipped Blair into a depression and he told Brown he would stand down before the next election. He was also in pain from a slipped disc, but to his credit he hid all of this as he campaigned for my re-election. Just days after my readmission we came together for the launch of our Olympic bid at the Royal Opera House. Mike Lee described Blair sweeping in just moments before the event and asking what we wanted him to emphasise. 'We gave him three points and he spoke without notes. He was superb,' wrote Mike in his book *The Race for the 2012 Olympics*. 'Ken's speech was particularly powerful. He focused on London's diversity and the regeneration of the East End and said it could be a model for the rest of the world. He spoke passionately and people felt it. You always hold your breath with Ken but he was particularly impressive that day.'

Lee felt that 'the relationship between Blair and Livingstone became one of the most fascinating elements of the bid. Blair . . . never let any differences with the mayor get in the way . . . of winning the vote in Singapore.' Mike quotes Blair: '"I've always got on fine personally with Ken. It's pretty hard not to like him. But there's no doubt that working closely with him on the 2012 bid helped heal wounds quicker than might have been the case. Like so many people involved with the bid, he was fantastic."'

As I launched the first neighbourhood policing team at the Stonebridge estate in February 2004 I said, 'My generation didn't get involved in crime. If you got caught causing vandalism you thought twice about doing it again.' But once police gave up the streets, kids could go for years without getting caught and believing they would always get away with it could progress from vandalism into a life of crime. Blair, who was present that day, chipped in to say he didn't know whether I'd be shocked but he agreed with every word I said.

At the start of the election Blair joined me at a children's nursery in Paddington, where he got a warm response with a deadpan 'I never had any doubt that Ken would turn out to be an excellent mayor.' As we waited in a side room I realised it was the first time we had been alone since October 1997, when I'd told him what I thought of his government. But for all our disagreements it was impossible to be with Blair without being charmed. The *Guardian*'s Jackie Ashley, who followed us that day, reported, 'If I hadn't seen it with my own eyes I wouldn't have believed it, but every second or third car that passes us beeps a horn or shouts a greeting to Ken. And every passer-by has something to say too. He laps it up, treating those who have a grumble and those who just want to shake his hand with equal good humour. He is a prince of the pavement.' She reported my views on the Saudi royal family and George W. Bush and my call for a 50 per cent tax rate on all earnings over £100,000 and was surprised when she resumed our interview 'after Mr Livingstone has had an hour or so to craft a cleverly evasive answer on tax. Except, of course, he hasn't bothered. He comes straight out with a call for a higher top rate.' When she asked me how this would appeal to the middle classes I said they'd pay a bit more tax but 'won't have to pay for private education for their kids and private health care, because as with the French, they would be happy to use state schools and state health care'.

*

Although Blair and I realised we had to make it work, his staff expected me to try to derail his premiership – as if I had the power to do so – and drafting the manifesto was a nightmare which tied up all my advisers with ten weeks of nit-picking negotiations. That it had been right to go back to Labour became clear when the government announced funding to build a new bridge across the Thames, gave the go-ahead to extend the Docklands Light Railway to City Airport and started discussing the possibility that I would be able to raise money on the bond markets to run larger projects. The only thing that went wrong was the 2003 New Year's Eve fireworks display. With control of the tube we kept stations open this time and hired a company to put on a display on the London Eye which could rival Sydney's. But as Big Ben struck midnight there was a technical fault and half of the fireworks failed to go off, reducing the display to three minutes. Knowing how our Olympic rivals could exploit this fiasco I said nothing publicly, but we didn't pay the firm for the fireworks that failed to go off, and hired a new team for the following year. That display was so stunning the BBC switched its New Year's Eve coverage from Scotland to London.

There were two controversial issues I could have put off until after the election: fares and the congestion charge. In 2000 I had promised to freeze bus fares and keep tube fares in line with inflation (as I had to do by law). Now bus passenger numbers were up a third, the fleet was 8,000 instead of 5,500 buses and the cost of running them was increasing with the price of oil so I decided to increase the fares before the election and then promise they wouldn't rise by more than inflation. The other issue was extending the congestion charge. There were only two other places in London that justified a charge – Heathrow Airport and Kensington & Chelsea. My mind was made up when the Assembly commissioned an opinion poll which showed 54 per cent of people in Kensington & Chelsea wanted it extended. But that didn't prevent a Chelsea tractor convoy outside my house in Cricklewood on a Saturday morning driving round the block tooting their horns with a woman's plummy voice exclaiming 'What a ghastly place to live!'

*

Simon Hughes had replaced Susan Kramer as Lib Dem candidate, Norris ran again for the Conservatives and we spent several weeks debating in a good-natured way. With timing to equal Tom's arrival eight weeks before the congestion charge came in, our daughter Mia was born twelve weeks before polling day. Sadly Emma's father had died four months earlier and to make home life even more stressful builders converting our loft into a study and installing solar panels were running late and we were without hot water for several days. Not the best preparation for an election, but I loved coming home to my giggling little girl every night.

The RMT planned a strike for election day, which wasn't surprising as Blair had caved in when they used the tactic in the 2001 general election. After all the effort I had put into building a working relationship with them I was furious. If I gave in a pre-election strike would become a political fixture for all time and the office of mayor would be a broken reed so I decided there would be no reward for strike action. In the past London Underground made derisory offers and the union struck until the offer was improved but we had broken the pattern of the past by making a serious offer in the 2004 pay negotiations. I also wanted to end annual strike threats with three- and four-year pay deals.

Other unions were livid with the RMT. The industrial muscle of tube workers could protect their wages and conditions but bus drivers were not in a strong position and a Tory mayor could roll back the pay increases we had given. For the first time in my life I was ready to call on workers to cross a picket line but the other unions forced the RMT to back down. After the election RMT called a strike to upstage other unions by demanding a four-day week, which would have meant a big increase in the fares paid by Londoners, many of whom were working six-day weeks. I decided to show the RMT executive that these tactics would win them nothing so I asked RMT members to cross the picket line and we managed to keep a reduced service running. Bob Crow strode into my office to say that I was a disgrace to the Labour movement but when I said his executive was behaving more like the mafia than a union he stormed out, leaving the union's president behind in embarrassed silence.

Once again the Police Federation called a meeting of all the candidates but this time only a few police turned up to hear Steve Norris complain that crime was soaring (even though crime was now falling for the second year in a row). John Stevens was furious and strode to the microphone saying, 'I'm not going to sit here and listen to those figures. They are from a Tory think tank, Civitas. Figures from the Met show that violent crime is down 5 per cent,' and then proceeded to tell Norris what he thought of his fiddling the figures. Glen Smyth, chairman of the Police Federation, warned that 'the candidates need to be sure that what they are saying [is] based on facts. There is no excuse for any of them to get it wrong.' Norris told the *Standard* that if he was elected he would not reappoint Stevens and until the end of his contract Stevens would only perform 'ceremonial tasks'.

*

After the Madrid rail bombings of March 2004 I told the press, 'There are people out there who want to take lives, in the hundreds and the thousands . . . these are people who celebrate death. We will be fools to assume we will always be able to stop terrorists.' Blunkett was appalled that there had been a press conference: 'There has to be a balance between telling the truth and reassurance. Otherwise people are jumpy without it having a good effect,' he told the *Sunday Telegraph*. I believed Londoners would have more confidence if we were honest with them about the risks.

Three weeks before polling day the police warned there had been an increase in electronic traffic suggesting that a terrorist group had been activated in London. Bizarrely, the US had switched their attentions to Iraq before destroying al-Qaeda and stabilising Afghanistan. According to Seth G. Jones's *In the Graveyard of Empires*, when Bin Laden left the caves of Tora Bora in December 2001, the CIA 'repeatedly requested an additional battalion of US army rangers to block Bin Laden's escape, but the US military relied on local Afghan forces. Some reports indicate that Bin Laden paid Afghans to let him through.'

I hadn't forgotten the warning from *Pravda*'s Yuri Sagadak in 1988 about the West's support for 'homicidal fanatics' fighting the Russians in Afghanistan. Released US files show the Russians were provoked into invading Afghanistan. In February 1979 Afghanistan was descending into chaos with the US ambassador kidnapped and killed. In March insurgents captured Herat, killing 100 Russian 'advisers' and their families, parading their heads on poles. On 30 March the Pentagon's Walter Slocombe told the White House there could be a benefit in 'sucking the Soviets into a Vietnamese quagmire' in Afghanistan and on 3 July President Carter authorised support for the mujahidin. The Soviets were alarmed by the shipment of rifles to the rebels and invaded. Having provoked the Soviet invasion, the CIA advised Carter that the Soviets' concern was the collapse of Afghanistan and it was 'unlikely the Soviet occupation is a pre-planned first step . . . of a highly articulated grand design for the rapid establishment of hegemonic control over all of South West Asia'. Carter's cynical ploy started the chain of events that led to 9/11, the London bombings and the deaths of our young men and women in Afghanistan that continue to this day.

Fearing an attack during the European and mayoral elections, my advisers discussed our plans. John Ross asked, 'What are you going to say when it happens?' I replied, 'I can't discuss this, John. It's inside my head but I really can't talk to anyone about it.' Polling day passed without bombs and the terrorist group was captured before they could act.

*

The election itself was an anti-climax. There was little media interest except when Norris was condemned by some of the newspapers for becoming chairman of the deeply unpopular construction firm Jarvis, which was responsible for the fatal Potters Bar train crash. Norris described the *Telegraph* as 'fascist and xenophobic' and the *Mail* and *Standard* hadn't forgiven him for describing Paul Dacre as a 'fuckwit', so in a tortuously worded editorial in the *Standard* they just about, and with great reservations, endorsed me. *The Economist*, which four years previously warned Londoners about my dangerous Red–Green coalition, now surprised themselves by backing me. After the result was announced, staff gathered to celebrate and within minutes Blair was on the phone from Washington talking enthusiastically about what we could achieve.

I had told Bob Kiley before the election that if I won I wanted to press ahead with the public transport schemes that had been on the drawing board for decades. Even if I wasn't re-elected in 2008 my successor would have to complete them. In 1967 a proposal to build a new tube called Crossrail to run from Heathrow through the City of London to the East End had been costed at just £300 million. There was also the proposal to build a new tube from Chelsea to Hackney which had been talked of since the Second World War, and more recent proposals to extend the East London Line down to Croydon and also for four new tram schemes and new extensions to the Docklands Light Railway and Croydon Tramlink.

In my eight years as mayor I must have met with a minister on average once every week, asking for support for various schemes or more powers and money to carry them out. I met transport ministers more than those from any other department but it always seemed that just as I was making headway the minister would move and I would have to begin again with their successor. Transport department officials were hostile to public transport schemes. They favoured road building and usually retired to a lucrative board position on some large construction firm as a reward. These pernicious, risk-averse civil servants finessed reasons why nothing could or should be done, fearing projects would be over budget and late and they would then be grilled by MPs and auditors. When I tried to persuade ministers to back Crossrail David Rowlands, the civil servant who headed the department, intervened to say there was no need to have a high-speed rail link from Heathrow into London as 'our studies show when businessmen arrive at Heathrow they don't go straight to work but like to go to their hotel and rest'.

The fiasco of the Jubilee Line extension, which opened just days before Millennium Eve and suffered huge delays for months before it worked properly, reinforced these fears so when a firm won the tender to extend the Docklands Light Railway to City Airport at a cost of £180 million nearly a year went by and the winning bidder's tender was due to expire in a few days. Faced with the embarrassment of starting the process all over again the government finally gave its permission to proceed. Frustrated by these delays, I wanted projects devolved to the Mayor's Office. We would raise funding on the bond markets and then build them. My hand was strengthened when the International Olympic Committee announced that London was on the shortlist for the Olympics but warned that 'rail public transport is often obsolete and considerable investments must be made to upgrade the existing system in terms of capacity and safety' if our bid was to have any chance of success against those of Paris and Madrid. (This was the main reason London was third-favourite behind those two.)

TfL's Jay Walder led the negotiations with the Treasury about funding the improvements that the IOC wanted but no progress had been made by the time I went on holiday to France in August 2004. If I hadn't been lying by the pool I would have fallen over when Jay phoned to say the Treasury was letting me take responsibility for the proposed rail projects and giving me power to borrow £2.9 billion from the bond markets without further reference to government. No local authority had been given this freedom before, but the sting in the tail was that I would have to increase the fares to service the debt. This meant breaking my promise not to raise fares faster than inflation, but given my contempt for Wilson and Callaghan – who cut investment rather than raise taxes – I took the deal. Now we had the money to build the East London Line, upgrade the North London Line and build a new Docklands Light Railway extension to Stratford International.

*

Barbara Cassani, having put together a credible bid in just eleven months and assembled a formidable team, had the integrity to recognise that when it came to lobbying IOC delegates Seb Coe would be more effective and stood down to make way for him. Neale Coleman, who advised on the Olympics, said he thought that I should go with him and Seb to the Athens games that August to lobby for votes. Before 2004, the only sporting event I'd ever attended had been a Test match at the Oval in 1972, where I'd fallen asleep over the course of a long hot afternoon. Now I was involved in Wembley, the Emirates Stadium and the Olympics. I started reading the sports pages for the first time in my life. When I went to the Athens games with Seb Coe I could smell the paint drying on the stadium. To keep each of the Athens suburban mayors happy the facilities were spread round the city so visitors spent half their time commuting from one site to another but Athens's legacy was three new underground lines and the removal of a lot of the advertising hoardings that hid the beauty of the city. The fear of an al-Qaeda attack ensured that there was a huge American security presence and Sir John insisted that my armed protection unit accompany me.

The mayor of Athens was a popular conservative, Dora Bako-gianni, who had been in office eighteen months and had survived an assassination attempt. Her socialist MP husband Pavlos had been assassinated in 1989. After his death she was elected in his constituency, where men still rode on donkeys while their wives walked in front in case there was a mine left over from the civil war (the donkeys being more valuable).

During the run-up to the games Dora had been driven mad by endless demands for extra money from the Athens Organising Committee and warned me that if London won the games I would have to chair the organising committee to control the costs. Dora had clashed with the chair of the Athens Organising Committee, Gianna Angelopoulos. She was fabulously wealthy even before she married an equally rich shipping magnate and smoked Churchillian-size cigars while her enormous diamond jewellery sparkled through the smoke. She had an expensive home in Chelsea but had built a new mansion in Athens specifically to entertain the presidents, prime ministers and royalty attending the games. And me.

At Gianna's mansion (which demonstrated that wealth is no guarantee of taste) I met the heart transplant surgeon Dr Magdi Yacoub, who had been an Olympic volunteer for years, looking very bored until we started talking about the problems of the NHS. At dinner I was the only unaccompanied person at a table of Greek millionaires and their young wives. One enquired, 'Are you by any chance related to the mayor of London?' The food had been prepared by a London catering firm and the entertainment had been flown in from America. There was not a single Greek speciality on the menu and I couldn't believe Gianna hadn't showcased everything great about Greece. I left early, puffing on a vast cigar, to be greeted by my bodyguard asking, 'Where's a *Standard* photographer when you need one?'

As well as a visit to the new Athens tube lines, Neale and Seb had scheduled several sporting events and to my surprise I got caught up in the passion of the games. Most competitors had spent a decade or more preparing for an event that in some cases lasts for only a few seconds; so much rides on those moments, as is obvious from the intensity visible on the athletes' faces. I watched boxer Amir Khan as he danced gracefully round his opponent, but I was less enthralled by the women's judo, which always seemed to result in either an immediate victory or a relentless war of attrition as they tried to wrench limbs off each other. As Neale and I watched Roger Federer play to an almost empty grandstand we realised the importance of getting ticket prices right. There was a similar problem with the hotels – the IOC had put me in one so overpriced that it was almost empty.

The five bidding cities each made a pitch to the IOC and sports journalists. I used mine to emphasise London's diversity. The Olympics in-house magazine *Around the Rings* said London 'appears to have come out the winner'. Cassani had created an amazing machine. We had biographies of all IOC members and officials so as we spotted them someone in our team would summarise in a whisper their weaknesses and interests as I bore down on them. We had such a good response that when I was next alone with Seb I said, 'I think we can win this,' and he agreed. It also helped that there were more British tourists watching the games than from any other nation.

The Olympic bid had started as a long shot in the hopes of getting more money for transport. Now the stakes were enormous. If we won, it could change the face of the East End. I knew that no mayor, regardless of party, could ever persuade any government to concede the billions needed to regenerate the East End, but now the Olympics gave me the chance. Back in London I told Manny Lewis and Tony Winterbottom at the LDA and my key advisers this was now the top priority but we must do nothing to alert our main rival Paris to the fact that we had a good chance. Despite the encouraging words in *Around the Rings*, most journalists doubted we could win and so did the rest of the world, and we needed to keep them thinking that way.

*

One point that had played well with the IOC was London's sheer diversity. Mayor Bloomberg said 200 different languages were spoken in New York schools but dropped that line after I said 300 were spoken in ours. London had come a long way since police in the 1950s would write reports after seeing a white woman out with a black man saying such a relationship was 'dangerous' and that black men 'were cunning, unprincipled crooks . . . accosting decent white women'. Employers like British Rail would tell black applicants all the jobs were filled and 'no coloureds or Irish' was regularly appended to small ads. But for thirty years political, religious, trade union and community leaders had made the case for tolerance and since 2000 the level of racist, anti-Semitic and homophobic crime in London had fallen every year.

London has attracted a large lesbian and gay community because it's more tolerant than many parts of Britain, but the ban on teachers discussing homosexuality in schools meant homophobia went unchallenged among teenagers. Gay men were still being beaten to death by teenage gangs. Building on the progress made by the GLC, I had been welcomed on stage by Kylie Minogue at the gay music festival Pride at Finsbury Park in July 2000 to announce that we intended to introduce civil partnerships in London. Although they carried no legal weight, I hoped our action would encourage government to make them do so. There was a flood of applications for the first ceremony, which took place on 5 September 2001 at Romney House. We made certain our first two couples were respectable and media-friendly, and when Ian Burford and Alexander Cannell talked about their thirty-eight years together there wasn't a dry eye in the room. The first lesbian couple, Linda Wilkinson and Carol Budd, later told me that the attitude of their families changed with this little bit of official recognition. Media coverage was positive – even the *Mail* didn't object. Four years later the government gave civil partnerships full legal status.

*

St Patrick's Day had never been officially recognised in Britain but during the 2000 mayoral election all candidates had promised the *Irish Post* that we would try to rival New York's grand parade on the Irish national day. Throughout the Troubles the Irish Counties Association organised a march but with the Irish community keeping its head down it was a very small event. Redmond organised support for a parade and with Blair's success in brokering a political solution to the problems of Northern Ireland we expected 10,000 people in Trafalgar Square in March 2002. At Westminster Cathedral for the start of the march the crowds were five times larger than that and the pavements were packed all the way to Trafalgar Square. As we marched there was a wave of euphoria and tears from Irish Londoners, finally able to celebrate their day. I could hear the pride in Redmond's voice as he phoned his Irish family. There were already 50,000 people in the square so the police closed neighbouring roads to cope with the overflow. It was an amazing day, but the *Evening Standard* ignored it.

Sadly they and the rest of the media didn't ignore London's Muslim community. As they had against Irish Londoners during the IRA bombing campaigns of the 1970s, the *Mail*, *Express* and *Telegraph* stirred up hostility to Muslims after 9/11 and the Met had to allocate police to protect mosques and other Muslim targets. There were votes to be had in Islamophobia, with the European right-wing parties competing to be the most vigorous in cracking down on 'the enemy within'. In the USA the chairman of the Republican National Committee wrote in the *Wall Street Journal*, 'We face a radical global movement of Islamic fascists held together by a to-talitarian ideology as deadly as the ones we faced in World War II or the Cold War.'

Historically, few Muslims had ever been recruited into the police, let alone MI5, so after 9/11 both organisations rushed to look for contacts and good intelligence in the Muslim community. One in ten Londoners is a Muslim of some variety, and our polling showed they came to London to be part of our society, not to transform it into Saudi Arabia with rain. But Londoners of Muslim origin were on average two and a half times less likely to find work. We had promoted tolerance for others. Now we had to protect London's Muslims.

The worst of the media depict Islam as a homogeneous threat, but there are huge differences among Muslims, with the vast majority of them practising tolerant and peaceful versions of Islam. But the intolerant, puritanical and backward-looking Wahhabi minority first registered in the West when Muhammad Ahmad bin Abd Allah led an uprising in Sudan and butchered General Gordon at Khartoum. The Saudi royal family won and still hold power in Saudi Arabia in alliance with the Wahhabi imams. In the 1950s Foreign Secretary Harold Macmillan wrote in his diaries that the Saudis were spreading Wahhabi influence around the world. 'The Saudis are bribing everyone, right and left, and are turning the whole Arab world upside down. If something could be done to stop this it would be the biggest possible contribution to peace.'

Most Sunnis wish to engage with the Western world and their leading theologian is Sheikh Yusuf al-Qaradawi, now in his eighties. As a young man al-Qaradawi was a member of Egypt's Muslim brotherhood opposing the military dictatorship but went into exile in Qatar forty years ago. Since then he has written over fifty books trying to reconcile Islam with democracy and human rights, in particular women's rights in contemporary Islam. As the leading Muslim critic of al-Qaeda, the *Sun* praised him as the 'true face of Islam' when he urged Muslims to donate blood to help the survivors of 9/11 and unite 'against those who terrorise innocents'. But in August 2004, when he arrived to address a conference at City Hall, the same paper screamed: 'The evil has landed' and 'Britain's welcome for devil'. The *Mail* warned, 'Cleric who backs child bombers is to visit Britain' and Tory leader Michael Howard demanded he be banned, though Qaradawi had visited Britain thirteen times during the Tories' eighteen years in power. When I met Qaradawi he was perplexed by the media attacks on him and made his views clear: 'Muslims have no right to punish homosexuals or to mistreat them,' he said, and 'The respectable and honest Muslim man does not beat his wife.' Also, 'Civilians should not be killed, or kept as hostages. Jews not in conflict with Muslims must not be killed. Anyone who commits these crimes has committed the sin of killing a soul which Allah has prohibited to kill . . . Islam recognises that Muslims, Christians and Jews are all people of the book.' He made clear these views in newspaper and television interviews but reiterated his belief that as the Palestinians have no aircraft or tanks he respected their right to be suicide bombers, a view that is widespread in the Muslim world. Although they had never opposed his previous visits to the UK, the Board of Deputies denounced my meeting with him. The Board had never condemned former Israeli prime minister Ariel Sharon, who was responsible for the massacres at the Palestinian refugee camps of Sabra and Chatila in Beirut, and first came to attention in 1953 when he led an illegal raid into Jordan which killed sixty-nine men, women and children in the village of Qibya. It's easy for someone like myself to oppose all acts of violence but unless we can end the injustice that drives people to take these desperate measures then our words will be ignored in the Arab world.

The *Sun* described me as a 'slimy twerp' but the *Independent* more intelligently wondered, 'So why the fuss now? The simple answer is politics. In today's heated climate over terror and Mullahs, there is nothing the popular press loves so much as a hate figure to arouse their outraged condemnation.' Many views attributed to Qaradawi are falsifications from a phoney website believed to be run by Saudi intelligence. A pro-Israel organisation, MEMRI, run by a former Mossad agent, has also been caught out for falsifying his views. In speeches he made while here he said that the UK is not a racist country, urged Muslims to play a positive role in the UK and warned them not to abuse the benefit system.

The security services, who know a real terrorist threat from a tabloid fabrication, actually wanted us to engage with al-Qaradawi and Special Branch believed his visit was important in preventing al-Qaeda from recruiting young British Muslims. An internal Special Branch report said 'Sheikh al-Qaradawi has a positive Muslim community impact in the fight against al-Qaeda propaganda in the UK. His support for Palestinian suicide bombers adds credibility to his condemnation for al-Qaeda in those sections of the community most susceptible to the blandishments of al-Qaeda terrorist propaganda.' The head of the Special Branch Muslim Contact Unit, Detective Inspector Bob Lambert, told Andrew Hosken: 'It became clear that most of the Muslim groups we were working with – those groups which were proving to be effective at the grass roots and in persuading young people not to get involved in dangerous activity – held City Hall and the Mayor in very high regard.'

Rejecting criticism from journalists like Nick Cohen and Martin Bright that we were 'appeasing radical Islam', Bob Lambert said,

'We were worried about young London Muslims who in some cases could have become al-Qaeda terrorists and supporters. Ken is part of an alliance which says to the same young people, "Look we can empathise with your grievances, the same grievances that al-Qaeda exploits for terrorist recruitment – we have the same grievances; you don't have to go down that road . . ." Where the mayor was useful was with his record of support for minorities, I think potentially, if anyone can, he is well placed to broker dialogue . . . Only through engagement can you hope to move people forward.'

After the row subsided I bumped into *Sun* editor Rebekah Wade and asked her what was the source of the misleading information they had been fed. 'American sources,' she replied cryptically. For all the manufactured controversy around this visit one fact remained: following my election in 2000 racist, anti-Semitic and homophobic incidents in London had declined each year. Even in 2006, when Israel's invasion of the Lebanon saw an upsurge in anti-Semitism in Britain and Europe, the Met recorded no increase in London.

This did not stop the right-wing attacks on multiculturalism. Bizarrely, Trevor Phillips, now chair of the Commission for Racial Equality, started arguing that 'discrimination may no longer be the main cause of inequality' and warned that 'Britain was sleepwalking to segregation' – even though the census showed that London's wards were becoming more mixed, not less.

*

My views on multiculturalism had crystallised when as GLC member for Stoke Newington I'd come to know the Orthodox Jewish community. Its members maintained a distinctive lifestyle expressed through their dress code and choice of food and schools. They married within their community while living side by side with old East Enders and newer arrivals from the Caribbean and Turkey. They participated in local politics and built thriving businesses and

Hackney was not diminished because they preserved their roots. Other Jews became so assimilated that they retained only a small part of their traditional culture. But between the Orthodox and the fully assimilated each Jew has made their own choice, and that is what I want for all our communities. In a hundred years some women will still be wearing the hijab, but already I meet London-born people from Muslim backgrounds who know nothing of the Koran. (The success of London's embrace of multiculturalism became clear in January 2010 from a study funded by George Soros. Muslims throughout western Europe were asked how patriotic they felt towards the country they lived in. Ninety per cent of Muslims in London and Leicester felt British but in Paris, where it is illegal even to record the percentage of Muslims in the population, only 45 per cent of Muslims felt truly French.)

When I first became mayor we were deluged with requests from cities around the world to twin with London but given how twinning often serves only to provide free trips for councillors I restricted it to our proper equivalents: New York, Paris, Berlin, Tokyo and Moscow, where exchanging information and good practice could bring real benefits. The mayor of Moscow wanted to establish an 'M6' of mayors modelled on the G7, but Rudy Giuliani seldom left New York and the governor of Tokyo didn't want links with cities which tolerated the mongrelisation of the races so we settled on the M4 – Berlin, London, Moscow and Paris. We also developed cultural links with Delhi, Dublin, Johannesburg and Kingston because of historical ties, but with so much going on during my first years as mayor I only managed to visit Dublin.

On my first trip to visit Mayor Giuliani to learn how he had cut crime I expected to find a hard-line right-winger, but he was in reality more like a one-nation Tory, socially liberal and tolerant. Over breakfast on Martin Luther King Day in January 2001 he worried that Clinton's 'welfare reforms' might throw many people on the streets as their benefit was ended after three years. He introduced his new police commissioner, who was rebuilding trust between police and the black community. New Yorkers I met said Giuliani had softened after his battle with prostate cancer. His fire commissioner was amazed that no London fire fighter had died in nearly a decade, but before he could visit London to find out why he died in the twin towers helping his men rescue the victims.

We also had meetings with businesses including a lunch in the restaurant at the top of the World Trade Center. Disappointed I couldn't see the view because we were in cloud, I promised myself I would come back. The British Consul in New York had been solemnly instructed that my visit had the same status as that of a cabinet minister. It was good to know that back in London they were concerned with really important issues like protocol.

I campaigned for the mayor of Berlin, Klaus Wowereit, in his election and was surprised at the level of security he had, but a previous mayor's car had been raked by machine-gun fire. As Klaus was the first openly gay German politician his Christian Democrat opponent bedecked Berlin with pictures of himself and his wife but to no avail. I avoided meeting the incumbent mayor of Paris (who was under investigation for corruption) until Bertrand Delanoë replaced him in 2001. Delanoë was the first socialist mayor of the city. He was also gay, which made for awkward meetings of the M4 when Yuri Luzhkov, Moscow's mayor, banned the city's annual Gay Pride march.

Bertrand, Klaus and myself were of the same generation, all of us led Red–Green coalitions and we became firm friends, but it was my relationship with Yuri Luzhkov which really paid off. In power since 1992 and winning over 90 per cent of the vote, his popularity was based on free travel for pensioners and a Moscow supplement to top up the low state pension. He built 50,000 new homes a year, half of which were given to key workers. He didn't think

I would get away with the congestion charge and was appalled when I told him that 95 per cent of all UK tax is collected by the British government. He exclaimed, 'That's worse than Russia under Stalin!' On my first visit I went to the reception where he launched Moscow's 2012 Olympic bid.

During the eight years John Ross spent in Moscow he made some good connections which paid off when Yuri asked Moscow Metro chiefs to look at the PPP proposals, which they denounced as dangerous. They also helped our negotiations with the company developing the Oyster travel card which did away with the need to queue for tickets and automatically charged the lowest possible fare for any journey. The contract was awarded by the government before I was elected and the company only wanted to provide monthly and annual tube passes, giving them a captive audience of better-off Londoners which they could then use as a market for other goods. I wanted a card that would benefit all Londoners who regularly used the city's public transport network, whatever their income. After months without progress I sent John to Moscow to ask if they would sell us a version of their travel card if I cancelled the Oyster deal. Now we had a fallback, the company gave in and began planning an Oyster card available to all.

*

In 2002 Yuri invited me to the annual commemoration in Moscow of the victory over Hitler. Few in the West understand the impact of the Second World War on Russia, where twenty-five million died and Nazi troops reached the outskirts of Moscow and Leningrad (now St Petersburg). The woman who ran the GLA's office in Moscow was not untypical in that she had lost every member of her family during the war. The two-day public holiday to remember the war dead also invokes the memory of Napoleon, who reached Moscow and, having occupied it, was stunned to see Muscovites burn their own city to the ground to deprive him of a base in which to shelter from the Russian winter, so forcing his disastrous retreat.

Winter had lifted and the trees were in leaf with glorious sunshine but instead of a bank holiday atmosphere the mood was sombre as grandparents brought their grandchildren to the eternal flame in Red Square and explained what the war was about. As the clock struck the hour there was total silence among the thousands of spectators. The silence went on for several minutes until I heard three soldiers marching the length of the square. One carried the threadbare old Soviet flag raised over the Reichstag when they took Berlin in 1945. The absolute silence continued until they completed their march and then the crowd erupted with roars as passionate as though the war had only just ended.

I joined Yuri Luzhkov later in a park where a vast crowd was listening to Tchaikovsky's 1812 Overture. Muscovites' pride in defeating both Napoleon and the Nazis was stirring and I was moved with them as they remembered the sacrifice their parents and ancestors made. Earlier I had visited the museum which commemorates the war, where I met Russian veterans from the Murmansk convoys and remembered my father's tales of their generosity as they shared the little they had with the visiting British sailors. I was overcome when the veterans gave me a posthumous medal and certificate in my father's honour. Because of the Cold War Britain did not give service medals to our sailors who risked their lives taking arms to Russia. This was resented by our seamen, so when I started celebrating Russian New Year in Trafalgar Square we held an annual reception for our convoy veterans.

*

As 2005 dawned everything was going right. The New Year's Eve fireworks display worked, Olympic plans were on schedule, the Oyster card had only minor glitches and was our second big IT scheme to come in on budget and on time, and as months passed without me screwing them, relations with government ministers relaxed. City Hall was bursting with the energy of people who wanted to turn London around; as one said, 'No matter our role we wanted to make a difference and wanted to do something right.' These weren't people who did the minimum and watched the clock. The lack of committee structure and my ability to make quick decisions meant the building was alive with new ideas and initiatives. Having built the organisation from scratch it was the most ethnically diverse public body in Britain, with the exception of the Commission for Racial Equality. Opening the staff café to the public meant that Londoners could come in to look around and in good weather sit in the amphitheatre for a range of entertainment. Every day I went home exhausted but enthused.

Apart from Kate Hoey saying that London did not deserve the Olympic Games, the only people giving me grief were the Board of Deputies of British Jews. They had always refused my offer to address them, so I didn't know what to expect when they sent a delegation. Coming straight to the point, they asked me to tone down my comments about Israel and gasped when I said I was already doing so and went on to explain why my opposition to Israel's policies had hardened.

I had believed that at the birth of Israel a small number of terrorists led by Menachem Begin and Yitzhak Shamir had murdered and driven Palestinians from their villages, so starting a spiral of violence thwarting the efforts of Israeli leaders to secure a lasting peace. But in 2004 I had read an interview with Professor Benny Morris of Ben-Gurion University, in *New Left Review*. As Israel's leading historian on the origins of Palestinian refugees, the Israeli army had let him see their confidential files.

He told the Israeli paper *Haaretz*:

There were far more Israeli acts of massacre than I had previously thought . . .

Also many cases of rape ... Units of the Haganah [predecessor to the Israeli army] were given operational orders that stated explicitly that they were to uproot the villagers, expel them and destroy the villages themselves ... The worst cases were Saliha (70–80 killed), Deir Yassin (100–110), Lod (250) ... Officers ... understood that the expulsion order they received permitted them to do these deeds ... No one was punished for these acts of murder, Ben-Gurion [Israel's first prime minister 1948–1954, 1955–1963] silenced the matter. He covered up the officers who did the massacres ... the commander of the northern front Moshe Carmel issued an order in writing to his units to expedite the removal of the Arab population. Carmel took this action immediately after a visit by Ben-Gurion ... There is no doubt in my mind that this order originated with Ben-Gurion. Just as the expulsion from the city of Lod which was signed by Yitzhak Rabin was issued immediately after Ben-Gurion visited the headquarters. From April 1948 Ben-Gurion is projecting a message of transfer. The officer core understands what is required of them.

Morris himself, who was once considered left-wing, justified these actions: 'Without the uprooting of the Palestinians, a Jewish state would not have arisen here ... there is no justification for acts of massacre. Those are war crimes. But in certain conditions, expulsion is not a war crime.' When the reporters asked him to justify the 'long and terrible column of the 50,000 people expelled from Lod' he replied that 'there are circumstances in history that justify ethnic cleansing. I know that this term is completely negative ... but when the choice is between ethnic cleansing and genocide – the annihilation of your people – I prefer ethnic cleansing ... a Jewish state would not have come into being without the uprooting of 700,000 Palestinians ... these are small war crimes.'

When the journalists asked if he believed that the remaining Arabs in Israel should be expelled Morris replied, 'I say not at this moment ... the world would not allow it, the Arab world would not allow it ... [but] the Israeli Arabs are a time bomb ... I think there is a clash of civilisations here ... the Arab world as it is today is Barbarian ... the phenomenon of the mass Muslim penetration into the West and their settlements there is creating a dangerous internal threat. A similar process took place in Rome. They let the Barbarians in and they toppled the empire from within . . . within the next twenty years there could be an atomic war here.'

For me, this interview blew away the lies that Palestinians had been told to flee by Arab governments which then invaded to prevent the creation of Israel. In his book about his father, Ramzy Baroud records, 'The ethnic cleansing of Palestine began . . . in December 1947 . . . [when] Zionist attacks on Palestinian areas resulted in the exodus of 75,000 people.' His father's town of Beit Daras 'came under heavy shelling in the first week of the war. The heaviest shelling was on March 27–28 1948 killing nine villagers and destroying large areas of the village's crops.' The first meeting of military commanders from the surrounding Arab states didn't even take place until 30 April, when they 'agreed to send three divisions . . . but only when the British Mandate ended on May 15th'.

These massacres (and rapes, which Morris also documented) meant Jews living in Arab countries would be driven out in retaliation – so why did Jews who had suffered genocide embark on ethnic cleansing? Zionism was conceived at a time when the concept of racial superiority was normal. The English had no doubt about their innate superiority, Germans believed anyone of German blood should be gathered into one great German nation, scientists hypothesised a hierarchy of races, many believed in sterilising the poor to improve their nation and in segregated America even in the 1950s interracial marriage with someone of Japanese origin was still illegal in California.

Born in a world where belief in race and blood was deep-rooted, the founding father of Zionism Theodore Herzl feared that anti-Semitism was inevitable, so his solution was the creation of a Jewish state to receive refugees. In his 1949 autobiography Chaim Weizmann, the first president of Israel, wrote in language that now sounds incredible that attempts to prevent Jewish refugees coming to Britain 'were natural phenomena . . . Whenever the quantity of Jews in any country reaches saturation point, that country reacts against them . . . this cannot be looked upon as anti-Semitism . . .'

Although Palestine was home to a thriving Arab community the Zionists spun the line that they were 'a people without a land' seeking to settle a 'land without people'. Once he had won the war, Ben-Gurion bragged, 'not one refugee will return. The old will die. The young will forget.' Now Israel's propaganda became the assertion that 'there are no Palestinians', merely Arabs who should be absorbed by the neighbouring states. When I visited Israel in 1986 I remember opinion polls showing that over 40 per cent of Israelis wanted to forcefully remove the remaining fifth of the population that was Arab. I told the Board of Deputies it would be easier to achieve peace if Israel comes to terms with the crimes committed at its birth. Sadly anyone questioning the injustice done to the Palestinians is denounced by hard-line supporters of Israel as anti-Semitic. Even the renting of a church hall by a Palestinian group in Britain to commemorate the Arab expulsion would be criticised in the *Jewish Chronicle*. Any Jew who questions Israel is dismissed as a self-hater or self-loathing Jew. My meeting with the Board of Deputies resolved nothing so we helped establish the London Jewish Forum to concentrate on issues where we could work together to improve life for London's Jewish community rather than endlessly debate the Middle East.

My problems on this front soon got worse. To celebrate the twentieth anniversary of Chris Smith coming out as the first openly gay MP we held a reception at City Hall. The *Standard* routinely ignored receptions at City Hall so I was surprised to find a photographer and reporter standing outside as I left. Smiling, I pointed out they had enough photographs of me and walked on. As the reporter announced he was from the *Standard* I joked:

'How awful for you. Have you thought about getting treatment?' Instead of recognising that I didn't want to be interviewed he pursued me, repeatedly barking the same question until he added, 'I'm only doing my job.' As I had told many journalists, I said that this was the standard defence of a concentration camp guard. He then said that he was Jewish, so I told him he shouldn't be working for the *Standard*. As the phrases 'behaving like a concentration camp guard' and 'jumped-up little Hitler' are common jibes in Britain, no journalist had ever complained before and I forgot about the matter.

Veronica Wadley went to work. To get it into the public domain, the transcript of my exchange with the reporter, whose name was Oliver Finegold, was leaked to the *Guardian*, where it was given the couple of paragraphs it deserved. The next morning the *Today* programme interviewed the chair of the Board of Deputies, who linked my comments to the rising tide of anti-Semitic incidents in Britain and Europe and wailed, 'Can nothing be done about this man?' Anti-Semitic incidents were indeed soaring in Britain and Europe but the BBC did not report that they had declined in London since I had been elected.

The *Standard* appeared with the headline 'Outrage at racist outburst by Mayor' and a double-page spread demanding that I apologise. The press kept the story going over the weekend until I was due to answer questions from the London Assembly. I said that 'if I could in anything I say relieve the pain anyone feels I would not hesitate to do so but it would require me to be a liar. I could apologise but why should I say words I do not believe in my heart?' For the first time seating arrangements were reversed so my back was towards the public. City Hall officials said Brian Coleman, the Tory Assembly chair, had instructed them to do so. The *Standard* said I had deliberately snubbed Holocaust survivors in the gallery by sitting with my back to them.

Acres of news space were devoted to demands for me to apologise. With the arrival of the IOC team for a three-day evaluation of London's bid, the press hypocritically ramped the story up while warning that my failure to apologise could cost us the Olympic Games. I said I wasn't going to discuss the issue while the IOC visit was under way but at Number 10 the Canadian IOC delegate Paul Henderson said, 'I don't think you should apologise,' and the Singapore delegate Ser Miang Ng was horrified: 'Your press are so disrespectful.' No other IOC member ever raised the issue and Israel's delegate Alex Gilady voted for London.

Over the next week the *Standard* filled page after page with the story, but a few voices of dissent broke through. Albert Scardino (the *Guardian*'s executive editor) said, 'It is past time for some high public official to stand up to the press rather than pander to it.' Andrew Alexander in the *Daily Mail* said, 'The issue has become one of freedom of speech . . . it does British Jewry's reputation no good to have the Deputies leading a campaign against freedom of speech [which] means . . . the right to irritate, annoy, dismay and shock.' Richard Ingrams in the *Observer* wrote, 'When it comes to sensitivity to attack, there is no one so sensitive as a journalist . . . [they] make a living from heaping abuse and ridicule on [those] whom . . . they do not approve . . . I urge [Livingstone] to stand firm.' Peter Hitchens in the *Mail on Sunday* said, 'Ken Livingstone is a cunning, nasty, narrow-minded, anti-British bigot who has done more damage to this country than almost anyone living . . . But it was not racist. Nor was it anti-Semitic. Nor should he apologise for the incident.'

Even firmer was the *Telegraph*'s Boris Johnson. 'Ken, whatever you do don't apologise . . . I speak as one who has been caught up in the modern mania for apology . . . it would be a surrender to media bullying . . . these words were not in themselves anti-Semitic . . . we have powerful newspapers that like to find some offence and then screech.' Both Blair and Tessa Jowell asked me to say I was sorry but I couldn't walk down the street without people urging me not to.

The media assumed I would give in and were shocked when I said at my weekly press conference I wouldn't. Adding:

No one in Britain is less qualified than [the *Daily Mail*] to complain about anti-Semitism. Their papers were . . . the leading advocates of anti-Semitism in Britain for half a century . . . even after the start of the Second World War they felt free to peddle the lie that Germany's Jews had brought the holocaust upon themselves. [While they] no longer smeared Jews as bringing crime and disease to the UK, it is only because they have moved on . . . pandering to racism against our citizens of black and Irish origin, they have now moved on and describe asylum seekers and Muslims in similar terms . . . The victims may change but the intolerance, hatred and fear pervade every issue of the papers. What was the motive of the Mail Group in whipping up this media firestorm? If the . . . journalist had expressed regret for his behaviour on the street I would have been happy to withdraw my comments and assure him I bore him no hard feelings.

Is it the case that . . . my words were so offensive they should never have been uttered? The *Jewish Chronicle* does not think so . . . on 7 February 2003 they published a letter accusing professors Hilary and Steven Rose of being Kapos (concentration camp inmates serving as guards). The Roses complained to the *Jewish Chronicle* and the Press Complaints Commission . . . [who] rejected the Roses' complaint . . . clearly the *Jewish Chronicle* . . . did not feel that this term diminished the holocaust. [For] an example of an inappropriate use of the term 'holocaust', we need look no further than the *Daily Mail* writer Quentin Letts, who described Labour MP Andrew Dismore as a 'holocaust bore' . . . Over the last two weeks my main concern has been that many Jewish Londoners have been disturbed by this whipped-out row . . . But . . . abdicating responsibility for one's actions by the excuse that 'I am only doing my job' is the thin end of an immoral wedge that at the other extreme leads to the crimes and horrors of Auschwitz, Rwanda and Bosnia . . . I have been deeply affected by the concern of Jewish people . . . that my comments downplayed the horror and magnitude of the holocaust.

I wish to say to those Londoners that my words were not intended to cause such offence and my view remains that the holocaust against the Jews was the greatest racial crime of the twentieth century ... Over the past two weeks the Daily Mail Group have worked hand in glove with the Chair of the London Assembly and his Conservative colleagues ... who have tried to widen this issue to include my views about the policies of the Israeli government ... Most Londoners would be surprised to discover that I can be removed from office and banned from public life for five years for breaching the Code of Conduct of the Standards Board of England which says that councillors 'must treat others with respect'. It has always been my view that respect has to be earned ... This code is a threat to freedom of speech. I have lost count of the number of times I have been approached by Londoners over the last two weeks and have been urged very forcefully not to apologise ... Not for the first time ... the views of ordinary people on the street are overwhelmingly at odds with much of the media.

The *Standard*'s Valentine Low wrote, 'I do not think I have ever seen such a loathsome fundamentally dishonest set of evasions and half truths.' In the same paper Norman Lebrecht wrote, 'Livingstone has stoked anti-Semitism in this city more than any politician since Oswald Mosley' and Trevor Phillips's CRE announced they were joining the Board of Deputies in referring me to the Standards Board. Months would pass before the issue was resolved and I was exonerated.

*

Sir John Stevens had restored the morale of the Met, rebuilt police numbers, reintroduced neighbourhood patrols and overseen the first consistent fall in crime in fifty years. The press loved his bluff, no-nonsense style and he retired in January 2005 to a chorus of approval. When I met with Met Police Authority Chair Toby Harris and Home Secretary David Blunkett we briefly considered former New York commissioner Bill Bratton as his replacement, but he came from a different legal system and had only just become commissioner in Los Angeles. It took only a few minutes to agree that Sir Ian Blair, the outstanding officer of his generation, was the obvious successor so we agreed Toby would proceed with the formalities.

Tony Blair's re-election in 2005 was no such formality and I was sent to the marginal seats. His miscalculation of the public mood over Iraq had made it tough going, with the Tories setting the agenda and Blair fighting for every vote. On *Ant and Dec's Saturday Night Takeaway* Blair was interviewed by the Geordie hosts, whose questions included 'Are you mad?' and 'If you make an ugly smell do people pretend not to notice because you are prime minister?' In the *Sun* Cherie praised Tony's fit body and hinted they had sex five times a night.

Only one adult in five voted for the government so the press proclaimed it a poor result. Blair had a majority of 66 seats on a vote down four million since 1997, despite a slightly improved turnout, but outside Britain, with three victories in a row, he was regarded as a commanding figure at the top of his game. That helped with the IOC vote, as did Seb Coe's immense standing in the IOC because of his refusal to join in Thatcher's boycott of the Moscow Olympics in 1980. Our third bit of luck was John Ross's contacts from his Moscow years. Everyone assumed the three Russian IOC members would vote for Paris but Mayor Luzhkov who controlled the remaining Olympic venues had huge influence on the Russian members. On a visit in early 2005 John realised we could win these three votes so went back with Keith Mills from the organising committee to pitch for their support. Keith now calculated we were a few votes ahead of Paris. It was essential not to alert Paris so Keith, Seb and myself told no one except Blair, who was to meet President Putin the following week. On his return he recalled Putin's opening line: 'I understand we are voting for London.'

Following the Salt Lake City Winter Olympics scandal where IOC delegates were paid money for their votes IOC boss Juan

Antonio Samaranch had introduced rules to prevent corruption which were rigorously enforced by his successor Jacques Rogge. IOC members were banned from visiting candidate cities on business or pleasure trips without IOC permission. Other cities had bribed delegates in the past. When I asked one mayor how his city had won a previous bid, 'given your laws on local government corruption are as tough as ours', he replied: 'I couldn't be involved so we left it to local businessmen to deal with that.' That said, Seb, Keith and I never once felt any IOC member was angling for a pay-off.

*

Before I left for Singapore in June 2005 for the IOC vote MI5 boss Eliza Manningham-Buller came to discuss the terrorist threat and how we would respond but after my allegations about MI5's dirty war in Northern Ireland in the 1970s the meeting had a surreal quality. I expressed surprise that since 9/11 we had prevented any attack on London and said, 'I'm beginning to think we might get away with it.' She cut me off with 'No, it's extremely serious out there.' As I reminisced about the KGB agent Yuri Sagadak Eliza schoolmarmishly asked, 'Did you notify MI5 about these approaches?' and was a bit put out when I said, 'I thought it would be a waste of time as you were bugging my phone.' I didn't believe her when she insisted that MI5 would never have done that and said I often picked up the home phone immediately after finishing a call and heard a playback of my conversation. However, given the *Guardian*'s 2009 exposé of phone tapping by newspapers, I may have blamed the wrong culprit.

I arrived in Singapore to find our slick operation in full swing. The UK High Commission threw everything behind the bid, which was running without a glitch. One of Seb's team was always at my elbow to brief me on IOC people as I prowled the lobbies and bars. Mike Lee had organised a slew of press conferences in which David Beckham stole the show with his 'bringing the games to my manor' line, and days were spent rehearsing our presentation. Barbara Cassani's inspired choice of David Magliano to head our marketing paid off when he found New Moon, a small film company, which produced the most shamelessly tear-jerking advertising pitch I've ever seen. Four adorable kids are shown catching a glimpse of the London 2012 games on their televisions and then go on to become Olympic champions themselves. Everyone who watched it was moved to tears.

Tony Blair was due to open the G8 summit in Gleneagles on the day of the vote but when Seb, London 2012 chair Craig Reedie and I went to see him, he simply said, 'What do I need to do?' We gave him a list of foreign leaders to phone but when Jacques Chirac said he was going to Singapore Blair said he would go too. Paris was on first so Chirac could address the IOC and still arrive in time for the G8 but London was on after lunch so Blair would have to do a video. Seb and Keith Mills had identified 35 of the 115 delegates we thought could be swung by one-to-one meetings with Blair, so between the press conference and working the receptions, Blair saw each of them in his hotel suite for a fifteen-minute chat. Given politicians' prima-donna tendencies, Blair earned my real respect as he sweated through two and a half days of this. Chirac flew in the night before the vote for the evening reception but he had lost a referendum and was beset with allegations of corruption and had the smell of death about him. People at the reception were more interested in meeting Victoria Beckham. Chirac's comment that 'the only worse food than British food was Finnish' antagonised the two Finnish delegates, but they were already voting for us.

Five cities were in the running: London, Paris, Madrid, New York and Moscow. There would be four rounds of voting, with the lowest-polling city eliminated each time. We knew it would be close but London was still the outsider and bookies' odds were so good I was tempted to borrow some money and bet on London but worried about charges of insider trading. There was a last-minute worry when we heard that Luc Besson and Steven Spielberg had directed videos for Paris and New York and Juan Samaranch was using his influence to swing support behind Madrid. John Ross and Neale went with me to meet Luzhkov in his hotel, where, without asking for anything in return, he said in the final ballot Moscow's votes would come to London. Samaranch had promised to switch some of Madrid's votes to Moscow on the first ballot so they were not humiliated and in return Moscow's votes would go to Madrid until they were eliminated. Unlike London and Paris, Madrid had no block of 'anti' votes to contend with, so we knew if Madrid knocked out Paris they would beat us in the final ballot.

For Luzhkov respect was important and we ensured he would have a meeting with Blair, who describes it in *A Journey*:

. . . the Russian delegation came in to see us, led by the mayor of Moscow. Ken Livingstone told me mysteriously that they were close, and that they had an understanding. He didn't give details and I thought it better not to ask. They trooped in looking very Russian . . . They sat down heavily, and looked at me. I looked at them. Then they smiled knowingly and nodded. Ken . . . looked at me and we both nodded at them. The nodding went on for some time until a conversation began that was, for me at least, entirely elliptical. The gist of it was that we all understood each other very well, that they were very true to their word and so were we, and they didn't like people who weren't (I got a bit uneasy at that). But since they were and we were, there was no need to say any more. After another round of knowing smiles and nodding, they trooped out. 'What the hell was all that about, Ken?' I asked when they had left. 'Don't worry your pretty head about it,' he said. 'I think it went well.'

Annoyed that so many cities, after winning the games, then wanted to revise their commitments, the IOC insisted that each bidding city sign the contract the day before the vote. As Craig Reedie, Simon Clegg and I signed the thick document we discovered that New York was refusing to sign because they wanted a bigger share of the television rights. Rogge warned that New York would be barred from the vote if they didn't sign and they gave in, but there was resentment as the Americans had pulled this stunt before.

I had joked I would be the last mayor standing in the hotel bars but was surprised how little the other mayors hung around. The rules meant I couldn't buy IOC delegates drinks but they got to know I would be easy to work with. On the night before the vote at a small party for IOC delegates who were campaigning for London (that, strangely, wasn't against the rules), I told Blair we should win but he was averse to counting chickens and rushed off to lobby one last delegate before catching his plane. I popped into the bar, where a Paris delegate told me that when Madrid was eliminated two-thirds of its votes would go to Paris, thus clinching victory. Knowing Madrid's votes would split equally between Paris and London, I told the BBC we expected to win by a few votes and staggered off to bed.

In the morning I felt detached as I showered while listening to the Paris bid and the hours dragged by in a combination of anti-climax and tension. I popped into Seb's room where he was amazingly relaxed, going over his speech and listening to jazz. As we waited to go in and deliver our presentation after lunch the stress was unbearable but it went perfectly. Seb spoke of inspiring youth and at the key point the young basketball player Amber Charles and thirty-six other East End kids of all complexions stood up, to much applause. In contrast to our rivals, politicians played a small role in the presentation except for Blair's video clip and another of Nelson Mandela endorsing our bid. Our emphasis was on athletes like Seb and the gold medal heptathlon winner at the Sydney Olympics, Denise Lewis, who wowed the (predominantly elderly and male) IOC members. After Moscow and New York were eliminated in the first two rounds I joined Keith, Tessa Jowell and Seb. We knew that if Madrid knocked out Paris they would win the final vote and we were elated when Madrid was narrowly eliminated in round three. There were hours to wait until the final ceremony so I went off for a swim.

As we filed into the hall to hear the IOC's decision we saw a huge crowd of television crews and photographers in front of the Paris delegation on the other side of the room and just three photographers in front of ours. Tessa and I sank into depression, convinced we had lost and that someone had leaked the result to the media. So much rode on the bid, with the possibility of changing the most impoverished part of London, that the thought of losing after coming so close was unbearable. As the ceremony dragged on I composed myself to cope with defeat, doing this so well that when Jacques Rogge announced 'The International Olympic Committee has the honour of announcing that the games of the 30th Olympiad are awarded to the city of . . . London' I remained grim-faced and rooted to the spot while everyone around leaped in the air and screamed. It wasn't until Denise Lewis sprang into my arms that I unfroze. Henry Kissinger came over and I made polite small talk while remembering how I had wanted him to die during the Vietnam war.

Seb and I broke away to commiserate with our opposite numbers from Paris. I knew Bertrand Delanoë had harboured the same hopes as I had for a run-down area of his own city and I felt genuinely sad for him as we hugged. The London delegation sailed off to a raucous party at one of Singapore's best restaurants while Seb and I spent an hour in back-to-back media interviews followed by the official contract signing with Simon Clegg and Craig Reedie. When Jacques Rogge and I exchanged the contracts he said, 'Enjoy tomorrow's newspaper coverage because after that it will be seven years of negative reporting before the games open.' Emma finally got through to me from a bar near London Bridge where GLA staff had gone to celebrate. She held the phone up so I could hear them scream 'We love you Ken' over and over again.

After the signing I went to the IOC's cocktail reception and commiserated with Alex Gilady, Israel's delegate, who was starting to get angry phone calls from Zionists demanding to know if he had voted for London. John Ross decided to miss his honorary doctorate ceremony at East London University as 'tonight's party will be the best I ever go to in my life' but by the time Seb, John, Princess Anne and I arrived everyone was plastered and we never caught up. Princess Anne had shown me the breakdown of voting and although we had finally won by 54 votes to 50, on the previous ballot Madrid with its 31 votes was only two behind Paris. If just two IOC members had switched and Madrid had got into the final round then they would certainly have won. Emma kept phoning from the different bars GLA staff had gone to, passing the phone round so everyone could scream their congratulations. I wanted very much to be in London. As I was about to leave, a British expat said, 'Mr Livingstone, I want you to come with me for the surprise of your life.' I said thanks but I was very tired. The man insisted: 'I want to take you to the best brothel in Singapore.' Usually there was always a press officer or member of staff with me to deal with situations like this but Matt the press officer was deep in conversation on the other side of the room and I couldn't see John Ross anywhere. Thanking the man for his kind offer, I went back to my hotel room where calls continued to come from increasingly inebriated friends and family. I lay on the bed channel-hopping to catch repeats of Rogge's announcement, overawed by the enormity of what we had won and knowing it would lock future governments into the transformation of the East End on a scale that would mean the benefits would still be flowing long after I was dead.

17

Tragedy

2005–2007

Next morning at breakfast there wasn't a Brit in sight. As I bounced into the press conference Mike Lee had organised, none of the other speakers was there until our triple-jump gold medallist Jonathan Edwards turned up. The early editions of the London papers that Thursday, 7 July, were overwhelmingly positive except for the *Daily Telegraph* – 'Victory party will leave capital with £4 billion headache' – and Alice Mills in *The Times* – 'You've got to be joking. £8 billion for years of misery and white elephants'. The *Mail* excelled itself with four articles. Edward Heathcoat-Amory demanded to know 'Who will pay for it all?' Tom Bower, Veronica Wadley's husband, asked, 'Golden cup or poisoned chalice?' Jonathan Foreman remembered 'Olympic cities brought to their knees by the games' and Alex Brummer warned 'Tube needs an Olympic effort'.

After an early lunch with Keith Mills I went off to buy presents for the family. It was morning in London and few of my staff were in early at City Hall but as I shopped on Orchard Road Joy Johnson phoned to say there was a power outage on the tube. As much of our tube infrastructure is antique I wasn't surprised, but having people trapped underground in July is dangerous. I cursed myself for not getting the last flight home the night before. John Ross phoned to say that his daughter had called to tell him something bad was happening on the tube and Joy called again to say that it could be bombs. I was desperate to get to the hotel but there was a huge queue at the cab rank. Fortunately an Australian reporter getting into a cab offered to drop me off. In the hotel lobby Simon Clegg was chatting to journalists so I took him aside and asked him to tell Seb there had been an attack and we expected many dead.

In my room the news channels were still speculating but speaking to City Hall I knew all the preparation had been worthwhile as our plans slipped into place. Our decision to devolve responsibility meant that no one was waiting for instructions to come down the line. Cleaning staff about to clock off turned around and took bottles of water down to the victims and just held and spoke to the wounded. Fearing she might be on her way to work, I phoned Emma but she was taking the morning off after a late night celebrating.

With everything working as planned I swam in the empty pool, finally deciding what I was going to say to the press about the attack. Back in my room John, Neale and my press officer Matt said local police feared a follow-up attack on the IOC headquarters and wanted Tessa and me to stay in our rooms. Watching television footage of the wreckage of the number 30 bus in Tavistock Square, I was surprised at the government's delay in admitting this was a terrorist attack. Had Blair been in Downing Street and I at City Hall there would have been a quicker public statement but with Blair in Gleneagles chairing the G8 and me sitting under police guard in a hotel room on the other side of the world the acknowledgement of what we were dealing with took longer than it should have. It was crucial that Blair and I said nothing to contradict each other so I waited until his press conference from the G8 was over before I went to speak to the journalists waiting in the lobby. After Redmond phoned with advice John, Neale, Matt and I took the lift down to the lobby where armed police had formed the reporters and camera crews into a square several layers deep. It felt like stepping into a brilliantly lit box lined with journalists.

After thanking the emergency services and TfL staff I continued:

I want to say one thing specifically to the world today. This was not a terrorist attack against the mighty and the powerful. It was not aimed at presidents or prime ministers. It was aimed at ordinary, working-class Londoners – black and white, Muslim and Christian, Hindu and Jew, young and old. It was an indiscriminate attempt to slaughter, irrespective of any considerations for age, for caste, for religion. That isn't an ideology, it isn't even a perverted faith, it is just an indiscriminate attempt at mass murder – and we know what the objective is. They seek to divide Londoners. They seek to turn Londoners against each other. I said yesterday to the IOC that the city of London is the greatest in the world because everybody lives side by side in harmony; Londoners will not be divided by this cowardly attack. They will stand together in solidarity alongside those who have been injured and those who have been bereaved and that is why I am proud to be the mayor of that city.

Finally, I wish to speak, through you, directly to those who came to London today to take life. I know that you personally do not fear to give your own life in exchange for taking others – that is why you are so dangerous. But I know you do fear that you may fail in your long-term objective to destroy our free society, and I can show you why you will fail. In the days that follow look at our airports, look at our sea ports and look at our railway stations, and even after your cowardly attack, you will see that people from the rest of Britain, people from around the world will arrive in London to become Londoners and to fulfil their dreams and achieve their potential. They choose to come to London, as so many have come before because they come to be free, they come to live the life they choose, they come to be able to be themselves. They flee you because you tell them how they should live. They don't want that and nothing you do, however many of us you kill, will stop that flight to our cities where freedom is strong and where people can live in harmony with one another. Whatever you do, however many you kill, you *will* fail.

Our planning undoubtedly saved lives and I had to take only one decision – whether to close the tube until Monday or run the maximum possible service the next day. Remembering tales of Londoners working through the Blitz we had to send the same message – this wasn't going to change the way we lived.

The police in Singapore were so concerned about another attack that Tessa and I weren't merely given outriders to the airport – every street was closed and emptied as far as the eye could see. We waited in silence in the VIP lounge with the High Commissioner and his staff where a few days earlier we had gossiped in anticipation of the vote. Once safely on the plane, our take-off was delayed until the pilot announced that the plane was unable to fly so we had to catnap in the business lounge until the first plane out in the morning.

*

I stepped off the plane at Heathrow to be met by the young Sean Connery lookalike who had provided me with armed protection after the office fire. When I asked if this was necessary he said, 'Your speech in Singapore makes you a target.' Simon Fletcher was waiting by the bulletproof car and briefed me as we sped back to London. When we hit a traffic jam the car mounted the pavement to drive round it. 'When the Commissioner says he wants to see you as soon as possible he means it,' said the driver.

I so wanted to see Emma and the children but there were briefings to bring me up to date and the news that Thelma Stober, one of my staff who worked at the LDA, had lost a leg in the bombings. The police were viewing all CCTV footage from the entire tube system to identify the bombers and their route as we didn't know if they had escaped to kill again. The new chair of the London Resilience Committee, Oldham East and Saddleworth MP Phil Woolas, complained that Sir Ian Blair wouldn't let him speak at the press conference and begged me to change his mind. Not unfairly, Sir Ian pointed out nobody knew who Woolas was. I wanted the clearest message of reassurance to avoid anything that might trigger a backlash against the Muslim community and, given Woolas's tendency to pander to the right, I backed Blair's decision.

Sir Ian, just five months in the job, was reassuring and detailed as he briefed journalists. I suspected the bombers' motivation was Britain's participation in the invasion of Iraq but the important thing was to hold London together rather than row with the prime minister so I said at the press conference:

All races and creeds and colours have come to this city where you can be yourself as long as you do not harm anyone else. You can live your life how you choose to do, rather than how anyone else tells you to do. That is what I think the bombers seek to destroy. They fear that. They fear a world in which the individual makes their own life choices and their own moral judgments. That is what they seek to snub out. But they will fail. I say to those who planned this dreadful attack, whether they are here in hiding or somewhere abroad, watch next week as we bury our dead and mourn them. But see also, in those same days, new people coming to this city to make it their home, calling themselves Londoners and doing it because of that freedom to be themselves.

Remembering that this week had begun with the huge Live 8 gig in Hyde Park through to winning the Olympics and Thursday's atrocities, I had no doubt these 'have been seven days no one will ever forget . . . Winston Churchill in his history of the Second World War titled the final volume *Triumph and Tragedy*. I think that typifies these seven days as no other sentiments could.'

After what seemed the longest day of my life, I was driven home but the children were asleep so I just stood looking at them, thankful they were safe. The next day in the playground they didn't notice my protection unit. The key image to send around the world was of me travelling on the tube to work, then it was on to visit hospitals to thank the staff and meet the survivors, going to mosques to re-assure a nervous community and inspecting the tube stations and Tavistock Square. The only victim I knew personally was Thelma.

As she talked in hospital about coming back to work I had nothing to say that matched her courage.

One of the surgeons at the London Hospital who operated on one victim after another said she had got through the day by focusing on her work but when she'd arrived home and seen my Singapore speech she had broken down. Like her, I only kept control by focusing on my role and as she spoke I felt the emotions I had buried start to take over and said, 'I'm sorry, I can't talk about it.' I still weep at the memories, but in the aftermath I didn't have that luxury.

*

Within twenty-four hours we had a reception centre in central London to provide advice and support and Tessa Jowell spent days there meeting victims, friends and relatives. In previous tragedies legal problems prevented victims and relatives getting payouts quickly from fund-raising appeals so years before I had asked Anthony Mayer to work with Howard Carter, head of law, and Anne McMeel, our director of finance, to ensure that the charity we had set up to receive donations could respond rapidly. Victims had money within a fortnight and all the money raised was paid out over the first year. Blair was so impressed by this compared to the snail's pace of the Criminal Injuries Compensation Board that he ordered it to pass part of its funding to us so that the money could be distributed quickly.

Police leave was cancelled and we called in officers from across the UK to have an overwhelming presence on the streets, both to deter further attacks and prevent any backlash. Harry Barlow devised the 'One London' campaign and the advertising industry gave it £3 million worth of space. The *Standard*, to its credit, helped us plaster London in banners emphasising the unity of the world's most diverse city and reprinted my Singapore speech which people displayed in their windows and at work. In the next three weeks the only incidents reported were one of graffiti in Stratford saying, 'Kill all the Muslims' and at a National Front march a man shouting abuse at a Muslim woman.

I started visiting the sites to meet staff but just as Bob Kiley and I were about to go into the tunnel at Edgware Road I was called back to Scotland Yard where the deputy commissioner, Paul Stephenson (three months in the job), told me what we most feared: the bombers were British.

As I went round the city meeting victims and relatives I was often asked to speak and sign books of remembrance. At the first of these what came to me was 'The city will endure. It is the future of the world.' We decided to commemorate the victims – one week after the bombings – in Trafalgar Square. Twenty-five thousand people came. As well as Denise Lewis and celebrities including Keira Knightley and Davina McCall, all faiths were represented including Chief Rabbi Dr Jonathan Sacks and Richard Chartres, the Bishop of London. The weather was perfect. The writer Ben Okri walked to the lectern and opened the evening by reading his poem 'Lines in Potentis', which celebrates London:

> One of the magic centres
> Of the world;
> One of the world's
> Dreaming places.
> Ought to point the way
> To the world.
> Here lives the great music
> Of humanity
> The harmonisation of different
> Histories, cultures, geniuses,
> And dreams.
> Ought to shine to the world

And tell everyone
That history, though unjust,
Can yield wiser outcomes.
And out of bloodiness
Can come love
Out of slave-trading
Can come a dance of souls
Out of division, unity;
Out of chaos, fiestas.
City of tradition, conquests,
And variety;
City of commerce and the famous river,
Tell everyone that the future
Is yet unmade.

. . .

Let the energy of commerce flow,
Let the vision of art heal.
Technology, provide the tools.
Workers of the world
Re-make the world
Under the guidance of inspiration
And wise laws.
Create the beautiful music
Our innermost happiness suggests.
Delight the future.
Create happy outcomes.

. . .

I want to tell everyone
Through trumpets plated with
The fragrance of roses
That a mysterious reason
Has brought us all together,
Here, now, under the all-seeing
Eye of the sun.

Seb and I walked out on stage together. I said that for Londoners during the Blitz a day in which 'only' fifty-two people had died
would have been a good day. 'We see the world gathered in one city,
living in harmony, as an example to all . . . People the world over
yearn to come to London to study, to work, to realise their dreams.'
I quoted Pericles, the first mayor of Athens over 2,000 years ago,
who said, 'In time all great things flow to the city, and the greatest of
those is the people who come.' Applause swelled from the audience
as I said the bombers hoped 'we would turn on each other like animals in a cage and they failed. Totally and utterly. There are places in
the world where that would have happened, but not here.'

That week in City Hall we had hosted veterans of the Second
World War and I recalled their words:

They told me how we had six years of bombs and some nights hundreds
died, some nights thousands died but when they came back they were not
bitter. They came back determined to build a better world and they gave
my generation all the things they never had and we will do the same. With
this example let us rebuild a better city. Let us lift our hearts rather than
worrying about who to blame or who to hate . . . We will never think about
the Olympics to come without thinking of those who lost their lives . . . In
seven years' time when these games begin, sitting in the seats in the front of
that stadium, cheering the 200 teams that will come from every nation will
be those who have been maimed but survived, and the relatives of those who
died . . . There are some people who want to talk about a clash of civilisations
but that is a false choice . . . Come to London and see the world together in
one city, living in harmony as an example to us all . . . I would also like to
congratulate Londoners – no panic and an incredible response of stoicism
and discipline that contributed to minimising casualties . . . There are places
where such things could have unleashed internal strife and physical violence.
In London the city stood together and we have not had any problems . . .

Showing how London would not be divided, the whole crowd
applauded Iqbal Sacranie of the Muslim Council of Britain as he

started walking to the lectern. ITN's Trevor McDonald brought another wave of applause as he talked about his childhood in the West Indies and how he and his classmates had 'looked longingly at this great distant metropolis'. Murziline Parchment, who handled Special Projects (i.e. anything really difficult), took me to the marquees to meet bereaved relatives and survivors. Remembering the long pain after Dad's death, I couldn't say their grief would end quickly because it wasn't true and we wouldn't want it to be true. I don't know if I gave any comfort but I felt useless and too drained to go back to my staff so I walked up Charing Cross Road to get the tube home. Confident the threat was over, Young Sean and his team said goodnight and peeled away.

*

The *Daily Mirror* captured the prevailing mood: 'The terrorists . . . were not representative of the vast majority of Muslims. The right-wingers who already threaten retaliation must be disowned as swiftly as Muslim leaders in Britain disowned the bombers.' Not everyone shared this view. The *Daily Mail*'s Simon Heffer sneered: 'Ken Livingstone gave a fine theatrical performance . . . but what does it say about our great capital city that it has such a silly, stinking hypocrite as its figurehead.' In the *Daily Telegraph* Charles Moore complained, 'If the Metropolitan Police really believe . . . the words "Islam" and "terrorism" must not be linked, then we have little hope of catching the killers.' Moore attacked Yusuf al-Qaradawi, although al-Qaradawi had denounced the bombings as 'evil acts characterised by barbarity and savagery, which are condemned by Islam in the strongest of terms, for Islam is extremely clear about the prohibition of taking human life'. In the *Spectator* Boris Johnson wrote, 'Islam is the problem . . . to any non-Muslim reader of the Koran, Islamophobia . . . seems a natural reaction.'

On 19 July at my first press conference after the bombings I was asked to respond to Tony Blair's views (reported in that day's *Mail*) that 'Islam is the main motivating force behind the murderous attacks in both Britain and Iraq' and that he was 'frustrated by what he sees as politically correct attempts . . . to explain away the bombings as a political protest against the invasion of Iraq'. At a press conference with Afghan president Hamid Karzai, Blair said the terrorists were simply using the war as 'an excuse . . . Let's be clear. If it wasn't that, it would be something else.' When MI5 boss Eliza Manningham-Buller told the Chilcot inquiry into the Iraq war that the intelligence services had warned Blair the war would lead to terrorist attacks on British soil, I no longer believed Blair was merely guilty of self-deception.

I told the press that the continuing abuses of suspected terrorists by American forces at their detention camp at Guantanamo Bay and in Baghdad's notorious Abu Ghraib prison fuelled anger against the West and remembered that the US had funded fundamentalists to attack the Russians in Afghanistan. 'This has been a terrible legacy. This will all have some impact on how these young men's minds were formed. This particular strand of extremism was funded by the West in Afghanistan . . . we gave no thought to the fact that when they stopped killing Russians they might start killing us.'

An ICM poll showed two-thirds believed the London bombings were linked to the war in Iraq and a leaked report from British intelligence in the *New York Times* warned that events in Iraq were fuelling 'terrorist-related activities in the UK'. An MI5 report posted on their website concluded that 'though they have a range of aspirations and causes Iraq is a dominant issue for a range of extremist groups and individuals in the UK and Europe'. It was leaked that Blair was told by Foreign Office diplomat Sir Michael Jay 'in explicit terms more than a year ago that the prime minister's foreign policy was a key driver of Islamic extremism'. The *Guardian* warned, 'One of the most unhelpful aspects of the government's response since the London bombings is the stubborn refusal of Tony Blair, in spite of all the evidence to the contrary, to acknowledge there is any connection between the attacks and the war.'

Ken Clarke, who was campaigning for the Tory leadership following Michael Howard's announcement of his resignation in the wake of the May election defeat, accused Blair of making us a main target for Islamic extremists. David Cameron, the eventual winner when the campaign finally ended seven months later, made a facile comparison with appeasement of Hitler in the 1930s, saying, 'If only, some argue, we withdraw from Iraq, or Israel made massive concessions, then we would assuage Jihadist anger. That argument . . . is as limited as the belief in the thirties that by allowing Germany to remilitarise the Rhineland or take over the Sudetenland, we would satisfy Nazi ambitions.'

Any doubt about the motive of the bombers was resolved with the posthumous broadcast from Mohammad Sidique Khan, the ringleader of the 7/7 bombers. 'While your democratically elected government continually perpetuate atrocities against my people all over the world, your support of them makes you directly responsible.' Accusing 'Western citizens' of electing governments that committed crimes against humanity, he went on, 'Until we feel security you will be our targets and until you stop the bombing, gassing and torture of my people we will not stop – now you will taste the reality of this situation.' On the first anniversary of the bombings al-Qaeda released a posthumous tape from Shahzad Tanweer, the Aldgate bomber, warning that attacks 'will continue until you pull your forces out of Afghanistan and Iraq and until you stop your financial and military support to America and Israel'.

There was a torrent of stories in the right-wing press demanding the expulsion of a few extremist imams such as Omar Bakri. These imams had only handfuls of followers but now they were transformed into some of the best-known people in Britain by media coverage. Andrew Gilligan in the *Standard* warned that ordinary Muslim schools were in danger of becoming Islamist madrasas. Boris Johnson in the *Telegraph* wrote, 'I've already had enough about how perfectly normal these young men were . . . If these four young men were perfectly normal Yorkshire men then what the hell is happening to this country . . . We have drifted on . . . and created a multicultural society . . . in which too many Britons have absolutely no sense of allegiance to this country or its institutions. It is a cultural calamity that will take decades to reverse and we must begin now . . .' Jeremy Clarkson in the *Sunday Times* revealed a great deal about himself by stating: 'Ken Livingstone has explained over and over again that Britain is now a multicultural, multiethnic society . . . Of course I'm sure Ken's headquarters are a veritable pick and mix of ethnical diversity . . . but in my world things are rather different . . . Pretty well all my friends are white and well-off . . . The only diversity in the office where I work is that three of the staff are left-handed. As a result I never meet any black or Asian people. So in this country at least I have no black or Asian friends. Not one . . . And what's more, we never get mixed ethnic groups in the Top Gear studio.' Melanie Phillips in the *Mail* said I blamed eighty years of Western intervention in Arab lands and accused Britain of betraying the Arabs after the First World War by denying them freedom in order to control their oil. 'By this bizarre interpretation of history Mr Livingstone lined himself up alongside such enemies of this country as the radical sheik Omar Bakri Mohammed . . . and the extremist group Al Muhajiroun.'

Responding to this torrent of Islamophobia Blair announced a crackdown on radical imams and an anti-terror bill allowing suspects to be detained for ninety days. Home Secretary Charles Clarke won the approval of the *Sun* by being prepared to rip up the Human Rights Act and ban fifteen Islamic groups he accused of supporting terror. Under this bill it would have been a crime to support Nelson Mandela and the ANC in their struggle against the apartheid regime and some lawyers said it might have meant a prison sentence for me when I met Sinn Fein had it been in force then. Opposition to the bill mounted, particularly from judges, and Peter Clarke, the Met's head of counter-terrorism, warned that anti-terrorist measures, such as stop and search, needed to be focused properly or we would alienate the Muslim community. For the first time, Blair was defeated in Parliament.

*

While everyone else focused on the bombings, senior civil servants plotted to take over the Olympics. Not expecting us to win, they took little interest in the detail of the legally binding contract the BOA and I had signed with the IOC. The mayor of Athens had told me I should chair the London Organising Committee of the Olympic Games (LOCOG) to control demands for more money, but I was talked out of this by Craig Reedie and Simon Clegg, who said it would be impossible to combine the role with the mayoralty. The obvious candidate was Seb Coe, who was completely focused on winning and then delivering a great games.

During negotiations with the IOC I heeded the advice Gerry Robinson and Charles Allen had given me when I'd been looking for someone to lead the bid: avoid day-to-day interference by civil servants and ministers. So we invested full legal control in an Olympic board of just four voting members – the mayor, the sports minister (then Tessa Jowell), Craig Reedie as chair of the BOA and Seb as chair of LOCOG. Seb would oversee the running of the games including ticket sales and sponsorship, but construction of the site would be run by the Olympic Development Authority (ODA). As the government was putting up the money they appointed the ODA board, but John Prescott and I had already agreed the chief executive of the ODA would be David Higgins – a successful Australian businessman who built the athletes' village in Sydney and turned round the dysfunctional regeneration agency English Partnerships.

The papers for the first meeting of the Olympic board had been sent out by civil servants who ignored our IOC contract and substituted a committee of senior civil servants to manage the project. I was so furious I couldn't get to sleep and as we assembled in the foyer of Tessa's department the head of the Government Office of Commerce introduced himself with a little lecture about how the Olympics had to be ready on time and to budget. I asked how many projects he'd worked on during his civil service career had been on time and to budget. Everybody else stopped talking while we waited for his answer, which never came.

Realising this was going to be a poisonous meeting, Tessa nervously opened by saying senior ministers had met and were strongly in favour of the civil service proposals. Trembling with anger, I pointed out that we had a legally binding contract with the IOC, that it could be changed only by the unanimous agreement of the four voting members present and the IOC and I had no intention of allowing civil servants to screw this up like every other government project. My views were echoed more amiably by Craig and Seb. The civil servants held back, leaving Tessa to make one last plea to give the proposals a trial, but Craig, in his affable manner, gently pointed out he had no intention of doing so and Seb suggested we move on to the next item. None of the civil servants spoke to me after the meeting.

On the evening of 20 July I was at Scotland Yard for Sir Ian's reception to thank officers for their performance during the bombings a fortnight earlier. It was an emotional evening, the officers were rightly proud and I specifically thanked Peter Clarke, who was flying out with his family for a well-earned holiday the next morning. That day I was to visit the reception centre for the victims of 7/7 to coincide with the first payments from the charity fund but just as I started lunch in my office word came through of more attempted suicide bombings at Shepherd's Bush, Warren Street and Oval tube stations and on a number 26 bus at Bethnal Green. All four detonators went off without igniting their bombs and the police were at the scenes within three to four minutes.

Peter Clarke took the first flight back while we speculated why the bombs hadn't gone off and how long we had before the bombers struck again. This time the tube system was back in operation in time to take commuters home. There was no panic but almost an air of taking it in our stride. I said, 'It's no surprise we have had another attempt to take life . . . we will get through this,' but I worried there could be a devastating impact on tourist numbers.

The Met threw everything into identifying the bombers before they could strike again. Knowing we would inevitably track them down, they had nothing to lose. With the huge pressure to catch them quickly a series of errors led to the shooting of Jean Charles de Menezes at Stockwell tube station. I believe one cause of this tragedy was the decision more than a decade earlier to save money by buying police radios that didn't work underground. Had Cressida Dick, the officer in command, been able to stay in contact with her officers on the train there might have been a different outcome. The next morning I was in a friend's garden when one of Sir Ian's staff phoned to tell me Jean Charles was not in fact one of the bombers. I sat in silence, completely cut off from my friends who continued chatting, unaware of this devastating news. In most jobs you can correct a mistake but if a surgeon or an armed officer makes a mistake someone usually dies.

Jean Charles was really the fifty-third victim of the London bombings, but I was shocked at how some right-wing papers exploited his death to attack Sir Ian. These same papers had slavishly supported police and denounced civil liberty campaigners when innocent people had been killed in the past.

The four bombers were caught within a week without further loss of life but I had real worries how we would cope if there were more attacks in a short space of time. Fortunately the small networks of al-Qaeda supporters had taken such a battering that they didn't have the capacity to launch attack after attack. July 2005 was the most intense month of my life. I was exhausted and glad to be spending a quiet fortnight in Devon.

*

The government accepted the situation on how the Olympics had to be organised, and allowed me to attend the cabinet sub-committee chaired by Jack Straw (there was resistance to the precedent of a non-minister attending committees). I bid for the Olympics to kick-start the regeneration of the East End, which had been neglected for forty years. There were plans for a vast new shopping centre at Stratford but this was stalled because of land ownership disputes. Now we had won the Olympics we proposed that a shopping centre development should become part of the Olympic site which would allow us to compulsorily purchase all the land needed for both the shopping centre and the Olympics. After the Olympic park and shopping centre were finished in 2012 the land between the Olympic site and the Thames would be available to build 40,000 homes and premises for 50,000 jobs.

We wanted to cut costs by developing the Olympics in parallel with the new shopping centre at Stratford but the partners included David and Simon Reuben, brothers described in the *Standard* as 'asset strippers of the most ruthless kind', a comment to which they objected. The Reubens had held minority shareholdings in the Paddington Hospital redevelopment which failed, and at the White City shopping development where their partners bought them out. The same pattern was repeating at Stratford. Sir Robin Wales, the leader of Newham Council, had met with the developers but made no progress.

The fabulously wealthy siblings had made their money from the privatisation of the Russian aluminium industry, an area John Ross had avoided because it was too dangerous: several participants had been murdered and an investigative journalist had his throat cut. Ownership of the land was divided between several developers. This delayed the project and forced us to spend £600 million on compulsory purchase, which would have cost each council taxpayer £250 (we might have got the money back after we sold the site). We were now eight months behind schedule and although Prescott and Tessa were nervous I was not going to be held to ransom and persuaded the LDA to make a compulsory purchase order for the whole site. The Reuben brothers counter bid to buy out other members of the consortium and have the site developed by Multiplex, the firm that was over a year late developing Wembley Stadium.

Luckily Frank Lowy, a refugee from Hitler who fought on the Israeli side in the 1948 war, was even richer. With dual Israeli–Australian citizenship he was the world's largest owner of shopping malls and rated David Higgins highly. Frank had bought the Reubens out of White City and I wanted him to do the same at Stratford. Fortunately the Reuben brothers were intensely private. Simon had only once in his life been quoted by a UK journalist after being stuck in the same room and forced to pass the time of day with him. To get the issue into the media I made a crude personal attack on them, which was an unpleasant thing to do but it put the Reubens in the spotlight they hated. They sold out to Frank, making a comfortable profit. Frank worked with us so that the Olympics stayed on schedule.

Barrie Segal, the campaigner against parking fines, referred my comments regarding the Reubens to the Standards Board but his complaint was dismissed on the grounds that my 'intention in making the criticisms . . . was to send a clear message that the public authorities would act robustly . . . to secure the achievement of the games and the redevelopment of Stratford. I conclude that this was a proper purpose and that Ken Livingstone's criticism was proportionate . . . Ken Livingstone had good reason to be strongly critical of his understanding of the Reuben brothers' conduct . . . The mayor merely concluded that they were disruptive "asset strippers".' As David Reuben's son put it: 'People who called [Livingstone] racist and anti-Semitic got the wrong end of the stick. He knew exactly what he was doing . . . He had already made his decision over who he wanted to develop that site and he was doing his best to make them win.'

David Higgins fulfilled all our hopes. Construction firms didn't want to bid for Olympic work because of the press coverage they would endure so we only had one bid for the stadium, but as problems arose David always came up with inventive solutions to keep costs down. Taking on board environmental concerns, his specifications cut the amount of concrete and steel used in stadia by half.

Our original plan was to appoint Margaret Ford to chair the ODA board (as chair of English Partnerships she worked with Higgins and Prescott) but Prescott was wowed by Jack Lemley, who had overseen the building of the Channel Tunnel. To appoint at this level based on performance in an interview is a big risk. Better to find out everything about someone before you have a final meeting just to ensure there is the right chemistry. Inevitably Lemley trod on Higgins's toes and Tessa and I had to make it clear to him what his role was. I wasn't persuaded by his assurances but the issue became immaterial when he unfortunately suffered a stroke during minor surgery. Tessa let him leave without fuss and was rewarded with a stinging stream of criticism.

I wanted redevelopment of the whole lower Lea Valley down to the Thames over the next twenty years so it would be stupid to build infrastructure for the Olympics but have to come back later to upgrade it to develop the rest of the lower Lea. Infrastructure capable of coping with the whole site meant increasing the Olympic budget and Minister of Communities and Local Government Yvette Cooper was far-sighted enough to agree. Our estimate for the Olympics was £4.2 billion but we hoped the private sector would pick up a chunk of that, leaving the taxpayer with £2.9 billion to find. As we had no access to most of the site and a fully worked-up scheme would have cost over £200 million this could not have been justified, given our bid was a long shot. The Olympic Board reviewed the whole site, which showed costs had risen by £1.1 billion.

No previous Olympics had ever paid VAT but Brown insisted on charging £836 million for the work. He also added a huge sum to cover emergencies and cost overruns, taking the budget up to £9.3 billion: £8.1 billion to construct the facilities and the site – though we planned to spend only £7.1 billion (the other £1.2 billion was set aside for security and transport costs). Fearing the contingency would encourage contractors to inflate their bids, I fought a losing battle to keep it at £8 billion. Blair was furious, believing Brown was doing this in order to restrict public spending elsewhere. I was determined to honour the promise that Londoners would pay only 38p a week extra on their council tax bills for the Olympics and Blair backed me so the final tally was £6.2 billion of government grants (plus £250 million from the LDA, which was also government grant) and £628 million from London council taxpayers. The National Lottery put in £2.2 billion. Even when investors pulled out of the media centre and athletes' village the budget only went up to £7.2 billion and the ODA is planning to hand back £850 million that we never needed.

*

The government was very secretive about the medals target we hoped our athletes would achieve in 2012. After the best medals haul for years in Athens we thought it was just possible to overtake Australia and come fourth after China, the USA and Russia. The government was so nervous it only admitted to the target after an FOI challenge in 2006. To everyone's surprise we came fourth in the Beijing games in 2008.

I was co-opted to a second cabinet committee preparing legislation to increase the mayor's powers. The government's line had been that we should wait at least two terms before reviewing mayoral powers but the government now saw that one way to achieve national targets on bus use, neighbourhood policing or house building was to work with me so improvements in London lifted the national average. David Miliband was the local government minister with responsibility for the bill increasing mayoral powers. I'd known David since he'd worked in my outer office at the GLC during school holidays when he was sixteen. He was a really nice kid and I was also impressed by his intelligence and knew he had a great future in politics. He played cricket with Bill Bush, worked for John McDonnell and our paths crossed as he rose under John Smith and Blair.

I wanted responsibility for housing, skills, training and recycling (London boroughs had the worst recycling rates in western Europe) along with several smaller bodies. But more powers for City Hall meant less for civil servants in Whitehall so they used every obstacle they could find to block me. What shocked me about the cabinet committees I now attended was the pitiful progress towards decision making. Each minister came briefed by civil servants to defend their department's interests with the dimmer ministers reading their briefs word for word. Decisions were always put off for more reports and studies. With committees filling ministers' time everything in government took far too long. In

America cabinet ministers are executive heads of their department with powers to appoint and decide. In setting up London's mayoralty as Britain's first executive political post Blair took a small step towards a system he would have liked for himself.

*

The only thing not going well was the aftermath of the Finegold affair, my flippant remark to that *Standard* journalist who had pursued me after Chris Smith's celebration. The Standards Board for England (SBE) was set up when Blair removed the power of the District Auditor to disbar councillors. The Standards Board built a new industry of rules and codes about proper conduct and language in public life. Still smarting from their failure to get my scalp over the incident when our friend Robin Hedges had fallen over a wall, they now referred me to another quango, the Adjudication Panel for England (APE), which had the power to remove me after a sort of low-grade court hearing.

For my appearance at APE on 13 December 2005 I had with me Tony Child, the solicitor who exposed Shirley Porter's gerrymandering. Tony believed this hearing was a blow to freedom of speech and that SBE authority did not extend once I was off duty. I said I was on duty 24/7 but his view of the law prevailed.

The panel of highly self-regarding bureaucrats no one had heard of (none of them had ever been elected to anything) included the chief executive of East Riding Council who had been awarded a £36,000 pay rise for cutting services. The uptight officer from the Standards Board oozed loathing from every pore, refusing to make eye contact throughout the proceedings.

I was out with Tom and Mia when the panel announced my 'conduct was unacceptable, was a breach of the Code and did damage to the reputation of his office' and they were suspending me for four weeks in March 2006. According to Andrew Hosken there

were 'whoops at the *Evening Standard* and even some high fives'.
In a signed editorial Wadley described me as a 'liar, a hypocrite, a
coward and arrogant'. Given that the charge against me was rudeness and nothing else, she must have a permanent irony by-pass.
When Murziline phoned to tell me the result I was stunned and by
the time I got home with the kids the huge scrum of journalists and
cameras outside the house reduced Mia to tears.

Simon, Tony and I had discussed what to do if APE suspended
me for a token day or two. My instinct was to appeal to the High
Court but with the costs and time involved I reluctantly decided I
would accept a brief suspension. But by overreaching themselves
and going for a month, APE left me with no choice but to appeal.
They made it an issue of free speech and I gained support across the
political spectrum with Billy Bragg, Ralph Steadman and Arthur
Smith organising a letter of protest. Tony Blair phoned to say 'This
is just bloody stupid' and briefed the press that the government
was thinking of abolishing the SBE. In the *Mail on Sunday* Peter
Hitchens wrote, 'I loathe almost everything [Ken] has ever done …
[but] just because, for once, this form of thought policing has been
applied to someone many of us rightly despise does not mean it is
not a very dangerous precedent.' The *Telegraph* added, 'We are certainly no fans of the Mayor of London, whom we find profligate,
prolix and an insufferable busybody. But it is for Londoners to sling
him out.' The *Guardian* pointed out the Board's inconsistency as
they had cleared a Tory councillor for saying 'Jews run everything
in Britain and particularly America' on the grounds that 'he did not
commit a criminal offence'.

From the moment we arrived at the High Court my confidence
soared as Justice Collins said he sympathised with me for doubt-
ing the good faith of the *Evening Standard* and that I was entitled
to take the view that their politics were very much to the right:
'They have obviously troubled him in the past and he was using

somewhat extreme language which perhaps he would not have used if he had not been caught on the hop.' Then, looking straight at the SBE lawyer, he said, 'I don't want anyone to suggest Mr Livingstone is anti-Semitic. There has never been any indication of that. That is absolutely clear. No one can think he was making a remark like that because of anti-Semitism.' Although my remarks were 'clearly offensive and intended to be so' that did not make it a breach of the Code of Conduct. Sensing the way things were going, the Board of Deputies denied there was a witch-hunt against me, and alleged I was 'really just trying to spin this and create a smokescreen to justify what he did'.

The following day Justice Collins said he would overturn the suspension regardless of the outcome of my appeal against APE. 'I have made it clear the suspension will be quashed whatever I decide on whether the panel's finding was correct,' he said, warning, 'It is not an easy case. There are certain ramifications, whatever I decide, which will affect other matters.' Tim Morshead, barrister for the SBE, said my remarks risked stoking religious tensions. 'Remarks like Ken Livingstone's, if unchecked, tend to endanger public confidence in local democracy.'

Two weeks later Justice Collins issued his ruling, in which he noted that I 'had been the target of the *Daily Mail* in particular, which was owned by Associated Newspapers which also owned the *Standard*. Mr Livingstone loathed and despised [Associated Newspapers] because of its past record of pre-war support for anti-Semitism and Nazism and what he regarded as its continuing racist bigotry, hatred and prejudice.'

The judge found for me on all the points, saying, 'freedom of speech does extend to abuse'. He ruled the SBE had 'failed to recognise the real distinction between the man and the office' and that I was off duty at the time and therefore not covered by the disciplinary code. He decided I could not be held responsible for having to challenge a miscarriage of justice and awarded the £250,000 costs against the SBE.

After my struggles with the judges at the GLC I thought it damning that senior judges were now better defenders of liberal values than the Labour government. The Board of Deputies said they 'had never been seeking the mayor's suspension'. The *Standard* moaned that this 'costly and unnecessary legal action' would not have been necessary 'had Mr Livingstone simply apologised for his remarks at the time'. With the case behind us I held a reception for the London Jewish Forum at City Hall where I said I was sorry if anyone had been upset and hoped if people had problems with me in future they would speak to me first.

The Standards Board was brought to a standstill by this ruling. The *Daily Telegraph* agreed the SBE had 'quickly attracted a reputation for intrusion and snooping out of all proportion to the problem . . . wasting tax payers' money on frivolous and malicious complaints'. Noting that one councillor was 'placed under investigation for using a loud hailer in campaigning', it revealed that 'the Board now employs more than one hundred people and spends £10 million annually [in 2004, investigating] 3,836 complaints'.

My belief that however bad the odds you should hang on until your enemies make a mistake was confirmed and it demolished one of New Labour's anti-libertarian excesses in the process. Many of the MPs who voted to set up the SBE to supervise councillors were at the same time busy abusing their expenses.

*

Although I won re-election promising to extend the congestion charge westwards, Tory Kensington & Chelsea and Westminster councils fought it and the *Standard* barely let a day go by without predicting disaster if it came to pass. The Tories whipped up petitions and protests but the papers never reported that the organiser was Gordon Taylor, a GLC Tory from Cutler's day. Although reporting was one-sided, Londoners were less so, with 41 per cent in favour of the extension and 43 per cent against.

The *Financial Times* reported a 'detailed independent assessment [by Oxford and Cambridge Universities] of the costs and benefits of congestion charging . . . The original congestion charge . . . increased road speeds more than expected, leading to big gains for the travelling public. Other studies have also found the zone had a broadly neutral impact on business and could find no evidence that the charge had affected employment, the number of businesses, turnover or profitability of companies inside the zone . . . the research found that the benefits of the westward extension were likely to exceed the costs by up to 50 per cent.' After the extension, retail spending inside the zone increased at three times the rate in the rest of the country. Boris Johnson's polls in 2009 showed 41 per cent of Londoners wanting to remove it and 45 per cent wanting to keep it.

Tories on Westminster Council who wore 'Hang Nelson Mandela' T-shirts during the Thatcher years also opposed the erection of a statue of Nelson Mandela in Trafalgar Square. It was the idea of campaigning journalist Donald Woods, with Sir Richard Attenborough raising the money. Ian Walters, who did a bust of Mandela for the GLC which still stands on the South Bank, was chosen by Mandela to be the sculptor. I liked the idea of two Nelsons in one square but at the public inquiry Westminster produced Professor Glynn Williams, of the Royal College of Art, to dismiss Walters's work as 'a mere husk . . . an empty shell . . . an adequate portrait but nothing more. A run of the mill mediocre model.' In portraiture, he said, the quality of art is usually overlooked in favour of a good likeness. Williams didn't mention that he lost to Walters in a competition for a statue of Harold Wilson in Huddersfield. I showed the inquiry photos of Williams's model, saying that 'it looks like Harold Wilson has been dead for several days, is starting to decompose while emerging out of a large pile of dog mess. For ordinary people like myself we want the statue to look like the person. We do not want to have to find someone with an art degree to explain what we are looking at.'

The planning inspector ruled against us and although Prescott could overrule the decision he was nervous and opted for a meeting with council leader Simon Milton and myself at which Milton indicated that Westminster Council wouldn't oppose the statue's erection in Parliament Square, which finally happened in 2009.

*

Bob Kiley had turned TfL into the most effective service I had ever dealt with. The National Audit Commission and the House of Commons Public Accounts Committee heaped praise on the transformation of London's bus system under Peter Hendy. Passenger numbers were up by 50 per cent since 2000, making us the only city in the world to achieve a shift from car usage to public transport.

But tensions grew between Bob and his head of finance Jay Walder. I was surprised, as Bob had brought Jay from New York and theirs was like a father–son relationship. Now Bob wanted to reorganise the finance department but with a £6 billion budget I feared splitting the finance operation could see costs spiralling before we knew what was happening. Neither Bob nor I was prepared to give in.

Having insisted on appointing senior management and determining salary levels, Bob had built an incredibly successful machine and his top staff could have doubled their salaries in the private sector. With his record of managing infrastructure I wanted to keep Bob, who was also a good friend and whose experience of the American mayoral system had shaped my own view about London's version. I reluctantly decided to back him but my advisers strongly disagreed and I changed my mind. Bob simply said, 'When a mayor and his transport commissioner disagree someone has to go and it isn't the mayor.' Bob agreed to stay as a consultant as I wanted his help negotiating the next seven-year financial deal on the PPP, and his advice was crucial in my negotiations on Olympics costs.

I met TfL's head of corporate services to discuss replacing Bob but said no when she suggested employing headhunters. Between Tim O'Toole, Jay Walder and Peter Hendy we had three outstanding people all capable of doing the job and I saw no point in spending £100,000 to have headhunters dredge up a couple of names to pad out the list. She replied that we would be overwhelmed with applicants but after I publicly said I doubted anyone could match our three internal candidates few outsiders applied. Tim asked what I wanted him to do but he was crucial in handling the PPP nightmare so I asked him to stay with the tube. The full TfL board chose Peter and Jay was soon snapped up as New York's transport commissioner.

*

That autumn saw a real breakthrough on environmental issues. We had drawn up strategies to improve the environment but my powers to enforce them were limited. The 20 per cent reduction in carbon emissions inside the congestion zone was a key reason for extending the zone westwards and we wanted a low-emission zone to improve air quality. Polluted air cut Londoners' lives by an average of eight months and caused appalling rates of childhood asthma on busy roads. And by getting rid of polluting vehicles we could reduce particulate levels in the atmosphere (which help trigger cancer).

Nicky Gavron and I were frustrated at the government's slow progress in tackling climate change. Blair said the right things but did nothing to reduce carbon emissions. Mark Watts worked on schemes to reduce London's emissions and Nicky invited mayors of the world's largest cities to exchange ideas. Mayors of several big cities, including Beijing, came to City Hall in October 2005 and agreed to set up the C20 (representing the world's twenty largest cities) to exchange best practice and combine our purchasing power.

While governments endlessly debated implementing the Kyoto treaty of 1997 and what should follow it at Copenhagen, city mayors faced day-to-day environmental dangers. This frustration was palpable worldwide so the C20 rapidly grew into the C40 and as our reputation spread the Clinton Foundation asked to work with us to reduce carbon emissions. I jumped at this but Redmond feared that with the levels of anger against the US we might not persuade other cities of Clinton's good intentions. It was not just Shanghai and Beijing but Bertrand Delanoë in Paris who said to me, 'I only agreed because *you* asked.'

With the cities on board, Mark, Simon, Nicky and I flew to Los Angeles to sign the deal with Clinton and debate climate change at UCLA with the mayors of San Francisco and LA, Gavin Newsom and Antonio Villaraigosa. One faction in the Clinton Foundation phoned to say that Blair was in town and asked could he speak at our meeting but another faction said Blair was too discredited because of his closeness to Bush. After hours of argument between the rival Clinton factions (confirming all I had read about decision making in the Clinton White House) Blair's staff said he would come if it helped and in the end it caused no problems at all.

Security was overwhelming, with speakers held in separate rooms until we went on stage. Blair had just met Governor Arnold Schwarzenegger to talk about climate change and Clinton joked that Arnie's poll ratings collapsed when he acted Republican but went up when he stole Democratic policies. Clinton told the audience, 'The fate of the planet that our children and grandchildren will inherit is in our hands and it is our responsibility to do something about this crisis.' I said that 'former President Clinton and his foundation [made] a real impact on one of the world's biggest problems, Aids . . . this new partnership will rapidly accelerate cities' response to global warming. Our aim is simple – to change the world.' The audience gasped when I said I would introduce a £25 daily charge for SUVs entering the congestion zone and was delighted when I attacked President Bush as a climate-change denier and pointed out he was only elected because term limits barred Clinton from standing again. To my surprise Blair praised my 'courage in raising issues of discrimination' at the GLC, saying he had doubts at the time but that I had been right. As Clinton and I signed the agreement Blair joked, 'Don't get too used to this.'

Before the meeting no one had been terribly interested in me but as we came off stage there was enthusiastic talk of working together in the future before I was ushered away so Blair and Clinton could have a private meeting. Mayor Villaraigosa was flown to the Labour party conference to join me in a session on the environment with David Miliband, Douglas Alexander and Tessa Jowell. David and Douglas disagreed when I called for restrictions on the growth of air traffic and the press were briefed there was no question of Labour preventing working-class people flying off on holidays. But in fact the richest 18 per cent of travellers take over half of all flights and the poorest 18 per cent just one-twentieth. The number of flights by people earning less than £14,000 has fallen to just seven million a year but those taken by people earning over £29,000 had increased to thirty-six million under Labour. The government had also suppressed figures showing that pollution from airlines had increased 85 per cent in fifteen years. As David and Douglas spoke, Villaraigosa's staff asked Simon, 'Don't you guys have media training over there?'

Clinton used charm even more effectively than Blair, who usually had an air of slight reserve. With Clinton it was full-on, over-whelming and completely captivating, making you feel you were the most important person in his world and you had grown up together. In a strange parallel with Blair and Brown, Al Gore was much more uptight. I met Gore when he came to London campaigning on climate change and I was impressed with his grasp of policy but like Brown he relied on arguments rather than charm.

Working with Clinton had huge benefits. Ira Magaziner, Clinton's former chief of staff, recruited an enthusiastic team based in C40 cities working to Mark at City Hall and turned up to give the GLA £170,000 a year to pay them. At dinner Ira recounted the nightmare of working in the White House under constant attacks from the Special Prosecutor appointed by the Republican Congress to investigate fraud allegations against the Clintons during the time Bill had been governor of Arkansas. The investigation was funded by Congress, but no money was available to help Clinton's staff's legal costs so by the time Ira finished at the White House he was broke.

*

I was flattered when Nobel Prize winner Dario Fo, author of *Accidental Death of an Anarchist*, asked me to support his campaign to become mayor of Milan, saying I was his role model and he would introduce a congestion charge. A virulent critic of Italian premier Silvio Berlusconi, he also denounced Blair as 'very crafty and he would fit in perfectly in Berlusconi's cabinet ... both he and Berlusconi are very similar. They are horrendous liars who have cheated the electorate. Italy has been ruined by Berlusconi, he's nothing short of a spiv, a travelling salesman.' Dario's wife had once been kidnapped and raped by fascists angry at his plays. I made a flying visit to his rally in Milan in a packed sports arena. Dario spent the entire eight hours on the stage singing, dancing and speaking even though he was seventy-nine. Sadly he didn't win, but the new mayor did introduce a congestion charge.

*

London was over-reliant on finance and business services so we built up tourism, culture and the research work in our universities by promoting them abroad and helping with planning applications. We were too dependent on Europe and America, where growth seldom exceeded 2 or 3 per cent a year. I wanted Chinese investment and the stock exchange wanted Chinese firms to list on it. China grew by 10 per cent a year with India catching up fast so I wanted to sell London to them as a twenty-first-century city by promoting its cultural diversity, business and education opportunities. London also has the largest Chinese community in Europe. But London still had an image of fog, bowler hats and bad food so we brought together the tourist agency Visit London and the inward investment organisation Think London and London Higher, which promoted our universities. Shanghai and Beijing wanted links with London so John Ross worked with the Freud Communications agency over months to plan the trip, taking people from business, culture and sport including Peter Kenyon of Chelsea FC. He also enlisted girl group Girls Aloud.

In spring 2006 Seb and I flew the seventy-strong delegation to China where Freud Communications had organised a concert and exhibition to showcase London. The trip started disastrously when after the ten-hour flight Seb and I went to the Olympic countdown clock in Tiananmen Square. The journalists accompanying us had decided to make human rights the issue rather than investing in London, and lobbed the innocuous question 'What do you think of the Square?' Tired, I didn't see the trap, simply saying it was very big. Pushed to expand, I recalled the poll tax riots when a Waterstones shop was burned down. 'In the same way that Trafalgar

Square has had an interesting history and not always a peaceful one, there is a very clear parallel.' Shouting that no one had died in the poll tax riots, they demanded I condemn the Tiananmen Square massacre. I had had no problems raising issues like Tibet with the Chinese ambassador but they resented being lectured on human rights, given the US actions in Vietnam and Iraq.

Saying, 'There is no such thing as one country with a perfect record,' I recalled eleven people demanding the vote were hacked to death and 400 injured by troops at the Peterloo massacre in Manchester in 1819, troops shot fourteen civilians dead on Bloody Sunday and in the only complete genocide in history we wiped out the population of Tasmania by paying British settlers £5 for the head of every Tasmanian they killed.

The right-wing press always go berserk when reminded of Britain's record so the *Telegraph* headline was 'Tiananmen? No one's perfect, says Livingstone.' Under the *Daily Mail* headline 'Ken is a nasty, ruthless political thug with a temper' Littlejohn said I was on a 'tax payer funded . . . jolly', denounced the Tiananmen massacre but added 'if ever there was a case for sending tanks and flame throwers into Trafalgar Square it was during the poll tax riots'. With recent revelations that Germans were tortured and starved to death by MI5 in London after the Second World War I explained we were 'not in a unique place where we can lecture other people in the world with clean hands ourselves. We never had them. Also I don't ask the mayor of Berlin about the war or the mayor of Paris about the Albigensian crusades.' The press were also annoyed when I cancelled a photo opportunity at the Great Wall for more talks on inward investment.

Seb and I visited the Olympic stadium and Olympic village, where I had never seen so many people working on a site: there was one builder per square metre. At lunch with Beijing mayor Wang Qishan we agreed to encourage tourism, business, trade and

educational and cultural exchanges between our cities. As a former
Red Guard and banker he had no plans to be mayor until his predecessor mishandled the SARS crisis. Something was lost in translation when Wang said I was siting the Olympics in 'a backward area'.
I had warmed to Wang when we met in London, although Chinese
delegates on the IOC voted for Paris and he had doubts about the
congestion charge but now he was considering it once Beijing's new
underground system was completed.

The Great Hall in Tiananmen Square was filled with business
people who laughed as I said, 'I am here because I am after your
money'. Whether it was to list on the London stock market, take
over failing companies or find a base for their European operations,
'your contribution is very welcome and we assume you will bring
your culture with you – it adds to our city's creativity'. As well as
business deals we wanted to reach the wider public so Freud organised a London exhibition in an inflatable dome. When it was
wrecked during a savage storm the Freud team worked through the
night to rehouse it. I was on tenterhooks in case it wasn't ready but
as Wang arrived for the opening no one would have known there
had been a problem. He was interested in two bicycles in front of
a screen showing what London streets looked like as you pedalled
through them. I invited him to get on and to the horror of his officials he pedalled away so fast that he became the only Chinese
leader I ever saw loosen his tie.

On my last night in Beijing I dined with China's richest new
entrepreneurs and was struck by how different they were from
their Western equivalents. With their enthusiasm for knowledge
and ideas they saw themselves making history, not just amassing
wealth. Fearing the potential for a demagogue to win power, they
warned against democracy while so many lived poorer lives outside cities. Only men who owned property were allowed to vote
in Britain before 1918. Votes for all only happened in Britain once

the vast majority had a stake in society.

The next morning we flew to Shanghai – a city of eighteen million people – where the mayor had decided to build a tube system as large as London's in just sixteen years. With four years until the opening of the World Expo in 2010 it was on time. With trains twice the size of London's, we could show the press what Crossrail would be like. Tim O'Toole was impressed with the speed of development, size of the stations and comfort of the trains as we launched their version of Poems on the Underground.

In Beijing the pollution was so bad you couldn't even see where the sun was through the yellow smog. Traffic in Shanghai was worse than London and Mayor Han was considering road pricing when their tube system was completed. Shanghai's response is to build a new environmentally sustainable city at Dongtan. The British engineering firm Arup were working on the scheme and also on our plan for 1,000 homes in Newham.

By Shanghai the tone of the press had changed. For most it was their first visit to China and anticipating an impoverished, fear-ridden police state they were amazed at the energy and bustle. As we were rushed from event to event the loudspeaker in the police car leading the convoy ordering the public to get out of our way was universally ignored – hardly a people living in fear of the police. Now the journalists saw the possibilities of China and they no longer glazed over as I said China's economy had grown faster than any in history. I told the *Observer*'s Frank Kane, 'China is already the second biggest economy, in real terms, after the USA, and they might overtake the Americans by 2025 so we've got to integrate Chinese people into our economic system, not shut them out. Even with the excesses of the Great Leap Forward and the Cultural Revolution, Mao's revolution improved Chinese life for the better by ending feudalism and warlordism. Deng Xiaoping's reforms had lifted 300 million people out of poverty and China is on the way towards being a modern society. This is completely unlike what happened in Russia where a small number of people stole assets from the state. The Communist party in China hasn't allowed that to happen so what you're left with is not the communism of Mao or the capitalism of the USA, but capitalism with Chinese characteristics.'

The journalists looked a bit sheepish when I said what I thought about their stunt at Tiananmen Square. None of them still believed it was a waste of money to open offices in these cities. We got commitments of inward investment worth £21 million and were in discussions with over 200 Chinese firms by 2008. In Shanghai we put on a fashion show to highlight London's leading designers and Girls Aloud performed. Huge crowds turned up to see Li Yuchun, the winner of China's *Pop Idol*, and the BBC crew was delighted when she said she thought of me as a 'kindly grandfather'.

*

Blair's premiership was now unravelling. In 2004, knowing that a recent minor heart scare and the purchase of a home in Bayswater would spark a media frenzy, he tried to defuse the issue of his retirement by announcing he would fight the 2005 election but would go before the end of that parliament. Once again short-term media tactics overcame the reservations of everyone around him. The media interest would have passed in a week or two but now he had started a debate about when he would quit. Privately he hoped to hang on to the end of 2008, giving Brown a few months to settle in before the next election. At the Labour party conference, after his announcement, I told him and Cherie this was a big mistake because his authority would ebb away.

Winning both the 2005 election and the Olympics revived his standing but rows over his anti-terror legislation saw his poll ratings fall and there was a lack of direction in government as loyalists started sucking up to Brown and Blair was besieged by the cash-for-honours scandal. Since 1925 it had been illegal to sell peerages as Lloyd George had done but the Scottish Nationalists were alleging that donors who gave over £1 million had all received a knighthood or peerage. Labour's treasurer, Jack Dromey, had been kept in the dark about £14 million of loans raised by Lord Levy from twelve businessmen including the boss of Capita, a healthcare privatiser, stockbroker Barry Townsley (who gave £10,000 to Frank Dobson's campaign), Lord Drayson (who gave £100,000 before receiving his peerage and a further £1 million before the election) and the property developer Sir David Garrard (who gave £2.4 million to Blair's city academies). These loans got around laws that Blair himself introduced declaring that all donations must be published. All parties gave honours to big donors but this seemed crude and obvious.

The investigation was led by Deputy Assistant Commissioner John Yates, who always got the sensitive cases. He was sent to meet the family of Jean Charles de Menezes in Brazil and oversaw the identification of British citizens killed in the Boxing Day tsunami. He rooted out corrupt police and investigated Jeffrey Archer, Neil and Christine Hamilton, Paul Burrell and the *Who Wants to Be a Millionaire?* 'cough at the right answer' fraud.

Lee Jasper told me the police were surprised by 'obstruction' at Number 10 and asked me to mention it to Blair. I said I would but I didn't, deciding that for a Labour mayor who sets the police budget to discuss a case with a Labour prime minister under investigation would be wrong. I remembered *Tribune* editor Mark Seddon saying a Labour donor had been phoned by a senior official at Number 10 urging him not to give money to my 2000 campaign. If civil servants had illegally lobbied donors then anything was possible.

Any doubts evaporated as I passed Lord Levy and Jonathan Powell (Blair's chief of staff) in Downing Street on my way to see Blair.

They looked hunted and terrified as they whispered to each other but the decision to prosecute or not had been transferred from the police to the Director of Public Prosecutions. Officers were furious when the DPP announced there wasn't enough evidence to prosecute, as the police believed they had found a prima facie case that honours had been traded and had evidence of an attempt to thwart their inquiry. They had considered interviewing Blair as a suspect but were told he would resign if they did.

By the May 2006 council elections Labour's vote was in meltdown. It was as though the government had a death wish. The NHS cash crisis worsened and some hospitals faced bankruptcy with health secretary Patricia Hewitt flayed alive in interviews. The press screamed that Home Secretary Charles Clarke had wrongly released rapists and murderers. Councillors I canvassed with asked if the government knew elections were on or even cared.

The final blow was the revelation of John Prescott's affair with one of his secretaries, and Labour had its worst result in years. Blair might have hung on but for Israel's invasion of the Lebanon. With appalling disregard for civilian casualties as Lebanon was laid waste Blair stubbornly refused to call for a ceasefire. Tessa Jowell despaired: 'Tony is completely isolated on this. No one in the parliamentary party supports his position. Even I don't agree with him.' This was the final straw and MPs began plotting a leadership challenge with Glenda Jackson prepared to be the stalking horse. Facing the kind of humiliation Heseltine had visited on Thatcher, Blair bought a last few months by saying he would quit within a year.

*

I was surprised when President Hugo Chavez of Venezuela asked to meet me during a European trip to meet oil companies in spring 2007. After visiting Number 10 in 1998 he said he was a convert to Blair's Third Way (between left and right), but then took control of Venezuela's oil and used it to pay for free health care, eliminate illiteracy and provide affordable food and medicines. A quarter of a million people blinded by cataracts had their sight restored by Cuban doctors and he gave £9 billion to his poorer neighbours (twice what the US spent in the region), allowing Argentina to pay off its IMF debt.

Chavez warned Blair in a speech, 'You have no moral right to tell anyone to respect international laws, as you have shown no respect for them, aligning yourself with [Bush] and trampling on the people of Iraq. Do you think we still live in the times of the British Empire . . . ?' Downing Street tried to stop the visit by saying it was private and they wouldn't be providing protection. Sir Ian Blair ignored Downing Street and provided the protection required but when I invited him to the lunch I was laying on for Chavez he said his life would become impossible if he was seen there.

There was a huge crowd waiting at Camden Town Hall but when I heard one of Chavez's staff had been floored by a Special Branch officer I worried he might fly home. Fortunately he laughed it off. The proceedings were broadcast live to Venezuela and after speaking for an hour and a half he asked me, 'How much longer have I got?' Not expecting him to take another hour and a half I gaily replied, 'As long as you like.' I and the audience, which included Bianca Jagger and Tariq Ali, then sat enthralled as Chavez extended his talk to three hours without once referring to a note, quoting George Bernard Shaw, Edgar Allan Poe and Pythagoras. You can't do that without revealing yourself. Here was an ordinary soldier who never expected to be president, excited he could change people's lives for the better. Starting with a history of Latin America's struggle for freedom, his speech was filled with diversions such as his enthusiasm for angiograms, which hadn't been available to Venezuelans before he funded them. He had no problem being both a committed Catholic and praising Castro.

He went on, 'I want to humbly offer support to the poorest people, who do not have resources for central heating in winter,' like the cheap heating oil provided under a programme in the USA run by Robert Kennedy's oldest son. The next day I told him we didn't use much heating oil in London but if he cut the price of our bus fuel we could give half-price fares to a quarter of a million people on income support and in return for the £14 million we would send experts to advise his local mayors on modernising their cities. Tories boycotted the meetings with Chavez, in contrast to their long-standing fêting of the murderous torturer General Pinochet.

Describing George W. Bush as 'an assassin responsible for genocide', the president told us of the failed American-backed coup against him in 2002. Following his decision to increase tax on the profits made by BP, Exxon and Shell from 16 to 30 per cent, US Assistant Secretary of State Otto Reich met Venezuelan billionaires and shortly afterwards generals besieged the presidential palace. To avoid bloodshed Chavez surrendered to them, but his support among the poor made the generals uncertain the coup would succeed so they refrained from killing him. Chavez said that three Americans were flown in to do the job, but that when the three assassins entered the room the sergeant guarding Chavez either had a change of heart or suspected he would be killed to ensure that there were no witnesses. He pointed his gun at the assassins saying he would kill them if they didn't leave, which they did. As people poured out of the slums to protest many were shot by the army before the coup collapsed. Bush refused to condemn the coup.

When I asked why he had given up the army for politics he recalled the military forays in pursuit of 'terrorists' who were really just peasants protesting. As he held a dying soldier in his arms he realised the stupidity of soldiers and peasants killing each other and joined other officers in a failed coup against President Pérez in 1992. As he surrendered he made a speech which electrified the poor. On his release from prison two years later he threw himself into politics full-time and won the presidential election in a landslide in 1998.

*

I always knew my most difficult election would be 2008. We had increased fares to build the East London Line and a new DLR line to Stratford International, and to upgrade the North London Line, so people had already felt the pain, but the new lines wouldn't open until after the election. I had increased council tax each year to recruit 7,000 extra police and 4,000 community officers and although crime was coming down it would still be too high in 2008. But our policies were having an effect: London overtook New York as the world's leading financial centre and, though only a year had passed since the bombings, our tourism campaign made 2006 our best-ever year for tourist numbers. I was reselected by the Labour party unopposed. My poll ratings were so high that the Tories couldn't find anyone willing to run against me so they announced a primary open to all Londoners. DJs Mike Read and Neil Fox were floated along with Michael Portillo, Zac Goldsmith, Jeremy Clarkson, Carol Thatcher, Sir Alan Sugar and Margot James, the first lesbian vice-chair of the Tory party, but only the actor Tom Conti came forward so they put off making their selection for a year. Veronica Wadley invited Seb Coe to lunch to persuade him to stand but he was committed to the Olympics. The press said that Brian Paddick might stand for the Lib Dems. Peter Stringfellow said he'd like to be mayor, 'but it does seem four years of very hard work so maybe I'd leave it to Ken Livingstone after all. He's not doing a bad job,' adding, 'I need all my energy for my twenty-four-year-old fiancée. I still think Jeffrey Archer would have made a brilliant mayor. He's been to prison – so what?'

The bill giving the mayor new powers lost momentum as Blair's power waned and David Miliband moved to Defra. David urged me to 'hold Ruth's feet to the fire' until she devolved real power over skills and training. He was referring to Ruth Kelly, the Secretary of State for Communities and Local Government. To get the rather reserved Ruth away from her civil servants I took her to the Cinnamon Club in Westminster and couldn't resist ordering a bottle of 'Nine Popes' wine for this devout Catholic but only managed to agree a messy compromise.

To improve the environment I set up Capital Standards, a unit that trained 600 borough council officers to crack down on littering, fly tipping, abandoned vehicles and graffiti, but five Tory boroughs (Bromley, Barnet, Redbridge, Enfield, Kensington) refused to take part. To tackle London's poor recycling rate (Newham recycled just 2 per cent of its waste and the best only 34 per cent) I proposed 208 recycling centres across London so we could recycle 50 per cent of our waste by 2012 and eventually 85 per cent. I had negotiated with Margaret Beckett at Defra but three of her officials thought recycling was a waste of time, preferring incinerators which emitted almost as much carbon as coal-fired power stations.

*

While the haggling was going on David asked me speak in his South Shields constituency so Simon and I travelled up on the train with him, his wife Louise and baby son. We had a great time and I saw he had the potential to be Brown's successor, and with David replacing Margaret at Defra I thought I would finally get control of recycling in London. I was shocked when he fell into line with his officials' position. After urging me to demand devolution I couldn't believe he was now taking the advice of three officials he had known for just a few weeks on what was politically acceptable in London. Even Tory council leaders privately said they didn't mind me taking over recycling. When we met David's office was filled with officials but when I challenged the lies of his staff about the 'benefits' of incineration David sided with them, almost jumping out of his seat to say, 'Attack me but please don't attack my officials.' I replied, 'They are not your officials. They have their own agenda and they're laughing behind your back because in a year or two you will be gone and they will still be here.'

That meeting changed my relationship with David. Listening to David talk about 'my officials' I recalled my own naivety on Lambeth Council where I'd got too close to officials and forgot the politics, but this was a forty-one-year-old cabinet minister making the mistakes I had made as a twenty-six-year-old councillor. The Thatcher–Blair years saw marginalisation of local government so that politicians now went straight into Parliament rather than learning the ropes on a council. When I raised the issue of David's capitulation with Blair he smiled and said, 'You mean the officials got to him?' but did nothing about it. David approved a new incinerator that would take Hammersmith and Chelsea's waste by road all the way to Bexley. I worked with local Tory leader Ian Clement to challenge this in court but we lost. London still has the worst recycling rate in Europe, with inefficient incinerators pumping out carbon. I am sure the officials will be on the boards of incinerator companies when they retire.

David's junior minister, Exeter MP Ben Bradshaw, campaigned for incinerators (referring to 'energy from waste') without mentioning the word 'incinerator'. David increased carbon emissions further by opposing my decision to block a desalination plant on the Thames. Thatcher's public spending cuts had prevented Thames Water replacing leaky pipes for seven years. After privatisation the new owners shelved fixing leaks while they were cutting the levels of fertiliser nitrites in our drinking water to avoid EU fines. Now over a quarter of all London's water was leaking away but instead of increasing the rate of replacement of leaky pipes or building a long-planned reservoir on the Thames (from which water stored in winter would be released in summer) Thames Water wanted a desalination plant costing £200 million. I feared the plant, which would use twice as much energy as fresh water treatment and pump 25,000 tonnes of carbon dioxide into the air each year, would be the first of many. I challenged the application in court. A House of Lords committee agreed that the desalination plant would cause significant pollution. Desalination is the most energy-intense way of providing water and in the run-up to our judicial challenge it had become clear that a reservoir was both cheaper and not environmentally damaging. During the heatwave of 1976, when I was chair of the GLC Environmental Panel, we avoided water rationing by putting the treated water from London's sewers into the drinking water system. We never announced it at the time but could do the same thing today if we ignored hysterical responses in the media.

*

My disappointment with David was nothing compared to my disgust at Trevor Phillips as head of the Commission for Racial Equality. Morale slumped inside the CRE as he cut the unit that took up cases of racial discrimination while increasing the size of his press team to raise his profile. He enjoyed headlines like the *Mail*'s: 'Cities where whites are the minority threaten stability, says race chief'. In an article in that paper Phillips warned that such cities 'would bring a risk of mistrust and fracture between rival groups'. He questioned the 'observation of minority religious holidays', and publication of 'information in multiple languages'. The *Guardian* reported his prediction that 'some districts are on the way to becoming fully fledged ghettoes – black holes into which no one goes without fear or trepidation and from which no one ever escapes undamaged . . . we are sleep walking our way to segregation'. Ignoring the fact that minorities already had their own identity, he warned against 'the dangers of multiculturalism, the doctrine which encourages different groups to develop their own identities'.

These views were challenged by research from Manchester University rejecting the myth that Muslims, for example, necessarily chose to live separately from non-Muslims. The censuses of 1991 and 2001 revealed mixed neighbourhoods had increased and there were only fourteen wards in Britain out of 8,850 where one ethnic minority comprised over half the population. In only 118 wards (under 1.5 per cent of the total) did non-white groups form a majority. 'The idea of no-go areas or apartheid does not stand up,' said researcher Ludi Simpson in the *Guardian*. 'More non-white residents leave areas where whites are a minority than do white residents. White flight is a misnomer.' The *Daily Mirror* reported that Asians now contributed 10 per cent of national wealth. Phillips also came under fire from his predecessor Lord Ouseley for 'grabbing headlines with controversial comments about race relations terminology'.

Phillips also gave ammunition to Islamophobia when under a *Daily Mail* headline 'Quit Britain if you want Shariah law' he was quoted as saying, 'We have one set of laws. They are decided on . . . by a parliament and that's the end of the story. If you want to have laws decided in another way you have to live somewhere else.' Forgetting he had referred my row with Oliver Finegold to the SBE he said that 'people had the right to give offence'.

Blair wound up the bodies campaigning for equality in race, gender and disability, merging them into the Equality and Human Rights Commission. We had been down this road before. Following GLC abolition Labour-run boroughs merged their women's, race and disability units and promptly sidelined the issues.

Once again Blair was pandering to the *Mail* and Phillips was being shoehorned in to head the unwieldy new organisation. I asked

Lee Jasper and my women's adviser Anni Marjoram to join the hundred-plus other groups and individuals, including the Labour MPs David Lammy and Keith Vaz, who were lobbying against this. We supported a demonstration against Phillips and the reforms but to no avail. When Blair conceded a separate committee to oversee disability issues I phoned the minister responsible, Alan Johnson, who was polite but wouldn't budge. I was already angry when he said, 'Look, if I concede a committee for blacks and Asians the next thing you know the transsexuals will want one.' Knowing he would never talk to me again if I told him what I thought of his comment, I put the phone down. (Phillips's leadership of the EHRC turned out to be disastrous and in 2010 a cross-party report from the Joint Committee on Human Rights blamed him for a failure to tackle human rights abuses, saying that his strategy was too vague and that his leadership was exclusive, cliquey and manipulative.)

*

Redmond had shown such energy in the campaign to block Phillips that I was amazed when he told me a huge tumour had grown round almost every organ in his abdomen. Redmond's father had died young and we talked about growing up with the ominous milestone of living beyond your father's age. Redmond's surgery took place a few days before Christmas 2006 and several surgeons worked in sequence to remove the tumour from around that organ in which they specialised. The operation lasted six hours and the eighth floor at City Hall was subdued as the minutes ticked slowly by. As his oldest friend, John Ross became more and more gloomy before we heard that the cancer had been successfully removed. When I visited Redmond in hospital on Christmas Eve he was weak but had recovered amazingly. We talked about the pattern of deaths in our families. Everyone in mine died of heart attacks or strokes, so I probably would too, I told him. I had no idea that within a year doctors would discover I was in the first stage of cancer.

*

Having eliminated his rivals, there was a sense both of inevitability and trepidation about Brown's rise to Number 10. We exchanged pleasantries when we bumped into each other at events, but he still refused to meet me and wouldn't allow a bed tax on London's four- and five-star hotels to fund a convention centre behind Centre Point, although the hotels wanted it. I told Simon Fletcher, 'I don't think he's going to meet me until he's actually prime minister,' but Ed Balls was the link and I was invited to seminars at Number 11 on banking and council powers. We had a public reconciliation of a kind at a nursery during the 2006 borough elections. When the press asked was he now going to be 'best friends with Mr Living-stone' he turned away without comment and chatted to four-year-olds. When asked could I work with him I replied, 'Always have.' There was no handshake for photographers and Tessa sat between us but the audience burst into applause as Brown called me a 'leader and a statesman'. The *Standard* reported 'what looked like genuine warmth' as I escorted Brown out and we chatted about being fathers. After nineteen years ignoring me, he knew we had to work together.

It was easy getting on with Ed Balls. He preferred to meet without officials so we did business over dinner near the House of Commons. As Brown's deputy in all but name he more than other ministers was in command of his department. After forty years of talk we needed £5 billion from government to build Crossrail. Over dinner in early 2007 Balls agreed that we had proved Crossrail could generate £10–15 billion in tax revenues for the Treasury. Asking when I needed the decision, I said by the end of the year. He replied it would happen but there might be nothing public until then, adding, 'It would help if you didn't denounce us for the delay.' Ever a stickler on expenses, GLA finance director Anne McMeel queried the bill as it included two bottles of wine and only reluctantly signed it off when I said that for a four-hour dinner London was going to get £5 billion in return.

*

Our decision to work with Clinton paid off when he persuaded energy service companies to cut prices for retrofitting buildings to be energy-efficient. Together with London fifteen cities agreed to retrofit all their public buildings within a decade. This increased the global market for retrofitting by 125 per cent and was the big announcement at the next C40 meeting in New York in May 2007.

I hadn't seen our host Mayor Bloomberg since the Olympic vote. The tenth-richest person in America, worth $18 billion, he was none the less pleasant and unpretentious with a nice, sly sense of humour. Pragmatic and effective, he was really a Democrat but had to stand as a Republican because the New York Democratic party was stitched up into rival camps.

I visited Bloomberg's Emergency Planning Center, an ultra-modern complex built because the rising temperature of the North Atlantic means that hurricanes will be more violent and a Category 3 hurricane would send two million New Yorkers fleeing to Bloomberg's shelters. No one knows when a hurricane of this strength will hit but it has huge potential implications for New York's status as a financial centre. At least New York was prepared, while I was still arguing with government about when to build a larger Thames Barrier further downriver. When I launched the London Flood Response plan at the C40 in May 2007 I said, 'When we opened the Thames Barrier in 1982 we raised it once or twice a year, a quarter-century on we are now raising it once or twice a month with government relying on the optimistic scenario the barrier could cope until the end of the century.' As it would take fifteen years to plan and build, and the ice caps are rapidly melting, I wanted it in place by 2050.

International civic meetings are usually just taxpayer-subsidised jollies but in New York thirty-four mayors representing a quarter of a billion people attended a serious discussion. I worried they might all speak on each issue but there was no grandstanding as they sat taking notes on subjects like anaerobic digestion. I opened the conference by saying, 'The fight to tackle climate change will be won or lost in cities,' and that mayors could not wait 'on the painfully slow progress of our governments while the window of opportunity for preventing catastrophic climate change disappears. No city can wall itself off from the consequences of climate change and no city can prevent catastrophic climate change on its own but together we can create a critical mass that puts the world on the path to tackling the biggest challenge ever faced by humanity.'

Ignoring the work of the conference, *The Times* merely reported that the 'Mayor of New York is Jewish. He is said to have snubbed his London counterpart who is in the Big Apple for a series of climate change events . . . Bloomberg is keen to keep his distance, said a source close to the billionaire. He will not be extending the hand of friendship.' Bloomberg asked me, 'What is all this crap in your papers about me snubbing you?' and was amazed when I explained the creative ability of British journalists. At a joint press conference in Central Park Bloomberg joked, 'The Mayor of London actually works for me. I have an apartment in London. I think I'm probably paying your salary, Ken, or probably a piece of it.' I announced TfL had begun trials with new energy-efficient LEDs in traffic lights; they were five times as expensive as existing lights but used only one-third of the power and lasted much longer. I said, 'If five or more cities placed one big order we expect the price to be cut by two-thirds as manufacturers would go into mass production.'

George David, chairman of industrial giant United Technologies, said efficient lighting and heating of buildings could cut New York's existing thirty-five power stations to twenty-four, adding that 'energy conservation is not only feasible but has attractive financial returns'. Charles Prince, chair of Citigroup, told delegates that 'cutting carbon emissions does not mean wearing a hair shirt and will ultimately save people money rather than cost them more'. A prototype hydrogen-fuelled bus was on display and I told the firm making it that when it went into production we would replace London's entire bus fleet.

Annoyed at continuing stories that he was snubbing me, Bloomberg opened the final press conference by praising the work I was doing. Bill Clinton announced he had persuaded four energy service companies to cut their costs dramatically. They would do energy audits of public buildings in the cities while five banks put up half a billion pounds in loans. Cities will repay the loans from lower energy bills. Clinton said, 'I'm very grateful for [the mayors'] leadership as we announce a significant step in the continuing efforts to combat climate change through a worldwide programme to make cities more energy-efficient.' I responded, 'This is the biggest single step to tackle climate change that has been taken by any layer of government anywhere in the world since the debate on climate change started. This scheme could not have been drawn up without President Clinton's involvement. No mayor could have mobilised this support. It is an incredible legacy for the protection of humanity and the well-being of all life on this planet.'

When all 900 public buildings in London are efficiently heated and lit it will cut carbon emissions by 50,000 tonnes a year and save millions a year in energy bills. In London buildings were never designed to keep the heat out (windows face west to catch the winter sun) and summer temperatures will rise to those of northern

Portugal by 2050. If we get runaway climate change it could be as bad as North Africa, with thousands dying in heatwaves. All buildings must be retrofitted for the conditions to come (creating in the process hundreds of thousands of jobs).

At a farewell dinner in the Time Warner building Clinton's speech electrified the audience and my heart sank when, as the applause subsided, he called me up to try to follow that. This had been a real breakthrough but it wasn't reported by any British national papers or BBC news programmes, only in the London evening papers and on London regional news.

*

Back in London I got caught up in Blair's 'farewell tour' in early 2007, following his announcement that he would be stepping down within a year. As the Northern Ireland peace process and the creation of a London mayor were wholly to Blair's credit, this ironically made me part of his legacy, which he acknowledged in a letter thanking me:

I am sure you will agree that working together, the GLA and central government have made a real positive difference to the lives of Londoners. From improving public transport – most notably London's bus network – to promoting adult skills, tackling crime and anti-social behaviour through neighbourhood policing, along with making our capital city a fairer and more tolerant place to live, the past seven years have seen a great record of achievement. You have also worked hard to promote London as an attractive city to invest in, creating jobs and helping to make London one of the world's most dynamic economies.

. . . The London Partnerships Register was another great initiative that promoted greater equality and paved the way for Civil Partnerships.

You have also been a strong advocate of taking action to tackle climate change, long before it became part of mainstream political debate. The congestion charge, controversial at first, has seen real results and your work with Mayors around the world will be important in the years to come in reducing carbon emissions.

And then there is the Olympics. No other achievement symbolises what a strong, modern and dynamic city we live in than London's successful Olympic bid. I know you were instrumental in London's campaign and I know you will do all you can to make it the best Olympics ever as 2012 fast approaches.

I also wanted to mention the tragic events of 7/7. Londoners showed a unity and strength on that terrible morning that we always knew was there but had not seen for many years. Your leadership in the wake of such horrific bombings, in the hours and days that followed, helped to set the tone for London's response.

With all good wishes

[adding in his own hand]

You have, despite my (wrong) misgivings, been an absolute pleasure to work with, and have, above all, entirely vindicated the decision to have an elected London mayor. Tony.

*

Brown became PM as his pet project of PPP imploded, with press reports that Metronet (responsible for two-thirds of the lines) had a £1.2 billion cost overrun. Four years into a £17 billion contract (which had been overpriced by 25 per cent) Metronet needed to borrow another £2 billion to stay solvent. The banks wanted me to guarantee the money if Metronet failed but the shareholders (Atkins, Balfour Beatty, Bombardier, EDF and Thames Water) privately said they had lost confidence in the management they had appointed and would not resist my forcing them into liquidation.

As noted, the five shareholders had awarded themselves the bulk of the work without competitive tender and naturally didn't penalise themselves for underperformance. When Brown forced the PPP on us, I was angry because we were paying through the nose for work Kiley could have done more cheaply but I never expected overpaid private sector managers to screw up so badly so quickly.

Their incompetence was exposed when a train derailed on the Central Line in July 2007, five weeks after Metronet had been warned that bales of tarpaulin could fall across the track if they were not secured. Eight hundred passengers were trapped in 100-degree heat and smoke during the rush hour for two hours before they were led to safety. Metronet was never going to be successful, so Tim O'Toole told them I would not underwrite their borrowing.

Metronet boss Graham Pimlott blamed Brown and Alistair Darling, even though the contract had complied with all their demands. Metronet had not examined the state of the tunnels and track because the shareholders believed they couldn't lose with such generous terms. The papers looked for someone to blame. Shriti Vadera, who had been Brown's adviser, said she had never been involved. Sir Steve Robson, head of the Treasury's privatisation unit, retired to a lucrative position on the board of Royal Bank of Scotland, where he did his bit towards the collapse of Britain's banking system. Professor David Currie, who claimed that PPP would save £3.3 billion, was now Lord Currie of Marylebone with a nice little earner chairing Ofcom. Denis Tunnicliffe, then managing director of London Underground, was a Labour peer comfortably remunerated as director of the Atomic Energy Authority and – alarmingly – the Rail and Safety Standards Board.

I met Brown forty-eight hours after I told Metronet that they were on their own. The news hadn't broken so Brown had no warning before we met with Tessa, Tim and Mayor Delanoë of Paris to lay wreaths on the second anniversary of the tube bombings. I took Brown to one side and told him Metronet was going into liquidation, leaving a bill of £2 billion. Brown just said: 'Someone better get in touch with the office.' Those were the only words we ever exchanged on the subject. I wanted government to pick up the bill so I told Joy Johnson and my staff that no one was to say 'we told you so'. Journalists pressed me to denounce Brown but I just droned on about 'working together to solve the problem'. The negotiations were with transport secretary Ruth Kelly, who tried to get me to drop my demand that any future problems from the PPP should be underwritten by government in exchange for an additional £130 million in that year's government grant. I walked out of the meeting and after a couple of days we got the £130 million without my accepting this as a full and final settlement.

*

Having always feared that 2008 would be a difficult election, I couldn't believe how well things were going. Research by the City of London concluded we had overtaken New York eighteen months previously as the world's leading financial centre. Twenty-eight of the world's top 500 companies now had their headquarters in London, only one behind New York, and we were handling a third of all foreign currency transactions. The Arnholt–GMI city brands index placed London top of thirty cities as 'a place to find a job, do business, obtain an educational qualification and for finding a community of people where one can fit in'. In the summer of 2007 London extended its lead over New York as the first choice for foreign companies listing on the world's exchanges and was winning the lion's share of foreign direct investment into Europe with 388 projects coming to London in twelve months.

Five years previously the *Lonely Planet* guide had written London off as a 'joyless, decaying city, where people are more likely to attack you than extend a welcome'. Now London was described as the best city in Europe, having 'enjoyed a dramatic renaissance . . . sailing high on a wave of determination, optimism and glee'. With 'more to offer tourists than any other European city' it was 'fashion forward, ethnically diverse and artistically pioneering . . . offering the best in history and tradition alongside glittering modern architecture'. The guide noted improvements in all areas from sightseeing and eating out to hotel accommodation and public transport. Tourism was 8 per cent up on a year previously.

*

The Tories were still in a mess in their search for a mayoral candidate anyone had heard of. John Major declined and David Cameron asked former BBC boss Greg Dyke if he would run against me as a joint Tory–Lib Dem candidate, prompting several Tories to say they would rather vote for me. Dyke turned them down, which wasn't a surprise as he had once been part of our left-wing caucus planning to take over the GLC. Prompted by LBC DJ Nick Ferrari I said, 'I want to reach out to David Cameron, I can feel his pain. If he wants a dual candidate I am happy to do it for him too.' CBI boss Sir Digby Jones had also been asked by Cameron to stand against me even though he was about to take a job in Brown's government.

The press were rather more interested in the sporting events we attracted to London. The American National Football League staged a match at Wembley between the New York Giants and Miami Dolphins, bringing a flood of American tourists to London. The American Basketball Association opened an office here following my visit to New York and held a pre-season exhibition game between Boston Celtics and Minnesota Timberwolves in the O2 arena. The American Hockey League and the world gymnastics championships also came to the O2. These events were worth between £5 million and £15 million each for London. The French daily *Le Figaro* proclaimed London 'The world capital of sport'. Even the *Standard* admitted: 'London has the newly built arenas to exploit the increasing globalisation of sport – often with Livingstone on hand to broker the deals.'

To cap it all, in 2007 the Tour de France held their Grand Départ in London for the first time. The idea came from Mike Hickford in TfL's cycling unit and after three years' planning two million people watched the event while spending £115 million in the city. On Saturday 7 July, as we were driven round the time trials route, Tour officials and Paris mayor Bertrand Delanoë were stunned by the size of the crowds. Everything went like a dream with perfect weather and not a single incident or accident. The Tour officials were a pleasure to work with – laid back and great company. The Grand Départ was a very egalitarian affair as the public mingled with cyclists as they prepared to race, and was a real boost to our plans for cycling in London. On Sunday morning on Tower Bridge I lowered the flag to start the Tour and watched the field cycle off. As I sat on the tube going home I thought we couldn't have a better run-up to the next election.

18

A New Messiah

2007–2008

The Tories' search for a big-name candidate was richly amusing. TV presenters Anne Robinson and Nick Ross were asked and declined. Cameron had groomed Nick Boles, from the Policy Exchange think tank, but he had cancer and couldn't stand. LBC's Nick Ferrari waited to know the Tory choice before deciding to stand as an independent. The hard right were appalled that the Tories might not find a credible candidate. Writing in the *Telegraph* the previous year, Charles Moore had warned:

London is not very English. More than 30 per cent of its inhabitants were not born in the country . . . a home for refugees . . . an adventure playground for Islamist terrorists. These people have very little experience of the wider Britain . . . In reality they are London citizens. London has almost become a city state . . . and we aren't quite sure what to do about it.

One person, unfortunately, who has had an idea is Ken Livingstone. He is the only truly successful Left-wing British politician of modern times. From the early 1980s he has understood how to exploit the ethnic resentments, pose as the champion of the oppressed, run against whatever is seen to be the establishment of the time.

Ken has combined hard line Left-wing politics – supporting the IRA and Castro, criticising Jews and attacking mainstream British culture – with a post-modern way of riding the latest trend . . . In the 1980s Ken was the champion of absurdly cheap tube fares.

After a long rant about the state of London today Moore called for a new mayor of London whose 'first gesture of London's reconciliation with its national hinterland should be something which for Ken Livingstone is blasphemy – a St George's Day parade'. I didn't have the heart to tell him the GLA had been celebrating St George's Day for years.

*

Ten days before the close of nominations in July 2007 Cameron's office told *The Times* that Boris Johnson was 'definitely considering it. He's not made a final decision but he's definitely not ruling it out. It's his own idea.' But Boris, disappointed not to be promoted into the shadow cabinet and ambitious to be Tory leader, wanted to stay in Parliament. He told the Press Association: 'I'm definitely not a candidate. It would be a fantastic job, but I'm greatly enjoying what I'm doing.' An hour later Tory HQ issued a statement in Boris's name saying, 'Being Mayor of London would be a fantastic job . . . I have been struck by the number of people urging me to run . . . There are huge obstacles – above all my . . . responsibility to my constituency.' The *Independent*'s Matthew Norman saw another obstacle: 'The mayor's salary is almost £150,000 compared to the £500,000 plus Boris would have to give up (on top of his MP's package and *Telegraph* income): he charges £10,000 for after-dinner speeches.'

Steve Norris said the idea 'smacks of a certain desperation . . . I find the whole prospect of Boris running hilarious'. Alexander Chancellor in the *Guardian* was enthusiastic. 'I will support him. I have no idea what kind of administrator he would be, but I don't think that's the most important thing . . . [Boris] is so clever and so popular . . . His own energy as he jogs and bicycles around the capital would be another kind of inspiration.' Kate Hoey said Boris 'would do quite well', adding, 'In theory I'm backing Mr Livingstone . . . but there's a feeling that the mayor is perhaps a kind of elected dictator.' I told the BBC, 'Londoners want a mayor who is their own person, not a party toady . . . As a candidate he would be brilliant . . . but I don't think Boris has held an administrative role and I am not sure whether the first one should be a city the size of London.'

By the end of the week, after he had talked privately to Cameron, a statement appeared on Boris's website saying he would stand but it was removed by aides, who said it was a mistake. Norris warned that 'he couldn't run a whelk stall'. That weekend papers recycled some of Boris's more memorable statements: 'Voting Tory will cause your wife to have bigger breasts and increase your chances of owning a BMW M3,' for example. The British Chamber of Commerce warned, 'Ken is a serious player and fights hard for London. Boris will have to rid himself of being seen as an eccentric figure if he is to have an impact.'

On Monday afternoon the media gathered outside City Hall. Boris, arriving late on his bicycle, announced, 'The opportunity is too great and the prize too wonderful to miss . . . I will put the smile back on London's face.' Asked his policies for London, Boris replied, 'It's a fantastic city.' Pressed for detail, he said, 'Wait and see.' Asked what I was doing wrong, he said, 'I'll get back to you on that.' Then, adding, 'This is a riot,' he cycled off. Not realising that City Hall is circular he was surprised to find he had ridden round into the journalists again. As Simon and I watched from my office Joy said, 'The only thing missing is you confronting him.' I had been tempted.

Boris's past was now fair game with *The Times* reporting on 17 July that while he 'was among those arrested after a restaurant window was broken at a Bullingdon Club dinner Mr Cameron, sensing trouble ahead, had left long before'. The *Sunday Mirror* had photographs of Boris on his mobile phone while driving with one hand on the wheel, reminding him that this could get him a £2,500 fine or community service order. Boris was unconcerned, writing that his hero was the mayor in the film *Jaws*: 'A gigantic fish is eating all your constituents and he decides to keep the beach open . . . I love his rationality . . . he was wrong . . . but heroically right in principle.'

That weekend John Ross and Redmond O'Neill had read fifteen years' worth of Boris's articles and checked his voting record. John said his writing showed he was deeply reactionary in all areas, with the sole exception of immigration. He had not bothered to vote to defend pensioners' free travel, he opposed the minimum wage, wanted new nuclear weapons, had not voted for Crossrail, voted against the right of unmarried couples (gay and straight) to adopt children and although he had the 567th-lowest voting record in the Commons he always supported fox hunting. Describing global warming as 'a new stone-age religion', he joked, 'There is not a lot we can do, we might as well enjoy our beautiful planet while we can.' Opposing large-scale house building in London, he wanted homes built in the north of the country instead. He was 'in favour of selection . . . so is every member of the British ruling classes . . . I believe passionately in academic inequality.' He wanted society to 'inculcate . . . Britishness especially into young Muslims . . . we should think again about the Jilbab . . . and we should probably scrap faith schools. We should forbid Imams from preaching sermons in anything but English . . . we cannot continue with the multicultural apartheid.'

Boris had been the most enthusiastic cheerleader for the Iraq war, saying that 'it was mesmerising in April 2003, to stand in Baghdad and look at the contrast between the Americans . . . and Iraqis, skinny and dark, badly dressed and fed . . . The Marines were taller and squarer . . . with better dentition. They looked like a master race.' His initial policy announcements were equally surreal. Ignoring the fact that house building in London had increased from 17,000 a year in 2000 to 27,000, he announced he would end my rule that half of all developments should be affordable housing on the ground that this was 'stifling development'. Overlooking the 50 per cent increase in bus ridership, he promised to scrap the mayor's powers to regulate buses and introduce the full privatisation of the bus service, which in the rest of the country had been a disaster.

Boris's biographer, Andrew Gimson, biked over six copies of his book. It was so funny and revealing that I read it twice. He quoted Martin Hammond, Boris's inspirational teacher, writing in a school report: 'I like his open friendliness of manner, and his ready wit . . . [he has] a finger in a wide variety of pies.' Hammond worried that he would 'fail to do justice to himself as a scholar'. Writing to Boris's father Stanley, Hammond warned, 'Boris did take on several large extra commitments . . . his regular academic responsibilities were sadly neglected . . . Boris really has adopted a disgracefully cavalier attitude to his classical studies . . . He honestly believes that it is churlish of us not to regard him as an exception, one who should be free of the network of obligation that binds everyone else.'

Little had changed in Hammond's next report in July 1982. 'Boris has still not been working at anything like the limit of his capacity . . . Boris is pretty impressive when success can be achieved by pure intelligence unaccompanied by hard work . . . [He] tends to sell himself short when an exercise requires intellectual preparation. He is, in fact, pretty idle about it all . . . Boris has something of a tendency to assume that success and honours will drop into his lap.' Boris's headmaster at Eton, Sir Eric Anderson, who also taught Blair at Fettes, told Gimson, 'Boris had some similarities with Blair as a boy – both of them opted to live on their wits rather than preparation. They both enjoyed performing. In both cases people found them life-enhancing and fun to have around, but also maddening.'

At Oxford Boris joined the Bullingdon Club and Gimson records a riotous night at La Paesana restaurant where they tried to debag DJ Tony Blackburn: 'There was a lot of shouting and suddenly a rubber plant hurtled across the room and landed in someone's meal.' Boris's politics were revealed in a long essay in which he explained that to win elections required a 'disciplined and deluded collection of stooges' who believe you will do a lot for them, but the 'brutal fact' is that the stooges will do more for the candidate – 'the relationship [being] founded on duplicity . . . the tragedy of the stooge is that even if he thinks this through, he wants so much to believe that his relationship with the candidate is special, that he shuts out the truth. The terrible art of the candidate is to coddle to the self-deception of the stooge.' Recognising there was no chance of a Tory being elected president of the Oxford Union, Boris put his strategy into practice by denying his Tory beliefs and claiming to support the SDP. Following his victory, he reverted to being a Tory. The one thing Boris was serious about was Israel and anti-Semitism, and Andrew Gimson recalls his anger when Boris's friend Darius Guppy made an anti-Semitic remark. Fellow student Frank Luntz recalls that his defence of Israel 'was not a popular thing to do . . . The Jewish students . . . just wanted to make him king.'

Gimson says, 'Boris pretends to be old-fashioned, partly in order to hide the fact that he really is old-fashioned. He most likely believes laundry is for women, but would never be foolish enough to say it. [He] has brought the art of masculine incompetence to such a pitch of perfection that women take pity on him.' He quoted Boris's first wife Allegra: 'He never had the time to wash laundry or buy shampoo and somehow he was terribly good at getting other people to do things. I ended up doing all his laundry.'

After coming down from Oxford he got a job at *The Times*, although Gimson was not surprised when he was sacked as 'the distinctive products of Boris's journalism had already emerged [at Oxford]. The powerful and amazing article, utterly convincing in its general drift, but weakened by cavalier treatment of mere facts.' Under pressure to file an article on Edward II and unable to reach the historian Colin Lucas for a comment, he made up a quote in his name which made Lucas a laughing stock among his fellow historians. When Boris was accused by the editor of *The Times* of inventing the quote he replied, 'So are most of the quotes in your paper.' Boris was one of only two trainee graduates sacked by the editor, the other being Toby Young.

Daily Telegraph editor Max Hastings gave Boris a second chance, sending him to Brussels to cover the EU. Gimson quotes fellow reporter Rory Watson saying, 'He made stories up,' including that the EU headquarters was to be blown up because of asbestos, overlooking the health risks of exploding asbestos (it is still there). The *Independent*'s David Usborne told Gimson that Boris 'was fundamentally intellectually dishonest, in my view. He was serving his masters in a very skilful way but I never felt he believed a word.' The *Independent*'s Sarah Helm added: 'Boris was a complete charlatan.'

Boris's anti-EU stories and florid style delighted the *Telegraph*'s readership and confirmed their prejudices. He became the *Telegraph*'s chief political columnist and carried the Tory flag in a safe Labour seat during the 1997 Labour landslide. *Telegraph* editor Charles Moore told Gimson he remembered Boris's 'maximum idleness'. Boris reached beyond the *Telegraph* when he appeared on *Have I Got News for You*, where Ian Hislop challenged him to justify a telephone conversation where he had discussed with Darius Guppy having a reporter beaten up. Although he lost his temper, his appearance was a great success and he became a regular. I never missed any episode he was in and roared with laughter when he couldn't answer a single question about the Tory party leader, Iain Duncan Smith. Boris was now a national character and moved on to become editor of the *Spectator*.

Having given his word of honour he would not stand for Parliament if he became editor of the *Spectator*, within two weeks he was applying for constituencies. Confronted by owner Conrad Black, Boris said, 'Oh God, I shouldn't have done this. You should fire me.' Gimson quotes *Spectator* colleague Stuart Reid: 'He's basically unreliable in terms of delivering copy or being around and he doesn't seem to bear grudges – it's impossible not to forgive him . . . If he wasn't a nice guy he'd be dead.' While journalists were forgiving, fellow MPs were not. Senior Tories anonymously told Gimson: '[He's] a blithering idiot. You never see him. I don't think I've ever seen him in the tea room.' Another said, 'I was staggered at his economic ignorance . . . He didn't make the reputation [on committee] he could have done for being able to do the nitty gritty. There was a laziness.' Iain Duncan Smith told Conrad Black, 'I'd like to have a talk with you about Boris. I suspect neither of us is getting full value.' Black told Gimson, 'He's so ineffably duplicitous, you never know.' Gimson says that when Boris entered Parliament he was told by Michael Portillo to 'focus on Parliament, stop being funny and resign from editing the *Spectator*. I can see why he rejected my suggestions. His journalism and television work have brought him money and fame. Devoting himself instead to mastering a shadow spokesman's brief would have been tedious and impoverishing. But if he calculated that he could leap from celebrity to leading the party he was wrong.' Boris preferred to be the *Spectator*'s motoring correspondent, describing the most powerful cars in sexual terms while driving at 160 mph on the M40. His ambition to be Tory leader was also undermined by the conflict between his personal behaviour and his view that 'the decay of marriage, the rise in illegitimacy are far more directly traceable to female emancipation, unemployment and the vast welfare state . . .'

As the Tories set out to choose their fifth leader in nine years with Ken Clarke, David Davis and Cameron as front runners, Cameron told the *Sun*: 'Boris phoned me up and said "If you don't stand [for the party leadership], then I will." That's when I thought

I've got to save the nation.' Boris was overtaken by a junior Etonian and Bullingdon Club member.

*

Many felt that with Boris as my opponent I would have a walk-over – but this was not a view I shared. Since the end of the Cold War and the demise of Reagan and Thatcher ideological differences had been blurred. In a world of celebrity, being witty on a TV sofa counted for more than political substance and turnout at general elections had dropped to just 60 per cent in 2001 from a high of 84 per cent in the 1950s. Polls showed that Boris was recognised by over 80 per cent of voters, which is the first step to winning. Trade union leaders shared my fear that he was a threat and started gearing up for a fight.

My poll ratings increased as people surged back to Labour when Blair quit and Brown managed the transition perfectly. His responses to the floods in Cumbria, an outbreak of foot and mouth and failed terrorist attacks in London and Glasgow were flawless. His holiday in Britain contrasted with Blair's extravagant holidays abroad as a guest of dubious figures like the Italian PM Silvio Berlusconi. By August Labour had a 10 per cent lead in the polls and Brown's personal lead over Cameron was 36 per cent.

In Number 10 at last, Brown finally asked to meet me. Afterwards I told Simon Fletcher, 'That wasn't as much fun as Blair.' He replied, 'But we got more done.' Brown planned to build three million new homes by ending Blair's ban on building council housing. Giving me £5 billion to build 50,000 homes and the power to draw up London's housing strategy and decide where to build meant that this would be London's biggest housing programme since the 1970s. Now I could stop boroughs agreeing housing schemes which had no affordable housing in them and insist on an increase in three-, four- and five-bedroom homes to 40 per cent of the total.

To see why I needed these powers I only had to look down from City Hall to an empty site owned by Southwark. The developer had plans for 386 homes but since 2000 the Lib Dem council had refused permission. Having lost the appeal, the Lib Dems refused to sell their part of the site, saying they wanted to build an opera house. A local Lib Dem told me, 'We are not having 600 new voters in a ward we only won by 205 votes.'

*

Mayor Delanoë of Paris invited Emma and me to the finish of the Tour de France that I had started in London three weeks earlier and, at four and three, Tom and Mia were now old enough to come. Bertrand had booked the exclusive Jules Verne restaurant in the Eiffel Tower and no one complained when he lit up a cigarette after lunch in the no-smoking restaurant. Tom and Mia loved the Paris Plage, where each August Bertrand closed the riverside road to traffic, turning the banks of the Seine into a beach with playgrounds, swimming pools, a circus and cafés. This had now grown so big and successful that thousands of Parisians were spending their August holiday in their home city. With London's South Bank a magnet for tourists, it was obvious we could do the same kind of thing along the Victoria Embankment so I started planners working on a Londres Plage which would open in 2010. I also saw Bertrand's new Vélib' bike-hire scheme in operation, and I asked TfL to start preparing a similar system for London. Jenny Jones led a TfL team to Paris to look at the details and on 31 August 2007 the *Standard* reported, 'TfL officials want it up and running within three years.'

*

My race adviser, Lee Jasper, had been working to respond to the demand of the UN that countries historically involved in the slave trade should apologise but Tony Blair feared that an apology could lead to demands for compensation and helped block an EU apology with the excuse that slavery was legal at the time. As London had raised the finance to fund the slave trade the UN hoped an apology by its mayor would pressure governments to do the same. A replica of the slave ship the *Zong* was moored outside the Tower of London. As I toured it, it was hard to believe that people had been crammed into such a small space and on the real *Zong* 133 slaves had been thrown overboard in 1781 as part of an insurance scam. UNESCO asked me to make the apology on 23 August – the anniversary of the successful slave rebellion in Haiti in 1791. At the ceremony in the chamber of City Hall I said:

As Mayor I offer an apology on behalf of London and its institutions for their role in the transatlantic slave trade. Some say that recognising such a crime is a form of – and I quote – 'national self-hate'. But the late senator Bobby Kennedy often quoted the French writer Albert Camus, who wrote, 'I should like to be able to love my country and still love justice.' Love of one's country and its achievements is based on reality, not denying it. A Britain that contributed Shakespeare, Newton and Darwin to human civilisation need fear comparison with no one. A British state that refuses to apologise for a crime on such a gigantic scale as the slave trade merely lowers our country in the opinion of the world . . . Estimates of the numbers transported range from ten to thirty million. As many as 5 per cent died in prisons before transportation and more than 10 per cent during the voyage – the direct murder of some two million people. Virginia made it lawful 'to kill and destroy such Negroes who absent themselves from service'. Branding and rape were commonplace . . . From 1707 punishment for rebellion included 'nailing them to the ground and applying fire by degrees from the feet and hands, burning them gradually up to the head'. In the rebellion in Antigua in 1736 five ringleaders were broken on the wheel, seventy-seven burned to death, six hung in cages to die of thirst. For 'lesser' crimes castration or chopping off half the foot were used . . . More than 1.5 million slaves were taken to the British Caribbean islands in the eighteenth century but at its end there were only 600,000 . . . If the murder of millions, and torture of millions more is not 'a crime against humanity' these words have no meaning. It was the racial murder of not just those who were transported but generations of enslaved African men, women and children. To justify this murder and torture black people had to be declared inferior or not human. We live with the consequences today.

Although I had read the statement several times, as the words to describe these horrors came out of my own mouth I was overwhelmed by the significance of the apology and what it meant for those present. Jesse Jackson came and stood by me before I could continue. UNESCO's Françoise Rivière said, 'You have distinguished yourself as the first high-visibility elected official to take such an historic stand.' The UN has now made 23 August the International Day of Remembrance of the Victims of Slavery.

*

Even though Redmond was still on an exhausting regime of chemotherapy he worked tirelessly to make the unveiling of Nelson Mandela's statue in Parliament Square on 29 August 2007 a moving and joyous success. The audience in Parliament Square was an eclectic mix of diplomats, anti-apartheid campaigners and politicians including Richard Attenborough, Jesse Jackson, Tony Benn, David Cameron, Ben Okri and Naomi Campbell. Given his view that 'South Africa under Mandela's leadership is a tyranny of black rule', Boris was quite rightly absent.

In 1987 Thatcher had said that Mandela was 'the leader of a typical terrorist organisation and anyone who thinks it will someday form the government of South Africa is living in cloud cuckoo land', but now as Mandela walked slowly into the square filled with 7,000 people there was complete silence with most of the audience in tears. Brown and I unveiled the statue and I said, 'This statue is placed here to demonstrate [that] the struggle of the South African people to overcome the tyranny of the racist apartheid state was itself a struggle for universal human rights ... There could be no more fitting place than this square which you will share with the American president who freed the slaves and the British prime minister who led a nation standing alone against the evil of Nazi ideology.' Mandela remembered first coming to Parliament Square in 1962 with Oliver Tambo and joking that 'we hoped that one day a statue of a black person would be erected here', alongside that of South African leader General Jan Smuts. He continued, 'Although this statue is of one man it should in actual fact symbolise all those who have resisted oppression, especially in my country ... We thank the British people once again for their relentless efforts in supporting us in the dark years.' The mood at the reception in Whitehall's banqueting suite was exhilarating and I couldn't resist telling foreign guests we were on the site where King Charles I had been beheaded.

*

At Labour's conference in September Bill Clinton praised the environmental lead London had given the world and I started my speech by predicting wrongly that it was an 'honour to be invited to give the first annual Boris Johnson memorial lecture'. Conference buzzed with rumours that Brown would call a snap election for the end of 2007 but I worried about getting voters out on a cold night in November. If Brown wanted a snap election I couldn't believe he hadn't begun planning before he took over. When I visited party headquarters, ministers were being photographed for the campaign and officials were booking advertising space.

At Tory conference Boris spoke before a live satellite link to Arnold Schwarzenegger, who was rolling his eyes during Boris's speech, saying, 'He's fumbling all over the place.' Mayor Bloomberg, who was at their conference before meeting me, said, 'Perhaps the acoustics were bad or my hearing's not what it was or perhaps [Boris] was talking rubbish.'

But George Osborne's promise to raise the threshold of inheritance tax to £1 million cut Labour's lead to 3 per cent and exposed a well-hidden flaw in Brown's character – indecisiveness. Brown dithered for days before announcing to derision that he had never intended to call an election that autumn. I always believed Brown knew what he wanted, pursued it relentlessly, crushing anyone in his way. But he lacked the ability to make a timely decision. His hesitation in nationalising the bankrupt Northern Rock bank was just the first of many delays on big decisions. As Labour's vote went down it dragged me with it and a YouGov poll cut my lead to just 6 per cent. To coincide with the start of an autumn election campaign we had planned to have Brown and Ruth Kelly with me at the announcement that work would finally start on the Crossrail network, but with the non-election fiasco there was a subdued mood.

*

In October I travelled to India to open offices in Delhi and Mumbai that would work to get Indian companies to invest in London, promote our universities to Indian students and increase tourism from India. I went with sixty-five business people in tow, representatives from four London universities and Seb Coe and his team, who were looking at India's preparations for the Commonwealth Games in 2010. With 10,000 Indian businesses in London and 230,000 Indian tourists visiting in 2006 (overtaking the Japanese) there were huge opportunities for London as India's economy was growing at 9 per cent a year. Meetings were planned with Tata Steel, ICICI Bank, BCCI finance house and others, and seminars were being held to discuss collaboration on stem-cell research. The press obsessed over the £740,000 cost of the trip but since our previous visit to China we had already seen £21 million of extra investment in London and were negotiating dozens of other schemes.

My first stop was at the Raj Ghat memorial to Mahatma Gandhi to scatter flower petals around the eternal flame. I also visited the Nizamuddin Dargah, the oldest mosque in Delhi, and the vast Swaminarayan temple at Akshardham. The papers couldn't resist pictures of me wearing turbans, silk wraps and no shoes at religious services. The following day the Indian media turned up in droves as we unveiled a fifty-two-foot-high mock-up of Big Ben on its way to Bollywood.

Instead of a mere mayor, Delhi had a chief minister, Sheila Dikshit, who sat in the national cabinet. If the Commonwealth Games were successful Delhi would bid for the 2020 Olympics so she was keen that our cities should learn from each other and was constructing an underground railway system to tackle Delhi's transport problems. She had planted millions of trees which in Delhi's climate grew so rapidly that from tall buildings it could feel as if you were in a forest with an occasional skyscraper poking up through the tree canopy. I met Dr Rajendra Pachauri, chair of the International Panel on Climate Change, and as we stood on his roof looking over the trees we discussed Lord Stern's prediction that we had barely a decade before global warming passed a catastrophic tipping point. Rajendra feared that we might have already passed it and at best had only a few years to avoid it.

The Freud agency and John Ross had covered everything in their planning of the trip. Peter Hendy was raising funds for orphans who lived round the main train stations, Chelsea boss Peter Kenyon and former player Graeme Le Saux were working to help young Indian footballers and Danny Boyle was on the Film London team. Pinching the idea from Rudy Giuliani, I had set up Film London in 2004 to help film makers overcome all the red tape which had prevented the blockbuster *Independence Day* from filming on Trafalgar Square. We arrived in Bollywood to agree a deal with the Film and TV Guild of India and to meet Indian superstar Amitabh Bachchan on the set of *Aladdin*. London has the largest Indian community outside India, so we wanted to increase the number of Indian films made in the city (forty were made there in 2006) and I hoped to sell the Olympic media centre to Indian film makers after 2012.

Afterwards I caught the train to Mumbai, but as Indians never see a politician on public transport seventy journalists turned up, dozens of police were needed to prevent me being pushed onto the track and Freud's people begged them not to use their batons to beat the journalists out of the way. As India's financial centre Mumbai wants to rival London and New York, but as a city of twenty million with appalling slums it has severe problems. The city is on a peninsula in the Indian Ocean, only a metre above sea level. In July 2005 nearly a metre of rain fell in twenty-four hours and a thousand people died. They need to relocate to higher land north of the city, but the mayor has limited powers and the state government views Mumbai as a cash cow. Complicating the city's problems still further, the financial centre is spread over many sites separated by grim traffic congestion. Businesses wanted a strong mayor but were frustrated by the bureaucracy.

To maximise the impact of our visit Freuds had arranged a cultural evening with Myleene Klass, performance poet Kat Francois and the cast of *Stomp*. Amitabh had started out as the angry young man of Indian film but was now treated as though he was India's monarch. He was our guest of honour, arriving with his daughter-in-law, a former Miss World, to receive a presentation for his contribution to film. He joked that if his popularity ever flagged he would just have to copy me and go for a ride on the train.

I had promised London's Sikh community that I would meet the chief minister of Punjab and visit Amritsar, the site of the massacre in 1919 where British soldiers fired on a peaceful demonstration, killing 1,200 people. The site has been a place of pilgrimage ever since and it was overpowering to stand by the well where people tried to save their lives by jumping down into it. Amritsar's great temple is the holiest site for Sikhs, a place of peace and beauty, so it jarred to see bullet holes in the walls from when it was stormed in June 1984 on the orders of Indira Gandhi, an act that led to her assassination four months later. Because of tensions with nearby Pakistan, politicians are accompanied by a jeep full of soldiers and throughout the night they sat outside my hotel room cradling their machine guns.

John's business team and Freud Communications had got so good at planning these visits that I was able to do forty-four separate meetings and events in the six days I was there. Business leaders on the trip were impressed, but it meant the only free time I had was an hour sunbathing by the pool before we left the country. London Chamber of Commerce & Industry chair Michael Cassidy wrote to his members that I was 'on the top of my form'. Even Veronica Wadley finally met me at the launch of the *Standard*'s annual London 'Influential's' ratings. As we stood side by side for a photo I felt her hand resting on my bottom, which was clearly a nervous response rather than an indication of desire, but she looked appalled when I pointed out that if I had done that to her it would be on the front page of her paper.

*

The fall in recorded crime in London was accelerating. Overall crime fell by 2.2 per cent in 2003, a further 4.3 per cent in 2004/5 and 4.4 per cent in 2006. We were heading for a 25 per cent cut in crime figures since they peaked at the beginning of the decade and if this trend continued we could cut crime by another 25 per cent during my third term. Murders had fallen from 222 in 2003 to 160 in 2007, rape was down by 25 per cent, gun crime was down by 22 per cent and GBH by 12 per cent in 2007. The Met's work led to a 20 per cent increase in juvenile convictions, but the *Standard* claimed that this proved crime was increasing. Knife crime had fallen by 18 per cent since 2004, but teenage stabbings and shootings, even with extra police, were rising. To tackle this we started several initiatives. After a young man named Richard Whelan was stabbed to death during a row on a bus in July 2005 Sir Ian and I launched the new Safer Transport Teams in Bexley the following March. Now 378 police would ride the buses in areas where young people congregated as schools came out. It cost £70 million a year but the results were dramatic with child crime cut by a fifth. We also doubled the Volunteer Police Cadets with units in each borough. A third of the cadets were from minorities and even included kids who had assaulted police officers. We wanted to divert them from crime and hundreds of police volunteered to be role models for them.

There were 170 known gangs in London so the Met established the Violent Crime Directorate to target guns, gangs and weapons, but we knew that the most important thing was to get kids off the streets. Institute for Public Policy Research studies showed kids who had been through uniformed youth clubs such as the Scouts or Sea Cadets were more likely to earn higher incomes later, achieve qualifications and were less likely to suffer depression. For years boroughs had underfunded youth activities. Part of the gap had been filled by religious groups, but for many kids in dysfunctional families who were excluded from school their poor self-image and lack of self-esteem led them into local gangs with the promise of quick money and the glamour of guns. The gang became an extended family; as one member said: 'When things happen people will be there to back you.' A MORI poll reported 29 per cent of pupils in London admitted to carrying a knife. With many families left behind in a society as unequal as London's, some kids robbed others so they could have the latest gadget. Being poor doesn't make anyone more likely to kill but being poor, unloved and brutalised might.

In April 2007 I had promised the boroughs we would match whatever money they put up to increase youth facilities in their areas. We used metal detectors at tube and train stations and I asked government to allow them to be installed in schools. I warned that too much film and music targeted at young people glorified violence and this was particularly so for black teenage boys who lacked a father figure at home. Reverend Nims Obunge, chief executive of the Peace Alliance, which created London's annual Week of Peace, said half the inmates at Feltham Young Offenders Institution were already fathers themselves. Instead of celebrities, sports personalities and rap stars he wanted role models who were successful in business and the professions. Nims said, 'I want to see doctors, lawyers and ordinary citizens acting as mentors.'

*

Despite our success in reducing the incidence of crime, there was only a small fall in the *fear* of crime among Londoners. This was largely the fault of the press. As we announced each year's improved figures the *Standard* would headline whichever offence had bucked the trend. Regional TV news followed the American newsroom adage of 'if it bleeds it leads' so often the 10.25 p.m. local headlines would lead with a criminal act while falling crime figures went unreported. Polling showed fear of crime differed among newspaper readerships, with *Mail* readers more fearful than most. Janice Turner in *The Times* wrote that the 'chief reason for leaving Britain . . . is crime'. Many journalists dismissed the falling crime figures as false. The tragedy of a teenage death was always given massive coverage and so more teenagers carried knives for self-defence, not realising the risk they ran that the weapons could be used against them by an assailant. The obsession with youth crime was not new, of course. When I was a kid stories about 'Teddy boys' meant that I ran away whenever I saw one. In the sixties media hysteria about clashes between mods and rockers at seaside resorts turned them into self-fulfilling prophecies. As papers lost interest, the clashes petered out.

We were desperate to identify the causes behind teenage violence but several long-term trends were at work. I grew up never knowing if police were about to come round the corner, and although our misdemeanours were small – bunking off school, stealing apples from a garden or climbing onto a building site at night – my mates and I often managed to get caught. We all believed the police would catch us if we did something really wrong. All that changed as soon as police were switched to patrolling in cars. With no one keeping an eye on them, kids could go from vandalism through petty crime to serious crime and became career criminals before they got caught. As I patrolled on foot with the neighbourhood police teams we had set up, kids were amazed that officers knew them by name; such close contact gave us a chance to divert the course of their lives.

Changes in the way schools were run didn't help. In fee-paying schools there was usually a good programme of physical exercise but in state schools most kids were given little opportunity to burn off their energy through sport. For non-academic boys the playing field is often where they win respect. As the time allocated to PE was cut in favour of the core curriculum, more boys dropped out of school altogether. The Inner London Education Authority had resources to tackle disruptive children, giving them a one-to-one relationship in a specialist unit until they could go back into the class. After the abolition of the ILEA these facilities closed, so some heads now simply expelled their most difficult pupils. Soon 80 per cent of children entering the criminal justice system had been excluded from school. Mainly illiterate and innumerate, they roamed the streets and joined local gangs.

But perhaps the biggest factor creating what Cameron describes as 'broken Britain' was that skilled working-class jobs were wiped out during the recessions of the 1970s and 1980s, leaving some families with no one in full-time employment. The end of council house building saw overcrowding and homelessness creating areas of poverty, hopelessness, high crime and the increasing polarisation of schools. These areas in London are often cheek-by-jowl with areas of gentrification and ostentatious prosperity, emphasising the exclusion of those left behind.

Lee Jasper wanted to divert kids from violence and worked with locals at the Brixton Base project which provided training in creative industries for young black people. Lee was having problems getting LDA funding for such an unorthodox project and asked if I wanted him to push this through. I agreed and went to see its groundbreaking work in rescuing young kids on the fringes of gangs. Lee became the unpaid patron of Brixton Base.

By autumn 2007 the government agreed our request to raise the age at which knives could be bought to eighteen but still resisted my call to ban replica handguns which could be converted for use as weapons. The Met introduced Operation Curb with police squads targeting gangs and identifying the five most violent young offenders in each borough. Daily reports on gang action came into Scotland Yard, including 'ceasefire summits' at which gangs met face to face with police chiefs and community leaders to try to end the violence. A third of gang members had been forced into joining and wanted out, but feared for themselves or their families, so the Trident unit and boroughs in South London planned to establish safe houses. We targeted gun suppliers by seizing their homes and cars. The Met also started a pilot scheme in Hammersmith which extended neighbourhood beat patrols to provide twenty-four-hour cover in difficult areas.

During 2007 twenty-seven teenagers were murdered in London. Sixteen of the victims were black (many from Zaire). Arrests had been made in twenty-three of the cases. There had been little response from the boroughs to our ideas about improving their youth facilities. Fortunately Ed Balls was the minister responsible and agreed to provide £57 million, matched by £20 million from the LDA, so we had £78 million to distribute and I hoped to get another £50 million from the European Social Fund by the end of 2008. The money would be offered to boroughs, with young people involved in deciding how to spend it.

The success of metal detectors at stations (Operation Shield) to seize knives, machetes, sharpened screwdrivers and guns led to 159 arrests and a 50 per cent reduction in muggings. Teenage stabbings dominated my meetings with Ian Blair but he was under constant attack from the media. For the *Telegraph* Sir Ian was a figure of 'New Labour' and 'politically correct' but he never expressed party views or even discussed politics. Sir John, Sir Ian and myself had all agreed on the need to change the culture of the Met. Although they had different styles, they were at one on policing issues. The 'PC' policies attributed to Sir Ian actually started under Sir John. The Metropolitan Police Authority met in the full glare of the media and two-thirds of its members were politicians, so each issue was fought over with Stevens and Blair pitched into a cauldron of nit picking and point scoring. Nothing prepared them for the transition from private meetings with the Home Secretary to public political squabbles. While the press saw Sir John as a no-nonsense traditional copper and were respectful, the *Telegraph* was determined to force Sir Ian from office, so any poorly expressed sentence was twisted into a screaming headline.

Sir Ian also had to cope with bruised egos when the MPA appointed Sir Paul Stephenson, chief constable of Lancashire, as his deputy. The situation deteriorated when Brian Paddick disagreed with Sir Ian's account of the shooting of de Menezes and when Tarique Ghaffur, who wanted to be the first Asian commissioner, wasn't promoted. The press ran stories of dissatisfaction among senior officers, including Ali Dizaei, whom Sir Ian had investigated for corruption. When the jury found him not guilty the press blamed Sir Ian and although we questioned Dizaei's integrity we could not get rid of him. He was jailed on another charge in February 2010. Policing needs a clear command structure and cannot have officers arguing the toss and going to industrial tribunals at the drop of a hat.

Senior officers were appointed by the MPA rather than the mayor (unlike in New York, where, when he became dissatisfied with the city's senior police officials, Giuliani brought in outsider Bill Bratton as commissioner, pensioned off the top twenty-three officials and appointed John Timoney, twenty-fourth in seniority, as deputy). The Met would work better if a new mayor appointed a commissioner and his deputy and assistant commissioners. At least Sir Ian was able to bring Anne McMeel over from City Hall to sort out Met finances, cut bureaucracy and increase front-line services.

*

At the November 2007 *Spectator* Awards Wadley vented her frustration with Boris, telling him, 'You've got to pull your finger out.' Peter Oborne reported, 'Cameron is tearing his hair out at Boris's lazy campaign.' The press also reported that George Osborne had given Boris a dressing-down because of his invisibility due to a heavy filming schedule with the BBC. Boris found time to write to the judge at the trial of Conrad Black urging that he be spared a jail sentence for defrauding shareholders but refused to release a copy of the letter. Asked at the Jewish Forum what he liked about London he said, 'Who would have dreamt you could go into Tesco and buy mangetout or your newsagent for mango juice?'

But others were working on Boris's behalf. Policy Exchange, a right-wing think tank, was led by Nick Boles, supported by Michael Gove and Francis Maude and chaired by Charles Moore from the *Telegraph*. It employed three former Tory Central Office staff and Dean Godson (formerly assistant to Conrad Black). Although claiming to be non-party-political, it campaigned against my decision to phase out the few Routemaster buses we had left because disabled people, parents with buggies and the elderly found them difficult to use, and was supported in this by Tories who had never been on a bus in their lives. Godson wrote, 'For the sake of 1,000 wheelchairs a day, six million Londoners will lose their beloved Routemasters' (we only had 140 Routemasters in a fleet of over 8,000). Godson's ignorance was shown when he warned, 'Journeys take longer on the new double-deckers because drivers must take the money.' No one told him that bus drivers had been taking money since the Tories started phasing out Routemasters in the 1970s to cut conductors' jobs.

The Routemaster was built in Southall specifically for use in London from 1956 and by the time production ended in 1968 2,876 had been built. In the 1970s about twenty people a year died after falling off the open platform. (I fell off twice myself, though luckily on both the occasions the cars that might have run me over stopped in time.) When Labour won control of the GLC in 1981 we kept the Routemasters but our plans for a new model were blocked by Thatcher. GLC abolition was followed by bus privatisation so when I became mayor there were only a few of the old buses left. We bought forty-nine old Routemasters and reintroduced conductors as a trial on two routes. The public were glad to have conductors back but the small improvement in journey time was not enough to persuade the Treasury to give us £600 million a year to reintroduce conductors on all buses.

When the Routemaster was designed, disabled people were stuck at home or in hospitals but now they lead active lives and go out to work. Elderly people go out more and one Londoner in ten found it impossible to climb onto a Routemaster. That didn't include people struggling with luggage or shopping or babies. I only understood the problem when I started taking Tom and Mia out in the buggy. London's buses had to be open to all, so reluctantly I agreed to replace Routemasters, keeping only two 'heritage' routes for tourists and bus enthusiasts. Forgetting the appalling Tory record on these buses, Policy Exchange and the *Standard* under Wadley whipped up a self-righteous campaign.

It was led by Andrew Gilligan, whose notoriety stemmed from his May 2003 *Today* programme report that a senior intelligence source claimed the dossier on Iraq's weapons of mass destruction had been 'sexed up'. Alastair Campbell furiously attacked the BBC, as the security services had been all too willing to tell Blair what he wanted to hear without pressure from Campbell. Fatally, Gilligan had over-egged his report. The senior intelligence source was scientist Dr David Kelly, who said he had met Gilligan but he couldn't be the source because he had not said what Gilligan reported. Unforgivably, Gilligan revealed Kelly's name to MPs, putting the shy and private Dr Kelly at the heart of a media firestorm that led to his suicide. An inquiry revealed that Gilligan had gone back and 'edited' his notes of the meeting with Kelly, creating two versions in only one of which was Alastair Campbell mentioned. This echoes MP Keith Vaz's claim that he sacked Gilligan as an intern because he had forged references on his CV.

He was described in 2004 by Elizabeth Day of the *Telegraph* as 'a man of contradictions . . . insecure yet arrogant, teetotal yet overindulgent, gentle yet controlling'. She quotes Gilligan saying that when he uses a word 'it means just what I choose it to mean' and that the Hutton inquiry into Dr Kelly's death should have concluded 'that most of my story was right'. Day believed this revealed a man 'who sets his own rules and lives by them with a desperate eccentricity'. Turning up at the *Telegraph* as most were leaving the office, he worked through the night 'filing late copy with hair-tearing frequency . . . He was incredibly retentive.' A former line manager recalls that 'he was incredibly arrogant and had an unshakeable belief in his own ability'. Day describes a furious row in which he threw his mobile phone and ended up in a police cell from which he was eventually rescued by newspaper executives who found him 'weeping like a baby and singing like a canary'. 'Gilligan did not seem to form close attachments with other people . . . There were no girlfriends or boyfriends.'

The government's Iraq dossier was cock and bull but Gilligan's duplicity cost Dr Kelly his life, allowed Blair off the hook, threatened the existence of the *Today* programme and forced Greg Dyke (one of the best director generals the BBC ever had) to resign. Boris organised a 'Save Gilligan' party and hired him on the *Spectator*. My first run-in with Gilligan was as we got the kids ready for school one morning. He stood on my doorstep demanding I ride with him on a Routemaster bus that the *Standard* had hired. He was speechless when I said I thought he was responsible for Kelly's death and didn't want him anywhere near my family. Gilligan never forgot this confrontation and in the *Standard* he attacked City Hall unremittingly. At the *Today* programme's fiftieth birthday party in 2007 Jim Naughtie warned me Gilligan 'is a very dangerous man'.

*

Tolerance was integral to my vision for London. Policy Exchange and the *Telegraph* were convinced that Islam posed a threat to our way of life and hated multiculturalism. Anthony Browne, director of Policy Exchange after Nick Boles, wrote that he lay awake at nights worried that British people could be wiped out by diseases from immigrants. Several commentators and minor intellectuals like Nick Cohen, Christopher Hitchens, Martin Bright, Oliver Kamm, Melanie Phillips, Michael Gove and my old friend John Ware became obsessed with Islam. Martin Amis said British

Muslims 'will have to suffer ... discriminatory stuff ... until they get tough with their children'. Former *Today* editor Rod Liddle warned that Islam is 'Fascistic, bigoted and medieval'.

This drift to the right was similar to what had happened during the Cold War, when, faced with a choice between capitalism and communism, some left-wingers not only threw their lot in with the right but concentrated their attack on socialists who advocated a middle path between the extremes. Venom poured forth from the *Telegraph* and Policy Exchange, and multiculturalism was depicted by Cameron as an enforced separation of different cultures rather than an expression of Britain's traditional live-and-let-live attitude.

In their determination to unseat me, nobody was safe. Channel 4's *Dispatches*, using gloomy lighting and sinister music to hide the lack of substance, claimed Seb Coe had exploited his position financially and was hired by companies bidding to host sporting events. Seb had done after-dinner speeches and advised on sporting events long before he joined the Olympic bid team, and after we won had not accepted payment when talking about the Olympics and always registered his income with the IOC and the House of Lords. Seb worried about his children and thought of resigning but Tessa Jowell and I begged him to stay.

Tory Assembly member Brian Coleman claimed he had seen Ian Blair 'the worse for wear at several functions', which I didn't believe for a moment. The *Telegraph* and Tories demanded Sir Ian resign because of the de Menezes shooting, although they had supported previous commissioners when innocent people had been shot. Polls showed Londoners by two to one wanted Sir Ian to stay. When Anne McMeel unearthed credit-card fraud by some officers, the papers again demanded Sir Ian's head, though I couldn't recall editors ever resigning when their reporters fiddled expenses or concocted alarmist stories.

The *Standard* also targeted Bob Kiley. I was unaware that Bob had a drink problem until 2005, when he phoned while Emma and I were in Barcelona. Bob had to take time off after an operation and had started drinking. He told me: 'I'm sorry to bother you but the *Standard* knows I have a drink problem. It's in hand and I'm getting treatment.' In his very open way Bob had wanted to issue a statement, but knowing how it would be blown out of all proportion I'd talked him out of it and the issue died. Now it was back. The *Standard* found out Bob was on his own at home and sent someone to interview him; because he was drunk they were able to get him to say he was overpaid.

Bob's drinking never affected his work and his advice on the Olympic budget was invaluable. I wanted to unleash him on the PPP companies to negotiate the next contracts but this was now impossible. Bob resigned and returned to America. That she would destroy a man's reputation to get at me showed Wadley to be despicable enough, but worse was to come. On 10 December 2007 the *Standard*'s front page screamed: 'Ken's aide and lost millions'. It claimed that '£2.5 million of City Hall money was channelled to organisations controlled by [Lee Jasper], his friends and his business associates', denounced the 'former street hustler at the heart of Livingstone's empire' and described Brixton Base as 'a vibrant hub for criminals and race adviser's cronies'. Gilligan also claimed the Black Londoners Forum was a mouthpiece promoting my administration and failed to say that it was funded jointly by City Hall and the London boroughs, which had a Tory majority. They were satisfied with its work and continued funding. Yvonne Thompson, who encouraged black women into business, was accused of doing nothing for her grant although she had organised twenty-three events that year. The story had been slanted to give the worst impression without giving grounds for Lee Jasper to sue.

Gilligan wrote that Joel O'Loughlin, who in the past had run a company with Lee, received an LDA grant for £295,000 for a project which had gone into liquidation. Gilligan implied Lee pushed the grant through, even though he had seen an email where Lee advised the LDA against the grant as he didn't think Joel could deliver the project. The *Standard* never once reported that Lee had opposed the grant.

The smears were repeated in the *Mail* and the *Mail*'s free sheets *Metro* and *London Light*. ITV's London regional news was circumspect but BBC regional TV reported the allegations. After working with Lee for two decades I knew he was honest. Lee left school without qualifications, became a single parent at twenty-three and raised his kids while studying at Manchester Poly. His ambitions were political, not financial. He used public transport and had lived in the same housing-association home for years. A sure sign of corruption is when a person moves into a mansion and starts driving an expensive car. That night Lee went on ITV's *London Tonight* and calmly explained the facts.

The next day Gilligan's headline was 'Taxpayers' cash used to attack Ken's rivals', above a story which 'revealed' that Lee and I had done everything possible to prevent Trevor Phillips taking over the government's new equalities organisation – this was hardly news to anyone who knew my differences with Phillips. The following day's headline screamed, 'Ken's £117,000 aide lives in £90pw council house'. Lee had never earned enough to buy his own home before I promoted him in 2004 and would have been mad to get a mortgage, given the insecurity of working for a politician.

The following Monday Gilligan claimed, 'Second Ken aide linked to City Hall cash scandal'. This story went back to 2004 when allegations were made against another of my advisers, Kumar Murshid. I'd taken these seriously because they were made by David Hencke in the *Guardian* and Kumar had resigned. Three years later Kumar was cleared by a court after an official in his charity admitted responsibility but Kumar was so disillusioned he left the Labour party. Kumar had been set up by enemies on Tower Hamlets Council who saw him as a threat because he had enough talent to lead the council. As he put it, only Asians who have been 'house trained' get to the top in Tower Hamlets. Gilligan recycled all the charges and buried away the acknowledgement that 'he stood trial but was acquitted'. Remembering Kumar, I wasn't going to sack Lee based on claims by a reporter of Gilligan's reputation.

On 11 December Gilligan claimed we had failed to answer his charges, which gave him the excuse to repeat them all. The *Standard* recycled the stories on 12, 13, 17, 18 and 30 December, adding smears from a former LDA secondee who had been forced to leave after complaints from co-workers.

*

Except for one piece in *The Times* only Mail Group titles had covered the story so the scale of coverage made me suspect their motives. They loathed my commitment to multiculturalism and in Boris they had a candidate who denounced it, but there was another issue at stake in all this. The mayor elected in 2008 would renew the contract for the daily *Metro* free sheet on the Underground. The contract had been rushed through before my first election and under it London Underground received just £1 million per year for allowing its distribution on the tube, which barely covered the cost of collecting discarded copies.

Metro was the brainchild of Lord Rothermere, the owner of the *Mail* and *Standard*, who came to City Hall to ask if I intended to renew when the contract ran out. I said we would let the contract through an open auction on the internet so that we got a bigger share of the profits. Rupert Murdoch was interested, as was Richard Desmond. A system of closed bids is always open to abuse and we were more likely to get Murdoch and Desmond committing to the costly process of bidding if it was an open auction.

Although other papers had not taken up Gilligan's smears, there was no such restraint on the part of Labour MP Kate Hoey. On 21 December Gilligan reported that Hoey had written to the Met urging an inquiry which gave the *Standard* the excuse to splash 'Police called in over City Hall scandal' on their front page. Gilligan claimed 'new allegations of fraud, violence and intimidation' over an LDA grant in 2002 to the Green Badge Taxi School, which trained taxi drivers from ethnic minorities who were taking the 'knowledge' exam. Hoey added lurid claims of threats between the taxi school and other tenants in the same block in her constituency. She said she had long been suspicious of the firm (though clearly not concerned enough to raise it with me). Our last private conversation had been when she'd come to me in tears in 2001 after being sacked as sports minister by Blair. I comforted her as best I could while she begged me not to give Tony Banks a job as my sports adviser. It never occurred to me Kate might have been angling for a job and I had no idea she had turned against me until she called me a 'dictator' in the run-up to congestion charging in 2003. I was also annoyed when she supported Paris for the Olympics. She refused to support me in the 2008 election and forty-eight hours before polling day announced she would be Boris's sports adviser if he won. Afterwards she said she couldn't remember who she voted for.

Gilligan's allegations had been raised months before by Tory Assembly member Richard Barnes and investigated and dismissed by Anthony Mayer and Martin Clarke, Anne McMeel's successor as GLA finance director. I asked them to look at them again and Manny Lewis at the LDA began a full investigation, which took time as inevitably some of the groups funded by the LDA had failed – not surprising as we funded projects in neighbourhoods where banks didn't invest, and many initiatives were led by people without formal qualifications. A group reaching out to kids on the periphery of gangs has to work with people in the local community.

The *Standard* never reported that every year 10 per cent of conventional firms in London also fail, and the LDA's failure rate was under a tenth of that.

Because he had nothing to hide, Lee rather naively kept his password on a post-it note stuck to his computer screen. Someone had downloaded the entire contents of Lee's computer going back years and passed them to the Tory group. After Anthony's first investigation cleared Lee the stolen files were passed to Gilligan, who combed through millions of words to find the few grants that failed and extract paragraphs and sentences out of context. For people seeing only the headlines or ubiquitous billboards screaming 'Mayor's aide and missing millions' it was enough to raise doubts.

*

Our Christmas was dampened when my medical check-up revealed a problem with my prostate and blood traces in my stool. Emma's medical also revealed that she might have breast cancer. I assumed the blood was just a matter of piles, the curse of anyone who has to sit for long periods, but I dreaded the problems associated with losing my prostate. Except for colds I'd been healthy all my life and averaged one day a year sick leave. Emma the same. We could not cope with two young children and an election if both of us were having chemotherapy at the same time. I didn't even discuss it with Simon, but I knew I might have to stand down.

With a sense of foreboding I turned up at University College Hospital to see a specialist and was elated to discover that it was a false alarm. As it can take twenty to twenty-five years for prostate cancer to develop, I would be in my eighties before there might be a problem. Emma's mammogram had also given misleading results. We were both in the clear. All that remained was for the hospital to check if I really had piles, so I dropped into UCH on 28 January on my way to City Hall.

Lying on the operating table as the microscopic camera relayed the image to the TV screen above my head, I saw three polyps silently growing. As the doctors snipped them out, they said they were probably benign but wouldn't know until they saw the lab results. Even if they were pre-cancerous, they had been caught in time and I just needed to have an annual check-up in case they recurred. It had taken barely an hour so before going back to work I went into the hospital canteen for a full English breakfast. I was amazed at the advances in cancer treatment in the forty years since I had worked at the Royal Marsden. Just twenty years earlier President Reagan had been in hospital for days for the same problem, and I smiled when I realised I was reminiscing about Reagan's rectum while eating my bacon and beans. One of the growths turned out to be pre-cancerous and without the check-ups I would have had full-blown cancer before knowing anything was wrong.

*

Emma and I were still waiting for our test results when we had the first debate of the campaign on ITV's *London Talking* with Boris for the Tories and Brian Paddick for the Lib Dems. Konnie Huq was in the chair. The *Morning Star* reported Boris's 'unfamiliarity with the issues' and criticism of his links to 'convicted fraudster Darius Guppy and disgraced media tycoon Conrad Black'. The *Standard* disagreed, just a little, saying Boris had clearly won with Paddick second and I 'appeared an angry old man . . . from a bygone era . . . Dressed in grey, he looked tired and every one of his sixty-two years. He became very angry very quickly . . . Ken, wounded by Boris's sharp journalistic probing, resorted to shouting to drown out his rival.' Paddick and I listened to Boris without interruption, in fact, but as I spoke Boris started bellowing over me. I was brought up not to interrupt others and was at a disadvantage up against the braying culture of the Bullingdon Club and Oxford

Union. Murdoch's *London Paper* reported that Konnie was forced to call for calm and quoted me as saying: 'Boris, you have got to let me answer. This is not the House of Commons, you just can't shout.'

*

Anthony Mayer's second investigation into Andrew Gilligan's allegations against Lee Jasper came to the same conclusion as the first – there was no corruption. Manny Lewis of the LDA had also investigated the allegations with the same result. When Tory Assembly member Richard Barnes raised them again Manny commissioned an internal enquiry overseen by the LDA's external auditors. When Manny came to see me with the results he was clear there had been no illegality, but we passed the report to the District Auditor to ensure it had been rigorous.

The Assembly called a session and asked me to answer briefly as they only had an hour. The cynicism was clear when I said I would stay for as long as it took to answer all questions and Labour proposed the meeting be extended and the Tories and the Lib Dems reluctantly had to agree. After several hours the *Guardian* concluded [Livingstone] had 'faced down his critics last night . . . the Mayor was grilled for more than two hours'. They reported my offer to 'phone Lee Jasper if you want and he will come down here and answer these questions himself'. I had pointed out the LDA operated with a much smaller team of lawyers compared with the seventy at the GLC who constantly monitored all our grants. My answers to the Assembly convinced most journalists this was just another Wadley witch-hunt so the issue receded.

A new front was then opened by Channel 4's *Dispatches* which told the *Observer* of 'incendiary claims that put the Mayor of London's personal and public life under intense scrutiny. Lawyers . . . have given Livingstone until Wednesday to respond to accusations.'

The *New Statesman*'s political editor Martin Bright had spent a year on this hatchet job and wanted me to respond in just a few days. If *Dispatches* had done a similar job on Boris that would have been one thing, but to attack one candidate just before the legal deadline which requires balanced coverage was outrageous. Complaining to Channel 4 was a waste of time as chief executive Luke Johnson had previously revealed I was his 'pet hate'.

Dispatches was Britain's most dubious documentary series. They had made programmes denying climate change and the existence of any link between HIV and Aids. Now they leaked claims to the press that I had a drink problem and had broken the law by using City Hall staff on my election campaign, but they did not allow me to preview the programme or be questioned live at the end. I sat down to watch it with a glass of Rioja and enjoyed it so much I immediately watched it again. After the leaks saying I might be forced to retire from public life it was bound to be a disappointment but the lack of substance wasn't obscured by Martin Bright at his most portentous. After thirty years of me being in the public eye, they couldn't find anyone who had ever seen me drunk but they claimed I was an alcoholic because I occasionally sipped a glass of whisky while being questioned by the Assembly for two and a half hours once a month – ignoring the fact that for centuries chancellors presenting their budgets to the House of Commons had sipped whisky or brandy to ease the strain on their voice. The *Telegraph* reported Brown's worry that I would lose the election. 'Concern over his drinking reached the highest levels of government,' they unctuously reported. The *Telegraph* also alleged that at the World Economic Summit in Davos I was 'apparently under the influence of alcohol. Tony Blair, David Miliband and Douglas Alexander were among those in the room.' The *Telegraph* failed to point out that I had two glasses of red wine while listening to long and worthy speeches by Blair and Bono at a charity fund-raiser. I also made the twenty-minute walk to my hotel over snow and ice without falling over.

The *Sun's* embittered political editor Trevor Kavanagh let his imagination rip, claiming I 'needed counselling from pals after turning up apparently drunk at a posh do for world leaders in Davos'. He concluded, 'I've known Ken as a manipulative, tinpot tyrant since . . . a Marxist coup more than thirty years ago [at the GLC] . . . I wouldn't trust this newt-loving egomaniac to walk a straight line – drunk or sober.'

Dispatches recycled Gilligan's claims with the added entertainment of getting passing shoppers to comment on the financial viability of LDA projects. Atma Singh claimed I was a stooge of the International Marxist Group. After being taught by Mo Mowlam, Atma had joined the IMG in 1981 where he met John Ross and Redmond O'Neill. Atma had once been on my side in the split in the Anti-Racist Alliance and was appointed as my adviser for Asian affairs.

On the day of the London bombings he was the only one of my advisers who did not come into work. He also failed to pass on messages from Special Branch. After he was confronted with this he went off sick, returning just before his sick pay entitlement ended. He told me he was well but then took sick leave again. After months with no contact he took a leaving package and disappeared until he popped up on *Dispatches*. Atma said that John and Redmond had illegally worked for my re-election but the advice of Tony Child, was that staff could work on my campaign in their own time.

Bright wrote that it was his 'duty to warn [Londoners that I was] a bully and a coward' but my poll ratings went up and *Dispatches* was quickly forgotten when BBC London revealed that a member of Lee's team failed to declare a free flight to Nigeria. Rosemary Emodi had worked hard trying to improve safety at the Notting

Hill Carnival, but it was a breach of the staff code and she had to resign. Rosemary's resignation prompted those newspapers which had ignored Wadley's campaign to suspect there might be something in it after all. Kate Hoey seized her chance. Working with Tory MP Greg Hands and Lib Dem MP Lynne Featherstone, she demanded a full police inquiry. Black groups said it was becoming difficult to raise funds with all the headlines about 'corruption'. Lee said he could no longer do his job because of Gilligan's coverage and asked me to refer his case to the police, so he was suspended on 15 February. I wrote to the officer leading the investigation asking him to extend it to cover Lee. He replied that after three months of investigation they could find no evidence of a crime being committed and Lee had no criminal case to answer so there was no evidence to justify an investigation into him. I believed these allegations had to be resolved so it was the only time I asked Sir Ian to overrule an investigating officer, which he reluctantly did.

Now Gilligan changed tack: 'One word we have quite deliberately never used about [Lee] is "corrupt" . . . Mr Jasper's alleged offences are not criminal. They are offences of misconduct in public office.' Gilligan overlooked the fact that misconduct in public office carries a maximum sentence of life imprisonment (and formerly the death penalty). Gilligan said, 'This is a matter for the District Auditor and the voters, not the Met.' In an interview in the *Independent* Gilligan admitted my 'stories have caused collateral damage, with other black organisations suddenly treated with mistrust by public bodies', going on to say, 'I'm afraid it's not our job to think about consequences like that.' Wadley sent hapless reporters to the mayoral debates to say the *Standard* had never alleged corruption, only misconduct. This was always greeted with laughter and disbelief by the audience. Gilligan couldn't help himself, however, and on 10 April 2008 referred to 'the mayor's waste and corruption'.

The Assembly had still not questioned Lee on the allegations.

When they raised them with me at Mayor's Questions, once again I told them that Lee was upstairs and ready to appear before them. The only time I had lost my temper with the Assembly was when they raised Bob Kiley's drink problem. Now I lost it again as I told them what I thought of their pathetic claim that they hadn't had enough time to read all the paperwork relating to Lee's non-existent case. It didn't stop members like Richard Barnes claiming in television interviews, 'A tide of corruption is lapping at the door of the mayor.'

The Assembly eventually agreed to interview Lee on 5 March. On the day before Gilligan filled the *Standard* with revelations of saucy emails Lee had sent to Karen Chouhan (a director of the Black Londoners Forum who had worked with Lee at the 1990 Trust). The previous November the Chouhans had been named 'Britain's brainiest family' after competing in the national finals of Nintendo's Big Brain Academy. Although there was no evidence of any financial or sexual impropriety Lee had made a stupid mistake. Taken on its own it would have justified a reprimand, but after the months of Gilligan's campaign he realised he couldn't continue working at the GLA and resigned.

*

The *Standard*'s attacks delayed preparations for my campaign but didn't have much impact on our policies. At the beginning of February our Low Emission Zone, covering 99 per cent of London, started on time. London has the worst air quality of any city in Europe, causing 3,000–5,000 premature deaths a year. We allowed plenty of time for lorries over twelve tonnes to fit converters, but the headlines drearily predicted 'that the lorry fee would wreck businesses', bring 'driver chaos' and – bizarrely – that the 'e-zone will add £750 to cost of removals'. But in the event there were no problems. Boris's website supported the low-emission zone to 'improve air quality' but, not having read his own material, in interviews he called the policy 'the most punitive, draconian fining regime in the whole of Europe'. Nearly two-thirds of Londoners supported the policy in opinion polls. To improve air quality further we planned to have 500 hybrid (part-electric, part-diesel-fuelled) buses by 2010 and from 2012 all new buses would be hybrid. I confirmed the congestion charge would go up to £25 a day for the worst-polluting vehicles (including many petrol-guzzling 4x4s). The German car maker Porsche decided to ask for a judicial review as they had neglected fuel efficiency and almost their entire range would be caught by the charge.

We took over the privatised Croydon Tram Link, which had been run for years with minimum service for maximum profit. Although bitterly opposed by the train operating companies, Ruth Kelly negotiated with me to transfer control of the Southern Rail franchise so I could set fares and timetables for their trains running in London. Government changed the law so that two new TfL board members would represent commuters from outside London. Finally, Steve Howes, representing the train companies, announced they would adopt the Oyster card by 2009 so that commuters could switch easily between over- and underground lines. We had built up reserves and balances of £1.5 billion so I cut bus fares to a 90p flat fare for anywhere to anywhere in greater London and froze them for 2008. Tube fare rises were held to inflation. A survey of travellers now rated London the best city in the world for transport and public transport use had increased by 20 per cent in just eight years. The C40 was close to agreeing a big reduction in the price of LED lights, which would have allowed us to replace all our street lighting over the next five years, and Honeywell and Dalkia got the job of retrofitting the first batch of our buildings, old police and fire stations, with energy-efficient lighting and improved insulation.

On 12 February 2008 *The Times* reported we were investing £75 million in our bike-hire scheme, which would start with 6,000 bikes in the summer of 2010 and quickly double. They would be free for the first hour, and cost £1 for each thirty minutes after that. Plans for twelve cycle 'super-highways' costing £400 million were reported in the *Guardian* on 9 February; the first would open in 2010 with five open before the Olympics. Boris continued with this policy but insisted the bike lanes had to be blue. The target was to increase cycling by 400 per cent by 2025. And on 5 March I met Tour de France organiser Christian Prudhomme, who was keen that London should host a stage of the Tour before 2010 and another Grand Départ after the Olympics.

We gave a grant of £5 million to a local community group, Boyz to Men, which steered vulnerable young men away from crime. This was the first grant from our £79 million budget for youth activities over the next two years. It was followed up by the Met's half-term-holiday weapons sweep, with metal detectors set up in parks, playgrounds and on public transport. Even with the election imminent I couldn't hide my opposition to the government's proposal to close another 200 post offices. The number of post offices in London had been halved to 667 so I launched a legal challenge.

*

Boris called for a referendum on the smoking ban without declaring that he was paid thousands for a speech to the Association of Tobacco Manufacturers. He also failed to declare that he owned a third of a television company, claiming it was an oversight. Boris agreed to pay rent for his offices when it was revealed the Shirayama Corporation was allowing his campaign to operate rent-free out of the building (the same offer I'd declined in 2000 because of their stated intention to build on the Jubilee Gardens site next door to County Hall). Boris was also forced to return a £25,000 donation from tax exile Lord Laidlaw. Most papers did not report any of these issues. In a poll of 185 fund managers, the *Standard* reported, Boris had a 35 per cent lead over me with most of his donations coming from rich financiers from equity houses, hedge funds and investment boutiques. Cameron and five other ex-Bullingdon members were among guests at a £1,000-a-head meal at Altitude on the twenty-ninth floor of Millbank Tower, where they raised £200,000 for Boris.

As in 2004, I left fund-raising to the Labour party, but I couldn't resist the Aquarium Gallery auction where artists including Marc-Quinn, Antony Gormley and Jamie Reid donated works, raising £35,000 for my campaign. Held back to the end was a Banksy piece showing two children declaring an oath of allegiance to a Tesco flag. Three very serious men, who didn't look like Labour supporters, with phones clamped to their ears took the bidding to £195,000 in just four minutes. In one evening we covered half the cost of my campaign.

*

I had previously had trouble with Prince Charles. We planned to extend the East London Line to Croydon but he worked behind the scenes to prevent it going through the Bishopsgate goods yard, which contained the listed Braithwaite Viaduct. This had been a derelict site since it was burned down in the 1960s, but English Heritage and the prince wanted it restored because it was the first goods yard of its type. We were able to preserve the viaduct's arches by running the East London Line along the top of them, but the prince's campaign caused a two-year delay.

Now Prince Charles intervened in the mayoral election. In a speech on 31 January 2008 he claimed that tall buildings 'pockmarked' the city. The *Telegraph* was delighted at this 'thinly veiled attack on the policies of Ken Livingstone'. I might have worried if anyone in London was likely to be influenced by the heir to the throne. Charles's former deputy private secretary, Mark Bolland, was blunter. 'I've always loathed Livingstone . . . Where on the planet outside Africa is there . . . a more brutal, bigoted and aggressive politician?' Madonna was another person whose vote I couldn't count on after she told *The Times*, 'The traffic is worse than ever. Now all Red Ken wants is roadworks going on everywhere. I would make it so that aspiring musicians wouldn't have to pay the congestion charge, or pay taxes. They should be exempt.' Gordon Ramsay called for me to be 'dropped in the Thames'.

All the environmental groups (but not Prince Charles) turned up for the first hustings of the campaign on green issues. I expected Boris to be torn apart but he joked, the audience laughed and he was not challenged once. Promising 'I'll teach Ken to ride a bike', he praised my bike-hire scheme and when I reminded him he had praised Bush for not signing the Kyoto Treaty he blustered, 'It is rubbish – stuff and nonsense.' This was Boris at his most effective: shaking his head, joking and getting away with it. That debate set the pattern. Every promise I made Boris endorsed. After thirty-five years of Tory attacks on pensioners' free travel, he endorsed my plan to make it a 24/7 service. He only disagreed with the western extension of the congestion charge, 50 per cent affordable housing targets and the construction of tall buildings. It was like being followed by an echo. He was also good at dealing with questions he knew nothing about. When asked if he supported 'contraction and convergence' he replied he had always believed in contracting and converging. Paddick got agitated, saying it was an unfair question, so the questioner explained it meant Western nations reducing their carbon emissions and the developing world increasing theirs until both converged at a point which was sustainable for humanity's future. Geoffrey Lean in the *Independent on Sunday* quoted Boris attacking wind farms 'crucifying our landscape . . . which, even when they are in motion, would barely pull a skin off a rice pudding'. Geoffrey added, 'Now he wants to provide more renewable energy.'

Although despised, politicians do acquire skills that can't be picked up overnight and Brian Paddick as an ex-police officer struggled. For someone born and brought up in London he was surprisingly brittle, wooden and old-fashioned. Unlike Boris, he got very personal, saying '[Ken is] a really nasty little man . . . very unpleasant.' Admitting he had seriously considered an approach from Cameron to be the Tory candidate, Paddick claimed he'd been 'more of a figurehead than Ken Livingstone' on the occasion of the London bombings.

Paddick was worse on *Question Time*, when, with Boris's wife Marina and her parents in the audience, he raised Boris's affair with Petronella Wyatt, telling him, 'You lied to your wife.' The audience gasped and I was dumbstruck. I had never seen a candidate raise the family life of another before and as Paddick had lived with his wife for five years before admitting he was gay he had no right to cast the first stone. Afterwards we joined Dimbleby for dinner where Marina's father Charles Wheeler quietly asked what I felt about Paddick's behaviour and was delighted when I said it was deplorable. A stilted evening was avoided when Paddick announced he wasn't staying because it was his birthday and the BBC wouldn't pay for champagne.

Once or twice during the campaign Boris's mask slipped. Challenged on his opposition to civil partnerships, he smashed his fist on the table shouting, 'Enough!', but this was not reported. After *Question Time* the cameras were still on us as a smiling Boris draped his arm around my shoulders and said, 'If you carry on talking about my grandfather I'm going to punch your lights out.' He was upset by my joke that although Boris was wooing Turkish Londoners by invoking his Turkish grandfather he didn't say that his grandfather was beaten to death by a mob because he was a British spy working against Atatürk. He also told the *Guardian*'s Jonathan Freedland, one of his critics, he was 'full of shit' and should stop spreading 'poison'.

*

YouGov gave Boris a lead of 13 per cent but most polls had us neck and neck. Worried that my defeat could lead to a leadership challenge against him, Brown pulled the whole Labour party machine into London. With the issue of Lee Jasper fading, Andrew Gilligan and the *Standard* switched to denying all the successes of the last eight years. The congestion charge hadn't worked, bus improvements were nothing to do with me, crime reduction figures were a fraud and our environmental policies were a sham. The *Standard*'s headlines claimed that the cost of the Olympics would more than double to £20 billion, that 'Suicide bomb backer runs Ken campaign' and that 'Ken talks to front for banned Tamil Tigers' (this was a meeting of the Tamil Forum in Harrow), all in stark contrast to 'Charmer Boris, a one-man Messiah' (as if there were any other sort). The *Standard* headline: 'Ken's adviser is linked to banned terror group' referred to TfL board member Dabinderjit Singh, who had spoken at a Sikh Federation rally in Trafalgar Square. In Gilligan's eyes this was enough to link him to a plane bomb that had killed 329 people in 1985. The story omitted to mention that Singh was chief auditor for the Ministry of Defence and therefore had the second-highest security clearance level possible.

The *Standard* didn't report that at a debate they organised for Boris at Cadogan Hall one of his supporters called journalist Yasmin Alibhai-Brown 'a cunt' and told her to 'go back to Uganda'. Michael Eboda, another speaker, was also racially abused and black people in the audience were 'pursued . . . and accused of being agents of Ken Livingstone'. Black police present were concerned at the 'intimidatory atmosphere'. Boris was forced to apologise that he had allowed Taki in the *Spectator* to write a column claiming the brains of black people were smaller than those of whites but compensated with a U-turn on *The Politics Show* when he raised 'concerns' about uncontrolled immigration. Boris ignored the claim by Rod Liddle that in a car in Uganda he had told the black driver, 'Let's get out and see some piccaninnies.'

The *Standard*'s coverage had by now become so demented that it was no longer having any effect on my campaign. What was having an effect was the state of the economy. With falling house prices and rising mortgage payments, the British economy slipped into recession. Even more damaging was the impending abolition of the 10p tax band, which would hit the poorest hardest. This had barely been noticed in Brown's budget a year earlier because it was linked to a 2p cut in income tax. The Institute for Fiscal Studies warned that 5.3 million families could lose out with those earning less than £18,000 seeing their tax double. The people worst hit were mainly Labour voters hanging on to low-paid jobs. When Alistair Darling's budget confirmed that the 10p tax band would go, voters realised what it would mean for them and my canvassers said it was playing badly on the doorstep. Characteristically and stubbornly, Brown insisted the poorest would really be better off and dug in until he was forced to introduce a compensation package a week before polling day on 1 May. YouGov's post-budget poll showed Labour's support at just 27 per cent and in London it was down to 24 per cent. Much later, Labour's pollster, Philip Gould, told me, 'After the March budget Labour's vote and yours just went off a cliff.' On 17 March YouGov gave Boris a 12 per cent lead and a MORI poll showed the *Standard*'s campaign on Lee and teenage killings had had an impact with voters thinking Boris more honest than me although I led among women, young voters and on all the issues except crime.

*

Blair sent a handwritten letter saying I could still win and we threw everything into the campaign. Even Neil Kinnock was wheeled out to endorse me, which I had never expected and which, from the look on his face, required a supreme effort. The successes of the last eight years were confirmed when in interviews I kept being asked, 'What was your biggest mistake?' If I had made a big mistake the press wouldn't have needed me to tell them what it was. The right now threw everything into the campaign too. Even after all these years I was still shocked by the nastiness I evoked, with the *Mail*'s Peter Oborne saying I was 'an almost habitual, pathological liar'. In the *Observer* Nick Cohen, a self-proclaimed left-wing intellectual who had become a crusader for the Iraq War, said that I had 'embraced the far right ... supported homophobes, misogynists and racists ... presided over ... corruption ... [supported] shady property developers', and urged a vote for Paddick. Littlejohn in the *Mail* said I was 'a cynical, rabble-rousing bigot who makes Enoch Powell look like a boy scout'.

I had just launched my manifesto on crime and policing when we got the shocking news that two teenagers had been murdered that day. I visited the parents of one of the victims, who was not involved in any gang but just in the wrong place at the wrong time. Thinking of my own children as I sat with the parents, I couldn't imagine how anyone could get though something like this.

I'd been looking forward to the Olympic Torch being run through London because in 2004 on the way to Athens the torch had brought huge crowds onto London's streets and in some places slowed the run to a walk. Unfortunately I woke to a bitterly cold and snowy April morning and everybody stayed home. My advisers were now really worried at how down and depressed I seemed so Mark Watts was sent to try and cheer me up in a coffee shop in West End Lane. He argued that the MORI poll still showed I had a chance to win and I grimly joked that Mark would be better off focusing his efforts on how to win the mayoralty back in 2012.

Although Boris spent most of his time talking about how bad crime was, on 16 April the Met reported crime had fallen by another 6 per cent in the last twelve months with robbery down 19 per cent, rape 16.7 per cent, murder 4.8 per cent, gun crime 1.4 per cent, violent crime 8 per cent, domestic violence 16.9 per cent, race crime 13.3 per cent and homophobic crime 17.1 per cent. Paddick said the figures were unreliable, though he'd earlier been quite happy to take credit for similar figures covering his patch in Lambeth. Boris claimed that there was huge under-reporting of crime, which would surprise anyone who read the *Mail*, and promised on LBC, 'I won't run again if I haven't made a huge reduction in crime. I intend to exceed 20 per cent.'

*

Given my awkward gaucheness during childhood and beyond, I was taken aback by press charges of arrogance. When I'd worked at Chester Beatty I'd always wished I could have the confidence of my mentor Tom Connors and had been in awe of the doctors there. After I joined the Labour party I was amazed to be elected a councillor and struggled to find my feet at Lambeth. I was a bit more confident at the GLC but felt like an apprentice to Tony Banks. I was always slightly bemused to be in these posts. I used to believe that those in power were somehow inherently different from the rest of the population, and certainly more able than me. As I came to work with ministers and eventually prime ministers and presidents I realised that was by no means true, but when I won a contest it was usually because I put my private life on hold to work harder and longer to convince the voters that my policies were the right ones, not because I was in some way better or cleverer than my opponents.

What the newspapers described as arrogance was really my refusal to buckle in the face of their hysterical campaigning.

Editors expect politicians, particularly Labour representatives, to back down as they ratchet up the noise; but even in the worst times strangers would stop me to say, 'Don't give in.' There was always more popular support for my policies than was ever reflected in the media.

The campaign was diverted for forty-eight hours when the BBC asked me about my three older children, Georgia, Lottie and Liam. I had so far done a pretty good job of keeping my kids out of the public eye, but inevitably they were briefly mentioned in a new biography, *Ken*, by Andrew Hosken, which was about to be published. The BBC jumped the gun and at the end of an interview on BBC London Tim Donovan let the cat out of the bag by asking about my family.

The same day Boris admitted he had taken cannabis and cocaine in his youth, allowing the papers to proclaim it a 'day of confessions'. The next day I was on a walkabout in Holloway and several nervous Labour party officials joined the scrum of photographers and camera crews who demanded I kiss each baby we passed. No one raised the issue until an elderly lady elbowed her way through the journalists to say, 'Mr Livingstone, I think you should have all the girlfriends you want.' The officials relaxed, the journalists drifted away, but *Mail* and *Telegraph* reporters stayed outside Jan and Liam's front door for another day before giving up. When Tessa Jowell asked why I hadn't told her about my children I reminded her that the Labour party leaked the information in 1999 to prevent me becoming mayor. She replied, 'Oh, yes, I think I remember that now.'

Although thousands of people, including one lobby correspondent whose children went to the same school, knew about my kids no one ever tried to make money by selling the story. I had taken them round Parliament, the zoo, museums, restaurants and local fêtes and we holidayed together every year. When Georgia's boyfriend reported a stolen bike the officer asked, 'Aren't you the boy going out with the Mayor's daughter?' I was amused when the *Standard* claimed to have 'known for some years about the Mayor's son and two daughters from another, earlier relationship, but chose not to publish the story'. The *Telegraph* said Georgia and Lottie were in their late thirties and early forties (actually they were seventeen and fifteen).

In the BBC interview I had said, 'There's a difference between private and secret and I think the media has got to understand that . . . I don't think anybody in this city is shocked about what consenting adults do. As long as you don't involve children, animals or vegetables they leave people to get on and live their own life in their own way.' I pointed out that over the years I had 'canvassed tens of thousands of people. On occasion they ask how the kids are and on a one-to-one I am happy to talk about that, but with the media I am not. My private life isn't my sole property. It's been shared with other people and they expect it to stay private.' In the *Sun* I was 'Bed Hopper Ken . . . randy Livingstone . . . dubbed Bed Ken'. They claimed I took all five children on holidays to Sardinia, an island which I have never visited. They asked, 'Do you know Ken Livingstone's secret family? Ring the *Sun* on 020 7782 4103.'

That it was right to keep them out of the public eye was confirmed by comments from Janet Street-Porter: 'Finding quality time for all his kids, who range in age from girls in their thirties to small toddlers, must be fiendishly difficult . . . I wonder, though, how the women fared. Were they left behind to bring up these kids by themselves? Now Livingstone has gone public they must be fearing unwelcome intrusion into their lives. They have been sacrificed on the altar of his ambition . . . I find his hypocrisy nauseating.' The *Mail*'s Amanda Platell added that the 'public surely has the right to ask . . . what kind of father he has been to his own offspring. There are legitimate personal questions . . . especially for one in charge of an £11 billion budget. Has he supported them all financially? How involved has he actually been in parenting his five children? How does he differ from the "baby fathers" whose serial philandering has blighted so many of London's poorer communities?' Edwina Currie speculated, 'Perhaps "come up and see my biggest newt" was a more successful chat up line than we all realised.' Carole Malone asked in the *News of the World* 'Weren't you shocked that there were three women in the world willing to have sex with [him]?' Martin Samuel in *The Times* complained, '[He] knocks five kids out in three relationships . . . and tells the world to mind its business . . . and not a peep from left or right.' Fortunately Georgia, Lottie and Liam were old enough to laugh at this crap, but no young child should be exposed to such vitriol and if we could have kept the existence of Tom and Mia secret we would have, but of course everyone at City Hall knew when Emma was pregnant.

*

Boris skipped many hustings, including *Time Out*'s, refused to appear on *Any Questions* or take part in a debate on the *Today* programme. Jonathan Freedland in the *Guardian* said that when the candidates have 'the chance to lay out a case that goes deeper than sound bites or photo ops, Ken goes to town – and Boris goes to pieces. Johnson can do the first sentence or two, but drill down any further and there is nothing there . . . His mouth moved up and down but no words would come out. He hit his obvious applause lines well enough . . . but has no real command. He looked uncomfortable too, clearly under strict orders from his handlers, led by the Australian election hard man Lynton Crosby, to say nothing that would get him into trouble – and therefore saying not much at all. The result was that Livingstone was able to make inroads in what was deeply hostile terrain, a *Standard*-run debate, in true blue, 4x4-driving Kensington and Chelsea.'

Boris's campaign organised a dozen protesters to follow me on walkabouts. When I arrived at Borough Market with TV presenter turned political commentator June Sarpong and the Green party's Siân Berry, they obscured our posters with theirs and shouted us down, and after they pushed the Greens' Jenny Jones around we cut the tour short before it became really violent. BBC London concentrated on Lee Jasper's resignation to the near-exclusion of any debate on policies and in the last studio interview with Boris asked him three times if he thought I was corrupt. When I was interviewed the following day I wasn't asked once about Boris's indiscretions or misdemeanours.

The final YouGov poll the day before the election gave Boris a 6 per cent lead but others showed us neck and neck. Since I didn't believe that online polling was as accurate as telephone polling, I threw everything into election day, starting in Stratford and working my way across London to end the evening in Brent. Local authority elections were taking place across the country. I was exhausted and fell asleep before results came in from councils outside London, so only when I turned on the radio at 7 a.m. on Friday morning did I learn that the Tories had 44 per cent to Labour's 24 per cent nationwide, our worst result since 1968. I knew immediately I couldn't overcome a 20 per cent Tory lead. The declaration wasn't due until that evening, but after telling Emma I didn't expect to win I went for a swim on the way into City Hall and began clearing my desk. John Ross was already packing up his office as Simon and the team drifted in to start clearing out.

*

Owing to a heavier-than-expected turnout the declaration was delayed until midnight. Early results showed me running 13 per cent ahead of the party nationally. While Boris did well in Bromley, Bexley, Havering and Hillingdon the Labour vote was up 20 per cent in Tower Hamlets, we hung on to our marginal Assembly seat in Enfield and to the Tories' surprise captured Harrow and Brent. At one point Boris's lead over me was down to 2 per cent but several Tory boroughs were still counting.

Brown phoned to commiserate and seemed genuinely upset, but whether this was because I was losing or because my loss might open up a leadership challenge to him wasn't clear. He said, 'We should think about working together on environmental issues in the future.' I said 'I would love to,' but given our differences on nuclear power and a third runway at Heathrow I added, 'We need to be certain we agree on the issues because we would both look fools if after a few months I resigned or you had to sack me.' 'Yes, I see what you mean,' he replied.

Backstage, before the formal announcement, Boris bounced over to say, 'This is not you. It's Brown's fault.' After the declaration and speeches I got Boris away from his staff alone in a side room. I said, 'I've got three bits of advice. The TfL team are the best transport officials in the world. Listen to Peter Hendy and Tim O'Toole and do what they tell you. There isn't anyone better. If you are now serious about tackling climate change then keep Mark Watts and his environment team. Mark knows everybody you need to work with. Finally, don't make decisions quickly. Take your time to work out what you want to do and who you want to bring in. I will make sure any of my staff stay to help during the transition if you want them.'

On the way to the lift Green leader Darren Johnson said it had been a real pleasure working with me and we had achieved a lot on environmental issues. Back upstairs my team drifted into my room but when Redmond proposed a toast to what we had achieved I knew I wouldn't be able to cope with their kindness. 'Thanks,' I said, 'but I just want to go home.'

19

Beyond Boris

2008–2011

Next morning I hired a van to remove my personal papers and was clearing the office when my son Liam phoned to ask how I was. I was overwhelmed with a sense of loss and tears rolled down my face. I spent the weekend with the kids and a very neglected garden but without warning every now and then I found myself quietly weeping. On Tuesday, Simon, Redmond, John, Mark and Murz came over and we sat in the garden looking at Mark's analysis of my vote compared with the vote for Labour Assembly candidates in each of London's 630 wards. I had run ahead of the Labour party vote in all wards – inner and outer, rich or poor, black or white, Muslim or Jewish. The team wanted me to make an early declaration that I would run again but I wanted to wait a couple of years until after the next general election. Redmond warned this would give New Labour time to build support for a rival so we compromised. I would let the unions, Labour Assembly members, party officials and the Greens know I would run in 2012 but wouldn't start campaigning until after the general election.

Mark's analysis showed that over half of Londoners voted for the Labour, Lib Dem, Green and Respect parties with the Tories, UKIP and BNP well behind. London had a progressive majority and to build links across those parties we set up Progressive London, open to anyone. At our first conference over 700 people came.

*

Boris tried to reassure staff by saying he was not a 'crazed neo-con', telling them, 'The differences between me and the previous mayor have been greatly exaggerated.' But he told Policy Exchange that he was 'the utensil that scraped Ken Livingstone from the soles of Londoners'. My first experience of Boris's pettiness came when I turned up at City Hall to discover my security pass had been blocked and I was only to be allowed in the building if accompanied by an official. When the DLR extension to Woolwich and the East London Line extension to Croydon were opened I wasn't invited to either ceremony. Tessa Jowell made sure I was invited to the unveiling of the Hyde Park memorial to the victims of the July bombings but in the eyes of City Hall I had become a non-person. Boris refused ever to appear on any platform with me and every attempt from radio and television to organise a debate was refused.

Boris had a busy first day, closing our office in Venezuela which we had opened to provide advice on how to improve their transport system in exchange for a cut in our bus fuel bill (this would cost Londoners £56 million during Boris's term). He also got rid of Mark Watts, which sent a bad sign to environmentalists, so every candidate Boris asked to be his environmental adviser declined. In the end he turned to Isabel Dedring, who led the team of analysts working on my Climate Change Action Plan. Boris wanted to chair the C40 but the only mayor supporting him was New York's Michael Bloomberg so Toronto's David Miller took over. Boris was allowed to be vice-chair but told he would not become chair when David Miller stood down. (Two years later Bloomberg got the job.) At the first conference call of the C40 executive Boris apparently lost interest after twenty minutes and asked if he could leave. He cut the environment programme by £139 million, saved £189,000 by getting rid of staff in the environment team and ended the London Schools Environment Awards but this did not stop the eco-friendly Prince Charles sending him a handwritten letter of 'warm regards'. This was followed up by handwritten memos on planning issues every few months and regular meetings.

As the answer to Boris's most frequently asked question – 'Whose responsibility is that?' – was 'Yours', it began to dawn on him that he was now the elected chief executive. When being briefed on crime trends for his first meeting with the Home Secretary he joked, 'The biggest crime is that I got elected on a platform of cutting crime when crime rates were already coming down under Ken.' He laughed but then looked embarrassed when he realised the City Hall staff present weren't laughing. Three weeks after the election it was announced that knife crime in London had fallen by 10 per cent. Because of the success of our use of knife scanners on the tube, offences were down from seventy a month to twenty.

On 10 July Andrew Gilligan wrote that stabbings had fallen by 8 per cent in the last year and wondered 'whether London child knife use is due to local fashion – a perverted teenaged copycat craze [and] the current media and political angst is actually fuelling that craze. Does all the coverage of knife crime reinforce kids' idea that London is a place where going unarmed is risky? Do TV pictures add a touch of glamour [to] dying young? I am not saying the press should stop reporting knife crime but I think we should describe the "epidemic" more precisely and the political response should aim to be a fairly low-key behind-the-scenes one.' Boris agreed in his *Telegraph* column of 6 October, saying, 'The more we talk about knife crime and the more we dramatise it the more some young people will . . . carry a knife as a mark of respect.' As media interest faded Gilligan reported on 3 November that there had been no stabbings for five weeks, adding, 'If there is a reduction in knife crime it won't be Boris's doing. He hadn't been around long enough.'

In the first six years I was mayor we had an average of seventeen teenage murders a year. This soared to twenty-six in 2007 with twenty-seven teenagers murdered in the first nine months of 2008 as press coverage became hysterical. I had been roundly denounced by the media for saying during the campaign what Gilligan and Boris were now saying after the election. No one can prove it but I believe all three of us were right to make the point that the media coverage encouraged more teenagers to carry a knife and led to more deaths.

*

When told he would have to attend the Beijing Olympics, Boris asked, 'Are you sure I have to go? I am supposed to be in France then.' I had planned to be there for the full three weeks and had got the city's mayor to let us use a historic pavilion in Beijing's equivalent of St James's Park. With a huge model of the East End showing sites for sale it would have been an amazing opportunity to showcase London and for British firms to secure sales contracts but since it would have to be paid for out of the mayor's budget, Boris scrapped it. He attended just the closing ceremony. Announcing he would fly economy, his staff lobbied BA for an upgrade which was refused.

The Chinese were aware of Boris's 2005 article in the *Telegraph* saying, 'We do not need to teach babies Mandarin ... The Chinese have an economy smaller than Italy's ... Chinese cultural influence is virtually nil, and unlikely to increase ... High Chinese culture and art are almost all imitative of Western forms ... It is hard to think of a single Chinese sport at the Olympics ... Ping pong ... originated at British upper-class dinner tables and was first called Whiff Whaff. And how many people do you know who can speak even a sentence of Chinese? ... The Chinese aren't even out of the paddock.'

He made things worse at the closing ceremony by shambling into the stadium with jacket undone, hands in his pockets, stomach hanging over his belt and forgetting to shake hands with Beijing's mayor or acknowledge the country's president. Not every nation is as relaxed as Britain about questions of dress and protocol and the contrast between Beijing's immaculately attired mayor striding forward respectfully and Boris looking as though he'd just got off his train at the wrong stop didn't play well. It got worse with his speech aimed at voters back home in which he recycled his views from the whiff-whaff article. The mayor of Beijing has not met Boris since.

*

Boris didn't trust the staff at City Hall so the GLA was forced to spend £465,000 to pay for a fifteen-strong team of 'consultants' (mainly from Tory Central Office) led by Nick Boles to oversee the transition. Boris refused to say who was paid what. The failure to consult existing staff had occasional humorous consequences. When Mayor Bloomberg paid a good-will visit he presented Boris with a crystal Tiffany apple. Boris didn't ask staff if there was a City Hall equivalent and, as Bloomberg said, 'Boris was not yet accustomed to the diplomatic niceties. He pulled out a shirt with a map of the tube on it. It was hilariously awful and I will never wear it.' Equally embarrassing was Boris's appearance on the *Today* programme where he was asked about the funding agreement for the Olympics that I had reached with the government and airily dismissed the question, saying, 'I rather doubt any such agreement exists.' I couldn't resist phoning the programme and relished pointing out that if Boris had bothered to check the briefing he would have been given the night before it would have been one of the documents he would be expected to read before appearing on the programme. Staff started to leave as they became bored by the lack of work.

Boris struggled to form an administration. Neither he nor Cameron had expected Boris to win when he'd been put up as a candidate so neither had given serious thought about what to next. As Boris had no management experience and was bored by detail, the Tories decided to bring in Tim Parker as the man to actually run the show while Boris did the public relations.

Parker was a fifty-two-year-old ruthless asset stripper from the private sector with a personal fortune of £75 million. He had 'downsized' the workforce at the AA, Kwik-Fit, Clarks Shoes and Kenwood, on one occasion turning up in his Porsche 911 to announce the job losses personally. He didn't know it but he was to be just one amongst many of Boris's appointments who wouldn't last ten minutes.

First to go was Barclays' Bob Diamond, who had agreed in the campaign to be chair of the mayor's fundraising committee for charitable causes. He was followed by James McGrath, Boris's thirty-four-year-old Australian chief political adviser, who was sacked after he said of 'West Indians' who didn't like Boris, 'Well let them go if they don't like it here.' Eleven days later Ray Lewis, whom Boris appointed to deal with youth crime, quit because of sexual and financial allegations (which he denied) and for saying he was a magistrate when he wasn't. Four days later Nick Boles quit and on 23 August Tim Parker was forced out when Westminster Council leader Simon Milton, who was another Boris adviser, told Boris, 'Either Parker goes or I do.' Boris had also made Bexley's Tory leader, Ian Clement, a deputy mayor. Clement was a down-to-earth, working-class Tory and he and I had worked together opposing the carbon-emitting incinerator the government was forcing on the borough so I was surprised to see him prosecuted for using a GLA credit card for non-business purposes.

This left Boris relying heavily on the old Westminster Council mafia that succeeded Lady Porter. As well as Simon Milton, who was made deputy mayor (he, not Parker, was to become the real 'number two'), fellow Westminster City councillor Kit

Malthouse was given responsibility for policing. The chief executive of the LDA, Manny Lewis, who had succeeded Mike Ward, was forced out and Westminster Council's chief executive Peter Rogers was put in charge. It was Milton, Malthouse and Rogers who had overseen the final settlement in Porter's gerrymandering case. Milton's then deputy, Malthouse, flew to Brussels on 21 April 2004 to meet in secret with Porter. After discussions lasting all day it was agreed Porter would pay just £12.3 million of the £48 million she owed Westminster taxpayers, even though Westminster had discovered £34 million of Porter family funds held in an account in Guernsey which they had had frozen. Instead of referring this squalid deal to the Standards Board for England, Peter Rogers had complained instead to the SBE that the leader of the Labour group on Westminster had brought the council into disrepute by leaking information to Andrew Hosken, the journalist pursuing Porter! Having this gang running City Hall did not fill me with confidence.

Although these were depicted by Boris as little local difficulties, his problem with his Olympic adviser David Ross threatened to engulf David Cameron. At just forty-three, Ross was already the eighty-seventh-richest Brit. While much of the money had come from his father, who had founded Ross Frozen Foods and ran Europe's largest fishing fleet, David had made his own fortune with Carphone Warehouse. Dividing his time between 'tax-efficient' Geneva and his ninety-room mansion at Nevill Holt estate, he had just spent £23 million on two grouse moors. He was known to the readers of the red tops for his relationship with Ali Cockayne, the former girlfriend of Will Carling; she was followed by Shelley Ross, a Stringfellows pole dancer who had rubbed shoulders with David and Samantha Cameron when she helped organise the 2006 Tory summer ball and brought in waitresses on roller skates clad in hot pants.

Although he had gone from prep school to being a boarder at Uppingham, where he made money employing future DJ Johnny Vaughan as his runner selling pens and cigarette lighters to the other boys, he affected an East End barrow-boy manner. As a close friend of Tory treasurer Lord Marland, Ross had been one of the Tories' biggest donors and had been considered as a possible Tory candidate for mayor. He was close enough to David Cameron to take him to see the England football team play in Germany and fly Cameron back and forth to Yorkshire in his private helicopter.

Boris had appointed Ross as his Olympic adviser, giving him a seat next to Seb Coe on the board of LOCOG and making him chair of the committee overseeing the Olympic legacy. In June he had produced a report, considered insubstantial, which warned that additional funding would be needed for the Olympics. Suddenly Ross was on the front pages of all the papers when it was revealed he had secretly used £162 million of his shares in Carphone Warehouse to secure loans from JP Morgan's private bank. This practice is allowed only if other shareholders on the board are informed, which he had failed to do for nearly two years. The press were unanimous in saying he had to go but Boris refused to sack him. A statement from the Mayor's Office said, 'All we have to go on is his firm saying it's an oversight' and Boris 'did not want to prejudge the issue' before any decision by the Financial Services Authority. As the press started exploring the links between him, Boris and Cameron, Ross announced he was resigning. Cameron said, 'He has done the right thing,' while Boris stated, 'Accepted with regret and sad to see him go.' His close friend Channel 4 boss Luke Johnson told the *Daily Telegraph* that Ross had been treated unfairly: 'Much of the criticism of David is based on envy . . . it is a pretty minor technical mistake.' Not for the first time or the last it seemed there was one rule for Boris and his class and another for the rest of us.

Boris strengthened his team with journalist Anthony Browne, yet another recruit from Policy Exchange, who had a rough ride when questioned by the Assembly about his article in the *Spectator* claiming that 'Islam really does want to conquer the world' and his fears that mass immigration could bring diseases that would wipe out the British people. Anthony Mayer was replaced as City Hall's chief executive by Barnet Council's chief executive Leo Boland. Trevor Phillips had initially created the post to undermine me with a rival power base but Anthony had worked closely with me and his civil-service contacts helped persuade government to devolve new powers to City Hall. With that work done it was becoming hard to justify the expense of having both a chief executive and a mayor, and I planned to abolish the post when Anthony retired. I was horrified that Boris paid off Anthony and appointed Boland at an increased salary of £250,000. However, it allowed Boris to share out the work so he could resume his old job as a columnist for the *Telegraph*. Two and a half years later Boris realised his mistake and abolished the post of chief executive, incurring a huge pay-off to Boland. Boris's failure to pick up the phone and just ask me if he really needed a chief executive cost Londoners nearly a million pounds.

*

Except for Peter Oborne, who said the arrangement was 'greedy and hubristic', no one reported that the Barclay Brothers, tax-exile owners of the *Daily Telegraph*, were paying Boris £250,000 to write a weekly column. This meant that Boris was in no position to ignore the *Telegraph*'s campaign for a new Routemaster, even though the five that were ordered cost £7.8 million and have still not been delivered at the time of writing. The *Telegraph* had also campaigned for Sir Ian Blair to be sacked and Boris obliged, even though such a major upheaval at the Met might slow the improvement in the crime figures. The new commissioner, Sir Paul

Stephenson, resigned after just two and a half years, further demoralising the Met.

Although Boris was on the *Telegraph*'s payroll, the paper oddly failed to include his parliamentary expenses in its 'Complete Expenses Files' supplement about MPs' manipulation of their allowances. However, the *Independent* reported Boris had claimed £85,299 on his second-home allowance between 2004 and 2008, even though his Henley constituency is only forty miles from Westminster.

The Barclay Brothers also helped Boris by employing Andrew Gilligan (at over £100,000 a year) as their 'London editor' so he could continue attacking me in the four years up to the 2012 mayoral election, none of which counted towards Boris's election costs. What I found more worrying was that Gilligan's twin obsessions – me and Islam – had taken over his whole life. With his frequent appearances at my public meetings, Gilligan seemed more like a stalker than a reporter and there was often an air of menace when he phoned to say, 'I'm running a story about you.' Worried what he might do if I won in 2012, I joked with friends about coming home to find him holding a blood-stained axe over the bodies of Emma and the kids.

Boris asked the *Telegraph*'s Patience Wheatcroft to chair a committee of Tory council leaders to investigate the allegations against Lee Jasper. Fearing a stitch-up, I was amazed when she reported there was no evidence of any illegality and that no rules had been broken. The *Standard* got round this problem by putting it to Wheatcroft that 'surely millions of pounds were wasted?' Of course, as a Tory she did think my policies were a waste of money and that allowed the *Standard* to run a 'millions wasted' headline and bury the news that nothing illegal had been discovered. BBC London followed the *Standard* and focused on the 'millions wasted' rather than the fact that Lee had been exonerated.

The police investigation continued but at Lee's interview in November 2008 officers dismissed the whole thing as 'just political'. After a thirty-two month investigation into all the *Standard*'s allegations police could find no evidence to charge any member of my staff or anyone at Brixton Base, the Green Badge Taxi School or any other of the organisations they looked at. The result of the inquiry was not released either by the Met or by the Mayor's Office. A report published in June 2009 after an eighteen-month investigation for the LDA by the law firm DLA Piper concluded Lee had not influenced funding decisions and there was no evidence of fraud or corruption. Two years after Manny and I referred the papers to the District Auditor he agreed there was no criminality and no rules had been broken but said he didn't approve of some grants or the way I ran my administration. Given how former DA Ian Pickwell had tried to fine me and the other Camden councillors £1 million for introducing a £60 minimum weekly wage in 1980, this wasn't terribly surprising.

*

After all the headlines and double-page spreads ('Hub for criminals', 'Lost City Hall millions', 'Mayor's aide and lost millions', 'Cash scandal', 'Ken and lost £500,000' and 'City Hall grants scandal') the police should have prosecuted Wadley and Gilligan for wasting their time. Between them they nearly killed the *Standard*. Wadley's negative *Daily Mail* style cost the *Standard* a quarter of its sales even before Murdoch's free sheet *London Paper* appeared. Wadley took the circulation down from 425,000 to 160,000. After the election the *Standard* was sold to Russian billionaire Alexander Lebedev for one pound. Wadley and Gilligan soon left the paper and the new editor Geordie Greig plastered London with adverts apologising for the abuses of the Wadley regime. Under Greig the paper was upbeat and circulation soared to 700,000: editorials said there had been no corruption or cronyism at City Hall. Wadley got her reward when Boris shoehorned her into the chair of the Arts Council England. When the Arts Council complained that she had no experience of the arts she pointed out that she went to the opera a lot.

The biggest reward was for Lord Rothermere. Boris scrapped my plans to have an open auction on the internet for the *Metro* contract and it was re-awarded to the Mail Group in a closed bid. The *Standard*'s campaign was a gross abuse of their power to ensure a favourable tendering process for one of their biggest money spinners. The GLA was legally barred from suing the *Standard* and Wadley knew neither Lee nor I could afford to do so privately, so she and Gilligan were free to peddle any line they chose, truthful or not. (The Press Complaints Commission remains spineless unless the victim is royal.) Later revelations of illegal phone tapping by Murdoch's papers demonstrate the need for either better regulation of the press or the provision of legal aid in libel cases.

Illegal bugging is not the sole preserve of the Murdoch press, of course. In April 2005 Paul Marshall, a civilian Met worker, admitted obtaining from police computers and then selling 'very personal and confidential details' of many people including me, Emma, Ricky Tomlinson and Bob Crow. The prosecution had no answer when the judge asked why those who had paid for this information were not also in the dock. At the same trial private investigator Steve Whittamore was another convicted of passing on confidential information to journalists. The *Guardian*'s James Robinson wrote in September 2010, 'A report by the information commissioner said more than 50 *Daily Mail* journalists bought material from Whittamore on 952 occasions. Other customers included the *Daily Mirror* (681 transactions), *News of the World* (228), *Sunday Times* (4) and *Observer* (103).' According to Nick Davies in his book *Flat Earth News*, Whittamore was paid over half a million pounds in three years. Except for a brief piece on the *Guardian* website, no paper reported this trial.

The press do more damage with the unremitting stream of poison spewed out by so many columnists. In this book I've included the worst things said about me by various columnists over the years because the gap left by having fewer good reporters is filled by hacks whose constant negativity and bile has played a big part in the collapse of trust in our institutions, not least the press itself, and the individuals that run them. It is right that wrongdoing and deceit should be exposed, but more often than not columnists fill the page with venom without making any attempt to find the truth.

Twenty-five years ago Thames Television and BBC London had resources to research and investigate allegations and the *Standard*'s slurs against me would have been challenged, but after decades of staff cuts BBC London could only repeat the lies (ITV was more cautious). The media must have resources for effective scrutiny of politics. Instead of undertaking independent research before interviewing a politician journalists too often rely on asking their opponents to suggest questions

*

Boris Johnson was a clear warning of what to expect from a government led by David Cameron with £2.4 billion of cuts in funding for transport, the cancellation of £3.5 billion of proposed transport investment and savage fare increases. Boris cancelled the Londres Plage and my plans to replace the buses in Oxford Street with a tram service. With the exception of the cycle-hire scheme, all transport projects which were not contractually committed were cancelled, including extensions of the DLR, trams and a new bridge over the Thames in East London. Almost all the cuts were in the suburbs and the cycle-hire scheme was restricted to the centre of London, and by the time it was introduced the cost had risen to £80 million (£12,000 for each bike and docking frame). Boris announced he was going ahead with the tube upgrade, the bike scheme and twelve new cycle routes, although we had started work on these years before. Staff became so demoralised that Boris invited tenders for 'well-being workshops' for them. Although I left a surplus of £1.5 billion in the GLA's £12 billion budget, Boris claimed a 'black hole' in finances to justify above-inflation fare increases. Fortunately, the first contracts to build Crossrail had been let and businesses had warned that there would be trouble if Crossrail did not go ahead. Three-quarters of businesses opposed his plan to close London's offices in China and India, which I'd opened during visits there in 2006 and 2007 to promote tourism and investment. In the first year we gained £21 million extra investment from China and were in negotiations with hundreds of firms that were interested in coming to London when Boris won, but without his backing little was achieved and the offices were wound down or closed.

As Boris didn't use the tube he had no idea of how quickly the service can deteriorate unless rigid control is maintained. At an early media event with Tim O'Toole from TfL Boris staggered up from the platform complaining the conditions were appalling. Tim replied, 'It's like that every morning in the rush hour.' The tube got worse with the loss of Tim just as the last PPP company, Tube Lines, collapsed. Instead of forcing them into liquidation as I had with Metronet, Boris paid £310 million to buy them out. His lack of interest in detail produced the worst-ever delays, cancellations and closures in the Underground's history.

As for his promise of a no-strike deal with the unions he did not even request a meeting with them to discuss it. He refuses to meet any transport union while there are unresolved issues, but if there were no issues to resolve then no meetings would be necessary. Boris also tore up his pledge not to cut tube ticket office opening hours and because he refused to meet the unions to discuss it, Londoners were forced to walk to work during the resultant strikes.

Boris's decisions to halve the size of the congestion zone, scrap the six-monthly checks on taxis to minimise emissions, drop the £25 excess charge on polluting 4x4s as a result of Porsche's application for a judicial review (meaning he had to pay Porsche £430,000 for their legal costs) and postponing the next stage of the low-emission zone have worsened London's air quality to such an extent that we risk being fined £300 million by the EU. The government has decided that any such fine will be paid by a £25 levy on each London council taxpayer. When we formulated these proposals we believed that 1,400 Londoners were dying prematurely each year because of air pollution with hundreds of thousands more suffering respiratory problems. New medical evidence now puts the figure of premature deaths at over 4,200 a year. It is extraordinary how little media coverage there is even though air pollution kills twice as many Londoners as alcohol abuse and thirteen times as many as traffic collisions.

Boris had an easier time with policing and the council tax. I left enough money in the budget to increase police and PCSO numbers to 36,000 during his first year. This did not stop Boris cutting police numbers by 455 but it did allow him to freeze the council tax. Unfortunately, the same measures that worsened London's air quality, plus spending nearly £8 million on five new Routemasters, resulted in the largest fare increases since the Law Lords overturned the GLC's Fares Fair policy in 1982. Although London already has the highest public transport fares in the world, Boris has agreed with government they should be increased each year by 2 per cent above inflation for the next twenty years. Fares will then be 50 per cent higher in real terms than they are today. Using the balances I left, Boris tried to put off big cuts in police numbers until after the

2012 election but nearly 1,000 police jobs were cut in 2010 and 1,900 are due to go after the Olympics.

*

For Boris, being elected mayor of London was a mixed blessing. It is the second-best job in English politics but it took him out of Parliament. Nothing had prepared him to run a £12 billion budget so a major screw-up could wreck his career and he could be out of Parliament and unable to contest the leadership if Cameron lost the next election. (Cameron kept Boris's father, Stanley, off the short-list for the June 2008 Henley by-election, fearing Stanley might step down and allow Boris to return to the Commons if Cameron's leadership became vulnerable.)

Boris's strategy was to take no risks so he didn't initiate any new schemes of his own. Boris's laziness meant that promotion of London was wound down and after his disastrous press conference with his 'youth deputy' Ray Lewis, in which he tried to defend Ray without knowing about allegations of sexual misconduct, only four further press conferences took place over the next three years. Media contact was restricted to stage-managed photo opportunities often involving charities. Boris's strategy was to try to depoliticise the role of mayor so he was never around for interview when fares were increased or police numbers were cut.

Watching Boris cancel investment in London was depressing, but even worse was his inability to spend the £5 billion I had got from Gordon Brown in order to build 50,000 affordable homes in three years. He fell so short of the target his staff made the figures unintelligible and claimed he would build the 50,000 homes over four years. In a city where every architect and builder was looking for work this was catastrophic mismanagement. He also scrapped the rule that half of homes in each development should be affordable and allowed boroughs to reduce their housing targets.

*

My defeat had put several people out of a job. My five political advisers were on fixed contracts that expired two days after the election. Environment adviser John Duffy and women's adviser Anni Marjoram retired but John Ross was immediately hired by Jiao Tong University in Shanghai as a visiting professor lecturing on globalisation. Mark Watts was snapped up to head a green team at Arup. Simon Fletcher and Redmond O'Neill worked on Progressive London. Emma, Maureen Charleson and Theresa Coates were permanent staff appointed by the Assembly on the understanding that following a change of mayor they would move to other GLA posts. Boris ratted on the deal and all were forced out. Boris's team told Gilligan I had added vast pay-offs totalling £1.6 million to eight of my advisers' contracts and the *Metro* reported that Emma was on £96,000 a year. Gilligan didn't report that employment law required the payment of a redundancy settlement and that the £1.6 million figure was arrived at by including total lifetime pension liabilities. Emma was employed on £35,000 but once our relationship began she agreed to stay on the same grade for the next six years.

As for me, after forty-six years as a workaholic, I could now take the kids to school and read the papers in the coffee shop. Tom and Mia were five and four, which is a wonderful age to be around children. During evenings spent at home I caught up with *The Wire*, *The West Wing*, *Mad Men* and *Battlestar Galactica*. My being around during the day meant Tom and Mia could finally have the puppy they wanted. Looking after Emma's sister's puppy for a week reminded me how much I'd enjoyed walking Mum's dogs as a teenager and so we got the children a seven-week-old yellow Labrador, which arrived just before Christmas. I lost the vote on what to call her, so she is Coco and not Cuba. Walking the dog once or twice a day meant I lost half a stone and Coco rapidly became a loved and loving member of the family rather than just a pet.

Emma, having been thrown out of City Hall, organised my speeches and trips to the cities I had not had time to visit as mayor. Most of my time was spent working on this book but LBC quickly signed me up to do a regular Saturday morning phone-in programme. I really enjoyed it, even though I kept showing myself up by announcing we were going to the weather report when it was really the travel slot, but when the sun was out on a big match day I had to work hard to get the calls. After I was selected as Labour's candidate for the 2012 mayoral election LBC decided to add David Mellor to the programme to ensure political balance. This was an inspired choice and worked so well that listening figures almost doubled.

I had approaches from head hunters saying they could get me on company boards but with my political views I could see too many problems so I said no. A year later civil engineering firm Parsons Brinckerhoff put me on their advisory board but just as I was getting into the swing of things they were taken over by the failed Metronet firm Balfour Beatty. Since I had crossed swords with them over the tube PPP I was thrown off the board when the takeover took place, so that was the end of that.

Although my presence at the 2008 Olympics was no longer necessary politically, the mayor of Beijing anyway had me flown out for the opening ceremony (probably the most expensive spectacle in human history) after Boris said he wasn't coming. John Ross, Redmond and I then spent a week in Caracas meeting Hugo Chavez and his finance minister. With a $50 billion surplus in their budget they wanted dramatic improvements in the capital's infrastructure and we met with Hugo's candidate for mayor to plan technical and professional support for the city. Sadly, he was defeated. Brown phoned from the closing ceremony in Beijing to say how disappointed he was that, given all my hard work, I wasn't there instead of Boris. He laughed when I said that I was in Caracas and was pleased that I had been at the opening ceremony. Brown hasn't spoken to me since. During the general election the Labour party ensured our paths never crossed while visiting marginal seats although Tom Watson, an MP close to Brown, had asked if I wanted to stand in the Ipswich by-election but I didn't want to leave London.

*

One advantage of my defeat was that Emma and I could finally get married. We hadn't wanted to do so while I was mayor for fear of the media spectacle it could generate and we also wanted to wait until Tom and Mia were old enough to take part along with Georgia (who had just made me a grandfather), Lottie, Liam and their half-sister Bertie. We got so caught up in the planning that I didn't notice that the date we had chosen clashed with the 2009 Labour Party Conference, so that put paid to our honeymoon. It also meant I would always be at conference on our wedding anniversary. Our wedding was small with just family and closest friends invited and only a handful of photographers turned up briefly. We held it in London Zoo's Mappin Terrace overlooked by wallabies and emus on the sunniest day of that autumn.

Redmond looked great and I assumed he had made a complete recovery from his operation three years earlier, so it was a shock when he told us after the wedding that a small growth had reappeared and he was going back into hospital to have it removed. He was in great spirits the night before the operation when he came round for a meal with Simon and other friends to talk about future plans. But Redmond's heart just stopped beating near the end of the operation. We were staggered and Mia reduced me to floods of tears when she said, 'Poor old Redwood, but you still have me Daddy.' Redmond had been at my side for twenty-two years and in all the struggles he had been loyal, funny, wonderful company and his advice was indispensable. Even if I were to win in 2012, being mayor would never be as much fun as before.

John Ross flew back from Shanghai for the funeral in Highgate Cemetery on a beautifully sunny autumn day. Hundreds of people gathered at the cemetery gates to follow the coffin, knowing Redmond would be delighted we were burying him within sight of Karl Marx's grave. I knew I wouldn't get through my speech unless I went first. The Venezuelan ambassador spoke next, followed by John's moving tribute to his best friend. Looking at the crowd I was moved to see so many of Redmond's colleagues paying their respects who had been celebrating my wedding alongside him just four weeks earlier.

*

Brown staggered on until the banking crisis of 2008 gave him the chance to give global leadership as he urged other governments to copy the rescue package for Britain's banks. For all his complicity in the policies that led to the crisis he was the right man in the right place at the right time. Brown's improved ratings counted for little, however, as the whole of Parliament was overwhelmed by scandal. MPs' expenses had changed in two ways since I had left the back benches. The cosy arrangement of expenses being 'a private matter between the House of Commons and its members' had been replaced by some proper rules and a backbench rebellion had increased expenses by 50 per cent. Some MPs, used to the lax old regime, 'overlooked' the new regulations, and although the previous £10,000 limit had just covered the mortgage on a second home there was now enough for everything from a duck house to a packet of HobNobs. There were a few saints who claimed nothing but hundreds including Boris, Cameron, Nick Clegg and Danny Alexander claimed the full amount. Sharper MPs like George Osborne and Boris used the whole allowance to buy the most expensive second home possible – a nice little asset to sell once they retired.

Although the *Telegraph* manipulated the release of information to maximise damage to the Labour party the impact on all three main parties was stunning. Labour, Tory and the Lib Dems together won only 57 per cent of the vote in the Euro elections as people registered their disgust by flocking to UKIP, the BNP and the Greens. Home Secretary Jacqui Smith and local government minister Hazel Blears undermined the Labour campaign by announcing their resignations from the cabinet and I was phoned by Margaret McDonagh asking me to lead the call for Brown's resignation. I was bemused. Margaret was the Labour Party general secretary who had expelled me from the party (although I had voted for her as she was the strongest candidate!). For all my doubts about Brown I wasn't going to help hand the party back to the Blairites so I phoned Ed Balls on his mobile to warn him.

*

The banking crisis triggered the worst recession since the 1930s but the greedy bankers were lucky that the anger against them was diverted by greedy MPs. Although Cameron had promised to match Labour's spending (pound for pound), the Tory strategy was to blame the recession on 'spending by Brown'. The truth is Britain had the lowest public debt of any large Western economy before the banking crisis. Our debt as a proportion of GDP was 40 per cent whereas in Germany, France and the USA it was over 60 per cent (in Italy and Japan over 100 per cent). Until the banking crisis government borrowing was just 2 per cent of GDP and this soared to 10 per cent only because of the banks. The financial sector in London was as large as New York's but New York was a small part of the US economy whereas London accounted for almost a fifth of the UK's output. Our economy was too dependent on the financial sector.

By blaming the crisis on Brown, Cameron and his shadow chancellor Osborne prevented a serious debate on what went wrong. If we compare the three decades that followed 1945 with the thirty years since Thatcher we see that under post-war governments inequality was slashed as progressive taxation shifted wealth from the rich to the average family. In the 1950s the top rate of tax was 98 per cent and it was still 80 per cent when Thatcher won in 1979. Public spending and trade union power grew throughout the thirty years of the post-war social democratic consensus and investment reached a peak of 20 per cent before the oil crisis in 1973. Salaries increased and holidays lengthened, there were reductions in the working day and women's wages were catching up with men's. Polling showed that the British were among the top two or three happiest nations.

Like Reagan, Thatcher argued that trade unions, taxation, regulation and public spending prevented the private sector investing and growing so she broke the power of the unions and cut regulation, and income tax to 40 per cent. The Treasury and the financial sector always wanted interest rates high enough to secure London's financial position, even though this made it more expensive to invest in manufacturing. The only time in the last century Britain had interest rates as low as 2 per cent was from the Great Depression through the Second World War until the defeat of the post-war Labour government. This allowed Britain to rebuild its manufacturing base, but these lessons were ignored by most chancellors, including Brown who kept British interest rates at 5 per cent while our European rivals' were usually two points lower.

Although the word privatisation had not appeared in Thatcher's 1979 manifesto, a pattern was clear as she carved her way through the public utilities. Whether it was BT, gas, electricity or water, prices increased dramatically while hundreds of thousands of skilled manual jobs with pensions were wiped out. Adam Smith said that one of the iron laws of economics is that no monopoly should be in private hands as it becomes a licence to steal. In the US one person in eight still lives in cities where the electricity supply has not been privatised and they pay 11 per cent less than other Americans for their energy. The higher prices charged by privatised companies have funded obscene salaries for senior executives and huge dividends for shareholders.

The mutually owned British building societies were encouraged to become private corporations. Each society that took this route either failed, like Northern Rock, or was taken over by a bank. None continues to exist independently. Taken together, the destruction of British manufacturing and privatisation eliminated most of the jobs the working class relied on and their loss added to the insecurity in working-class communities.

Post-war governments encouraged companies to implement final-salary pension schemes (paying up to two-thirds of a person's final salary until death) with tax relief on contributions and investments. Covering 12 million people, they were a tempting target for Nigel Lawson, the chancellor whose 1988 budget reduced the assets of pension funds to grab an extra £1 billion in tax. Companies were encouraged to take 'holidays' from making contributions, which was fine while the stock market boomed but when it turned down companies complained they couldn't meet their pension obligations and started closing their final-salary schemes to new employees. When Thatcher came to power companies were putting over 11 per cent of their wage bill into pension schemes; this was cut to 6 per cent within ten years. In 1993 another Tory chancellor, Norman Lamont, raided pension funds by cutting tax credits and under Labour Brown cut tax relief for pension funds from £7 billion in 1996 to just £3 billion by 2002 despite a warning from accountants Arthur Andersen that this was a risky strategy.

To tackle the looming pension crisis Brown proposed replacing existing benefit and pension schemes with a tax benefit for all pensions which would allow everyone to accumulate a pension 'pot' of up to £1.4 million, producing up to £65,000 a year. For the 10,000 people with pension pots above the £1.4 million level there would be a tax surcharge. The backlash from big business is recounted in Robert Peston's *Who Runs Britain*. In September 2003 Niall FitzGerald of Unilever, Martin Broughton of BAT, Sir Christopher Hogg of GlaxoSmithKline, Lord Browne of BP, Arun Sarin of Vodafone, Sir John Bond of HSBC and others met Blair to warn that their highest-paid staff would be transferred out of Britain if this went ahead. They also threatened that unless the richest could benefit from company pension schemes they would be closed down for all. Although Blair and Brown backed down they were more resolute in resisting the demands of pensioners and trade unions to restore the link between the state pension and earnings. When Thatcher broke the link state pensions were cut in real terms by a third.

*

Blair continued Thatcher's tax policy and her hostility to trade unions so after three decades the proportion of GDP paid in wages was cut from 67 per cent to just 54. Public sector investment (which averaged 5.5 per cent before Thatcher) was cut to just 1 per cent, creeping up to 1.5 per cent under Blair. The neo-liberals always promised this would unleash dynamic growth in the private sector but even before the banking crisis private sector investment was running at only 16 per cent. Thatcher gave the private sector all it demanded but it was never able to equal the levels of investment, job creation or exports seen in the thirty years of post-war progressive politics. The country lost most of its manufacturing to foreign competitors as interest rates were kept high to benefit the financial sector. In Germany tax policy remained redistributive, trade unions were involved in setting industrial policy and investment was consistently higher. But Britain was not unique. Under President Eisenhower's Republican US administration in the 1950s the top rate of tax was 90 per cent, which funded public sector investment across America. In 1980 Reagan cut tax and public spending and broke the unions. As in the UK, the rich got richer but investment never again reached the levels of 1945 to 1975.

Cameron talks about 'broken Britain' without acknowledging who broke it. Thirty-five years ago working-class men had jobs which paid enough for them to support a family and could look forward to a modest pension and an improving quality of life. More important, their children could look forward to the same. That world was swept away by Thatcher's policies. As well as wiping out jobs in manufacturing and by privatisation, breaking the power of the unions in the private sector allowed corporations to take away their employees' pension rights and job security.

As I travel round the capital I meet communities in both inner and outer London where people live in a state of insecurity with the real prospect that their standard of living will continue to worsen for the rest of their lives. Middle-class students leaving university also face insecurity and a potential standard of living that will not match that of their parents. New jobs are being created in countries that have prioritised investment such as China, India and Brazil, while in Britain, the USA and most of Europe investment has sunk to its lowest level since the Great Depression. Today the economies of America and Europe have just crept back to where they were before the banking crisis of 2008. In the UK where public spending cuts were deeper and faster than elsewhere we are still nowhere near recovering the ground we have lost.

Ignoring the lessons of history, the Tory-led coalition that came to power in 2010 is now using the deficit as an excuse to reduce the size of the state, but why would a strategy that failed to deliver higher investment after 1980 do so now when competition from other nations is growing? China's GDP has increased by 40 per cent since the banking crisis and will overtake that of the US as early as 2017.

By 2050 China, India and the USA, in that order, will control over half the global economy. Brazil will push Japan into fifth place and Indonesia and Mexico will leap ahead of Germany and the UK. These changes are caused by one factor above all others: the level of investment. As the banking crisis tipped the West into recession US and British private sector investment collapsed (to just 10 per cent in the UK) and the small increase in government investment barely registered. China was able to increase investment from 43 to 46 per cent of GDP because the government told banks to increase loans to businesses. Britain's bailed-out banks have contemptuously ignored all pleas to increase loans to businesses, restoring their own financial position and bonuses instead.

Public anger at bankers' bonuses has prompted verbal criticism from ministers but no action of any serious nature. But banks in Britain and the US have always put their own interests first. During the Second World War Montagu Norman, Governor of the Bank of England, didn't tell the government he was transferring a large part of Britain's gold reserves (held at the Bank of International Settlements in Basel) to Nazi Germany on the grounds the war shouldn't interfere with financial obligations. Churchill's fury when he discovered this may explain why he did not repeal Labour's nationalisation of the Bank of England when he returned to power.

Bankers have abused their powers before. Arthur Schlesinger's *The Age of Jackson* describes the Bank of America's 'deliberate creation of a panic in order to blackmail the government' in the USA in the early nineteenth century. The bank's boss Nicholas Biddle 'plainly preferred . . . a speculative economy with quick expansion, huge gains and huge risks . . . willing to take the chance of depression . . . for the opportunities of boom'. President Jackson warned that people 'are in constant danger of losing their fair influence in the government . . . from the multitude of corporations with exclusive privileges . . . Unless you become more watchful . . . you will find control of your dearest interests has passed into the hands of these corporations.' George Bancroft, Navy secretary under Jacksonian president James K. Polk, said of the banks that 'no man or body of men ought ever to be invested with such exorbitant powers that, in the case of misdemeanour, the guilty cannot be arraigned without plunging the country into distress', while the radical clergyman Reverend Theophilus Fisk warned that 'the moment a spirit of speculation can be excited, the banks increase the flame by pouring oil upon it . . . they add to the distress a thousand fold'.

Schlesinger records Democrats warning, 'The rich plunder the poor, slow and legal . . . Privileged orders through history – the priesthood, the nobility, now the banking system – showed how every age had known its own form of institutionalised robbery by a minority operating through the state.' Chief Justice Taney warned 'against the unnecessary accumulation of power over persons and property in any hands. And no hands are less worthy to be trusted with it than those of a moneyed corporation.' These 200-year-old words could equally well be describing the current banking crisis. Every society is divided between those with wealth and power and those without. On those occasions in history when the wealthy and powerful have ruled benignly, it was only because they feared harsher policies might radicalise the masses.

*

Why, then, with the experience of post-war Britain, was Blair's government such a disappointment? Inheriting a benign economy from Ken Clarke just as the Tories were having a collective mental breakdown gave Blair the chance to lead a great reforming government to equal those of the Liberals in 1906 and Attlee in 1945. Yet with the exception of the peace deal in Northern Ireland and the creation of the London mayoralty the other progressive measures of Blair's first term – such as the minimum wage and Scottish and Welsh devolution – were the legacy of John Smith.

One reason Blair failed to transform Britain can be found in Alastair Campbell's diaries. Blair was obsessed with the media. No one in his team worked on a strategy for government or planned what Britain should look like in twenty years' time. Among the inner core of Blair, Brown, Mandelson and Campbell no one had been a minister or even chaired a council committee. None of them had ever run anything. Blair admits he spent his first term learning how to do the job, which is a luxury no government can afford. Campbell records how Blair's eyes would shift to the garden when officials discussed the details of NHS or welfare reform. It isn't essential for a prime minister to master detail as long as they have people they trust to master it for them. Brown could have filled that role but spent his time blocking Blair's Thatcherite schemes (and was right to do so).

Blair wasn't a Tory cuckoo in the Labour nest but with his comfortable background of public school, Oxford and the Bar he was ignorant of working-class life and knew little about economics. He preferred the company of the rich to that of trade union leaders and some believe Blair's pursuit of wealth after leaving office is because he was also seduced by their world. But journalist Hugo Young's notes record Labour peer David Puttnam already warning in February 1998 that Blair 'is very interested in money . . . could get any job he wanted. He could get a lot of pay with a private jet attached [possibly as] boss of News International or boss of a merged Glaxo and Smith Kline . . . A few years in that job could get him £20 million in the bank.' Puttnam kept repeating that 'Blair was very aspirational . . . He could become President of Europe . . . and fulfil his even grander ambitions – having got his money.' No one obsessed with wealth is going to preside over a shift of power and wealth from rich to poor. We need to bear in mind Jesus' words that 'you cannot serve two masters, God and Mammon' when choosing Labour's leaders.

Blair's second term was overwhelmed by Iraq but if he believed before then that Saddam was a threat he didn't mention it once during the 2001 election campaign. I had hoped Blair would be a restraining influence on Bush because Anji Hunter told me just before Blair flew to Washington for his first meeting with Bush: 'With Europe so hostile they are so desperate and isolated we will have huge influence on them.' Blair's personality made this unlikely. He never once said no to my requests. It was always 'I'll get back to you' or 'Let me look into it', but he never did. If he couldn't say no to my face he was never going to stand up to a fanatical US president. With the single exception of his persuading Bush not to bomb Al Jazeera TV, Blair was an echo not a conscience. He ignored security warnings that invading Iraq would make us vulnerable to terrorist attacks and after the July 2005 bombings denied the connection completely, saying the problem was purely to do with Islam.

Prime Minister Brown seemed like a breath of fresh air but Campbell had been right in his jibe about the new PM's 'psychological flaws'. As chancellor, Brown could hide away, making only the occasional set-piece speech, but being leader put him in a relentless media spotlight. The warnings were there in his student days. Brown was seventeen and already at university in 1968 as students occupied and marched and only twenty when Jimmy Reid led the workers' occupation of Govan shipyard, but although he was a committed Labour activist he took no part in any of these activities and always went to college wearing a jacket and tie. I don't know anyone else of my generation who was so stuck in the forms and rigidities of the 1950s.

Ignoring the previous two centuries of growth and recession, Brown claimed to have eliminated the economic cycle of boom and bust. Rather than challenge the Tory complaint that under Labour public spending was too high, he pandered to the *Mail* by stating that 'never again will Labour tax and spend for the sake of it'. He never said which chancellor had increased taxes just for the sake of it. More damaging was his 'golden rule' of keeping government debt below 40 per cent of GDP, which prevented the building of homes for rent and the modernisation of the transport system. Instead he fell back on his unwieldy private-finance initiatives and public–private partnerships, although these meant a much greater and longer financial burden on the public.

The thirteen years of Blair and Brown were Labour's greatest lost opportunity but their New Labour project was just a cross between a marketing exercise and an attempt to stifle any dissent. Life was sucked out of the Labour party as decisions were dragged up to the caucus around Blair and Brown. Vetting procedures stopped local parties selecting candidates they wanted as MPs and local councillors. Safe Labour seats became gifts with which Blair and Brown rewarded their supporters. The right of ordinary members to set policy was replaced by the charade of policy forums where dissenting voices were ignored. Annual conference was transformed from being a parliament of the left into media puffs for ministers.

*

The biggest shock for those Labour MPs elected in the 1997 landslide was the announcement that the Bank of England was being given control of interest rates. Blair and Brown decided this without the agreement of Labour's NEC, the PLP or even the cabinet. At the first meeting of the PLP Dennis Skinner and I pointed out the danger of allowing bankers the power to increase interest rates to deflate the economy or refuse to reduce interest rates to avoid recession. The Carter presidency was derailed by the refusal of the Federal Reserve to expand the economy in the late 1970s and the sound economy Labour inherited from Ken Clarke was partly because he repeatedly refused the Bank of England's demand to increase interest rates. As the economy is managed by decisions on taxes, public spending and interest rates it is barmy to have bankers taking the interest-rate decisions while second-guessing what the chancellor will do on spending and taxes.

MPs rapidly discovered this was not a one-off. At meetings of the PLP MPs were not allowed to vote on Blair's and Brown's policies. MPs who voted against the whip were marginalised and the obsequious promoted. Because they no longer faced reselection by local parties most MPs were concerned only to get the approval of Blair rather than that of their voters or party members. Had reselection of MPs still been in place Blair could never have led us into Iraq. Labour MPs were reduced to a stage army, wheeled on to push through policies that hadn't even been voted on in cabinet. I remembered fondly when Neil Kinnock told those MPs who wanted me disciplined for my views on Ireland, 'Ken Livingstone has the right to be wrong.' Labour MPs could not even publicly express disagreement without being denounced for endangering Labour's chances at the next election.

*

There is a long-standing myth about the talent and impartiality of the British civil service. I believed there was a golden age in the past but reading Harold Macmillan's diary of his struggles to overcome civil service opposition to building 300,000 homes changed my mind. In my dealings the civil service were determined not just to avoid taking risks but to avoid making any change at all. Transport officials opposed every project we wanted in London and they got utility companies in to lobby transport minister John Spellar so he had already decided against our plans to reduce roadworks before I was able to make my pitch.

Civil servants also lied to ministers to stop projects. Once we won the Olympics I needed a decision to build a new sewer from the site to Beckton sewage works, east of Stratford, because a sudden downpour could spew millions of gallons of raw sewage into the Lower Lea just downwind from the stadium. The junior minister said he had been told it wasn't possible to build a tunnel in time. I pointed out we were removing the pylons on site by building a tunnel to take electricity underground and were building a longer tunnel under the Thames to take the DLR extension to Woolwich, so his officials were lying. No officials spoke up but in the months that followed civil servants stalled a decision for over a year. When government gave the go-ahead, it was too late for it to be ready before the games. The same civil servants who had said the tunnel couldn't be built were asked to prepare a scheme about what to do if there was a flood of raw sewage during the games.

Another area where I failed to overcome civil servants was control of the South Bank Concert Halls, which had been built and managed by the GLC until abolition. Every culture secretary I lobbied from Chris Smith through Tessa Jowell and James Purnell to Andy Burnham wouldn't pass control back to London. There would be uproar if this happened in Edinburgh or Cardiff. Tony Banks had broken the grip of the middle-class arts establishment back in GLC days but it was back with a vengeance. I was allowed to nominate one person to the twelve-member board of the South Bank Centre and that was the only black person appointed. All other appointments to the board were made by the incumbents and when I asked the vice-chair when they intended to appoint another black or Asian Londoner he said they had found a black person worth interviewing but 'they weren't ready'.

Junior ministers don't upset civil servants because each year the head of the civil service writes a report on the abilities of ministers. This is sent to the prime minister for his information when considering promotions or sackings. Aberdeen North MP Bob Hughes, a minister in the 1974 Labour government, told me he was at his desk each day ploughing through the endless stream of red boxes until he came down with flu. Coming back to work, he was surprised to find no backlog of boxes and realised he was just being kept busy. Chris Mullin's recent diaries show little has changed.

*

MPs were kept in line with the mantra that only Blair could have won the election and only mindless loyalty could secure re-election. This rubbish was demolished by the distinguished pollster Robert Worcester in his book *Explaining Labour's Landslide*, in which he demonstrated that not only would John Smith have won by a landslide but so would Neil Kinnock. Far from being the brilliant campaign talked up by spin doctors, Worcester showed how over a million voters who had supported Labour in 1992 abstained in 1997 and Labour's support fell from 54 to 44 per cent as voters focused on Labour's ideology-lite campaign. When Blair was re-elected in 2001 another three million voters deserted Labour and turn-out collapsed to under 60 per cent. The voters had rumbled New Labour and the only reason we were saved was that the Tory party was going through a period of insanity.

Party membership declined by half but nothing better reveals how brutally the Labour party had been gutted than comparing the 2010 Labour leadership election with that of 1976 when Callaghan, Foot, Healey, Jenkins, Benn and Crosland fought to succeed Wilson. All these men, their politics and personalities, were known to the public, but after sixteen years of control freakery, with every speech or article vetted to remove any trace of independent thought, few people had any idea who Labour's candidates were in 2010, let alone what they believed. Even lifelong activists struggled to work out which Miliband or which Ed might be the more radical.

Yet for all this, the Tories failed to win the election of 2010. At the Tory conference in 2009 their poll lead gave Osborne and Cameron the confidence to give a glimpse of their cuts agenda, but as Labour closed the gap Osborne was kept from public view. At elections, though politicians evade and dissemble, they seldom directly lie, but as the prospect of a majority slipped away the Tories panicked, promising the Education Maintenance Allowance would be kept and that there were no plans to raise VAT or reform the NHS. Finally, when asked on television by Andrew Marr, Cameron said that 'any minister who brings me cuts in front-line services will be sent away'. The crime of the angry student who smashes a window pales next to the enormity of Cameron's fraud.

Nevertheless, for Labour to win the next election we must learn the right lessons. Tens of thousands of people have joined the Labour party since our defeat but they will want to play a real part in politics, not just be canvassing fodder. The vetting of candidates has turned MPs into an all-graduate cadre but only 25 per cent of the general public have degrees. This cultural gap between MPs and voters is made worse because the same has happened in the media. Three-quarters of the British people see almost no one in Parliament or the media with whom they feel they can identify. Local parties must once again be free to select the candidates they want.

Party members and trade unionists must have a decisive say in our policies. Believing that working-class voters had nowhere else to go, Blair and Brown took them for granted while they focused on winning over the middle class, but every Labour majority government has to win the support of both working- and middle-class voters. We have to show both classes we have an economic policy that will work for them. This needs a clear break with New Labour's failure. All the candidates for Labour leader invoked *The Spirit Level* by Richard Wilkinson and Kate Pickett. The book, the result of twenty-five years of work, shows that almost all that is wrong in today's society is rooted in the increasing inequality of wealth.

Whether it is crime, drug addiction, teenage pregnancy or poor schooling, those countries that do best are those in which income differences are the narrowest. Because Blair refused to redistribute wealth and despite the fact that SureStart and other community programmes spent billions targeting the poorest, inequalities still increased. Cameron and Osborne will now widen that gap to US levels and bring US levels of social disaster to British towns and cities as whole communities get left behind.

However much more Cameron widens the wealth gap, it won't be enough for the super rich. The top 1 per cent have seen their income multiplied ten times in real terms in thirty years but still bewail the 50 per cent tax rate and threaten to go elsewhere. But I remember the multimillionaire Robert Maxwell, who still felt the need to steal pensions from his workers at the Mirror Group, and Conrad Black, who lived a millionaire lifestyle yet still stole from his shareholders so he could live like a billionaire. As Japan became the world's second-largest economy the bosses who ran Japanese corporations were earning between a fifth and a tenth of their US equivalents because Japanese do not measure status merely by income. The next Labour government must recognise the super-rich always want more and not pander to them.

Given that a third of the population will never be able to afford to buy their own home, a fair society requires homes to rent. But Blair's lack of council experience allowed him to be taken in by the horror stories of slum estates and he refused to let local councils build homes for rent. Tenants on run-down estates were told their homes would only be modernised if they voted to opt out of council control. Labour lost Camden in 2006 when home improvements were cancelled because tenants had the temerity to vote to remain council tenants (Blair used his MP's allowance to pay for a makeover of his constituency home before he resigned). In London waiting lists doubled to 800,000 – one Londoner in ten. Ed Balls calculated that building an extra 100,000 homes a year would create jobs for three-quarters of a million people. Public spending is lowered as health improves and children who have their own bedroom do their homework better, increasing educational attainment.

Blair also upheld Thatcher's anti-union laws while taking no steps to eliminate the abuses and greed of great corporations. This left workers weak and subject to intimidation by the more ruthless employers. Having no experience of industrial action, Blair simply bought the *Daily Mail* line, even promising business that there would be no return to the mass picketing seen in the Grunwick dispute in the 1970s. Blair either knew nothing of the poorly paid Asian women at Grunwick who went on strike after years of intimidation, or he simply didn't care. After the right to vote, the right to strike is our second-most important right and had that right been restored to all it would have reduced the corporate abuses and greed that have damaged our economy over the last thirty years. There is a reason why in every dictatorship, of left or right, trade union rights are crushed.

No democracy is as centralised as Britain's and we should devolve services like the NHS and further and higher education to local and regional government. Building a local management is cheaper than trying to micro-manage the whole country from Whitehall. If London were an independent city-state we would just scrape into the G20 at G19 with more people than half the nations in the UN, yet almost every aspect of running London is decided in Whitehall. Just 7 per cent of London's GDP is run by the mayor and even there government sets targets and often the mayor can proceed only with its agreement. This causes inefficiency and waste and stunts the development of local skills and expertise. We should at least devolve power to the same extent as the US and Germany so that a majority of both taxation and spending occurs at local and regional levels. This would allow people to gain experience of managing government on a smaller scale before they end up running the whole country.

The next Labour government will have to rebuild our economy along fairer lines while economic power shifts from the West, but this is an opportunity not a problem. When I opened offices in China and India I was struck by the preference of Chinese and Indian firms to base themselves in London and the UK. Although language, our legal system and cultural life are attractive factors, what matters most is our tolerance. The French parliament has unanimously voted to ban the hijab, the Swiss in a referendum have banned the construction of any further minarets (as they already have three) and across Europe there are growing demands to restrict immigration and raise barriers against foreign trade. Against that background London stands out as a beacon of tolerance.

*

For 500 years the West, via first Europe and then the US, has run the world on its own terms. With China overtaking the US by the end of this decade the yuan could displace the dollar as the main global reserve currency in the 2020s – risking a political backlash within the US. Since Reagan and Thatcher the neglect of investment in Britain and the USA has meant the failure to modernise industry and impoverished the working class in both nations. Watching secure, well-paid jobs, pensions and good-quality social provision wiped out in little more than a generation has fed the anger that President Obama described as 'clinging onto guns and bibles' and in Britain shows up as support for the BNP and the English Defence League.

But the end of US dominance will not mean an equally dominant China. No one nation will ever again dominate the world as Britain and the US have. The world will have several major economic powers with shifting alliances. Nor will there be a dominant culture. Around the world young people who have access to PCs and smartphones surf the internet to pick and choose what they want from the different cultures on offer. This mix-and-match future is one in which the quality of the offer will matter more than its national origin.

For the West to respond by raising barriers would be self-defeating. We have to learn what has worked and what hasn't in the past thirty years. When I opened our office in Shanghai the local woman we appointed to run it told me that for nine years her school day started at seven in the morning and ended at six at night. In China the biggest item in the family budget is not food, housing or leisure but supplementary education for their children. With India, Brazil and others following down this path we have to increase our levels of investment and spending on education to stay in the race.

There are other changes needed. Britain played second fiddle to the US in the Cold War, spending 30 per cent more on the military than the European average – money which could have gone into modernising our industry. We now know Stalin had no plan for world domination but wanted a ring of puppet states around his borders as a barrier to neighbouring US bases. It was Washington that was set on global domination. The US State Department's War and Peace Studies Project at the end of the Second World War identified a 'world area . . . essential for the security and prosperity of the US . . . [The US must aim] to secure the limitation of any exercise of sovereignty by foreign nations that constitutes a threat [to this world area which included the Americas, British Empire and Far East].' The US objective was 'an integrated policy to achieve military and economic supremacy for the United States', recognising that since 'the British Empire as it existed in the past will never reappear . . . the United States may have to take its place', though Britain would be brought in as a 'junior partner'.

As colonies gained independence US military spending increased so that today 48 per cent of all the military spending in the world is by the US. Not only has this undermined its economy but it has allowed the military to scatter bases and arms production in marginal US constituencies so that it is difficult to cut military spending because of the threat to jobs and votes.

*

The collapse of the Soviet Union removed the justification for military spending so a new enemy was needed. In 1996 Samuel P. Huntington in his book *The Clash of Civilizations* warned of conflict between the West and Islam. Huntington also predicted a clash with China, but as China has nuclear weapons and is willing to prop up the US budget deficit by buying trillions of dollars the US decided to pick on the easier target. This followed the tradition of Western interference in Muslim lands. In the First World War Britain used Lawrence of Arabia to promise the Arabs that if they fought for our side they would be given an independent Arab nation. Britain had also secretly promised Zionist bankers funding our war effort that they would aid the creation of a Jewish homeland. After the war Britain's determination to retain control of Middle East oil meant both pledges were betrayed with Britain and France creating artificial and unstable medieval dictatorships.

In the 1950s when Mossadegh was elected in Iran and Nasser came to power in Egypt, rather than work with them to build modern, viable states the US and UK undermined them, working with the most reactionary strands of Islam from the Saudi royal family through the Gulf tribal despotisms to the Afghan mujahidin. Progressive figures were marginalised or eliminated because in democracies Arabs would have demanded a fairer share of their oil wealth. To control the oil Britain kept a tight grip on Iraq, botched the invasion of Egypt in 1956 and continued interfering in the region through to the invasion of Iraq in 2003. American and Saudi cash overthrew the Afghan communists but gave no help to create a viable state afterwards, so the Taliban came to power using weapons the West had either supplied or funded via the Pakistani ISI.

Western cynicism was clear as air strikes drove the Taliban from power and Osama bin Laden was allowed to escape because Bush was concentrating on planning the invasion of Iraq. In *Overcoming the Bush Legacy in Iraq and Afghanistan* the BBC's resident Afghan correspondent Deepak Tripathi wrote that intelligence reports showed a convoy of about 'a thousand Taliban and al Qaeda fighters escaped to Tora Bora . . . on November 13 2001, the same day Kabul fell to the Northern Alliance. Osama bin Laden was thought to be in the convoy . . . When the bombing of Tora Bora commenced on November 16, the convoy of al Qaeda and Taliban leaders had come and gone.' There were two routes from Tora Bora to Pakistan but 'American planes bombed only one route and 600 Taliban and al Qaeda fighters and many senior leaders escaped via the second route. The much publicised siege of Tora Bora came too late in December 2001 . . . Reports from the area said that top al Qaeda leaders had been airlifted by mysterious looking black helicopters and that al Qaeda was even paying off the pro-American militia to let its operatives escape.'

When Saddam Hussein came to power he was given lists of Iraqi communists by the CIA and trade union leaders by MI6 so he could kill them. When he invaded Iran in 1980, which led to a million deaths over eight years of war, he was funded and supported by the West. In every sense he was seen as a Western asset who could be used against Iran – until he invaded Kuwait. In 2008 Bush set aside $300 million to fund attacks on Iran by terrorist groups. This project has continued under Obama.

This meddling in Muslim nations eventually claimed the lives of nearly 3,000 Americans in September 2001 and fifty-two Londoners in July 2005. The human and financial cost to both the West and the Muslim world of not allowing Muslim nations to develop in their own way massively outweighs the lower price we have perhaps paid for our oil and, until the Arab Spring of 2011, has fostered the most intolerant and backward forces in Islam by propping up medieval and military dictators. We must recognise the right of Muslims to run their own countries or live with the consequences.

Inevitably these conflicts have led to the demonisation of Islam and Muslims generally. A Cardiff University analysis of the British press from 2000 to 2008 found two-thirds of all stories about Muslims depicted them as either 'a threat . . . a problem, or both'. As mayor I commissioned a survey of media coverage of Muslims in one week in 2006 which showed 91 per cent of stories about Islam were negative. The stereotype of Muslims as either super-rich oil sheikhs or fanatical terrorists leads to intolerance, discrimination and physical attacks. A few extreme imams do not define a community any more than Christians are defined by the Baptist minister in the US who regretted that more Londoners did not die in the 7 July bombings because we allow homosexuality in our city or Jews are defined by the Rabbi who said a 'thousand Arab lives aren't worth a Jewish fingernail'. But whereas most people have never heard of the Baptist or the Rabbi, the *Today* programme turned Abu Izzadeen into a national figure by giving him twelve minutes of airtime to rant on.

Every religion produces its fundamentalist fringe but the teachings of Rabbi Hillel, Jesus Christ and the Prophet Muhammad are remarkably similar in their advocacy of tolerance and the acceptance of diversity, but in the West few know much about the life of Muhammad as most newspaper stories about Islam concern only terrorism. In all the hundreds of such articles I read in my eight years as mayor I recall none that analysed his final sermon, given just a few weeks before his death. Knowing this would be his farewell address, he set out how he believed God intended Muslims to live, saying, 'All mankind is from Adam and Eve, an Arab has no superiority over a non-Arab, nor a non-Arab any superiority over an Arab. Also a white has no superiority over a black nor a black any superiority over a white.' He goes on to say that God created humanity 'from a male and a female and have formed you into tribes and nations so that you may get to know one another. Not so that you may fight or oppress or occupy or convert or terrorise but so that you may get to know one another.'

This was not the view of Islam that had formed in the mind of Anders Breivik as he set out to kill seventy-seven people in Oslo and on Utøya island in Norway in July 2011. In his long manifesto, which he sent to members of the British National Party, the English Defence League and the Stop Islamisation of Europe Group, he extensively quoted the *Daily Mail*'s Melanie Phillips and her bizarre view that London has become Londonistan. Phillips is just one of many commentators who, like Nick Cohen in the *Observer*, Andrew Gilligan in the *Telegraph* and Richard Littlejohn in the *Mail*, earn their money by lazily caricaturing Islam and Muslims. Breivik cited Phillips and others in his rambling Manifesto, and this general stew of hatred will continue to have disastrous consequences in Europe.

In the aftermath of the killings, Thorbjørn Jagland, the chairman of the Nobel Peace Prize Committee and former prime minister of Norway, told the *Observer*, 'We have to be very careful how we are discussing these issues, what words are used.' He urged the use of the word diversity rather than multiculturalism and warned, 'We also need to stop using "Islamic terrorism" which indicates that terrorism is about Islam. We should be saying that terrorism is terrorism and not linked to religion.' Certainly the vast majority of terrorist attacks in recent years have been from the far right and in Britain since 9/11 the police have caught several far-right activists amassing guns and bomb-making equipment in preparation for attacks, but these individuals never receive the same coverage as Muslims caught planning terror.

Jagland singled out David Cameron, who he warned was 'playing with fire' following his speech in Munich in spring 2011 when he declared that multiculturalism had failed. The speech was immediately praised by the BNP and the French National Front. Cameron's Munich speech was not just an attempt to divert attention from his government's economic policies. He has pandered to Islamophobia before. Quoted in the *Sun* in 2006, he said, 'If someone wants to see Sharia law they should think of going to live in another country.'

From his background of Eton, Oxford and his millionaire's enclave at Chipping Norton it may appear as though Cameron feels that multiculturalism forces us to live apart, but it isn't so in London. On page 505 I wrote of how Hackney was enriched by the way Orthodox Jews had preserved their culture whilst other Jews have left this distinctive culture behind but London is enriched by Jews in all their diversity. Similarly, many Muslims live devout lives while others have grown up as ignorant of the contents of the Koran as many Anglicans are of the Bible. The George Soros-funded study of Muslim attitudes across Europe showed that in Frankfurt barely a quarter considered themselves German, in Paris nearly half felt French but in London and Leicester 90 per cent felt themselves to be British. Muslims came to Britain as others have before them to become English not to change us. The Soros study shows British tolerance has worked. If Cameron wants to help integrate Muslims in our society he should focus on punishing employers who discriminate and reverse his cuts in teaching English as a second language.

*

The biggest challenge humankind faces today is climate change. In the run-up to the Copenhagen conference in 2009 I had no doubt that, whatever posturing there might be right up to the deadline, there would surely be a deal aimed at stabilising carbon emissions to keep the global increase in temperature to two degrees centigrade. For the British two degrees of warming might seem quite attractive but the increasingly frequent extreme weather events in vulnerable areas that are causing floods, forest fires, drought and desertification are happening with an increase in global temperature of under one degree. Today's violent weather is the result of carbon emissions in the 1970s and 1980s and earlier, so even with a deal at Copenhagen our climate would have continued to become more volatile for another thirty years.

The *Guardian* asked 250 climate scientists how much they thought the world's temperature would increase by. Only one said two degrees. The others split between three, four and five. In 2007 the Intergovernmental Panel on Climate Change warned that 'at current rates of global warming, the earth will be uninhabitable by the end of the twenty-first century'. The difference between today's temperatures and the last ice age is just six degrees. In his book *Six Degrees* Mark Lynas spells out the implications of each one-degree increase. An increase of six degrees could lead to the death of 95 per cent of all life on the planet. Scientists point out that such catastrophes have occurred before. Following them, it took millions of years for the planet to recover. Even with urgent measures to reduce carbon emissions there is a real danger that by the end of the century the human population will have been reduced to just a few hundred million living around the Poles. Privately some experts in this field talk of an optimistic scenario where two billion people survive by the end of the century. Today there are seven billion people on earth.

With Republicans controlling the House of Representatives

there will be no serious effort made to reduce emissions in the USA. Fortunately China's new Five-Year Plan is a step towards creating a sustainable economy with renewable energy. Although no serious scientist disputes climate change, given how little we know about 'tipping points' and 'feedback loops' we have little idea how quickly temperatures will increase. I fear things will become much worse much quicker than most politicians anticipate, and believe that the collapse of human civilisation by the end of the century is possible. Although many leaders like Blair and Clinton said the right things while in office, they weren't prepared to make the changes needed for fear of losing votes. But City Hall's Climate Change Action Plan showed we could cut carbon emissions by 60 per cent in just twenty years by eliminating waste and generating energy locally. When I lost the election I was still struggling to persuade the government that London needed a new and bigger Thames Barrier a bit further out to sea if we were to avoid catastrophic flooding by the middle of the century. Ministers clung to the hope we could muddle through until 2100.

*

In the summer of 2010, as Oona King and I both sought the Labour nomination for the 2012 mayoral election, we took part in over twenty debates across London. While there was little that divided us on the issue of running City Hall, we disagreed fundamentally on the role of the Blair government. As our comments became sharper I felt the tide turning my way. I won the nomination and Ed Miliband was also elected as Labour leader because he was prepared to acknowledge the failures of the last government. We both know we need to win back those voters who became disillusioned not just because of the wars but because we failed to tackle the deeply unfair inequalities of wealth in Britain.

The challenges facing Ed Miliband, Labour's new leader, are not contradictory. To rebuild our economy on fairer lines while adapting to the shift of economic power to the East and preparing for climate change can be achieved only by a fairer distribution of resources within and between nations, and by planning and co-operation on a massive scale. It is in Labour's core values which have always been based around fairness, redistribution, cooperation and planning that we will find the answer to these problems. Many of the thousands of new members who have joined or rejoined the party since Brown lost may believe that Labour's greatest achievements are in its past and all we can hope for is to reverse the damage being done by the Tories. I believe that, if we have confidence in our core beliefs, our greatest achievements still lie ahead. London can play a key role in this task. New York is the only other city in the world where a third of the population was born in a foreign country. London is also the only city in Europe that matches American levels of productivity and competitiveness. London's diversity makes it a bridge between the old powers and economies and those that are emerging. Its tolerance and dynamism can act as a template for the future of humanity as we rise to tackle the challenges we all face together.

Acknowledgements

After the 2008 mayoral election my first idea was to spend a year writing a book about the eight years of my mayoralty, but the publishers I spoke to wanted me to include something about the GLC years and make it more autobiographical. Once I started writing though, it slowly but naturally grew into a full autobiography. There were so many gaps in my knowledge about my parents and grandparents and I realised that one day my children might want to know more about why I did what I did, and I might either be dead or too senile to remember, so the book is really for them.

As well as being a record of my life and political upheavals I have tried to recapture the very different Britain and London in which I grew up. Also, to understand me, my children need to know the ideas and people that changed me.

I am lucky that *Guardian* journalist John Carvel wrote a biography of me, *Citizen Ken*, in 1984, updated it in 1986 and did a much fuller version, *Turn Again, Livingstone*, in 1999. John interviewed many people, now dead, and I have been able to include their comments only because of his original work. I've also been helped by the work of the *Today* reporter, Andrew Hosken, who wrote *Ken: The Ups and Downs of Ken Livingstone* in 2008. Andrew spent the best part of a year tracking down people I had lost touch with thus saving me a similar effort. There are many other books I have drawn on, such as *Nightmare!*, the account of the 2000 mayoral election by Mark D'Arcy and Rory MacLean, all of which have made my task much easier. It would not have been possible to understand what was going on inside the Blair and Brown governments without the revelations in Alastair Campbell's diaries and Andrew Rawnsley's *Servants of the People* and *The End of the Party*.

Usually a politician does a deal with a publisher based on a spiced- up outline of the book they intend to write, but I didn't want to waste a lot of time arguing with a publisher about what I could or couldn't say, so I decided to write it and then let publishers decide if they wished to risk publishing it. That this was the right thing to do was clear when one publisher who had offered me an advance immediately withdrew the offer once they saw the manuscript.

Faber and Faber were always keen to publish the book and came up with the title once they had read it. My editor Neil Belton's enthusiasm for the book over these three years never wavered and it's been a real pleasure to work with him and his team. So my thanks to all at Faber especially Neil, Kate Ward, Kate Burton, Lisa Baker, Anna Pallai, Donna Payne, Pedro Nelson; and to copy editor Trevor Horwood for his unceasing hard work, proofreaders Merlin Cox and Peter McAdie, and indexer Sarah Ereira. Also, thanks as always to my agent Jonathan Lloyd. I would like to apologise to all those people who have helped me throughout my political career who don't get a mention in the book because nothing went wrong. So thank you to those.

The most significant help through these last three years has been my wife Emma who patiently typed the book whilst confined to the attic as I rambled on dictating the words to her. As well as being able to type as fast as I compose she was a brilliant check on my tendency to assume everybody understands the jargon and practices of politicians. She also made sure I didn't forget my feelings and emotions thus making the book more accessible and readable than it might otherwise have been.

I came of age politically at a time when politics was about class and ideas rather than presentation and how easily a politician could emote on the daytime TV sofa and I have never felt comfortable with politicians using their families as a campaign tool. The people who have been part of my private life since I became leader of the GLC never wished to be in the media and we went to great lengths to avoid being splashed all over the papers. Where I write of my private life over these last thirty years what I have written has been agreed with the people who shared it.

Ken Livingstone, September 2011

Index

INDEX

Bush, Bill: arrest and release, 243–4; career, 146, 156, 480, 545; GLC Labour leadership elections, 152, 168; on Kinnock leadership, 271; relationship with Ken, 146–7, 190, 216, 288; voluntary organisation funding, 213; vote analysis, 192–3

Bush, George W.: Afghanistan invasion, 455; Afghanistan strategy, 672; Blair relationship, 475, 553, 661; environment policies, 554; Iran policy, 672; Iraq invasion, 475, 661, 672; state visit (2003), 488; Venezuelan coup attempt, 564

Butler, David, 301

Byers, Stephen, 430, 445

C40, 553, 555, 572, 619, 634

Cable, Vince, 130–1

Callaghan, Jim: budgets, 37; economic policies, 143, 228, 497; election question (1978), 142, 145; government unpopularity, 135; Labour leadership election (1976), 665; Labour leadership in opposition, 148, 155; Kenyan Asians policy, 70–1, 141; political career, 140–1; poll ratings (1977), 141; poll ratings (1979), 145; 'winter of discontent', 143

Calwell, Arthur, 75

Camber Sands, 19

Camden Council: housing programme, 139–40, 149–50; Ken's position, 139–40, 151; Labour loss (2006), 667; minimum wage settlement, 143–4, 150, 206–7

Cameron, David: on banking crisis, 653; on 'broken Britain', 600, 657; Conservative leadership election, 588–9; cuts, 645, 666; on London bombings, 536; London mayoral candidate selection, 579, 581, 582, 583, 623, 637; Mandela statue, 592; MP's allowances, 652; on multiculturalism, 607, 675; relationship with Boris, 588–9, 648; Ross affair, 639–40; support for Boris's London mayoral campaign, 603, 621; wealth gap, 667

Cameron, Ken, 210

Cameron, Samantha, 639

Camfield, Barry, 395

Campaign for Labour Party Democracy (CLPD), 302, 375

Campaign for Nuclear Disarmament (CND), 103

Campbell, Alastair: background and career, 347–8; on Blair, 363, 660; Blair's inner circle, 346; on Brown, 661; on Clause Four, 345, 349; on Dobson, 401–2; on 'fanatics' and 'long-gamers', 342; influence, 369; Iraq dossier, 605; on Kinnock's view of Blair, 350–1; London mayoral candidate selection, 385, 392, 393, 397–8, 400, 401–2; on New Labour economic policy, 362; on spinning, 376

Campbell, Beatrix, 175

Campbell, David, 456

Campbell, Duncan, 214–15, 283

Campbell, Mr (tailor and politician), 4–5

Campbell, Naomi, 592

Canary Wharf bombing (1996), 356

Canavan, Dennis, 344, 389

Cancer Research UK, 82

Candler, David, 146

Cannell, Alexander, 501

Capelin, Arthur, 211

Capita, 472, 476–7, 561

Capital Radio, 243

Capital Standards, 566

carbon emissions, 552–3, 574, 618–19

Cardoen, Carlos, 332

Carlisle, John, 263

Carlton TV, 467

Carmel, Moshe, 511

Caro, Robert, 469–70

Carr, Ewan, 85

Carr, John, 202, 211–12, 393

Carr, Robert, 134

Carter, Howard, 461, 530

Carter, Jimmy, 292, 494, 662

Carter, Patrick, 482

Carvel, John: on anti-Livingstone press coverage, 178; biographies of Ken, 1, 385; on Blair's view of Ken, 385; on Goodwin, 124; Jenkin leaked letters, 242; on Ken's babyhood, 8; on Ken's education, 22; on Ken's parents, 1; on Ken's political views, 97; on Ken's sister, 16; on Ken's supporters, 154, 166; on Kinnock's view of Ken, 271

Cashman, Michael, 375

Cassani, Barbara, 481, 496, 497, 499, 520

Cassidy, Michael, 380, 597

Castle, Barbara, 77, 101, 111, 113, 141

Castro, Fidel, 270, 563

censorship, film, 105–7

Centre for Policy Studies, 192

Chamberlain, Joseph, 232

Chancellor, Alexander, 582

Channel 4, 615

Chaplin, Ina, 128

Chapman, Christine: divorce, 183; holidays, 140, 151, 181; Ken's father's death, 93; life with Ken, 112, 137–8; marriage, 112, 158; relationship with Ken, 90–1, 112, 158, 179, 183; relationship with Ken's mother, 140; separation from Ken, 158, 178, 179; teaching career, 107, 112, 158; view of NF, 134

Chapman, Honor, 485

Chapple, Frank, 171

Charles, Amber, 522

Charles, Prince, 43, 176, 186, 621–2, 634–5

Charleson, Maureen: background and career, 288; at City Hall, 421, 432, 649; Ken's mayoral

[685]

Tribune Group, 289

Streatham, 21B Shrubbery Road, 9–10

Streatham constituency, 4–5, 9

Street-Porter, Janet, 267, 629

Stringfellow, Peter, 486, 565

Stubbs, William, 244

Suetonius, 216

Suez crisis (1956), 22

Sugar, Alan, 413, 565

Sun: abuse of Ken, 504, 616; on Blair, 518; on
Boris, 588; on congestion charge, 476, 477;
on GLC, 248; on homosexuality, 286; on
Islam, 537, 675; on Ken as leader of GLC,
169, 249; Ken's column, 323, 334; on Ken's
private life, 182, 183, 389, 629; on Ken's views
on Ireland, 187–8, 224, 296, 298; on May Day
demonstrations, 418; on Qaradawi, 503

Sunday Business Post, Dublin, 99

Sunday Express, 171, 462

Sunday Mirror, 182, 419, 583

Sunday Telegraph, 171, 392, 421, 472, 493

Sunday Times: buying confidential material, 644;
Clarkson on multiculturalism, 537; on Ken's
election as mayor, 421; on Ken's private life,
390; on Kiley's view of Ken, 442; on London
mayoral elections, 391, 402; on MI5 and Ken,
356; on Olympic Games, 479; on Peach's
death, 177; serialisation question, 334; Young's
column, 227

Sunni Islam, 502–3

Sure Start, 667

Swaffield, Sir James, 125, 171–2, 176, 202, 209,
213

Snyder, Michael, 470

Taki, 625

Taliban, 672

Tambo, Oliver, 593

Taney, Chief Justice, 659

Tanweer, Shahzad, 536

Tatchell, Peter, 120, 233

Tate Modern, 427

Tatham, Jean, 106

Taylor, Cyril, 181

Taylor, Sir Godfrey, 263, 266, 267

Taylor, Gordon, 550

Taylor, Teddy, 358

Teather, Sarah, 487

Tebbit, Norman: drinking, 334; election campaign
(1987), 287; fares policy, 203; GLC abolition,
245; on 'loony left' councils, 278; Maplin
airport policy, 109; relationship with Ken, 359;
unemployment policy, 293

Telstar, 33

Temple-Morris, Peter, 76, 83

Ten Alps, 436

Teviot, Baron Charlie, 246

Texaco, 474

Thames Barrier, 108, 256–8, 572–3, 677

Thames Energy, 484

Thames TV, 189, 190, 257, 645

Thames Water, 567–8, 576

Thamesmead housing estate, 256

That Was The Week That Was, 32

Thatcher, Carol, 332, 565

Thatcher, Denis, 236

Thatcher, Margaret: advice to Ken, 422; anti-
union laws, 314, 654, 668; benefit cuts, 177;
Blair's praise for, 350; character, 351; civil
service relations, 358; Cold War, 184, 283, 312;
Conservative leadership, 137, 140, 322, 562;
council house policy, 150; deregulation of City
firms, 447, 654; election (1979), 111, 133, 142,
143, 145, 146, 160, 170, 375, 654; election
(1983), 230, 231, 300; election (1987), 287;
fares policy, 196, 203; GLC abolition, 230,
231–2, 234–6, 237, 240, 241–2, 249, 264, 396,
438; ILEA abolition threat, 153; immigration
views, 138–9; LDDC, 88; local government
policies, 130, 157, 158, 249, 255, 438, 567; on
Mandela, 592; Master of the Rolls, 262; miners'
strike, 250–1; Northern Ireland policies, 185–7,
224–5, 295–6, 299; Olympics boycott (1980),
518; pensions policy, 656; police numbers,
414, 451; poll tax, 321; press coverage, 226;
privatisations, 305, 654; Routemasters, 604;
school milk, 89; taxation policy, 158, 286, 361,
448, 654, 656; warnings on left-wing policies,
169; Zircon affair, 283–4

Thatcher, Mark, 332

Thatcher and Friends (Ross), 300

Thieu, President, 74

Think London, 556

Thomas, Clifford, 21

Thomas, George, 75

Thompson, Yvonne, 608

Thomson, Peter, 360

Three Horseshoes pub, 188–9

Thurley, Simon, 457

Time Out, 175, 201, 226

Times: on bike-hire scheme, 619–20; on
Bloomberg and Ken, 573; on Boris, 582, 583,
586–7; on congestion charge, 472; on crime,
599; on film censorship, 106; on GLC Labour
leadership, 152; on Ken as mayor, 421, 422; on
Ken's finances, 416–17; on Ken's private life,
389, 630; on Ken's views on Ireland, 187; on
LCC, 233; on Olympic Games, 525; on PPP,
444, 483; on roadworks, 622

Timms, Stephen, 304

Timoney, John, 603

tobacco advertising, 370–1

Today newspaper, 348

Today programme (BBC): Abu Izzadeen on,